Changing the Paradigm of Energy Geopolitics

Changing the Paradigm of Energy Geopolitics

Security, Resources, and Pathways in Light of Global Challenges

Edited by
João Simões, Francisco José Leandro, Eduardo Caetano de Sousa, and Roopinder Oberoi

PETER LANG
Lausanne • Berlin • Bruxelles • Chennai • New York • Oxford

Library of Congress Cataloging-in-Publication Data

Names: Simões, João, 1982–editor. | Leandro, Francisco José, editor. | Sousa, Eduardo Manuel Vicente Caetano de, editor. | Oberoi, Roopinder, editor.
Title: Changing the paradigm of energy geopolitics : security, resources and pathways in light of global challenges / edited by João Simões, Francisco José Leandro, Eduardo Caetano de Sousa, and Roopinder Oberoi.
Description: New York : Peter Lang, [2023] | Includes bibliographical references.
Identifiers: LCCN 2022052354 (print) | LCCN 2022052355 (ebook) | ISBN 9781433191350 (hardback) | ISBN 9781433191367 (ebook) | ISBN 9781433191374 (epub) | ISBN 9781433191381 (mobi)
Subjects: LCSH: Energy policy. | Geopolitics.
Classification: LCC HD9502.A2 C445 2023 (print) | LCC HD9502.A2 (ebook) | DDC 333.79—dc23/eng/20230104
LC record available at https://lccn.loc.gov/2022052354
LC ebook record available at https://lccn.loc.gov/2022052355
DOI 10.3726/b18776

Bibliographic information published by the **Deutsche Nationalbibliothek.**
The German National Library lists this publication in the German National Bibliography; detailed bibliographic data is available on the Internet at http://dnb.d-nb.de.

Cover design by Peter Lang Group AG

ISBN 9781433191350 (hardcover)
ISBN 9781433191367 (ebook)
ISBN 9781433191374 (epub)
DOI 10.3726/b18776

Peter Lang Group AG, Lausanne
Published by Peter Lang Publishing Inc., New York, USA
info@peterlang.com - www.peterlang.com

Changing the Paradigm of Energy Geopolitics

Security, Resources, and Pathways in Light of Global Challenges

Edited by
João Simões, Francisco José Leandro, Eduardo Caetano de Sousa, and Roopinder Oberoi

PETER LANG
Lausanne • Berlin • Bruxelles • Chennai • New York • Oxford

Library of Congress Cataloging-in-Publication Data

Names: Simões, João, 1982–editor. | Leandro, Francisco José, editor. | Sousa, Eduardo Manuel Vicente Caetano de, editor. | Oberoi, Roopinder, editor.
Title: Changing the paradigm of energy geopolitics : security, resources and pathways in light of global challenges / edited by João Simões, Francisco José Leandro, Eduardo Caetano de Sousa, and Roopinder Oberoi.
Description: New York : Peter Lang, [2023] | Includes bibliographical references.
Identifiers: LCCN 2022052354 (print) | LCCN 2022052355 (ebook) | ISBN 9781433191350 (hardback) | ISBN 9781433191367 (ebook) | ISBN 9781433191374 (epub) | ISBN 9781433191381 (mobi)
Subjects: LCSH: Energy policy. | Geopolitics.
Classification: LCC HD9502.A2 C445 2023 (print) | LCC HD9502.A2 (ebook) | DDC 333.79—dc23/eng/20230104
LC record available at https://lccn.loc.gov/2022052354
LC ebook record available at https://lccn.loc.gov/2022052355
DOI 10.3726/b18776

Bibliographic information published by the **Deutsche Nationalbibliothek.**
The German National Library lists this publication in the German National Bibliography; detailed bibliographic data is available on the Internet at http://dnb.d-nb.de.

Cover design by Peter Lang Group AG

ISBN 9781433191350 (hardcover)
ISBN 9781433191367 (ebook)
ISBN 9781433191374 (epub)
DOI 10.3726/b18776

Peter Lang Group AG, Lausanne
Published by Peter Lang Publishing Inc., New York, USA
info@peterlang.com - www.peterlang.com

Table of Contents

Part II

List of Figures

List of Tables

Foreword

THIJS VAN DE GRAAF

We live in times of profound change and uncertainty. A combination of technological, political, and economic shifts is reshaping the international order. New digital technologies are upending our personal lives as much as they are transforming the world economy. The rapidly warming climate is dangerously approaching irreversible tipping points. Shifts in the global balance of power are coinciding with increased geopolitical competition. Even a global systemic shock like the pandemic, which shut down much of the world, has not canceled or reversed these megatrends. On the contrary, in many ways, it even catalyzed or accelerated them.

As the post-Covid world slowly shifts into a "new normal," energy continues to make international headlines. Just as the UN climate conference kicked off in Glasgow in October 2021, an energy crisis took hold of global energy markets. Soaring gas prices in Europe coincided with lower-than-usual gas deliveries from Russia, which amassed troops along the borders of Ukraine. Coal shortages contributed to blackouts in China and reportedly led government officials to instruct state-owned energy companies to secure energy supplies at any cost. Rising oil prices prompted a release of strategic oil reserves from the United States in coordination with other major economies. These events are a stark reminder of the persistent centrality of fossil fuels to the geopolitics of energy.

Yet, in the background, the tectonic plates of our energy system are profoundly changing. Renewable energy such as wind and solar was once referred to as "alternative" energy, too expensive to expand beyond niche markets. Today, that perception has fundamentally changed. As oil company BP noted even before the COVID-19 pandemic, renewables are penetrating the global energy system more quickly than any fuel ever seen in history.[1] This is so across *all* of its scenarios. In its Rapid Transition Scenario, which is largely aligned with the 2°C goal of the Paris Agreement, the growth of renewables would be "literally off-the-charts relative to anything seen in history."[2]

Renewables now form the leading edge of a global energy transformation. The growth of renewables is dominated by wind and solar power, aided by at least three major forces: falling costs of production, policies to combat climate change and air pollution, and rising social and investor pressure for change. Renewables are growing fastest in the power sector, but they are increasingly also finding their way to other end-use sectors such as transport, buildings and industry thanks to cost reductions in technologies such as batteries, heat pumps and electrolyzers (to produce hydrogen).

The world has transitioned to new energy sources before, from wood to coal and from coal to oil. Each shift has brought changes to the geopolitical map of the world. Coal and steam power, for example, were essential pillars of the British Empire in the nineteenth century whereas control over oil production and trade formed the bedrock of American power in the twentieth century. In a similar vein, the from fossil fuels to renewables will create effects that reverberate well beyond the energy sector, and shape the outlook of the twenty-first century world order.

There are at least four reasons to believe that a renewable-powered world will be very different from the fossil fuel powered world as we have known it for the past 150 years. First, fossil fuels are concentrated in specific geographic locations, while renewables are much more dispersed. In fact, renewables (wind, solar, biomass, geothermal, hydro, ocean energy) are available in one form or another in most countries. Second, renewables take the form of infinite flows (of wind, water, sun, and warmth from the Earth's crust) rather than finite stocks of energy, which means they cannot be exhausted and are harder to disrupt. Third, while fossil fuels give way to centralized systems of energy production, renewables can be deployed at almost any scale and lend themselves better to decentralized forms of energy production and consumption. Fourth, the operating costs for fossil fuels are sensitive to underlying changes in fuel prices, which tend to be cyclical. Modern renewables, by contrast, have nearly zero marginal costs, and some of them, like solar and wind, are on technological learning curves (i.e., they enjoy cost reductions of nearly 20 % for every doubling of capacity).

The energy transition is often talked about in the future tense, as something that might or will happen in the next few decades. In reality, the transition is already well underway and even shows signs of accelerating. Over the past 5 years, renewables at a compound annual rate of more than 12.5 % while gas increased at a rate of 2.9 %, both much faster than total energy consumption growth of 1.6 %. By contrast, oil consumption grew more slowly than consumption as a whole (+1.4 %) and coal consumption fell (-0.5 %).

The geopolitical effects of the energy transition will be felt early on. Consider the massive impact coal had on the nineteenth-century world order, and you will be surprised to learn that coal only surpassed wood as the world's primary energy source by around 1900. Similarly, it was not until the 1950s until oil overtook coal as the world's primary energy source. By that time, of course, the two devastating World Wars had underscored the critical importance of petroleum for the security and wealth of nations.

All of this implies that we do not have to wait until the point where renewables overtake fossil fuels in the world's energy mix to see the contours of this new energy order. In fact, many countries are already recalibrating their foreign and strategic policies to the clean energy transition—whether it is the oil kingdoms of the Persian Gulf planning for life beyond oil (e.g., Saudi Arabia's Vision 2030), India's leadership in setting up the International Solar Alliance, China's bid for technology leadership in electric mobility, Japan's search for new energy trading partners to import hydrogen, or the critical materials strategies that all major nations have developed.

The present volume is a particularly welcome exploration of the shifting geopolitics of energy at this time of profound change.

Thijs Van de Graaf

Ghent, Belgium, February 2022

Notes

1 BP, Energy Outlook 2019, p. 107.

2 Ibid.

Acknowledgments

An edited volume is far more than just a product of its editors' imagination. It is a culmination of every contributor's generosity and expertise. We therefore, first and foremost, offer our deepest appreciation to all the authors for not only penning every page that helps this book project to materialize, but more importantly for enlightening and stimulating us intellectually. Indeed, we have all benefitted tremendously through this project.

Also indispensable to an academic project of this nature is the peer review process, and we would therefore like to express particular gratitude to all the reviewers for offering time and expertise to meticulously review every chapter. Without them, this book would not be what it is:

Anton Tugushev, *City University of Hong Kong, Hong Kong*
Flavius Caba-Maria, *Middle East Political and Economic Institute, Romania*
Jamie P. Halsall, *University of Huddersfield, UK*
Jason Lee Carter, *City University of Macau, Macau*
Paulo Duarte, *University of Minho, Portugal*
Pedro Steenhagen, *Getulio Vargas Foundation, Brazil*
Priscilla Roberts, *City University of Macau, Macau*
Richard Ghiasy, *The Hague Centre for Strategic Studies, the Netherlands*
Susann Handke, *Independent Scholar, the Netherlands*
Tom Baxter, *China Dialogue, United Kingdom.*

To City University of Macau, we are grateful for their institutional support, and for providing an encouraging and nurturing environment that allows new ideas and new projects to flourish. In particular, we would like to express our gratitude to the University's project officer, Ms. Yong Qi, for her professionalism, dedication, and unwavering support. She has been instrumental in managing and coordinating between the numerous individuals and organizations involved in the project.

We also wish to express our recognition for the work done by the English proofreader and copy-editor, Professor Gershom Tse. We thank him for his exceptional qualities which have greatly improved the final work, and for always being there for us.

Last but not least, we would like to thank Peter Lang our publisher for supporting and giving impetus to this editorial project from the very first day, and for cheering us on every step of the way. We are also deeply grateful for their contractual flexibility, without which we could not have been able to complete all necessary revisions as a result of the war in Ukraine.

As we acknowledge these friends and colleagues with great pleasure and fondness, we also recognize that a mere page or two of gratitude will not suffice to thank everyone who deserves to be thanked. Nevertheless, for every bit of support and encouragement we have received throughout this project, we offer our heartfelt appreciation and gratitude.

About the Cover Photo

Access to energy is an increasing priority in countries and regions worldwide, particularly those with rising demographic and economic development. Climate change has brought a new level of concern about such energy provision, requiring a comprehensive shift of mentalities and procedures regarding energy production, access, and use.

Highly densified areas and intensive economies face such a paradigm shift in the first degree, with environmental crises forcing governments to act to protect their citizens, in addition to taking care of their natural resources and goods. However, such a shift should be of broad concern to all communities, regardless of potential short-term environmental risks.

The cover photo illustrates a paradigm shift in Faial Island of the Azores archipelago, located on the Atlantic Ocean, despite its pristine environment and low energy consumption.

In Azores, multiple sources of energy are used. Although some of these are traditional energy sources, the use of environmentally friendly energy sources, such as geothermic, solar, and wind, is increasing. Environmental protection also means conserving the landscape and its visual quality. The cover photo also highlights that wind turbines have been built on such landscapes to help them cope with environmental protection concerns in addition to creating new signs and visual paradigms of contemporary societies for the future.

Francisco Ricarte
Macau, November 23, 2021

Introduction: Muse of Fire—Energy, Geopolitics, and Decarbonization

It is the purpose and wish of this manuscript that the collection of research contained among its pages not only shares but also inspires discussions toward intellectual advancement. At the same time, and perhaps more importantly, the authors of this collection have stayed mindful of the possibilities that their depictions and analyses might deviate from reality—this latter point has been particularly pertinent, as during the 20 or so months that this manuscript was being prepared, the world also experienced the outbreak and eventual escalation to global pandemic of COVID-19, in addition to a change in U.S. administration, Brexit and its aftermath, the 2021 United Nations Climate Change Conference (COP26), the energy crisis of late 2021, and the appalling invasion of Ukraine that Russia launched on February 24, 2022. These happenings have all had significant impact on every one of us, especially in terms of energy security, global energy markets, and the global transitions toward greener, more sustainable energy sources. As the aforementioned turmoils continue to unfold, some of the authors have made revisions accordingly, and we have all been reminded of the ever-evolving and ever-dynamic nature of the world that we inhabit. We therefore cannot afford to be complacent about conclusions drawn in the past. This is especially true during uncertain times.

By a similar token, geopolitics no longer has a singular classical view, one that used to stem from an intertwined vision shared by imperial powers, where sovereign states were the only entities of reference. This view, though outdated, retains certain relevance, as it has indeed influenced and steered international relations toward a space-power paradigm where states are perceived as living spaces, and the international order is only expressible in terms of states (Lebensraum). The view did however evolve: during Cold War and post–Cold War geopolitics, even though states continued to be the key subject, other aspects such as bipolarism began to be introduced.

Contemporary geopolitical debates are, on the other hand, driven by critical geopolitics (i.e., spaces of political actions) and further broadened by hybrid or meta-geopolitics. Critical geopolitics encompasses not only uni-, bi-, and multi-polarism, but also a global order comprising multiple actors, as well as the spatial constructions of national identity and political spaces. The visions of critical geopolitics are multidimensional, intertwined, and competitive: geo-economics,[1] transnationalism,[2] globalism[3] and digitalization (Geopolitics 2.0), geopolitics of feminism and gender, as well as energy and sustainability. Hybrid (or meta-) geopolitics, on the other hand, combines traditional views with new multidimensional geopolitical views on space-power relationships, and empires, states, regional realms, cities, outer space, and the cyberspace are all regarded as determinants of state power.

The world today is undergoing varying degrees and scales of transformations on multiple, inter-related, and intertwined fronts: digitalization, social transformations, energy transitions, and climate change as well as the countering responses, etc. Such transformations in turn induce new scientific, technological, and industrial capabilities, heavily influencing the models through which societies are organized and ways that states in the international system will interact with each other. Geopolitics seeks to understand and explain all such development, variables and parameters, conditions, power dynamics, and scenarios by tracking and analyzing them in the context of the international system.

Framed within contemporary geopolitical debates is the geopolitics of energy. Energy, as a fundamental part of the gamut of human experiences, has direct impact on the dynamics, development, and lives in human societies. It is a resource that forms the axes along which economies evolve. In fact, it is "a contributing factor to economic growth," and "has traditionally been a source of international rivalry and conflict" (Mirtchev, 2021, p. 190). Energy therefore plays a deciding role in dictating the power relations among public and private actors across the world and is especially relevant to both sovereign states and actors in the international system. For those sovereign states, energy security is a crucial matter of national concern.

It is up to every state to defend its own national interests. In terms of ensuring energy security, a sovereign state must deploy a combination of energy (re)sources, production, and capabilities, as well as broader regional energy strategies, within the economic and political arenas that it is in and/or has integrated into. Energy security is highly dependent on regional planning, as well as infrastructural, spatial, and network arrangements, as energy production and trade are not only a protracted multi-partner enterprise but also an intertwined spatial cooperation between cities, regions, states, and sovereign neighbors. Regional cross-border cooperations may prove especially important and beneficial for long-term sustainability and productivity.

Energy security is nevertheless more than just a political narrative; it is a multidimensional concept whose meaning has in fact expanded over time. Traditional definitions of energy security used to focus on the stability of energy flows from source to consumer and the dynamics of the energy markets. Contemporarily, on the other hand, energy security can also refer to environmental and other social concerns such as energy poverty. Energy security therefore needs synergetic inter-sectorial visions, ranging from capital flows, flows of ideas and people, to education, technologies, taxation, and international cooperation. It also depends on such human social capital as social skills, technical know-how, innovative abilities, and constructivist education on global governance.

A significant part of contemporary energy security concerns environmental impacts and the sustainability of economic development. The term "sustainable development" was defined in 1987 in a World Commission on Environment and Development report entitled "Our Common Future" (also known as the Brundtland Report) as "development that meets the needs of the present without compromising the ability of future generations to meet their own needs." The concept therefore reconciles economic development with social and environmental balance, and part of sustainable development requires that human societies transition away from their current dependence on fossil fuel energy sources, toward greener, renewable energy sources.

The world's current energy mix sits on two unbalanced trios: The first trio comprises conventional fossil fuels—coal, oil, and natural gas—which together accounts for around 80 % of global energy consumptions; the second trio involves low-carbon energy sources—hydropower, nuclear, and various renewable sources. To rectify the imbalance between the two, we must expand the low-carbon trio and shrink the conventional trio—this is and will be at the core of current and future energy policies and strategies.

For example, hybridizing renewable technologies and resources (e.g., solar and wind power) may be a cost-effective strategy. Not only has solar and wind power's individual reliability increased over time, but hybridizing them can also pave the way for further devising integrated schemes of renewable energy sources. In addition, smart energy management is now at the forefront of technology and can be expected to redefine the energy markets—the coming decades will likely witness the development of smart homes, communities, workplaces, industries, cities, even countries. However, such environmental concerns, sustainability considerations, and innovations as well as related-issues including the transfer and protection of intellectual properties, all add layers of complexity to not only energy geopolitics but geopolitical analysis in general. This is not least because energy transitions require more than mere technological innovations; they do not just span decades, but they are complex processes that need to grapple with issues arising from the increasing decentralization of energy production, the emergence of new energy (re)sources and their management, as well as volatility of the energy markets and any necessary adjustments in response. Further adding to the complexity is that, because societies' departure from fossil fuels will not happen overnight but rather entails a gradual, transitional process, during the interim en route to carbon neutrality, we must not neglect the fact that conventional fossil fuels will still play an important role of protecting the energy markets and consumers from turmoil and major disruptions to energy supply.

Ultimately, to achieve true net-zero carbon, sustainability and environmental concerns need to not only be incorporated into development plans but be given precedence of consideration. Energy transitions will also have a higher chance of success if more urgency can be induced among the next generations. Nonetheless, despite all the obstacles facing energy geopolitics, our collective efforts toward building a carbon-neutral future must not be fazed, as the alternative is not an option: If we fail to act on reducing, and eventually eliminating our dependence on fossil fuels, humankind will face dire consequences.

Energy and geopolitics—the backbone of this volume—will each be difficult to untether from the other. Geopolitics of energy might have traditionally focused on energy security, risks, and underlying threats, as well as issues relating to state sovereignty and inherent strategies. Current energy geopolitics, however, has expanded and now also revolves around energy resources and their utilization on both the local and global levels, as well as any latent complexity in the energy-induced power relations between states, international organizations, NGOs, large multinational companies, and even non-state actors, directly linking not only the general interests of individual states but also the relations, balance, domination, subjection, and cooperation between them. What energy geopolitics attempts to do, essentially, is to resolve energy-related disputes and restore geostrategic balances among actors on the international stage, through analyzing issues relating to energy production, supply, transmission, trade, as well as energy security, dependence, risks, threats, capacities, and impact on the environment.

At the core of such complex geopolitical analysis of the world's energy landscape are not only the direct interests of both regional and global powers, their respective foreign, security, and defense policies, but also global trade and economy, all of which contributing to the challenges facing today's global community. As Ladislaw and Tsafos explain:

> Competition and the struggle for influence are likely to be hallmarks of the global energy landscape for the future but that does not mean shared interests and principles of energy security have disappeared. These are massive technological and geostrategic considerations that the energy security community has not coherently addressed but it must do so sooner rather than later. (2019, p. 8)

In this context, geopolitics will continue to be significantly driven by concerns of energy security, energy geopolitics will tend to orient toward group energy models and systems that cross geographic, political, and social realities and are also interdependent, and interdependence and sustainability will assume an increasingly important position in the decision-making of all levels of the international system. What geopolitics of energy must utilize are premises and vectors that bridge—rather than divide—people(s), progress, and policies, through fair, objective means that resolve, instead of create, problems, and what needs to be developed are essential energy resources and technologies that are not only comprehensive but also complementary of each other.

Current uncertain times and volatility across the world have been compelling us to rethink and reassess our societies and the global community in terms of energy and geopolitics. In particular, the armed conflict in Ukraine has prompted us to reconsider energy security on the national, regional, and global scales: if a positive could be derived out of this horrendous conflict, it would be that it has given us a renewed sense of urgency to take decisive steps to decarbonize the world's economies, to move away from fossil fuel dependence, and to plan and deploy energy strategies toward reducing global greenhouse gas emissions, limiting global warming, and building resilient, sustainable economies. Such energy strategies must be robust but at the same time flexible against changing circumstances, and must therefore comprise two concurrent levels: energy security at the state level, complemented or backed by the regional economic and political integrations of states.

The reevaluation of our energy resources and landscape had in fact started even before the invasion of Ukraine, when a confluence of adverse factors such as the fast post-COVID economic recovery, liberalization of the energy markets, and extreme weather conditions had led to a global energy crisis in late 2021 (European Union Institute for Security Studies, 2022). A sudden imbalance between supply and demand, soaring natural gas and electricity prices in Europe, blackouts in China, and a resurgence of coal demand ensued. This very crisis has highlighted the pressing need to balance each dimension of the oft-discussed energy trilemma—security, affordability, and sustainability.

Since the beginning of the twenty-first century, the world has already taken steps to transition away from fossil fuels, but concerns regarding the sustainability of the planet and threats from environmental degradation have also continued to grow and mount, and, though the current energy horizon embraces new technologies, its contours remain undefined and the paradigms are still uncertain. Such is the reality of the international system, and we attempt to examine its current issues with a "lens of the future," in the hope of offering a better grasp of the challenges ahead.

Transitioning toward cleaner energy and incorporating artificial intelligence will be at the core of the fifth industrial revolution. Given that we have witnessed in recent years tremendous technological development as well as a more electrified, digitalized, and decentralized future energy scenario, it is also quite predictable that geopolitical disputes may grow and the direct interests of both regional and world powers may clash, as all compete and struggle for control of new technologies and domination over other actors. The road toward a sustainable planet will be an obstacle course, full of agents and stakeholders with vested interests. However, we should keep in mind that:

> A failure to appreciate the unintended consequences of various efforts to reach net-zero will not only have security and economic implications; it will also undermine the energy transition itself. If people come to believe that ambitious plans to tackle climate change endanger energy reliability or affordability or the security of energy supplies, the transition will slow. Fossil fuels might eventually fade. The politics—and geopolitics—of energy will not. (Bordoff & O'Sullivan, 2022, p. 69)

In the aftermath of the COVID-19 pandemic, the International Energy Agency released its flagship report "World Energy Outlook 2021," which, though predicting that the emergence of a new global energy economy has already been underway, states that the transformation toward carbon neutrality still has a long way to go:

> In 2020, even while economies bent under the weight of Covid-19 lockdowns, renewable sources of energy such as wind and solar PV continued to grow rapidly, and electric vehicles set new sales records. The new energy economy will be more electrified, efficient, interconnected and clean. Its emergence is the product of a virtuous circle of policy action and technology innovation, and its momentum is now sustained by lower costs. In most markets, solar PV or wind now represents the cheapest available source of new electricity generation. Clean energy technology is becoming a major new area for investment and employment—and a dynamic arena for international collaboration and competition. [...] The rapid but uneven economic recovery from last year's Covid-induced recession is putting major strains on parts of today's energy system, sparking sharp price rises in natural gas, coal and electricity markets. For all the advances being made by renewables and electric mobility, 2021 is seeing a large rebound in coal and oil use. Largely for this reason, it is also seeing the second-largest annual increase in CO_2 emissions in history. (International Energy Agency, 2021, p. 15)

What the world in fact needs is a revitalization of global partnerships in energy governance. Major energy consumers and producers must build trust and advance a new energy paradigm, gathering world leaders such as China, the United States, the European Union, India, Brazil, Russia, Japan, the African Union, as well as regional economic and cooperation communities around the world to form not only partnerships but a global alliance engaged in dialogue over energy sustainability. If they can and are willing to take the lead, other actors will follow suit.

Ultimately, it is imperative that all actors and stakeholders continue to have comprehensive, multidisciplinary discussions—even debate—over energy and geopolitics. This volume has set out to do just that: to induce these discussions, and to collect timely, enlightening chapters that will unveil new, emerging pathways to transform our relationship with energy in the coming decades, as well as their geopolitical implications in light of security and environmental challenges. The authors of these pages may not always be in agreement, but they share a vision to build analytical models that demonstrate the implications of the new challenges in energy, security, and the environment. Several case studies from around the world further illustrate the intricacies of energy transitions at the national level, and the combination of global, regional and other multidisciplinary perspectives on energy transitions provides a valuable context for further discourse.

These topics should be of great interest to all actors of the international system—in particular, states as well as the industrial and energy sectors—as they explain the necessity of adopting far-seeing approaches and methodologies in the face of an ever-changing reality. The ideas, proposals, and scenarios formulated, developed, presented, and referenced throughout these pages, as well as the various experiences and geographies will shed light on the challenges ahead and pathways toward decarbonizing the global economy. To guide the discussions and debates which at once contain both precise and broad ideas, proposals, and concepts, we pose the following question as the structural basis of the book: *How, and to what extent, will the multiple dimensions of the ongoing energy transitions affect existing fundamental geopolitical issues, and what new dynamics may result from the decarbonization process of the planet?*

STRUCTURE OF THE BOOK

This book contains 21 chapters divided into three parts, plus the conclusion. Part I frames the discussions that follow in the next two parts of the book. There are two chapters in Part I. In Chapter 1, Majia Nadesan and Jennifer Keahey make a pathbreaking assessment of current energy policies by drawing comparisons between the roles of resources in international affairs since at least the second half of the nineteenth century, showing how energy extraction in the past has resonated with contemporary geopolitics. In Chapter 2, Cátia Miriam Costa and Ana Teresa Santos combine analysis of scientific discourse with bibliometric data and discuss whether scientific discourse has evolved in response to changes in political discourse on energy and energy geopolitics in the last two decades. This chapter sheds light on the leading producers of scientific discourse, their geographic distribution, and identifies new trends in research topics.

Part II offers a broader understanding on the geopolitical implications of energy transformations by collecting a diverse set of global, regional, and national perspectives. This part contains 13 chapters. In Chapter 3, through analyzing Chinese investments and cooperation mechanisms under the Belt and Road Initiative, Rui Pereira and Carla Fernandes evaluate how the People's Republic of China is contributing to global energy transitions. In Chapter 4, Evgeniia (Jen) Sidorova examines the potential of energy cooperation between China and Russia and between Russia and the EU by comparing the concepts of energopower and biopower that have been created and framed by each of these actors. In Chapter 5, Javad Keypour looks at the impacts of the EU's current decarbonization and political concerns regarding relations with its major natural gas supplier, Russia, and the factors that will shape the direction of EU-Russia gas relations in the coming decades.

The expected move away from Russian energy imports is analyzed by Susann Handke in Chapter 6. The author supports that the quest for independence from Russian energy supplies will be a permanent feature of European energy policies, which in fact corresponds with the principles on which the Energy Union is based. Still in the realms of Russian energy dependence, in Chapter 7 Alexandros-Cătălin Bakos delves into the economic sanctions levied by the United States in connection with the Nord Stream 2 pipeline. Acknowledging the actual context of the Russian invasion of Ukraine, which has put the future operationalization of the pipeline at stake, the author critically analyzes Washington's claims that the imposition of sanctions has had the role of safeguarding Europe's energy security. The principal axes of the United States' energy revolution and economic instruments are pointed out in Chapter 8. Fernanda Delgado, João Victor Marques Cardoso, and Victor Gaspar Filho argue that the Biden administration hopes to establish tools to influence the rest of the world by raising climate ambitions while guaranteeing the stability of the oil and gas markets.

Chapter 9 analyzes the geopolitical impact of the EU's carbon border adjustment mechanism (CBAM) as a normative and regulatory tool to incentivize environmental policy reforms in non-EU countries. In particular, Alaz Munzur, Katharina Koch, and Jennifer Winter look toward how the draft CBAM regulation was received by public and private stakeholders in China, Russia, and Turkey. In Chapter 10, Ana Isabel Xavier explores the security and defense actorness of the European Union and the extent of the institutional narrative of sustainability and resilience adapted to the military field. In Chapter 11, Roberto Álvaro-Hermana, Jorge Fernández-Gómez, Macarena Larrea-Basterra, and

Jaime Menéndez-Sánchez, in a case-study setting, show how the EU's Green Deal is expected to become an effective geopolitical tool to fight climate change in the coming years, facilitating investments in energy infrastructures and cooperation in research and development activities around low-carbon technologies. Jorge Tavares da Silva in Chapter 12 analyzes the effects caused by Chinese investment in the Islamic Republic of Pakistan, a regional geopolitical game-changer who brings structural changes, strategic motivations, and new regional security risks.

The next three chapters of Part II present national case studies on energy transitions, discussing the geopolitical implications as well as the challenges and constraints that energy policies and decision-makers face: in Chapter 13, Venkatesh Dutta and Roopinder Oberoi describe India's major reform of energy systems and the bottlenecks in transition to a low-carbon economy; in Chapter 14, Paulo Zagalo examines the role of Angola, a leading African oil producer, and Mozambique, an emerging gas supplier, in the new global energy trends and their strategies toward decarbonization; in Chapter 15, Gerardo Rabinovich explains the intricacies of the energy transitions in Argentina, taking into consideration the challenges of integration in the Southern Cone of America, and access to technology and financing.

Part III discusses new patterns of policies and drivers that establish pathways for sustainable energy transitions. This part contains six chapters. In Chapter 16, Sara Pugliese reviews bilateral trade and association agreement, macro-regional, and multilateral agreements, and assesses whether the EU is assuming a leadership role in drawing up effective international energy regulation. Chapter 17 scrutinizes the main policy and legal prerequisites of the hydrogen economy in the European Union. The authors Javad Keypour, Tanel Kerikmäe, and Archil Chochia meticulously demonstrate that to achieve the EU's hydrogen goals requires critical policymaking that facilitates investment and removes barriers pertaining to hydrogen storage and transportation. In Chapter 18, Gianmatteo Sabatino explores how the evolution of a legal framework for the development of circular economy has shaped new legal structures in both public and private law, with special emphasis on the analysis of the European Union and the Chinese context. In Chapter 19, Gabriela Benatti, Antônio Buainain, Marcelo Pereira da Cunha, and Pedro Cavalcante Filho reflect upon the institutional dynamics and results of Brazil's National Program for the Production and Use of Biofuels, launched in 2004 as part of the Brazilian government's strategy to foster bioenergy production while promoting regional development. In Chapter 20, Dipta Majumder and Ferdous Rahman discuss the policy-level readiness of Bangladesh to promote renewable energy and the challenges facing its implementation. In Chapter 21, Lisha Fu, Nicole Minfui Chong, and Faustina Fu Yip use Russia as a case study to investigate Generation Z's evolving attitude toward the environment. In particular, this chapter examines how the incorporation and use of technology in education has allowed this cohort to become instigators of social innovations, especially in response to environmental changes.

Finally, in Conclusion, the editors frame the changing paradigms of energy geopolitics in the broader picture of a world in change, offer some concluding remarks, as well as suggest new questions for future research. Indeed, this book has not ended the debate around the new geopolitical ramifications resulting from the ongoing energy transitions and the decarbonization of the planet. The editors are fully aware that the book's scope and depth of analysis can only be limited at best, and, more importantly, energy geopolitics will continue to induce and invite tremendous public interest, concern, and discussions. New volumes on this topic must include the challenges of global energy governance in a multipolar world, the new interdependencies arising from global energy transformations and major infrastructure development programs, as well as the role of energy diplomacy in a time of transitions. In addition, the horrific events unfolding in the sovereign state of Ukraine, appalled by the violent scenes of an armed conflict, will push for more invigorated efforts for global energy transformations whose future extent we cannot possibly ascertain in full at present.

To reduce the possibility of bias in our academic discussion, the editors have gathered the works of 38 authors from 19 different nationalities, 19 male and 19 female, representing 22 institutions across four continents. Of the 21 chapters presented in Parts I, II and III, 10 are single-authored and 11 are offered in co-authorship. Moreover, every chapter in this Peter Lang research project was fully peer reviewed by not only the editors but also a number of identified external qualified reviewers. Furthermore, the views, ideas, and opinions expressed in this manuscript are attributable to their respective authors but not their professional affiliations or any other organizations, and should therefore be understood as purely academic information.

One last note: the editors would like to express their heartfelt appreciation to all of the authors, who generously gave their time and shared their knowledge to this collective endeavor, in particular during such challenging times that we have found ourselves in, as everyone's personal and professional lives have been deeply, irreversibly affected, in more ways than one.

September 2022
The Editors
João Simões
Francisco José Leandro
Eduardo Caetano de Sousa
Roopinder Oberoi

NOTES

1 "[A] new geopolitical order dominated by geo-economic questions and issues, a world where the globalization of economic activity and global flows of trade, investment, commodities and images are re-making states, sovereignty and the geographical structure of the planet" (Ó Tuathail et al., 1998, p. 2).

2 "[T]he "new geopolitics" describes a world dominated no longer by territorial struggles between competing blocs but by emerging transnational problems like terrorism, nuclear proliferation and clashing civilizations" (Ó Tuathail et al., 1998, p. 2).

3 The planet earth "is more important than ever as states and peoples struggle to deal with environmental degradation, resource depletion, transnational pollution and global warming. For the environmentally minded intellectual and policy maker, the "new geopolitics" is not geoeconomics but ecological politics or ecopolitics" (Ó Tuathail et al., 1998, p. 2).

REFERENCES

Bordoff, J., & O'Sullivan, M. (2022). Green upheaval: The new geopolitics of energy. *Foreign Affairs*. https://www.foreignaffairs.com/articles/world/2021-11-30/geopolitics-energy-green-upheaval

European Union Institute for Security Studies. (2022). *Europe's energy crisis conundrum: Origins, impacts and way forward*. Publications Office. https://doi.org/10.2815/262906

International Energy Agency. (2021). *World Energy Outlook 2021*.

Ladislaw, S., & Tsafos, N. (2019, September 13). *Energy spheres of influence*. Center for Strategic and International Studies. https://www.csis.org/analysis/energy-spheres-influence

Mirtchev, A. (2021). *The Prologue: The alternative energy megatrend in the age of great power competition*. Post Hill Press.

Ó Tuathail, G., Dalby, S., & Routledge, P. (Eds.). (1998). *The geopolitics reader*. Routledge.

PART 1

CHAPTER 1

Energy Neomercantilism and Regenerative Alternatives

MAJIA NADESAN AND JENNIFER KEAHEY

INTRODUCTION

Over human history, energy access and control have shaped the conditions of everyday life, from early dependence upon solar beneficence to the captured energy from steam and coal that fueled the industrial revolution. As a vital force, energy has the potential to nurture as well as destroy life. For example, coal enabled the industrial revolution but wrought unprecedented atmospheric perils for populations, as illustrated by nineteenth-century London's toxic fogs. More recently, cheap oil underpinned industrial expansion in the twentieth century, enabling mass production and market expansion, but within a global system characterized by non-equitable extractive relationships among and within nations. Nuclear often is heralded as a renewable energy source, but the Chernobyl nuclear disaster in 1986 and the Fukushima disaster of 2011 illustrate its capacities for catastrophic failures. All energy systems present trade-offs—for example, renewables such as solar and wind energy rely on limited mineral resources that are highly polluting when refined—but there exists a growing gap between a failing status quo and the technological possibilities for improving the conditions of life for humanity.

Many people lack access to basic energy while many others rely on aging energy infrastructures that are vulnerable to catastrophic risks (see Nadesan, 2016). While technological innovations open scope for improving reliable access, authentic institutional commitments to access, health and safety are needed. Energy policy would ideally be organized around long-term social and ecological sustainability goals that are grounded in community needs and aspirations, rather than being summarily imposed by detached and remote decision-makers. Democratic inputs by multiple stakeholders regarding sustainable energy objectives and the means for achieving them under local conditions are key for building resilient and sustainable systems. However, this nominal model of energy democracy confronts serious institutional constraints, including the challenges of incorporating citizen input and competing national energy priorities. Of particular concern is the geopolitical risk posed by a zero-sum energy paradigm described here as "state neomercantilism." Subsequent to the market collapse in 2008, the world system began shifting from a neoliberal to a neomercantilist formation, with powerful nations like Russia, China, and the United States "vying for political influence and control over natural resources" (Ziegler & Menon, 2014, p. 17). The geopolitical risk posed by this zero-sum paradigm is contributing to energy poverty and political instability at a time when climate change threatens human survival.

In this chapter, we identify regenerative energy movements that offer meaningful alternatives to the destructive status quo. Examining the intersection of renewable energy and energy democracy with Green Economy and Earth Charter principles, we identify a "regenerative" logic for improving energy access and reducing risks. Although there is no doubt that population and resource pressures are driving forces for zero-sum interactions, we find that the greatest barrier to social transformation derives from the "*forms* of thinking and doing" that frame decision-making and ground institutional policies and expectations. Therefore, we begin the chapter by unpacking the logic of energy neomercantilism.

The following section focuses on the historicized animation of energy extraction in late nineteenth-century neomercantilism, whose strategic deployments resonate with contemporary geopolitics. In rhythm with the imperial past, neomercantilism is prompting new global alliances, with competing nations and their privileged corporations engaged in a struggle to control territory and coveted resources. According to Ziegler and Menon (2014, p. 20) this "twenty-first century Great Game" resembles the nineteenth-century struggle for influence between Britain and Russia. If the iconic representation for the paradigm of neomercantilism is the chess board, memorialized in Zbigniew Brzezinski's (1998) book on the subject, our analysis illustrates how this paradigm plays out on the gameboard of *Risk*, where players deploy army units to secure imperial power. In short, we show that the extractive and calculative logic of energy neomercantilism (re)produces energy assemblages that are prone to catastrophic failures.

DISCUSSION: EXTRACTION AND THE COLLAPSE OF NEOLIBERALISM

Extraction, or the process of removing something, especially by force, according to the Cambridge Dictionary, has undergirded global capitalism since its emergence. Extraction is encoded within social relations of production, or more specifically, the rationally detached logic of resource utilization that inscribe economic formulations of labor as *surplus value*. Although extraction relationally organizes people and non-human materialities under the logical rubric of capitalism, the specific forms whereby extraction is thought and enacted are historically variable and not limited to this particular economic system. While it applies more generally to human societies, extraction can be considered a bio-social logic that produces deeply hierarchical and invasive social ecologies. Linked to the expansion of civilizations, extractive social ecologies produce destructive energies that seed their own demise, for as Jared Diamond evocatively describes in the book *Collapse: How Societies Choose to Fail or Succeed* (2011), extractive social ecologies destroy biodiversity, making them prone to collapse. Extractive societies may rapidly grow, but in so doing, they inevitably confront resource depletion and internal strife, largely resulting from entrenched social inequalities.

Extractive civilizations respond to resource pressures by innovating technology and securing new territory through warfare. Within the empires of the ancient world system, food, energy, and water were particularly powerful drivers of conflict; within the modern-colonial world system of the early twentieth century, food, energy, and water contributed significantly to the militarist insurgence of both world wars; and in the present geopolitical milieu of resource depletion and global climate change, food, water, and energy lie at the heart of neomercantilist resurgence.

Conflict over energy was particularly pervasive across the twentieth century. Historic parallels between our own circumstances in the early 2020s and those prevailing in the late 1800s are instructive. Empowered by wealth extracted from the slave-based sugar, cotton, coal and oil economies of the eighteenth and nineteenth centuries, turn-of-the-twentieth-century industrialists began perceiving a finite geopolitical terrain. Accordingly, the political and economic world system shifted to a governance logic described as "neomercantile" or economic nationalist in formation (Palmer & Colton, 1984, p. 605). The three key features of neomercantilism are: (1) international rivalry; (2) capital accumulation; and (3) capital investment (Fay, 1966, pp. 44–45). If capital exacerbated rivalries among imperial European states and their emerging nationalist corporations one century ago, it also resulted in a state of constant warfare and cyclical destruction.

Early twentieth-century energy neomercantilism violated the liberal market pact of the preceding century. While publicly repudiating the free trade policies that had enabled its consolidation of power, nationalist capital worked to undermine the more populist and progressive values of the European Enlightenment, including the democratic concepts of national sovereignty and community and individual self-determination (Foster et al., 2010). This shift was inexplicably connected to the surge of fossil fuel technologies, which reshaped imperial warfare along modern lines resulting in the mass devastation of two World Wars in a span of less than 30 years. After World War II, allied forces assembled a post-war order that sought to learn from the past by pursuing a state-led model of economic modernization in accordance with the logic of mid-century Keynesian economics (Terra et al., 2021).

Regulated capital and state investment promised democratization and enhanced global connection. However, these reforms failed to consider critiques to the dominant western philosophy of modernization; namely, its continued reliance upon a colonial-mercantilist logic. Indeed, this era of state-led public growth relied upon techno-rational systems of control that detached functionaries from their actions, serving to reinforce "geographies of extraction" and power, especially with respect to energy resources (Sassen, n.d.). It should perhaps come as no surprise that labor became stripped of its hard-won influence during the latter half of the twentieth century (e.g., see Saez et al., 2016), when a generation of neoliberal economists within the International Monetary Fund (IMF) and the World Bank (WB) laid the groundwork for the resurgence of a neoliberal capitalist world order dominated by Anglo-American interests.

By the 1980s, economic stagnation and rising energy prices prompted regulatory reforms aimed at unleashing capital and the global flows of resources. Neoliberalism represented a return to a laissez-faire market logic, cloaking a seemingly liberal, yet deeply extractive, colonial world system. Prioritizing economic growth above all else, neoliberalism reshaped the political ethos in Great Britain and the United States, first through the Thatcher-Reagan alliance then continued through the Blair-Clinton alliance of the 1990s (Tooze, 2018). The collapse of the Soviet Union in 1991 brought an end to Cold War divisions, unleashing a wave of free-market triumphalism that further halted progress in relation to labor rights and social welfare. Brokering free trade agreements, neoliberal forces lifted regulatory constraints that had held post–WWII capital in check. In a similar vein as the Industrial Revolution of the nineteenth century, the Telecommunications Revolution of the late twentieth century enabled capital to develop global trade networks that extracted wealth through increasingly ephemeral financial instruments.

As case in point, early twenty-first-century markets deployed exchange trade funds (ETFs) to ease speculation on future contracts and reduce financial risk for investors. In practice, however, ETFs exacerbated speculative-driven demand, creating bubbles in energy and other key market commodities, as illustrated by the 2008–2009 "food bubble" that impoverished millions of people when investors fled the housing-backed securities thronging commodity markets (Kaufman, 2010). Newly industrializing nations were particularly vulnerable to commodity bubbles, given their semi-peripheral position in the world system. Situated as the central pivot of a highly unequal global economy, these nations both bought raw goods from impoverished peripheral societies and sold manufactured goods to the wealthy core, making them most susceptible to plunging commodity prices. In 2015, when core nations were recovering from the Great Recession of 2008, commodity deflation in coal, oil, and minerals caused economic havoc in the semi-peripheral sphere, devaluing currencies in Indonesia, Brazil, South Africa, Kazakhstan, Vietnam, and Turkey, among other nations (Ostroukh et al., 2015). After 50 years of neoliberal globalization, neomercantilist retrenchment is again occurring. Not only did the contradictions wrought by neoliberal extractive circulations result in the 2008–2009 housing market collapse, but the hollowing out of the global middle-class has fed an emotional economy of resentment, engendering a resurgence in fascist movements and a return to authoritarian politics. The rejection of neoliberalism may have begun as a populist response to the consolidated power of global capital; however, as in the early twentieth century, capital has responded to this challenge by undermining democratic progress. If capital has benefitted from the rise of "strongman" politicians who deflect attention from corporate malfeasance by stirring up xenophobic and racist sentiments, the COVID-19 pandemic has super-charged capitalist accumulation. In the United States, billionaires increased their wealth by nearly two-thirds, with Elon Musk alone increasing his empire by nearly $300 billion (U.S.) dollars over the course of the pandemic (Peterson-Withorn, 2021).

Contemporary neomercantilism may operate in accordance with the imperialist logic of the late nineteenth century, but this time around, the stakes are even higher. According to Michael Klare (2018), the imperial race to seize endless frontiers have been replaced by a neo-imperial "race for what's left." Upon the twenty-first-century horizon looms the perfect storm of the Anthropocene, with climate change, resource depletion, population pressure, engendering unprecedented risks to human and interspecies survival. Klare argues that this race has produced a "new global tinderbox" characterized by an accelerating arms race that blurs old distinctions between war and peace as battles are fought using trade wars, cyberattacks and other non-traditional means. Within the energy sector, emergent neomercantilism has further empowered a centralized and profit-seeking energy sector closely aligned with powerful financial firms that once claimed to speak for the public good but whose largesse is primarily enjoyed by global elites (Slater, 2015).

The renewed economic concentration of wealth in the contemporary era has sparked interest in C. Wright Mills' (1956) argument for the existence of power elites. Billionaire wealth gains under the pandemic are the latest iteration of a decades-long pattern of economic consolidation; indeed, the World Inequality Report indicates that the top one percent of the global population captured 27 % of growth in wealth between 1980 and 2016 (Alvaredo et al., 2018). Vitali and colleagues (2011) offer critical insight into this consolidation of power, with their analysis revealing a core group of 1,318 corporations who now own the 43,000 largest corporations in the world. A "super entity" of 147 corporations, mainly in finance, have secured interconnected ownership across firms, meaning that less than one percent of the world's corporations have captured 40 % of the entire network.

Henry Farrell and Abraham L. Newman (2019, p. 44) argue that the forces of neoliberal globalization transformed the regulated capital economy of the mid-twentieth century, by "moving the action away from multilateral interstate negotiations and toward networks of private actors." They contend that global economic networks engender state coercion and therefore have significant security consequences. Through their research, these authors demonstrate how the "topography of the economic networks of interdependence intersects with domestic institutions and norms to shape coercive authority," with special emphasis on financial interest, communications, supply chains, and the internet (p. 44). In the current neomercantilist context, the centralization of finance and decision-making power has engendered a collusion of state and corporate interests, as policymakers replace the neoliberal ethos of "governing from a distance" with more consolidated forms of "sovereign" power that enable authoritarian leaders to maximize executive, legislative, and juridical control. Endless "crises" add urgency to the institutional and cultural trajectories supporting the centralization of power, especially through technocratic and hyper-rationalized mechanisms of crisis management. New surveillance and information-management tools stand ready to assist authoritarian efforts to re-establish direct surveillance and control over far-flung resources and populations in crisis.

The power and influence levied by financial and energy firms is facilitated by powerful state conceptions of national security. By narrowly defining security in terms of institutional preservation, these states effectively ignore catastrophic risks posed by key operations. This logic of security encourages states to invest in risky "innovative" technologies. As described by the sociologist Ulrich Beck and cited in Jeffries (2006), decision-makers claim a rational calculus of control over hazards, yet engender instability and irrationality in practice by failing to acknowledge the complexities institutionalized risk has created, rendering "a situation where normal instruments of calculating, anticipating and colonising the future don't work anymore." In a 2011 interview with *The Asahi Shimbun* news in Japan, Beck described the governance of nuclear risk as a "system of organized irresponsibility" where no entity assumes responsibility for catastrophic consequences (cited in Ohno, 2011). Not only are known hazards ignored by both industry and government, but in cases where ignorance is impossible, technocratic systems largely perform a facade of governance by producing weak risk-management plans that fail to foresee destructive outcomes.

These moves are undermining socio-legal systems designed to protect public interests. The recent U.S. case of Pacific Gas & Electric (PG&E) illustrates the corruption of democracy in the wake of catastrophic energy governance failures. In 2020, this California-based IOU, pleaded guilty to involuntary manslaughter after a 2018 blaze ignited by its long-neglected electrical grid killed 84 and displaced thousands more (Blunt & Gold, 2019). In the months following the disaster, state governor, Gavin Newsom protected PG&E from consequence by signing legislation that would protect the firm's financial interests. While an independent auditor found that the firm had known that its grid was unsafe, but purposively placed bonuses and profits above safety, PG&E was not held accountable for its actions (Kelly, 2017). When the court went to trial, the presiding judge helped PG&E time its bankruptcy to receive relief funds that the federal U.S. government had designated to assist the victims of the fire (Penn & Eavis, 2020). As PG&E prepared for bankruptcy, its CEO walked away with a 2.5-million-dollar severance package.

The most visible alternative to the western oil complex comes from state-owned energy enterprises that were largely, although not exclusively, institutionalized as anti-colonial enterprises in the twentieth century. Unfortunately, these state enterprises often simply re-inscribe the hierarchical and rationalized governing logics of imperial Europe, over time becoming behemoths that reproduce colonialism in practice. Naná de Graaff's (2011) study of the expansion and integration of national oil companies between 1997 and 2007 found increased integration of corporate relations between state-owned and private energy companies, in large part due to a process of transnationalization. Defined as an increase in transactions across national borders that involve at least one non-state actor, transnationalization has resulted in increased integration of the national oil companies into the global energy market. This shift has been made possible through their interdependencies with privately owned companies and their increased involvement in financial markets.

In the current context of energy neomercantilism, state-owned enterprises both collaborate and compete with private energy corporations across many energy sectors. With China's Sinopec (n.d.), we see the type of hybridization that can occur as state enterprises sell off their equity to private investors. Despite their control over substantial oil supplies, state enterprises do not control global commodity markets, and still must operate within a global financial system mediated primarily by the U.S. dollar. Efforts to conduct oil sales in national currencies are underway and may somewhat erode U.S. hegemony, but replacing one system of centralized and extractive control for another neither promises ecological improvements, nor the pursuit of self-governance and happiness.

Whether neoliberal or neomercantile in formation, the global economy relies upon an extractive logic that assumes limitless horizons for conquest and expansion. In concert with the freewheeling colonial markets and reactionary empires of the eighteenth and nineteenth centuries, twentieth- and twenty-first-century economies have adopted neoliberal globalization and neomercantile exploitation. The short-lived Keynesian experiment of the mid-twentieth century did not profoundly differ from what had come before, for it simply sought to regulate capitalism rather than transform its extractive logic of top-down organization, centralized control, and rationalized management. Indeed, the Keynesian world system of the post–WWII era espoused a universal and linear approach to economic modernization, with First World capitalists and Second World Soviets cold warring in a race to impose their vision of a singular political economy upon a socially and culturally diverse Third World (Foster at al., 2010).

In the following section, we explore regenerative alternatives to the warring impulses of extractivism. We begin with coverage of two global movements that have articulated regenerative principles in an effort to guide transitions to sustainability: the Green Economy Coalition and the Earth Charter. Next, we examine efforts to enact renewable energy and energy democracy in practice. As we discuss, alternative energy initiatives are falling short in terms of meeting regenerative principles. Nevertheless, a growing array of socially just and environmentally sustainable energy movements are challenging business-as-usual. By replacing the extractive logic of universality with the regenerative logic of pluriversality, diverse energy ecologies may yet change the paradigm of energy geopolitics.

In 1992, the world's leaders assembled at the Rio Earth Summit to discuss strategies for enacting transitions to sustainability, in accordance with the Brundtland Report, *Our Common Future* (WCED, 1987). Published by the World Commission on Environment and Development, this report concluded with a call for a global charter that would establish norms for sustainable development. At the time of the Rio Summit, the global economy was in the thrust of a neoliberal revolution, dually fueled by Anglo-American politics and the collapse of the Soviet Union. However, it also was a unique moment of global openness, with former enemies coming together to establish peace. In this vein, Mikhail Gorbachev arrived in Rio with a vision for establishing the foundations for peaceful, globally just, and sustainable future.

In *Manifesto for the Earth* (2006) Gorbachev explains his rationale for guiding the Soviet Union toward social and environmental reform. As a child growing up in a region of Russia "that had witnessed countless invasions," Gorbachev grew up in desperate poverty, experiencing a famine in 1933 that had been unleashed by Stalin through the collectivization of farms and destruction of peasant life (p. 9). Approximately half the people in his village starved to death, including three family members. Not only did subsequent Stalinist purges target his grandfathers, but his father was sent to the war front when Hitler invaded the Soviet Union. It is perhaps no surprise that Gorbachev turned to nature for solace, and as an ardent environmentalist, he had come into power in 1985 with the intention to heal his nation. Two scant years into his administration, the Chernobyl disaster occurred, urging Gorbachev to deepen his commitment to environmental conservation. Having achieved the impossible goal of bringing an end to the Cold War, Gorbachev entered Rio with a vision for peace, social justice, and sustainability. While the Summit failed to arrive at meaningful consensus, he later worked with Maurice Strong, the Secretary General of the Rio Summit, to bring their environmental organizations together on this project (Earth Charter, n.d.). In 1997, an Earth Charter Commission formed, bringing radical activists, religious leaders, and scholars from around the world together on a consensus building project to construct intercultural values around global sustainability.

The Commission published the Earth Charter in 2000. Perhaps the only global document to have been constructed with the active input of marginalized peoples from every world region, the Charter preamble emphasizes the import of unity in diversity, stating:

> We stand at a critical moment in Earth's history, a time when humanity must choose its future. As the world becomes increasingly interdependent and fragile, the future at once holds great peril and great promise. To move forward we must recognize that in the midst of a magnificent diversity of cultures and life forms we are one human family and one Earth community with a common destiny. We must join together to bring forth a sustainable global society founded on respect for nature, universal human rights, economic justice, and a culture of peace. Towards this end, it is imperative that we, the peoples of Earth, declare our responsibility to one another, to the greater community of life, and to future generations. (p. 1)

The Earth Charter's 16 principles are grouped under four interdependent values, namely:

- Respect and care for the community of life
  1. Respect Earth and life in all its diversity.
  2. Care for the community of life with understanding, compassion, and love.
  3. Build democratic societies that are just, participatory, sustainable, and peaceful.
  4. Secure Earth's bounty and beauty for present and future generations.

- Ecological integrity
  5. Protect and restore the integrity of Earth's ecological systems...
  6. Prevent harm...when knowledge is limited, apply a precautionary approach.
  7. Adopt patterns of production...that safeguard Earth's regenerative capacities ...
  8. Advance the study of ecological sustainability and promote open exchange...
- Social and economic justice
  9. Eradicate poverty as an ethical, social, and environmental imperative.
  10. Ensure that economic activities and institutions at all levels promote human development in an equitable and sustainable manner.
  11. Affirm gender equality and equity as prerequisites...
  12. Uphold the right of all, without discrimination, to a natural and social environment...attention to the rights of indigenous peoples and minorities.
- Democracy nonviolence, and peace
  13. Strengthen democratic institutions at all levels...
  14. Integrate into formal education...[sustainable] knowledge, values, and skills...
  15. Treat all living beings with respect and consideration.
  16. Promote a culture of tolerance, nonviolence, and peace.

Under the Earth Charter principle 7, the document goes onto consider the role of energy, stating the need "act with constraint and efficiency when using energy and rely increasingly on renewable energy sources such as solar and wind" (p. 2). Rather than centering economic growth, the Charter emphasizes democratic institutions and "the equitable distribution of wealth within and among nations" (p. 3). In short, the Earth Charter moves beyond the extractive logic of capital to embrace a regenerative logic of unity in diversity, achieved through an awareness of the fragile interdependence of all life.

The Green Economy Coalition (GEC, 2020) is another global coalition that comprises more than 50 organizations from every world region, ranging from non-profit and non-governmental organizations to green businesses and sustainability research institutes. It emerged in the 2008 when the United Nations Education Program (UNEP) promoted the development of a global economy based upon a Green New Deal. According to Levidow (2018) the "UNEP soon abandoned its early vision, instead favouring market instruments and public-private partnerships" (p. 199). However, in the wake of the global recession, it subsequently returned to the concept of a global Green New Deal when preparing for the RIO+20 summit in 2012. In a review of the GEC's principles, Levidow argues that its agenda both overlaps with the socialist proposals made by the World Social Forum and the capitalist proposals made by the OECD, in part by relying on the development of efficient technologies capable of reconciling conflicting capitalist and socialist approaches. Although its inconsistencies have caused skeptics to raise concerns regarding the GEC's tendency to oversimplify challenges by maintaining an assumption of limitless renewable horizons, the director of the coalition nevertheless recognizes that economic growth must be rooted in core values upheld by authentic institutions in order to prevent green economies from becoming corrupted by greed. In this vein, the GEC (2020) offers five essential principles of an imagined green economy:

1. The Well-being Principle: A green economy enables all people to create and enjoy prosperity.
2. The Justice Principle: The green economy promotes equity within and between generations.
3. The Planetary Boundaries Principle: The green economy safeguards, restores and invests in nature.
4. The Efficiency and Sufficiency Principle: The green economy is geared to support sustainable consumption and production.
5. The Good Governance Principle: The green economy is guided by integrated, accountable and resilient institutions.

Given the overlap between capitalist and socialist ideals and potential for irreconcilable disputes among stakeholders who may interpret green economy in profoundly different ways, the principle of good governance is essential for their equitable adjudication. Thus, a deeper reading of this principle is illustrative:

- An inclusive green economy is evidence-based—its norms and institutions are interdisciplinary, deploying both sound science and economics along with local knowledge for adaptive strategy.
- It is supported by institutions that are integrated, collaborative and coherent—horizontally across sectors and vertically across governance levels—and with adequate capacity to meet their respective roles in effective, efficient and accountable ways.
- It requires public participation, prior informed consent, transparency, social dialogue, democratic accountability, and freedom from vested interests in all institutions—public, private and civil society—so that enlightened leadership is complemented by societal demand.
- It promotes devolved decision-making for local economies and management of natural systems while maintaining strong common, centralized standards, procedures, and compliance systems.

- It builds a financial system with the purpose of delivering well-being and sustainability, set up in ways that safely serve the interests of society.

Although less forceful than the Earth Charter in its rejection of extractive logic, these imaginings nevertheless posit energy as multidimensional, with Russell and colleagues (2011) arguing that the GEC affords both physical and social power (Russell et al., 2011). Indeed, the normative concept of "energy democracy" arises from this convergence of physical and social power. Given the moral and philosophical scaffolding provided by these two green movements, a critical question arises: what are the possibilities for actualizing these regenerative values in practice? It is to this subject that we now turn.

To begin, it does appear that the energy sector is pivoting, however incrementally, to renewable energy. In 2019, renewables were estimated to account for approximately 26 % of global electricity generation (Matthews et al., 2021). Projected energy supply is anticipated to fall short of demand, exacerbating energy challenges including "affordability, energy security and reducing emissions," according to OPEC's Secretary General, Mohammed Barkindo (cited in Matthews et al., 2021, p. A8). At the same time, demand for oil, coal and natural gas skyrocketed worldwide in late 2021 as these energy sources remain integral to critical infrastructures (IEA, 2021). Thus, efforts to green electricity grids while also shifting to electric vehicles could very well result in worldwide energy shortages if states continue to fall short in providing the substantial support needed for renewable transitions. Currently, financial investments in renewable energy are severely lagging, with expenditures needing to grow from the global $1.1 trillion in 2021 to $3.4 trillion annually through 2030 (Matthews et al., 2021, p. A8). Yet, the semi-peripheral nations of the Global South, upon which the world economic system pivots, lack the funds for necessary investment, a point made by South African environment minister Barbara Creecy's $750 billion climate bill to support renewable transitions (Dalton, 2021). This evidence suggests that the market is a grossly insufficient stopgap for funding the necessary investments in renewables, despite its claims to the contrary. Moreover, regenerative investments are not merely a matter of finance for renewable technologies, for transitions to sustainability hinge on developing democratic and socially just supply and utilization networks.

The regenerative logic embedded in the Earth Charter and GEC remind us that there also is an urgent need to revisit the socio-ecological relations of production, distribution, and consumption. While sustainable models for finance generation do exist, the question is whether these can work at scale. For example, the public banking model provides a framework for generating the credit necessary to finance energy transitions. Public banking emphasizes fiscal stimulus rather than monetary policy as the primary mechanism for injecting credit into the economy (see Brown, 2013). Whereas monetary policy entails government transfers of credit to powerful banking systems, fiscal policy entails direct investment in public infrastructure, such as roads, dams, and public schools. In the U.S., a "New Deal" type of fiscal stimulus program has been proposed as a path toward a green energy transition in the form of the "Green New Deal." However, state-led infrastructural investments historically have been heavy-handed and costly, making it unclear whether a Green New Deal is ecologically and socially viable in the absence of local consultations and considerations.

National and international funding programs are required for funding sustainable energy innovations and transitions, but if there is to be any hope to establish unity in diversity, decision-making about research priorities and energy policy must be highly localized and participative. Ideally, regenerative fiscal investments would operate as a multilayered grant program, targeting (1) risk assessments of current energy infrastructures and options; (2) research redressing resource and technological constraints, such as those posed by energy storage; (3) community-led energy-infrastructural development; and (3) community-embedded social-cultural initiatives aimed at promoting just and democratic transitions. Therefore, regenerative fiscal investments must be simultaneously supported by fiscal stimulus and grounded in the needs and local contingencies of communities, rather than being conceived and implemented from afar.

Despite rising commodity prices, the cost to build and operate large-scale wind and solar plants are now less than coal or gas-fired power plants in nearly half of the world, according to a current financial analysis (Mathis, 2021). Even with these efficiencies, renewables face considerable sustainability challenges that cannot be easily solved with public banking. In particular, technological challenges derive from basic resource limits and from the unreflexive conflation of renewables and sustainability. Currently, global supply chains for mining rare-earths are adopting what has been described as "byproduct economies" whereby the mining costs are covered by other operations, as illustrated by the case of Baotou Steel (Hui, 2021). This Chinese state-owned iron and steel operation produces byproducts that contain rare-earths, which it then passes on to subsidiaries such as China Northern Rare Earth. The U.S. and European approaches also rely increasingly on byproduct economies. While the integration of layering ventures in byproduct economies enable efficiencies of scale, these can impinge against the sustainability of renewables, as they are fundamentally anchored in extractive assemblages whose operations are not adequately attuned to social-ecological considerations, including basic resource constraints. Young et al. (2021) argue that supplies of the raw materials for battery inputs, such as lithium, nickel, cobalt, manganese and graphite, is less than one-third of demand expected by 2030. In 2021, prices for lithium carbonate, one of two key compounds used in battery production, more than doubled in price, costing in U.S. dollars $14,386 a metric ton in August, up from $6,124 in December (Wilmot, 2021). Likewise, the promise of green hydrogen as a means of decarbonizing heavy industry also faces basic resource limits, such as the need for platinum required for the cathodes in electrolyzers (Young et al., 2021). Assuming a green capitalist perspective, these authors recommend for renewables a "portfolio of strategic and tactical responses" including securing supply through building resiliency in supply chains, especially through long-term contracts, owning supply chain origins, promoting innovation, broadening and seeding markets, and acting collectively. However, the emphases that these authors place on "extracting value" and "arbitraging options" are precisely grounded in the neomercantile extractive logic this chapter rejects.

In important respects, the race for rare-earth resources echoes early twentieth-century efforts to secure oil in the mad scramble that culminated in WWI. China plans on building one of the world's largest rare-earth companies, the China Rare-Earth Group to be based in Jiangxi province, while the U.S. is relying on an agreement with Australia's Lynas Rare Earths Ltd. for these resources (Zhai, 2021). The strategic importance afforded these resources belies green capitalist claims of limitless horizons. Moreover, development of sustainable supply chains requires long-term commitment to sustainable partnerships up and down supply chains, and this cannot occur if energy networks continue to value extraction and geopolitical arbitrage above sustainable community practices.

Regenerative alternatives must simultaneously confront the challenge of resource limits and the mandate of sustainable community relationships and democratic practices. Mining is historically and industry prone to externalizing although frameworks of corporate responsibility in contemporary mining operations often involve increased community input and considerations of environmental stewardship. Yet, too often the inherently extractive commodity chains behind "renewables" are ignored. Responsible and community-involved stewardship of mineral resources necessary is critical for sustainable renewable technologies.

Local involvement should also be mandated in energy transition planning. The contingencies of energy ownership, mix, and distribution preclude a single best solution, but there are clear "sustainability" benefits for creating energy systems that are inclusive and adaptable. Energy planning from this regenerative alternative therefore requires some localization of decision-making about energy futures, but also extensive state investment. Patricia Mann (2016) argues optimistically that a new global movement could be founded on green energy microproduction, an energy Internet for sharing on postcapitalist grids, and efforts to generate more sustainable community relationships and practices.

Kacper Szulecki explains that energy democracy needs to be seen in terms of "the demand for increased accountability and democratization of a sector that was previously not seen as requiring public involvement, and was (is) most often depoliticized" (Szulecki, 2018, p. 27). Szulecki draws on Rosanvallon's "democracy of proximity" (2011, p. 171), which posits forms of direct engagement as necessary for combatting detached and technocratic energy governance. At the very least, engagement can be fostered by legislating policies or otherwise enacting protocols that require transparent and inclusive risks assessments of entire supply chain impacts on ecologies and communities. While this framework acknowledges inevitable conflicts of interests, it emphasizes authentic stakeholder involvement and reflexivity concerning "the moral implications of our collective energy decisions" (Sovacool & Dworking, 2015, p. 435). However, in "Grasping for energy democracy," Shelley Welton (2018) points out that lack of clarity regarding the precise operationalization of energy democracy complicates democratizing energy law as distinct interpretations demand divergent legal changes. Welton observes that typically energy democracy is framed in relation "consumer choice," "local control" and "access to process" (pp. 581–582). While these are in line with regenerative logic, each of these operationalizations has the potential to narrow participation and deflect attention from broader reflection on grid-wide changes, as discussed below.

Consumer choice models of energy democratization often operate by disrupting regional energy provider monopolies through deregulation of energy markets. This approach to broadening consumer participation by enabling more options has been enacted in the U.S. and Japan with varying results. An analysis of U.S. Energy Information Administration data published in 2021 found that U.S. consumers who purchased energy from retail companies after deregulation ended up paying $19.2 billion more than they would have if they had remained with incumbent utilities (Patterson & McGinty, 2021). In Japan, deregulation has created a crowded market of energy suppliers and led to the creation of new energy exchanges, such as Enechange, an energy-switching website that enables consumers to shop energy suppliers (Romero, 2018). However, Enechange founder and CEO, Yohei Kiguchi, observed that approximately 95 % of customers switched providers based on price rather than the desire for a greener energy source. This evidence suggests that energy affordability emerges as an important, if not *the* most important value criterion in consumer choice-based models. However, the deregulation of energy markets is not alone sufficient to deliver that outcome. If consumer choice promoted deregulation in the U.S., ultimately causing consumers to experience rising costs, the Japanese case demonstrates that price is not a sufficient factor in driving democratization, let alone sustainability.

Local control of energy is another often-cited approach toward increasing energy democracy. Yet the very meanings of local control and due process in energy decision-making are conceptualized in varying ways depending upon the scale of analysis and across urban and rural settings. Local energy cooperatives represent one approach to decentralization of energy control that can be implemented in both rural and urban environments. A U.S. example is Cooperative Energy Futures (CEF, 2021). This Minnesota-based energy co-op, which defines energy democracy in relation to a socially just and sustainable future characterized by reliable and affordable clean energy, shared ownership, and access to the jobs and wealth created by local energy systems. Institutionally, it is designed to operate in collaboration with energy system partners and local governments to combat climate change while protecting human and environmental health. The co-op aims to "uplift" communities that are most impacted by pollution and economic injustice. Favoring solar, it seeks installation sites that are already developed spaces, such as commercial rooftops and parking lots. CEF's efforts illustrate the potential of energy cooperatives to democratize energy systems, but while cooperative models enable more direct decision-making, such localized operations do not address higher level energy issues, including the sustainability challenges occurring within complex energy supply chains that produce and distribute solar panels.

Although community-based energy production is a necessary component for building redundancy and resilience into energy grids, state-backed investment remains critical for ensuring that solar panels and other energy technologies are available and affordable. Public funding for developing and evaluative alternative energy production should be extensive, transparent, and subject to democratic review processes. Although models for regenerative alternatives are contingently materialized by the considerations of place and community, they are unified by similar objectives, including efforts to detach from corporate and state dependency, delinking from the neomercantile world system, and—most importantly given the current conditions of planetary existence—they aim to find workable and just solutions from without and within.

In terms of this latter point, regenerative energy movements emphasize the urgency of revisiting underlying logics that reproduce and strengthen neoliberal and neomercantile paradigms that reproduce modern-colonial and modern-imperialist world systems. At the heart of the problem is the faulty logic of extraction, and its manifestations in inequitable and unsustainable capitalist accumulation. In *The Limits to Capital*, David Harvey (2018) articulates the internal contradictions of capitalism by laying bare the problem of an economic system that demands limitless growth in a world of finite resources. Yet the problem lies not only in the logic of surplus value, for Ulrich Beck's (1992) analysis of institutionalized risk reminds us of the faulty logic of instrumental rationality, which presupposes disconnected minds and bodies in a world of homogenous knowing and enforced separateness. When energy corporations like PG&E are not held accountable for the 84 deaths that resulted from their negligence, when its CEO is rewarded with a $2.5 million dollar severance package while families go homeless, and when the presiding judge over the case enables the firm to secure access to funds meant for fire victims, it is clear that the system has become pathologically corrupt. Although PG&E pled guilty to 87 counts of manslaughter, there were no consequences because technically, no one was to blame in in a world where rationalized governance results in organized irresponsiblity.

The solutions offered by regenerative energy movements provide critical insight into alternative ways of knowing, being, and doing that offer scope for transformative energy futures. Indeed, two global movements have developed a clear set of regenerative standards that point the direction forward. The values espoused by GEC may be most attractive to pragmatic sustainability actors who are seeking to scale up energy sustainability; however, this model runs the risk of neomercantilist cooptation, given its greater economistic focus and hazy principles that may be interpreted to support extractive interests. The Earth Charter may be harder to scale up in a world system where capital holds all the cards and powerful states are engaged in a race to the bottom. Yet the Earth Charter—conceived of during a rare moment of global *glasnost* and co-developed by a diverse Commission representing the interests of marginalized and indigenous people around the world—is resoundingly clear in its regenerative logic.

Like those involved in writing the twenty-first-century Earth Charter, we contend that unity in diversity can only be achieved by cultivating respect for all life and its self-determination, establishing democratic, transparent, and accountable institutions, and centering responsibility in practice. Numerous energy movements are emerging in an attempt to pivot the twenty-first-century economy toward more just and sustainable pathways, but given current authoritarian trends and global power elite consolidations, these regenerative pivots are unlikely to occur without a critical mass of families and communities who—facing the perfect storm of climate change—reject unjust energy assemblages that are so wantonly poisoning air, water, and food, and setting homes ablaze, in the mad scramble for power and profit.

CONCLUSION

The key questions that this chapter answers are what logics are driving conventional energy biopolitics across space and time and what alternatives do regenerative energy movements offer? While the solutions posed by these alternatives are multifaceted, our review of regenerative energy uncovers the common goal of ecological and social sustainability. Within the radical spaces of regenerative energy practice, a combination of structural and ethical logics informs the construction of multi-stakeholder practices grounded in the opportunities and constraints of place, participatory dialogue, community collaboration, and consensus building. The regenerative logics identified in this chapter exemplify the right of all beings to exist in relational connection through the establishment of democratic institutions and sustainable systems that work with, rather than against, the interconnected web of bio-physical and socio-ecological life. The spark of interrelational connectivity that regenerative energy alternatives promise are nascent and fraught with existential challenges, but in the liminal cracks of an increasingly unstable world system, alternative, sustainable, and democratic energy movements are converging in critical conscious along the road toward more responsible futures.

REFERENCES

Alvaredo, F., Chancel, L., Piketty, T., Saez, E., & Zucman, G. (2018). *World inequality report: Executive summary.* World Inequality Lab. https://wir2018.wid.world/files/download/wir2018-summary-english.pdf

Beck, U. (1992). *Risk society: Toward a new modernity* (M. Ritter, Trans.). Sage.

Blunt, K., & Gold, R. (2019, July 10). PG&E knew for years that its lines could spark wildfires, and didn't fix them. *The Wall Street Journal.* https://www.wsj.com/articles/pg-e-knew-for-years-its-lines-could-spark-wildfires-and-didnt-fix-them-11562768885

Brown, E. (2013). *The public bank solution: From austerity to prosperity.* Third Millennium Press.

Brzezinski, Z. (1998). *The grand chessboard: American primacy and its geostrategic imperatives.* Basic Books.

CEF. (n.d.). *Cooperative Energy Futures does things differently.* Cooperative Energy Futures. Retrieved November 24, 2021, from https://www.cooperativeenergyfutures.com/

Dalton, M. (2021, October 19). Poor nations want trillions to fund climate goals. *The Wall Street Journal*, pp. A1–A8.

deGraaff, N. (2011). A global energy network? The expansion and integration of non-triad national oil companies. *Global Networks, 11*(2), 262–283.

Diamond, J. (2011). *Collapse: How societies choose to fail or succeed.* Penguin.

Earth Charter. (n.d.). *History. Earth Charter.* Retrieved November 26, 2021, from https://earthcharter.org/about-the-earth-charter/history/

Earth Charter. (2000). *The Earth Charter.* Retrieved October 22, 2021, from https://earthcharter.org/about-the-earth-charter/

Farrell, H., & Newman, A. L. (2019). Weaponized interdependence: How global economic networks shape state coercion. *International Security, 44*(1), 42–79. doi:10.1162/ISEC_a_00351

Fay, S. (1966). *Before Sarajevo: The origins of the world war* (Vol. 1). Free Press Macmillan.

Foster, J. B., Clark, B., & York, R. (2010). *The ecological rift: Capitalism's war on the earth.* Monthly Review Press.

Green Economy Coalition. (2020, June 7). *The 5 principles of green economy.* https://www.greeneconomycoalition.org/news-and-resources/the-5-principles-of-green-economy

Gorbachev, M. (2006). *Manifesto for the earth: Action now for peace, global justice, and a sustainable future.* Clariview Books.

Harvey, D. (2018). *The limits to capital.* Verso.

Hui, M. (2021, July 12). *A new US-Europe rare earths supply chain is using a "very Chinese model" to counter China*. Quartz. https://qz.com/2031880/us-eu-rare-earth-chain-uses-china-model-to-hedge-china-dominance/

International Energy Agency. (2021, April 20). *Global carbon dioxide emissions are set for their second-biggest increase in history*. https://www.iea.org/news/global-carbon-dioxide-emissions-are-set-for-their-second-biggest-increase-in-history

Jeffries, S. (2006, February 11). Risky business: The world is out of control, sociologist Ulrich Beck tells Stuart Jeffries. *The Guardian*. https://www.theguardian.com/books/2006/feb/11/society.politics.

Kaufman, F. (2010, July). The food bubble. *Harpers Magazine*, pp. 27–38.

Kelly, D. (2017, February 14). *An unethical culture that bred death*. LawRoom. http://blog.lawroom.com/corruption/an-unethical-culture-that-bred-death/

Klare, M. T. (2018, October 2018). *This is not your mother's cold war*. The Nation. https://www.thenation.com/article/archive/this-is-not-your-mothers-cold-war/

Levidow, L. (2018). Green economy. In N. Castree, J. Hulme, & J. D. Proctor (Eds.), *Routledge companion to environmental studies* (pp. 199–204). Routledge.

Mann, P. S. (2016). On the precipice with Naomi Klein, Karl Marx, and the Pope: Towards a post-capitalist energy commons and beyond. *Radical Philosophy Review, 19*(3), 621–652.

Mathis, W. (2021, June 23). *Building new renewables is cheaper than burning fossil fuels*. Bloomberg. https://www.bloomberg.com/news/articles/2021-06-23/building-new-renewables-cheaper-than-running-fossil-fuel-plants

Matthews, C. M., Eaton, C., & Faucon, B. (2021, October 18). Energy crisis pressures renewables. *The Wall Street Journal*, pp. A1, A8.

Mills, C. R. (1956). *The power elite*. Oxford University Press.

Nadesan, M. (2016). *Crisis communication, liberal democracy and ecological sustainability*. Lexington.

Ohno, H. (2011, July 7). *Interview/ Ulrich Beck: System of organized irresponsibility behind the Fukushima crisis*. The Asahi Shimbun. http://www.asahi.com/english/TKY201107060307.html

Ostroukh, A., Albanese, C., & Cox, J. (2015, August 20). More victims in emerging market currencies selloff. *The Wall Street Journal*, p. C3.

Palmer, R., & Colton, J. (1984). *A history of the modern world since 1815*. Alfred A. Knopf.

Patterson, S., & McGinty, T. (2021, March 8). Deregulation aimed to lower home-power bills. For many, it didn't. *The Wall Street Journal*. https://www.wsj.com/articles/electricity-deregulation-utility-retail-energy-bills-11615213623?mod=hp_lista_pos4

Penn, I., & Eavis, P. (2020, June 19). PG&E's plan to resolve bankruptcy wins court approval. *The New York Times*. https://www.nytimes.com/2020/06/19/business/energy-environment/pge-bankruptcy-court-approval.html

Peterson-Withorn, C. (2021, November 7). *Led by Elon Musk's crazy gains, American billionares have added nearly $2 trillion to their fortunes during the pandemic*. Ezzaworld. https://www.ezzaworlddtv.com/led-by-elon-musks-crazy-gains-american-billionaires-have-added-nearly-2-trillion-to-their-fortunes-during-the-pandemic/

Romero, T. (2018, July 24). *As Japan deregulates electricity, this startup lets consumers compare suppliers*. TechinAsia. https://www.techinasia.com/talk/yohei-kiguchi-enechange

Rosanvallon, P. (2011). *Democratic legitimacy: Impartiality, reflexivity, proximity*. Princeton University Press.

Russell, E., Allison, J., Finger, T., Brown, J., Balogh, B., & Carlson, W. (2011). The nature of power: Synthesizing the history of technology and environmental history. *Technology and Culture*, *52*(2), 246–259.

Saez, E., Piketty, T., & Zucman, G. (2016, December 6). *Economic growth in the United States: A tale of two countries*. Washington Center for Equitable Growth. https://equitablegrowth.org/economic-growth-in-the-united-states-a-tale-of-two-countries/

Sassen, S. (n.d.). *Geographies of extraction*. UrbanNext.net. Retrieved November 24, 2021, from https://architizer.com/blog/inspiration/stories/saskia-sassen-geographies-of-extraction/

Sinopec. (n.d.). *About Sinopec Group*. Sinopec. Retrieved November 24, 2021, from http://www.sinopecgroup.com/group/en/companyprofile/AboutSinopecGroup/

Slater, J. (2015, January 19). *Richest 1% will own more than all the rest by 2016*. Oxfam. Retrieved January 19, 2016, from http://www.oxfam.org.uk/blogs/2015/01/richest-1-per-cent-will-own-more-than-all-the-rest-by-2016

Sovacool, B. K., & Dworkin, M. H. (2015). Energy justice: Conceptual insights and practical applications. *Applied Energy*, *142*(C), 435–444.

Szulecki, K. (2018). Conceptualizing energy democracy. *Environmental Politics*, *27*(1), 21–41. https://doi.org/10.1080/09644016.2017.1387294

Terra, F. H. B., Filho, F., & Fonseca, P. C. D. (2021). Keynes on state and economic development. *Review of Political Economy*, *33*(1), 88–102. https://doi.org/10.1080/09538259.2020.1823072

Tooze, A. (2018). Neoliberalism's world order. *Dissent*, *65*(3), 132–136.

Vitali, S., Glattfelder, J. B., & Battiston, S. (2011) The network of global corporate control. *PLOS One*, 6(10), Article e259945. https://doi.org/10.1371/journal.pone.0025995

Welton, S. (2018) Grasping for energy democracy. *Michigan Law Review*, *116*(4), 581–644.

Wilmot, S. (2021, September 3). Lithium booms as EV sales rev up: Price of a metal compound needed for electric automobiles has more than doubled this year. *The Wall Street Journal*, p. B10.

Young, D., Hutchinson, R., & Reeves, M. (2021, July 8). *The green economy has a resource-scarcity problem*. Harvard Business Review. https://hbr.org/2021/07/the-green-economy-has-a-resource-scarcity-problem

Zhai, K. (2021, December 4–5). China to create national rare-earths giant. *The Wall Street Journal*, p. B3.

Ziegler, C. E., & Menon R. (2014). Neomercantilism and great-power energy competition in Central Asia and the Caspian. *Strategic Studies Quarterly*, *8*(2), 17–41.

CHAPTER 2

Scientific Discourse About Energy Geopolitics: Changing Paradigms or Simply Adapting to New Times?

CÁTIA MIRIAM COSTA AND ANA TERESA SANTOS

INTRODUCTION

Energy became a hot topic in international politics, bringing up several issues centered on energy security concerns and the need for an energy transition to meet climate change demands. According to the U.S. Energy Information Administration (EIA), demand is expected to rise by 50 % by 2050, owing primarily to non-OECD economic growth and population growth, particularly in Asia (Nalley & LaRose, 2021). Currently, fossil fuels meet 80 % of global energy demand (REN21, 2021). However, due to the rapid depletion of fossil fuel reserves and the negative environmental consequences, research into green and renewable energy sources has emerged. This chapter will examine how scientific discourse has changed over the last two decades and whether research topics reflect the context of climate change, energy transition, and the political debate about energy.

Indeed, there has been a surge of interest in the energy transition in recent decades, prompting a slew of other reviews and analyses. Nevertheless, while some narratives have covered key areas such as energy policy (Jenkins et al., 2016), energy resources (Evans et al., 2012), and sustainable development (Dincer & Acar, 2015), to the best of our knowledge, no contributions have covered the field of energy geopolitics.

The core place easily explains the attention received by the energy sector it has when addressing societies' lives. Energy is central for producing, exchanging and maintaining the societies' living standards (Palle, 2021). So, the change of energy paradigm impacts the economy and society as well as in public policies, resulting many times in the shifting of power balance domestically and internationally. The confrontation of discourses over energy in the public sphere during the last decades diversified. The scientific field was one of the most significant and dynamic. The study of some national cases or regional cases contribute to understanding better this relation between scientific discourse, public sphere/media discourse and political discourse.

The Russian case is particularly interesting in this dialogue because the political power announces a clear reception of the scientific discourse about the human-generated climate change and the need for a new energy paradigm in the Medvedev presidency, moving to a very different discourse after 2012, under Putin presidency, who turned the energy into a national issue (Tynkkynen & Tynkkynen, 2018). The study of the U.S. situation is also significant, where there is the confrontation between negationists of climate change and the defenders of the human-generated climate change in political and scientific discourses. Finally, in the EU case, the debate over energy supply diversification (Hofmann & Staeger, 2018) and the full reception of the principle of the human-generated climate crisis, driving to a direct intervention in the way energy was produced and distributed, penetrated political discourse. Accordingly, with this trend, many national parliaments became the floor for debate about public policies and confrontation over different energy development conceptions, inclusively responding to civil society demands for a further discussion about "energy democracy" (Williams & Sovacool, 2020).

Energy has a determinant role in human development and how humans relate to the environment (Urbina, 2022). Therefore, managing energy resources and transportation became one of the most significant concerns of political powers. The turn to more energy-intensive economies directly impacted the international order and contributed to the complexification of this international order (Oatley, 2021). Consequently, any change in the energy production and use paradigm will result in readjustments of the international order and open new geopolitical perspectives on the place and role each state plays in international politics. In the last decades, climate change has become a central issue and compelled states to action and to look for alternatives concerning energy. The direct connection between sustainable growth, development, and energy became evident (Ali et al., 2020; Silva et al., 2022). Accordingly, political agenda-setting based on energy concern emerged. Economic growth and development, the economic decarbonization and energy production and distribution to fight the climate crisis entered the domestic and international political discourse. Simultaneously, the scientific discourse also grew, diversified in authorship and topics.

In this chapter, we identify the most relevant scientific journals, the centers of research producing scientific discourse on this topic and the issues receiving increased attention from researchers. This study seeks to answer the following primary questions: has scientific discourse about energy geopolitics shifted in terms of the source of its production or the topics deemed most important? Is scientific discourse changing in response to changes in political discourse on energy and energy geopolitics? We use the Scopus database as the resource for the scientific discourse and analyze the past two decades, focusing on the discourse production combining the analysis of scientific discourse with bibliometric data. This chapter addresses these questions in two folds: the identity of scientific discourse producers and the analysis of scientific discourse itself.

THE INCREASING RATE OF SCIENTIFIC PRODUCTION OVER ENERGY

The evidence for this article is drawn from the Scopus database (Boyle & Sherman, 2008; Moed et al., 2011; Mongeon & Paul-Hus, 2016; Thelwall & Sud, 2022). Scopus is the world's largest database of peer-reviewed literature, with over 26,000 serial titles and more than 94.8 thousand affiliation profiles (*Why Choose Scopus—Scopus Benefits | Elsevier Solutions*, 2021). It includes journals from the Social Sciences, Arts and Humanities, and Science, Technology, and Medicine. Bibliometric materials can and have been used to map emerging trends related to contemporary societal challenges, from radical wireless technologies (e.g., Mendonça et al., 2022) to governance concepts like the "circular economy" (e.g., de Jesus et al., 2018). Our approach is to bring insights from the quantitative studies of science to the understanding the global debates regarding energy.

The search strategy was to include the terms "geopolitics" and "energy" in the title, keyword, or abstract. We also restricted our search until 2021 because it was the most recent year with completed records. This search yielded 2,006 documents, including 1,566 research articles, 151 books, 202 book chapters, 86 conference papers, and one conference review (see Figure 2.1). We retrieved articles' titles, authors, journals, years, abstracts, and affiliation addresses. The analysis excluded editorial, erratum, letter notes, retracted, review, and short survey documents.

Even though all 2,006 documents were published in 958 different scientific journals and books, there were 383 journals, 55 conference proceedings, 135 books and 110 book chapters publishing only 1 article and 114 journals, 6 conference proceedings, 3 books and 25 book chapters issuing two items with these expressions. These numbers suggest that not all journals are equally interested in

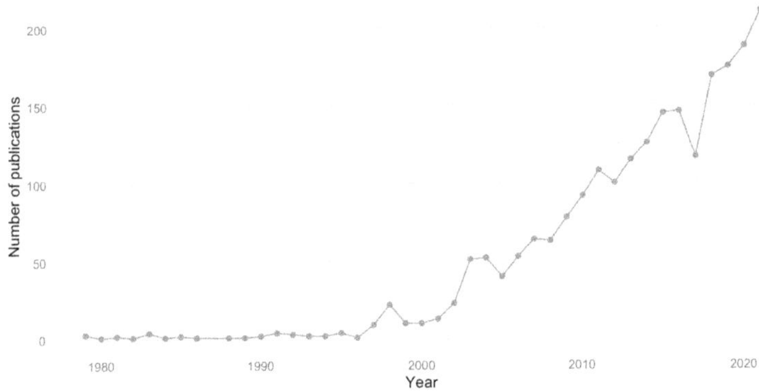

Figure 2.1: Number of papers published per year with the expression "geopolitics" and/or "energy"

Source: Authors' own elaboration (data retrieved from Scopus).

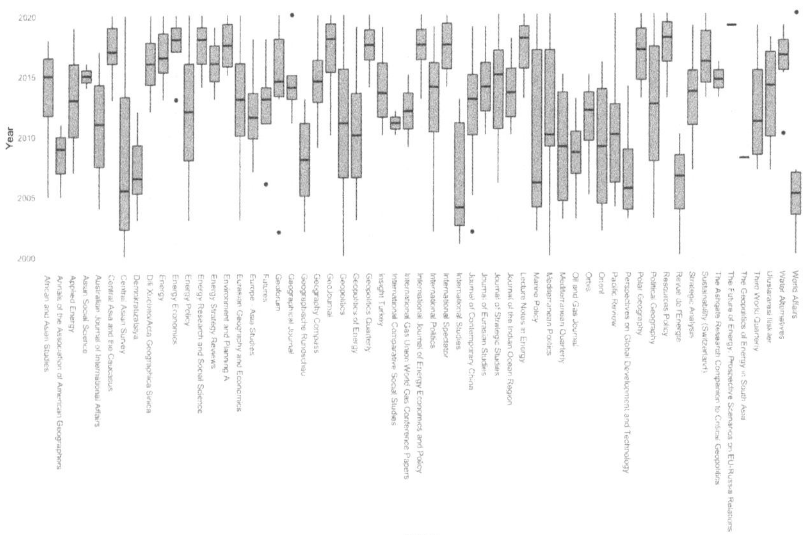

Figure 2.2: Distribution of the number of articles published by each journal through the years

Source: Authors' own elaboration (data retrieved from Scopus).

these terms and that their interest varies over time. Figure 2.2 depicts the number of articles published per journal over a 20-year period to demonstrate how the number of articles published has changed over time. Only journals with at least five articles published between 2000 and 2020 were considered for a range of 59 journals.

Figure 2.3: Frequency of authors affiliated per country

Source: Authors' own elaboration (data retrieved from Scopus).

There were clearly more journals publishing articles after 2010. Figure 2.2 depicts 41 items from 2001 to 2010 and 57 source titles from 2011 to 2020, indicating a rising interest in these topics. The authors of 1,992 documents were retrieved, and their affiliation was considered. Figure 2.3 shows the number of authors affiliated with each country over two time periods: blue between 2001 and 2010 and green between 2011 and 2020. The darker the colors, the more authors affiliated with local institutions.

Prior to 2010, most of the documents were written by academics affiliated with U.S. institutions. However, after 2011, the United Kingdom and China increased the number of authors they hosted, and many other authors from other affiliations contributed to this subject. These new countries are from the Southern Hemisphere and East Europe.

THE MOST PROMINENT JOURNALS AND NEW CONTRIBUTORS

Aside from increasing the number of scientific publications in the field, some journals continue to publish and bring new knowledge about the subject. Figure 2.4 compares the top 12 journals regarding the number of manuscripts containing these expressions published over two ten-year periods (2001–2010 vs. 2011–2020).

Among the top 12 journals identified, only five were found to be familiar to both periods: *Geopolitics*, *Energy Policy*, *Political Geography*, *Eurasian Geography*

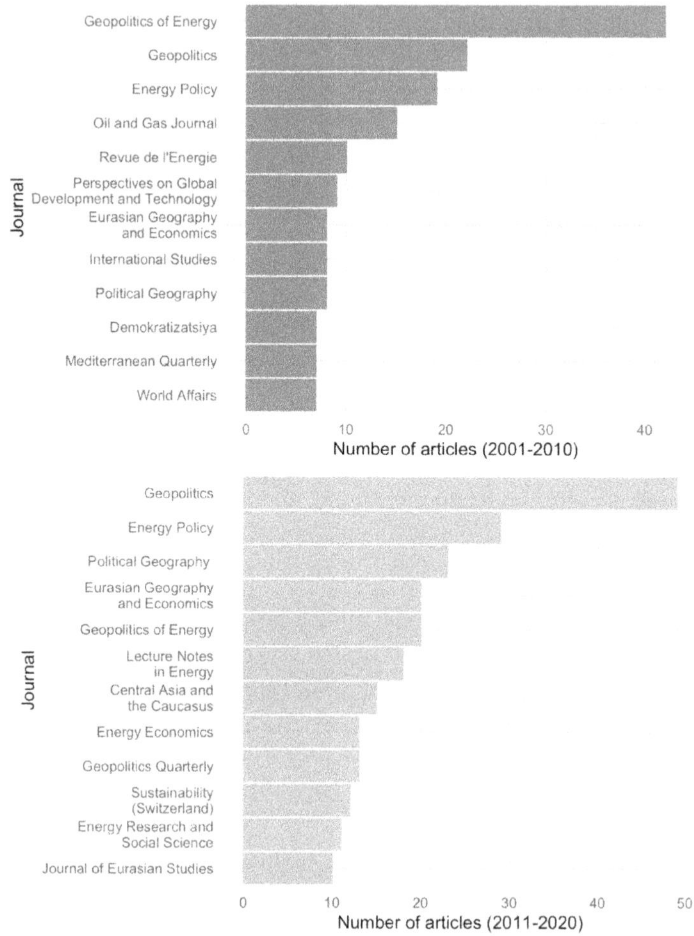

Figure 2.4: Frequency of articles published by the journal top 12 in the time periods between 2001 and 2010 and between 2011 and 2020

Source: Authors' own elaboration (data retrieved from Scopus).

and Economics and *Geopolitics of Energy*. They also increase the number of articles published with one or both expressions of interest in the latest decade, reinforcing the importance of the topics except for *Geopolitics of Energy*. This journal is the only one that has published fewer articles since 2011, indicating a drop in interest. In the second decade, six journals began publishing manuscripts with the words of interest after 2012, and one in 2010. They were all included in the top 12 most prolific publishers.

Along with the growing number of authors publishing in these fields, many institutions hosting researchers with similar interests have grown. Considering

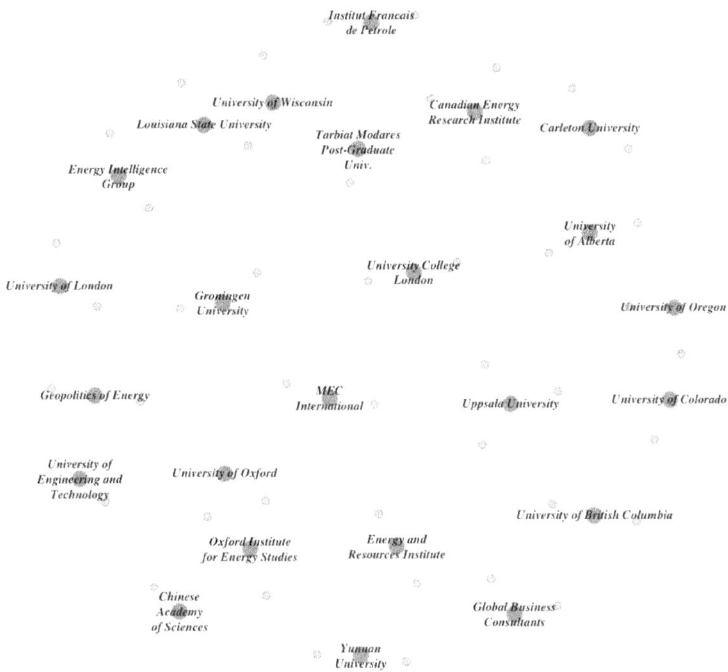

Figure 2.5: Institutions connected to the manuscripts published between 2001 and 2010
Source: Authors' own elaboration (data retrieved from Scopus).

only the five journals shared by both decades, as identified in Figure 2.4, the institutions hosting authors responsible for at least two publications are depicted in Figures 2.5 and 2.6, respectively, for 2001 to 2010 and 2011 to 2020. The number of articles published with one or both expressions of interest in the latest decade also increased, reinforcing the importance of the topics except for *Geopolitics of Energy*. This journal is the only one that has published fewer articles since 2011, indicating a drop in interest. In the second decade, six journals began publishing manuscripts with the words of interest after 2012, and one in 2010. They were all included in the top 12 most prolific publishers.

Along with the growing number of authors publishing in these fields, many institutions hosting researchers with similar interests have grown. Therefore, considering only the five journals shared by both decades, as identified in Figure 2.4, the institutions hosting authors responsible for at least two publications are depicted in Figures 2.5 and 2.6, respectively, for 2001 to 2010 and 2011 to 2020.

There is evidence that the number of institutions is increasing. Figure 2.5 depicts 24 institutions that hosted authors who published at least two publications between 2001 and 2020, whereas Figure 2.6 depicts the number of institutions

Figure 2.6: Institutions connected to the manuscripts published between 2011 and 2020
Source: Authors' own elaboration (data retrieved from Scopus).

increasing for 33 institutions over the next decade. In the first decade, only four institutions had more than two publications (actually 3). The following decade revealed 11 institutions with more than two publications: seven with three, three with four manuscripts, and one with five. Global Business Consultants, the University of British Columbia, the University College London, the University of Colorado, and the University of Oxford were the only five institutions found to be common between the two time periods. The number of publications at the last three institutions increased from two in the first decade to three in the second.

CONTEMPORARY DEVELOPMENTS IN THE DISCOURSE

Various topics have piqued the interest of researchers over the last two decades, and they have been addressed in manuscripts that have been published. Figure 2.7 depicts the evolution of 16 expressions with the most significant changes in the frequency of usage that we discovered.

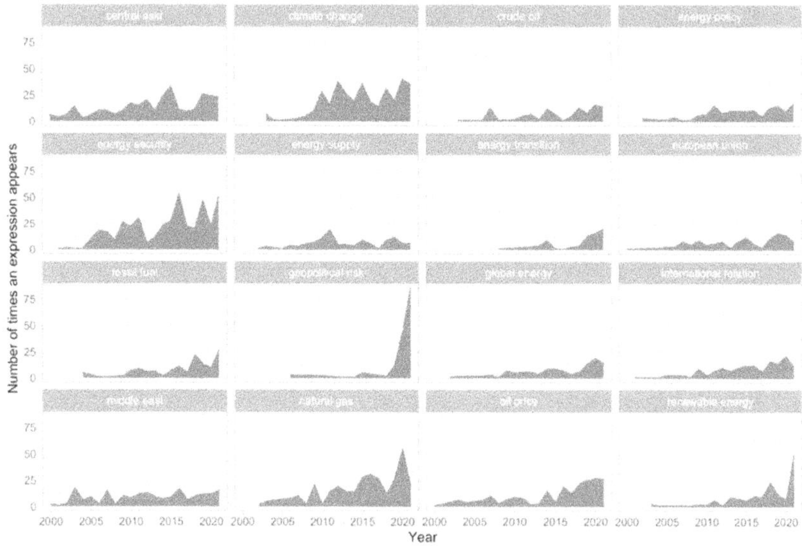

Figure 2.7: Evolution of frequency of some expressions used in the 20 journals

Source: Authors' own elaboration (data retrieved from Scopus)

Although some expressions revealed to have a modest increase, such as "crude oil," "energy policy," and "energy supply," others showed to be increasing simultaneously. For instance, "natural gas," "renewable energy," and "energy security" proved to have a considerable increase being used more than 50 times in some years. this concern with "clean energy" and "energy security" is evident in the EU political discourse. The security issue became progressively associated with the diversification of energy suppliers (Strigunov et al., 2022). The dependence on a supplier was pointed out as one of the significant fragilities of the EU energy public policy (Tichý, 2020).

Although intriguing, the rising trend and many instances of "geopolitical risk" in 2020 can be somehow justified by the evolution of the energy market and the rearrangements for supply and transportation. Along with these developments, many other concepts related to the central ones, such as "energy" and "geopolitics," were added over time. For instance, in the MENA, U.S. power diminished, and, simultaneously, other powers entered the equation (e.g., Russia, Cina, Iran and Turkey). The Arab Spring brought more substantial involvement of some of these powers, like the Russian Federation's case (Strigunov et al., 2022). As for China, the international project Belt & Road also brought a new discourse for energy issues and a replacement of this discourse in the international sphere (Costa, 2020). Therefore, the rise of "clean energy" seen as the future and as the way for sustainable growth and development did not end the concern with fossil and not clean energies, such as oil and gas. Part of the disagreements and geopolitical alignments over energy is still about the supply and transportation of not clean energies. As some authors refer to, multipolarity is increasing in many regional areas; political power disputes result from this situation (Strigunov et al., 2022).

Figures 2.8 and 2.9 were created to understand the occurrence of words and their relationships.

In this network of the words of the abstract, there is some significant clustering. They are organized into some word families that tend to go together. Words like "shortage," "price," and "import" can be found near the word "oil." Concerns about the energy crisis caused by fossil dependency can be found in words related to "energy," such as "supply" and "source." The word "security" is also visibly linked to "oil" and "energy," emphasizing the concern about the availability of energy sources and oil at a reasonable price. Surrounding "gas" occurs "natural" referring to the fossil fuel classified as clean, "demand" about the consumption and some regional words like both "EU" and "27" suggesting a reference to the European Union formed by the current 27 countries, "Europe" and "Russia" due to the increasing dependence of Europe and EU on Russian natural gas. Some authors highlight that the debate over energy intensified during and after the turning of the millennium (Tichý, 2020). The economic rise of Russia and the energy disputes with the western neighbors (production and channels for supply) partially explain this trend. Furthermore, the political and military instability

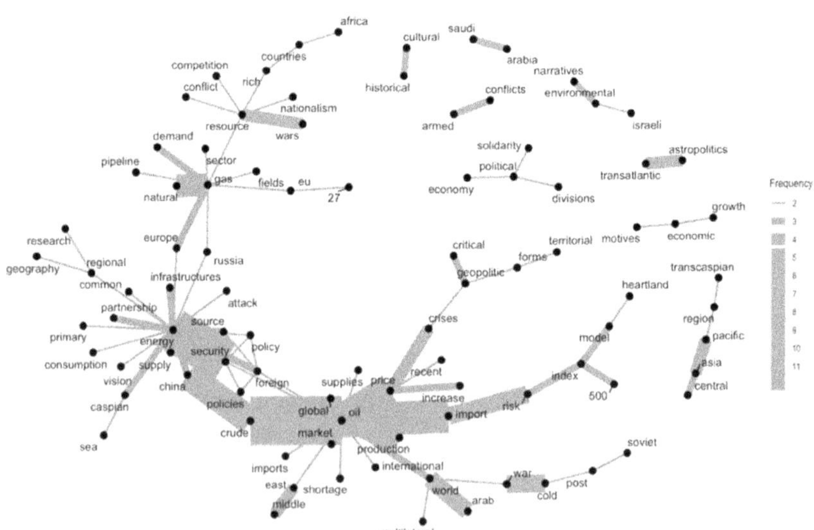

Figure 2.8: Network of co-occurring words in the abstracts published between 2001 and 2010

Source: Authors' own elaboration (data retrieved from Scopus).

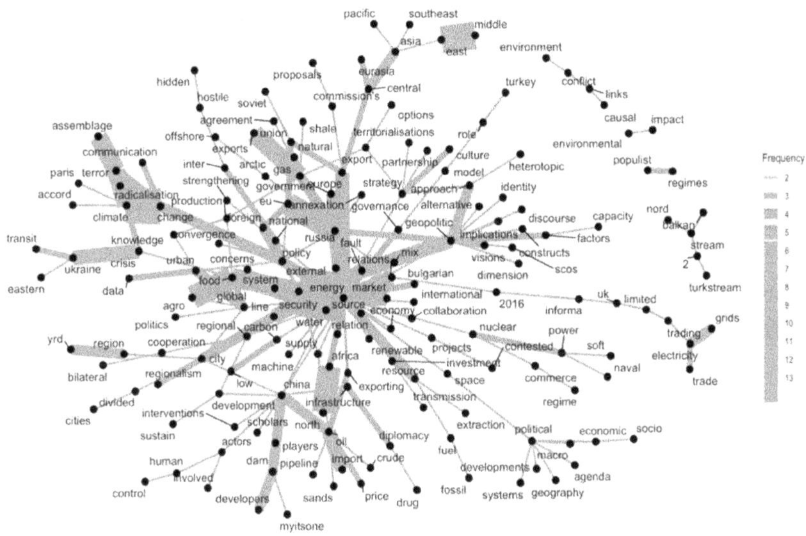

Figure 2.9: Network of co-occurring words in the abstracts published between 2011 and 2020
Source: Authors' own elaboration (data retrieved from Scopus).

in Ukraine, after the self-proclamation for the independence of some Eastern territories and the Russian Federation's direct support and involvement in this confrontation, raised more concern in the EU and more turbulence in the relations with the Russian State. Since 2014, with Crimea's annexation, the relations between the EU and Russian Federation deteriorated even more, and the EU saw the diversification of energy supply as an issue that was more than emergent; it was an urgent problem to solve.

A final cluster is associated with the word "resource," which is linked to two disturbing words, "wars" and "conflict." It is interesting to note that some studies carried out about the geopolitical implications of energy focus on the ways to reduce tensions created by the need for more energy supply. Gosh particularly suggests the signing of financial and political instruments that allow to solve the problems coming from energy resources competition peacefully (Ghosh, 2022).

Word clusters are reorganized between 2011 and 2020, and some words, such as "energy," "politics," "Russia," "Europe," and "gas," become highly connected, which evidences the rise of energy production, commercialization and transportation as one of the main issues in a so-called transition period from carbon-intensive energy and clean energy. A decade ago, some of them were the clusters' focal points. However, two words remain at the heart of clusters: "oil" and "geopolitics." They were both surrounded by new ideas. Along with "oil," "price" frequently appears, as it is a current concern for European countries. Concerning "geopolitics," concepts such as "visions," "implications," and "factors" are also addressed. As new clusters, one may be associated with "crisis" and "Ukraine," one with "nuclear" and "power," and one with "change" and other concepts such as "climate" and "terror," which result from particular attention to the competition for energy and also to the disruptive situations resulting from this competition.

CONCLUSION

The field of energy geopolitics has experienced exponential growth in publications since at least the year 2000. Between 2001 and 2020, 59 journals were found to have published at least five manuscripts, increasing from 41 between 2001 and 2010 to 57 between 2011 and 2020. The geographical distribution of the producers also increased in the second decade, with an increase in the number of authors in the United Kingdom, China, and other Southern Hemisphere and East European countries. These results point out to a multipolarization of the scientific discourse geographically speaking.

Five journals were discovered to be among the top 12 most-published journals in both decades. In addition, the data gathered indicated five institutions that stood out for producing manuscripts during both time periods and 28 newcomers to the list of leading producers of scientific discourse with two publications in the last decade.

The energy geopolitics discourse has also evolved to express widespread concern about geopolitical risk. Over the years, many other ideas and concepts were added as the main topics were developed. For example, both "Ukraine" and "crisis," as well as "nuclear" and "power," became frequently used terms, which also reflect the political concerns and discourse in the recent years. The field's development will continue in the coming years, and it will be crucial to track the concepts that will gain traction.

Nonetheless, the study has several implications for the field by taking stock in this manner. It gives readers an overview of two decades of research output and a concise summary of the field's key trends. It may also serve as a solid foundation for interested scholars to broaden their collaboration networks to include a more diverse group of collaborators, potentially increasing the relevance of field analyses. Finally, the findings of this study can assist new researchers in the field in gaining a better understanding of global trends and critical institutions.

REFERENCES

Ali, Q., Raza, A., Narjis, S., Saeed, S., & Khan, M. T. I. (2020). Potential of renewable energy, agriculture, and financial sector for the economic growth: Evidence from politically free, partly free and not free countries. *Renewable Energy*, *162*, 934–947. https://doi.org/10.1016/J.RENENE.2020.08.055

Boyle, F., & Sherman, D. (2008). Scopus™: The product and its development. *The Serials Librarian*, *49*(3), 147–153. https://doi.org/10.1300/J123V49N03_12

Costa, C. M. (2020). The words of the belt and Road Initiative: A chinese discourse for the world? In F. Leandro & P. Duarte (Eds.), *The Belt and Road Initiative: An old archetype of a new development model* (pp. 23–44). Palgrave Macmillan. https://doi.org/10.1007/978-981-15-2564-3_2

de Jesus, A., Antunes, P., Santos, R., & Mendonça, S. (2018). Eco-innovation in the transition to a circular economy: An analytical literature review. *Journal of Cleaner Production*, *172*, 2999–3018. https://doi.org/10.1016/J.JCLEPRO.2017.11.111

Dincer, I., & Acar, C. (2015). A review on clean energy solutions for better sustainability. *International Journal of Energy Research*, *39*(5), 585–606. https://doi.org/10.1002/ER.3329

Evans, A., Strezov, V., & Evans, T. J. (2012). Assessment of utility energy storage options for increased renewable energy penetration. *Renewable and Sustainable Energy Reviews*, *16*(6), 4141–4147. https://doi.org/10.1016/J.RSER.2012.03.048

Ghosh, S. (2022). Renewable energy and CO_2 emissions: The economics and geopolitical implications, experiences from the BRICS nations. *International Journal of Energy Sector Management*. Advance online publication. https://doi.org/10.1108/IJESM-08-2021-0024

Hofmann, S. C., & Staeger, U. (2018). Frame contestation and collective securitisation: The case of EU energy policy. *West European Politics*, *42*(2), 323–345. https://doi.org/10.1080/01402382.2018.1510197

Jenkins, K., McCauley, D., Heffron, R., Stephan, H., & Rehner, R. (2016). Energy justice: A conceptual review. *Energy Research & Social Science*, *11*, 174–182. https://doi.org/10.1016/J.ERSS.2015.10.004

Mendonça, S., Damásio, B., Charlita de Freitas, L., Oliveira, L., Cichy, M., & Nicita, A. (2022). The rise of 5G technologies and systems: A quantitative analysis of knowledge production. *Telecommunications Policy*, *46*(4), 102327. https://doi.org/10.1016/J.TELPOL.2022.102327

Moed, H. F., Aisati, M., & Plume, A. (2011). Studying scientific migration in Scopus. *Scientometrics*, *94*, 929–942. https://doi.org/10.1007/s11192-012-0783-9

Mongeon, P., & Paul-Hus, A. (2016). The journal coverage of web of science and scopus: A comparative analysis. *Scientometrics*, *106*, 213–228. https://doi.org/10.1007/s11192-015-1765-5

Nalley, S., & LaRose, A. (2021). *International Energy Outlook 2021 (IEO2021)*. https://www.eia.gov/outlooks/ieo/pdf/IEO2021_ReleasePresentation.pdf

Oatley, T. (2021). Energy and the complexity of international order. *Global Environmental Politics*, *21*(4), 20–41. https://doi.org/10.1162/GLEP_A_00637

Palle, A. (2021). Bringing geopolitics to energy transition research. *Energy Research & Social Science*, *81*, 102233. https://doi.org/10.1016/J.ERSS.2021.102233

REN21. (2021). *Renewables 2021 Global Status Report*.

Silva, J., Távora, G., & Mendonça, S. (2022). *Taking stock of storage innovation: Electric battery patenting in the context of the renewable energy and electric mobility usage sectors*. Mimeo.

Strigunov, K. S., Manoilo, A. v., Rozhin, B. A., & Simons, G. (2022). Energy market wars as a factor of military-political escalation in Eastern Mediterranean region: A Russian perspective. *Cogent Social Sciences*, *8*(1). https://doi.org/10.1080/23311886.2021.2005878

Thelwall, M., & Sud, P. (2022). Scopus 1900–2020: Growth in articles, abstracts, countries, fields, and journals. *Quantitative Science Studies*, *3*, 1–17. https://doi.org/10.1162/QSS_A_00177

Tichý, L. (2020). EU political discourse on the energy security relations with Russia. *European Political Science, 19*(4), 603–621. https://doi.org/10.1057/S41304-019-00229-X/TABLES/9

Tynkkynen, V. P., & Tynkkynen, N. (2018). Climate denial revisited: (Re)contextualising Russian public discourse on climate change during Putin 2.0. *Europe-Asia Studies, 70*(7), 1103–1120. https://doi.org/10.1080/09668136.2018.1472218

Urbina, A. (2022). Solar electricity and globalization. In *Sustainable solar electricity* (pp. 267–288). Springer. https://doi.org/10.1007/978-3-030-91771-5_12

Why choose Scopus—Scopus benefits | Elsevier solutions. (2021). https://www.elsevier.com/solutions/scopus/why-choose-scopus

Williams, L., & Sovacool, B. K. (2020). Energy democracy, dissent and discourse in the party politics of shale gas in the United Kingdom. *Environmental Politics, 29*(7), 1239–1263. https://doi.org/10.1080/09644016.2020.1740555

Part II

CHAPTER 3

China's Energy Geopolitics and the Belt and Road Initiative: The Green Energy Cooperation[1]

RUI PEREIRA AND CARLA FERNANDES

INTRODUCTION

The People's Republic of China (PRC)'s energy geopolitics has traditionally been focused on securing access to fossil fuel supplies, particularly oil. China has been a net importer of oil products since 1993, with a rapid and progressive increase in external dependence, and since 2018 has been the second world's largest crude oil importer. This excessive reliance on oil imports, combined with its high energy intensity and coal dependence, leads to efficiency and pollution challenges, which forces changes in China's energy security (*nengyuan anquan*) strategies and, subsequently, in energy geopolitics.

With a high reliance on fossil fuels, the PRC is undergoing an energy revolution,[2] transforming its energy structure and investing in the production and consumption of renewable energy. This revolution, in turn, has implications for Chinese energy geopolitics, with a gradual shift from quantitative strategic goals (e.g., increasing the amount of imported oil) to qualitative goals (e.g., improving and diversifying transport infrastructure and industries, and production and energy development on a national and international scale).

The investments made in the energy sector under the Belt and Road Initiative (BRI) must be framed within this framework, as this global project reinforced the initiatives developed by the Going Out strategy (*Zou chuqu*) launched in 2002, with regard to investment, development, exploration, and production of energy abroad (Fernandes, 2020). The BRI also came to support the strengthening of the qualitative goals of China's security of supply strategies, with the diversification of the supply sources and transport routes, by contemplating an update and a transformation of electricity networks; the construction and improvement of oil, gas pipelines, and transport and communication infrastructures (ports, roads, and railways) that will allow the recreation of the old Silk Road into a current "Energy Route" (Fernandes, 2019).

This Initiative, also known as "One Belt One Road" (OBOR), or just "New Silk Road," was announced by Chinese President Xi Jinping in Kazakhstan in October 2013. According to China's State Council Information Office (2021), the BRI is a long-term transcontinental policy and investment program aimed at developing infrastructure and accelerating the economic integration of countries along the route. Building on the ancient Silk Road, which linked ancient China to Asia, Africa, and Europe through trade and cultural exchange routes, this new Silk Road currently connects China to all continents. In terms of organization, this platform for international cooperation and development comprises two projects: the first by land, the "Silk Road Economic Belt," which mainly links China to Europe via Central Asia and Russia, to the Persian Gulf and the Mediterranean Sea through Central and Western Asia, and to the Southeast and South Asia and the Indian Ocean; and the second by sea, the "21st Century Maritime Silk Road," is projected from coastal ports of China via the Indian Ocean to Europe through the South China Sea and to the South Pacific via the South China Sea (NDRC, 2015).

Energy cooperation is the main cornerstone of the BRI, translated "in the joint contribution and shared benefits, to achieve common development and prosperity in the energy sector for participating countries through mutually beneficial cooperation" (NEA, 2019). Since 2017, green cooperation has been one of the main objectives of this Initiative, embodied in "cooperation in clean energy and energy efficiency, to face climate change, guarantee universal access to modern energy services at affordable, reliable, and sustainable prices" (NEA, 2019).

Energy cooperation has been investigated in a variety of ways within the context of the BRI, ranging from energy relations between China and the countries along the BRI, as a whole (Fernandes, 2020), to institutions (Andrews-Speed et al., 2021), investments (Shi & Yao, 2019) or analysis of some of the BRI countries (Fernandes, 2021; Xu et al., 2021). From the effects on the reduction of CO_2 emissions (Gu & Zhou, 2020; Hou et al., 2020), to the potential of infrastructure development (Dwyer, 2020), energy, and sustainability (Abdul et al., 2018), addressing also the risks and the potential of this global project (Fernandes, 2021). However, despite several studies highlighting the advantages of energy cooperation being applied to clean energies, such as onshore and offshore wind energy (Zhou et al., 2012), solar (Chen et al., 2019), and hydroelectric (Han & Webber,

2020), there is still few research developed on investments made in renewable energy projects in this Initiative (Fernandes, 2021; Lin & Bega, 2021; Lin et al., 2020). There are also few studies linking these same investments to the energy transition. Thus, we propose in this article to analyze energy cooperation with countries that participate in this initiative, to contribute to the enrichment of the literature, and to fill research gaps.

For the Chinese government, energy cooperation is based on the principles of equality, reciprocity, and mutual benefits, translated into "bilateral and multilateral efforts, within the scope of South-South cooperation, to promote economic and social development through foreign aid, humanitarian assistance, and other means" (China's State Council Information Office, 2021). Bearing in mind the importance of this cooperation, we will examine the "means" that promote the exploration, development, and production of energy, considered as the necessary driving force for the "progress of human civilization (…), for the economy, for people's lives, for national security and the survival and development of humanity" (China's State Council Information Office, 2020). Given the importance of energy for China's energy security,[3] we focused our analysis on energy investments made in the BRI countries between 2013 and 2021, in order to verify whether there is a change in the pattern of these investments, namely in energy sources, regions, and countries. To fulfill our objective, we will use a mixed empirical approach, with an analysis of the strategic objectives presented in the official Chinese documents and reports on the BRI. To analyze investments in the energy sector, we will use statistical data from the Chinese Ministry of Commerce, the Boston University Global Development Policy Center, the Green Finance & Development Center from FISF Fudan University, and the Belt and Road Energy Cooperation of National Energy Administration, evaluating possible changes throughout the analysis, in terms of energy sources with greater investment, as well as the main regions and countries in this Initiative. We observe that data on energy investments in this Initiative vary from source to source and are frequently ambiguous. Another challenge in this study is the large number of countries and regions involved in this Initiative, which forces us to limit our analysis to the major investments.

This article is organized into three sections, the first of which analyzes China's energy panorama and energy cooperation strategies. The following section describes the BRI Energy Initiative and analyzes and discusses the evolution of the Chinese investment in the energy sector. The last section presents some concluding remarks.

FROM OIL INSECURITY TO CLEAN ENERGIES

China is a country of contrasts in terms of energy, being, simultaneously, the largest consumer and the world's largest producer and importer of energy.[4] It is also the world's largest polluter[5] and the largest contributor to the increase in energy production and the development of clean energy technology (EIA, 2020). This disparity is due, on one hand, to being a country with vast energy resources, having the largest oil and gas reserves and the second-largest coal reserves in Asia-Pacific (BP, 2021, pp. 16, 34, 46). On the other hand, its consumption is constantly growing and exceeds the internal production of primary energy. China continues to rely heavily on fossil fuels for power generation, with 57.7 % coming from coal,[6] 20 % from petroleum, and 8 % from natural gas, making it the world's largest emitter of greenhouse gases (see Figure 3.1). However, China is making progress in energy production, with a notable increase in endogenous production in gas and renewable energy production. It has transformed its energy structure and developed the largest hydropower, solar photovoltaics, and wind capacity in the world, with 13 % of total primary energy consumption coming from renewable sources, of which 8 % are from hydroelectricity in 2019 (EIA, 2020).

At the same time, in the last decade, while remaining dependent on fossil energy imports, especially oil and gas (the latter since 2007), energy import

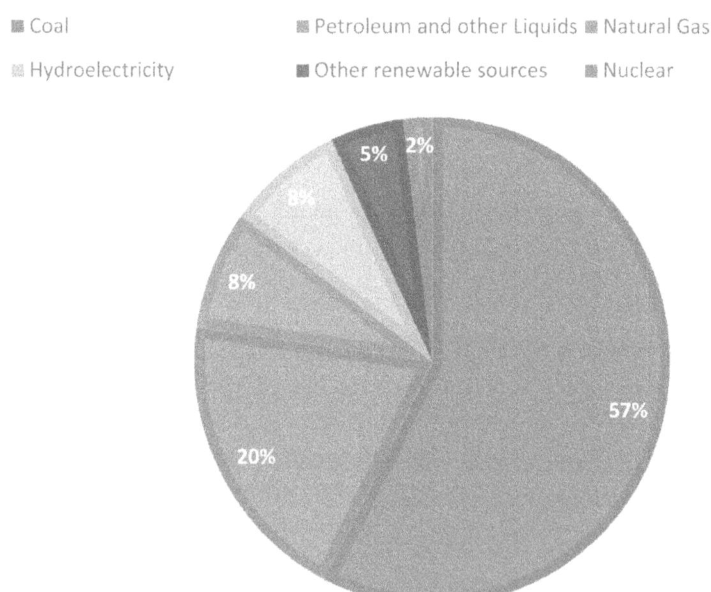

Figure 3.1: China's total primary consumption by fuel type, 2019

Source: Authors' own elaboration (data retrieved from EIA, 2020).

dependence presents numerous challenges to China's energy security, being the largest oil and liquefied natural gas (LNG) importer in the world (EIA, 2020) since 2017 and 2019 respectively. Despite the government's goal of reducing foreign oil dependence to around 62 %, 70 % of its oil consumption is still imported, with the projection that this figure could rise to 80 % (Wang et al., 2018). Gas, as a cleaner fuel than coal, has become an increasingly important transitional energy in China's energy mix, with 4.6 trillion cubic feet (Tcf) currently (7 % above 2018 consumption levels) coming primarily from LNG (62 %), with the remainder coming from pipelines (38 %) (EIA, 2020). China has diversified its import sources, particularly from neighboring countries, with the increasing importance of Russian import, both in oil and gas (see Figures 3.2 and 3.3).

This transformation is a cornerstone of the "New Energy Era" promoted by the Chinese government as an "Energy Revolution" since 2012. At a conference of China's Central Leading Group for Financial and Economic Affairs Commission in June 2014, General Secretary Xi Jinping proposed that China initiate an energy revolution. The revolution encompasses the demand, supply, technology, and the energy system as a whole, as well as strengthening international cooperation and guiding China's energy reforms. The Chinese government published its Energy Production and Consumption Revolution Strategy (2016–2030) in December 2016, outlining the specific actions required to promote the energy

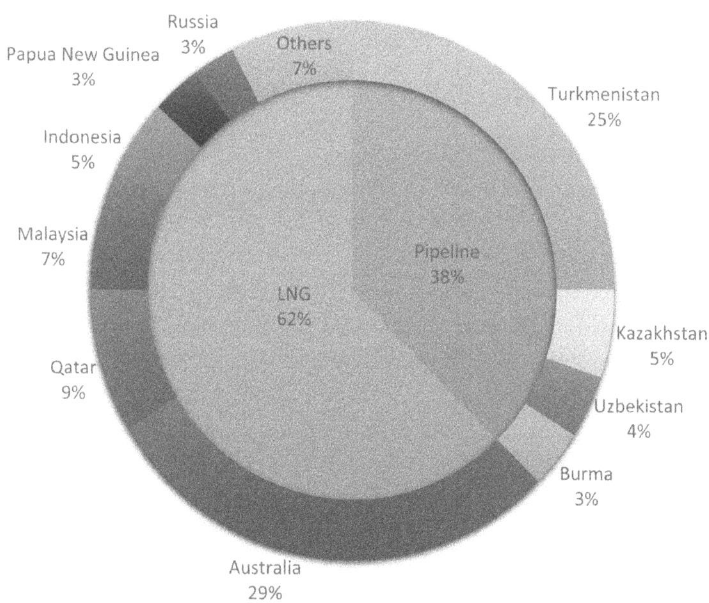

Figure 3.2: China gas imports by region and country, 2019

Source: Authors' own elaboration (data retrieved from EIA, 2020).

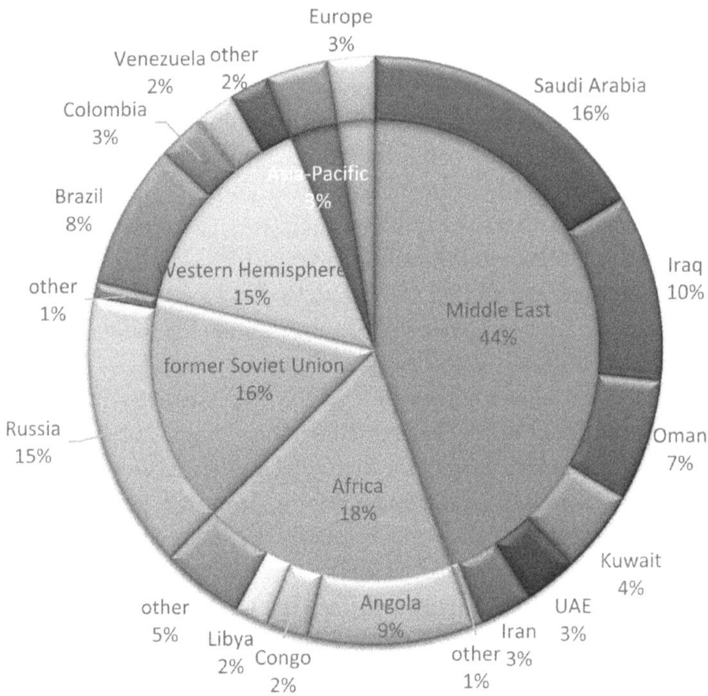

Note: Total may not equal 100% because of independent rounding.

Figure 3.3: China's crude oil imports by source, 2019

Source: Authors' own elaboration (data retrieved from EIA, 2020).

revolution that President Xi had mentioned. This concept was presented for the first time by President Hu Jintao in the report of the 18th CPC National Congress, establishing, as an objective of energy security, the increase in energy production, energy conservation, the reduction and alteration of consumption, and the promotion of clean energy and new low-carbon industries (Xinhua, 2012). Subsequently, Xi Jinping further elaborated on this objective in the energy security strategy "Four Reforms and One Cooperation," presented at the conference of the Leading Group for Financial and Economic Affairs of the Central Committee of the Chinese Communist Party on June 13, 2014 (China's State Council Information Office, 2020). The four reforms comprise (1) the improvement of the energy consumption structure by containing unnecessary consumption; (2) building a more diversified energy supply structure; (3) the development of energy technologies to upgrade the industry; and (4) optimization of the energy system for faster growth of the energy sector.

In the report of the 19th CPC National Congress of October 2017 (People's Republic of China, 2017)[7] Xi Jinping emphasized that China should put quality first and prioritize performance; through supply-side structural reform and working hard to achieve better quality, higher efficiency, and stronger drivers of economic growth. In this "New Era," he also underscored the need to impose new requirements for China to "deepen its study of the energy revolution" and follow the paths that other countries have already passed to "achieve China's energy revolution." In this new roadmap introduced by the 19th, CPC China must build a clean, low-carbon, safe and efficient energy system passing from coal to oil and gas, followed by a switch from oil and gas to renewable energy.

The PRC is attempting to actively contribute to global energy governance, stabilize the global energy market and strengthen international cooperation in response to climate change through cooperation (NEA, 2020). It is also supporting the formulation of responses to global climate change based on the Paris Agreement, focusing, among other measures, on the development of renewable energy, being currently the largest renewable energy market, the largest clean energy equipment manufacturer in the world, and one of the largest investors in the clean energy sector in several countries (China's State Council Information Office, 2020).

In September 2020, at the 75th United Nations Assembly in New York, President Xi Jinping announced that he would adopt tougher climate targets to achieve carbon neutrality by 2060. Afterward, in December of that year, he proposed more ambitious measures to reduce carbon intensity by 2030, reducing carbon dioxide emissions per unit of GDP by more than 65 % compared to 2005 levels and increasing the share of non-fossil fuels in primary energy consumption to around 25 % (Xinhua, 2021, March 16).

China's commitment to achieving carbon neutrality by 2060 is part of the national strategy to build an ecological civilization (*shengtai wenming*) based on the sustainable environmental, economic and social development of China and the world.[8] It also represents not only a technical change in the definition of energy and environmental policy, but also a set of systemic, broad and profound reforms with an impact on the Chinese economy and society. To ensure energy security and accessibility for its citizens and simultaneously achieve these goals, the PRC will have to transform its entire economy over the next 40 years, through a profound reform process similar to the one that industrialized the economy after 1978 (EIA, 2020). In energy terms, it will imply changes in global energy production and trade flows, in particular, in the increase in the production of clean energy needed to combat climate change and change the current energy paradigm. In terms of investment abroad, it also represents a shift in priorities in the energy sector, with a focus on clean energy.

The 14th Five-Year Plan period (14FYP) (2021–2025) will be critical for China to meet the 2060 target, being fundamental for China to accelerate the country's energy revolution while actively working toward the global green and low-carbon energy transition, and engaging in the cooperation and promotion efforts of renewable energy globally. On March 22, 2022, the National Development and Reform Commission (NDRC) and the National Energy Administration (NEA) published the 14FYP for the energy sector, setting out an overall direction, as well as specific tasks and targets, for the coming five years. This plan, that distinguishes itself from the previous by name,[9] instead of being an "energy development plan," is called 14FYP for a "modern energy system," and sets five goals to achieve this "clean, low carbon, safe and highly efficient": it stipulates that the country must strive for "safer and more solid" energy security, achieve a "remarkably effective" energy transition, "significantly" increase energy efficiency, "obviously" improve innovation capabilities and "continuously" improve general energy service levels (NDRC & NEA, 2022). This initiative shows how the Chinese energy system also needs to be reconfigured to accommodate the changing energy mix. In this context, the role of coal was also mentioned, by not defending a simply abandoned source, but using it as a link between the old and the new system, adapting to the new energy challenges imposed by the Russia-Ukraine war and the energy crisis felt since 2021, which shook the Chinese energy system. With regard to energy cooperation, this plan proposes to improve the international energy cooperation mechanism in the field of new energy storage, build a cooperation platform and expand the field of cooperation, promote international cooperation in new energy storage technologies and industries, and achieve high-quality introduction and high-level development of new energy storage technologies and industries.

THE BRI AND ENERGY COOPERATION

According to official information presented in Belt and Road Portal (Liu, 2022) on January 14, 2022, 147 countries and 32 international organizations had signed cooperation agreements for the BRI, however, several countries did not confirm having signed a full memorandum of understanding for cooperating under the BRI framework. These include Russia, Austria, D.R. Congo, Dominica, Niger, and Benin (see Table 3.1).

These countries, including China, account for one-third of global trade and GDP, as well as nearly two-thirds of the world's population (Ruta, 2018). To Gu and Zhou (2020), they are the world's major energy production bases, with abundant renewable energy resource endowment, providing a solid foundation for renewable energy development. Vietnam, Kazakhstan, and Mongolia, for

Table 3.1: Countries of the Belt and Road Initiative

Continents	Countries
Sub-Saharan Africa	Angola; Benin*; Botswana; Burundi; Cape Verde; Cameroon; Chad; Comoros*; Dem. Rep. Congo; Rep. Congo*; Côte d'Ivoire; Equatorial Guinea; Eritrea; Ethiopia; Gabon; Gambia; Ghana; Guinea; Guinea-Bissau; Kenya; Lesotho; Liberia; Madagascar; Mali; Mauritania; Mozambique; Namibia; Niger*; Nigeria; Rwanda; Senegal; Seychelles; Sierra Leone; Somalia; South Africa; South Sudan; Sudan; Tanzania; Togo; Uganda; Zambia; Zimbabwe
Europe & Central Asia	Albania; Armenia; Austria*; Azerbaijan; Belarus; Bosnia and Herzegovina; Bulgaria; Croatia; Cyprus; Czech Republic; Estonia; Georgia; Greece; Hungary; Italy; Kazakhstan; Kyrgyzstan; Latvia; Lithuania**; Luxembourg; Moldova; Montenegro; North Macedonia; Poland; Portugal; Romania; Russian Federation*; Serbia; Slovak Republic; Slovenia; Tajikistan; Turkey; Ukraine; Uzbekistan;
East Asia & Pacific	Brunei Darussalam; China; Cook Islands; Cambodia; Fiji; Indonesia; Kiribati; Korea; Lao PDR; Malaysia; Micronesia; Mongolia; Myanmar; New Zealand; Niue; Papua New Guinea; Philippines; Samoa; Singapore; Solomon Islands; Thailand; East Timor; Tonga; Vanuatu; Vietnam;
Middle East & North Africa	Bahrain; Algeria; Djibouti; Egypt; Iran; Iraq; Kuwait; Lebanon; Libya; Malta; Morocco; Oman; Qatar; Saudi Arabia; Syrian; Tunisia; United Arab Emirates; Yemen
Latin America & Caribbean	Antigua and Barbuda; Barbados; Bolivia; Chile; Costa Rica; Cuba; Dominica*; Dominican Republic; Ecuador; El Salvador; Grenada; Guyana; Jamaica; Nicaragua; Panama; Peru; Suriname; Trinidad and Tobago; Uruguay; Venezuela;
South Asia	Afghanistan; Bangladesh; Maldives; Nepal; Pakistan; Sri Lanka;

* Countries that did not confirm having signed an MoU under the BRI.
** In May 2021, Lithuania pulled out of the 17+1 platform, a vehicle to discuss BRI with eastern and southeastern European countries.
Source: Adapted from Liu (2022).

example, have abundant wind energy resources, while Uzbekistan, India, and Pakistan have extensive solar energy reserves.

In terms of energy, they can be divided into three groups: importers, exporters and transit countries, although some may assume these three categories simultaneously. The first comprises the importing countries from south and central Asia and central and eastern Europe, such as Thailand, Laos, and Bangladesh. The second group includes exporting countries mainly from central and Southeast Asia, the Middle East & North Africa, such as Russia, Kazakhstan, Saudi

Arabia, Iran, and Indonesia. In turn, the third group is made of countries along the transport routes, such as Pakistan, Myanmar, and Kazakhstan.

Beijing has been strengthening relations with these three groups through intense energy diplomacy, which combines different actions that involve visits by senior government officials, financial support, the signing of memoranda of understanding (MoU), and the establishment of Strategic Partnerships (*zhanlue huoban guanxi*). It has also supported Chinese companies, financially and diplomatically, to invest in these same countries in sectors identified as priorities by the government, particularly in the energy sector (Fernandes, 2021).

Traditionally, China's energy cooperation was oriented toward the security of supply, especially oil, to diversify transport routes and suppliers and access to new technologies and know-how. At present, it also integrates the Chinese government's concerns "with increasingly critical global problems, such as climate change, environmental risks and challenges and energy and resource constraints" (China's State Council Information Office, 2020). In this way, in addition to promoting the domestic use of clean, low-carbon energy, the PRC cooperates with a large number of countries in the process of shifting toward low-carbon growth and the use and production of new energy sources. This evolution in cooperation represents, at the same time, the expansion of the challenges to energy security, as well as the PRC's commitment to global energy governance. In particular, in supporting the international community to achieve the goals set by the United Nations for Sustainable Development of "ensuring access to cheap, reliable, sustainable and renewable energy for all" (NDRC, 2017a).

The Chinese government pursues its energy policy to have a solid and sustained economic and social development, while contributing to world energy security, addressing global climate change and boosting global economic growth. In this sense, it has made the development of renewable energies, namely hydro, solar, wind, nuclear, and geothermal energy, the construction of transmission, transformation, and distribution networks and the expansion of access to energy, a national and global priority (China's State Council Information Office, 2021).

As mentioned, energy cooperation is one of the main features of BRI, whose principles to be developed have been identified in several strategic documents. In 2017, the National Development and Reform Commission of the State Council of China (NDRC) and the NEA presented the "Vision and Actions on jointly Building Silk Road Economic Belt and 21st-Century Maritime Silk Road." This white paper identifies six principles: openness, mutual benefit, market orientation, safety, respect for the environment and harmony. It also identifies the priorities of this same cooperation, including policy coordination, access to trade, energy investment, energy production capacity, energy infrastructure connectivity, sustainability, and governance (NDRC, 2017b).

Partly as a response to the increasing international criticism on China, for its alleged promotion of dependence on fossil fuels in developing nations and investing in environmentally damaging infrastructure projects, as a way of supporting the global energy transition over the past years, the Chinese government has been emphasizing on developing a "green" and "high-quality" Belt and Road Initiative. In this context, the Ministry of Environmental Protection[10] published the "Guidance on Promoting Green Belt and Road" in 2017, a document that "stresses the relevance of the "ecological civilization," "green development concepts," "principles of resource efficiency and environmental friendliness" within the five goals of the Belt and Road Initiative." It has also drafted two more documents, the "Vision for Maritime Cooperation under the Belt and Road Initiative" (NDRC, 2017b) and the "China's Arctic Policy" (China's State Council Information Office, 2018), where, alongside these principles, green cooperation was highlighted, in particular for the generation of renewable energy, emphasizing that its investment projects will be used to promote the Paris Agreement and the 2030 Sustainable Development Goals, and are motivated by the need to "share the ecological civilization philosophy and achieve sustainable development" (BRIGC, 2022).

Chinese cooperation in the energy sector in the BRI countries takes place on two levels: the first revolves around bilateral investment agreements between China and the BRI member countries and between companies on both sides; while on the second level China establishes several multilateral cooperation platforms to reinforce the importance of energy cooperation in this initiative. In this sense, the Belt and Road Energy Partnership (BREP) was created on October 2018, during the Belt and Road Energy Ministerial Conference in Suzhou. Officially launched in April of the following year, it is made up of 30 member countries that share the same challenges to global energy development (People's Republic of China, 2021). BREP aims to contribute to six objectives: (1) to facilitate communication and coordination among participating countries in energy policy, development planning, laws and regulations; (2) to strengthen infrastructure connectivity, facilitate energy trade and contribute to the development of an open and stable global energy market; (3) to improve energy investment and cooperation in industrial capacity building, reducing investment barriers, improving the investment environment and reducing project-financing costs across the energy industry value chain along the BRI; (4) to facilitate cooperation in innovation and dissemination of advanced technologies throughout the energy industry, while protecting intellectual property; (5) to promote cooperation on clean energy and energy efficiency to address climate change, ensure universal access to affordable, reliable and sustainable modern energy services; and (6) to improve cooperation in capacity building and training of people (NEA, 2019).

The BRI International Green Development Coalition (BRIGC) was also created in 2019, after the second Belt and Road Forum, in order to strengthen multilateral cooperation. The BRIGC is overseen by China's Ministry of Ecology and Environment, and since it was initiated more than 100 international and Chinese partner institutions were included, such as environment ministries of 25 countries that may host BRI projects, eight intergovernmental organizations, including several UN agencies and over 60 non-governmental organizations and research institutes along with 30 companies (IISD, 2019).

It is important not to think of the Belt and Road as a unified, coherent strategy, but rather as a fragmented collection of bilateral arrangements made on different terms. This is illustrated by the fact that governments receiving Chinese loans are not always sure which authority in China they are dealing with. In fact, 15 different Chinese government ministries claim some responsibility for Belt and Road projects, and Chinese provinces have their own competing agendas, businesses, and projects. In addition, Chinese diplomats sign up client governments to major projects to demonstrate loyalty to the party as opposed to promoting a viable project and even the Chinese central government is still unable to produce a list of which projects are part of the BRI and which are not (Yu & Wallace, 2021).

This is part of a wider issue of the opaque nature of the Belt and Road and the loans on which it is built. The Chinese government has never published detailed information about the size and terms of Belt and Road loans, and this absence of information feeds confusion and mistrust. Many countries have put projects on hold or canceled them outright: of the 52 coal-fired power plants planned for development through the BRI between 2014 and 2020, 25 were shelved and eight were canceled (Economy, 2022).

Following the COVID-19 pandemic, Chinese state banks directed more support to projects at home, echoing the behavior of much of the rest of the world. Internationally, China has drawn in the scope of its ambitions to projects along its enormous border and in Southeast Asia. Investments abroad have declined considerably since a peak in 2015 (Yu & Wallace, 2021).

CHINA ENERGY BRI INVESTMENTS

In this section, we will analyze the level of investment of China in the energy sector under the BRI framework, from 2013 until the end of 2021. To begin with, it is important to note that investments related to the energy sector constitute (together with transport) most of China's BRI engagement (see Figure 3.4). The only period we saw a change in this investment pattern was 2020 and 2021, under the effects of the pandemic restrictions. In those years, there was a reduction in investments in these sectors, respectively, of 67 % and 65 %, which was counterbalanced by an increase in the sector of health (Nedopil, 2022, p. 11).

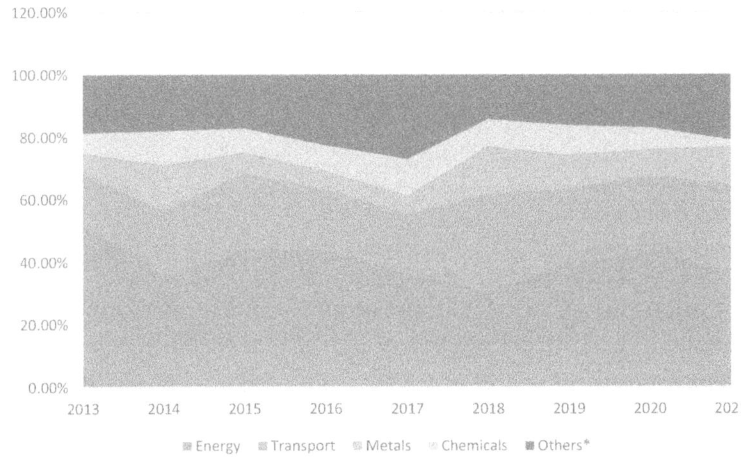

Figure 3.4: Main sectors of investment in the BRI, 2013–2021

* Includes Health, Logistics, Real Estate, Utilities, others

Source: Authors' own elaboration (data retrieved from Nedopil, 2022, p. 12).

As mentioned by Wu Hao et al. (2020), infrastructure development is one of the four areas of energy cooperation within the BRI, in addition to diversifying energy production, expanding international energy technology cooperation, and sustaining global energy governance. The BRI's focus on infrastructure is on the energy and transport sector, which is especially related to the strategy of security of supply and diversification of energy sources. The development of new infrastructures for land transport of energy allows for the protection of energy flows to China as well as some BRI importing countries, avoiding the challenges that the domain of maritime imports implies for supply security, namely the Malacca Strait and the South China Sea.

It is interesting to note that the primacy of these two sectors predated the launch of the BRI in 2013, as they were the priority investments in the Chinese energy security strategy (Fernandes, 2013). This initiative reinforced the priority of investment in these sectors in other geographic areas, in line with the objectives of the previous Going Out strategy, as well as China's supply energy security strategy. In this way, at the beginning of the BRI, we saw the completion of many projects that were already being developed or planned to be executed, such as the Pakistan energy corridor that later came to be dominated in the China-Pakistan Economic Corridor (CPEC) and the Power of Siberia gas pipeline with Russia. CPEC includes a wide range of infrastructure projects, such as roads, railways, pipelines and optical cables, with more than half of the investment in this corridor going to energy projects, as mentioned in Table 3.2. In the twenty-first-century maritime route, in line with China's previous String of Pearls strategy, priority

Table 3.2: Energy Projects Under CPEC

Project Name	MW	Status
Sahiwal Coal-fired Power Plant	1,320	Completed
China Hub Coal Power Project, Hub Balochistan	1,320	Completed
Engro Thar Coal Power Project	660	Completed
Quaid-e-Azam Solar Park (Bahawalpur)	400/600	Completed
Hydro China Dawood Wind Farm, Gharo, Thatta	50	Completed
Wind Farm, Jhimpir, Thatta	100	Completed
Sachal Wind Farm, Jhimpir, Thatta	50	Completed
Three Gorges Second and Third Wind Power Project	100	Completed
Matiari to Lahore ±660 kV HVDC Transmission Line Project	4,000	Completed
Thar Coal Block-I 7.8 mtpa & Power Plant (2×660MW) (Shanghai Electric)	1,320	Under construction
HUBCO Thar Coal Power Project (Thar Energy)	330	Under construction
HUBCO ThalNova Thar Coal Power Project	330	Under construction
Suki Kinari Hydropower Project, KP	870	Under construction

Source: CPEC Authority Office (2022).

was given to the construction of ports, such as the development of the Port of Gwadar in Pakistan, or the construction of the ports of Piraeus in Greece, the Lamu, and the Mombasa in Kenya, as well as in Djibouti in the Horn of Africa (Fernandes, 2021).

In 2021, total engagement in the energy sector reached about US$22.3 billion, around a 14 % year-over-year decrease, compared to more than US$26.1 billion in engagement in 2020 and almost US$44.8 billion in 2019 (see Figure 3.5). For 2022, although some encouraging signs are already taking place, the year should continue to be dominated by COVID-19 uncertainty. This is also a recognition

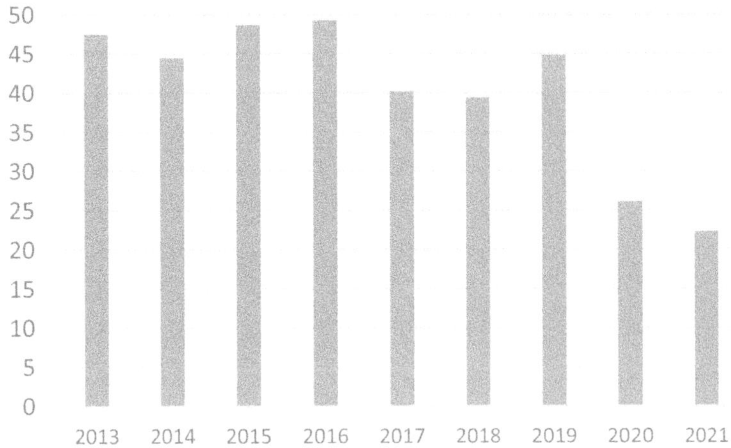

Figure 3.5: Chinese energy investments in countries of BRI from 2013 to 2021 in billion U.S. dollars

Source: Authors' own elaboration (data retrieved from Textor, 2022).

of the Chinese Ministry of Commerce (MOFCOM), which put a brake on fast overseas expansion in its 14th Five-Year Plan (FYP) for 2021 to 2025: it plans for China to invest US$550 billion (that includes non-BRI countries), down 25 % from US$740 billion in the 2016–2020 period. Nevertheless, with a resurgent post-COVID19 world, there is both more scope and demand for overseas finance, yet unlikely to the same level as in the late 2010s (Nedopil, 2022).

Traditionally, the major players for BRI investments in the energy sector have been SOE's (State-Owned Enterprises). Among them, Power Construction Corp (Power China), China Petroleum and Chemical (Sinopec), China Energy Engineering, China National Petroleum Corp (CNPC), China National Offshore Oil (CNOOC), and China Three Georges stand out.

As it was already mentioned, bearing in mind priority given in China to the security of supply, investments of Chinese companies abroad were traditionally made in projects of fossil fuels. As a result, during the first years of BRI, investments in the energy sector were dominated by oil and coal. From Figure 3.6, in 2013, oil and coal together represented 59.98 % of total investments. In 2015, coal alone represented 42.5 % of total investments in the energy sector and, in 2018, oil concentrated 37.08 % of the total that year.

The year of 2021 marks a turning point in Chinese energy investments, with investments in renewable sources (wind and solar) at the same level as those made in oil, both with 31 %. Natural gas continues to be a transition source, occupying 22 % of the total. It is interesting to note that 2021 also marks the year with no indication of investments in the coal sector (see Figure 3.6).

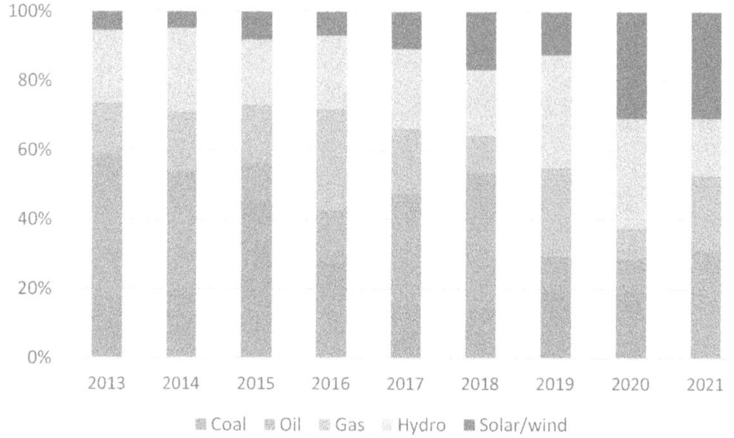

Figure 3.6: Chinese energy investments in the Belt and Road Initiative, 2013–2021, in percentage

Source: Authors' own elaboration (data retrieved from Nedopil, 2022).

According to Nedopil (2021b), between the second half of 2014 and the end of 2020, 52 coal-fired power projects abroad had been announced with Chinese financial participation. Of these projects, only one came on stream: the 1.3 GW Payra Patuakhali coal-fired power plant in Kalapara, Bangladesh, in the first half of 2020. Simultaneously, 25 of the projects announced since 2014 were shelved and eight closed or canceled. On the other hand, in 2021, no Chinese support was announced for the construction of new coal plants abroad.[11] Although these figures correspond to President Ji Xiping's stated goal, it is still too early to tell how much will be continued and how real the fact that Chinese companies have not participated in coal investments abroad will be. However, it remains a watershed moment in the history of Chinese investment, particularly in the BRI.

There are multiple explanations for this change, which marks a fundamental stage in the global energy transition, given that the PRC is the largest consumer and largest investor in coal production in the world. In geopolitical and energy terms, two factors influenced this change. The first is the fact that several BRI countries (e.g., Pakistan, Bangladesh) have announced the phasing out of new investments in coal (Lo, 2020), following the objective expressed by most countries of promoting post-pandemic green recovery and energy transition to low carbon. Secondly, this shift to green energy is in line with the goal also announced by President Xi Jinping at the 76th United Nations General Assembly in September 2021, to stop building new coal-fired power projects abroad, offering in return support for the development of green and low-carbon energy (Xinhua, 2021, September 22).

Lastly, the other greatest change of pattern between 2013 and 2021 was the increasing importance of hydro and solar energy. The trend of increasing shares of renewable energy investments in the BRI has accelerated since 2017, when only 35 % of BRI investments went to hydro, solar and wind projects. In 2020, 60.75 % of BRI investments went into these sectors, a strong relative increase (Nedopil, 2021a). The bet on renewable energies over fossil energies is due to a variety of factors. For instance, solar and wind energy have become more competitive in comparison to fossil energy, with the costs of producing and purchasing solar energy panels falling significantly year on year. According to the International Renewable Energy Agency (IRENA), in 2020, the costs of "solar power fell by 16 %, onshore wind by 13 percent, offshore wind by 9 percent, and solar PV by 7 percent." This agency also predicts that in 2022 the global cost of renewables will continue to decline, with the onshore wind being 20–27 % cheaper than the new coal-based power generation option (IRENA, 2021).

In addition to becoming financially more attractive, the "opportunity" factor also contributed to the increase in investments in renewable energies by Chinese companies abroad. After several years of investing in the domestic energy market, especially in wind energy, Chinese companies found themselves with the challenge of domestic overcapacity accompanied by the government's slowdown in the use of wind farms.[12] In line with the desire of BRI countries to contribute to the energy transition to clean energy, Chinese companies have gone abroad as a way to overcome the investment capacity challenges at home (Fernandes, 2020; Geng, 2021).[13]

Another relevant issue for this increase in investment abroad in clean energy is the set of guidelines launched since the BRI Vision in 2015, with great emphasis on green and low-carbon development, as well as biodiversity protection. Since then, and as mentioned earlier, a set of annual policy recommendations have been released by the China Council for International Cooperation on Environment and Development (CCICED) on greening the BRI, which has received the endorsement of President Xi Jinping. The Chinese government guidelines indicated in the "Guidelines for Greening Overseas Investment and Cooperation" issued in 2020, encourage companies to carry out measures to prevent ecological and environmental risks and to improve ecological and environmental management capacity in the implementation phase of their projects. In addition, they must follow host country's rules and standards and take reasonable and necessary steps to reduce or mitigate adverse environmental impacts.

Regarding the main energy investment areas, the data displays that these were not evenly distributed among all regions, with Asia being the main region since the creation of this initiative, particularly East Asia (see Figure 3.7). One of the explanations for the supremacy of Asia is due to the bet on the "strategy

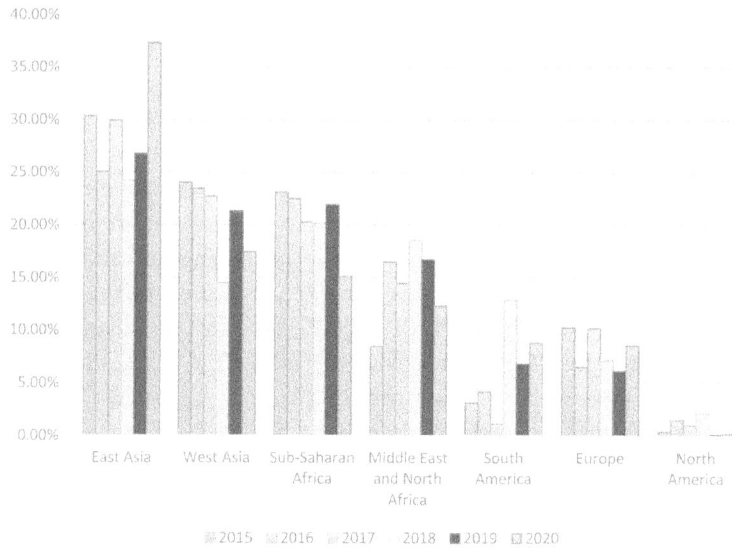

Figure 3.7: BRI investments in different regions, 2015–2020, in percentage

Source: Authors' own elaboration (data retrieved from Nedopil, 2021a).

for energy security through proximity," investing in neighboring Asian countries (Fernandes, 2013, 2019).

In addition to the diversity in geography, the predominance of investments in developing and emerging markets is another feature of BRI energy investments, where projects avoid bidding more easily and contracting is made directly to energy companies. Albeit there are also some successful investments in advanced energy markets, especially in southern and western Europe, that have targeted a broader range of European countries (e.g., Portugal, Greece, United Kingdom) and entered multiple energy sectors, particularly energy infrastructure and renewable energies.

The analysis of investments by region shows that, despite variations from year to year, Asia continues to be the main investment area, particularly East Asia. Due to the pandemic, there was a decrease in investments in the Middle East and North Africa between 2019 and 2020. With an opposite variation, in 2021 there was a return to this geographical area, with greater investment in them, to the detriment of investments in Asia (see Figure 3.8).

Traditionally, Southeast Asia is also one of China's main energy investment areas in the Asian region (Fernandes, 2013), especially in the coal sector. Africa, on the contrary, although it maintains the traditional investments in the gas and oil sector, and as we can see in Figure 3.9, there is a greater predominance of renewable energies (wind, hydro and solar).

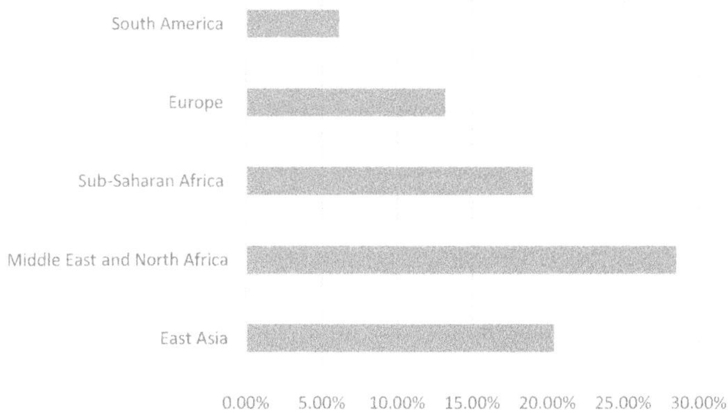

Figure 3.8: Investments in BRI by region, 2021, in percentage

Source: Authors' own elaboration (data retrieved from Nedopil, 2022).

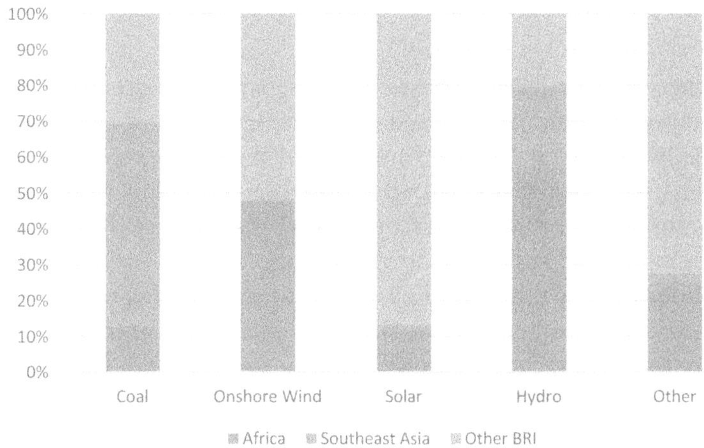

Figure 3.9: Investment in all BRI countries by fuel type, 2013–2020

Source: Authors' own elaboration (data retrieved from Ma, 2022).

Analyzing Chinese energy engagement in different BRI countries, we find that Iraq was the country that received by far the most energy investments in 2021, followed by Indonesia (see Figure 3.10). With this result, Iraq moved up to be the third-most important partner in the BRI for energy engagement between 2013 and 2021, after Pakistan and the Russian Federation. In 2020, the ranking was different, as it was led by Vietnam, Indonesia, Pakistan, and Chile. It is important to note that Bangladesh, Egypt, Peru, Uzbekistan, and Nigeria saw BRI investments more than double in the first half of 2021 compared to the first half of 2020. Vietnam continued to be a major beneficiary of Chinese financing and investment in 2021.

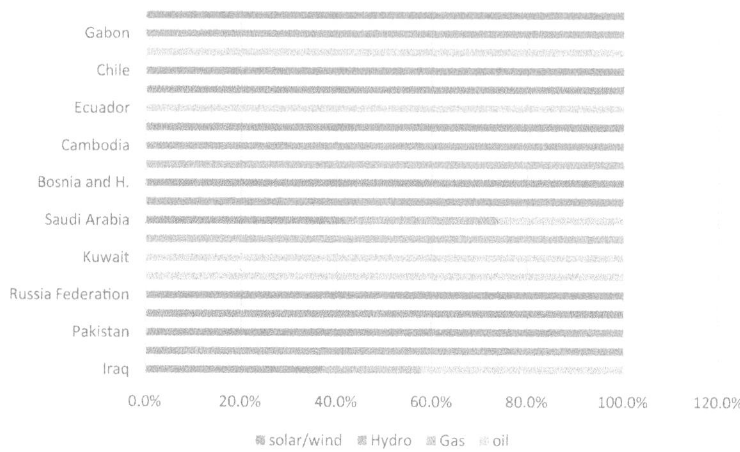

Figure 3.10: Chinese investment in the BRI energy sector by main countries, 2013–2020
Source: Authors' own elaboration (data retrieved from Nedopil, 2022).

Over the past years, Pakistan has been the largest recipient of both coal-related (followed closely by Indonesia) and hydropower-related investments. Overall, Pakistan attracted more than 47 % of renewable energy investments (41 % of which were in hydropower), while Russia and the United Arab Emirates predominantly received fossil fuel-related energy investments (Nedopil, 2021b). The changes mentioned in terms of sources are also reflected in the country analyses, with Iraq, Tanzania, Kuwait, Ecuador, and Uganda being the largest recipients of oil investments by 2021. In terms of gas, Iraq is, once again, in first, followed by the Russian Federation, Uzbekistan, and Thailand. Finally, in terms of renewable energy, Indonesia, Pakistan, Nepal, Cambodia, and Gabon received the most investments in hydropower, while Ukraine, Chile, Nigeria, Egypt, and Vietnam were the main recipients of solar and wind energy.

CONCLUSION

The PRC's white paper "Energy in China's New Era" highlights, in the introduction, the importance that energy has for national security and the progress of human civilization. For China, as the world's largest energy consumer, it is vital to have stable and secure supplies of energy. Since China became an energy importer in 1993, the main improvement has undoubtedly been a large bet on the consumption, production, and development of clean energies. As part of the energy revolution, this bet had implications for Chinese energy geopolitics, with a gradual shift from quantitative strategic objectives to qualitative objectives.

That is, from the import of oil, the PRC also became concerned with improving and diversifying transport infrastructure and industries, production, and energy development in Chinese territory and in other countries. It is in this context that the BRI should be inserted, a global project with energy cooperation as one of its main characteristics.

President Xi's carbon-neutral 2060 target represents a turning point in the global energy transition, but in many ways builds on past policies and international cooperation for sustainable low-carbon development. Although China has still a difficult and challenging path to follow in order to fulfill this ambitious goal, the focus on energy transition, which became increasingly clear since 2017, is now a reality and should be intensified in the coming years.

From our analysis of investments made in the BRI energy sector from 2013 until the end of 2021, there is an ongoing change of pattern, with the increasing share of renewables (particularly hydro, wind, and solar) in the energy mix, currently on par with oil. The lack of investments in new coal projects in 2021 is also particularly significant, but it is still to be confirmed if it will be maintained in the future.

Bearing in mind the nature and objectives of BRI, this reorientation can also be regarded as the Chinese contribution to the energy transition efforts on a global scale. However, it is important to underline that more studies will be needed in order to confirm the tendency of "greening" the BRI. The post-pandemic years will be fundamental to consolidate this tendency, most importantly until the end of this decade. And, of course, the outcome of the ongoing Russian military intervention in Ukraine, including possible changes in the world economic order, will also determine future decisions on energy policy from the PRC, eventually contributing for the reinforcement of investments in energy renewables (both in China and in BRI countries), as a more viable, cleaner and safe alternative to fossil fuels.

NOTES

1 This chapter obtained FCT funding from the IPRI-UN Multiannual project, under Reference UIDB/04627/2020.

2 According to the report of the Communist Party of China's 19th National Congress in 2017, China's economy has transitioned from a period of rapid growth to one of high-quality development. It stated that China must concentrate on improving the supply system and strengthening the economy in terms of quality. Quality energy is an essential component of the supply system and a key goal of the energy revolution (People's Republic of China, 2017).

3 The importance of energy to China can be seen in the preamble of the white paper Energy in China's New Era published in December 2020 "Energy is the foundation and driving force for the progress of human civilization. It matters to the economy, to people's lives, to national security, and to the survival and development of humanity. It is of vital importance in advancing social and economic development and public welfare" (China's State Council Information Office, 2020).

4 China's primary energy production in 2019 reached 3.97 billion tons of standard coal, making it the world's largest energy producer (NEA, 2020).

5 The PRC is the biggest environmental polluter on the planet, with 90 % of the production of greenhouse gas emissions coming from its energy sector (International Energy Agency, 2021, p. 13).

6 Reducing coal consumption is a goal for all major global consumers, as well as for China. China coal consumption has been progressively reduced, in 2009 it represented 70 % of their power generation mix (Fernandes, 2013, p. 4). However, according to estimates of China's National Bureau of Statistics, after several years of declines, China's coal consumption grew by 1 % each year in 2018 and 2019, based on physical volume (more than 4.3 billion short tons in 2019) (EIA, 2020).

7 During the congress, the Constitution of China Communist Party was amended to include a new guiding ideology called Xi Jinping Thought on Socialism with Chinese Characteristics for a New Era (People's Republic of China, 2017).

8 The concept of ecological civilization is considered the main ideological frame of reference for Chinese environmental and climate policies and actions at different levels of government. It was included in the Chinese constitution in 2018 and serves as a vision of sustainable development with Chinese characteristics and refers to Chinese philosophical and civilization traditions (Kuhn, 2019).

9 For Yin Ming beyond this difference, while the 13th FYP focuses on the new energy security strategy of four revolutions and one cooperation, focusing on task deployment, the 14th FYP is task-oriented oriented to this energy security strategy. For more details, see Yin Ming (2022). 解析《"十四五"现代能源体系规划》(Analysis of the "14th Five-Year Plan of the Modern Energy System"), https://mp.weixin.qq.com/s/2tdt7ReLGYY9zmiyUxSWqg. See also NEA (2022). 《"十四五"新型储能发展实施方案》解读(Interpretation of the "14th Five-Year Implementation Plan for the Development of New Energy Storage"), http://www.nea.gov.cn/2022-03/21/c_1310523223.htm.

10 Currently the Ministry of Ecology and Environment.

11 According to Lin and Schmidt (2022), between 2019 and 2020, Chinese-backed coal plants worth $47 billion were canceled, mothballed, or shelved. Through the first part of this year, China had not financed any new coal plants overseas, and only three Chinese-financed projects moved forward through pre-construction phases of development in 2021.

12 While some provincial governments such as Guangdong and Zhejiang will continue to subsidize offshore wind farms, the central government has removed direct subsidies for most renewable projects. According to Diana Xia (2021) China intends to increase offshore wind capacity by 5x-6x between 2021 and 2025, compared to end-of-2020 levels. Nonetheless, we anticipate that the remaining installations will be pushed back to 2024–2025 due to concerns about project returns in the absence of central-level subsidies.

13 China faces several challenges in its transition from renewable to clean energy. It continues, as mentioned before, with an economy still highly dependent on coal, which implies the need

for considerable costs to transfer this capacity to other energy sources, such as natural gas and renewable energy. Furthermore, the construction of solar panels and wind farms in China has outpaced upgrades to its electricity grid, generating a large amount of waste. To increase the challenges, even with the great development of renewable energy production in the territory, there are still no failures in the transmission system between provinces, with the areas with the greatest wind and solar potential in China located in western areas, such as predominant regions of Xinjiang Uyghur and Inner Mongolia, as well as Gansu Province, far from the densely populated and energy-hungry eastern regions.

REFERENCES

Abdul, A., Liu, X., Amin, W., Ozturk, I., Rehman, O., & Sarwar, S. (2018). Energy and ecological sustainability: Challenges and panoramas in Belt and Road Initiative countries. *Sustainability, 10(8)*, 2743–2721.

Andrews-Speed, P., Yao, L., & Shi, X. (2021). ASEAN electricity market integration: How can belt and road initiative bring new life to it? *The Singapore Economic Review, 66*(1), 85–103.

BP. (2021). *Statistical Review of World Energy 2021.* Statistical Review of World Energy. https://www.bp.com/content/dam/bp/business-sites/en/global/corporate/pdfs/energy-economics/statistical-review/bp-stats-review-2021-full-report.pdf

BRIGC. (2022). *BRIGC.* Retrieved from Belt and Road Initiative International Green Development Coalition (BRIGC). http://en.brigc.net/

Chen, S., Lu, X., Miao, Y., Deng, Y., Nielsen, C.P., Elbot, N., Wang, Y., Logan, K. G., McElroy, M. B., & Hao, J. (2019). The potential of photovoltaics to power the Belt and Road Initiative. *Joule, 3(8)*, 1895–1912. https://doi.org/10.1016/j.joule.2019.06.006

China's State Council Information Office. (2018). *China's Arctic Policy.* Retrieved January 12, 2021, from https://english.www.gov.cn/archive/white_paper/2018/01/26/content_281476026660336.htm

China's State Council Information Office. (2020). *Energy in China's new era.* Retrieved January 12, 2021, from http://english.www.gov.cn/archive/whitepaper/202012/21/content_WS5fe0572bc6d0f725769423cb.html

China's State Council Information Office. (2021). *China's international development cooperation in the new era.* Retrieved October 13, 2021, from http://obor.nea.gov.cn/detail/15030.html

CPEC Authority Office. (2022). *Energy projects under CPEC.* Retrieved January 14, 2022, from China-Pakistan Economic Corridor. http://cpec.gov.pk/energy

Dwyer, M. B. (2020, April). "They will not automatically benefit": The politics of infrastructure development in Laos's Northern Economic Corridor. *Political Geography, 78*, 102118. https://doi.org/10.1016/j.polgeo.2019.102118

Economy, E. (2022, January/February). Xi Jinping's New World Order. *Foreign Affairs, 101*(1), 52–67. ISSN 00157120.

EIA. (2020). *China energy analysis.* U.S. Energy Information Administration. Retrieved October 12, 2021, from https://www.eia.gov/international/content/analysis/countries_long/China/china.pdf

Fernandes, C. (2013). *China Hoje. Relações Internacionais e necessidades energéticas. As relações com a comunidade dos países de Língua Portuguesa.* Faculdade de Ciências Sociais e Humanas da Universidade de Lisboa.

Fernandes, C. (2019). China energy security and portuguese speaking countries. In F. Ilhéu, P. Duarte, & F. Leandro (Eds.), *The new Silk Road and the Portuguese speaking countries in the New World context* (pp. 121–135). Suma Oriental.

Fernandes, C. (2020). China-Africa energy cooperation: From fossil to "clean" energies. *Ralações Internacionais*, *65*, 27–41. https://doi.org/10.23906/ri2020.65a03

Fernandes, C. (2021). China energy security and Portugal in Belt and Road Iniciative. In S. Gaspar & I. Rodrigues (Eds.), *The presence of China and the China diaspora in Portugal and Portuguese speak countries* (pp. 127–150). Brill.

Geng, Q. (2021). The Belt and Road Initiative and its implications for global renewable energy development. *Current Sustainable Renewable Energy Report*, *8*, 40–49. https://doi.org/10.1007/s40518-020-00172-2

Gu, A., & Zhou, X. (2020, April 6). Emission reduction effects of the green energy investment projects of China in Belt and Road Initiative countries. *Ecosystem Health and Sustainability*, *6*(1). https://doi.org/10.1080/20964129.2020.1747947

Han, X., & Webber, M. (2020, March). From Chinese dam building in Africa to the Belt and Road Initiative: Assembling infrastructure projects and their linkages. *Political Geography*, *77*. https://doi.org/10.1016/j.polgeo.2019.102102

Hou, J., Deng, X., Springer, C., & Teng, F. (2020, April 6). A global analysis of CO_2 and non-CO_2 GHG emissions embodied in trade with Belt and Road Initiative countries. *Ecosystem Health and Sustainability*, *6*(1). https://doi.org/10.1080/20964129.2020.1761888

IISD. (2019, April 25). *Coalition aims to build sustainability into Belt and Road Initiative projects.* Retrieved October 2021, from https://www.iisd.org/articles/coalition-aims-build-sustainability-belt-and-road-initiative-projects

International Energy Agency. (2021). *An energy sector. Roadmap to carbon neutrality in China.* Retrieved October 12, 2021, from https://iea.blob.core.windows.net/assets/6689062e-43fc-40c8-9659-01cf96150318/AnenergysectorroadmaptocarbonneutralityinChina.pdf

International Renewable Energy Agency. (2021). *Renewable power generation costs in 2020.* https://www.irena.org/-/media/Files/IRENA/Agency/Publication/2021/Jun/IRENA_Power_Generation_Costs_2020.pdf?la=en&hash=755CB6E57667D53B629967EC7F9BE57A55D1CD78

Kuhn, B. (2019, August 26). *Ecological civilisation in China.* Retrieved October 1, 2021, from Dialogue of Civilizations Research Institute. https://doc-research.org/2019/08/ecological-civilisation-china-berthold/

Lin, B., Bae, N., & Bega, F. (2020). China's Belt & Road Initiative nuclear export: Implications for energy cooperation. *Energy Policy*, *142*, 111519. https://doi.org/10.1016/j.enpol.2020.111519

Lin, B., & Bega, F. (2021). China's Belt & Road Initiative coal power cooperation: Transitioning toward low-carbon development. *Energy Policy*, *156*, 112438. https://doi.org/10.1016/j.enpol.2021.112438

Lin, A., & Schmidt, J. (2022). *China announces it will not build new coal plants abroad.* Retrieved April 9, 2022, from Natural Resources Defense Council. https://www.nrdc.org/experts/alvin-lin/china-announces-it-will-not-build-new-coal-plants-abroad-0

Liu, M. (2022, February 6). *已同中国签订共建"一带一路"合作文件的国家一览* (*A list of the countries that have signed cooperation documents with China to jointly build the Belt and Road*). Retrieved from 中国一带一路网 (Belt and Road Portal). https://www.yidaiyilu.gov.cn/xwzx/roll/77298.htm

Lo, J. (2020, December 16). *Pakistan signals coal power exit, in potential model for China's belt and road.* Retrieved October 12, 2021, from https://www.climatechangenews.com/2020/12/16/pakistan-signals-coal-power-exit-potential-model-chinas-belt-road/

Ma, Z. (2022, February 17). *China committed to phase out overseas coal investment. New database tracks progress.* Retrieved February 25, 2022, from https://www.wri.org/insights/china-phasing-out-overseas-coal-investment-track-progress

National Energy Adminstration. (2019, April 25). *Cooperation principles and concrete actions of the belt and road energy partnership (BREP).* Retrieved October 3, 2021, from Belt and Road Energy Cooperation. http://obor.nea.gov.cn/detail/8210.html

National Energy Adminstration. (2020, December 31). *新时代中国能源在高质量发展道路上奋勇前进 (In the new era, China's energy is advancing bravely on the road of high-quality development).* Retrieved January 6, 2021, from . http://www.nea.gov.cn/2020-12/31/c_139631430.htm

NDRC. (2015). *Vision and actions on jointly building Silk Road economic belt and 21st-century maritime Silk Road.* Ministry of Foreign Affairs and Ministry of Commerce of the People's Republic of China. Retrieved March 14, 2021, from https://www.fmprc.gov.cn/mfa_eng/zxxx_662805/t1249618.shtml

NDRC. (2017a). *Energy supply and consumption revolution strategy (2016–2030).* Retrieved October 29, 2019, from http://www.sdpc.gov.cn/gzdt/201704/t20170425_845304.html

NDRC. (2017b). *Vision and actions on energy cooperation in jointly building Silk Road economic belt and 21st-century maritime Silk Road.* Beijing. Retrieved June 4, 2021, from http://obor.nea.gov.cn/detail/669.html

NDRC & NEA. (2022, March 22). *"十四五"现代能源体系规划 ("14th Five-Year" modern energy system planning).* Retrieved April 10, 2022, from National Energy Administration. https://www.ndrc.gov.cn/xxgk/zcfb/ghwb/202203/P020220322582066837126.pdf

Nedopil, C. (2021a). *China's Investments in the Belt and Road Initiative (BRI) in 2020.* Green BRI Center, International Institute of Green Finance (IIGF). Retrieved January 2022, from https://greenfdc.org/wp-content/uploads/2021/01/China-BRI-Investment-Report-2020.pdf

Nedopil, C. (2021b). *Coal phase-out in the Belt and Road Initiative (BRI): An analysis of Chinese-backed coal power from 2014–2020. Green BRI Center.* International Institute of Green Finance. https://greenfdc.org/wp-content/uploads/2021/06/Christoph_NEDOPIL_Wang_2021_Coal-phase-out-in-the-Belt-and-Road-Initiative-BRI_Fin.pdf

Nedopil, C. (2022). China Belt and Road Initiative (BRI) Investment Report 2021. Green Finance & Development Center, FISF Fudan University. https://greenfdc.org/brief-china-belt-and-road-initiative-bri-investment-report-2021/

People's Republic of China. (2017). *Full text of Xi Jinping's report at 19th CPC National Congress.* https://www.mfa.gov.cn/ce/ceil/eng/zt/19thCPCNationalCongress/W020171120127269060039.pdf

People's Republic of China. (2021). *Outline of the 14th Five-Year Plan (2021–2025) for national economic and social development and vision 2035 of the People's Republic of China.* https://www.fujian.gov.cn/english/news/202108/t20210809_5665713.htm

Ruta, M. (2018, May 4). *Three opportunities and three risks of the Belt and Road Initiative.* https://blogs.worldbank.org/trade/three-opportunities-and-three-risks-belt-and-road-initiative

Shi, X., & Yao, L. (2019). Prospect of China's energy investment in Southeast Asia under the Belt and Road Initiative: A sense of ownership perspective. *Energy Strategy Reviews, 25*, 56–64.

Textor, C. (2022, February 22). *Chinese BRI investment volume in energy sector 2013–2021.* https://www.statista.com/statistics/1275027/china-energy-investment-volume-in-belt-and-road-countries/

Wang, Q., Li, S., & Li, R. (2018, November). China's dependency on foreign oil will exceed 80% by 2030: Developing a novel NMGM-ARIMA to forecast China's foreign oil dependence from two dimensions. *Energy*, 163(15), 151–167. https://doi.org/10.1016/j.energy.2018.08.127

Wu, H., Syed, M. A., Asad, A., Iqbal, S., Zahoor, H., & Maqsoo, A. (2020). The impact of Energy Cooperation and the role of the One Belt and Road Initiative in revolutionizing the geopolitics of energy among regional economic powers: An analysis of infrastructure development and project management. *Complexity*. https://doi.org/10.1155/2020/8820021

Xia, D. (2021, November 23). *China's 2022 wind power growth to stay strong despite subsidy end.* Retrieved April 9, 2022, from FitchRating. https://www.fitchratings.com/research/corporate-finance/china-2022-wind-power-growth-to-stay-strong-despite-subsidy-end-23-11-2021

Xinhua. (2012, November 19). *Full text of Hu Jintao's report at 18th Party Congress.* http://en.people.cn/90785/8024777.html

Xinhua. (2021, March 16). *Xi Focus: Walk the talk—Xi leads China in fight for carbon-neutral future.* XInhuaNet. Retrieved March 7, 2021, from http://www.xinhuanet.com/english/2021-03/16/c_139814792.htm

Xinhua. (2021, September 22). Xi Focus: China to stop building new coal-fired power projects abroad. *Xinhua*. Retrieved October 14, 2021, from http://www.news.cn/english/2021-09/22/c_1310201218.htm

Xu, Q., Yu, J., Shi, X., & Collinson, E. (2021). The potential of energy cooperation between China and Australia under the Belt and Road Initiative. *Economic and Political Studies*. https://doi.org/10.1080/20954816.2021.1951482

Yu, J., & Wallace, J. (2021, September 13). *What is China's Belt and Road Initiative (BRI)?* Retrieved January 8, 2022, from Chatam House. https://www.chathamhouse.org/2021/09/what-chinas-belt-and-road-initiative-bri

Zhou, Y., Luckow, P., Smith, S.J., & Clarke, L.E. (2012). Evaluation of global onshore wind energy potential and generation costs. *Environmental Science & Technology*, *46*, 7857–7864. https://doi.org/10.1021/es204706m

CHAPTER 4

The Energopower and Biopower Relations in Russia, China and the EU and Their Impacts on Russia-China and Russia-EU Energy Trade Before and After the War in Ukraine[1]

EVGENIIA (JEN) SIDOROVA

INTRODUCTION

Russian Arctic natural gas appears to be a promising source of hydrocarbon energy for Asian customers. In January 2020, the Russian government passed legislation creating $300 billion in new incentives for new infrastructure development in the Arctic Ocean. Russia's minister of the Far East and the Arctic, Alexander Kozlov, stated that those incentives resulted in three new massive offshore oil projects (Staalesen, 2020). Russia's state-owned energy companies are also expected to significantly increase their onshore Arctic development. Some authors predict Russia is more likely to look to the East—Japan and China, and India—for expertise and investment (Henderson & Mitrova, 2016; Shagina, 2020).

Arctic LNG 2 is the ongoing Novatek LNG project, supplied by the Utrenneye field. The field is located in the Gydan Peninsula in the Yamal-Nenets Autonomous District, approximately 70 km across Ob Bay from Yamal LNG (Novatek, 2021). The project participants include NOVATEK (60 %) (Russia),

TotalEnergies (France) (10 %), China National Petroleum Corporation (CNPC) (China) (10 %), CNOOC (China) (10 %) and the Japan Arctic LNG consortium of Mitsui & Co, Ltd. and JOGMEC (10 %) (Novatek, 2021). Capital expenditure for the full project is estimated at $21.3 billion. The Yamal-Nenets LNG projects have certain comparative advantages, including shorter transportation routes to the Asia-Pacific region; winter costs for LNG in the Yamal-Nenets Autonomous area will be 10–15 % lower than Middle Eastern LNG projects; Russia has set a zero-export duty for LNG supplies, to encourage construction of LNG plants (Steblyanskaya et al., 2021).

Before the Russian invasion of Ukraine, Russia was also actively collaborating with the European partners. Nord Stream 2 is an underwater twin pipeline that would transport natural gas from Narva Bay, Russia to Germany (Wettengel, 2021). The two new lines will link the Russian Bovanenkovo gas field on the Yamal Peninsula to European markets (Lang & Westphal, 2017). The pipeline system's total capacity is set to double to 110 billion cubic meters following Nord Stream 2's completion. The pipeline could help Germany meet its emissions-reduction goals (Wettengel, 2021).

Nord Stream 2 was conceptualized as a political and economic project due to the Russian monopolization of German and EU markets; yet, because of the war in Ukraine and fragmentation of state interests within the EU, the pipeline discussion is inherently politicized (Lang & Westphal, 2017). Germany has an interest in being active in framing European energy interests and the energy union (Lang & Westphal, 2017), and due to its historically close energy trade with Russia, its energy policy needs closer attention. The Russian invasion of Ukraine also caused debates in Germany/the EU regarding the continuation of energy trade with Russia.

The time framework of this article includes the period from 2011, when President Vladimir Putin announced a pivot to Asia (Shagina, 2020) to May 2022, after the Russian invasion of Ukraine. We used qualitative research methodology based on the analysis of the secondary data (academic peer-reviewed sources and news articles). The first section of this chapter includes the examination of gaps in the current literature on the Sino-Russian and EU-Russian energy trade cooperation. The next section describes the theoretical framework that we applied to the case studies of Russia, China/Asia-Pacific Region (APR) and the EU/Europe. In the following Discussion section, we examine current Sino-Russian and the EU-Russian energy trade relations. Then, we analyze the Russian, Chinese and EU/German domestic/regional energy policies by applying the theoretical framework. In the analysis and implications section we answer the main research questions about the distinction of the Russian perception of energopower from Chinese and the EU, and how this distinction would influence energy trade dynamics in Russia-China and Russia-the EU cooperation/conflict. In the conclusion we provide the summary of analysis and suggest future directions for further developments in this particular topic.

THE RUSSIAN-CHINESE AND RUSSIAN-EU ENERGY TRADE COOPERATION: GAPS

Even though Chinese investors cooperate with Russian on Arctic LNG, the prospects for China's engagement in the development of the Russian Arctic is under-studied in the literature (Tianming & Erokhin, 2021). Both China and Russia do not accept the legitimacy of neoliberal political and ideological norms and values that support global governance structures (Wilson, 2015). These values and norms are also symbolized by the soft power tactics of Western actors, which Russia and China view as threats of domestic penetration and subversion (Wilson, 2015). Yet, Russia—as well as China—presents itself as a norm enforcer rather than outlining a different set of rules that challenge the international system (Wilson, 2015). Would Russia and China build their energy alliance on possessing non-European norms and values?

Also, as it was noted by Wilson (2015), both Russia and China do not accept neoliberal norms and values, but Wilson does not identify why they prefer having separate worldviews. In other words, in the discussion on whether Russia (and China) would cooperate in the Arctic, there is not much emphasis on how their non-European norms and values were constructed; these norms and values are taken as given. Both Russia and China are interested in energy trade with the EU as well as with one another. Realist and liberal international relations (IR) theories cannot explain why Russia's ideas and interests do not take rules, values and norms into account. Nor do they explain why Russia and China undermine global governance despite their compliance with international order. As Kuteleva (2020) notes, the current discussion on Russian energy relations with other states is dominated by realist and liberal approaches. In this regard, it is important to seek or answers beyond the mainstream IR framework by utilizing constructivist and poststructuralist approaches and methodologies (Kuteleva, 2020).

THEORETICAL FRAMEWORK

To answer these questions, this study applies social constructivist theory and the Foucauldian concepts of biopolitics and energopower to the current domestic and regional frameworks in Russia, the EU and China. We argue that investigating state-society links and power dynamics in energy production and trade relationships would help to identify how norms and values affect energy trade. We will apply IR poststructuralist and constructivist approaches. Constructivist theory argues that states possess distinct identities, which are framed by actors' socialization and participation in collective knowledge (Wendt, as cited in Fierke, 2016). States' behavior cannot be separated from a context of normative meaning, and concepts such as energy, cooperation, society and power are inherently socially constructed categories (Fierke, 2016). Thus, in order to understand what drives states' motivations and beliefs, it is important to understand historical and social contexts.

By applying the governmentality approach to the case studies of Russia, China/APR and the EU/Europe, this study argues that in their decisions regarding energy trade, the APR, Russia and the European states follow the logic of rationality and pragmatism, and they have special modes of governance to exercise power over their populations. We will examine how the energopower and biopower function and operate in Russia, China and the EU in the content of Russian energy production, and how these modes of governance interact with one another. By examining modes of governance, this study will analyze the existing Russian energy trade relations with China and the EU and suggest potential scenarios of future partnerships in Russian Arctic energy development given the ongoing war in Ukraine.

The poststructuralist approach challenges dominant understandings and interpretations of world politics, which are both arbitrary, in the way that they only represent one possibility among a range, and they are also nonarbitrary, in the sense that social and historical practices shaped the dominant ways of making the world that have real impacts upon our lives (Bleiker & Campbell, 2016/2021). For example, realism neglects the importance of new transnational actors (i.e., the EU), issues and relationships as well as the voices of marginalized peoples and perspectives (Bleiker & Campbell, 2016/2021). In this regard, it is essential to analyze the state perceptions of energy trade between Russia, the EU and China, and the impact of these perceptions on Russia-EU and Russia-China energy trade relations.

Michel Foucault's governmentality (government and rationality) is the art of governing subjects as population and managing political space, as well as an examination of how political rationalities and technologies of government evolved from the seventeenth century onward (Wohl, 2016). Governmentality is not centered on how an already existing policy issue can be managed, but how particular modes of governance and their technologies of power happened to be primary solutions to certain problems of governance in a specific historical and geopolitical setting (Wohl, 2016). Governments of modern states have political reason, which is not dominated by discourses of sovereignty and legitimacy (Foucault, 2016). Biopolitics is the governmental practice that manages the life of individuals, a set of living beings forming a population (Burchell et al., 2008). Biopolitics and biopower are new understanding of power, located beyond the traditional concepts of sovereignty and law (Genel, 2006). Boyer (2014) suggests that biopower as an exercise of governmental power is the management of life and population. By studying energy governmentality, it is possible to better understand what kind of power, truths, and identities the energy industry is building (Tynkkynen, 2016).

Energopower, introduced by Dominic Boyer, refers to the harnessing of electricity and fuel (Boyer, 2014; Hasberg, 2019). Energopower does not replace the concept of biopower, but it puts emphasis on the need to examine the essential function of energy in "the organization and dynamics of political forces across different scales" (Szeman, 2014). Scholars use the concept of energopower to analyze how energy is used to govern populations and produce subjectivities (Allan et al., 2021). For example, the OPEC oil crisis in 1973, and reorganization of power in global energy production led to the decline of the U.S. as an oil superpower (Szeman, 2014).

Tynkkynen (2019) argues that the materialities, spatialities, and infrastructure related to energy constitute a form of agency. Actor–network theory posits that materialities, such as infrastructure or the natural environment, produce both inertia and action due to the social norms and practices that are tied to them. A question posed by the governmentality literature, therefore, is how both the conscious and unconscious "truth" interpreted by leading discourses is produced as part of governments' exercise of power (Mills, 1997, pp. 2–8, as cited in Tynkkynen, 2019). Therefore, in the context of this study, dominant discourses that shape ideas and interests of as states and other actors emerge while these actors exercise their energopower.

RUSSIA-THE ASIA-PACIFIC REGION (APR): WHY FOCUSING ONLY ON CHINA?

In light of worsened relations with the EU, Russia planned its "Pivot to Asia" by increasing energy exports to the APR (Tagnizadeh-Hesary et al., 2021). Japan, the Republic of Korea, China and India are the main consumers of natural gas in the region (Pyatkova, 2018). Yet as transportation costs increase with distance and the existence/absence of a land border with Russia, geography factor can ensure or diminish the energy security of an importing country (Tagnizadeh-Hesary et al., 2021). In this regard, China is the most natural market for Russia as they share borders. In comparison, constructing gas and oil pipelines to India would involve higher risks, involving reliance on the countries between India and Russia (Tagnizadeh-Hesary et al., 2021).

Besides geography, there are other reasons why the APR countries (besides China) are not actively engaged in energy trade relations with Russia. Japan has pre-existing trade relations with other energy exporting countries. Despite its investment in the Sakhalin-1 project, Japan is more interested in Middle Eastern energy, notably Qatar and Saudi Arabia. These countries supply substantial shares of Japan's energy market (Suganuma, 2011; Yennie-Lindgren, 2018). India is also involved in the Sakhalin-1 project and the Vankor oil field (Bhagwat, 2020). However, as of January 2020, Russia is still working on improving energy supply routes from Russia to Indian partners (Bhagwat, 2020).

The Asian countries know that Russia's foreign policy has shifted toward the East only because its bilateral relations with the West worsened. Such a predictable strategy diminishes Russia's role as a trade partner (Shagina, 2020). For a long time, Russia was absent in the APR affairs, and was largely viewed by Asian countries as a "distant neighbour" (Shagina, 2020). Hence, Japan and India do not perceive Russia as a stable and serious energy supplier, but rather as a possible diversification option in the foreseeable future.

In 2022, China is a main energy partner with Russia, and currently, China is the only viable option for Russia-APR projects. As Sorensen and Klimenko (2017) note, one anonymous scholar defined this situation well: "China understands that Russia plays a game. Now China is the only horse Russia can find. Russia will ride the China horse to find a better one." China needs energy imports and can exploit Russia's sanctions issue, but it is also concerned about its important relationship with the U.S. and does not fully trust the Kremlin (Henderson & Mitrova, 2016).

CHINA AND RUSSIAN ARCTIC ENERGY PROJECTS

Chinese-Russian cooperation in the Arctic has not advanced much in recent years and, except for partnering on the Arctic LNG-2 project on the Yamal Peninsula, there are still not many real outcomes (Sorensen & Klimenko, 2017). Nevertheless, China is often considered a key partner in Russian LNG initiatives (Tianming & Erokhin, 2021).

On one hand, Chinese-Russian Arctic energy cooperation is a match made in heaven. China is attempting to use clean energy and phasing out coal to address minimal energy efficiency and environmental protection (Tang et al., 2017 as cited in Steblyanskaya et al., 2021). It is beneficial for China to diversify its sources of oil and gas to safely sustain its economic growth (Fu, 2016). While China imports vast amounts of energy, a large share of these imports consists of clean energy only (Tang et al., 2015 as cited in Steblyanskaya et al., 2021). After the Ukraine crisis, China became a new export market for Russian hydrocarbons and arms sales, the main provider of state-of-art technology, and a viable alternative to Western markets. Russia surpassed Saudi Arabia as China's largest oil supplier and is slated to become Beijing's major natural gas supplier (Shagina, 2020).

On the other hand, Arctic energy development is not the main priority for the Chinese government. Alexeeva and Lasserre (2018) argue that China has been quite cautious about Russia's "pivot to the East" strategy. When providing an overview of initiatives and priorities relating to China's foreign and defense policy in 2014–2015, Chinese President Xi Jinping rarely referred to Russia specifically or spoke about Sino-Russian partnership outside of the mutual cooperation within BRIC (Brazil, Russia, India and China) and other international organizations (Gabuev, 2015, as cited in Alexeeva & Lasserre, 2018). Furthermore, Russia and China have differing priorities for the Arctic.

Russia is prioritizing hydrocarbon extraction and renewable energy development as one of its main goals during its Arctic Council chairing (2021–2023) (Bouffard & Lackenbauer, 2021). The Arctic is not a top priority in Chinese foreign policy or efforts to secure and diversify its energy supply through the Belt and Road Initiative (BRI)—where regions such as Africa, the Middle East and Central Asia are more in focus (Sorensen & Klimenko, 2017). A part of the BRI focused on Central Asia is China's Silk Road Economic Belt (SREB), launched in 2013 (Shagina, 2020). By 2017, China's bilateral trade with Central Asia reached $30 billion, more than its trade with Russia ($18 billion). Chinese economic power in Central Asia has weakened Russian political influence in this region and created a quasi-Chinese dominance, which shows the potential for submission under the impact of China's financial strength (Henderson & Mitrova, 2016). Since the Soviet era, Russia has viewed Central Asia as within Moscow's sphere of influence, and the BRI threatens Russian geopolitical interests (Shagina, 2020). Therefore, broader Chinese infrastructure plans such as BRI do not correspond with Russia's interests and needs, and intimidate Moscow geopolitically (Henderson & Mitrova, 2016; Shagina, 2020).

As an Arctic superpower, Russia is not willing to share its Arctic dominance with anyone (Sorensen & Klimenko, 2017). As Bouffard and Lackenbauer (2021) state, the Russian goal is to dominate the region by encouraging other Arctic stakeholders to adopt and repeat the language and narratives that Russia supports, particularly Russia's self-view as the biggest, toughest, most progressed—and most legitimate—Arctic player. Unlike Russia, China wants to transform the region into an international space as opposed to a regional one (Sorensen & Klimenko, 2017). Thus, China and Russia have different level of geopolitical ambitions, which could be supported or weakened by a potential energy alliance.

Russia wants to discover new markets for its energy supplies but is hesitant to tolerate too much reliance on China (Henderson & Mitrova, 2016). If Russia could create space within the Chinese energy import agenda, then a mutually advantageous partnership will develop. If either connection should fail, however, Russia, rather than China, will experience the worst outcomes (Henderson & Mitrova, 2016). Russia will have to accept the fact that there is intense competition for market share in the Chinese energy industry (Henderson & Mitrova, 2016).

Chinese interest in the Arctic is driven by access to energy resources and the potential of building polar research capacity (Sorensen & Klimenko, 2017). Nevertheless, Russian companies, who were mostly dependent on Western drilling equipment and technology for Arctic oil and gas exploration, are updating their current technical expertise on resource extraction, though the Russians hesitate to share their skills, experience and expertise with the Chinese (Alexeeva & Lasserre, 2018). This hesitance to share knowledge does not correlate with the Chinese plans as the Chinese government is not interested in investing in ventures where Chinese firms have no opportunity to learn about engineering, design, and drilling activities in the Arctic region (Alexeeva & Lasserre, 2018). Therefore, it is still challenging for both parties to find a common ground due to geopolitical, technological and economic reasons.

IMPLICATIONS OF THE RUSSIAN INVASION OF UKRAINE ON SINO-RUSSIAN ENERGY TRADE

Similar to Russia, China views energy as a strategic source (South China Morning Post, 2022), not much as a market commodity. As discussed above, the Chinese strategic approach toward energy policy results in the view of China as a stable strategic partner in energy trade by Russia. After the invasion, Russia relocated its energy supplies from the Western partners to the Eastern. After the war started, the Shell employees at the Sakhalin-2 project in Russia were removed over the weekend to be relocated back as Shell moved forward with an exit (Bloomberg News, 2022a). The Chinese companies CNOOC, CNPC and Sinopec Group have been involved in joint discussions with Shell over the company's 27.5 % holding in the Sakhalin-2 liquefied natural gas venture after the European firm said it would exit Russian operations following the Russian invasion (Bloomberg News, 2022a). In April 14 Putin called on "to redirect our exports gradually to the rapidly growing markets of the South and the East," particularly to China, the world's largest energy market, and India, the world's third largest (Bradsheer, 2022). Russia wants to ship LNG to Asia via the Northern Sea Route, over the top of Russia from Western Siberia to China via the Arctic Ocean. The Kremlin has given its full backing to a new private-sector company, Novatek, which has pioneered the development of LNG from the Yamal Peninsula (Gustafson, 2022). Therefore, the Western partners will soon be replaced by the Chinese and Indian companies as expected by Moscow.

The Russian dependency on Beijing has enormously amplified. As a result of exit of the Western companies from Russia, Sino-Russian energy trade increased by 60 % after the invasion (South China Morning Post, 2022). Beijing and Moscow signed energy agreements in February 2022 worth an estimated US$117.5 billion (South China Morning Post, 2022). The deliveries have been made through the Power of Siberia pipeline as part of the contract between Gazprom and CNPC (The Economic Times, 2022). Russia already sends gas to China via its Power of Siberia pipeline, which began pumping supplies in 2019, and by shipping LNG. It exported 16.5 billion bcm of gas to China in 2021 (China Briefing, 2022). Additionally, Russia is currently planning to develop the Power of Siberia-2 pipeline to deliver an extra 5 bcm/year of gas to China (Bloomberg News, 2022a). The construction of the pipeline, however, is expected to conclude only by 2030 (Bloomberg News, 2022a). The Power of Siberia network is not connected to pipelines that send gas to Europe, which has faced surging gas prices due to tight supplies, one of several points of tension with Moscow (China Briefing, 2022). Eventually, Russia may be able to connect its western and eastern pipeline systems, allowing it to reroute current European gas flows to Asia (Evans, 2022). Yet, it is unlikely to happen (Evans, 2022).

RUSSIA-THE EU-EUROPE RELATIONS

Since the Ukraine crisis in 2014 and combat in eastern Ukraine, energy cooperation with Russia has come under increased qualitative political criticism in the EU (Cebotari, 2022). The war in Ukraine made these trade interactions particularly fragile, as the Ukrainian transit pipeline is a crucial and indispensable corridor for EU gas imports from Russia (Siddi, 2020; Cebotari, 2022). For both Russia and the EU, the Ukraine crisis and the subsequent Russian invasion of Ukraine were a culmination of growing mutual frustration (Haukkala, 2015; Cebotari, 2022). Despite the emergence of trade cooperation between EU and Russia, both parties have not experienced stability in their economic partnership.

The key question on Russia-EU energy relations is whether the EU should be treated as a single independent actor or if Europe should be viewed as a region with multiple independent state interests? As Veebel (2015) states, EU members have fragmented interests and positions regarding trade interactions with Russia. For example, Finland, Hungary, Greece, Lithuania, Netherlands, Poland and Slovakia strongly rely on Russian energy while other EU countries do not or to a lesser extent (International Energy Agency, 2022a). Russia is a main exporter of crude oil, natural gas and solid fossil fuels. Thereby, any potential disruption of energy supplies from Russia to Europe might pose a threat to some European countries. Yet, Poland and the Baltic states see EU-Russia energy trade relations as a source of political pressure from the Russian government (Siddi, 2020).

In addition, interactions between individual EU members and Russia are asymmetric because some EU countries such as Hungary and Slovakia depend on Russian oil imports more than others and because of this, the EU cannot permanently ban all Russian oil imports (Horton & Palumbo, 2022). The Nord Stream 2 pipeline completion, though, means that Russia no longer has to rely on Ukraine's gas infrastructure to deliver gas supplies to European customers (Euronews, 2021; Siddi, 2020).

ENERGOPOWER AND BIOPOWER CONCEPTS IN THE RUSSIAN ENERGY CONTEXT

Russia's semi-authoritarianism affects its Arctic energy strategy by turning Arctic energy development into a geopolitical game with the purpose of keeping the stability and order required for regime survival. The political regime's survival relies on Russian political elite (Markowitz, 2020). Strategic decisions regarding the Arctic, and military actions in particular, aim to demonstrate Moscow's ability to project power (Markowitz, 2020). Nuclear icebreakers, Arctic military units and training, and military bases along the Northern Sea Route protect Russian strategic security interests across the Arctic shelves (Markowitz, 2020). Due to unstable oil prices and reliance on resource extraction (Tynkkynen, 2019), the government can only hope that energy prices will go up in unforeseen future (Markowitz, 2020).

Sergunin and Konyshev (2019), similarly, argue that Russia has important strategic interests in the Arctic region, including opening up the Northern Sea Route, protecting natural environment and modernizing the industrial base. The policymaking mechanism has improved after the chaotic 1990s, yet it is still unclear how federal and regional governments divide control and jurisdiction over the Russian Arctic (Sergunin & Konyshev, 2019). The federal government attempts to control all policies (Sergunin & Konyshev, 2019). Thus, Arctic policy in Russia is very centralized and mostly implemented by the central government.

Arctic energy policy belongs entirely to Moscow, and it is part of federal mega projects. Salonen (2021) characterizes mega projects as large programs implemented through public-private partnerships, which prioritize selected territories and industries. Renewable energy resources are also part of Russia's national goals, and as Salonen (2021) argues, climate change, including melting permafrost and the need for renewable energy in the Arctic constitute new challenges for Russia, in addition to issues with energy exports. Some renewable energy projects (for example, the Tiksi wind project in the Sakha Republic launched in late 2016) are subnational jurisdiction but, it is unclear how Moscow will divide responsibilities between the center and periphery regarding "green" energy programs (Salonen, 2021). The Russian state shapes and frames the entire concept of sustainable development and legitimizes this idea (Andreassen, 2016).

Instead of navigating environmental challenges and giving space to bottom-up green energy firms, Russia's elite focuses on launching a state-controlled renewable energy industry to evade the green threat that may challenge Russia's hydrocarbon exports in the medium term (Smeets, 2018). The neopatrimonial power structure (the hierarchical distribution of resources that gave rise to patron-client networks based around an influential individual or group [Francisco, 2010]) in Russia fundamentally restricts a rapid renewable energy transition (Smeets, 2018).

Bouffard and Lackenbauer (2021) argue that Russia's chairing the Arctic Council aims to legitimize its goals and objectives in the Arctic region. The importance of the Arctic in Russian national strategy and the centrality of Russia in circumpolar relations and enhanced accessibility to undiscovered oil and gas resources in the Circumpolar North (Bouffard & Lackenbauer, 2021) would mean that Russia includes hydrocarbon resources as part of its geopolitical agenda.

Does Russia have enough capacity to develop Arctic energy markets? As Vatansever (2017) argues, Russia has developed substantial surplus pipeline capacity, which is likely to remain in the near future. Yet, some authors disagree that Russian energy exports will grow. Meynkhard (2020) emphasizes that Russian energy development includes unique factors that include long distances between regions, a cold climate, and cheap hydrocarbon resources. These factors deeply affect the development of electricity and heat supply systems in the Russian Arctic. Combined with changing foreign energy markets, these factors cause high uncertainties regarding the further growth of Russian energy exports (Meynkhard, 2020).

Energy power has been transformed into an instrument for identity construction in Russia—a hydrocarbon culture in the making (Tynkkynen, 2019). Tynkkynen (2019) introduces the concept of Russian energopower as the combination of identity construction and material interests of Russia based on energy exports. They argue to understand how energopower works, it is crucial to identify what kind of material power, discursive truths, and cultural-political identities are constructed in and around energy flows and entangled materialities, and how these forms of political power shape the perception of energy as a societal phenomenon (Tynkkynen, 2019).

As Kuteleva (2000) states, in projecting energy superpower into the concept of Russia's "greatpowerness," Putin's government undertook a conscious identity-construction strategy. The energy superpower discourse survived the oil price rise of the mid-2000s and occupied a visible space in Putin's political agenda in the 2010s (Kuteleva, 2020). Russia's energy diplomacy toward the EU results from the conflict between the discourse of energy superpower and the discourse of raw-material producer (Kuteleva, 2020). Thus, to build cooperative and productive energy trade partnerships with Russia, the European states must take into account the material factors of Russia's energy trade and Russian institutional settings and energy regulations, as well as several figurative meanings that energy resources acquire in Russia (Kuteleva, 2020).

Russia and the EU perceive energy distinctly. The European Community felt a compelling need to lock Russia into an institutional market-based economic agreement that would make the economic and political changes in the country permanent (Haukkala, 2015). Russia repeatedly pushed for more trade discounts and a more substantial long-term vision in the form of free trade capacity than was envisioned in the Commission's original negotiating strategy (Haukkala, 2015). Putin's centralization of power meant that Russia started distancing from the set of "European values" commonly agreed upon at the beginning of the 1990s (Haukkala, 2015). The emergence of the Eurasian Customs Union (ECU) between Russia, Belarus and Kazakhstan in 2010 was a move to counter the EU's rising power in the post-Soviet countries (Haukkala, 2015).

Resource nationalism in Russia, developed during and after Vladimir Putin's second term, strongly and negatively affected the liberal market path promoted by the EU (Kuzemko, 2014). In the 1990s, the EU attempted to build free and fair markets underpinned by the rule of law, and Russia demonstrated its incompliance by rejecting the all-important Energy Charter Treaties (Kuzemko, 2014). A liberal market path determines the presence and stability of international energy market institutions, and more importantly, EU energy security (Kuzemko, 2014). The dominance of state-owned energy companies in Russia undermines and jeopardizes the existence of liberal market energy governance (Kuzemko, 2014).

From the EU liberal market perspective, energy is a commodity, tradable and replaceable, and less as a public good or strategic asset as it is in Russia. This has tended to increase the relevance of economic over political analysis (Cherp & Jewell, 2011, as cited in Kuzemko, 2014). Resource nationalism also means that energy plays a large socioeconomic role in country's development (Kuzemko, 2014). Thus, energopower in Russia should be understood as the exercise of governmental power through state-owned energy corporations.

Energopower in Russia plays an important role in biopolitics. According to Tynkkynen (2016), post-Soviet Russia is a case study of a state where, stemming from the Soviet-era strategies and rules, the goals of both the social welfare state and classical liberalism have come together to form contemporary biopolitical practices. Thus, governmental concern over energy production and trade stems from both the biopolitical goals of ensuring the (bio)security of the population, as well as control over populations and economic growth by maintaining energy flowing in grids and pipelines (Tynkkynen, 2016).

The links between energopower and biopolitical objectives (i.e., that physically and mentally fit bodies serve economic and military and other patriotic ends) are visible in the social responsibility program, "Gazprom–for Children" (Tynkkynen, 2016). This program is dominated by local-level sports sponsorship and infrastructure construction projects carried out by Gazprom and its regional daughters (Tynkkynen, 2016). The ability of major energy corporations in post-socialist Russia to formulate what is worth knowing, what is the truth, is exceptionally strong (Tynkkynen, 2016). Its unique form of corporate governmentality can thus be defined as a marriage between the energy superpower ideal and military Great Power identity that are constructed with the help of sports metaphors, values, and infrastructure (Tynkkynen, 2016).

In the Arctic energy context, biopolitics (socioeconomic development) of northern territories in the Russian Arctic is strongly tied with energopower (hydrocarbon energy production). Tysiachniouk and Petrov (2018) argue Moscow demonstrates paternalism that is also exacerbated by weak civil society in energy development. Fragile civil society results in weakly developed benefit-sharing agreements that assist local and indigenous communities and protect local and indigenous rights to land and traditional resources. Even though most oil and gas companies committed to signing benefit-sharing agreements, underdeveloped civil society institutions undermine benefit-sharing policies. Companies struggle to build local institutional capacities and human capital in local indigenous communities in the region (Tysiachniouk & Petrov, 2018). Patrimonialism and weak civil society intertwined with the strategic nature of Arctic energy supplies characterize existing Russian energopower and biopolitics.

IMPLICATIONS OF THE RUSSIAN INVASION OF UKRAINE ON RUSSIAN PERCEPTION ON ENERGOPOWER AND BIOPOWER

After the invasion of Ukraine, Russia demonstrates its energopower by using state-owned companies to manipulate Eastern European countries by shutting down the gas supplies. In May 2022, Russia stopped shipments of natural gas to Poland and Bulgaria over payment issues (Rapoza, 2022). President Putin ordered Gazprom to accept payment in rubles. Due to the sanctions, Russia's Central Bank dollar and euro accounts abroad have been frozen (Rapoza, 2022). Yet, in March 2022, it was announced that Poland had begun receiving Russian fuel from its allies. The gas is being ordered by Italy and France and supplied through pipelines crossing Poland (Bloomberg News, 2022b). It was reported that in order to reduce dependence on Russian gas, a natural gas pipeline between the Greek-Bulgarian borders is expected to be finished by June 2022, which is supposed to provide the two countries and their neighbors with access to new grid connections (Euronews with AP, 2022).

The EU countries accused Russian of blackmailing as Moscow asked the EU buyers to pay using Russian currency (Armstrong, 2022). Polish and Bulgarian officials reported that Gazprom issued a statement stating it had halted supplies to Poland and Bulgaria due to payments not being delivered in rubles (Ellyatt, 2022). Nevertheless, these supplies might only be a short-term solution for eastern Europe and would not reduce energy dependency on Russia completely.

To start with, substituting Russian oil and coal imports will likely not pose a major problem. Sufficient world market capacity exists from other oil and coal exporting countries to make up the shortfall. The greater challenge is to find short-run substitutes for Russian gas (Bachmann et al., 2022). Russian gas imports already decreased substantially in the second half of 2021 and especially in the first months of 2022. On the EU level, its import share fell from about 40 % to 20–30 % (Zachmann et al., 2021). Utilizing energopower by using energy as a weapon is an old game for Russia. "Putin's got this weapon, and he's using it," said Natasha Lindstaedt, a professor of government at the University of Essex and the author of Democratic Decay and Authoritarian Resurgence (Ray, 2022). She also mentioned: "Not the military weapons he's using in the war, but the weapon of everyone being dependent on his country's natural resources" (Ray, 2022). This is not the first time Russia weaponized its energy supplies; due to price disputes, Russia cut supplies to Ukraine in 2006, 2008–2009 and 2014 (Kirby, 2022).

Therefore, energy blackmailing was a predictable move from the Russian side. The question is whether the Eastern European countries could start transitioning toward other energy sources before the war. Knowing about previous Putin's blackmailing strategies in negotiations with Ukraine, eastern Europe, along with the EU, in general, could have prepared to the possible energy shutdown.

ENERGOPOWER AND BIOPOWER CONCEPTS IN THE CHINESE CONTEXT

According to Leung (2011), energy policy is a means, not an end, for the Chinese government. Energy serves major national goals and objectives and corresponds with Chinese values (Leung, 2011). The Communist Party of China's (CPC) key domestic concern is stimulating economic progress while maintaining political and social stability (Leung, 2011). Post-Mao China is a non-communist nation, ruled by a communist party, the CPC (Leung, 2011). To maintain the CPC's political legitimacy as an authority, it must meet citizens' economic and patriotic expectations: economic development, increases in living standards, territorial sovereignty, and China's superpower ambitions (Leung, 2011). China has "an unwritten social contract between the party and the people whereby the people do not compete with the party for political power as long as the party looks after their economic fortunes" (Breslin, p. 749, as cited in Leung, 2011). Oil demand in China is closely connected to Chinese heavy industry's need for energy. China is the second-largest oil consumer in the world (International Energy Agency, 2022b) Similar to Russia, energy plays a large role in Chinese society as a strategic socioeconomic asset. The tremendous growth of oil demand in China is linked to increased living standards in the country. The party and the people are more closely interconnected in semi-authoritarian states, and unlike the democratic European states, the Chinese government has to maintain its political legitimacy to remain in power.

The view of Chinese leaders toward energy security has seen a sea change. In the 1990s, Beijing wanted to maintain self-sufficiency of oil, synonymous with the U.S. claim of "energy independence" in the Obama era, and issued oil import bans in 1994 and 1998, respectively, (Wang, 1999; International Energy Agency, 2000, as cited in Leung, 2011). As Leung notes (2011), despite attempts to maintain oil self-sufficiency by issuing import bans in 1994 and 1998, the Chinese leaders eventually had to support security of oil imports. Energy policy measures included construction of transnational oil pipelines, bilateral oil deals, and investment in overseas oil fields; all of these share a higher strategic goal—diversification of oil sources (Leung, 2011). In China, governmental guidelines, especially those relating to Five-Year Plans, generate a new and complex environment that provides companies an entirely new roadmap of approaches to pursue larger market shares and profits (Lau et al., 2019).

The ubiquity of government and the relative consistency of most Five-Year Plans create a quite reliable and stable business environment, at least for Chinese firms or system-relevant non-Chinese firms. On the other hand, any business approach defined by quarterly earnings and shareholder profits will have restricted benefits in China for the foreseeable future because the government's plans are intrinsically long term, multidimensional and complex (Lau et al., 2019). Senior managers of Chinese companies focus not only on maximizing profits but on the economic development of China (Lau et al., 2019). This means that, perceived as engines of economic growth, firms will (be compelled to) carry corporate responsibility toward socioeconomic improvement of the Chinese people (Lau et al., 2019). Hence, Chinese firms aim to reach broader and long-term socioeconomic goals, improving the well-being of Chinese citizens. The clean energy transition does not only mean development of renewable energy sources, but rather, rejection of coal as an energy source.

IMPLICATIONS OF WAR IN UKRAINE FOR CHINA

Similar to Russia, China views energy as a strategic source (South China Morning Post, 2022), not much as a market commodity. As discussed above, the Chinese strategic approach toward energy policy results in the view of China as a stable strategic partner in the energy trade with Russia. After the invasion, Russia relocated its energy supplies from the Western partners to the Eastern. After the war started, the Shell employees at the Sakhalin-2 project in Russia were removed over the weekend to be relocated back as Shell moved forward with an exit (Bloomberg News, 2022a). The Chinese companies CNOOC, CNPC and Sinopec Group have been involved in joint discussions with Shell over its 27.5 % holding in the Sakhalin-2 liquefied natural gas venture after the European firm said it would exit Russian operations following the Ukraine invasion (Bloomberg News, 2022a). On April 14, Putin called on "to redirect our exports gradually to the rapidly growing markets of the South and the East," particularly to China, the world's largest energy market, and India, the world's third largest (Bradsheer, 2022). Russia wants to ship LNG to Asia via the Northern Sea Route, over the top of Russia from Western Siberia to China via the Arctic Ocean. The Kremlin has given its full backing to a new private-sector company, Novatek, which has pioneered LNG development from the Yamal Peninsula (Gustafson, 2022). Therefore, the Western partners will soon be replaced by the Chinese and Indian companies, as expected by Moscow.

The Russian dependency on Beijing has enormously amplified. As a result of the exit of the Western companies from Russia, the Sino-Russian energy trade increased by 60 % after the invasion (South China Morning Post, 2022). Beijing and Moscow signed energy agreements in February 2022 worth an estimated US$117.5 billion (South China Morning Post, 2022). The deliveries have been made through the Power of Siberia pipeline as part of the contract between Gazprom and China National Petroleum Corporation (CNPC) (The Economic Times, 2022). Russia already sends gas to China via its Power of Siberia pipeline, which began pumping supplies in 2019, and by shipping LNG. It exported 16.5 billion bcm of gas to China in 2021 (China Briefing, 2022).

Additionally, Russia is planning to develop the Power of Siberia-2 pipeline to deliver an extra 5 bcm/year of gas to China (Bloomberg News, 2022a). However, the construction of the pipeline is expected to conclude only by 2030 (Bloomberg News, 2022a). The Power of Siberia network is not connected to pipelines that send gas to Europe, which has faced surging gas prices due to tight supplies, one of several points of tension with Moscow (China Briefing, 2022). The PoS infrastructure does not have enough capacity to transfer gas supplies to China—its only customer.

ENERGOPOWER AND BIOPOWER IN THE EU AND GERMAN CONTEXT

As energy is viewed as an economic commodity in Europe (Kuzemko, 2014), price is a crucial element of energy security in Europe, and an incentive for European integration. The movement toward a unified European market is an outcome of the liberalization of gas markets (Maltby, 2013). The key stakeholders in the development of a single European energy market are supranational institutions, national energy champions and private energy companies (Maltby, 2013). Markets deliver energy security up to a certain level (Gillessen et al., 2019).

According to Solorio and Jorgens (2020), the EU members have tended to establish a common EU renewable energy policy because of functional needs (renewable energy systems advantages for domestic security systems), and value-based objectives (alleged EU international leadership on climate change). With renewable energy policy, member states prefer to delegate their legal authority to the EU, following the soft modes of governance approach (Solorio & Jorgens, 2020).

With non-renewable energy resources, a focus on clean energy and climate change mitigation also shapes the EU direction toward managing efficient use of natural resources, maintaining rational use of energy sources, and providing high standards of environmental protection (European Commission, 2022). However, as Maltby (2013) and Gillessen et al. (2019) note, the internal EU non-renewable energy market legislation shows bilateral and EU actions tend to follow independent approaches, specifically in foreign energy trade. For instance, the development of Russian-supported extensive gas pipeline projects such as Nord Stream reveal the importance of member state preferences within the EU, and the impact of their security and economic interests, comparative to the EU's goals of diversification of energy supply, which both Russian-supported projects' challenge (Maltby, 2013). The European Commission is in the process of developing the energy union strategy, which aims at building an energy union that gives EU consumers—households and businesses—secure, sustainable, competitive, and affordable energy (European Commission, 2021). The major challenge for the energy union is to establish Europeanization as opposed to maintaining member state sovereignty in the energy sector (Szulecki et al., 2016).

Member states are not especially willing to give up their energy sovereignty as energy policy is a component of national security, and states are reluctant to hand over this element of their sovereignty (Tichy, 2019). As energy security is ultimately a public good, member states retain their sovereign rights to decide on their respective energy mixes. Also, the distinct structures of domestic energy sectors and the related requirements for energy resource composition are key factors preventing a unified energy policy of the EU (Tichy, 2019). Therefore, rather than having a consensual and consolidated energy policy, it would be more appropriate to say that the EU is still in the process of shaping such a policy, which inherently also influences the EU's interactions with key energy suppliers (Tichy, 2019).

The liberalization of the EU energy market has had a significant influence on the political economy of the German energy sector as Germany has used market-based approaches to manage its energy policy (International Energy Agency, 2022c). Germany's natural gas market constitutes a unique case because of its privatized organization, fragmentation, segmentation, and the multiple actors involved (Westphal, 2016). Liberalization began at the end of 1990s and has since then been a reason for debates between member states and the Commission, as the extent and promptness of adopting the Commission's guidelines relies on the member states (Westphal, 2016). The liberalization of the energy market is as an outcome of the creation of a single market, and crucially, it was initiated during a time when energy prices were very low and not related to security concerns (Westphal, 2016).

Due to Germany's central location in Europe, it is an essential transit country for long-distance transportation of natural gas (Gillessen et al., 2019). Pipeline development is capital intensive and is challenged by payback times of up to several decades (Gillessen et al., 2019).

Biopolitics and energopower discourses in Germany are primarily situated within energy transition debates (Schwarz, 2020). The German energy security increases significantly due to reducing gas demand because of the *Energiewende* (Gillessen et al., 2019). Even situations with a complete outage of Russian gas supply or empty gas storages are manageable from a grid perspective as long as other gas suppliers compensate missing gas quantities (Gillessen et al., 2019).

As Kalkbrenner and Roosen (2016) note, Germany's energy transition process is not only an economic and technological process but also a societal and political transformation (citizens can decide for themselves whether renewable energy plants are needed in their local areas). When it comes to citizen acceptance of energy sources such as wind power, as Langer et al. (2018) and Zoellner et al. (2008) note, civil society involvement and activism plays a crucial role in acceptance. Citizen participation in a wind energy project positively influences acceptance. Energy cooperatives are an important tool to financially involve citizens in wind energy programs and willingness of local citizens to participate in a renewable energy project is a decisive factor (Kalkbrenner & Roosen, 2016; Langer et al., 2018). If residents thought that their local authorities supported the project, they were more likely to accept the project (Zoellner et al., 2008). As Zoellner et al. (2008) argue, active community engagement arranged as cooperation of the local communities and operating companies is key to successful renewable energy projects implementation. The combination of liberal democracy and high level of civil engagement intertwined with responsibility of operating companies makes state-society dynamics more equal as opposed to patrimonial nature of Russian and Chinese energopowers.

EU-GERMAN-RUSSIAN RELATIONS AND THE IMPACT OF WAR IN UKRAINE

As an energy embargo on Russia as an outcome of the war in Ukraine seems inevitable, the EU contemplates an urgent transition to renewable energy such as wind and solar power. It is expected that the energy transition will reduce dependency on Russian energy by two-thirds in 2022 and will eliminate it over five years (Gabbatiss, 2022). The president of the European Commission, Ursula von der Leyen, stated that "[t]he quicker we switch to renewables and hydrogen, combined with more energy efficiency, the quicker we will be truly independent and master our energy system" (Turrentine, 2022).

One obvious outcome of the war in Ukraine for Germany is the shift in energy perception. As opposed to the previous perception of energy as a commodity in the market, for Germany, energopower has turned into a policy tool, and energy has become the domain of strategic national policy. In April 2022, global observers speculated whether Germany was planning to nationalize Gazprom Germania or not (Kachenhoff & Eckert, 2022). After the Russian invasion, Russia's Gazprom announced it was quitting its business in Germany without explanation (Kachenhoff & Eckert, 2022). However, Bundesnetzagentur, Germany's network regulator, which took control of Gazprom Germania, announced that the company has not been nationalized (Reuters, 2022). Therefore, the nationalization of the German energy industry is still a topic of debate.

Even the threats of sanctions toward the energy sector do not stop Russia from committing war crimes and genocide in Ukraine. This is a human rights issue that comes into play. The European leaders declared that war atrocities in Ukraine constitute an important factor in energy trade with Russia. The atrocities in Ukraine made it unlikely that sanctions on Russia would ever be lifted even if Russia left Ukraine or a ceasefire agreement (Cohen, 2022). French President Emmanuel Macron said, "It is very clear that there are indications of war crimes. What happened in Bucha dictates a new package of sanctions" (Cohen, 2022). Thus, the energy sector collided with human rights issues, and this trend makes the EU partners less and less likely to purchase Russian energy.

The war in Ukraine might also result in the unification of the EU energy policy. Some German companies, despite the war, are still willing to buy Russian gas by using the rouble currency, as per Putin's request. For example, Germany's

Uniper has been negotiating with Russian Gazprom and the German government to pay in roubles for Russian gas deliveries (Slav, 2022a). Similarly, the German company VNG, a top natural gas buyer, has opened an account with Gazprombank for payments for Russian gas under Moscow's new terms (Slav, 2022b).

Yet, the EU energy ministers had accepted that paying in roubles through the mechanism set out by Russia would breach sanctions imposed by the bloc after Russia's invasion of Ukraine (Boffey, 2022; Slav, 2022a). The German Foreign Minister Annalena Baerbock has said Berlin was prepared to support a slow, EU-wide embargo on Russian oil imports (DW, 2022). Hence, this is where the perception of energy as a market commodity (by Uniper) clashes with the EU energy policy (i.e., economic sanctions). Thus, despite the lack of a unified energy policy, the EU is on the same page regarding the Russian oil embargo.

ANALYSIS AND IMPLICATIONS

Russia and China have similar relations between energopower and biopolitics/biopower. Both view energy trade and/or energy production as a socioeconomic asset closely linked to the well-being of their population. As an energy producer, Russia sees the presence of Arctic gas as an opportunity to establish itself as a regional power. As an energy consumer, China is seeking sources of clean energy elsewhere as part of its BRI. China needs access to Arctic politics and governance, but it might be more interested global competition than in regional competition. Chinese participation in the global economy is largely dependent on energy supplies. Nevertheless, energy plays a crucial role in Russian and Chinese strategic goals and actions geopolitically despite the difference in ambitions. Thus, energopower in both states is an entirely strategic concept and guides national geopolitical agendas. In chairing the Arctic Council, the Russian government has already declared that LNG production in the Arctic and renewable energy production (i.e., wind power in Tiksi) will be prioritized.

The presence of state-owned companies in Russia and China results in more participation in biopolitics through corporate social responsibility. The patrimonial relationship between state corporations and society is explicitly demonstrated through the Gazprom support of youth sport programs. The underdeveloped nature of benefit-sharing agreements between communities and state corporations in Russia is caused by paternalistic character of state-society relations and fragile civil society. Chinese companies rely on the long-term Chinese Communist Party's plans and must be forward-looking. CPR carries the responsibility toward Chinese citizens through enhancing their living standards, including transportation and infrastructure development. To fulfill these objectives, China needs energy. Similar to Russia, business approaches do not work quite well in Chinese energy policy due to the strategic role of energy in society.

Thus, Chinese and Russian energopower-biopower narratives share similarities based on organization of their political systems because of the patrimonial character of state-owned cooperation, the role of energy as a strategic asset, and energy supplies as the main driving force of geopolitical ambitions. Despite the distinction in energy trade roles (consumer versus producer), Chinese and Russian energy goals and ambitions could align. This could help both overcome challenges including the lack of Chinese interest in the Arctic energy; reluctance of Russia to share expertise in Arctic drilling technologies with other states; and China's larger geopolitical ambitions, which include the contested dominance of Central Asian markets. China and Russia's energopower concepts are more similar to the one shaped by the EU.

How have these energopower narratives been created? Russia's paternalistic mentality developed after President Putin's second term as the Russian government emphasized its separation from European values and norms. The hydrocarbon prices boom in the mid-to-late 2000s ultimately resulted in renationalization of the Russian energy sector, predetermining the Russian domestic economy's dependency on energy exports. Nationalization of energy sources in Russia did not correspond well with liberalization of energy markets in the EU. As the EU is interested in energy as a commodity, there is a clash between state-owned and privately owned companies that perceive the role of energy distinctly. This distinction determines their goals in energy trade as the European companies are profit-oriented, whereas Chinese and Russian companies view energy as an asset. This might mean that, at least theoretically, there is the compatibility of Russian and Chinese goals and objectives related to energopower and biopolitics.

After the beginning of the war in Ukraine, Russia does not have much of choice in terms of energy imports. There is also a possibility that the Kremlin strategically calculated the risks of losing Western partners in energy trade with an option of reorienting its supplies toward China and India.

In energy trade and production, the EU operates in an exceptionally distinct geopolitical realm. Fragmented energy interests in the EU itself also do not serve the European Union's goals. The role of the energy union in the EC is still quite small and mostly regulates the energy transition. The energopower in the EU is a component of national sovereignty as each country decides what works the best for their energy security strategies. In this regard, it makes sense to examine energopower and biopower linkages in Germany, potentially revealing the German goals toward Nord Stream 2.

Germany and Russia have a long history of energy trade cooperation, enhanced by Schroeder-Putin's close personal relationships. Nevertheless, Germany is transitioning toward more renewable energy projects. Unlike Russia, German success in the energy transition is determined by citizen participation and willingness to accept renewable sources such as wind power plants. Energy transition discourses (*Energiewende*) are dominated by the discussion of citizen involvement; renewable energy development is understood as a social and political transformation as opposed to a national energy strategy. Energopower in Germany is decentralized, and society is an essential agent in energy governance.

What does it mean for the Russian Arctic energy strategies and Nord Stream 2? By applying a constructivist lens, we argue that the relationships between energopower and biopower can impact the creation and framing of rules, norms, and values in each respective actor. Constructitivism argues that state identities and interests are not taken for granted but rather developed as process of interactions. Ideas, norms and values are shaped by intersubjective meanings of concepts such as power, energy, society, state and social responsibility. China and Russia's similarities in terms of their nationalized industries, centralized policy approaches and patrimonial structures of energopower mean that both actors operate in the same geopolitical realm where energy supplies guide and rule national policy strategies. In comparison, the EU energy strategy is fragmentized and driven by climate change mitigation/adaptation trends and energy transition topics. As energy is part of the national sovereignty issue, Russia would have to treat each state in Europe as an independent actor. At this moment, Germany is the most interested partner in Nord Stream 2 project. Active civil society involvement in Germany and other liberal democratic EU states is another factor in EU energy policy. As long as Germany is reliant on Russian gas supplies, the EU-Russia energy trade might continue even during the Russian-Ukrainian conflict.

After the Russian invasion of Ukraine, some German gas buyers, such as VNG, complied with Moscow's new terms. Yet, Russian atrocities in Bucha, Mariupol and other parts of Ukraine immediately caused heated debates in the EU regarding the importance of human rights. As a result, the European politicians, particularly the French President Emmanuel Macron, urged the EU to hold Russia accountable for its war crimes. As a result, the European Commission warned European gas buyers that conceding to the Russian rules would violate EU sanctions against Russia (Slav, 2022b). Hence, human rights issues play a crucial role in the EU political agenda, yet, some European buyers still might view the Russian gas merely as a market commodity in high demand.

Russian Arctic LNG is not China's main priority, but energy supplies from these projects could enhance larger Chinese geopolitical ambitions. The LNG projects also appear to be more stable as China is the only customer. While Russia is still quite interested in an energy partnership with China (as it is the only horse to ride), China might establish energy trade agreements with other states (i.e., the U.S.). If China's agreements with other states fall through, then Russian-Chinese energy cooperation in the Arctic is a match made in heaven.

CONCLUSION

Why does the Russian perception of energopower differ compared to China and the EU? How would this distinction in norms and values potentially impact energy trade dynamics in the Russian Arctic? This chapter attempts to understand the Russian-Chinese-EU energy relations at the ideational level by analyzing how energopower operates in each of these respective actors, how energopower influences biopower and how the energopower-biopower link informs the creation of ideas.

This book chapter examined the potential of energy cooperation between Russia and China and Russia and the EU by comparing the concepts of energopower and biopower that have been created and framed by each of these respective actors (Table 4.1). Russia has several Arctic LNG projects, and Moscow is looking to cooperate with Chinese investors as part of its pivot to Asia. Other Asian states, including Japan and India, are slightly interested in Arctic gas but remain relatively lukewarm toward Russian Arctic hydrocarbon resources. Energy plays a strategic role in Russia by contributing to socioeconomic development and legitimizing the Russian role as a great regional power in the Circumpolar North. Nord Stream 2 is another Russian energy project in which Russia hopes to overcome its dependency on transit across Ukraine. The war in Ukraine has negatively influenced fragile Russia-EU relations, but some European states such as Germany, Finland and the Baltic states are still quite reliant on Russian gas. Russia is thus in between two (or multiple) trade partnerships, which are determined by the difference in norms, values and rules. As the literature indicated, both Russia and China share a distinct set of norms and values which do not entirely correspond with the European. Despite being interested in the EU-promoted clean energy and renewable energy transition, both Russia and China mainly focus on hydrocarbon resources as China aims to remove coal production from its energy supply. The Russian elite, in turn, hopes that the energy transition would be slow and complementary to existing hydrocarbon development. In this regard, it is essential to analyze how this distinction in terms of Russian and Chinese energy governance and related to their norms and values have been constructed. In order to discover the energy governance modes, we looked at each of these actors' energy policy through the lens of energopower and biopower conceptualizations. As it was noted that the EU actors prefer having fragmented energy policies, we focused on the case study of Germany and its energy transition. Yet, the war in Ukraine also allowed the EU to develop a unified opinion regarding the proposal of a phased-in embargo on Russian oil imports.

The analysis revealed that China and Russia exist in a similar geopolitical realm in the exercise of energopower: state-owned companies, patrimonialism, the weak role of civil society in industry-society interactions and the lack of focus

Table 4.1: The Energopower and Biopower Relations in Russia, China and the EU and Their Impacts on Russia-China and Russia-EU Energy Trade

Actor	The notion of energopower	Perception of relations between energopower-biopower in energy trade with Russia	Implications for Russian-Chinese and Russian-EU energy trade (Arctic LNGs and Nord Stream 2)
Russia	Energy as a strategic asset, an element of socioeconomic development, after the invasion—as an economic and political weapon. Energy development is a strategic goal.	Corporate responsibility, youth sport programs development; socioeconomic development is tied to the ideas of hydrocarbon extraction; paternalism in benefit-sharing agreements; weak civil society	Compatibility of goals and objectives related to energopower and biopolitics with China. State-owned Russian companies and private owned companies in Europe possess distinct values and goals.
China	Energy as a strategic asset, an element of socioeconomic development and by being intertwined with infrastructure development is part of global geopolitical ambitions	A business approach has limited success in the Chinese context because state agendas are long term and multidimensional. Maximizing not only profits but socioeconomic improvement	Russian Arctic LNG is not the main priority for China but energy supplies from these projects could enhance Chinese geopolitical ambitions. Russian LNG also appears to be more stable as China is the only customer.

Table 4.1: Continued

Actor	The notion of energopower	Perception of relations between energopower-biopower in energy trade with Russia	Implications for Russian-Chinese and Russian-EU energy trade (Arctic LNGs and Nord Stream 2)
The EU	Energy as a commodity; Liberalization of energy markets in EU and Germany; after the invasion—the EU emphasis on the importance of human rights over the gas supplies from Russia.	Commodification of social life; neoliberalism; privatization; transition to clean renewable energy; active citizen involvement into renewable energy development; after the invasion—keeping Russia accountable for war crimes.	Russia should treat the EU states as independent fragmented actors with their own political agendas. Germany is still reliant on Russian hydrocarbon energy supplies, but it slowly makes energy transition; even given the negative position of Germany toward the invasion, the German-Russian gas trade may still continue.

Source: Author's own elaboration.

on renewable energy. Unlike neoliberal EU members, Russia and China do not make their energy policy decisions based on cost-benefit analysis or the willingness of citizens to participate in policy implementation. Energy plays a role of a strategic asset. Despite the difference in positions (consumer-producer) and strategic ambitions (regional power vs. global power), China and Russia have a high compatibility potential in energy partnerships. Their similar mindsets could even help overcome challenges, such as competition for political and economic dominance in Central Asia.

The fragmented nature of EU energy policies can be explained by energy security, part of national sovereignty. As the EU members slowly transition toward renewable energy development, would it be possible for influential actors such as Germany to stop being reliant on Russian gas? The answer is hidden in the possibility of completing the social and political transformation of the EU mindset in the energy transition. The Green Revolution would mean that the EU (and other regional actors) will altogether refuse to buy hydrocarbon resources from oil and gas producers, including Russia and the Middle East. How would Russia react to this transition? It could be accurate that China would remain it is the only loyal customer.

The further developments in this topic should address the impacts of energy transition in the EU/the West on the energy producing countries in eastern Europe and Central Asia. The studies of political implications of energy transition in the EU/the West analyzed through the lens of poststructuralism would be particularly captivating.

NOTE

1 The author would like to thank Dr. Jennifer Winter, Dr. Galina Belolyubskaya, and Dr. Katharina Koch for their valuable feedback and support, as well as the anonymous reviewers for their valuable feedback.

REFERENCES

Alexeeva, O., & Lasserre, F. (2018). An analysis on Sino-Russian cooperation in the Arctic in the BRI era. *Advances in Polar Sciences*, *29*(4), 269–282.

Allan, J., Lemaadel, M., & Lakhal, H. (2021). Oppressive energopolitics in Africa's last colony: Energy, subjectivities, and resistance. *Antipode*, *54*(1), 44–63. https://doi.org/10.1111/anti.12765

Andreassen, N. (2016). Arctic energy development in Russia—How "sustainability" can fit?. *Energy Research & Social Science*, *16*, 78–88.

Armstrong, P. (2022, May 4). *The surprising resiliency of Russia's economy (and why it won't last)*. CBC. https://www.cbc.ca/news/business/russian-economy-sanctions-analysis-1.6440166

Bhagwat, J. (2020). Russia and India in the Arctic: A case for greater synergy. *Social and Economic Development*, *58*.

Bleiker, R., & Campbell, D. (2021). Poststructuralism. In T. Dunne, M. Kurki & S. Smith (Eds.), *International relations theories: Discipline and diversity* (pp. 196–218). Oxford University Press. (Original work published 2016)

Ruediger Bachmann & David Baqaee & Christian Bayer & Moritz Kuhn & Andreas Löschel & Benjamin Moll & Andreas Peichl & Karen Pittel & Moritz Schularick, 2022. "What if? The Economic Effects for Germany of a Stop of Energy Imports from Russia," EconPol Policy Reports 36, ifo Institute - Leibniz Institute for Economic Research at the University of Munich.

Bloomberg News. (2022a, April 21). *China energy giants in talks for Shell's Russian gas stake*. https://www.bloomberg.com/news/articles/2022-04-21/china-state-energy-giants-in-talks-for-shell-s-russian-gas-stake

Bloomberg News. (2022b, May 4). *Cut off by Moscow, Poland gets Russian gas from its allies*. https://www.bnnbloomberg.ca/cut-off-by-moscow-poland-gets-russian-gas-from-its-allies-1.1761053

Boffey, D. (2022, May 2). EU faces crunch point over Russia's gas payment demands. *The Guardian*. https://www.theguardian.com/business/2022/may/02/eu-to-reject-moscow-demands-to-pay-roubles-for-russian-gas

Bouffard, T., & Lackenbauer, P. W. (2021, March 30). The development of the Russian Arctic Council chairmanship: A strategic plan of preparation and pursuit. *Strategic Perspectives*, North American and Arctic Defense Security Network. https://www.naadsn.ca/wp-content/uploads/2021/04/Strategic-Perspectives-Russian-Arctic-Council-Chairmanship-TB-PWL-mar-2021.pdf

Boyer, D. (2014). Energopower: An introduction. *Anthropological Quarterly*, *87*(2), 309–333.

Bradsheer, K. (2022, May 3). Russia could sell more energy to Asia. *The New York Times*. https://www.nytimes.com/2022/05/03/business/russia-china-energy-ukraine.html

Burchell, G., Davidson, A., & Foucault, M. (2008). *The birth of biopolitics: Lectures at the Collège de France, 1978–1979*. Springer.

Cebotari, L. (2022). EU-Russia energy relations: Problems and perspectives. *Proceedings of the International Conference on Business Excellence*, *16*(1), 1001–1014.

China Briefing. (2022, April 14). *Russia's pivot to China—Geopolitics, trade, and development in the wake of the Ukraine conflict*. China Briefing. https://www.china-briefing.com/news/russias-pivot-to-china-geopolitics-trade-development-in-the-wake-of-the-ukraine-conflict/

Cohen M. (2022, April 8). Why Bucha is a turning point—And why that's so ominous. *New Republic*. https://newrepublic.com/article/166051/bucha-ukraine-war-crimes

DW. (2022). Germany ready to support EU ban on Russian oil. *DW*. https://www.dw.com/en/germany-ready-to-support-eu-ban-on-russian-oil/a-61654275

Economic Times, The. (2022, May 4). *Russian gas supplies to China soar by 60 pc in 2022*. https://economictimes.indiatimes.com/news/international/world-news/russian-gas-supplies-to-china-soar-by-60-pc-in-2022/articleshow/91300453.cms

Ellyatt, H. (2022, April 29). *Russia accused of "blackmail" after halting gas supplies to two European countries*. CNBC. https://apnews.com/article/russia-ukraine-covid-health-business-germany-274aae7fd9dfa88bab1dd26200db9423

Evans, D. (2022, April 22). *Europe strives to end dependency on Russian gas*. China Dialogue. Retrieved from https://chinadialogue.net/en/energy/europe-strives-to-end-dependency-on-russian-gas/

Euronews. (2021). *Nord Stream 2 construction completed, but Ukraine pledges to continue fight*. https://www.euronews.com/2021/09/10/nord-stream-2-construction-completed-but-ukraine-pledges-to-continue-fight

Euronews with AP. (2022, April 30). *Eastern Europe teams up to reduce EU's dependence on Russian gas*. https://www.euronews.com/2022/04/30/eastern-europe-teams-up-to-reduce-eu-s-dependence-on-russian-gas

European Commission. (2021). *Energy union*. https://ec.europa.eu/energy/topics/energy-strategy/energy-union/

European Commission. (2022). *In focus: Engaging with energy partners in a changing world*. Retrieved from https://ec.europa.eu/info/news/focus-global-energy-partners-and-eu-2022-jun-14_en

Fierke, K. M. (2016). Constructivism. In T. Dunne, M. Kurki, & S. Smith (Eds.), *International relations theories: Discipline and diversity* (pp. 161–178). Oxford University Press.

Foucault, M. (2016). *The punitive society: Lectures at the Collège de France, 1972–1973*. Springer.

Fu, K. C. (2016). 7 Russia's energy policy in the Arctic region and China's opportunities. In *Challenges of the Changing Arctic* (pp. 103–124). Brill Nijhoff.

Gabbatiss J. (2022, May 20). *In-depth Q&A: How the EU plans to end its reliance on Russian fossil fuels.* Retrieved from https://www.carbonbrief.org/in-depth-qa-how-the-eu-plans-to-end-its-reliance-on-russian-fossil-fuels/

Genel, K. (2006). The question of biopower: Foucault and Agamben. *Rethinking Marxism, 18*(1), 43–62.

Gillessen, B., Heinrichs, H., Hake, J. F., & Allelein, H. J. (2019). Energy security in context of transforming energy systems: A case study for natural gas transport in Germany. *Energy Procedia, 158*, 3339–3345.

Gustafson, T. (2022, April 6). *Go east? Why China's not going to save Russia's energy exports anytime soon.* Fortune. https://fortune.com/2022/04/06/china-buys-russia-energy-exports-oil-gas-coal-ukraine-sanctions-thane-gustafson/

Hasberg, K. S. (2019). From Foucauldian biopower to infopower and energopower: A review of Colin Koopman's and Dominic Boyer's novel conceptualizations of power. *Le foucaldien, 5*(7), 1–16.

Haukkala, H. (2015). From cooperative to contested Europe? The conflict in Ukraine as a culmination of a long-term crisis in EU-Russia relations. *Journal of Contemporary European Studies, 23*(1), 25–40.

Henderson, J., & Mitrova, T. (2016). *Energy relations between Russia and China: Playing chess with the dragon.* Oxford Institute of Energy Studies.

International Energy Agency, World Energy Outlook 2002, Paris 2002, pp 249.

International Energy Agency. (2022a). *Energy Fact Sheet: Why does Russian oil and gas matter.* Retrieved from https://www.iea.org/articles/energy-fact-sheet-why-does-russian-oil-and-gas-matter

International Energy Agency. (2022b). *An energy sector roadmap to carbon neutrality in China.* Retrieved from https://www.iea.org/reports/an-energy-sector-roadmap-to-carbon-neutrality-in-china

International Energy Agency. (2022c). *Germany.* Retrieved from https://www.iea.org/countries/germany

Kachenhoff, Tom, & Eckert, Vera. 2022. (2022, April 8). German energy regulator to sustain Gazprom Germania operations. Reuters. https://www.reuters.com/business/energy/german-energy-regulator-sustain-gazprom-germania-operations-2022-04-08/

Kalkbrenner, B. J., & Roosen, J. (2016). Citizens' willingness to participate in local renewable energy projects: The role of community and trust in Germany. *Energy Research & Social Science, 13*, 60–70.

Kirby, P. (2022, October 31). *Russia's gas fight with Ukraine.* BBC News. https://www.bbc.com/news/world-europe-29521564

Kuteleva, A. (2020). Discursive politics of energy in EU-Russia relations: Russia as an "energy superpower" and a "raw-material appendage." *Problems of Post-Communism, 67*(1), 78–92.

Kuzemko, C. (2014). Ideas, power and change: Explaining EU-Russia energy relations. *Journal of European Public Policy, 21*(1), 58–75.

Lang, K. O., & Westphal, K. (2017). *Nord Stream 2: A political and economic contextualisation.* SWP.

Langer, K., Decker, T., Roosen, J., & Menrad, K. (2018). Factors influencing citizens' acceptance and non-acceptance of wind energy in Germany. *Journal of Cleaner Production, 175*, 133–144.

Lau, C. L., Bergman, Z., & Bergman, M. M. (2019). Environmental protection and corporate responsibility: The perspectives of senior managers and CxOs in China. *Sustainability, 11*(13), 3610.

Leung, G. C. (2011). China's energy security: Perception and reality. *Energy Policy*, *39*(3), 1330–1337.

Maltby, T. (2013). European Union energy policy integration: A case of European Commission policy entrepreneurship and increasing supranationalism. *Energy Policy*, *55*, 435–444.

Markowitz, J. N. (2020). *Perils of plenty: Arctic resource competition and the return of the great game*. Oxford University Press.

Meynkhard, A. (2020). Long-term prospects for the development energy complex of Russia. *International Journal of Energy Economics and Policy*, *10*(3), 224.

Novatek. (2021). Project Arctic LNG. Novatek website. https://www.novatek.ru/en/

Pyatkova, N. (2018). The future of Russian LNG on the world gas markets. In *E3S web of conferences* (Vol. 58, p. 03005). EDP Sciences.

Rapoza, K. (2022, May 4). *Why Russia's natural gas leverage won't last much longer*. Forbes. https://www.forbes.com/sites/kenrapoza/2022/05/04/why-russias-natural-gas-leverage-wont-last-much-longer/?sh=7603fe3b5542

Ray, S. (2022, May 2). *Europe scrambles for long-term fix after Putin cuts off gas*. AjJazeera. https://www.aljazeera.com/economy/2022/5/2/europe-scrambles-for-longterm-fix-after-putin-cuts-off-gas

Reuters. (2022, April 14). Gazprom Germania has not been nationalised—German regulator. https://www.reuters.com/business/energy/gazprom-germania-has-not-been-nationalised-german-regulator-2022-04-14/

Schwarz, L. (2020). Empowered but powerless? Reassessing the citizens' power dynamics of the German energy transition. In Energy Research & Social Science (Vol. 63, p. 101405). Elsevier BV. https://doi.org/10.1016/j.erss.2019.101405

Salonen, H. (2021). All habits die hard: Exploring the path dependence and lock-ins of outdated energy systems in the Russian Arctic. *Energy Research & Social Science*, *78*, 102–149.

Sergunin, A., & Konyshev, V. (2019). Forging Russia's Arctic strategy: Actors and decision-making. *The Polar Journal*, *9*(1), 75–93.

Shagina, M. (2020). Russia's pivot to Asia: Between rhetoric and substance. *Orbis (Philadelphia)*, *64*(3), 447–460. https://doi.org/10.1016/j.orbis.2020.05.007

Siddi, M. (2020). EU-Russia energy relations. In M. Knodt & J. Kemmerzell (Eds.), *Handbook of Energy Governance in Europe* (pp. 1–25). Springer.

Slav, I. (2022a, May 3). *Germany's uniper looks to buy Russian gas in Euro-to-Ruble scheme*. Oil Price. https://oilprice.com/Latest-Energy-News/World-News/Germanys-Uniper-Looks-To-Buy-Russian-Gas-In-Euro-To-Ruble-Scheme.html

Slav, I. (2022b, May 10). *Top German gas buyer concedes to Russian payment scheme*. Oil Price. https://oilprice.com/Energy/Natural-Gas/Top-German-Gas-Buyer-Concedes-To-Russian-Payment-Scheme.html

Smeets, N. (2018). The Green Menace: Unraveling Russia's elite discourse on enabling and constraining factors of renewable energy policies. *Energy Research & Social Science*, *40*, 244–256.

Solorio, I., & Jörgens, H. (2020). Contested energy transition? Europeanization and authority turns in EU renewable energy policy. *Journal of European Integration*, *42*(1), 77–93.

South China Morning Post. (2022, May 2). Russian natural gas exports to China jump 60 percent in first 4 months. https://www.scmp.com/news/china/diplomacy/article/3176280/russian-natural-gas-exports-china-jump-60-cent-first-4-months

Sorensen, C. T. N., & Klimenko, E. (2017). *Drivers and challenges in China-Russia cooperation in the Arctic*. Forsvaret.

Staalesen, A. (2020, October 22). *Top Moscow officials at odds over Arctic shipping*. Barents Observer. https://thebarentsobserver.com/en/arctic/2020/10/top-moscow-officials-odds-over-putins-command-arctic-shipping.

Steblyanskaya, A., Qingchao, X., Razmanova, S., Steblyanskiy, N., & Denisov, A. (2021). China and Russia Energy Strategy Development: Arctic LNG. *International Journal of Energy Economics and Policy, 11*(4), 450–460.

Suganuma, K. (2011). Economic effects of foreign direct investment on the Sakhalin region from 1995 to 2005. *Far Eastern Studies, 10*, 1–23.

Szeman, I. (2014). On energopolitics. *Anthropological Quarterly, 87*, 457–468.

Szulecki, K., Fischer, S., Gullberg, A. T., & Sartor, O. (2016). Shaping the "Energy Union": Between national positions and governance innovation in EU energy and climate policy. *Climate Policy, 16*(5), 548–567.

Taghizadeh-Hesary, F., Rasoulinezhad, E., Yoshino, N., Sarker, T., & Mirza, N. (2021). Determinants of the Russia and Asia-Pacific energy trade. *Energy Strategy Reviews, 38*, 100681.

Tianming, G., & Erokhin, V. (2021). China-Russia collaboration in shipping and marine engineering as one of the key factors of secure navigation along the NSR. *China's Arctic Engagement, 9*, 234.

Tichý, L. (2019). *EU-Russia energy relations*. Springer International.

Turrentine J., (2022, May 3). *How we can help Europe end its reliance on Russian gas*. NRDC. https://www.nrdc.org/stories/how-we-can-help-europe-end-its-reliance-russian-gas.

Tynkkynen, V. P. (2016). Energy as power—Gazprom, gas infrastructure, and geo-governmentality in Putin's Russia. *Slavic Review*, 75(2), 374–395.

Tynkkynen, V. P. (2019). *The energy of Russia: Hydrocarbon culture and climate change*. Edward Elgar.

Tysiachniouk, M. S., & Petrov, A. N. (2018). Benefit sharing in the Arctic energy sector: Perspectives on corporate policies and practices in Northern Russia and Alaska. *Energy Research & Social Science, 39*, 29–34.

Vatansever, A. (2017). Is Russia building too many pipelines? Explaining Russia's oil and gas export strategy. *Energy Policy, 108*, 1–11.

Veebel, V., & Markus, R. (2015). Lessons from the EU-Russia sanctions 2014–2015. *Baltic Journal of Law & Politics, 8*(1), 165–194.

Wang, Henry. (1999). China's Oil Industry and Market. Elsevier.

Westphal, K. (2016). Germany and the EU-Russia energy dialogue. In *The EU-Russian energy dialogue* (pp. 109–134). Routledge.

Wettengel, J. (2021, September 9). *Gas pipeline Nord Stream 2 links Germany to Russia, but splits Europe*. https://www.cleanenergywire.org/factsheets/gas-pipeline-nord-stream-2-links-germany-russia-splits-europe

Wilson, J. L. (2015). Russia and China respond to soft power: Interpretation and readaptation of a Western construct. *Politics, 35*(3–4), 287–300.

Wohl, S. (2016). Gendering governmentality and European integration theory. In G. Abels & H. MacRae (Eds.), *Gendering European integration theory: Engaging new dialogues* (pp. 237–255). Barbara Budrich.

Yennie-Lindgren, W. (2018). New dynamics in Japan–Russia energy relations 2011–2017. *Journal of Eurasian Studies, 9*(2), 152–162.

Zachmann, G., Sgaravatti, G., & McWilliams, B. (2021). European natural gas imports. *Bruegel Datasets*. https://www.bruegel.org/publications/datasets/european-natural-gas-imports/

Zoellner, J., Schweizer-Ries, P., & Wemheuer, C. (2008). Public acceptance of renewable energies: Results from case studies in Germany. *Energy Policy, 36*(11), 4136–4141.

CHAPTER 5

The Energy Transition Geopolitical Outlook for the European Union: Will Russian Gas Decline?[1]

JAVAD KEYPOUR

INTRODUCTION

The European Union (EU) has been traditionally known as a net energy importer as its domestic energy resources do not suffice for its demand. While the EU has been importing oil from different origins, the 1968 Soviet-Austria gas deal set the stage for gas to flow to Europe from the east. After the Soviet Union collapsed, both sides expanded their gas relations, and Russia became the dominant natural gas supplier of Europe (Gazprom, 2021). While under the post–Cold War rapprochement paradigm, bilateral gas relations were growing, the Russia-Ukraine gas disputes in 2006 and 2009 raised concerns about the Russian gas reliability and accentuated the geopolitical aspects of EU energy security. Consequently, Russian gas was viewed as a twofold threat: geopolitical leverage that the Kremlin applied to bully the Union to influence the neighbors (Collins, 2017; Smith 2009) and a threat against member states' energy security, considering the EU's low resilience against gas interruptions in general (Richter & Holz, 2015; Ruban, 2013).

Nevertheless, as attention to climate issues increased, these geopolitical concerns were sidelined, though not forgotten. By the Energy Union initiative of 2015, the security of supply was amalgamated with environmental goals. Juncker's Commission aimed at accelerating the fundamental modernization of Europe's entire economy inside and enhancing the EU's global leadership in climate policies outside of the Union, as Maroš Šefčovič, the former European Commission Vice President for the Energy Union and EU Space Policy asserted (European Commission, 2017). It paved the way for the EU Green Deal of 2019 that accentuated the importance of the climate frame further, targeting the transformation of the EU into a climate-neutral economy by 2050. This objective builds on the commitments made by the EU under the Paris Agreement to reduce greenhouse gas emissions by at least 40 % by 2030 compared to 1990. Although the EU has remained dependent on Russian gas for up to 43.6 % of its imports in 2020 (Eurostat, 2021), the energy transition necessitated reducing Russian gas consumption in the EU's 2050 perspective.

Hydrocarbon resources have long been viewed as affecting the international system by causing interstate conflicts and cooperation. This could mean that any significant change in such interactions, like the energy transition, inevitably changes the international and regional energy relations, for example, the EU-Russia gas relations. While the energy transition implications were still being debated among scholars, Russia's invasion of Ukraine has once again brought security of supply concerns under the limelight. This made the projections of future relations even more complicated. In fact, two distinctive vectors will run the EU-Russia gas relations in the energy transition era; the climate-based and the security of supply considerations. This chapter aims to discuss the outcomes of these vectors' interactions on forming bilateral gas relations. Thus, we formulate our research question: How will the geopolitics of EU-Russia gas relations change in the energy transition era?

To this end, we begin by clarifying the critical enshrined theoretical terms and background concepts to avoid any distortion in answering our research question. Then, we discuss the EU-Russia gas relations before and after 2030 as a mid-term perspective targeted by some EU plans, that is, the Fit for 55 and REPowerEU. Then, the 2030–2050 perspective is projected by analyzing the two actors' behavior, Russia and EU, separately and in correlation to each other. Finally, the conclusion shows that while Russian gas exports to the EU may fall in the 2030 vision, it must become decarbonized despite the technical and regulatory requirements and challenges to remain in the EU market. The geopolitical outcomes of the energy transition on bilateral relations are also highly path-dependent, as will be discussed. The writing of this chapter was concluded in March 2022.

RESEARCH FRAMEWORK

Not wishing to get lost in the quagmire of definitions, we must frame a clarified lexicon of energy within the research framework. The first necessary definition is energy security. Although a consensus on defining energy security has not yet been reached among scholars and policymakers, most of the rendered definitions have overlapping elements, easing the selection (Ang et al., 2015). Therefore, we will adhere to a widely used four-component definition, asserting that energy security is minimizing the risks associated with *availability* (or elements relating to geological existence), *accessibility* (or geopolitical elements), *acceptability* (or environmental and societal elements), and *affordability* (or economic elements) of energy supply (APERC, 2007). These components are by no means isolated categories but are subject to a complex interplay forming a unified definition (Kruyt et al., 2011).

Another concept is energy geopolitics. Like energy security, geopolitics has consistently appeared in security studies and national strategy under various definitions. It has often been used interchangeably with "great power rivalry" and "international relations"; however, they are not the same (Vakulchuk et al., 2020). Generally, geopolitical analysis "focuses on using natural resources and the impact of geographic characteristics in national and foreign policy" (Campos and Fernandes, 2017). Given that the definition of geopolitics is deeply affected by the context under analysis, energy geopolitics analyzes how energy—as a critical element of the states' geography—may influence international relations. By this definition, energy is not limited solely to resources but includes a broad spectrum of issues, such as the location of energy supply and demand centers, transit routes, or even energy prices. We mainly focus on the EU member states and Russia as the main actors within the energy geopolitics sphere for our research. However, non-state actors like energy companies and the EU bodies have been considered whenever necessary, considering that energy is a shared competence according to the Treaty on the Functioning of the European Union (TFEU).

Even though energy security and energy geopolitics have been inextricably linked, it is crucial not to confuse them. As mentioned before, the second component of the rendered definition of energy security, accessibility, implies the geopolitical considerations of energy. In other words, it focuses on the uneven geographical distribution of fossil fuel deposits and whether policies to integrate markets can help bridge differences of political and economic interest between fossil energy consuming and producing states (Pakiam, 2011). Thus, it is not accidental that oil and gas supply geopolitics have been traditionally classified under the hard, or military–security, dimension of risks and uncertainties associated with energy security (Hippel et al., 2011). Nevertheless, energy security has a broader perspective as it covers the geological, economic, societal, and environmental dimensions of energy in our acquired definition; these aspects may sometimes have political and geopolitical effects on energy, but not always.

The geopolitical aspects of EU-Russia gas relations became more sensitive in the 2000s due to two gas disputes with Ukraine showing the EU's vulnerabilities of supply security. Therefore, reducing energy dependence on Russian gas and increasing control over energy transit routes and pipelines were two main geopolitical options for the EU (Casier, 2011). Meanwhile, renewables development was perceived not only as a matter of climate change movement but also for strengthening the EU's energy security; it gradually replaces the existing system with a more self-dependent and less vulnerable one (Keypour & Ahmadzada, 2021). However, the Ukraine war in 2022 has drastically intensified the geopolitical concerns over Russian gas, and the Commission urged immediate dependence reduction by proposing the REPowerEU Plan. Thus, the energy transition geopolitical impacts of EU-Russia gas relations should be interpreted considering the REPowerEU proposal.

The geopolitical consequences of energy transition can be examined from different perspectives. Scholten and colleagues (2020) expect fossil fuel-exporting countries like Russia may experience economic instability as they lose a significant portion of their export earnings, which causes internal political instability and impacts Russia-EU gas relations. In an analogy resembling the role of oil in a fossil fuel-oriented geopolitical system, Hache (2018) sees the unequal distribution of new materials needed to produce renewable energy equipment as a new source of geopolitical power, which complicates global energy geopolitics. Energy transition also increases electrification and digitalization across all energy sectors facilitating decentralization of energy supply, which may have political consequences like cyber threats, civil unrest, and separatism (Griffiths, 2019; Scholten et al., 2020). These analyses on *indirect* consequences of energy transition have been criticized by Overland (2019); however, our analysis focuses on the geopolitical effects of a *direct* factor in bilateral relations, that is, natural gas. Thus, in this chapter, we focus specifically on the geopolitical consequences of expected fluctuations in the share and importance of gas in the EU energy mix in the transition era.

Assessing the geopolitical consequences of the energy transition on EU-Russia gas relations is not straightforward as it entails long-term projection, that is, until 2050. While the ongoing policymaking around energy transition has kept it volatile, the Commission's urge for quick Russian gas decline within the REPowerEU has intensified the uncertainties. Therefore, to make a more precise prediction, one can divide the forecast period into two parts: before and after 2030, since the Commission has seen 2030 as the stepping stone in energy policymaking. The extent to which the EU succeeds in accomplishing its climate decisions by 2030 and the situation in that year will directly impact the way forward. Predictions also look more realistic for such a perspective as it comes in less than a decade, and the possibility of transiting from the status quo to 2030 targets can be assessed more accurately.

Last but no less important, the energy transition is path-dependent, meaning that it is affected by different kinds of interactions between the involved actors, regimes, and landscapes (Sovacool, 2016). However, a few publications have distinguished between the geopolitics of the transitional phase and a world where energy transition has been accomplished, focusing on the former (Vakulchuk et al., 2020). This chapter will focus on the geopolitics of EU-Russia gas relations in the transition era rather than the endpoint. Since different sectors in different EU member states will rarely react uniformly, different geopolitical outcomes and inconstant rates of change are expected. Thus, our research will be developed using some simplifying assumptions, as follows.

FIT FOR 55 AND THE EU-RUSSIA GAS RELATIONS IN THE 2030 PERSPECTIVE

The 2030 vision has been defined as a turning point that the European Commission has targeted in its two major policy packages, the Fit for 55 plan and the REPowerEU. While the former proposal aims at decarbonization in the wake of climate change efforts, the latter wants to reduce dependence on Russian gas. Thus, the EU-Russia gas relations in the transition era should be addressed considering both initiatives. While the first section tries to realize how decarbonization can be potentially perceived as a driving force for reducing natural gas consumption in the main EU member states, the second section evaluates the operationality of the REPowerEU rendered measures for reducing Russian gas consumption.

FIT FOR 55 IMPLICATIONS FOR EU-RUSSIA GAS RELATIONS IN THE 2030 PERSPECTIVE

The question of EU-Russia gas relations in the transition era can be addressed by analyzing the trends of Russian gas share in the EU market in coming years under the impact of member states' decarbonization policies. However, the EU gas market is not an integrated structure as it was in the 1990s but a fragmented market consisting of different groups and actors who have different interests and diverse time frames for decision-making due to market liberalization (Stern, 2017). Furthermore, EU member states experience different levels of dependence on Russian gas, from zero (like Portugal) to 100 % (like Finland) of their gas demand. Additionally, their perceptions of Russian gas have been formed differently, and in some cases even opposite, especially before the recent Ukraine war. Unlike Finland, which did not show any significant intention to reduce its dependency, or Germany, which aimed to commence the controversial Nord Stream 2 pipeline, Poland has been known as the foremost opponent of Russian gas. Siddi (2020) has already shown that the EU member states' stance on Russian gas is strongly inspired by ideational factors, that is, how a member state constructs the identity-based "Russian Other" rather than the Russian gas share in the fuel mix. For instance, despite its negligible share, Russian gas was perceived as a severe threat in the pre-Brexit UK gas market (Williams & Sovacool, 2019).

Since the 15 member states importing Russian gas are not on the same level regarding perception and dependence on Russian gas, and this is expected to continue, one can assume the EU-Russia gas relationship is influenced by the behavior of major EU gas importers, that is, member states where 80 % of Russia's total gas exports to the Union end. Table 5.1 indicates how much exported Russian gas ended in each member state in 2019. Considering this table, the six states of Poland, Austria, the Czech Republic, Italy, France, and Germany (hereinafter the PACIFG states) consume more than 80 % of the total Russian gas exported to the Union. Thus, this chapter will focus on PACIFG-Russia gas relation.

In order to assess changes in Russian gas shares in the PACIFG states, we focus on three main sectors, namely residential (including domestic, commercial, and public services), industrial, and heat and electricity generation. This assumption is not far from the truth, as Table 5.2 shows that the transportation, energy, and non-energy industrial sectors do not have a significant share of gas consumption, and this situation is unlikely to change in the future. For instance, complete decarbonization of the transportation sector by 2030 or even 2050 looks ambitious, and even so, the application of gas in this sector will take a small portion of liquified natural gas (LNG) fueled heavy fleets (Eyl-Mazzega & Mathieu, 2020).

Table 5.1: The Share of Russian Gas Ending in Each Member State at the End of 2019

State	DE	IT	FR	PL	AT	CZ	NL	HU	SK	EL	FL	BG	HR	LV
State share of total Russian gas exports (%)	32.99	24.96	8.02	6.03	4.38	4.21	3.14	3.01	2.55	2.04	1.78	1.65	1.46	0.91
State	RO	BE	LT	EE	SL	IE	ES	PT	SE	LU	MT	CY	DE	
State share of total Russian gas exports (%)	0.82	0.81	0.68	0.68	0.27	0.26	0.04	0.00	0.00	0.00	0.00	0.00	0.00	

Source: Authors' own elaboration (data retrieved from http://statistica.com, https://www.gazprom-international.com, https://www.bp.com/, and https://www.entsog.eu).

Table 5.2: Gas Consumption in Different Sectors in PACIFG States (%)

		DE	IT	FR	PL	AT	CZ
Gross heat and production	Power	14.97	32.32	13.14	13.19	17.85	8.96
	Heat	9.41	9.41	6.02	6.45	12.71	14.59
Energy sector		1.94	2.52	1.48	8.68	3.25	1.37
Final non-energy consumption (industry)		4.54	1.05	3.16	11.06	4.63	1.36
Industry		25.75	14.01	27.97	23.11	34.85	28.30
Transportation		1.04	1.88	0.43	2.29	3.27	1.35
Residential		42.11	38.09	46.19	29.47	23.07	41.37
Other sectors		0.24	0.71	1.59	5.76	0.37	2.71
Total		100	100	100	100	100	100

Source: Authors' own elaboration (data retrieved from Eurostat, 2021, June 8)

RESIDENTIAL SECTOR

The majority of the EU's residential energy consumption (more than 63 % in 2019) is dedicated to heating and cooling (Eurostat, 2021). Figure 5.1 indicates that district heating plays a significant role in the central and eastern Europe (CEE) region's heat supply conversely to the rest of Europe, especially in Poland and the Czech Republic. These heating facilities are not efficient, as studies imply potential heat savings of up to 25 % compared to the baseline. While Table 5.2 shows that the residential sector is the main natural gas consumer in the PACIFG states, except in Austria, the central heating systems still provide heat mainly using coal-fired boilers, resulting in a considerable carbon footprint and energy waste (Mathiesen et al., 2019). Thus, it stands to reason that if decarbonization of the residential sector is aimed in the CEE region, especially in Poland and Czechia, it should start from central heating systems optimization but not from natural gas replacement.

Figure 5.2 shows that while Poland and the Czech Republic have pursued a policy of replacing coal with gas in their household sector, the share of gas in Austria, France, Germany, and Italy's residential sector, where district heating does not play a significant role, has generally declined over the past two decades. However, Germany and France tried to replace coal with natural gas following the gas price fall in 2014 (EEGAS, 2021). Under the current situation, the climate policies could imply reducing the share of gas and replacing it with other sources, such as converting existing residential heating systems to renewable systems like heat pumps, although it is time-consuming and costly (Barnes, 2021).

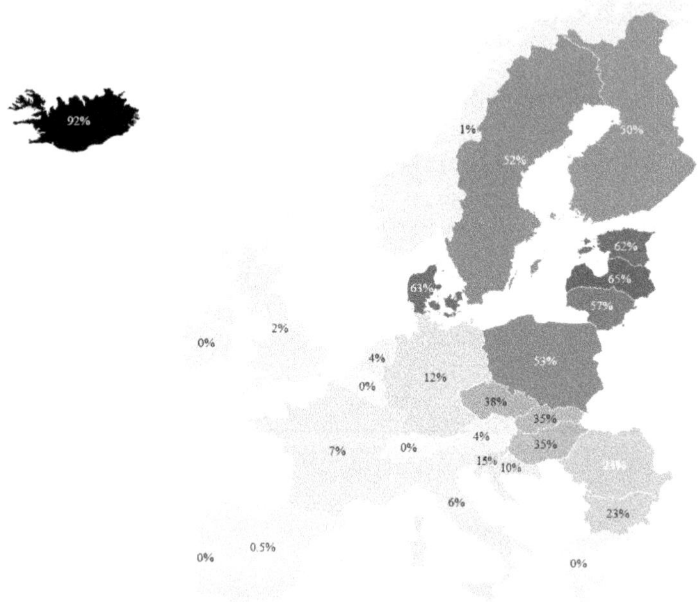

Figure 5.1: Share of district heating in total H/D demand

Source: Authors' own elaboration (data retrieved from European Commission, 2017).

Figure 5.2: Share of coal (left) and natural gas (right) in the heat mix of PACIFG states

Source: Authors' own elaboration (data retrieved from Eurostat, 2021, June 8).

POWER GENERATION AND THE INDUSTRIAL SECTOR

Figure 5.3 shows the share of gas in the fuel mix of the power generation sector among the PACIFG states. The share of gas in the power plant fuel portfolio in the five countries of Austria, the Czech Republic, Germany, Poland, and France is less than 20 %. Since Austria and France's power generation is heavily reliant on renewables and nuclear energy (more than 70 %), they are not under severe

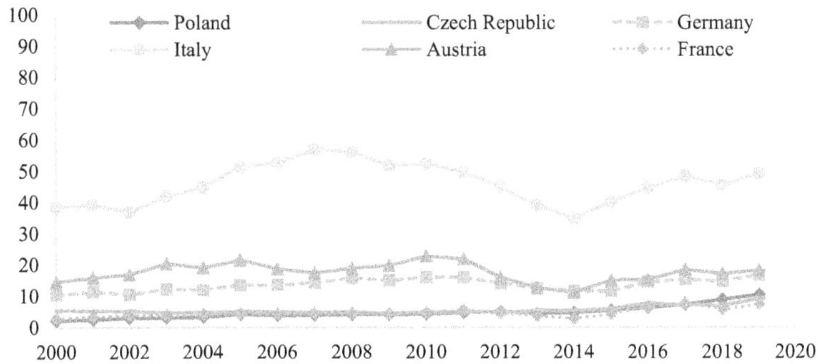

Figure 5.3: Natural gas share in the fuel mix of the power generation sector in PACIFG states
Source: Authors' own elaboration (data retrieved from Eurostat, 2021, June 8)

pressure for electricity decarbonization through gas consumption reduction. In contrast, the role of renewables in Italy's power generation is not at the same level as in Austria. Since Italy's share of coal in power generation is less than 7 %, natural gas can be targeted by the decarbonization policies.

Counter-wise, major concerns come from coal in Poland and Germany, whereas nuclear energy is also sensitive for Germany. Both countries are determined to change this situation. Germany has planned to shut down its nuclear and coal-fired power plants by 2022 and 2038, respectively (Zhu et al., 2021), while it may rethink this decision due to the recent reducing Russian gas import intentions. Therefore, focusing on coal replacement with renewable seems a more logical policy in these two states, pursuing climate considerations.

The situation in the Czech Republic is unique. While the country is one of the three most coal-intensive countries in Europe, it has slightly increased its power production capacity using renewables and gas. Prague has also expanded its nuclear capacity significantly to decarbonize the sector despite the criticism of its neighbors (Mišík, 2015). The public backs the nuclear energy extension policy so strongly that the share of other energy carriers is practically defined based on nuclear energy usage (Osička et al., 2020). Thus, decarbonization of power generation in Czech entails coal reduction rather than natural gas, while it seems Prague will have a new incentive for insisting on its nuclear power policy due to the current political situation.

When it comes to industrial gas consumption, the lack of options for the high-temperature process heat needed in industry and feedstock makes it challenging to change the current fuel and feedstock pattern rapidly (Westphal, 2020). Technically, hydrogen has been considered a possible alternative to the industrial use of natural gas in the future. For this purpose, in addition to the EU hydrogen strategy, some member states, like Germany, have developed their hydrogen strategies to increase the share of hydrogen with fossil fuels (Gielen et al., 2020). At the same time, the EU's hydrogen targets are so ambitious that a gradual replacement, that is, by using the hydrogen-natural gas mixture, seems unavoidable. For instance, Snam Italy plans to modify its natural gas network for hydrogen transmission (Zhu et al., 2021). Considering a gradual transition from natural gas to hydrogen and the required investment for developing an independent hydrogen network infrastructure (including the necessary electrolyzers, networks, and appliance optimization), it is unlikely that hydrogen will be able to dramatically change the state of industrial gas consumption in the 2030 perspective.

REPOWEREU IMPLICATIONS FOR THE EU-RUSSIA GAS RELATIONS IN THE 2030 PERSPECTIVE

In the aftermath of the Ukraine war, two major proposals, International Energy Agency's (IEA) 10-Point Plan (IEA, 2022) and the European Commission's REPowerEU (European Union 2022), have outlined how the idea of a rapid shift from Russian gas can be implemented. These proposals recommend substituting Russian gas with LNG, optimizing energy consumption, and promoting renewables. Below the question is addressed in if these instructions are operational within the asserted timeframe[2] or even compatible with the spirit of the green transition.

Diversification of Gas Sources

REPowerEU has defined a magnificent burden on LNG, that is, 50 bcm on a yearly base, to compensate the Russian gas mainly by importing from Qatar, the USA, Egypt, and West Africa by 2023. The first implication of this decision is economical as it entails 62 % expansion for the 81.4 billion cubic meter EU LNG market in a year, according to BP (2021). Such a massive change in the global LNG market structure will hike the price; Asian and European buyers have to compete over the LNG to take a higher share from the market. The envisaged measure in REPowerEU, that is, "the continuation of discussions with global gas buyers in Asia," seems too general to prevent the price growth for the already tight LNG market.[3]

A rapid shift to the LNG has environmental consequences as well. In the U.S. LNG case, as it originates from not-so-environmentally friendly shale resources whose carbon footprint is not even well-measured, higher import means that the EU is getting far from its climate goals. On one occasion, concern over the climate risks of the U.S. loose regulation of methane flaring led France to deny a requested permit to import American LNG before, which means such climate concerns are significant (Kolbe and Finley, 2021). Although it is not the first time that the EU prioritizes its security of supply to environmental considerations,[4] it looks more sensitive now, given the EU Green Deal. The LNG price spike will have environmental consequences as it decreases Asians' tendency for coal replacement, considering that switching just 20 % of coal-fired power in Asia to gas can potentially save 680 million tonnes (mt)/yr of CO_2 (equivalent to annual Germany's emission) (Ellinas, 2022). It raises questions about the EU's full commitment to being a global leader in the climate movement.

Additionally, the lack of LNG terminals and interconnectors refrains the EU's ability to substitute Russian gas (Cox, 2022). The biggest EU-Russian gas consumer, Germany, does not have any operational LNG terminal, although it is projected to fast-track constructing Wilhelmshaven and Brunsbüttel terminals by 2024. However, the struck long-term LNG importing from Qatar may result in Germany's gas lock-in (France24, 2022). Additionally, the reverse flow interconnectors should be strengthened to operationalize the unutilized Iberian LNG capacity for the rest of the EU. However, these solutions need time and investment, making them unrealistic to become operational in a year, as REPowerEU targets. In addition to that, REPowerEU stipulates that the "new cross border infrastructure should be hydrogen compatible" (European Union, 2022, p. 8), which will put an extra financial burden on the projects.[5] This could return gas projects to the EU's projects of common interest (PCI) list, although oil and natural gas infrastructure were supposed to be no longer eligible to be supported, as the commissioner for energy Kadri Simson stated before (European Commission, 2020).

Renewable Promotion

The REPowerEU sets ambitious goals for hydrogen among other renewable sources; 15 mt of renewable hydrogen on top of the 5.6 mt foreseen under Fit for 55. This is expected to moderate 25–50 bcm per year of imported Russian gas. However, this goal is clearly ambitious, if not unattainable, as it follows. According to the EU hydrogen strategy, the European Commission has already targeted 40 GW installed electrolyzer capacity and production of up to 10 million tons of renewable hydrogen in the 2030 vision. The strategy also stipulated the need for establishing 40 GW electrolyzers in the Eastern and Southern neighborhood, of which one-fourth was supposed to be located in Ukraine according to Hydrogen Europe's paper "2×40GW." Achieving this goal depended on developing renewable energy infrastructure in southeastern Ukraine (Lenivova, 2022). Since the region was deeply damaged in the war, such a goal does not look achievable.

Moreover, considering the natural gas price growth and carbon price decline after the Ukraine war (S&P, 2022), Norway and North Africa's potential for low-carbon hydrogen export are expected to decrease and cannot be accounted for stiffly. Under such circumstances, increasing renewable hydrogen production capacity for 10 mt more than the hydrogen strategy seems questionable.

Additionally, REPowerEU demands rapid action to remove the "lengthy administrative procedures" (p. 9) to facilitate investment in renewables and related infrastructures. However, the experience has shown that such organizational and policy reforms take time to be implemented and result in tangible impacts. Renewables should also be receipted by society favorably, which requires time per se. Particularly, studies show that some EU member states, like the Baltic states, are still involved with social barriers to renewable development, like the not in my backyard (NIMBY) syndrome (Lu et al., 2020).

Energy Efficiency Enhancement

Like renewables development, energy efficiency has already been enshrined in the EU agenda since the 1990s, and even the vast majority of member states seem to agree that state steering is vital to accelerate business in this profitable area. Although Article 194 of the TFEU aims at promoting energy efficiency and energy saving in the Union, it recognizes the member states' right in planning for the general structure of their energy system. Therefore, different member states prioritize the efficiency enhancement diversely and attach diverging urgency and immediacy to energy saving, while the existing EU legal frameworks cannot force the member states to move at the same speed. As a result, despite providing incentives to member states to develop Energy Efficiency Accreditation Plans (EEOS), 12 member states have not prepared it yet. It stands to reason that the non-binding REPowerEU is not expected to act legally as a game-changer.

Energy efficiency enhancement should be treated delicately and as a socially-sensitive area of policymaking since it impacts the energy price. The percentage of the population in the EU who are not able to heat their homes is still significant; 34 million people are affected by energy poverty and have difficulties to afford heating their houses in the winter (European Commission, 2021). This situation is more severe in some member states: Bulgaria (27 %), Lithuania (23 %), Cyprus (21 %), Portugal, and Greece (both 17 %). While energy poverty is intensified by the low efficiency of buildings and low income, these low-income households can become stuck in a vicious cycle of energy poverty. This means they cannot afford energy-efficient homes and home appliances, resulting in increased consumption of costly energy that ends up being wasted, which is not affordable either (Council of Europe Development Bank [CEB], 2019). Even wealthy member states like Denmark and the pre-Brexit UK have faced challenges operationalizing the

EEOSs due to concerns over increasing costs (Fawcett et al., 2019). This requires designing required policies delicately, but not quickly, as the REPowerEU depicts. One can claim that energy efficiency enhancement is more time-consuming than renewable development, as experience has proven (Szulecki & Westphal, 2016).

EU-RUSSIA GAS RELATIONS: THE WAY AHEAD IN 2030 PERSPECTIVE

While the EU's climate obligations could push the member states to reduce natural gas imports from Russia, the advent of the Ukraine war consolidated the EU's persistence. However, one can say that the replaceability of Russian gas in the short run, that is, by 2023, is highly curtailed by factors like the EU's lack of adequate infrastructure, global LNG market constraints, time-consuming essence of and energy-saving projects, and renewables development. Moreover, the EU ended this winter with a lower gas storage level than the previous years, as Russia has reduced its gas supply to the EU since July 2021. Therefore, to avoid a gas shortage in the next autumn-winter, the EU must refill the storage, especially because one-third of winter gas consumption is met via storage uptake. The EU must import more gas in the coming summer and needs a less volatile price. This will also reduce Europe's maneuverability for Russian gas replacement (Fulwood et al., 2022).

When it comes to the 2030 vision, the EU has to weigh up the pros and cons of a rapid shift from Russian gas. The Fit for 55 goals requires steep coal phase-out (especially in the CEE), which will not leave room for a radical reduction in dependence on Russian gas considering the gradual growth of renewables. Imposing rigid environmental standards on the U.S. LNG import or nuclear power plant closure policy squeezes the freedom of choices for major member states. However, the geopolitical concerns over Russian gas necessitate moderate policies, for instance, suspending nuclear power plants closure or coal phase-out. The EU still needs to loosen its climate considerations to entirely eliminate Russian gas from its fuel mix. It also means that the gas infrastructure projects should remain on the PCI list. The construction of interconnectors, LNG terminals, and alternative gas routes like the Baltic pipeline[6] should also be accelerated.

The energy price growth seems inevitable under a rapid shift from the Russian gas policy. Energy price growth creates a vicious cycle that slows down consumption optimization in the building sector, as described in section 2-2-3. It intensifies the energy poverty in the EU and jeopardizes social welfare, especially for more vulnerable social classes. Additionally, replacing LNG with Russian gas in the largest EU market, Germany, means more expensive gas, putting extra pressure on German industries and domestic consumers. Thus, the European Commission must adopt policies to avoid catastrophic consequences, especially because the Union's GDP growth has already slowed by 0.5 % since last fall due to rising gas prices (European Union, 2022). This may extend the use of coal in the EU's conversely to the primary climate goals, as it has already happened.

Stepping against climate policies and the energy prices growth necessitate a robust discourse for convincing the public. This discourse must be capable of justifying the EU's decisions costs, for instance, by relying upon solidarity with Ukraine or the urgency of expelling the Russian threat through gas import reduction. Nevertheless, the Ukraine political crisis will not last forever, and public opinion may become moderated over time under the economic pressure of higher energy prices. The energy companies' lobbies may get the upper hand gradually, especially those whose sunk investments become stranded (like Nord Stream 2). The whispers of reducing the speed of the "shift from Russian gas" policy may consequently emerge. In addition, Coal phase-out suspension may also complicate the situation provoking environmental groups' opposition who support COP 26 goals commitment. These factors could erode the power of Russian gas shift supportive discourse.

Last but no less important, the legal frameworks do not allow enforcing member states to converge on their energy policies. Articles 194(2) and 192(2) of the TFEU allow member states to independently formulate their energy policies and energy mix, even if common environmental concerns arise. This means that member states can continue decreasing or increasing their gas imports from Russia according to their individual energy and decarbonization policymaking considerations. In other words, member states' decarbonization plans may differ, which has implications for their Russian gas importation levels as well. Some member states may follow their policies in greening their energy mix, unlike others, who may intend to offset carbon emissions to meet 2030 targets. Under such circumstances, the REPowerEU is not expected to be applied as an extraordinary tool, especially as a non-binding package.

Considering the analysis mentioned above, one can conclude that the Russian gas share in the EU's energy mix in the 2030 perspective is highly dependent on the member states' decisions. Their tendency for loosening their environmental considerations on one side and the pace of energy efficiency enhancement, renewable development, and infrastructure development for replacing natural gas from other resources, on the other hand, will form bilateral relations. The complementary policies should also manage the economic consequences of the shift and make them tolerable. However, different member states will probably follow diverse routes. For instance, Poland is expected to take more severe actions for importing LNG or Norwegian gas in the short term. Italy also has great potential to replace its Russian gas consumption if its infrastructures are strengthened.

Russian gas reduction is an immutable goal for the EU and seems achievable to a high extent; however, total elimination will cost economically and for the EU's climate global leadership.

EU-RUSSIA GAS RELATIONS: THE 2030–2050 PERSPECTIVE

Contrary to the bilateral gas relations in the 2030 perspective, projecting for 2050 is more challenging, considering that energy transition is highly path-dependent. If Russian gas is entirely removed from the EU fuel mix by 2030, talking about the 2050 gas relations seems non-existing ab initio. Thus, we assume the opposite scenario where the EU-Russia gas relations after 2030 will be formed by the extent to which they are prepared to adopt deep or lenient decarbonization afterward. The EU can prepare infrastructures and legal bases for renewable promotion in the current decade to make a subsequent leap afterward. The status of the EU-Russia political relationship is the other important factor, for which it is almost impossible to render precise estimates. Thus, by focusing on the first factor, our analytical framework is framed to understand which factors may preserve or decrease Russian gas consumption in the EU market from 2030 onwards.

2030–2050 EU-RUSSIA GAS RELATIONS: AN EU PERSPECTIVE

The European Commission (2020, p. 5) has rendered three different scenarios for decarbonization:

- Strong electricity use (full electrification) with (renewable) electricity;
- Strong methane end-use, based on biomethane;
- Strong hydrogen end-use, based on green hydrogen.

Ideally, a combined full electrification-high energy efficiency enhancement scenario can lead the EU to achieve its carbon neutrality aims by 2050 if clean energy is used for electricity generation (Nam & Jin, 2021). The full electrification scenario would require a different investment and social costs than gas decarbonization. Electrification could mean a paradigm shift from the geopolitics of pipelines to the political choice of grid communities in which the relationship between these communities would be influenced by various factors, including two main opposite technical and political factors. From a technical perspective, the connection between these main centers could help their stability, especially since the network's reliance on renewables and energy storage alone for more than 50 % is not enough to maintain network stability (Zheng, 2021). On the other hand, political concerns of network dependency may encourage the centers to stay independent from their neighbors. Such political considerations have already encouraged the Baltic states to desynchronize their power grids from Russia's Integrated Power System/Unified Power System (IPS/UPS). This would reduce the alleged risk that third parties could use our dependence on the IPS/UPS and the respective frequency area (Elering, 2021). Therefore, a techno-political trade-off can always define the final decision on electricity exchange and the establishment of network connectivity.[7]

Nevertheless, as some sectors like aviation, shipping, and some industries are hard to electrify, the use of gas will probably not drop to zero. In central heating, gas phase-out is also likely to be much slower, although the development of smart grids and the optimization of heating systems in CEE could pave the way for the development of electrification and decentralized renewables (Stern, 2017). This could mean that the two other scenarios may look more viable based on using other gases like hydrogen or green gas. Given that the predicted share of hydrogen in the EU energy mix 2050 is 13–14 % according to the EU hydrogen strategy, the total biomass and renewable hydrogen production by 2050 will not exceed 150 billion cubic meters. This could mean other gases like decarbonized natural gas and low-carbon hydrogen will still be needed to safeguard EU energy security in the transition era in the 2050 vision, even though their role will decrease over time (Stern, 2020).

This gradual gas phase-out will allow the EU to steadily construct the required electrolyzers and optimize the existing transmission networks for hydrogen and biomethane purposes. Adopting appropriate policies is necessary to regulate the pace of this transition so that neither will existing gas facilities become stranded assets nor will the continued use of gas delay the achievement of climate goals. However, this does not mean Russian gas can remain in the EU's energy mix due to different reasons. First, the EU's investment in its domestic biogas potential can narrow the field for Russian gas imports. There are currently 12,000 biogas sites in 12 European countries with a production capacity of 18 billion cubic meters per year. The cost of biomethane production is currently eight times more than that of natural gas. However, biomethane has clear advantages, considering externalities in terms of CO_2 footprint, territorial development, energy security, agroecological transition, and replacement of fossil fuels in the transport sector. This capacity can be increased by adopting restrictive policies on fossil fuels during the transition period (Eyl-Mazzega & Mathieu, 2020; Stern, 2017).

Another limiting factor for gas consumption is economic considerations of supply-demand dynamics. Declining demand will reduce gas undertakings to invest in natural gas infrastructures and lower existing gas facilities' load factors. A steady replacement of hydrogen can minimize natural gas undertaking losses. However, legal frameworks need to be revised to establish hybrid natural gas transmission system operators (TSOs), that is, those gas undertakings that can enter the hydrogen industry as well (see Chapter 17, this volume). Nevertheless, the emergence of hybrid TSOs will not undo the investment decrease in the gas industry since even these TSOs do not want their facilities to become stranded assets under a declining demand trend. The consequences of supply-demand interaction will accelerate shrinking gas demand, shift transmission facilities or appliances to hydrogen, and narrow the Russian gas market.

The EU's approach in defining two crucial and correlated concepts of negative emission and life cycle assessment (LCA) is also determining. While some non-zero-carbon sectors are unavoidable in 2050, the abstract idea of *negative emissions* can favor natural gas in these sectors. This could mean that the carbon dioxide removed from the atmosphere through technical means by the gas undertakings is accounted in the total emission calculation for the gas supplied. Similarly, while natural gas production, including gas flaring, leaves a carbon footprint, mitigation through negative emission allegedly results in greener gas production. One can produce low-carbon hydrogen from this gas combined with carbon capture and storage (CCS). Such hydrogen can be claimed clean as renewable hydrogen if its carbon footprint is assessed in its life cycle and carbon dioxide removal is done proportionally.

Nevertheless, such a claim is still challenged from different angles. So far, no unique definition of green gas exists, even from different suppliers. Thus, it may refer to a direct reduction of greenhouse gas emissions in the supply chain or offsetting greenhouse gas emissions with alternative projects outside the suppliers' core activity (Belyi, 2021). Additionally, technical issues of carbon measurement still exist as it is not always clear how to assess the carbon footprint of a specific production procedure. For instance, estimations on carbon emission from U.S. shale resources vary in different sources (Stern, 2017). Even if such technical issues are solved, LCA has not been officially formulated to render a straightforward and unanimously accepted carbon accounting method (Brander et al., 2021). Under such circumstances, gas may rapidly lose its market to energy forms that can be granted a guarantee of origin, like renewable hydrogen. If not regulated properly, the gas market can be distorted by different treatments on imported natural gas from various sources.

Ultimately, the discursive battle between renewables and gas should not be neglected. While renewable development needs higher social support, as mentioned in section 2-2-2, natural gas needs also to be recognized by the public as an energy carrier compatible with EU climate goals, given that public refusal to accept it as a less pollutant fuel in comparison with coal resulted in its global failure in playing "the bridge fuel" role in the 2010s (Stern, 2017). Russian gas role in post-2030 depends highly on the extent it is received by society. Finally, assuming the necessity of natural gas decarbonization in the transition era, for instance, for producing low-carbon hydrogen, the competitiveness and acceptability of CCS are vital. CCS projects can only be implemented in offshore areas like Norway and the North Sea because currently, setting up such facilities near population centers is socially problematic, especially in the two leading gas-consuming member states, Italy and Germany (Zhu et al., 2021; Fevre, 2019). Such barriers to CCS can delay the use of low-carbon hydrogen and limit Russian gas consumption in the hydrogen industry.

As a result, while Russian gas imports reduction in the EU market seems inevitable, the decrement pace depends on different factors. In addition to these EU-side factors, Moscow's decisions about its energy exports and the capacity it makes operational to adapt to the EU's new energy demand forms will influence the two sides' collaboration. Therefore, the viability of Russian plans will be scrutinized in the next section.

2030–2050 EU-RUSSIA GAS RELATIONS: A RUSSIAN PERSPECTIVE

Russia adjusted its Paris Agreement commitments relying on forestry rather than fossil fuel sector optimization and set not-so-ambitious climate goals compared to its carbon emission levels (Seliverstov & Gudkov, 2016). Meanwhile, skeptical viewpoints about the anthropogenic nature of climate change have grown among Russian politicians and society[8] (Poberezhskaya, 2019). Kremlin published the Concept for the Development of Hydrogen Energy in Russia (hereinafter, the Concept) in which the energy transition is addressed as a threat to Russia's fuel and energy complex, and therefore, to its economy, entities, and international investments in the EU, the Asia-Pacific, and the U.S. (Government of Russian Federation, 2021). In the same document, Russia aims to realize its hydrogen production potential to act as a major competitor for other countries in hydrogen export. It also plans to create three hydrogen clusters or hubs: the Northwest cluster (export to the EU), the Eastern cluster (export to Asia-Pacific), and the Arctic cluster (supply). The document also leaves open the possibility of a fourth Southern cluster and spells out three phases of development (Government of Russian Federation, 2021):

- Stage 1 (2021–2024): Reach 0.2 million metric tons of exports by creating hydrogen clusters and a research ecosystem, developing technologies and manufacturing of industrial products for hydrogen, implementing pilot projects, and creating domestic demand for hydrogen.

- Stage 2 (2025–2035): Reach 2 million metric tons of exports by launching commercial projects for hydrogen production, particularly large, export-oriented production facilities. Continue to expand and integrate hydrogen energy into the domestic market. Scale up the production and export of domestically produced hydrogen equipment.
- Stage 3 (2036–2050): Develop into a major player in the global hydrogen energy market on a large scale. Export 15–50 million metric tons to the global market by 2050.

Russia's ability to achieve these goals can be assessed based on its renewable and low-carbon hydrogen potential. As a country that meets 87 % of its energy demand with fossil fuels, it is not unexpected that renewables have never been developed in Russia despite the great potential for exporting renewable electricity.[9] Current plans aim to increase the renewables share to 5 %–11 % in the 2030 energy mix (Government of Russian Federation, 2020); however, this requires conquering major economic and legal obstacles. Russia's offshore wind farms look attractive, whereas they are more capital intensive than either solar or onshore wind; one 250 MW project costs about $1 billion—more than the entire Russian investment in renewables to date (Gustafson, 2021, p. 122). Russia cannot attract Western investment in the Arctic wind plans because of sanctions which the new sanctions wave will intensify. Moreover, the development plans must comply with the equipment localization for renewable energy, smart grids, and numerous import substitution programs. The local content criterion is a considerable obstacle for renewable development; 65 % of the equipment of wind farms and small hydro and 70 % of solar power plants should be provided from the local market, which will grow to 80 % in the long term. These high levels failed many tenders in wind farm development, for little to no Russian-made equipment has been proposed (Henderson & Mitrova 2020, p. 104). Thus, one may not have high expectations for renewable electricity production, resulting in greener hydrogen production in the short term.

Some scholars found the idea of importing low-carbon hydrogen and decarbonized natural gas from Russia beneficial for EU-Russia energy relations (Konoplyanik, 2021). However, natural gas production, one of Russia's major carbon emission sources, has flared 24 billion cubic meters of associated petroleum gas in 2020 (or 17 % of world gas flaring), ranking it as the first in the world (EIA, 2021). This is expected to impact Russia's hydrogen export plans adversely, considering that previous flare reduction plans have not been achieved but only postponed (Taherifard et al., 2019). Technical barriers should not be overlooked either. Low-carbon hydrogen produced via steam reforming requires CCS to remove CO_2, but there are no CCS demonstration projects, effective state support system, or an adequate emissions tax on CO_2 in Russia (Tcvetkov & Cherepovitsyn,

2016). Instead, Gazprom has been focusing on the pyrolysis method that splits methane molecules into hydrogen and solid carbon, leaving no CO_2, needless to CCS (Neuymin, 2020). However, it does not look achievable until beyond 2030 at best due to investment and regulation requirements. The same is expected from nuclear-based hydrogen, which Rosatom, the state atomic energy corporation, is working on (Zabanova and Westphal, 2021).

Even if low-carbon hydrogen is produced inside Russia, transportation will remain problematic. In October 2019, Eurogas Secretary General James Watson said that the Nord Stream 2 gas pipeline, when completed, could potentially transport as much as 80 % hydrogen. Nevertheless, no studies have been undertaken to verify such an idea technically, according to Gazprom (Zabanova & Westphal, 2021), and the current political situation between Russia and the West overshadows more ambiguities. Other methods, including liquefied or compressed gas, as well as in a bound state in the form of ammonia or liquid organic carriers, are considered priority methods for large-scale transportation of hydrogen and were addressed by the Concept; however, the document did not mention how these strategies will be realized.

As a result, one can say Russian gas share in the EU market will be squeezed even more beyond 2030, if not cut before that. While Russia's technical ability for producing decarbonized gas will be declined under the economic sanctions, the regulatory and political barriers will restrain it in the following, despite its high potential for exporting decarbonized gas or hydrogen.

THE GEOPOLITICAL CONSEQUENCES OF EU-RUSSIA GAS RELATIONS FORM IN THE TRANSITION ERA

As discussed, Russian gas exports to the EU may still be needed in 2030–2050; however, this should be decarbonized gas, complying with the regulations or in the low-carbon hydrogen form. This implies that, in the transition era, Moscow's control of gas flow will become a less effective geopolitical power instrument over time. In the same vein, one may ask if gas will lose its political importance so much as to become depoliticized in EU-Russia bilateral energy relations resulting in energy relations detente as Bazilian and colleagues (2020) have already asked.

To address this question, the depoliticization concept should be clarified. Heinrich and Szulecki (2017, p. 47) define depoliticization as a procedure that shifts the responsibility for policymaking from the government and its institutions to either quasi-independent or wholly independent bodies. If securitization makes room for human agency intervention in energy policymaking on

the pretext of a constructed threat existence, depoliticization can be regarded as foreclosing others' choices to perceive energy from a more technocratic vision (Bues & Gailing, 2016; Healy & Barry, 2017). Thus, depoliticization could imply a lower potential for tension around the gas relations. Nevertheless, the energy transition implications will not necessarily depoliticize Russian gas, as discussed in the following.

First, while the decline of natural gas imports from Russia does not remove it entirely, decarbonized gas or low-carbon hydrogen will have to play a vital role in the sectors where gas is hard to replace, like refineries and perhaps the maritime and freight transport segments (Eyl-Mazzega & Mathieu, 2020). The political atmosphere is currently too unstable to predict the 2050 pathway; however, the rapid shift from Russian gas may become decelerated in the following and slightly open a room for decarbonized Russian gas. This will maintain corresponding interest groups' positions and preserve their lobbying positions in the European decision-making structure, even though weaker than before. Recalling the fact that the EU member states' stance on Russian gas is forged by the ideational factor but not its share in the fuel mix, one can assume that lower Russian gas consumption will not guarantee its depoliticization.

One can also argue that the current form of EU-Russia gas relations is not a complex interdependence decreasing the tension, but a security dilemma. Thus, each side tends to prevent the relationship from becoming asymmetric to its detriment. Otherwise, an asymmetric relationship might encourage one party to put more effort into security or a securitized area where it already has relative superiority. Similarly, Krickovic (2015) has shown that trade between two sides becomes prone to tensions when they know it will not continue in the future, as the EU-Russia gas relationship in the transition era could exemplify. Thus, declining gas imports may potentially raise tensions between the two sides or spread security concerns to other areas of cooperation.

Additionally, the discursive aspect of depoliticization should not be neglected. Relying on an identity-based background, securitization applies linguistic tools to construct a threat from a subject that is not necessarily one. Depoliticization is the opposite procedure; however, it uses the same tools, inter alia, discursive and regulatory or institutional ones (Keypour & Ahmadzada, 2021). Thus, the depoliticization of EU-Russia gas relations requires discursive measures simultaneously with adopting appropriate EU regulations for replacing renewables with gas. On the other hand, the EU's narrative to implement its energy policies in the transition era may even politicize energy transition, for instance, if the Union takes a stance as a superior, rendering the only correct transition model and imposing its narrative on others (Romanova, 2021).

CONCLUSION

This chapter discusses the future of EU-Russia gas relations during the transition period. Considering some simplifying assumptions, the level of these relations is dependent on the decisions of the six major Russian gas importing member states, Poland, Austria, the Czech Republic, Italy, France, and Germany. It can be divided into two periods: until and after 2030. The pure climate considerations entail these states phase-out coal, enhance energy efficiency and expand renewable capacity. This is expected to be accompanied by nuclear dismantling in some cases like Germany. Thus, making a significant change in the natural gas consumption and import from Russia is problematic in a brief period, unless political reasons can fuel the motivation for a rapid shift from Russian gas.

The war in Ukraine has already provided this political motivation for the EU to take off from the current level of Russian gas dependence. While this research shows that REPowerEU's goal of reducing dependence upon two-thirds in a year is not achievable, total Russian gas elimination is possible in the 2030 perspective, although costly. The EU should plan to moderate the adverse impacts of the high energy price, especially as it has to replace more LNG with Russian gas. This research also indicates that the EU's coal consumption will grow (temporarily) since renewable capacity growth, including hydrogen, will not suffice to safeguard the security of the energy supply. Thus, the EU's insistency on such a goal undermines the EU's global climate leadership's credibility and burdens extra cost on the Union contrary to a climate-running energy transition scenario.

On the one hand, the level of gas relations from 2030 onwards depends on preparations made in the coming decade to replace other energy carriers with gas in the Union. Under full electrification and proper energy optimization scenario, the structure of the electricity system can be decentralized, which implies restructuring electricity markets to form grid communities. Then, gas pipeline geopolitics may be replaced by the political choice of grid communities. This could mean that the connection of energy and electricity systems between the EU and Russia will depend on a trade-off between technical, environmental, and political considerations.

Nevertheless, as it is challenging to electrify all sectors, gas consumption seems to be inevitable during the transition period. Under the pressure of alternatives such as biomethane, renewables, and batteries and the development of smart grids, natural gas must be decarbonized and consumed in a downward trend. However, the continuation of gas consumption after 2030 requires persuasive narratives which convince society to accept decarbonized (Russian) gas and related technologies, including CCS. Although the political environment is currently too volatile for a long-term prediction, such a narrative seems difficult to be forge and receive, especially considering the war in Ukraine consequences. Additionally, the way the EU makes regulations about negative pollution and LCA of carbon emission can accelerate or procrastinate the decline of natural gas consumption.

On the other hand, the continuation of Russian gas imports also depends on Russia's ability to comply with European standards on decarbonized gas or low-carbon hydrogen, if politically possible. Commercializing specific CO_2-free hydrogen production technologies, for example, methane pyrolysis or nuclear hydrogen production can be beneficial. At the same time, solutions need to be found to overcome the challenges of hydrogen transportation since utilizing the existing natural gas networks for hydrogen has not been technically verified yet. Russian policymakers have lagged in developing appropriate strategies in response to global energy shifts. This provokes uncertainties around the future of hydrogen export to the EU, despite the solutions rendered.

While Moscow's control of gas flow will become a less effective geopolitical power instrument, especially from 2030 onwards, the results of this study show that it will not necessarily depoliticize gas. This is because depoliticization requires discursive prerequisites in addition to regulations. Hence, an inappropriate narrative may even politicize energy transition, mainly because fading trades are generally prone to tension, for example, EU-Russia gas relations. Although future bilateral energy relations are difficult to estimate now, the remained energy ties may result in new geopolitical considerations. Alternatively, those sectors that continue to import decarbonized Russian gas may preserve a certain level of energy geopolitics.

Lastly, but not less important, metaphorically, the energy transition does not occur in a vacuum. The actors and their interactions are a part of the energy transition, and ironically, they affect the formation of the energy scene at the end of the transition. It is like a chessboard where the actors make decisions based on their observations and perceptions of the changing scene. Hence, a static analysis that portrays Russia or any other player as bystanders watching the EU reduce its dependence on Russian gas may not be accurate. While a flawed perception of transition may push Russia to make a hurried decision accelerating what it wants to avoid happening, lagging behind other actors may turn Moscow into a big loser. Similarly, suppose the EU embraces decarbonization without preparing alternatives to Russian gas. In that case, it will jeopardize its energy security, whereas acting hesitantly in decision-making may result in a fossil fuel lock-in. Therefore, how the two sides' strategic agents perceive the change, plan to maximize their benefits, and then implement their thoughts are crucial.

NOTES

1 The author would like to express his deep gratitude to Ms. Nina Dalai Milan for her constructive advice and valuable critiques, especially about Russian energy strategy, in this research.
2 IEA's plan claims to bring down gas imports from Russia by over one-third by 2023, with additional temporary options to deepen these cuts to well over half while still lowering emissions. Nevertheless, it has an additional fuel-switching option in the power sector to replace coal with natural gas to accelerate the Russian gas import cut, which is not obviously climate-friendly. The REPowerEU wants to cut Russian gas supplies by two-thirds before the end of 2022 and cut it entirely by 2030. Thus, both proposals promise to reduce the Russian gas share by one to two-thirds in a year and remove it until 2030. Because the European Commission proposed it, we focus mainly on REPowerEU, even though it is not binding on member states.
3 It is worth mentioning that the REPowerEU has addressed Russian pipeline gas export to the EU but not its LNG. Given that Russia has exported 14.1 bcm LNG to the EU in 2021 (BP, 2021), replacing Russian LNG will further stimulate the price. Consequently, Moscow can overflow its LNG on the Asian market, benefiting from a higher price. This may look contradictory to the aim of sanctions, that is, curtailing the economic power of the Russian war machine.
4 For instance, while the EU has closely coordinated with countries like Colombia in reducing the carbon footprint, Colombia remains the single largest exporter of coal to the EU as a whole. Different scholars like (Maas et al., 2015) and (Kamphof et al., 2017) have perceived this as a dual standard.
5 It is not easy to interpret the "hydrogen compatibility" technically since the standards of hydrogen transmission systems have not been codified unanimously in the Union yet. Even in the available standards, the safety requirements of a hydrogen-natural gas mixture are different from pure hydrogen, while one may perceive the former system as "compatible" with hydrogen. Thus, there is no unique operational interpretation of this concept for different member states yet.
6 Baltic Pipe project is a 900 km natural gas pipeline project intended to supply 3 bcm gas annually from the Norwegian gas system in the North Sea to Poland, via Denmark, expected to be launched by October 2022 (https://www.nsenergybusiness.com/projects/baltic-pipe-project/).
7 The intention of the EU to import electricity from third countries will also be affected by the cleanness of the source. The EU may impose a carbon tax on electricity or even other products as it is currently working on relevant regulations. For further information, see https://ec.europa.eu/commission/presscorner/detail/en/qanda_21_3661.
8 For instance, during "Russia's energy week" in 2018, President Putin stated: "We are witnessing global warming, but we do not understand the reasons for this warming because there are still no answers. Moreover, the so-called anthropogenic emissions, most likely, are not the main cause of this warming; it may be changes of a global nature" (RIA Novosti, 2018). Since the 1990s, Russian media has propagated a narrative that bad things may happen because of climate change; however, Russia will not be affected (Tynkkynen, 2020).
9 According to the U.S. Energy Information Administration (EIA 2021), Russia's energy mix in 2019 was natural gas (52 %), oil (23 %), coal (12 %), nuclear (7 %), and renewables (7 %). However, the share of non-hydro renewables was negligible. Also, Russia's power generation comes from fossil fuels (59.3 %), nuclear (21 %), hydro (19.1 %) and renewables (0.6 %). This makes Russian power generation less pollutant than countries like Poland, Germany, Australia, Chile, the USA, and southern Africa based on the gr.CO_2/KWh indicator (Mitrova & Melnikov, 2019).

REFERENCES

Ang, B. W., Choong, W. L., & Ng, T. S. (2015). Energy security: Definitions, dimensions and indexes. *Renewable and Sustainable Energy Reviews*, *42*, 1077–1093. https://doi.org/10.1016/j.rser.2014.10.064

APERC. (2007). *Quest for energy security in the 21st century: Resources and constraints*. https://aperc.or.jp/file/2010/9/26/APERC_2007_A_Quest_for_Energy_Security.pdf

Barnes, A. (2021). Regulation of hydrogen markets—Are concerns about "lock-in" effects valid? In OIES (Ed.), *The role of hydrogen in the energy transition* (pp. 26–31). The Oxford Institute for Energy Studies.

Bazilian, M., Bradshaw, M., Gabriel, J., Goldthau, A., & Westphal, K. (2019). *Four scenarios of the energy transition: Drivers, consequences, and implications for geopolitics. WIREs Climate Change*, *11*(2). https://doi.org/10.1002/wcc.625Belyi

Belyi, A., Piebalgs, A., & Conti, I. (2021). *How green is "Green LNG"?* Florence School of Regulation.

BP. (2021). *Statistical review of world energy 2021* [Statistical report].

Brander, M., Ascui, F., Scott, V., & Tett, S. (2021). Carbon accounting for negative emissions technologies. *Climate Policy*, *21*(5), 699–717. https://doi.org/10.1080/14693062.2021.1878009

Bues, A., & Gailing, L. (2016). Energy transitions and power: Between governmentality and depoliticization. In *Conceptualizing Germany's energy transition* (pp. 69–91). Palgrave Macmillan. https://doi.org/10.1057/978-1-137-50593-4_5

Campos, A., & Fernandes, C. (2017). *The geopolitics of energy*. In P. Fernandes, C. Ferreira, & R. Teresa (Eds.), *Geopolitics of energy and energy security* (Vol. 24, pp. 23–40). Instituto da Defesa Nacional.

Casier, T. (2011). Russia's energy leverage over the EU: Myth or reality? *Perspectives on European Politics and Society*, *12*(4), 493–508.

CEB. (2019). *Energy poverty in Europe*.

Collins, G. (2017). *Russia's use of the "energy weapon" in Europe* (Issue Brief No. 07.18.17). Rice University's Baker Institute for Public Policy.

Cox, E. (2022, March 1). *Can LNG Replace Russian Gas in Europe?* Retrieved March 8, 2022, from https://www.maritime-executive.com/editorials/can-lng-replace-russian-gas-in-europe

EEGAS. (2021, December 2). *EEGAS*. https://eegas.com/price_chart1.htm

EIA. 2021. *Country analysis executive summary: Russia* [Executive summary]. https://www.eia.gov/international/content/analysis/countries_long/Russia/russia.pdf

Elering. (2021, December 12). *Synchronisation with continental Europe*. https://elering.ee/en/synchronization-continental-europe

Ellinas, C. (2022, March 21). Shell unveils LNG outlook amid heightened uncertainty. *Natural Gas World*, p. 38.

European Commission. (2017, February 1). *Europe's energy transition is well underway*. https://ec.europa.eu/commission/presscorner/detail/en/IP_17_161

European Commission. (2017). *Mapping and analyses of the current and future (2020–2030) heating/cooling fuel deployment (fossil/renewables)* [Project report].

European Commission. (2020, December 15). *European Commission*. December 15. Retrieved March 25, 2022, from https://ec.europa.eu/commission/presscorner/detail/en/IP_20_2394

European Commission. (2020). *Impact of the use of the biomethane and hydrogen potential on trans-European infrastructure*.

European Commission. (2021). *"Fit for 55": Delivering the EU's 2030 Climate Target on the way to climate neutrality* (COM [2021] 550 final). https://eur-lex.europa.eu/legal-content/EN/TXT/PDF/?uri=CELEX:52021DC0550&from=EN

European Union. (2022, March 8). *EUR-Lex.* Retrieved March 14, 2022, from https://eur-lex.europa.eu/legal-content/EN/TXT/?uri=COM%3A2022%3A108%3AFIN

Eurostat. (2021, December 11). *Energy consumption in households.* https://ec.europa.eu/eurostat/statistics-explained/index.php?title=Energy_consumption_in_households

Eurostat. (2021, June 8). *Eurostat.* Retrieved October 1, 2021, from https://ec.europa.eu/eurostat/statistics-explained/images/8/86/Oil_and_gas_partners_-_details_2021.xlsx

Eyl-Mazzega, M.-A., & Mathieu, C. (2020). The European Union and the energy transition. In *The geopolitics of the global energy transition* (pp. 27–46). Springer International. https://doi.org/10.1007/978-3-030-39066-2_2

Fawcett, T., Rosenow, J., & Bertoldi, P. (2019). Energy efficiency obligation schemes: Their future in the EU. *Energy Efficiency, 12*, 57–71.

Fevre, C. (2019). *The future of gas networks—Key issues for debate.* Oxford Institute for Energy Studies.

France24. (2022, March 21). *Germany to "fast-track" gas terminals as part of Qatar deal.* Retrieved March 25, 2022, from https://www.france24.com/en/live-news/20220321-germany-to-fast-track-gas-terminals-as-part-of-qatar-deal

Fulwood, M., Sharples, J., & Henderson, J. (2022). *Ukraine invasion what this means for the European gas market.* Oxford Institute for Energy Studies.

Gazprom. (2021, December 8). *Foreign partners.* http://www.gazpromexport.ru/en/partners/austria/

Gielen, D., Medlock III, K., & Bazilian, M. (2020, May 15). *Steel, hydrogen and renewables: Strange bedfellows? Maybe not….* Retrieved December 18, 2021, from https://www.forbes.com/sites/thebakersinstitute/2020/05/15/steel-hydrogen-and-renewables-strange-bedfellows-maybe-not/?sh=66dc1096188e

Government of Russian Federation. (2020). *Energy strategy of the Russian Federation for the period up to 2035* [Official document]. https://docs.cntd.ru/document/565068231

Government of Russian Federation. (2021). *Concept for the development of hydrogen power engineering in the Russian Federation* [Official document]. http://static.government.ru/media/files/5JFns1CDAKqYKzZ0mnRADAw2NqcVsexl.pdf

Griffiths, S. (2019). Energy diplomacy in a time of energy transition. *Energy Strategy Reviews, 26*, 10386.

Gustafson, T. (2021). *Russia in the age of climate change.* Harvard University Press.

Hache, E. (2018). Do renewable energies improve energy security in the long run? *International Economics, 156*, 127–135.

Healy, N., & Barry, J. (2017). Politicizing energy justice and energy system transitions: Fossil fuel divestment and a "just transition." *Energy Policy, 108*, 451–459. https://doi.org/10.1016/j.enpol.2017.06.014

Heinrich, A., & Szulecki, K. (2017). Energy securitisation: Applying the Copenhagen school's framework to energy. In *Energy security in Europe* (pp. 33–59). Springer International. https://doi.org/10.1007/978-3-319-64964-1_2

Henderson, J., & Mitrova, T. (2020). Implications of the global energy transition on Russia. In *The geopolitics of the global energy transition* (pp. 93–114). Springer International. https://doi.org/10.1007/978-3-030-39066-2_5

Hippel, D., Suzuki, T., Williams, J., Savage, T., & Hayes, P. (2011). Evaluating the energy security impacts of energy policies. In B. K. Sovacool (Ed.), *The Routledge handbook of energy security* (pp. 74–95). Routledge.

Horton, J., & Palumbo, D. (2022, January 26). *Russia sanctions: What impact have they had on its oil and gas exports?* Retrieved September 18, 2021, from https://www.bbc.com/news/58888451

IEA. (2022). *A 10-point plan to reduce the European Union's reliance on Russian natural gas.* https://iea.blob.core.windows.net/assets/1af70a5f-9059-47b4-a2dd-1b479918f3cb/A10-PointPlan-toReducetheEuropeanUnionsRelianceonRussianNaturalGas.pdf

Kamphof, R., Bonenkamp, T., Selleslaghs, J., & Hosli, M. (2017). External competences in energy and climate change. In R. Leal-Arcas & J. Wouters (Eds.), *Research handbook on EU energy law and policy* (p. 44). Edward Elgar.

Keypour, J., & Ahmadzada, U. (2021). Consolidating EU energy security by relying on energy de-politicisation. *European Security, 31*, 135–157.

Kolbe, P., & Finley, M. (2021). Winners and losers in an uneven energy transition. In OIES (Ed.), *The geopolitics of energy: Out with the Old and in with the New?* (pp. 41–45). Oxford Institute for Energy Studies.

Konoplyanik, A. (2021). Gas decarbonisation in Europe: Clean hydrogen as the new prospective area for Russia-EU cooperation. *Oil, Gas & Energy Law Journal (OGEL).* http://www.ogel.org/article.asp?key=3960

Krickovic, A. (2015). When interdependence produces conflict: EU-Russia energy relations as a security dilemma. *Contemporary Security Policy, 36* (1), 3–26.

Kruyt, B., van Vuuren, D., de Vries, B., & Groenenberg, H. (2011). Indicators for energy security. In B.K. Sovacool (Ed.), *The Routledge handbook of energy security* (p. 292). Routledge.

Lenivova, V. (2022). *Potential development of renewable hydrogen imports to European markets until 2030* [Analytical report]. Oxford Institute for Energy Studies.

Lu, J., Ren, L., Yao, S., Rong, D., Skare, M., & Streimikis, J. (2020). Renewable energy barriers and coping strategies: Evidence from the Baltic states. *Sustainable Development, 28* (1), 352–367.

Maas, E., van Schaik, L., & Kamphof, R. (2015). *EU and Colombia: Climate partnership beyond aid and trade* (Policy Brief). Clingendael Policy Brief.

Mathiesen, B. V., Bertelsen, N., Schneider, N. C. A., García, L. S., Paardekooper, S., Thellufsen, J. Z., & Djørup, S. R. (2019). *Towards a decarbonised heating and cooling sector in Europe: Unlocking the potential of energy efficiency and district energy.* Aalborg Universitet.

Mišík, M. (2015). The influence of perception on the preferences of the new member states of the European Union. The case of energy policy. *Comparative European Politics, 2* (13), 198–221.

Mitrova, T., & Melnikov, Y. (2019). Energy transition in Russia. *Energy Transitions, 3*, 73–80.

Nam, E., & Jin, T. (2021). Mitigating carbon emissions by energy transition, energy efficiency, and electrification: Difference between regulation indicators and empirical data. *Journal of Cleaner Production, 300*, 126962.

Neuymin, K. (2020, September 18). *Views and perspectives from Russian side on decarbonization and on the EU hydrogen and energy system integration strategies.* Retrieved December 21, 2021, from https://minenergo.gov.ru/system/download/14646/129013

Overland, I. (2019). The geopolitics of renewable energy: Debunking four emerging myths. *Energy Research & Social Science, 49*, 36–40.

Osička, J., Kemmerzell, J., Zoll, M., Lehotský, L., Černoch, F., & Knodt, M. (2020). What's next for the European coal heartland? Exploring the future of coal as presented in German, Polish and Czech press. *Energy Research & Social Science*, *61*, 101316.

Pakiam, G. (2011). The industrial dimension of energy security. In B.K. Sovacool (Ed.), *The Routledge handbook of energy security* (pp. 250–274). Routledge.

Poberezhskaya, M. (2019, December 11). Talking about climate change in Russia. *Russian Analytical Digest*, pp. 8–11.

RIA Novosti. (2018, November 3). *Putin said that the global climate problem cannot be solved without the United States*. Retrieved December 22, 2021, from https://ria.ru/20181003/1529899296.html

Richter, P., & Holz, F. (2015). All quiet on the eastern front? Disruption scenarios of Russian natural gas supply to Europe. *Energy Policy*, *80*, 177–189.

Romanova, T. (2021). Russia's political discourse on the EU's energy transition (2014–2019) and its effect on EU-Russia energy relations. *Energy Policy*, *154*, 112309.

Ruban, R. (2013). *The European natural gas supply, under particular consideration of gas transit* (1st ed.). viademica.verlag.

S&P. (2022, March 7). *Commodity Tracker: 5 charts to watch this week*. Retrieved March 15, 2022, from https://www.spglobal.com/commodity-insights/en/market-insights/blogs/energy-transition/030722-russia-ukraine-impact-gas-lng-coal-renewable-energy

Scholten, D., Bazilian, M., Overland, I., & Westphal, K. (2020). The geopolitics of renewables: New board, new game. *Energy Policy*, *138*, 111059.

Seliverstov, S., & Gudkov, I. (2016). Energy law in the Russia. In M. Roggenkamp, C. Redgwell, A. Ronne, & I. del Guayo (Eds.), *Energy law in Europe: National, EU and international regulation* (pp. 1137–1217). Oxford University Press.

Siddi, M. (2020). Theorising conflict and cooperation in EU-Russia energy relations: Ideas, identities and material factors in the Nord Stream 2 debate. *East European Politics*, *36* (4), 544–563.

Smith, K. (2009). *Security implications of Russian energy policies*. Centre for European Policy Studies.

Sovacool, B. K. (2016). How long will it take? Conceptualizing the temporal dynamics of energy transitions. *Energy Research & Social Science*, *13*, 202–215. https://doi.org/10.1016/j.erss.2015.12.020

Stern, J. (2017). *The future of gas in decarbonising European energy markets: The need for a new approach*. Oxford Institute for Energy Studies.

Stern, J. (2020). The role of gases in the European energy transition. *Russian Journal of Economics*, *6*, 390–405.

Szulecki, K., & Westphal, K. (2016). Taking security seriously in EU energy governance: Crimean shock and the energy union. In K. Szulecki (Ed.), *Energy security in Europe* (pp. 177–202). Palgrave.

Taherifard, A., Mahdavi, R., Sahebhonar, H., Keypour, J., & Kamali, M. (2019). *Associated petroleum gase flaring reduction in Iran*. Talab.

Tcvetkov, P., & Cherepovitsyn, A. (2016). Prospects of CCS projects implementation in Russia: Environmental protection and economic opportunities. *Journal of Ecological Engineering*, *17*(2), 24–32.

Tynkkynen, V. (2020). Could Russia embrace an energy transition? *Current History*, *119*(819), 270–274.

Vakulchuk, R., Overland, I., & Scholten, D. (2020). Renewable energy and geopolitics: A review. *Renewable and Sustainable Energy Reviews*, *122*, 109547.

Westphal, K. (2020). German-Russian gas relations in face of the energy transition. *Russian Journal of Economics*, *6*, 406–423.

Williams, L., & Sovacool, B. (2019). The discursive politics of "fracking": Frames, storylines, and the anticipatory contestation of shale gas development in the United Kingdom. *Global Environmental Change*, *58*, 101935.

Zabanova, Y., & Westphal, K. (2021). *Russia in the global hydrogen race* [Commentary]. German Institute for International and Security Affairs. https://www.swp-berlin.org/en/publication/russia-in-the-global-hydrogen-race

Zheng, Z. (2021). Improving grid interconnection to support climate change mitigation. In OIES (Ed.), *The geopolitics of energy: Out with the Old and in with the New?* (pp. 22–26). Oxford Institute for Energy Studies.

Zhu, Z., Zhang W., & Liu W. (2021). *The future of natural gas in a deeply decarbonized world.* Energy Future Initiative.

CHAPTER 6

Governing the Energy Union: The Quest for a Secure, Low-Carbon Future for the EU

SUSANN HANDKE

INTRODUCTION

In the twilight of the fossil age, the German government initiated the fast construction of infrastructure to receive seaborne supplies of liquid natural gas (hereafter LNG). In May 2022, new floating LNG terminals were installed along the German coast of the North Sea. The first terminals were expected to be operational by early 2023. These activities were a response to the unprovoked war that the Russian Federation (Russia) started by invading Ukraine on February 24, 2022. Negotiations about LNG supplies were ongoing with producers in the Middle East, North America, and Africa, in order to replace Russian pipeline gas imports.

Yet, the Germany's first terminals to handle LNG are also an investment in the future. Steffi Lemke, the German minister for environmental affairs and member of the ruling coalition party The Greens, emphasized that these new installations would also be able to process green hydrogen[1] supplies. The German Federal government demanded this intended, non-fossil usability when it set the conditions for the accelerated construction of the terminals (The Federal Government, 2022). Thus, emergency measures to secure the supply of fossil fuels simultaneously anticipate a climate-neutral future that will rely on other fuels.

With its decision to terminate pipeline-bound imports of Russian natural gas as soon as possible and its forward-looking implementation, the German government followed the approach of the European Union (EU): The EU is moving away from Russian energy supplies, while also trying to speed up the shift to renewable energy sources. To coordinate this endeavor, the European Commission, the Union's governing body, presented the REPowerEU Plan in early March 2022 (European Commission, 2022).

After Russia's attack on Ukraine, EU policymakers and stakeholders in the energy business had no doubt that this war was a watershed for the perception of energy security in the EU. They re-assessed the threat that the Union's reliance on imports from Russia posed to the member states' economic and political room for maneuver. The REPowerEU Plan is testimony of their swift and far-reaching choices to ensure stable energy supplies to the EU.

The purpose of this chapter is to study the evolution of EU-Russia gas relations in order to obtain valuable insights into the undertaking of enhancing the Union's energy security during the transition to climate neutrality. No doubt, energy security concerns loom large in the current transitional period when energy generation processes are shifting from the predominant use of fossil fuels to renewable energy sources. During this period, the components of energy security—such as the physical availability, economic affordability, and environmental and social sustainability of energy supplies—pertain to a variety of fuels, supply arrangements, and geopolitical theaters.

Given the recent flurry of activity, it seems that the thinking about energy security in Europe quickly adjusted when the Russian invasion of Ukraine began. However, the invasion in 2022 was only the culmination of a decades-long process in which several instances of disagreement about energy governance and conflicts in the bilateral relations re-contextualized the concept of energy security. The development of Russia's gas trade and export to western and eastern Europe is most revealing in this regard.

This chapter assesses EU-Russia gas relations in the twenty-first century and focuses on three crucial episodes that contributed to growing concerns on the European side. The matters that are specifically discussed are the conflict about the Energy Charter Treaty's Transit Protocol, the European Commission's decision regarding Gazprom's approach to eastern EU member states, and disagreements on the nature of the Nord Stream 2 project. The analysis of these episodes shows that the perception of energy security relates to the market structure, rules that apply to vital energy assets, and the governance of the supply infrastructure.

Since about 2006, legal conflicts and political debates about these three elements have shaped the concept of energy security in the context of EU-Russia gas relations. To study EU-Russia gas relations and develop its argument, the chapter chooses an interdisciplinary approach, relying on legal and infrastructure scholarship. The chapter assesses the evolution of EU-Russia gas relations in their spatial-functional, legal, and politico-economic context. Thus, it links the gas relations to the obduracy of infrastructure, the regulation and ownership of energy assets, and the structure of the gas sector. The chapter explores how the interrelationship between these elements contributed to the conceptualization of energy security in the EU in the context of the relations with Russia. Since the analysis focuses on these elements, it is possible to specify domestic factors that lead to the securitization of energy. By accepting that energy securitization is a continuous process (Wilson, 2019, p. 119), this approach is able to trace the evolution of the concept of energy security in the EU during the past two decades.

The chapter argues that the incompatibility of practices that govern the physical gas supply infrastructure, together with diverging approaches to the control of vital energy assets and market regulation, contextualized increasingly contentious political relations. Eventually, the move away from Russian energy imports, as suggested by the REPowerEU Plan, corresponds with the principles of the Energy Union,[2] a policy strategy that seeks to comprehensively imagine the Union's energy future on the path to climate neutrality (European Commission, 2015).

This chapter structures its analysis as follows. The next section gives an overview of the evolution of EU-Russia gas relations. Then, the third section discusses the above-mentioned three episodes of legal issues and political debates that contributed to changing perceptions of energy security in the context of EU-Russia gas relations. Section four builds on the findings of the previous sections and presents a conceptualization of energy security. This conceptualization is informed by the historical lessons that the EU can infer from its decades-long, difficult relationship with Russia. The section explains how the resultant conceptualization of energy security can form a point of departure for the low-carbon transition of the EU energy sector. Section five concludes.

TOWARD EU-RUSSIAN GAS RELATIONS IN THE TWENTY-FIRST CENTURY

A vast system of gas pipelines traverses thousands of kilometers from western Siberia to Europe. Since the 1960s, its incremental growth has been facilitating vital economic interests on both ends of the pipes. Yet, more often than not political frictions in the bilateral relations led to concerns about undue dependence and vulnerabilities that this infrastructure creates. This section shows that EU-Russia gas relations are rooted at the intersection of geopolitics (sub-section "Political Frictions, Ill-Fated Energy Cooperation") as well as governance and infrastructure (sub-section "Divergent Legacies and Hidden Integration"). However, gas cooperation, applicable rules, and bilateral political relations never really developed in lockstep.

Political Frictions, Ill-Fated Energy Cooperation

In his speech at the 2007 edition of the annual Munich Security Conference, NATO Secretary General Jaap de Hoop Scheffer was deeply disappointed at President Vladimir Putin's remarks and asked, "who can be worried that democracy and the rule of law is coming closer to somebody's borders?" (NATO, 2007). Indeed, Putin had alleged that "NATO has put its frontline forces on our borders" and that "NATO expansion" was "a serious provocation that reduces the level of mutual trust" (President of Russia, 2007).

No doubt, the geography of Russia's engagement with the West had changed after NATO's enlargement in the 1990s and the 2004 EU enlargement, when ten eastern European countries—the Czech Republic, Estonia, Hungary, Latvia, Lithuania, Poland, Slovakia, and Slovenia—became EU member states.[3] However, at the same time attempts were made to formalize the relations with Russia, institutionalize dialogue formats, and foster trust building. Russia also endorsed these efforts by signing the 1994 EU-Russia Partnership and Cooperation Agreement and 1997 NATO-Russia Founding Act.

By the mid-2000s, little was left of the optimism about establishing an order of security and cooperation in Europe that after the Fall of the Berlin Wall had inspired an entire generation of politicians. On both sides, diverging experiences with the post–Cold War situation, domestically and internationally, contributed to the changed mood.

The years after the collapse of the Soviet Union 1991 were constitutive for the nature of bilateral political relations between the EU and Russia in the twenty-first century. Conflict was not inevitable. However, the domestic political situation in Russia and the impact of the economic crisis at the end of the 1990s on society and the political discourse were detrimental to EU-Russia relations.

From the mid-1990s onward, the domestic political debate in Russia increasingly featured nationalistic ideas and populist arguments. The manipulative rigor of Russia's media, especially the TV, amplified popular grievances and distrust among the people (Ostrovsky, 2015). An anti-democratic, anti-Western sentiment grew during the economic crisis toward the end of the decade. It brought new elites to power, led by Vladimir Putin. These developments provided the conditions for increasing domestic suppression after the turn of the century (Gessen, 2018).

The post-Soviet experience of a market transition that ended in a socioeconomic disaster proved to be a challenging foundation for relations with the EU, where at the same vital economic sectors were liberalized in order to strengthen the internal market and foster the overall integration project. Russia's economy took a different trajectory. After the economic crisis, the Russian state maintained and regained control of vital energy assets, led by the inner circle of the political leadership. During the early 2000s, the divergent choices on both sides became tangible in bilateral energy affairs (see "Divergent Legacies and Hidden Integration").

Russia's approach to deal with domestic dissent, beginning with the first war in Chechnya, caused increasing disillusionment in the EU. The list of criticisms expanded; and after the turn of the century it also included foreign policy issues. They concerned Russia's interference in domestic affairs of former Soviet republics and, in particular, its response to the "colorful" revolutions in Georgia and Ukraine. The EU and its member states condemned the war against Georgia in 2008; and Russia's covert military action against Ukraine in 2014 was met with sanctions. Still, EU-Russia gas relations remained unscathed. Business as usual was still hugely beneficial for both sides.

From the outset, parties involved in the gas relations did their utmost to avoid derailing trade arrangements as a result of political disagreements. In 1967, for instance, the first pipeline that crossed the Iron Curtain finally linked Ukrainian gas fields with a town near the Austrian-Czechoslovakian border. The first gas deliveries were due to arrive in Austria in September 1968, shortly after Warsaw Pact forces had invaded Czechoslovakia to end the reformist policies of the Prague Spring. Other western governments had urged Austria to at least delay the scheduled deliveries, but Austria feared the consequences of a major conflict with the Soviet Union if the cooperation was halted. Only one year later, in June 1969, the West-German government began negotiations with the Soviet leadership about gas exports to Germany via Austria, while Soviet-Italian talks also made good progress (Högselius, 2013, pp. 92, 112, 125). This pattern of separating politics from gas trade helped to endure many bilateral conflicts for more than 50 years, while reaping the benefits of unimpeded gas flows.

After the dissolution of the Soviet Union, the EU tried to institutionalize its cooperation with Russia in order to stabilize the bilateral economic relations. Agreements and platforms for dialogue aimed to shape the relations, relying on market mechanisms, enforceable rules, and mutual investments. Since the mid-2000s, Russia has explicitly been rejecting this approach. Numerous political frictions with the EU indicated deep-rooted hostility. Yet, both sides chose to expand their gas cooperation.

Only in 2022, after the Russian invasion of Ukraine, the EU announced a phase-out of fossil fuel imports from Russia. Arguably, by then the securitization of energy in the EU had reached an alarming level. The next sub-section shows that, in the end, terminating the extensive energy cooperation with Russia might have been inevitable, mainly because governance choices in the past two decades had put both sides on increasingly divergent trajectories.

Divergent Legacies and Hidden Integration

Domestic gas production in the EU declined after the turn of the century. Subsequently, the import of Russian natural gas increased considerably during the 2010s, and so did the Union's reliance on gas from Russia. In 2021, the EU imported 155 billion cubic meters (bcm) of natural gas from Russia—140 bcm were delivered via pipeline and 15 bcm as LNG. Thus, 45 % of the Union's total gas imports originated from Russia, and almost 40 % of its total gas consumption (IEA, 2022, p. 4).

The previous sub-section showed that maintaining these extensive gas trade relations did not contribute to a substantial improvement of the political relations between Russia and its western partners. Difference about the governance of vital economic sectors, such as energy, were at the basis of many disagreements.

After 2000, the geographic and regulatory context of Russian gas transport to its customers in western, central, and eastern Europe changed profoundly. The reasons are twofold. First, the integration and liberalization of EU member states' gas sectors required ever more far-reaching legislation that eventually led to the unbundling of the business components of producing, transporting, and selling natural gas. This will be discussed in more detail below.

Second, after former socialist countries in central and eastern Europe became EU member states EU-Russia gas relations entailed two legacies. There was the gas cooperation that was initiated by the Soviet Union and western European companies in the 1960s; and there was the legacy of central and eastern European countries' involuntary participation in the construction of the pipelines in exchange for gas supplies. Hence, decades after the end of the Cold War Europe's geography and history contextualize the gas cooperation with Russia in a way that rules hardly can address, as section three will show.

No doubt, geography is an important factor. After all, the infrastructure that enables the trade relations traverses rivers, tundra, mountains, and plains from Urengoy in western Siberia to Ushhorod in Transcarpathia. Large parts of this extensive pipeline system were built before the dissolution of the Soviet Union (see Table 6.1).

The initial Soviet-Austrian gas contract was signed in June 1968. The first pipeline to transport gas to Austria was finished in 1967. However, the fields that supplied the gas were not the vast discoveries in Siberia but well known and much smaller fields in western Ukraine (Högselius, 2013, pp. 89–90). Linking the Ukrainian-Austrian pipeline with Siberia required a huge effort, as thousands of kilometers of pipeline still had to be built before the Soviet Union could live up to the contracts with Austrian and West-German counterparts, ensuring substantial long-term gas supplies (Högselius, 2013, pp. 135–136).

Table 6.1: Development of EU-Russia (Gas) Relations

Year	Energy infrastructure and governance	Major developments in EU-Russia (gas) relations
1967	Completion of **Dolyna-Ushhorod-Western border of the USSR pipeline** (Bratstvo/Brotherhood pipeline system), first gas delivered to Austria in 1968	
1978	**Orenburg-Western border pipeline** (Soyuz pipeline system)	
1983	**Urengoy-Western border pipeline** (Bratstvo/Brotherhood pipeline system)	
1988	**Yamburg-Western border pipeline (Progress pipeline)**	
1989		Fall of the Berlin Wall
1991		Dissolution of the Soviet Union
1994	**Energy Charter Treaty** **Yamal-Europe pipeline** (start of construction; first gas delivered in 1997; pipeline was fully commissioned in 2006)	First war in Chechnya (until 1996)
1998	**First EU gas sector liberalization legislation**	
1999		Second war in Chechnya (until 2009)
2003	**Second EU gas sector liberalization legislation** **arrest of Mikhail Khodorkovsky, chairman of YUKOS**	
2004		EU eastern enlargement
2006	YUKOS broken up Gazprom obtains majority stake in Sakhalin-2 gas project	Major gas supply crisis in Ukraine
2008		Russian invasion in Georgia
2009	**Third EU energy package**, including legislation to strengthen liberalization and integration of gas sector **Russia withdraws from Energy Charter process**	Major gas supply crisis in Ukraine
2011	**Nord Stream 1** **Energy Community Treaty**	
2014		Russia illegally occupies and annexes Crimea; begins covert military action in eastern Ukraine

(Continued)

Table 6.1: Continued

Year	Energy infrastructure and governance	Major developments in EU-Russia (gas) relations
2015	**Energy Union** construction of **Nord Stream 2** agreed	
2018	**European Commission's Gazprom decision**	
2021	Nord Stream 2 completed	
2022	Nord Stream 2 permission proceedings halted by German federal government (22 February) **REPowerEU Plan** (8 March)	Russia recognizes the so-called People's Republics of Donetsk and Lugansk on the territory of Ukraine (21 February) **Russian invasion in Ukraine** (24 February)

Source: Author's own elaboration.

The Soviet Union neither had the technical and financial means nor an adequate workforce to realize a project that would become the longest pipeline in the world. Thus, in 1974 the Soviet leadership signed an agreement with the leaders of Bulgaria, Czechoslovakia, the GDR (East Germany), Poland, and Hungary to jointly built the pipeline and additional infrastructure in exchange for decades of gas supplies. The leaders of the socialist satellite states had no choice but to agree to this new socialist mega-project. They were obliged to send tens of thousands of workers and provide the material for the construction of residential buildings and transport infrastructure, while the pipeline components and machinery came from western Europe and Japan. The construction works lasted throughout the 1970s and 1980s, creating the Bratstvo and Soyuz pipeline systems that transport gas from Siberia and Central Asia westward.

Before the dissolution of the Soviet Union, the construction of the pipeline systems and the trade relations established two modes of gas grid integration in Europe. The socialist central and eastern European countries' participation in the pipeline construction brought these countries closer to the Soviet Union. At the same time, western European countries began to build pipelines that linked them with other import routes, mainly because they pursued a strategy that sought to balance imports from the Soviet Union with supplies from other gas exporters to hedge against sudden cut offs. Thus, the transcontinental links between the Soviet Union were complemented with intra-European links to transport Siberian gas to Germany, France, and Italy, and new links from Algeria and Norway to western Europe to diversify supplies. In the 1980s, eastern European countries were neither allowed nor able to consider alternative supplies (Högselius, 2013, pp. 231–232).

Understanding the history of two different patterns of trade relations and two forms of hidden integration in Europe is important for analyzing the regulatory difficulties that emerged after the turn of the century. The transcontinental pipelines created socio-technical landscapes—massive physical and technological links that carry institutional arrangements (Bouzarovski et al., 2015, pp. 218, 220). These rules and practices shape legacies that are part of the physical links and persist, mainly because obduracy is an important feature of networked infrastructure (Johnson, 2017). The gas infrastructure that was created toward the end of the Cold War added a layer on top of Europe's natural geography—an "infrastructured geography of natural gas" that can only be changed "with huge effort and at enormous costs" (Högselius, 2013, p. 235).

For decades, the gas infrastructure was governed differently in western and central-eastern Europe. After the dissolution of the Soviet Union and the Warsaw Pact, the post-socialist countries were aware of the need to reduce their reliance on Russia. However, these countries were unable to finance construction works that would help them to significantly diversify their gas supplies; and potential external investors found the required investment not commercially viable (Stern & Yafimava, 2017, p. 25). As a result, the infrastructure continued to operate against a backdrop of unabated dependence and a legacy of these countries' unconsenting participation in the establishment of physical links, symbolizing a past they struggled to relinquish. When the countries became EU members, this aspect of their energy relations with Russia considerably affected the Union's securitization of energy.

The 1990s were a transitional, open-ended period in the gas relations between the EU and Russia. As Russia began to implement market reforms, new institutions and rules were needed to guide the gas relations, especially the gas transit through now independent former Soviet republics. The transcontinental gas infrastructure was in an institutional limbo. New pipelines, such as the Yamal-Europe pipeline, were planned to diversify transport routes. In an environment driven by market forces, new infrastructure projects required rules on investment and access. The 1994 Energy Charter Treaty was an attempt to fill this void. It was signed in 1994 and entered into force in 1998 (International Energy Charter, 2019).

The institutionalization of the energy relations between Russia and the EU coincided with far-reaching changes in the European energy sector. Around the turn of the century, the EU moved to liberalize the energy sector by restructuring energy companies and creating a Union-wide market for natural gas. Indeed, for decades the integration of member states' economies has been an important vehicle for strengthening the political cohesion of the Union. Since the adoption of the

Single European Act in 1986 (European Communities, 1987), various economic sectors were identified as suitable for the implementation of integration policies. The term of "cohesion" points to the political aspect of EU market integration. Although the plans faced considerable resistance among member states and economic stakeholders, a political settlement between France and Germany helped to convince other member states to support these efforts. This move was one of those fundamental alignments that have been shaping the European project since its commencement. Subsequently, national perceptions and positions among the EU member states evolved as the liberalization and market integration proceeded (Eising & Jakob 2001, p. 743)

In 1998, legislation to apply liberalization and integration policies to the European gas sector was adopted, aiming to restructure the member states' domestic gas sectors and facilitate cross-border gas trade to establish an Union-wide internal market. To implement this long-term project, numerous legal, economic, and technical problems had to be solved. Previous integration processes in the gas sector followed the deployment of infrastructure outside formal institutionalization. They were "hidden" forms of integration (Misa & Schot, 2005). With the new laws, European legislators essentially sought to replace the two "hidden" forms of integration in the European gas grid.

During the second half of the 2000s, the EU incrementally dovetailed its energy and climate policies. Given the enormous economic and technical task, the European Commission had to adjust its legal approach several times. In 2003, the second legislative package was adopted, while the debate about the path to market integration continued. The adoption of the Third Energy Package in 2009 constituted the third round of integration legislation. It strengthened market integration efforts.

The EU also pursued ambitious policies to mitigate climate change. In 2008, the so-called 20-20-20 by 2020 Strategy was announced (European Commission, 2008). The related legislative package was enacted in 2009. By the year 2020, the EU aimed to reduce its greenhouse gas emissions by 20 %. Renewables should achieve a 20 % share in EU energy consumption; and the EU should consume 20 % less energy. The announcement of the Energy Union in 2015 was a milestone in dovetailing of EU energy and climate policies. Energy security, solidarity, and trust form one of five dimensions that guide EU legislators (European Commission, 2015, p. 4).

By that time, relations with Russia had already noticeably worsened. After 2000, the Russian government reversed previous tentative market reforms. Around the year 2003, it was clear that Russia's transition from a socialist state-economy to a liberal market economy had stalled. The fall of Mikhail Khodorkovksy and the dismantling of his company YUKOS marked a new era in Russian energy affairs. The country's economic and political development took a turn toward a crony-driven kleptocracy in which most valuable companies were controlled by the state and administered by the ruling elite.

Russian authorities re-assessed projects in the gas and oil sector that were jointly conducted with western companies and transferred more shares to the Russian companies. The Shell's Sakhalin 2 project is a case in point. By the mid-2000s, the Russian government seemed less concerned about the investment climate, as the commodity boom helped to stabilize the Russian economy (Yergin, 2021, p. 77). Russia could afford to play hardball in its energy relations, especially with Ukraine. Gas supply crises, especially the disruptions in 2006 and 2009, also alarmed customers and governments in the EU. Building a pipeline through the Baltic Sea, directly connecting Russia and Germany, seemed to be a good solution to the frequent hiccups in Russian-Ukrainian gas relations.

To sum up, the EU embarked on an ambitious reorganization of the member states' energy sector, both in terms of market structure and long-term fuel use, while the relations with Russia, the Union's dominant gas supplier, became increasingly complicated. The reasons were threefold. First, the accession of eastern European countries to the EU changed the security of supply equation. Second, both sides chose approaches to govern the gas sector that proved mutually incompatible. Third, political and energy-related divergences increasingly strained bilateral relations. The next section describes three episodes in EU-Russia gas relations that manifested the growing estrangement.

UNAMBIGUOUS TRANSIT RULES, AN INNOVATIVE DECISION, AND AN UNNECESSARY PIPELINE

From 2000 onward, episodes of disagreement exemplified the underlying reasons for the decline of EU-Russia gas relations. They concern the Energy Charter Treaty's Transit Protocol and the rules that are applicable to Russian gas supplies to EU member states. The contention generally centered around EU rules that altered the structure of the EU gas market. The potential violation of rules that govern EU energy transport networks also informed the legal part of the Nord Stream 2 debate. The political conflict among EU members about Nord Stream 2 was the culmination of the interaction between infrastructure, rules, and market arrangements. This section briefly reviews how these three episodes of disagreement unfolded over the course of two decades.

Transit Politics

In mid-2009, the Russia government decided to withdraw from the Energy Charter Treaty (ECT). The withdrawal became effective on October 19, 2009. At the time, this decision might only have been of great significance for the relatively small community of investment lawyers. Moreover, the news about Russia's withdrawal from the ECT paled in comparison with events that took place months before the decision, such as Russia's war against Georgia and another gas crisis in Ukraine.

Yet, the Russian government's withdrawal from the ECT was nothing less than the country's deliberate and official abandonment of the shared European energy governance structure. The reasons that informed this decision point to a profound divergence between the EU and the Russian ruling elite regarding the governance of energy affairs.

The ECT was signed in Lisbon in 1994 and entered into force in 1998. It aimed to foster investment protection, enable non-discriminatory trade of energy materials, facilitate the settlement of disputes, and enhance energy efficiency. Article 2 ECT obliges the parties to "promote access to international markets on commercial terms, and generally to develop an open and competitive market" for energy supplies. The EU and its member states are parties to the Treaty; and Russia, as one of few large energy producers, also signed the Treaty.

However, from the outset Russia made the ratification of the Treaty conditional on adjustments to the Transit Protocol. Since 2000, Russian leaders, policymakers, and parliamentarians repeatedly presented proposals for amendments to the ECT or even called for an entirely new treaty (Westphal, 2011, p. 4). In essence, Russian grievances focused on the provisions that governed the transit of oil and gas through pipelines, especially with respect to the gas supply infrastructure.

The transit provisions in Article 7 (1) ECT stipulate that the parties have to enable the transit of energy "consistent with the principle of freedom of transit and without distinction as to the origin, destination or ownership" of these resources, "without imposing any unreasonable delays, restrictions or charges."

Russia's reasons for refusing the ECT's transit provisions were twofold. First, Russian leaders and Gazprom did not accept the process of unbundling vertical integrated energy companies. In other words, the separation of business activities that pertain to the gas production, sale of gas, and transport of supplies to customers should not interfere with Gazprom's business model. However, with each liberalization round EU legislators chose ever more rigorous rules to delineate this separation. Second, especially after the EU enlargement and given the legal nature of the EU as one market, Gazprom envisioned many transit risks in eastern European member states and the post-Soviet space (Konoplyanik, 2009, pp. 455–462). From its complaints against the nature of an integrated EU gas market, it is discernable that Gazprom does not embrace the fact that independent network regulators as well as national and EU enforcement would ensure the functioning of the market. Thus, Gazprom's concerns revealed a distrust of EU institutions. Both Gazprom and the Russian government treated the EU internal market with ambivalence.

Assessments by Russian analysts of the disagreements between the EU and Russia as well as proposals to change the ECT show that Russia would have preferred a reversal of both European integration and EU gas market liberalization. Russia would rather deal with individual European states and vertically integrated companies that buy its gas. Furthermore, Russia was open to assets swaps, but did not want to drop long-term supply contracts (Konoplyanik, 2009, p. 471; Westphal, 5). Yet, both business practice contradicted the EU market rules.

This episode clarifies the reasons for disagreement between the EU and Russia regarding the governance of energy affairs. Section two has shown that the creation of the single gas market was a crucial project for the integration of the member states' economies; and the Commission pursued the integration project despite formidable resistance in many member states. The efforts seemed worthwhile because of the economic benefits that a large, competitive market can provide. The incompatibility of Russia's preferences with the Union's vision was obvious. The application of ECT transit rules would end Gazprom's monopoly on gas exports. Moreover, it would change the governance of the vast pipeline system on Russian territory. Gazprom would thus be forced to abandon the non-cost-based operation of Russia's gas sector and cross-subsidizing its subsidiaries (Konoplyanik, 2009, pp. 475–476). Neither side was willing to give in. Russia's withdrawal from the ECT ended the debate about a shared, rules-based energy future on the continent. The following episodes also relate to the incompatibility of governance approaches.

Investigating the Gas Supplier

Gazprom has a dominant position in the gas supply of central and eastern European member states. This reality was known when the post-socialist countries acceded to the EU. However, at the time it was thought that effectively mitigating Gazprom's dominance in these countries' gas supply would be too expensive and almost unfeasible (see section "Divergent Legacies and Hidden Integration").

In 2018, the European Commission chose a creative approach to ameliorate the effects of Gazprom's dominance in central and eastern Europe. After an investigation of Gazprom's practices in central and eastern Europa, the European Commission took a legally binding decision. that corrected the disruptive effects of the company's control of the pipelines. The European Commission concluded that Gazprom's control of the infrastructure and central provisions in its supply contracts constituted an abuse of a dominant position. As a result, the European Commission could have issued a fine for violating EU law. However, Gazprom agreed to four commitments that would mitigate the effects of its dominant position in the gas supply of the post-socialist EU member states. The European Commission accepted these commitments.

They address four concerns that the European Commission had raised. First, EU member states in the east can re-sell gas across borders. Second, these countries can choose the delivery points for contracted Russia gas deliveries. Third, if countries only receive Russian gas they can request price changes based on the rates at liquid hubs in western Europe markets. Fourth, the European Commission will monitor future gas contract and can decide on the inclusion of unrelated undertakings in the contracts (European Commission, 2018).

This decision illustrates an important aspect of the interaction between governance and infrastructure. Obviously, the lopsided import infrastructure reduces the effectiveness of EU market integration. Yet, by adjusting the legal context of the infrastructure the European Commission's decision helped to alleviate exclusionary effects of the physical linkages.

The decision was a milestone in the governance of the EU gas market and the Union's stance on Gazprom's practices in the EU. The investigation could have helped Gazprom to adapt to rapidly changing international business practices. But the Russian government saw the investigation as politically driven. In an attempt to protect Gazprom from the EU antitrust proceedings, President Putin, by decree, tried to impede the collection of evidence (Sartori, 2013, pp. 10, 13). By offering commitments, Gazprom avoided the worst-case scenario of moving on to court proceedings. However, the underlying incompatible governance approaches that characterize Russia's gas sector and the EU internal market remained. The debate about Nord Stream 2 continued this high-stake infrastructure saga.

The Undercurrent of Directly Linking Russia and Germany

Contentious issues of controlling the transit to Gazprom's customers that had shaped the dispute about the Transit Protocol resurfaced in the debate about the Nord Stream 2 pipeline. In this third episode of divergent governance approaches, the legal aspects of the issue at hand were overshadowed by the political controversy about this pipeline. The debate about this project highlighted concerns that had mounted in EU-Russia gas relations. Despite Russia's covert military actions in eastern Ukraine and the annexation of Crimea, the German government agreed to support the pipeline project that would create an additional direct gas pipeline on the ground of the Baltic Sea.

However, the European Commission made clear that Nord Stream 2 would not contribute to the security of supply of the EU (Euractiv, 2021). Researchers at the DIW, the German Institute for Economic Research, concluded that neither Germany nor Europe suffered from gas supply gaps that at the time or in the future would necessitate putting Nord Stream 2 into operation (Holz & Kemfert, 2021, p. 17).

The project had driven a wedge between the western European member states that endorsed the pipeline, and Poland and the Baltic states. Russian analysts saw this as sign of a "crisis in solidarity" among member states who seemed to pursue diverging energy interests (Starikovs, 2017, p. 10), while some suggested that the completion of Nord Stream 2 could make a "considerable contribution to European energy security;" and it would reduce "military tensions" between NATO and Russia in the Baltic region, as the need to operate the pipeline would preclude a military conflict in the region (Zhiznin & Timokhov, 2019, p. 38).

It was not possible to deal with the pipeline based on existing legislation. In 2019, an amendment to the Gas Directive was adopted that sought to "address obstacles to the completion of the internal market in natural gas which result from the non-application of Union market rules to gas transmission lines to and from third countries" (EU Gas Directive, 2019). This amendment closed a legal loophole that the design of Nord Stream 2 intended to exploit. However, it seemed that the intricate issues pertaining to the project could only be solved through negotiations (Zafoschnig, 2019, p. 161). By that time, EU-Russia gas relations were at a critical juncture. Eventually, the German government stopped the permission proceedings after Russia officially recognized the two puppet "people's republics" in eastern Ukraine in February 2022.

Concluding Remarks

The three episodes exemplified the differences in governing energy affairs and how these differences increasingly affected EU-Russia gas relations. After 2010, the European Commission and EU legislators displayed a firm resolve to enforce EU rules and protect the common market. Thus, after the deterioration of bilateral political relations and Russia's rejection of EU energy rules, both the EU executive and legislative branches acted decisively. At the same time, political disagreements and conflicts between the EU and Russia further increased in number and severity.

Until 2022, the reliability of Russian gas supplies was hardly questioned. Yet, after Russia's invasion of Ukraine the Union's dependence on these supplies was regarded as a threat. Energy securitization increased tremendously, given the prolonged incompatibility of energy governance in the EU and Russia and severe political conflicts. For the EU, dependence on Russian energy supplies was no longer acceptable.

INFRASTRUCTURE, ENERGY SECURITY, AND CLIMATE NEUTRALITY

Initially, the EU addressed legal loopholes in the governance of vital gas infrastructure to respond security of gas supply issues that resulted from the Union's dependence on Russia and increasingly fraught bilateral relations. This was no longer possible when European gas customers faced a more immediate supply threat and Russia's unprovoked war in the Union's vicinity.

In the winter of 2022, gas storage levels in western Europe were historically low, especially at facilities that Gazprom subsidiaries ran. Months before the Russian invasion in Ukraine, alarm bells rang when investigative journalists, policymakers, and people involved in the energy sector pointed to Gazprom's reluctance to refill storage facilities that it owned in the Netherlands and Germany (Hecking, 2021; Van Dijk, 2021). The gas infrastructure in these two countries is the backbone of the industrial core region of western and central Europe. Furthermore, millions of residential customers use gas for heating.

In October 2021, President Vladimir Putin promised that Gazprom would start filling its storages, but Gazprom did not act on this promise. Suspicion grew by the end of 2021 that with the reduced supplies Gazprom wanted to accelerate the deployment of Nord Stream 2. This move had already been suggested by Russian media outlets months ago and would be intended to force the EU to acknowledge that only Russian supplies can guarantee the Union's energy security (Gurkov, 2021; Hecking, 2021).

The Russian invasion of Ukraine ended the proceedings in Germany regarding the permission for putting Nord Stream 2 into operation. Furthermore, only a month after the beginning of the war the European Commission presented a proposal for legislation aiming to enhance gas security by requiring minimum gas storage levels in the Union (European Commission, 2022). The legislative process went smoothly on a fast track. It was expected that the legally binding regulation would be adopted before the summer in order to have the legislation in force in the second half of 2022 (Euractiv, 2021).

The thrust of the proposed regulation offers new governance tools to enhance the security of gas supply. Most importantly, the regulation will require a mandatory minimum level of gas in storage facilities of up to 90 %. Further, the member states agreed on a mandatory certification of storage system operators in order to "ensure that potential security of supply risks resulting from influence over the critical storage infrastructure can be excluded" (European Commission, 2022, p. 2). Hence, when confronted with the weaponization of gas infrastructure the European Commission and the member states opted to interfere with the management of essential assets.

Obviously, there is an link between the willingness to have foreign companies control energy assets and the nature of the political regime in the companies' home country, if the issue at hand concerns an important partner in energy affairs. The swift action to secure gas storage capacity was reminiscent of the fast adoption of the EU investment screening regulation in 2017.

At that time, this legislative act was a response to efforts by Chinese state-owned electricity companies, in particular China State Grid, to acquire shares in European electricity generation and transmission companies. These activities coincided with a deterioration of the relations between the EU and China. Under the country's current leadership, the EU considers China as an "economic competitor in the pursuit of technological leadership" as well as "a systemic rival promoting alternative models of governance" (European Commission and High Representative of the Union for Foreign Affairs and Security Policy, 2019, p. 1). Thus, in the late 2010s it was no longer conceivable that Chinese state-owned enterprises should be allowed to acquire (further) assets in the EU energy sector.

Exercising caution seems to be reasonable, when growing political conflicts can easily affect energy cooperation and reliance on long-term infrastructure arrangements. The third section's account on infrastructure and governance explained this interrelationship. The response to a potential extension of Chinese involvement in European energy infrastructure as well as the Union's handling of gas storage facilities after the beginning of the Russian invasion prove that security considerations interact with the control of energy assets and infrastructure, when the political mood in bilateral relations changes.

This insight is vital for the transition to climate neutrality and the evaluation of China's role in the industrial complex that is emerging with the rising demand for renewable energy. China dominates the global production of several critical minerals that are vital inputs for components for low-carbon energy generation. Chinese firms account for 40 %–70 % of global copper, lithium, and cobalt refining and almost 90 % of rare-earths processing (IEA, 2021, pp. 31–32, 165). China Rare-Earth Group, a recently created state-owned "megafirm," controls 60 %–70 % of the country's rare-earth production, which is equivalent to about 30 %–40 % of global supply (Vekasi, 2022). Moreover, China currently supplies 70 % of the solar modules and 50 % of the wind turbines that are deployed worldwide (Wood Mackenzie, 2022).

In addition, during the energy transition the importance of the electricity sector will increase. In this regard, not only physical transmission lines should be considered as critical infrastructure where third-party involvement can lead to the securitization of energy. The dominance in the production and supply of components that are used in relay stations and other installations as well as the quest for a prevalent position in introducing new international technological standards in the electricity sector are issues that also warrant attention. Chinese activities in the manufacturing of essential components and international standard-setting bodies have been increasing for years. The goal of Chinese companies is twofold. They try to dominate sectors that drive the global energy transition and the innovation of technologies that will shape this industrial transformation, especially in the electricity sector (Handke, 2022, pp. 213–220).

As mentioned above, accelerating the deployment of green energy technologies to substitute Russian gas is one of the REPowerEU Plan's objectives. For the EU to succeed, it is important that lessons from its energy relations with Russia inform the approach to energy partnerships that will foster the Union's transition to climate neutrality. Section three concluded that the incompatibility of governance approaches, primarily pertaining to the regulation of infrastructure and the ownership of energy assets, is a crucial factor in the securitization of energy when the number of political conflicts or their intensity increase.

Accordingly, a comparison between EU energy governance and the characteristics of China's energy sector can help to assess the potential for an increased securitization of energy in the bilateral relations. Five aspects provide some insights—i.e., economic policy goals that pertain to the energy sector and low-carbon transition, governance structures, the nature of the economy, the structure of the energy sector, and the role of regulatory oversight (see Table 6.2).

To be sure, this section does not intend to provide an in-depth assessment of the prospects for future energy cooperation between the EU and China. It aims to help evaluate developments that will most likely influence energy security concerns on the EU side. Sections two and three demonstrated that early warning signs, such as Russia's rejection of the ECT's transit provisions, hinted at ingrained attitudes that would eventually confirm the mutual incompatibility of governance approaches in Russia and the EU. This incompatibility, over the years, led to a securitization of energy affairs. Thus, the following brief overview of energy governance in the EU and China tries to detect traces of early warning signs that deserve further scrutiny to fully appreciate changes in the degree of energy securitization.

When assessing the susceptibility of energy cooperation between the EU and China to the securitization of energy in the EU, the overview of governance arrangements helps to identify a number of differences. Some of them point to incompatible governance approaches. Thus, they constitute early warning signs. Three potential issues of concern stand out. They relate to the openness of the economy, regulation of economic affairs and legal certainty, as well as the stability of the trajectory toward climate neutrality.

First, given China's above-mentioned dominance in the renewables supply chain its economy's openness is decisive for fruitful relations with the EU throughout the transition to climate neutrality. However, with President Xi Jinping's economic policies China transitioned from the opening up and reform period to

Table 6.2: Overview of EU and China's Energy Governance

	European Union	China
Policy goals	• Energy Union (five dimensions) • European Green Deal, climate neutrality by 2050	• Building a "great modern socialist country," common prosperity • Dual circulation • Climate pledges: peak in greenhouse gas emissions before 2030; carbon neutrality by 2060
Governance structure	• Legislation to implement Energy Union and EU Climate Law • Regional and transregional cooperation mechanisms • National legislation and policy implementation	• Centralized policymaking (see five-year-plan, long-term strategies) • Local implementation • Party system as control mechanism
Economy	• Social market economy	• Party-screened economy (market does not determine outcomes) • Industrial policy, Made in China 2025
Energy sector	• Liberalized	• Dominated by a few large state-owned enterprises • Regulatory capture
Regulatory oversight	• European Commission • ACER and national regulators	• Weak • Campaign-style policy implementation

Source: Author's own elaboration

a new era (Hadano, 2022; Minzner, 2018). Xi's policies create a redistributive, inward-looking political economy, to establish a great modern socialist country by the mid-twenty-first century by pursuing common prosperity and organizing the economy in a dual-circulation mode (Chang & Wang, 2020; Nagai, 2017; Wu, 2022).

The goal of operating the economy in a dual-circulation mode is most consequential for global energy and climate cooperation. It entails a reduced dependence on foreign trade and investment, while Chinese companies and banks will remain engaged in activities abroad. By doing so, China's domestic economic development should be shielded from harmful external impacts.

Second, for the pursuit of long-term projects in the realm of the low-carbon energy transition the regulation of economic affairs and legal certainty in China matter greatly. Yet, the Chinese economy is party-screened. The market does not determine outcomes; and the influence of the party-state on economic affairs is tangible. Recent regulatory campaigns against the country's sprawling technology sector and educational services are examples for how party objectives guide decisions. The party-state's interference in economic affairs is increasingly abrupt and arbitrary.

Furthermore, the party leadership seeks to foster the development of certain industries, as outlined in the "Made in China 2025" strategy. This industrial policy of "grand steerage" that is enormous in scope and unprecedented in Chinese history forms a big gamble (Naughton, 2020, p. 52; 2021, p. 96). Hence, the current governance approach causes a sense of legal uncertainty, while large sums of money are spent on extraordinary industrial policies.

The Chinese energy sector, especially the electricity sector, is marred by serious structural shortcomings. Central planning, based on five-year plans and sector-specific plans, is usually re-interpreted according to provincial and local needs in the course of the implementation process. Much of the central policymaking rigor is lost on the plans' way downstream, as local preferences and rent-seeking often prevail. The party-based control mechanisms are only effectuated when regime security is threatened.

Moreover, the electricity sector is dominated by a few power generation companies and two large transmission companies. State Grid controls about 80 % of China's power transmission business and is peerless even at a global level (Xu, 2017). In 2003, the State Electricity Regulatory Commission was established to oversee the sector. However, in 2013 its responsibilities were transferred to other bodies within the central government's bureaucracy. From the outset, the commission lacked authority and autonomy to fulfill its oversight tasks (Tsai, 2014). The understaffed and underresourced regulator was no match for influential industry actors. No further efforts were made to create independent industry regulators.

Third, the transition to climate neutrality needs to be guided by a clear policy trajectory. The leadership has not yet detailed China's path. Recent climate pledges—such as having emissions peak before 2030 and achieving carbon neutrality by 2060—were expected to inform the current 14th Five Year Plan and related energy policies. However, thus far efforts to stabilize or even reduce greenhouse gas emissions are hardly detectable in the policy planning for the coming years (Handke, 2021, pp. 31–34; You, 2022). On this basis, it is difficult to anticipate the development of China's energy sector and elaborate cooperation strategies.

Accordingly, when engaging in energy relations with China three issues are hardly guaranteed that determine the EU approach to achieve climate neutrality—i.e., reciprocity in economic affairs, legal certainty, and sustainability. Pursuant to Article 119 (1) of the Treaty on the Functioning of the European Union, EU member states adopt economic policies "in accordance with the principle of an open market economy with free competition." The operation of the EU energy sector is rules based and overseen by an independent regulator at EU level, the Agency for the Cooperation of Energy Regulators, and national regulators, while the European Commission enforces EU competition and state aid rules.

The European Commission increasingly takes the lead in proposing energy and climate legislation, such as the Clean Energy for all Europeans package, the legislative acts that implement the Energy Union (European Commission, n. d.). The member states transpose this legislation into domestic law, while regional intergovernmental groupings, such as the Pentalateral Forum in western and central Europe, deal with technical matters of interconnecting the electricity and gas sectors. These forums cooperate closely in a depoliticized manner to support the further integration of the energy sector (Handke, 2018).

Finally, the EU goal of achieving climate neutrality by 2050 is irreversible and legally binding, pursuant to Article 1 of the European Climate Law (2021). Article 4 (1) of the European Climate Law stipulates the legally binding goal of reducing net greenhouse gas emissions by at least 55 % by 2030, compared to 1990 levels. The implementation of these goals is guided by the dimensions of the Energy Union (1) energy security, solidarity, and trust; (2) a fully integrated European energy market; (3) energy efficiency contributing to moderation of demand; (4) the decarbonization of the economy; and (5) research, innovation, and competitiveness (European Commission, 2015, p. 4). Hence, the far-reaching transition to climate neutrality unfolds within the framework of the treaties that govern the EU and secondary legislation.

To sum up, when trying to achieve climate neutrality the EU is increasingly dependent on China. With respect to China's economy, early warning signs need to be taken seriously, as they point incompatibility in governance approaches—i.e., the lack of openness, absence of legal certainty, and inconclusiveness regarding the path to climate neutrality. Since Chinese companies are already present in the EU energy sector, the differences in domestic governance can result in a securitization of energy in the relations with China, as soon as bilateral political relations further deteriorate.

CONCLUSION

The securitization of energy is a continuum. This chapter examined the securitization in the course of EU-Russia gas relations during the twenty-first century. Its findings are useful lessons for the transition to climate neutrality. By relying on legal and infrastructure scholarship, the chapter was able to assess domestic developments that influence the securitization of energy. Incompatibility of practices that govern the physical gas supply infrastructure, together with diverging approaches to the control of vital energy assets and market regulation, contextualized increasingly contentious relations. Serious political conflicts between the EU and Russia eventually securitized energy on the EU side.

On the path to climate neutrality, the EU is confronted with the abrupt unraveling of its relations with Russia, its most important supplier of fossil fuels. The transition to climate neutrality of the EU member states' energy sectors will neither be linear nor easily projectable, as Germany's sudden need for the construction of new fossil infrastructure exemplified. Still, the legislation and principles that institutionalize the Energy Union form a powerful tool to guide EU policymakers and economic stakeholders toward a secure, low-carbon energy future. This framework needs to direct the transition to climate neutrality from the outset. New fuels, technologies, and requirements for the low-carbon transition of the electricity sector put China in a dominant position. The lessons from Union's relations with Russia help to assess dependence, control of networked infrastructure and vital supplies, as well as the consequences of political frictions.

Energy security belongs to one of the dimensions that form the basis of the Energy Union. The legislation to implement the Energy Union requires member states to regularly reassess, update, and present their energy and climate plans. No doubt, the EU also needs to continuously evaluate its external energy affairs. Studying the evolution of EU-Russia gas relations in the early twenty-first century is enlightening. It provides valuable insights into the process of securitizing energy and shows which developments are likely to be early warning signs.

NOTES

1 Green hydrogen points to the generation of hydrogen based on renewable energy sources.

2 The Energy Union was announced in February 2015. It entails a dovetailing of EU energy and climate policies and, at the time, anticipated the climate goals that are enshrined in the Paris Agreement. It forms the basic policy document of EU energy and climate legislation that is currently in force.

3 Bulgaria and Romania joined the EU in 2007, and Croatia in 2013.

REFERENCES

Bouzarovski, S., Bradshaw, M., & Wochnik, A. (2015). Making territory through infrastructure: The governance of natural gas transit in Europe. *Geoforum*, *64*, 217–228. https://doi.org/10.1016/j.geoforum.2015.06.022

Chang, X., & Wang, K. (2020, May 15). 中共中央政治局常务委员会召开会议：中共中央总书记习近平主持会议 (Zhonggong zhongyang zhengzhi ju changwu weiyuan hui zhaokai huiyi: Zhonggong zhongyang zong shuji Xi Jinping zhuchi huiyi) [The Standing committee of the Politburo convenes: The general secretary of the Chinese Communist Party Xi Jinping chairs the meeting]. 人民日报 (*Renmin ribao*). http://cpc.people.com.cn/n1/2020/0515/c64094-31709627.html

Eising, R., & Jabko, N. (2001). Moving targets: National interests and electricity liberalization in the European Union. *Comparative Political Studies*, *34*, 742–767.

Euractiv. (2021, February 24). *EU says it does not need Nord Stream 2, but only Germany can block it*. https://www.euractiv.com/section/global-europe/news/eu-says-it-does-not-need-nord-stream-2-but-only-germany-can-block-it/

European Climate Law. (2021). Regulation (EU) 2021/1119 of the European Parliament and of the Council establishing the framework for achieving climate neutrality and amending Regulations (EC) No. 401/2009 and (EU) 2018/1999, OJ L 243/1, 9.7.2021, pp. 1–17.

European Commission. (n.d.). *Clean energy for all Europeans package*. https://ec.europa.eu/energy/en/topics/energy-strategy-and-energy-union/clean-energy-all-europeans

European Commission. (2008, January 23). 20 20 by 2020: Europe's climate change opportunity. COM 30 final, pp. 1–12.

European Commission. (2015, February 25). Energy Union package: A framework strategy for a resilient Energy Union with a forward-looking climate change policy. COM 80 final, pp. 1–21.

European Commission. (2018, May 24). *Antitrust: Commission imposes binding obligations on Gazprom to enable free flow of gas at competitive prices in central and eastern European gas markets* [Press release]. https://ec.europa.eu/commission/presscorner/detail/en/IP_18_3921

European Commission. (2022, March 23). Proposal for a regulation of the European Parliament and of the Council amending Regulation (EU) 2017/1938 of the European Parliament and of the Council concerning measures to safeguard the security of gas supply and regulation (EC) no. 715/2009 of the European Parliament and of the Council on conditions for access to natural gas transmission networks. COM 135 final, pp. 1–32.

European Commission and High Representative of the Union for Foreign Affairs and Security Policy. (2019, March 12). EU-China: A strategic outlook. JOIN 5 final, pp. 1–11.

European Communities. (1987). *Single European Act*, OJ L 169/1.

European Union Gas Directive. (2019). Directive (EU) 2019/692 of the European Parliament and of the Council amending Directive 2009/73/EC concerning common rules for the internal market in natural gas, OJ L 117/1, 3.5.2019, pp. 1–7.

Federal Government, The. (2022, May 12). *Steffi Lemke zum LNG-Beschleunigungsgesetz und zur dramatischen Beschleunigung für den Klimaschutz* [*Steffi Lemke on the LNG Acceleration Act and on the dramatic acceleration of climate protection measures*]. https://www.bmuv.de/interview/steffi-lemke-zum-lng-beschleunigungsgesetz-und-zur-dramatischen-beschleunigung-fuer-den-klimaschutz

Gessen, M. (2018). *The future is history: How totalitarianism reclaimed Russia*. Granta.

Gurkov, A. (2021, July 9). *Gazprom zeigt Europa seine Marktmacht* [*Gazprom demonstrates Europe its market power*]. DW. https://www.dw.com/de/gazprom-zeigt-europa-seine-marktmacht/a-58216903

Hadano, T. (2022, March 11). *As Xi forges own path, China plays down Deng's economic policy*. Nikkei Asia. https://asia.nikkei.com/Politics/China-People-s-Congress/As-Xi-forges-own-path-China-plays-down-Deng-s-economic-policy

Handke, S. (2018). Renewables and the core of the Energy Union: How the Pentalateral Forum facilitates the energy transition in western Europe. In D. Scholten (Ed.), *The geopolitics of renewables* (pp. 277–303). Springer.

Handke, S. (2021). *Regulating post-Paris climate cooperation: The geopolitics of transparency, flexibility, and common timeframes* (Clingendael International Energy Programme Research Paper No. 2). https://www.clingendaelenergy.com/inc/upload/files/CIEP-Paper-202102-web.pdf, pp. 1–47.

Handke, S. (2022). Harmonising oversight of the EU low-carbon power transition: With an eye to sustainability, energy justice and security. In B. Vanheusden, T. Iliopoulos, & A. Vanhellemont (Eds.), *Harmonisation in EU environmental and energy law* (pp. 207–236). Intersentia.

Hecking, C. (2021, December 10). *Gazprom füllt die deutschen Gasspeicher nicht auf* [*Gazprom does not refill German gas storages*]. Spiegel. https://www.spiegel.de/wirtschaft/unternehmen/gazprom-fuellt-deutsche-gasspeicher-nicht-auf-a-a76e5e8a-ba67-4d86-8846-6af453c5df5e

Högselius, P. (2013). *Red gas: Russia and the origins of European energy dependence*. Palgrave Macmillan.

Holz, F., & Kemfert, C. (2021, January). Die kurz- und langfristige Bedarfsentwicklung im deutschen und europäischen Erdgasmarkt: Stellungnahme zur Fertigstellung und Inbetriebnahme des Nord Stream 2 Pipeline-Projekts [Short-term and long-term development of demand in the German and European market for natural gas: Statement on the completion and operationalization of the Nord Stream 2 project]. *Politikberatung kompakt*, *162*, 1–18. https://www.econstor.eu/bitstream/10419/233021/1/1751464210.pdf

International Energy Charter. (2019, February 18). *The energy charter treaty*. https://www.energycharter.org/process/energy-charter-treaty-1994/energy-charter-treaty/

International Energy Agency. (2021, May). The role of critical minerals in clean energy transitions [Flagship report]. https://www.iea.org/reports/the-role-of-critical-minerals-in-clean-energy-transitions, pp. 1–283.

International Energy Agency. (2022, March 3). *A 10-point plan to reduce the European Union's reliance on Russian natural gas* [Fuel report]. https://iea.blob.core.windows.net/assets/1af70a5f-9059-47b4-a2dd-1b479918f3cb/A10-PointPlantoReducetheEuropeanUnionsRelianceonRussianNaturalGas.pdf, pp. 1–11

Johnson, C. (2017). Mobile energy and obdurate infrastructure: Distant carbon and the making of modern Europe. In S. Bouzarovski, M. J. Pasqualetti, & V. Castán Broto (Eds.), *The Routledge research companion to energy geographies* (pp. 95–105). Routledge.

Konoplyanik, A. A. (2009). Gas Transit in Eurasia: Transit Issues between Russia and the European Union and the Role of the Energy Charter. In Journal of Energy & Natural Resources Law (Vol. 27, Issue 3, pp. 445–486). Informa UK Limited. https://doi.org/10.1080/02646811.2009.11435224

Minzner, C. (2018). *End of an era: How China's authoritarian revival is undermining its rise*. Oxford University Press.

Misa, T., & Schot, J. (2005). Introduction. *History and Technology*, *21*(1), 1–19.

Nagai, O. (2017, October 18). *China's Xi outlines vision of "great modern socialist country."* Nikkei Asia. https://asia.nikkei.com/Economy/China-s-Xi-outlines-vision-of-great-modern-socialist-country

NATO. (2007, February 9). Speech by NATO Secretary General, Jaap de Hoop Scheffer at the Munich Conference of Security Policy, NATO. https://www.nato.int/cps/en/natohq/opinions_8107.htm?selectedLocale=en

Naughton, B. (2020). Grand steerage. In T. Fingar & J. C. Oi (Eds.), *Fateful decisions: Choices that will shape China's future* (pp. 51–81). Stanford University Press.

Naughton, B. (2021). *The rise of China's industrial policy, 1978 to 2020*. Universidad Nacional Autónoma de México.

Ostrovsky, A. (2015). *The invention of Russia: The journey from Gorbachev's freedom to Putin's war*. Atlantic Book.

President of Russia. (2007, February 10). *Speech and the following discussion at the Munich Conference on Security Policy*. http://en.kremlin.ru/events/president/transcripts/24034

Sartori, N. (2013, January). The European Commission vs. Gazprom: An issue of fair competition or a foreign policy quarrel? (IAI Working Papers No. 3). https://www.jstor.org/stable/resrep09733?seq=1

Starikovs, A. (2017). "Северного потока-2": Дилеммность европейских энергетических интересов ["Nord Stream 2": The dilemma of European energy interests]. *Науковедение*, *9*(6), 1–11.

Stern J., & Yafimava, K. (2017). *The EU competition investigation of Gazprom's sales in central and eastern Europe: A detailed analysis of the commitments and the way forward* (OIES Paper No. 121). https://www.oxfordenergy.org/wpcms/wp-content/uploads/2017/07/The-EU-Competition-investigation-of-Gazproms-sales-in-central-and-eastern-Europe-a-detailed-analysis-of-the-commitments-and-the-way-forward-NG-121.pdf, pp 1–40.

Tsai, C. (2014). Regulating China's power sector: Creating an independent regulator without autonomy. *The China Quarterly*, *218*, 452–473.

Van Dijk, B. (2021, August 3). *Toenemende zorgen over gastoevoer naar Nederland* [*Growing concerns about the gas supply to the Netherlands*]. https://fd.nl/ondernemen/1406914/toenemende-zorgen-over-gastoevoer-naar-nederland-txe2caWCAzcp.

Vekasi, K. (2022, March 29). *Chinese rare earth consolidation a cause for concern*. East Asia Forum. https://www.eastasiaforum.org/2022/03/30/chinese-rare-earth-consolidation-a-cause-for-concern/

Westphal, K. (2011). The Energy Charter Treaty revisited: The Russian proposal for an international energy convention and Energy Charter Treaty. *SWP Comments*, *8*, 1–8.

Wilson, J. D. (2019). A securitisation approach to international energy politics. *Energy Research and Social Science*, *49*, 114–125.

Wood Mackenzie. (2022, February 17). *China's renewables boom year poses major challenges to western markets*. https://www.woodmac.com/press-releases/chinas-renewables-boom-year-poses-major-challenges-to-western-markets/

Wu, G. (2022, March 31). *China's common prosperity program: Causes, challenges, and implications* [Asia Society report]. https://asiasociety.org/sites/default/files/2022-03/ASPI_ChinaCommonProsp_report_fin.pdf, pp. 1–20.

Xu, Y. (2017). *Sinews of power: The politics of the State Grid Corporation of China*. Oxford University Press.

Yergin, D. (2021). *The new map: Energy, climate, and the clash of nations*. Penguin Books.

You, X. (2022, March 29). *Analysis: What does China's coal push mean for its climate goals?* [Carbon Brief]. https://www.carbonbrief.org/analysis-what-does-chinas-coal-push-mean-for-its-climate-goals/

Zafoschnig, N. (2019). The "Lex Nord Stream 2" and its Potential Impact. In Review of Central and East European Law (Vol. 44, Issue 2, pp. 148–161). Brill. https://doi.org/10.1163/15730352-04402002

Zhiznin, S. Z., & Timokhov, V. M. (2019). Экономические и геополитические аспекты "Северного потока-2" [Economic and geopolitical aspects of "Nord Stream 2"]. *Балтийский регион*, *11*(3), 25–42. https://doi.org/10.5922/2079-8555-2019-3-2

CHAPTER 7

Nord Stream 2 and Energy Security in Europe: The Impact of Economic Sanctions[1]

ALEXANDROS-CĂTĂLIN BAKOS

INTRODUCTION

As Tim Marshall (2019, p. 18) pointed out, "[e]nergy as political power will be deployed time and again in the coming years [...]." This is one of the phrases used by him in his seminal work, *The Revenge of Geography*, to describe the power that Russia has over states that are dependent on it for their energy needs, such as Germany, Ukraine, and Poland. In other words, the energy security of such states is heavily dependent on good, or at least acceptable, relations with Russia. Trying not to antagonize Russia is the baseline from which some of these states approach their relations with Moscow. What happens, then, if the United States—(still) the sole global superpower, at this moment, in the eyes of many, such as Beckley (2018) and Brooks and Wohlforth (2016, pp. 7–53)—enters this equation? And what happens if it does this by trying to leverage its own power against Russian influence? How? By imposing sanctions against Nord Stream 2, a pipeline that was supposed to answer the increasing demand for gas in Europe.

At the moment, however, the future of this pipeline is in serious doubt after the invasion of Ukraine by Russia. Even Germany, Nord Stream 2's strongest proponent, has taken a step back, essentially halting the future operation of Nord Stream 2 (Palacio, 2022), at least for the time being. This is in stark contrast to Berlin's position so far of strongly defending the completion of the pipeline and its future operation despite fears of Russian influence in eastern Europe

(Palacio, 2022). Technically, the approach was to halt the certification process of the pipeline since it had already been completed (Politico, 2022b). However, the change in Germany's approach is justified and even understandable. The issue has dynamically evolved from one mainly revolving around energy security (as will be further explained below) to one pinning energy security against territorial sovereignty (that of Ukraine). Halting Nord Stream 2 was seen as a response to Russian aggression in Ukraine, something that was supposed to urge Moscow to stop its military advances (among other measures, of course).

It is in this context that Marshall's position becomes clear—Nord Stream 2 had heavy geopolitical implications even before Russia's acts in Ukraine. This is especially true at the present moment, as Nord Stream 2 is being used as leverage against Russian aggression. Of course, simply halting this project will not stop the invasion (Financial Times, 2022a), and it is not the aim of this chapter to analyze the aggression itself and its broader consequences. The focus is on Nord Stream 2 and how the whole issue contributed to or hindered the attainment of energy security in Europe when looking at this context from the perspective of economic sanctions.

Initially, Nord Stream 2 was a project in which, alongside Gazprom, companies from five major European economies were involved: Engie (France), OMV (Austria), Shell (the United Kingdom), Uniper, and Wintershall DEA (Germany). At this moment, however, it is unclear how the involved companies will choose to continue their involvement in the project. For instance, Shell (Politico, 2022c) and Uniper (Financial Times, 2022b) have already decided to exit the joint venture. The future of the pipeline is uncertain at the moment—it is even unclear whether Germany only suspended the certification process pending further developments or whether it halted it altogether (Congressional Research Service, 2022). However, for the purposes of the present work, it will be assumed that Nord Stream 2 will not become operational since it is hard to envision, at least for the time being, further developments that will resume the operation of the pipeline.

It is in this context that the present chapter will seek to assess the impact that economic sanctions have on energy security in Europe. The analysis will look at the energy security needs of Europe, Russia's role in satisfying them, and the impact that economic sanctions (imposed mainly by the United States) may have in this complex, multifaceted scenario.

In fact, energy security and energy markets have always been at the forefront of (geo)politics. Along with economic and energy security arguments, political ones have arisen (although it is quite debatable to what extent *energy security* is not, in fact, a political concept). European Union (EU)-Russia energy relations represent a perfect example of this geopolitical influence, owing to the dependence of the EU on Russia for its energy supply needs (Szulecki & Westphal,

2018, pp. 193–194). One of the situations in which such a geopolitical tension has recently played out concerns the *Nord Stream 2* gas pipeline. The pipeline was supposed to deliver an additional 55 bcm of gas to the EU (Nord Stream 2, n.d.). The problem is that internal divisions arose within Europe regarding the impact of the Nord Stream 2 pipeline, even before the Ukrainian invasion. Some states, such as Germany, tried to push the project forward, arguing that the operation of the pipeline would contribute to energy security in Europe. Others, like Ukraine and Poland, opposed the project from the beginning. They argued that the project would bypass them and the current revenue that they derive from gas transition costs.

Not only was there intra-Europe opposition to the project, but Washington's involvement in the already existing political tensions had spurred a variety of reactions from all actors, complicating the issue even further. Initially, Washington seemed to take a step back concerning the Nord Stream 2 pipeline after Joe Biden's election as President of the United States (Shagina & Westphal, 2021). This appears to contrast the hawkish approach seen during the Trump administration. However, during that era, divisions on both sides of the political spectrum could be said to be more apparent—even if some of the sanctions passed during those times were a result of bipartisanship (Mackinnon et al., 2021). In any case, the narrative changed once again with the Russia-Ukraine border issue (right before the invasion), as Joe Biden essentially threatened that the United States would take steps to prevent *Nord Stream 2* from functioning—the exact terms used by the President of the United States were that "there will be no longer a Nord Stream 2," without expanding at the moment upon the way in which that would occur (WION, 2022). One of the ways in which Washington got involved in the whole affair, looking to influence its development, was through the use of economic sanctions (Tsafos, 2021). These also included restrictive measures addressed to third parties getting involved in the Nord Stream 2 consortium. While initially partly withdrawn, sanctions against Nord Stream 2 were reimposed following Russian aggression in Ukraine (Congressional Research Service, 2022). In fact, Nord Stream 2 AG was expressly added to the United States Department of Treasury's Foreign Assets Control Specially Designated Nationals List (U.S. Department of Treasury, 2022). In simpler words, there is a clear legal prohibition under U.S. law—at least against U.S. nationals—from doing business with Nord Stream 2 AG (Openhoff, 2022).

It is in this context that this chapter focuses on the impact that such restrictive measures can have on the development and, subsequently, the operation of the pipeline. However, it also looks at the reasoning behind the sanctions in order to better understand if there is a divergence between the aim stated by the United States and the less apparent but practically grounded reason for their imposition. In this chapter, we also seek to answer a more abstract but perhaps more important question: Can the sanctions imposed by Washington affect energy security in Europe? It is important, therefore, to focus on the implementation of such restrictive measures against the economic operators developing and operating the pipeline (and their business partners). As such, the most important question that arises in this context, and which we will attempt to answer in this chapter, is the following: Can the imposition of sanctions on the Nord Stream 2 consortium/ other involved third parties affect energy security in Europe? Of course, asking this question in isolation is no longer practically feasible. Recent developments, as mentioned in the beginning, clearly show that the issue is not about energy security anymore. Considerations of Ukrainian territorial sovereignty have come to the fore. However, since this chapter is only indirectly concerned with that matter, the analysis focuses exclusively on the impact that sanctions can have on the energy security in Europe. As such, for the purposes of the present discussion, there is a clear separation of the impact of sanctions before the Ukrainian invasion (when they were mostly concerned with energy security) and after the Russian aggression that is unfolding at the moment. In the latter case, sanctions also become relevant in the context of Ukraine's territorial sovereignty (although, to a certain—though not the same—extent, one could argue that they were also relevant in this respect before).

To answer the main question, we will start by looking at the present status of the Nord Stream 2 project and the types of sanctions that are currently levied against, and in connection to, the Nord Stream 2 consortium (the economic operators involved in developing and operating the pipeline). We will then move on to uncover the concept of energy security and how it applies specifically to Europe, especially in the context of Nord Stream 2. A brief overview of the existing tensions and of the conflicting arguments will be given, showing how the concept of energy security becomes fluid and politicized based on the interests of the involved stakeholders. For instance, Poland and Ukraine argued in opposition to Germany (which, as mentioned earlier, changed its position) and Russia, with the latter two having the strongest interests in operationalizing Nord Stream 2. We will also look at Washington's arguments for getting involved in the affair, showing how, according to official declarations, its policies might point to concern about energy security in Europe. At the same time, certain acts *on the ground* point in the opposite direction. After having clarified the complexity raised by the concept of *energy security* in Europe, we will move on to the specific issue of economic sanctions levied against the Nord Stream 2 consortium and other involved third parties. In this case, we will analyze both the declaratory purpose of these restrictive measures and their practical and potential impacts. We will demonstrate how tension also exists between the declared *liberal* aim of the sanctions (to induce the target(s) to change policies that may have an adverse effect, in this case, on energy security) and the more cynical but realistic *realpolitik* impact of these sanctions.

HOW DID WE GET HERE, AND WHAT IS THE CURRENT STATUS OF THE NORD STREAM 2 PROJECT?

It is important to start by saying that the *Nord Stream 2* project was supposed to bring gas directly from Russia to Germany (and, subsequently, Europe) through the Baltic Sea (Gazprom, 2021). According to official information found on Gazprom's (one of the major parties in the Nord Stream 2 consortium) website,

> Nord Stream 2 is a new export gas pipeline running from Russia to Europe across the Baltic Sea. The decision to build Nord Steam 2 was based on the successful experience in building and operating the Nord Stream gas pipeline. The new pipeline, similar to the one in operation, will establish a direct link between Gazprom and the European consumers. It will also ensure a highly reliable supply of Russian gas to Europe. This is particularly important now when Europe sees a decline in domestic gas production and an increasing demand for imported gas. (Gazprom, n.d.)

This official statement by itself sheds light on the majority of interests involved in this project—first and foremost, those of Russia and Germany and then, of course, those of European states (or at least Western European states, although this can be debated). Finally, according to the official narrative, as found on Gazprom's website (Gazprom, 2021), Nord Stream 2 was supposed to be beneficial to energy (gas) security in Europe, ensuring a supply of gas to the continent. Indeed, it is generally accepted that security of supply constitutes one of the major elements of the concept of energy security (Szulecki, 2018, pp. 1–4). However, what is not immediately apparent (or at least not directly apparent) from the above-quoted statement is the range of other, rather divergent, interests—for example, those of Eastern European states, such as Ukraine and Poland, who, even before the invasion, had much to lose if Nord Stream 2 were to become operational. More specifically, the Ukrainian-Polish gas pipeline would have become irrelevant, thus leading to a decrease in the revenue that those two states would otherwise have earned from transit fees (Temnycky, 2021). Of course, this does not necessarily mean that operationalizing Nord Stream 2 would have automatically rendered the Ukrainian-Polish pipeline obsolete, as this outcome would have depended on a number of factors. For instance, Moscow had incentives to use both pipelines since doing so would lead to an increase in its own revenues. Then, there is the future demand for gas in Europe. If it increases, it might have made more sense for both pipelines to remain operational (Temnycky, 2021). However, it must be pointed out that it is not entirely clear, nor does there seem to be any consensus on how gas demands in Europe will increase in the future. Thus, it is unclear whether Nord Stream 2 would have filled any gaps or not (Wattenegel, 2021). Also, these developments depend on the impact that the energy transition would have on European markets (Zuey, 2020, p. 365).

Finally, one of the most important pieces to this puzzle needs to be mentioned: the United States' involvement in this affair cannot be understated. At first glance, Nord Stream 2 may have seemed like a regional affair affecting only regional interests. After all, it concerns a market (the gas market), which is traditionally considered to have a regional scope (Van de Graaf, 2013, pp. 55, 73), unlike oil, for example, which has a global impact (Van de Graaf, 2013, p. 73). However, it can be argued that the gas market is also becoming globalized (Proedrou, 2018, p. 157), especially with the advent of liquified natural gas (LNG). However, gas delivered via a pipeline still involves a regional market (as long as one does not see it as competing against LNG, something which would complicate the picture). So, why did the United States get involved, then? At first glance, the arguments are geopolitical and based on security threats that Russia may pose to Europe. Given how events unfolded over the past couple of months, this makes sense. Furthermore, the United States cited several reasons for its opposition to Nord Stream 2: increased European energy dependence on Russia, depriving Ukraine and Poland (traditional U.S. allies or at least states in which the United States has certain interests) of transit fees derived from the Ukrainian-Polish pipeline, or the possibility of Russia cutting gas supplies to eastern Ukraine during winter period (The Economist, 2021b). Other arguments brought by Washington against Nord Stream 2 concerned the reality of European energy demands—specifically, the fact that the operation of the pipeline would not fill in a gap in the energy needs of the continent—and the border conundrum between Ukraine and Russia (The Economist, 2021b).

To be fair, there is some merit to Washington's argument that Nord Stream 2 would have given Moscow additional leverage over Europe (especially eastern Europe) in terms of the latter being dependent on Russia for their gas needs and, as such, more geopolitical power (The Economist, 2021a; Zolotova, 2021). While it would be farfetched to go as far as to say that the Nord Stream 2 pipeline would have given Russia a definitive advantage in a so-called quest for regional domination, such a claim does bring to memory a quote from Halford Mackinder's (widely known as the father of geopolitics) well-known thesis: "who rules East Europe commands the Heartland; whoever rules the Heartland commands the World-Island; whoever rules the World-Island commands the World" (Mackinder, 1942, p. 106). Essentially, the Heartland represents the area where the continental masses of Eurasia converge (Ismailov & Papaya, 2010), and whoever controls this area could be considered as having the *most advantageous geopolitical location* (Ismailov & Papaya, 2010). Moreover, as mentioned earlier, while it would be farfetched to even think of Nord Stream 2 as giving Moscow such an advantage, a grand strategy toward other powers (in this case, Washington's strategy toward Moscow) is developed with an overview spanning decades, not mere moments, which would allow for an identification of patterns (Gaddis, 2018, pp. 112–113). In this context, it is easier to understand the American approach. It also helps to look at the leveraging of economic power by Moscow in order to attain other gains—military (especially at the moment) or economic, for example—as Moscow did with Ukraine, for instance, when it tried to obtain an extension of the lease to the Black Sea fleet base (this happened in 2010, before Russia annexed Crimea; McMaster, 2020, p. 58).

These are all valid reasons for concern with the project and its possible operation. However, what is immediately striking is that there seems to be more to this issue than a simple U.S. concern with energy security in Europe and the security of Ukraine. In fact, the United States is interested in the European gas market, as it sees it as a hub for exporting its LNG (Zengerle, 2021). This is because the concept of energy security can be easily manipulated, as it will be shown below. Any party that has certain interests can hide between a desire to safeguard energy security when, in fact, it seeks to reach other, hidden, goals.

Finally, it is also important to consider another actor that has a stake in the project and which needs to balance different interests: the EU. For the purposes of the present discussion, it is quite difficult to pinpoint what the interests of the EU were, at least before the Ukrainian invasion (ever since, there seems to be more convergence; Balfour, 2022), given that its member states themselves had conflicting interests (e.g., Germany and Poland). In a 2021 briefing of the European Parliament, these potentially diverging interests were acknowledged:

> Germany's energy sector also sees the pipeline as a viable commercial project. Some opponents point to the environmental impact of the pipeline's construction, as well as the contradiction between the EU's climate goals and long-term investments in fossil fuel import infrastructure. However, the pipeline's geopolitical implications are its most controversial aspect. Critics, including several EU Member States, describe Nord Stream 2 as a Kremlin project to export malign Russian influence as well as gas to Europe. They note that, combined with the new TurkStream pipeline delivering Russian gas to south-eastern Europe, it will eventually enable Russia to starve Ukraine's ailing economy of much needed transit fee revenue. The pipeline looks set to perpetuate Russia's stranglehold on EU energy markets and compromise European strategic autonomy. (European Parliament, 2021)

So, what is the present status of the pipeline, and, more importantly, are there any economic sanctions that are presently levied against the actors involved with the project or against their business partners? The construction of the pipeline was completed in September 2021 (Soldatkin, 2021). However, this does not mean that the pipeline is operational. In fact, there are still some legal and administrative hurdles that have to be overcome. One of those hurdles is that the project still needs to be certified, and the Nord Stream 2 consortium needs to register a German subsidiary that would subsequently apply for an operating license (The Economist, 2021b). As mentioned earlier, though, Germany has suspended this process as a reaction to Russian hostilities in Ukraine.

Concerning sanctions imposed against the Nord Stream 2 consortium, the pendulum seems to be swinging back and forth. This is also true of sanctions designed to prevent the project from moving forward (e.g., secondary sanctions imposed against business partners that are engaged with the consortium; McDougall et al., 2020). In May of 2021, the United States agreed to withdraw almost all sanctions imposed against Nord Stream 2 (and involved business partners; Marineau, 2021), with Germany promising in July of the same year to react if Russia were to use its influence or if it were to engage in aggressive behavior toward Ukraine (Geopolitical Futures, 2021). In the meantime, however, at the end of November 2021, some sanctions were reimposed in connection with the pipeline. Specifically, these sanctions targeted a Russian company and two vessels involved in the project (Reuters, 2021). Moreover, insurers seemed to fear even further sanctions in connection with the project (Cohn & Ridley, 2021). This was before the Ukrainian invasion. Currently, Nord Stream 2 is subject to strict sanctions, and Germany's position, at least for the time being, is not favorable to the operationalization of the pipeline.

ENERGY SECURITY IN EUROPE AND THE CONTRIBUTION OF THE NORD STREAM 2 PIPELINE TO ACHIEVING IT

This section deals with the concept of energy security in Europe in detail and seeks to explain if, and to what extent, the gas that would have been delivered to Europe via Nord Stream 2 would have actually contributed to or hindered the attainment of energy security on the continent—or at least in the EU. In a recent EU Parliament briefing, a great deal of attention was given to the impact that the pipeline could have had on energy security in the EU.

There are two views that the briefing addresses. The first view is one mainly propounded by Nord Stream 2 AG (the consortium of companies involved in the project) and, implicitly, Germany, the two actors with the most at stake in the completion and operation of the pipeline. According to this view (at least initially), Nord Stream 2 would contribute to energy security in Europe. This view is based on the prediction that the EU's demand for natural gas will increase by 120 bcm by 2035 (European Parliament, 2021). However, the operational capacity of Nord Stream 2 would not have exceeded 55 bcm. Therefore, not only is

Nord Stream 2 necessary to fill in the ever-growing demand gap, but it would not even be sufficient. Additionally, while this would not have necessarily led to a diversification of suppliers, it would have led to a diversification of supply routes, which could have benefitted other EU member states, such as the Czech Republic (European Parliament, 2021).

The European Parliament's briefing, however, also raises questions concerning the negative impact that Nord Stream 2 may have had on energy security (specifically, security of supply). This view is shared by the European Commission, which points to an increased dependence on Russia. This increased dependency would lead to a negative impact on security of supply in the EU (European Parliament, 2021). In other words, instead of diversifying sources and suppliers, the EU would have deepened an already-complicated relationship with its main gas supplier. Another argument raised by the EU Commission was related to Nord Stream 2's capacity to fill in the ensuing gaps that would arise in the future owing to increased demand. In fact, the existing pipelines transporting gas from Russia to Europe and to Turkey have a capacity of nearly 300 bcm, whereas only two-thirds of that was used in 2019 (European Parliament, 2021).

Finally, as aptly pointed out by the European Commission, the Ukrainian risk (namely, that Nord Stream 2 would allow Moscow to bypass existing Ukrainian pipelines when delivering gas to Europe) was more than an altruistic concern for the security of Ukraine. It would also have a negative impact on EU energy security:

> [I]f Nord Stream 2 is intended to replace, rather than supplement the Ukrainian route, that is worrying from an energy security perspective, as it would leave Europe with three main supply routes (the Nord Stream pipelines, Yamal and—once interconnecting pipelines are in place—TurkStream), instead of four at present, resulting in less flexibility rather than more. (European Parliament, 2021)

No discussion on energy security in Europe, in general, and in the EU, in particular, would be complete in the context of the present volume without also focusing on the impact that the energy transition may have on already existing energy sources and supplies. Of course, this complicates the picture even more from one point of view. At the same time, it might also shed additional light on the practical benefits that Nord Stream 2 may have brought about.

Policy-wise, the EU seeks to move away from fossil fuels and rely instead on renewable sources of energy. A practical application of this policy is that, by 2030, the bloc should rely on renewable sources of energy for at least 32 % of its energy mix. This is according to the recast *Renewable Energy Directive* (EU Directive 2018/2001), which establishes a *binding* target of 32 % reliance on renewable energy sources in the EU's energy consumption by 2030. According to Article 3 of the Directive, "[EU] Member States shall collectively ensure that the share of energy from renewable sources in the Union's gross final consumption of energy in 2030 is at least 32 %." In practice, however, things are a little more complicated. The move toward renewable energy sources will not be as smooth as envisioned. The situation on the ground shows that there are different perceptions in the EU as to what constitutes energy security and, more importantly, the role of renewables in it. For instance, as shown by Mata Pérez et al. (2019), there are two broad positions, or clusters, formed around different EU member states and their approaches to the future role of renewables in attaining their energy security needs.

There are states that are particularly concerned with diversifying their supply of gas, owing especially to their dependence on Russian gas; they also tend to have a short- to medium-term view of attaining their supply needs, thus considering the switch to renewable energy sources of lower importance than avoiding shocks (both concerning supply and price; Mata Pérez et al., 2019, p. 2). These tend to be Eastern European states, such as Poland and other Visegrad group members.

In the other category are EU states that are developed economically and whose consumers are relatively insensitive to increases in prices that may be brought about by the switch to more environmentally friendly energy sources; such states may also find business opportunities in the switch to renewable energy sources (Mata Pérez et al., 2019, p. 2). For these states, switching to renewable energy sources not only serves an environmental (and perhaps business) purpose but also has the added benefit that this will beneficially contribute to energy security in the EU. Since it will diversify their energy mix, it will also decrease their reliance on current suppliers (Mata Pérez et al., 2019, p. 2). These states are mostly Western European.

At the same time, it is important to point out that Nord Stream 2 created divisions, not along the traditional lines mentioned above, as opponents to Nord Stream 2 come from both groups mentioned in the previous paragraph. For instance, alongside the Baltic states' opposition to the operationalization of the pipeline, one could also see states such as the United Kingdom and Ireland (LSM.lv, 2021).

In this light, it is doubtful whether Nord Stream 2 would actually have brought tangible benefits to energy security in Europe and in the EU in particular. Looking at the sometimes diverging interests of the two clusters of states mentioned earlier, Nord Stream 2's operation may have affected states in each of the two categories. In other words, we may be looking at a point of convergence in this regard, thus raising doubts as to the pipeline's impact on energy security. States in the first cluster stand to lose because of their continued reliance on Russian gas and, thus, a lack of diversification of suppliers and supply routes. Perhaps there could even be a reduction in supply routes, if one were to take into consideration the EU's Parliament position concerning the risk to Ukrainian routes. The states in the second category may also have stood to lose from the impact of Nord Stream 2 on energy security in Europe for the same reasons concerning a lack of diversification. In this case, the picture is also complicated by the unknown demand needs of such states. To what extent will renewables acquire a larger share of the market? As such, how much does Nord Stream 2 AG's assessment of future (gas) demand reflect the real situation? It is hard to answer this question, especially when looking almost a decade into the future.

All these considerations are further complicated by the fact that alternative energy sources (from different suppliers), such as LNG, are not readily available. For instance, the LNG terminal at Brunsbuettel faces major investment problems. Even if those obstacles were to be overcome, it would only become operational by the end of 2022 at the earliest (Bloomberg, 2021).

At the same time, it is quite difficult to simply accept that Nord Stream 2 would not have contributed to energy security in the EU just because it stems from (and might have increased reliance on) Russia. This seems to be the strongest argument used by its detractors, together with the risk of giving Moscow an additional incentive to abuse its position. However, as antitrust economists, lawyers, and policymakers are already aware, big does not necessarily mean bad (of course, this is open to debate, but the point remains that a great number of people in that field share that view). A dominant position does not automatically translate to abuse (Dunne, 2020). At the same time, it makes complete sense to prepare against such outcomes, and Germany's promise to attempt to avoid them is justified in light of how current events are unfolding. However, from preparing to such outcomes to completely opposing Nord Stream 2 is a long way to go (at least if one ignores the Ukrainian invasion and analyses the facts as they were before the invasion occurred).

It is also important to remind the reader that the concept of energy security is quite broad, sometimes to the point of becoming vague. As such, one can manipulate that concept according to their own interests. However, if one were to reduce *energy security* to its essential characteristics (or to its narrowest understanding), there seems to be a consensus that it refers to the possibility for a state to secure its energy needs at an affordable price (Chester, 2010, pp. 887–895; Mata Pérez et al., 2019, p. 2, fn 4; Szulecki, 2018, p. 5). In other words, security of supply seems to be the common denominator. In this case, does Nord Stream 2 still seem to have been as antagonistic to energy security as it seemed initially? A definitive answer is still very hard to offer, but it would have increased the energy supply. Furthermore, as long as Eastern European interests would not have been affected, it may even have fit the definition of energy security as understood in a narrow sense. Of course, it is hard to argue this anymore, although not exclusively because of Nord Stream 2. Because of this, checks were, and are, needed to prevent possible risks that may arise. One such risk is a possible Russian abuse of its position, which happened. And this is what led to the suspension of the project and possibly its cancelation. Put differently, Nord Stream 2 could have contributed in a beneficial way to security of energy supply in the EU had it not been for Moscow abusing its position.

ECONOMIC SANCTIONS IMPOSED AGAINST AND CONCERNING NORD STREAM 2

At this point, the question that needs to be answered here is the following: *Will the imposition of sanctions related to the Nord Stream 2 pipeline by the United States affect energy security in Europe and, more specifically, in the EU, and if so, to what extent*?

As seen in the previous section, answering this question is not straightforward. Firstly, there is no clear answer as to what constitutes energy security in the EU or, more generally, Europe. Secondly, even if there can somehow be an answer, it will not be possible to clearly pinpoint the essence of energy security and its main elements. That is why the EU's Parliament briefing aptly shows how conflicting answers can be given to this question. As such, we will take the last stance taken in the previous section, namely that it would have been possible for Nord Stream 2 to contribute to energy security—at least in the EU—if the term *energy security* is understood as security of energy supply at affordable prices. This assumption also implies that Russia would not abuse its power. Since Russia, however, abused its position, this complicated matters further and led to the suspension (or even cancelation) of the project. Thus, checks and balances were in place to react to this, as Germany promised. As such, it is assumed in the present discussion that Nord Stream 2 could have contributed to energy security in Europe if the invasion had not taken place without necessarily reaching a definite conclusion on this point.

So, how did sanctions impact the construction and future operation of Nord Stream 2? Or, if this is still difficult to pinpoint, what was their purpose? What was Washington trying to achieve? Apparently, the ideal result would have been the prevention of the eventual operation of the pipeline (The Economist, 2021a). This was also evident from U.S. Secretary of State Anthony Blinken's declaration back in May 2021, when sanctions were waived:

> *Today's actions demonstrate the Administration's commitment to energy security in Europe, consistent with the President's pledge to rebuild relationships with our allies and partners in Europe. We will continue to oppose the completion of this project, which would weaken European energy security and that of Ukraine and Eastern flank NATO and EU countries. Our opposition to the Nord Stream 2 pipeline is unwavering. Though we may not always agree,*

ong, and our position is in line with our commitment to strengthen our ...nships as a matter of national security, according to an official statement ... States Department of State. (Blinken, 2021a)

... interesting to note, however, is that the sanctions imposed in late N... ...r 2021 were justified under the Protecting Europe's Energy Security Act (PE...A) of 2019:

Today's report is in line with the United States' continuing opposition to the Nord Stream 2 pipeline and the U.S. Government's continued compliance with PEESA. With today's action, the Administration has now sanctioned 8 persons and identified 17 of their vessels as blocked property pursuant to PEESA in connection with Nord Stream 2. Even as the Administration continues to oppose the Nord Stream 2 pipeline, including via our sanctions, we continue to work with Germany and other allies and partners to reduce the risks posed by the pipeline to Ukraine and frontline NATO and EU countries and to push back against harmful Russian activities, including in the energy sphere, according to a press report stemming from the Department of State. (Blinken, 2021b)

What comes across from the above is that the declared reason—even the legal justification—for the imposition of sanctions connected to Nord Stream 2 was, during those moments, the safeguarding of Europe's energy security. However, as already demonstrated, the fluidity of this concept allows different stakeholders to decide what energy security means for them and, in turn, to selectively address the parts of energy security that suit their interests. Compare the American approach to what European energy security means and that of the European Parliament. At no point did the Department of State acknowledge, or even accept, the possibility that Nord Stream 2 may also have had a positive impact on energy security in Europe—at least as it concerns security of supply. It is also important to mention that neither the PEESA nor the guidance that is available regarding this act (U.S. Department of State, 2021) contains any indication as to what may actually be considered *European energy security*. In other words, there is no objective way of assessing what can be considered *European energy security* under the U.S. legal framework applicable to the issue. This leads to even more questions regarding the real reasons behind the imposition of sanctions concerning Nord Stream 2.

Moreover, shortly after the PEESA was enacted, a member of the European Parliament asked the EU Commission, among others, about the latter's stance on this U.S. act (European Parliament, 2020a). The Commission's answer to this question shows that the European bloc may not necessarily have considered the U.S. act as beneficial to Europe's energy security:

The Commission is aware of the Bill introduced to the United States (US) Congress, cited as 'Protecting Europe's Energy Security Clarification Act of 2020' and is closely monitoring developments. As a matter of principle, (as indicated in the response to Question E-001783/2020), the EU opposes the imposition of sanctions against EU

> companies conducting legitimate business [footnote omitted] and systematically conveys this message to the US. The Commission's objective has always been to ensure that if built Nord Stream 2, as well as the Turkish Stream pipeline, operate in a transparent and non-discriminatory way with the appropriate degree of regulatory oversight, in line with key principles of international law and EU energy law. (European Parliament, 2020b)

In other words, one can see the same stance here as evidenced earlier by Germany—that is, Nord Stream 2, per se, should not necessarily have been considered detrimental to Europe's energy security, as long as appropriate checks and balances would have been in place to prevent abuse on Russia's part. However, the United States seems to have had a different opinion from the beginning. It seems to have considered Nord Stream 2 as damaging to European stakeholders' interests by default. In other words, there seems to be a clear disconnect between the stated aim—protecting Europe's energy security—and the real aim, which was to completely stop Nord Stream 2 from becoming operational.

In fairness to U.S. policies and lawmakers, the act did deal with European, and not necessarily EU, energy security, hence the heavy focus on Ukrainian interests and the risks that may have been brought about by Nord Stream 2 concerning the former's energy security. However, it is not as if the European Parliament's briefing did not address this issue also or as if the EU or Germany were not concerned with preventing Russia's abuse of its position. In fact, the EU itself has been a respondent in investment arbitral proceedings (the way disputes between foreign investors and host states or host regional economic integration organizations, such as the EU, are settled) brought by Nord Stream 2 AG. The latter brought the claim against the EU for extension of the EU rules on the separation of gas producers and gas distributors (avoiding vertical integration; *Nord Stream 2 AG v. the European Union*, PCA Case No. 2020–7, July 3, 2020). This change was done via the amendment of the EU's Gas Directive (*Directive 2009/73/EC of the European Parliament and of the Council (…) concerning common rules for the internal market in natural gas (…)*). The intended purpose, according to Nord Stream 2 AG, was for this legal act to also apply to Nord Stream 2

Another interesting aspect is that the strategy of European states in which the Nord Stream 2 consortium companies are located was not necessarily opposed to the imposition of sanctions, even before the Ukrainian invasion (at least not vehemently). Even Germany, perhaps Nord Stream 2's strongest supporter behind Russia, seems to have accepted the imposition of sanctions if certain lines were to be crossed (for instance, if Russia were to weaponize energy or invade Ukraine; Puglierin, 2022), which happened and to which Germany reacted. Austria, on the other hand, seemed rather opposed to sanctions imposed against Nord Stream 2 by the EU before the invasion. This could be because of several factors, including Vienna's dependence on Russian gas and its vested interest in OMV, a consortium partner in Nord Stream 2 (Reuters, 2022). France and the United Kingdom (the two other states that are home to Nord Stream 2 consortium companies) seemed to have a stronger stance regarding sanctions targeting Nord Stream 2—again, even before the Russian invasion (Politico, 2022a; Clean Energy Wire, 2022).

CONCLUSION

U.S. sanctions could not stop Nord Stream 2 from being finalized, although this was their clear aim. They did not seem to be able to stop the pipeline from becoming operational, at least not before the Ukrainian invasion. In this case, it is not the sanctions themselves that halted the project but the newfound political will of states such as Germany. Before the Russian aggression in Ukraine, a few legal and administrative hurdles had remained to be overcome. At that moment, it seemed like a matter of time before Russian gas would be delivered to Europe via this pipeline. However, the reason for which the sanctions themselves did not reach the stated aim was complicated, and specific reasons are hard to pinpoint. One could venture to say that Germany's interest and deep involvement in the Nord Stream 2 project could have acted as a counterweight (Colibasanu, 2022). It is possible that the United States took a diplomatic step back, considering its relationship with Germany as more important than doing everything in its power to prevent the operation of the pipeline. Again, this supposition is based on events as they unfolded before the invasion of Ukraine by Russia.

However, if the precise impact of sanctions cannot be pinpointed, it was possible to show that their declared aim was apparently different from their real, practical aim. Of course, the present situation involving Ukraine's territorial sovereignty complicates matters. However, in the moments before the invasion unfolded and especially in those moments in which what transpired had been unlikely, the U.S. position raised questions. This was evident from the way in which the U.S. policymakers approached the concept of *European energy security*. They insisted on the negative impact that the Nord Stream 2 pipeline might have had on this type of interest while completely ignoring the possible benefits. The U.S. position was unlike that of the European Parliament (and, to a certain extent, the European Commission), which took a much more balanced approach to the issue. The EU bloc essentially accepted the risks (e.g., the risk of Russian abuse, which materialized) but also considered the benefits. The EU went as far as possible to look at possible checks and balances to prevent abuse on Russia's part or at least take some concrete steps in that direction. Moreover, Brussels also showed how, practically, it would pursue this—for example, via the amendment of the EU's Gas Directive so that it applied to Nord Stream 2 AG and ensured that no vertical integration could be attained by the latter in the European gas sector.

It is very difficult, at this point, to look a decade into the future and predict whether Gazprom's promise that Nord Stream 2 would simply bridge a widening gap between demand and supply would have materialized. Current events raise questions about the future operationalization of Nord Stream 2 and EU-Russia energy relations. What is clear is that the United States was attempting to completely prevent the operation of Nord Stream 2, choosing to focus only on the risks while overlooking possible benefits. To that extent, it is doubtful whether its acts could have safeguarded European energy security. In fact, one could reasonably ask whether Washington's acts would have reduced European energy security. The conclusion of this chapter shows that this is a real possibility—at least as long as one assumes that energy security means access to adequate and affordable energy. Of course, whether those acts had other benefits is a pertinent question. However, strictly in terms of energy security and judging them on their merits (referring to the moment at which they occurred), there seems to be less clarity.

NOTE

1 The author would like to thank the anonymous reviewers for their comments and suggestions. All the mistakes are, of course, the author's responsibility.

REFERENCES

Balfour, R. (Carnegie Europe) (2022, March 8). *What Russia's war in Ukraine means for Europe*. Retrieved March 14, 2022, from https://carnegieeurope.eu/strategiceurope/86587

Beckley, M. (2018). *Unrivaled: Why America will remain the world's sole superpower*. Cornell University Press.

Blinken, A. J. (2021a, May 19). *Nord Stream 2 and European energy security*. Retrieved December 6, 2021, from https://www.state.gov/nord-stream-2-and-european-energy-security

Blinken, A. J. (2021b, November 22). *Imposition of further sanctions in connection with Nord Stream 2*. Retrieved December 6, 2021, from https://www.state.gov/imposition-of-further-sanctions-in-connection-with-nord-stream-2

Bloomberg. (2021, December 30). *German gas terminal faces headwinds as major investor steps back*. Retrieved February 16, 2022, from https://www.bloomberg.com/news/articles/2021-12-30/german-lng-terminal-faces-headwinds-as-major-investor-steps-back

Brooks, S. G., & Wohlforth, W. C. (2016). The rise and fall of the great powers in the twenty-first century: China's rise and the fate of America's global position. *International Security*, *40*(3), 7–53. https://doi.org/10.1162/isec_a_00225

Chester, L. (2010). Conceptualising energy security and making explicit its polysemic nature. *Energy Policy*, *38*, 887.

Clean Energy Wire. (2022, January 25). *UK calls for end to Nord Stream 2 in event of Russian attack on Ukraine*. Retrieved February 16, 2022, from https://www.cleanenergywire.org/news/uk-calls-end-nord-stream-2-event-russian-attack-ukraine

Cohn, C., & Ridley, K. (2021, December 1). *Analysis: European insurers fear sanctions coming down Nord Stream 2 pipe*. Reuters. Retrieved December 5, 2021, from https://www.reuters.com/markets/commodities/european-insurers-fear-sanctions-coming-down-nord-stream-2-pipe-2021-12-01/

Colibasanu, A. (2022, February 9). *How Germany's energy needs limit sanctions on Russia*. Retrieved February 11, 2022, from https://geopoliticalfutures.com/how-germanys-energy-needs-limit-sanctions-on-russia

Congressional Research Service. (2022, March 10). *Russia's Nord Stream 2 natural gas pipeline to Germany halted*. Retrieved March 14, 2022, from https://crsreports.congress.gov/product/pdf/IF/IF11138

Dunne, N. (2020, December 11). *The antitrust anticonsensus*. Project Syndicate. Retrieved December 6, 2021, from https://www.project-syndicate.org/onpoint/antitrust-competition-law-end-of-old-consensus-by-niamh-dunne-2020-12

Economist, The. (2021a, July 15). *Why Nord Stream 2 is the world's most controversial energy project*. Retrieved December 5, 2021, from https://www-economist-com.eu1.proxy.openathens.net/the-economist-explains/2021/07/14/why-nord-stream-2-is-the-worlds-most-controversial-energy-project

Economist, The. (2021b, December 4). *Nord Stream 2 could still sabotage German-American relations*. Retrieved December 5, 2021, from https://www-economist-com.eu1.proxy.openathens.net/europe/2021/12/04/nord-stream-2-could-still-sabotage-german-american-relations

European Parliament. (2020a, May 27). *Question for written answer E-003209/2020 to the Commission. Subject: 2019 US law on protecting Europe's security of energy supply*. Retrieved December 6, 2021, from https://www.europarl.europa.eu/doceo/document/E-9-2020-003209_EN.html

European Parliament. (2020b, September 11). *Answer given by Ms. Simson on behalf of the European Commission* (Question reference: E-003209/2020). Retrieved December 6, 2021, from https://www.europarl.europa.eu/doceo/document/E-9-2020-003209-ASW_EN.html

European Parliament. (2021, July). *The Nord Stream 2 pipeline. Economic, environmental and geopolitical issues*. Retrieved December 5, 2021, from https://www.europarl.europa.eu/RegData/etudes/BRIE/2021/690705/EPRS_BRI(2021)690705_EN.pdf

Financial Times. (2022a, February 23). *Germany's Nord Stream 2 decision shows sanctions on Russia haven't worked*. Retrieved March 14, 2022, from https://www.ft.com/content/3d5b851a-02eb-4bd6-b7a4-1cda74b108f5

Financial Times. (2022b, March 8). *Uniper takes €1bn Nord Stream 2 hit and signals shift from Russian gas*. Retrieved March 14, 2022, from https://www.ft.com/content/e1baff27-1032-47ee-8bbf-630a1c05c999

Francisco, A. (2010). Neopatrimonialism in Contemporary African Politics. E-International Relations. https://www.e-ir.info/2010/01/24/to-what-extent-can-neopatrimonialism-be-considered-significant-in-contemporary-african-politics/

Gaddis, J. L. (2018). *On grand strategy*. Penguin.

Gazprom. (n.d). *Nord Stream 2. A new export gas pipeline running from Russia to Europe across the Baltic Sea*. Retrieved December 5, 2021, from https://www.gazprom.com/projects/nord-stream2

Geopolitical Futures. (2021, August 27). *Nord Stream 2 nears completion*. Retrieved December 5, 2021, from https://geopoliticalfutures.com/nord-stream-2-nears-completion

Ismailov, E., & Papava, V. (2010). *Rethinking Central Asia*. Central Asia-Caucausus Institute Silk Road Studies Program. http://www.silkroadstudies.org/resources/pdf/Monographs/2010_MONO_Ismailov-Papava_Rethinking-Central-Eurasia.pdf

LSM.lv. (2021, August 2). *Baltic states and other condemn Nord Stream 2 pipeline*. Retrieved February 16, 2022, from https://eng.lsm.lv/article/politics/diplomacy/baltic-states-and-others-condemn-nord-stream-2-pipeline.a415295/

Mackinder, H. J. (1942). *Democratic ideals and reality. A study in the politics of reconstruction*. National Defense University Press.

Mackinnon, A., Gramer, R., & Detsch, J. (2021, July 23). *The Russian pipeline that turned into a lightning rod. How Nord Stream 2 made everyone in Washington mad at one another.* Foreign Policy. https://foreignpolicy.com/2021/07/23/nord-stream-2-pipeline-russia-us-ted-cruz/

Marineau, S. (2021, August 4). *What the lifting of US Sanctions means for the Nord Stream 2 pipeline*. The Conversation. Retrieved December 5, 2021, from https://theconversation.com/what-the-lifting-of-us-sanctions-means-for-the-nord-stream-2-pipeline-165275

Marshall, T. (2019). *Revenge of geography*. Elliott and Thompson.

Mata Pérez, M. de la E., Scholten, D., & Smith Stegen, K. (2019). The multi-speed energy transition in Europe: Opportunities and challenges for EU energy security. *Energy Strategy Reviews*, *26*, 100415. https://doi.org/10.1016/j.esr.2019.100415

McDougall, K., Reisinger, S. H., & Greewood, S. (2022, November 6). *Update on US sanctions in respect of Nord Stream 2 and Turkstream pipelines*. Norton Rose Fulbright. https://www.nortonrosefulbright.com/en/knowledge/publications/542bab55/us-house-approves-nord-stream-2-and-turkstream-sanctions-adoption-appears-likely

McMaster, H. R. (2020). *Battlegrounds. The fight to defend the free world* (William Collins); *Nord Stream 2 AG v. the European Union* (July 3, 2020). PCA Case No. 2020–07. Claimant Memorial of July 3, 2020. https://www.italaw.com/cases/8187

Nord Stream 2. (n.d.). *Fact Sheet: The Nord Stream 2 project*. Retrieved December 6, 2021, from https://www.nord-stream2.com/media/documents/pdf/en/2018/07/factsheet-project-en.pdf

Openhoff. (2022, February 24). *Ukraine conflict: European Union and the USA impose sanctions against Russia*. Retrieved March 14, 2022, from https://www.oppenhoff.eu/en/news-detail/ukraine-conflict-european-union-and-usa-impose-sanctions-against-russia

Palacio, A. (2022, March 14). *Germany awakens*. Project Syndicate. Retrieved March 14, 2022, from https://www.project-syndicate.org/commentary/german-policy-shift-after-russia-invasion-of-ukraine-by-ana-palacio-2022-03

Politico. (2022a, January 28). *Nord Stream 2 could be hit in Russia sanctions, France says*. Retrieved February 16, 2022, from https://www.politico.eu/article/nord-stream-2-russia-sanctions-french-foreign-minister-le-drian/

Politico. (2022b, February 22). *Germany shelves Nord Stream 2 pipeline*. Retrieved March 14, 2022, from https://www.politico.eu/article/germany-to-stop-nord-stream-2/

Politico. (2022c, February 28). *Shell to divest from Gazprom, Nord Stream 2*. Retrieved March 14, 2022, from https://www.politico.eu/article/shell-to-divest-from-gazprom-nord-stream-2/

Proedrou, F. (2018). *Energy policy and security under climate* change. Palgrave Macmillan.

Protecting Europe's Energy Security Act (PEESA) (Sec. 7503 of FY2020 NDAA), as amended (by FY2021 NDAA Sec. 1242). (n.d.). https://www.state.gov/wp-content/uploads/2021/04/PEESA-Sec.7503-of-FY2020-NDAA-as-amended-by-FY2021-NDAA-Sec.-1242.pdf

Puglierin, J. (2022, January 19). *Sanctions in the pipeline: Germany's troubles over Russia and Nord Stream 2.* European Council on Foreign Relations. Retrieved February 16, 2022, from https://ecfr.eu/article/sanctions-in-the-pipeline-germanys-troubles-over-russia-and-nord-stream-2/

Reuters. (2021, 23 November). *U.S. imposes further sanctions in connection with Nord Stream 2 gas pipeline.* Retrieved December 5, 2021, from https://www.reuters.com/business/energy/us-imposes-further-sanctions-connection-with-nord-stream-2-gas-pipeline-2021-11-22/

Reuters. (2022, 12 February). *Austria resists including Nord Stream 2 in EU package of Russia sanctions.* Retrieved February 16, from https://www.reuters.com/world/europe/austria-resists-including-nord-stream-2-eu-package-russia-sanctions-2022-02-11/

Shagina, M., & Westphal, K. (2021, July 28). *Nord Stream 2 and the energy security dilemma. Opportunities, options and obstacles for a grand bargain.* German Institute for International and Security Affairs, SWP Comment 2021/C 46. Retrieved November 3, 2021, from https://www.swp-berlin.org/en/publication/nord-stream-2-and-the-energy-security-dilemma

Soldatkin, V. (2021, September 10). *Russia completes Nord Stream 2 construction, gas flows yet to start.* Reuters. Retrieved December 5, 2021, from https://www.reuters.com/business/energy/russias-gazprom-says-it-has-completed-nord-stream-2-construction-2021-09-10/

Szulecki, K. (2018). The multiple faces of energy security: An introduction. In *Energy security in Europe. divergent perceptions and policy challenges.* Palgrave Macmillan.

Szulecki, K., & Westphal, K. (2018). Taking security seriously in EU energy governance: Crimean shock and the energy union. In K. Szulecki (Ed.), *Energy security in Europe. divergent perceptions and policy challenges.* Palgrave Macmillan.

Temnycky, M. (2021, July 12). *Nord Stream 2 and the tangled interests of Germany, Poland, and Ukraine.* Wilson Center, Focus Ukraine. Retrieved December 5, 2021, from https://www.wilsoncenter.org/blog-post/nord-stream-2-and-tangled-interests-germany-poland-and-ukraine

Tsafos, N. (2021, August 4). *Beyond Nord Stream 2.* Center for Strategic & International Studies. Retrieved December 6, 2021, from https://www.csis.org/analysis/beyond-nord-stream-2

U.S. Department of State. (2021, April 9). *Protecting Europe's Energy Security Act (PEESA), as amended, guidance.* Retrieved December 6, 2021, from https://www.state.gov/protecting-europes-energy-security-act-peesa/

U.S. Department of Treasury. (2022, February 23). *PEESA designations; issuance of Russia-related general license.* Retrieved March 14, 2022, from https://home.treasury.gov/policy-issues/financial-sanctions/recent-actions/20220223_33

Van de Graaf, T. (2013). *The politics and institutions of global energy governance.* Palgrave Macmillan.

Wattenegel, J. (2021, September 9). *Gas pipeline Nord Stream 2 links Germany to Russia, but splits Europe.* Clean Energy Wire. Retrieved December 5, 2021, from https://www.cleanenergywire.org/factsheets/gas-pipeline-nord-stream-2-links-germany-russia-splits-europe

WION (2022, February 8). *Biden pledges "No Nord Stream 2 if Russia invades Ukraine."* Retrieved February 16, 2022, from https://www.youtube.com/watch?v=62J5Nf18I_U

Zengerle, P. (2021, June 7). *Blinken: U.S. able to mitigate Nord Stream 2 pipeline effects.* Reuters. Retrieved December 5, 2021, from https://www.reuters.com/business/energy/blinken-us-working-with-germany-mitigate-nord-stream-2-effects-2021-06-07

Zolotova, E. (2021, November 17). *Is Russia planning another assault in Ukraine?* Geopolitical Futures. Retrieved December 5, 2021, from https://geopoliticalfutures.com/is-russia-planning-another-assault-in-ukraine

Zuev, V. (2020). Setting up a global system for sustainable energy governance. In M. Hafner & S. Tagliapietra (Eds.), *The geopolitics of the global energy transition.* Springer.

CHAPTER 8

The COVID-19 Pandemic and the Energy Transition: The Geopolitics of Energy Envisaged by American Politics

FERNANDA DELGADO, JOÃO MARQUES CARDOSO,
AND VICTOR GASPAR FILHO

INTRODUCTION

In this chapter, we intend to explore the COVID-19 pandemic as a phenomenon that consolidates the energy transition in the United States (U.S.) as a path to both economic recovery and climate crisis mitigation. The pandemic, according to the International Monetary Fund's (2021) World Economic Outlook, triggered global economy and trade volume to shrink by 3.1 % and 8.2 %, respectively, in 2020, with advanced economies, including that of the U.S., weakening by more than the global average. Regarding energy data, the 70th BP Statistical Review of World Energy (2021) points out that the pandemic dramatically impacted energy markets in 2020. Primary energy consumption and carbon emissions from energy experienced the largest decline rates seen since the Second World War, falling by 4.5 % and 6.3 %, respectively (BP, 2021). Almost three-quarters of the net decline in energy demand net was represented by oil, whose production fell by 6.6 million barrels per day (b/d) and whose consumption was reduced by 9.1 million b/d (BP, 2021). The U.S. contributed more than any other country to the decline of the global energy supply and demand, as the country's oil demand was reduced by 2.3 million b/d, and its oil supply fell by 600,000 b/d (BP, 2021). Notwithstanding the concerning effect on the fundamentals of the supply and demand of the petroleum market, the markets for renewable energy sources, such as wind, solar, and hydropower, grew, making the U.S. the world's second-largest contributor of renewable power. Thus, the global COVID-19 infection has significantly impacted the economic trajectory and oil market of the U.S. However, as this work aims to show, the pandemic also encouraged U.S. policymakers to fill the gap between policies concerned with economic growth and the transition to a low-carbon future. In this regard, the energy market is crucial to mitigating carbon emissions and providing solutions.

Following a qualitative analysis of U.S. documents issued in 2021, we intend to point out the most significant measures taken by the American federal government during the first months of the Joe Biden and Kamala Harris administration to determine the scale of the energy transition and the role of fossil fuels (oil, natural gas, and coal) in the energy sector the following years. Through a case study on the American policy during President Joe Biden's administration, the authors target the principal axes of the country's energy revolution and economic instruments. Through a comprehensive analysis of Joe Biden's first year in office, we present an overview of the most notable actions taken by the U.S. federal government to foster the energy transition while recovering from the economic impacts of the COVID-19 pandemic and tackling the global climate crisis by encouraging the use of renewable sources and low-carbon energy solutions. We infer that it is possible to identify such convergence of domestic and foreign policies proposed for the energy sector by the Biden administration. However, a significant gap is also analyzed regarding domestic policies discouraging investments in fossil fuels to impose political pressure on oil-producing countries to enhance crude oil production and ease escalating fuel prices. The authors believe that the analysis of the first year of the administration will aid future discussions on the American approach to the energy transition during Joe Biden's term as president.

The work presented in the current chapter is based on a selection of executive orders, federal plans submitted to congress, and documents from two multilateral meetings held in 2021 to discuss the challenges facing the energy transition according to reports from specialized institutions such as the International Energy Agency (IEA).

The government documents analyzed were the Executive Order on Addressing the Threat to the Domestic Supply Chain from Reliance on Critical Minerals from Foreign Adversaries (Exec. Order No. 13953, 2020), the Executive Order on America's Supply Chains (Exec. Order No, 14017, 2021), the Executive Order on Climate-Related Financial Risk (Exec. Order No. 14030, 2021), and Executive Order on Tackling the Climate Crisis at Home and Abroad (Exec. Order No. 140082021, 2021). We also analyze the following communiqués and press releases of the above-mentioned international meetings: Carbis Bay G7 Summit Communique (G7, 2021), Brussels Summit Communiqué (North Atlantic Treaty Organization, 2021), FACT SHEET: President Biden and G7 Leaders

Launch Build Back Better World (B3W) Partnership (White House, 2021, June 12), Leaders' Summit on Climate (U.S. Department of State, 2021a, b). Data from the Paris Agreement (United Nations Framework Convention on Climate Change, 2015) are also presented in the chapter.

Associations with climate risks are identified throughout the analyzed material. Circumstantial measures in the documents that appear to be designed to circumvent the current economic crisis are meant to be durable and developed over the following years and decades. Most of the documents mention a whole-of-government approach to climate and energy matters. When not explicitly mentioned, several agencies and departments tasked with carrying out domestic and international efforts regarding the subjects are listed.

THE ALIGNMENT OF CLIMATE AND ENERGY IN U.S. POLICY

During Joe Biden's presidential campaign, he announced that, if elected, he would invite world leaders for a virtual summit on climate, which took place in April 2021. Forty international leaders met after the U.S. returned to the Paris Agreement. According to John Kerry, the U.S. special presidential envoy for climate, the Leaders' Summit on Climate gathered a diverse group of countries, including oil-producing, biodiverse-rich, landlocked, and small developing island states. Each country brought its own capacities and demands to curb GHG emissions and to adapt to the irreversible effects of climate change, considering that the Earth's temperature has already increased by around 1.2°C compared to pre-industrial levels, and the margin to limit this increase to 1.5°C, as Kerry mentioned, is very narrow, thus requiring more ambitious goals and effective plans (Kerry, 2021). During the summit, developed countries such as Japan and Canada announced more elaborate ambitions to reduce their greenhouse gas (GHG) emissions by 40 % by 2030. The U.S., in turn, stated that it would lower its carbon emissions by 50 %–52 % by 2030 (Kerry, 2021).

Considering the efforts for carbon neutrality, the climate agenda is also an energy agenda calling for the transition from fossil fuels to clean and renewable energy sources. However, the negative effects of this transition on fossil fuels' value chains and the high global dependence on them will make it difficult to achieve. Challenges will arise in terms of employment generation, access to electricity, gender equality in the energy sector, and each country's specificities regarding available energy sources, consumers' choices, and access to financing. In this sense, the COVID-19 pandemic has strengthened the social justice element of the energy transition, as the economic recovery and the energy security objectives might be given more importance than the climate agenda.

According to Batini et al. (2021), the impacts triggered by the pandemic are driving governments to adopt economic recovery measures. However, these measures might not be completely aligned with climate goals because stimulus packages continue to fund non-climate-friendly industries and promote oil consumption (Batini et al., 2021). Thus, the challenge is to align climate goals with a just energy transition that leaves no country or community behind. Green projects help mitigate GHG emissions and develop nature-based negative emissions technologies while creating jobs and delivering high short-term financial returns. Batini et al. (2021) estimated investment multipliers to quantify the impact on GDP of green stimuli measures. Accordingly, the total increase in GDP is many times greater than the original increase in green spending, as every dollar spent on carbon-neutral activities generates more than a dollar's worth of economic activity (Batini et al., 2021). Compared to fossil fuel energy investments, green spending multipliers are about two to seven times greater, depending on the sector, technology, and horizon (Batini et al., 2021).

The U.S. documents analyzed in this chapter indicate that the U.S. government recognizes the risk imposed on the fossil fuels market by the energy transition and seeks different ways to mitigate potential adverse impacts. Different types of financing have been proposed to alleviate the shift away from fossil fuels and adapt to the new conditions while avoiding climate-related supply chain disruptions (Exec. Order No. 14030, 2021).

For instance, the Jobs Plan (White House, 2021, March 31) is designed to mobilize over USD 2 trillion over the next decade. The amount to be invested in the clean energy sector is around USD 27 billion, which includes eliminating tax preferences for fossil fuels, as well as a proposal for restoring payments from major industry polluters (White House, 2021, March 31). At the same time, the plan proposes that the federal government will be responsible for boosting the economy through federal procurements aimed primarily at critical technologies, citing advanced nuclear reactors and nuclear fuel; USD 46 billion will be allocated for this purpose. Furthermore, the transition proposed by the government is followed by investments in sectors associated with the climate crisis, such as carbon capture, usage, and storage (CCUS). In terms of electric vehicles, it is mentioned that the American electric vehicle market is only a third as large as its Chinese counterpart; thus, USD 174 billion is to be invested in the sector according to the document (Jobs Plan, 2021).

The Jobs Plan mentions the Recovery Act proposed in 2009, when Joe Biden was vice president during the Barack Obama administration. It can be suggested that the two measures taken by the federal government after different crises are linked. A parallel can also be drawn between the current expectation for American manufacturing to overcome the COVID-19 crisis and how American industry fueled the economy during and after World War II.

"Build Back Better"[1] has become a motto of the federal government for different climate and energy transition measures taken as part of domestic policies. In this context, there is also an ambition for reshoring and nearshoring supply chains, as well as developing new ones, even if they are redundant. The Build Back Better campaign aims to reduce the risks imposed on supply chains, especially if they are climate-related. Thus, supply chains for critical minerals, especially rare-earth elements, are mentioned in governmental documents (Exec. Order No. 14017, 2021). There is continuity in the initiatives established during Donald Trump's administration, thus maintaining the previous president's evocation of the National Emergencies Act to make the U.S. less dependent on the critical minerals sector (Exec. Order No. 13953, 2020).

U.S. internal policies and strategies are envisaged significantly impact on foreign policy, even when they are not conceived to do so. However, the size of the country's economy and its importance to global flows and value chains turn domestic policies into matters of international concern. The Executive Order on Tackling the Climate Crisis at Home and Abroad (Exec. Order No. 14008, 2021) recognizes that even though the U.S. is experiencing a crisis because of the pandemic, there is an even graver crisis posed by climate change that risks people's health, the economy, and even the habitability of the planet. According to this analysis, U.S. national policies impact other international arenas for discussion and negotiation.

For instance, at the North Atlantic Treaty Organization (NATO)[2] meeting in Brussels, the Alliance recognized climate change as a threat multiplier capable of imposing risks to international security. Of note, the climate and energy debate has reached the realm of the armed forces and is recognized by the Alliance as a current defining challenge. NATO has put forth a proposal on GHG emissions to achieve the net-zero goal by 2050, which involves all 30 member countries (North Atlantic Treaty Organization, 2021).

The seven wealthiest nations in the world, referred to collectively as G7,[3] in turn, published a communiqué after its 2021 meeting to discuss climate change and energy transition according to the IEA's (20211) Roadmap to Net Zero by 2050. The group aims to decarbonize its economies per the agency's recommendations. The most pressing measure to be taken by G7 is to move away from coal (which is recognized as the leading cause of GHG emissions) and eliminate inefficient fossil fuel subsidies by 2025. The G7 document also expresses concern that the pandemic undermines progress toward the United Nations' Sustainable Development Goals (Group of Seven, 2021).

During the same G7 meeting, the Build Back Better World (B3W) initiative, aligned with U.S. domestic policy, was proposed for foreign investment in infrastructure by the G7 countries. Climate is one of the pillars of this initiative, which aims to reduce the need for infrastructure in developing countries. The USD 40 trillion gap between developed and developing countries was aggravated by the COVID-19 pandemic, according to the U.S. government (Group of Seven, 2021).

In this sense, considering the world's finance gaps, during the Leaders' Summit on Climate, Joe Biden announced an intention to triple green public investments toward developing nations by 2024 to help developing countries achieve their climate goals. This financial flow is viable due to the direct involvement of U.S. government agencies such as the U.S. Agency for International Development (USAID), Millennium Challenge Corporation, and the U.S. Trade and Development Agency (USTDA) (White House, 2021, June 12). Furthermore, this endeavor has a geopolitical component, as the B3W initiative is said to be the West's response to the Chinese Belt and Road Initiative (Porto, 2021). Considering the competition between the two most powerful countries in the world, the U.S. Jobs Plan is also intended to help the U.S. outperform China, as China's ambitions are seen as a threat comparable to the climate crisis (White House, 2021, March 31).

THE CHALLENGE AHEAD BY SOURCES AND TECHNOLOGIES

According to the IEA, coal-fired generation contracted 3 % in 2019 and declined further 4.6 % in 2020 (IEA, 2021c). Nevertheless, higher natural gas prices, especially throughout the third quarter of 2021, have driven hydrocarbon-dependent countries to return to using coal (IEA, 2021c). This is the case of major carbon emitters, including the U.S. and China. Coal-fired generation increased by nearly 15 % in the first half of 2021 compared to the first semester of 2020. Moreover, final investment decisions regarding this capacity slightly increased in Asia; however, final investment decisions are 80 % lower today than five years ago (IEA, 2021c).

Following the IEA's Net-Zero Scenario (NZS), unabated coal-powered plants in advanced economies will be halted by 2030, and the remaining plants will be phased out by 2040 to reach net-zero emissions by 2050. In the U.S., coal-fired generation decreased by 20 % in 2020; however, generation rose by 36 % in the first five months of 2021 compared to the same period in 2020 (IEA, 2021c). The weekly share of coal in U.S. electricity generation peaked at 30 % in February 2021 during the cold wave (IEA, 2021c). The U.S. is not committed to phasing out its use of coal, and this is in alignment with the COP26 final communiqué, which adopts the term phase-down in expenses of phase-out measures. In other words, "phase-down" focus on the gradual and slow process for decommissioning coal-fired power plants, instead of a global commitment to "phase out" and stop burning coal in a precise timeframe. Recent commitments for phasing out coal from 18 countries cover only 4.1 % of global coal-fired generation and 1.2 %

of global energy-related carbon dioxide (CO_2) emissions (IEA, 2021c). In this sense, the IEA's recommendations are retrofitted to CCUS to prevent plants from becoming stranded assets and adhere to developing countries' energy security and energy access goals (IEA, 2021b). Another recommendation is to co-fire coal with low-carbon fuels such as ammonia or sustainable bioenergy in recently built plants (IEA, 2021c).

Regarding natural gas, power generation from this energy source contracted 2 % in 2020 but natural gas still represented 24 % of all global power (IEA, 2021i). According to the IEA, the share of natural gas in the electric matrix in the U.S. decreased from 44 % in July 2020 to 35 % at the end of 2020, remaining between 33 % and 34 % in the first months of 2021. These decreases are due to rebounded prices, the considerable reduction of final investment decisions, and higher renewables power generation (IEA, 2021i). Owing to the move away from coal, unabated gas-powered plants are envisaged to expand in the short term, though the increase in the renewable share by 2030 might reverse this trend (IEA, 2021i). The relevance of natural gas to the U.S. economy has deepened with the shale revolution, which guaranteed energy security and less dependency on fossil fuels imports. In the last decade, natural gas production in the U.S. has grown by 5.2 % yearly, increasing from 575.2 billion cubic meters (bcm) in 2010 to 930 bcm in 2019 (BP, 2021). Similarly, gas imports decreased by 3.1 % per annum (from 102.3 bcm to 74.7 bcm), and exports increased by 15.5 % per annum (from 30.7 bcm to 122.8 bcm) (BP, 2021). Therefore, the country's shift from a gas net importer to a net exporter granted the U.S. a position of energy security that it has not given up.

The IEA's recommendations for transitioning to low-carbon solutions also include using CCUS technologies to reduce emissions while natural gas maintains its critical role as a flexible resource in the energy system (IEA, 2021b). Most gas-fired plant projects with CCUS are currently under development in the U.S. and the UK (IEA, 2021b). Another recommendation is to retrofit existing plants to co-fire with hydrogen. For example, the 1.2-gigawatt (GW) facility of American integrated energy company Entergy is expected to co-fire up to 30 % and start operations in 2026. Moreover, in terms of CCUS projects, the U.S. Department of Energy (DOE) announced in April 2021 that USD 75 million in funding would be spent on developing this technology (IEA, 2021b).

CCUS technology is an alternative resource to economic assets and environmental impacts from coal- or natural gas-fired power plants. Since early 2020, governments and industries have invested more than USD 18 billion in CCUS projects and programs (IEA, 2021b). The IEA (2021b) highlights the Petra Nova Project. This project started operations in 2017 in Texas and captured 1.4 million tonnes (Mt) of CO_2 per year from a coal-powered plant. Although carbon usage aided the recovery of oil and gas mature fields, the negative impacts of

COVID-19 on oil prices halted the project's operations in May 2020 (IEA, 2021b). Today, only one commercial energy facility in the world is equipped with CCUS technology—namely, the Boundary Dam, which has been in operation in Canada since 2014 is (IEA, 2021b). This technology's evolution is slow because of the high operating costs of CCUS-equipped energy plants compared to unabated plants. Thus, CCUS-equipped plants require tax credits, feed-in tariffs, public procurement measures, and capital grant funding. At the same time, methods for linking CCUS facilities with industrial use must be utilized to improve efficiency and provide a viable revenue stream. Thus, according to the IEA, including CCUS in sustainable recovery packages will foster emissions reduction while boosting deployment (IEA, 2021b).

According to the IEA, 30 new CCUS projects with the capacity to capture a total of 30 Mt of CO_2 annually were announced since January 2020. Such projects are possible primarily because of incentives from the U.S. government to expand tax credits, stimulate CO_2 storage in a geological formation, and utilize CO_2 for oil recovery and other industrial uses (IEA, 2021b). Furthermore, the Infrastructure and Jobs Act, recently approved by the United States Congress, allocated USD 9 billion to CCUS (IEA, 2021b). In sum, more than 40 energy projects equipped with CCUS technology are under development, a quarter of which are being developed in the U.S. These include:

- Cal Capture at Elk Hills natural gas-powered plant, funded by the DOE along with the Electric Power Research Institute (NS Energy Business, 2020);
- San Juan Generating Station in New Mexico, an 847 MW coal plant, whose retrofitting with CCUS technology would keep the plant open beyond 2022 and avoid the loss of 1,500 jobs and USD 53 million in annual tax revenues (Proctor, 2020);
- Coyote Clean Power Project, which generates 280 MW of clean power annually while capturing and storing 855,000 tons of CO_2 per year (Coyote Energy, n.d.);
- Gerald Gentleman Station, a coal-fired power plant in Nebraska that will utilize solvent-based CO_2 capture technology (Nebraska Public Power District, 2019); and
- Project Tundra, designed to retrofit a two-unit coal-based power plant in North Dakota (IEA, 2021b; Project Tundra, n.d.).

The pandemic affected the fossil fuels market and the economic viability of related technologies such as CCUS (IEA, 2021b). However, according to BP's 70th Statistical Review of World Energy, power generation using renewable sources performed well even during the worst periods of the pandemic, thus revealing the resilience of renewable resources in the energy market (BP, 2021). Since 2015, renewable resources have represented 60 % of the growth in power generation. The leading sources of renewable energy are solar and wind power, whose costs have fallen by 55 % and 40 %, respectively, and whose generation has increased to 800 GW in the last five years, averaging 18 % growth per year (IEA, 2021g). The leading country in this regard is China, which contributed almost half of the 238 GW global additional capacity of solar and wind in 2020 (IEA, 2021g).

According to the IEA, renewable electricity generation rose by around 7 % in 2020, reaching a 28.6 % share in global electricity generation, which is the highest level ever (IEA, 2021g). Solar photovoltaic (PV) generation was 156 terawatt-hours (TWh) high, reaching a total of 821 TWh. Meanwhile, onshore wind power increased by 144 TWh (an 11 % increase), and offshore wind power increased by 25 TWh (a 29 % increase). These values translate to 1,592 TWh of wind power generated in 2020 in total (IEA, 2021g). Together, solar PV and wind power accounted for about 60 % of the increase in renewables generation, while hydro accounted for 25 %, and bioenergy contributed 15 %. Renewable capacity additions increased by 46 % from 2019 to 2020, being 192 % high in wind and 25 % high in solar PV (IEA, 2021g).

Solar PV accounted for 3.1 % of global electricity generation, making it the third-most utilized renewable source of electricity behind onshore wind and hydropower (IEA, 2021h). China was responsible for a 75 % increase in annual solar PV installations, representing an additional capacity of 48 GW; this is less than the 53 GW capacity in 2017, which is the highest capacity recorded to date (IEA, 2021h). Cost reductions and new targets under the 14th Five Year Plan, along with new auctions and subsidies for residential systems, are expected to boost solar PV expansion in China (IEA, 2021h). In the U.S., developers completed projects before the production tax credit expired, which has been extended and has propelled capacity deployment (IEA, 2021h). Due to corporate demand reinforced by power purchase agreements and declining costs, the U.S. capacity increased by 45 % in 2020, reaching 19 GW and breaking the previous record of 15 GW set in 2015 (IEA, 2021h). The U.S. installed 5.7 GW of solar PV in Q2 of 2021, reaching 108.7 GWdc, which is enough to supply power to 18 million people (Solar Energy Industries Association, 2021). The industry is expected to continuously break such records for the next three years before the phase-down of the investment tax credit is finalized (Solar Energy Industries Association, 2021).

Wind power generation increased by almost 170 TWh (11 % high) in 2020, which is similar to the increase achieved in 2019 (IEA, 2021j). The onshore wind capacity increased by 108 GW, doubling the 2019 capacity (IEA, 2021j). The conditions for public support scheme in China and in the U.S. were responsible for such unprecedented results, making American and Chinese developers to rush to meet deadlines and accounting both countries 79 % of global wind deployment (IEA, 2021j). China tripled its 2019 growth to 69 GW, while the U.S. generated almost 17 GW, nearly twice as much as it had generated in 2019 (IEA, 2021j). This growth is expected to slow down in upcoming years because projects eligible for full tax credits will be limited. The global offshore wind capacity increased by only 6 GW, which was also the growth rate recorded in 2019. China was responsible for half of this output; the European Union and the UK were responsible for the other half (IEA, 2021j). In the U.S., multiple projects in Maryland, New York, New Jersey, and North Carolina may lead to the first American offshore wind farms (IEA, 2021j).

In sum, the renewable industry adapted well to market conditions during the pandemic, which encouraged governments to commit to applying renewable technologies application quickly. However, the requirement of renewables deployment to the IEA's NZS is more than 60 % generation by 2030, which will require an average increase of nearly 12 % per year (IEA, 2021g). The NZS requires a net capacity addition of 630 GW of solar PV (from the current capacity of 134 GW) to achieve 6,970 TWh of generation in 2030 (from the current generation of 820 TWh), which translates to an annual growth rate of 24 % (IEA, 2021g). The NZS also requires annual capacity additions of 310 GW of onshore wind and 80 GW of offshore wind to achieve 8,000 TWh of generation in 2030, corresponding to an 18 % annual generation growth rate (IEA, 2021g).

These projections represent an opportunity for countries to boost renewable deployment as part of their economic stimulus packages and to offer clean and affordable electricity while creating jobs and fostering sustainable development. The IEA recommends long-term goals, policy stability, and adaptation to market conditions to ensure investor confidence and attract investments and competition as the energy policy shifts toward less subsidy-driven deployment. As renewable shares increase, policies should also ensure flexibility in power systems, as undesired long-term effects of distributed solar PV to the electricity markets could create burdens for power distribution companies.

Hydropower is another important traditional renewable energy source. According to the IEA, hydropower generation increased by 3 % in 2020, reaching 4,418 TWh as capacity additions rebounded during this year (21 GW high) after decreasing over the five consecutive previous years. Almost 60 % of the addition occurred in China (12.1 GW from 4.2 GW in 2019), which has led all countries in hydropower generation since 1996 (IEA, 2021e). The U.S., in turn, deployed only 0.3 GW of hydropower in 2020 after a 0.2-GW decline the year before (IEA, 2021e). Hydropower is the most significant renewable source of electricity, and more hydropower is currently generated than all other forms of renewable energy combined. In the NZS, hydropower will provide 5,870 TWh in 2030; an average of 48 GW should be added to the grid annually, and the average annual generation must be increased by 3 % to meet this target (IEA, 2021e). These expectations are related to projects under construction in China, India, Ethiopia, and Southeast Asia. The hydro fleet in North America is the oldest in the world. The average hydropower plant in North America is 50 years old, and nearly 70 % of American plants are at least 40 years old. Meanwhile, the global average age of hydropower plants is 32 years (IEA, 2021e). Thus, North American plants require modernization and refurbishments to improve equipment performance, and their flexibility must be increased through digitalization.

According to data collected by the IEA, bioenergy electricity generation increased by 8 % (53 TWh) in 2020, reaching 718 TWh, and a capacity addition of 9 GW was achieved in the same year (IEA, 2021a). In the last five years, the capacity has increased by an average of 8 GW per year due to policies such as feed-in tariffs. The NZS calls for the generation of 1,400 TWh (7 % annual growth) and a 15-GW annual addition of new capacity by 2030 (IEA, 2021a). Whether electricity generation from bioenergy will be sufficiently increased relies on timing, sustainability, and the effective implementation of existing and planned policies. Since this source is less competitive than wind and solar power on a cost-per-unit-of-energy basis, policies changed from fixed feed-in tariffs. Furthermore, certificates for competitive auction frameworks in countries like China, Japan, Germany, and the UK might decrease deployment forecasts. Other advantages could capitalize public policies since bioenergy is a dispatchable source to meet the always changing electricity demands of the societies, complementing intermittent wind and solar generation while increasing grid reliability and enhancing bioenergy's role in waste management to reduce municipal solid waste, agricultural residues, and co-firing coal plants.

The Biofuture Platform,[4] whose leadership shifted from Brazil to the U.S. in 2021, recommends embedding the low-carbon bioeconomy in broad economic recovery programs to ensure the continuity of successful policy mechanisms, support producers considering related COVID-driven economic losses, reassess fossil fuels, require bioeconomy investments and targets as part of aid packages in sectors such as transport and chemicals, and integrate sustainability-rewarding mechanisms into policy frameworks (Biofuture Platform, 2021).

Other alternative renewable energy sources could be considered part of the path to net-zero emissions in the U.S., but this would require economic and research efforts. This is a case of geothermal and ocean power. Geothermal electricity generation increased by 2 % in 2020, and 200 MW of capacity was added, which is less than the 500 MW annual average addition observed over the last five years (IEA, 2021d). The additions have come from Turkey, Indonesia, and Kenya. The NZS requires a 13 % annual increase in generation and a 3.6 GW annual capacity addition by 2030. Therefore, policies must be implemented to cope with the costs and predevelopment risks associated with the achievement of these goals (IEA, 2021d). Ocean power electricity generation increased by 33 % (400 GWh), from 1.2 TWh in 2019 to 1.6 TWh in 2020 (IEA, 2021f). However, the IEA's NZS calls for annual increases of 27 TWh and 1 GW of capacity addition by 2030 (IEA, 2021f). Marine projects from 10 kW to 1 MW have been deployed in the UK, Canada, Australia, China, and Denmark; these projects alone increased the total annual capacity by 200 MW in 2020 (IEA, 2021f). However, this technology lacks the commissioning of large-scale projects and requires political support for research, development, and demonstration in this field (IEA, 2021f).

Finally, even though nuclear power is a non-renewable resource because it includes uranium, it is a reliable and accessible low-carbon energy source that can be utilized to keep the global temperature increase below 1.5°C. According to the IEA (2021k), nuclear power is the second most important low-carbon source of electricity in the world. Between 2005 and 2020, its global capacity grew from 398 GW to 415 GW, and investments in nuclear power reached USD 37 billion in 2020 (IEA, 2021k). During the same period, the highest capacity addition occurred in 2018, when 11.2 GW were connected to the grid; China and Russia were the global leaders in terms of grid connections and new constructions (IEA, 2021k). In the U.S., nuclear energy produces nearly 20 % of the country's power and 52 % of its clean energy (Office of Nuclear Energy, 2020). However, the number of reactors in the U.S. decreased to 94 in 2020 after two units ceased operations; eight more are scheduled to close by 2025 owing to the increasing availability and decreasing prices of natural gas (Office of Nuclear Energy, 2020). This current trend may cause a 10 % reduction in the nuclear power capacity in the U.S. and damage the DOE's objective of using all available energy sources to boost hydrogen production.

In this sense, nuclear power is a reliable source for producing both electricity and clean hydrogen, whose growing demand is expected to transform steel manufacturing, synthetic fuels production, and transportation. Differently from non-OECD countries like China, Russia, India, and the United Arab Emirates (which are investing in new-build projects) and other OECD countries like France and Canada (which are refurbishing existing plants to meet climate goals), the U.S. lacks a clear policy (IEA, 2021k). While the federal administration considers nuclear power a clean energy source, not all state-level policies reflect this. The 2021 infrastructure bill encompasses investments in advanced reactors like small nuclear reactors to provide electricity to remote communities, replace coal-powered plants, and produce low-carbon hydrogen. Recently, the DOE awarded USD 8.5 million on projects concerned with the commercialization of advanced nuclear technologies, and more than USD 215 million has been spent for this purpose since 2017 through the Office of Nuclear Energy (2021).

Nuclear power also contributes to the environment and the economy by mitigating emissions, minimizing land footprints, creating jobs, fostering technological innovation, and promoting economic growth. According to Batini et al. (2021), spending on nuclear energy is more persistent than non-climate-friendly energy expenditures, as nuclear energy's output effect is about six times larger than that of fossil fuels. Nuclear energy employs more workers than renewable resources at the local level and pays higher salaries than the wind and solar sectors by about one-third (Batini et al., 2021).

CONCLUSION

Owing to the COVID-19 pandemic's impact on energy markets and the economy, U.S. policies targeting economic recovery and climate crisis mitigation merged under the common objective of transitioning the energy sector to renewable and low-carbon solutions. According to the documents analyzed in this chapter, the measures prescribed for the most important sectors in the U.S. in 2021 cannot be detached from the impacts of the pandemic. The country has adopted a whole-of-government approach to promote recovery from the economic slowdown and regain the previous pace of the energy transition. However, the federal propositions also aim to implement new efforts that were not in place before the crisis to rebuild the economy by investing in the energy sector.

As discussed in several documents seen in this chapter, the funds allocated by the federal government are to be implemented according to different timescales. The outcomes of the investments provided in the first year of the Biden administration can only be assessed throughout the next few years.

Several challenges to the advancement of renewable and clean sources in power generation are addressed in the current analysis, which considers each one attributes, and significant efforts are required to enhance capacity additions, improve regulations, and reduce costs, according to each country objective in terms of energy transition. Furthermore, while a substantial growth of investment in renewables has been observed, fossil fuels remain a prominent energy source, and the U.S. continues to depend heavily on natural gas and coal power, as well as oil products for transport and industry sectors, to guarantee economic growth and the capacity to balance challenging purposes from great powers like China. In this context, the effects of COVID-19 on the energy transition represent geopolitical challenges to the position of the U.S. in the international system and its dubious strategies to foster renewable sources while maintaining a stable supply of fossil fuels.

Despite significant efforts to transition to renewable energies, the U.S. is still heavily reliant on fossil fuels. Phenomena such as the 2021 cold wave illustrate how dependent the country is on pollutant fuels and how difficult it will be to achieve its decarbonization goals. Thus, fossil fuels will maintain their prominent role in the country's energy mix throughout the energy transition. Resolving this issue will require improvements in the efficiency of low-carbon technologies such as CCUS. This way, thermal power plants can undergo retrofitting, meaning that current workers can keep their jobs while new opportunities are created in the growing renewable energy market.

Despite the negative impacts of the COVID-19 pandemic, it has bolstered the energy transition as a path to achieve economic recovery while tackling the climate crisis. Such argument weakens the argument that a low-carbon future would undermine economic growth and social development. In fact, especially in the U.S., efforts to tackle the climate crisis are related to the energy transition, as well as its positive effects on investments, jobs creation, and economic growth.

NOTES

1 Build Back Better refers to a USD 1.7 trillion federal government plan directed to improve social safety and climate change measures. The government hopes to guarantee public spending on infrastructure and economic recovery while preserving social protection, education, and healthcare programs. It also hopes to achieve its climate goals, such as the goal to cut emissions in half by 2030.

2 NATO was created in 1949 to provide collective security to Western countries against the Soviet Union. Even though the Cold War has ended, this military organization still plays a relevant role in 30 European and North American countries in terms of security, military, and defense technology subjects.

3 The Group of Seven includes Canada, France, Germany, Italy, Japan, the United Kingdom, and the United States.

4 The Biofuture Platform is an alliance comprising 21 countries (Argentina, Brazil, Canada, China, Denmark, Egypt, Finland, France, India, Indonesia, Italy, Morocco, Mozambique, Netherlands, Paraguay, Philippines, Portugal, the United Kingdom, the United States, and Uruguay) concerned with bioenergy's role in sustainable development. This alliance creates projects and strengthens the dialogue among policymakers to foster bioenergy deployment.

REFERENCES

Batini, N., Di Serio, M., Fragetta, M., Melina, G., & Waldron, A. (2021). *Building back better: How big are green spending multipliers?* International Monetary Fund. https://www.elibrary.imf.org/view/journals/001/2021/087/article-A001-en.xml

Biofuture Platform. (2020, August 12). *Five core Biofuture principles for post-COVID bioeconomy recovery and acceleration.* http://www.biofutureplatform.org/post/biofuture-platform-launches-five-principles-for-post-covid-bioeconomy-recovery-and-acceleration

BP. (2021). *Statistical review of world energy* (70th ed.). Retrieved August 11, 2021, from https://www.bp.com/content/dam/bp/business-sites/en/global/corporate/pdfs/energy-economics/statistical-review/bp-stats-review-2021-full-report.pdf

Coyote Energy. (n.d.). https://coyote.energy/

Exec. Order 13953 (Executive order on addressing the threat to the domestic supply chain from reliance on critical minerals from foreign adversaries), 3 C.F.R. (2020).

Exec. Order 14017 (Executive order on America's supply chains), 3 C.F.R. (2021).

Exec. Order 14030 (Executive order on climate-related financial risk), 3 C.F.R. (2021).

Exec. Order 14008 (Executive order on tackling the climate crisis at home and abroad), 3 C.F.R. (2021).

Group of Seven. (2021). *Carbis Bay G7 Summit Communique*. https://assets.publishing.service.gov.uk/government/uploads/system/uploads/attachment_data/file/1001128/Carbis_Bay_G7_Summit_Communique__PDF__430KB__25_pages_.pdf

International Energy Agency. (2021a). *Bioenergy power generation*. https://www.iea.org/reports/bioenergy-power-generation

International Energy Agency. (2021b). *CCUS in power*. https://www.iea.org/reports/ccus-in-power

International Energy Agency. (2021c). *Coal-fired power*. https://www.iea.org/reports/coal-fired-power

International Energy Agency. (2021d). *Geothermal power*. https://www.iea.org/reports/geothermal-power

International Energy Agency. (2021e). *Hydropower*. https://www.iea.org/reports/hydropower

International Energy Agency. (2021f). *Ocean power*. https://www.iea.org/reports/ocean-power

International Energy Agency. (2021g). *Renewable power*. https://www.iea.org/reports/renewable-power

International Energy Agency. (2021h). *Solar PV*. https://www.iea.org/reports/solar-pv

International Energy Agency. (2021i). *Natural gas-fired power*. https://www.iea.org/reports/natural-gas-fired-power

International Energy Agency. (2021j). *Wind power*. https://www.iea.org/reports/wind-power

International Energy Agency. (2021k). *Nuclear power*. https://www.iea.org/reports/nuclear-power

International Energy Agency. (2021l). *Net zero by 2050: A roadmap for the global energy sector*. https://www.iea.org/reports/net-zero-by-2050

International Monetary Fund. (2021). *World economic outlook*. https://www.imf.org/en/Publications/WEO/Issues/2021/10/12/world-economic-outlook-october-2021

Kerry, J. (2021). *John Kerry on the urgency of global climate action*. Chatham House. https://chathamhouse.soutron.net/Portal/DownloadImageFile.ashx?fieldValueId=5931

Nebraska Public Power District. (2019). *Department of Energy awards funding for Phase II of carbon capture study for Gentleman Station*. Retrieved October 1, 2019, from https://www.nppd.com/press-releases/department-of-energy-awards-funding-for-phase-ii-of-carbon-capture-study-for-gentleman-station

North Atlantic Treaty Organization. (2021). *Brussels Summit Communiqué*. https://www.nato.int/cps/en/natohq/news_185000.htm

NS Energy Business. (2020). *Fluor wins FEED contract for CRC's Cal Capture project in US*. Retrieved July 22, 2020, from https://www.nsenergybusiness.com/news/fluor-crcs-cal-capture-project/#

Office of Nuclear Energy. (2020). *Could hydrogen help save nuclear?* Retrieved June 24, 2020, from https://www.energy.gov/ne/articles/could-hydrogen-help-save-nuclear

Office of Nuclear Energy. (2021). *DOE awards $8.5 million to advance promising nuclear technologies.* Retrieved November 18, 2021, from https://www.energy.gov/ne/articles/doe-awards-85-million-advance-promising-nuclear-technologies

Porto, L. F. (2021, July 2). *O plano do G7 para contrapor a China no desenvolvimento de infraestrutura global. Open Democracy.* https://www.opendemocracy.net/pt/plano-g7-para-contrapor-china-desenvolvimento-infraestrutura-global/

Proctor, D. (2020). *DOE supports CCUS retrofit for San Juan coal plant.* Retrieved October 6, 2020, from https://www.powermag.com/doe-supports-ccus-retrofit-for-san-juan-coal-plant/

Project Tundra. (n.d). https://www.projecttundrand.com/

Solar Energy Industries Association. (2021). *U.S. solar market insight.* Retrieved September 14, 2021, from https://www.seia.org/us-solar-market-insight

United Nations Framework Convention on Climate Change. (2015). *The Paris agreement.* https://unfccc.int/process-and-meetings/the-paris-agreement/the-paris-agreement

U.S. Department of State. (2021a). *Leaders' summit on climate: Day 1.* Retrieved April 30, 2021, from https://www.state.gov/leaders-summit-on-climate/day-1/

U.S. Department of State (2021b). *Leaders' summit on climate: Day 2.* Retrieved April 30, 2021, from https://www.state.gov/leaders-summit-on-climate/day-2/

White House. (2021, March 31). *FACT SHEET: The American Jobs Plan* [Press release]. https://www.whitehouse.gov/briefing-room/statements-releases/2021/03/31/fact-sheet-the-american-jobs-plan/

White House. (2021, June 12). *FACT SHEET: President Biden and G7 Leaders Launch Build Back Better World (B3W) Partnership* [Press release]. https://www.whitehouse.gov/briefing-room/statements-releases/2021/06/12/fact-sheet-president-biden-and-g7-leaders-launch-build-back-better-world-b3w-partnership/

CHAPTER 9

Geopolitical Implications of the European Union's Carbon Border Adjustment Mechanism

ALAZ MUNZUR, KATHARINA KOCH, AND JENNIFER WINTER

INTRODUCTION

The Paris Agreement is an outcome-focused environmental treaty, which aims to keep the global average temperature increase below 2°C, preferably 1.5, compared to pre-industrial levels (United Nations, 2021). However, it does not prescribe how signatories should achieve this outcome. The targets and measures are voluntary and vary widely across countries. Numerous industrialized countries have implemented emissions-reduction policies in the absence of concerted global action. Such disproportionate emissions-reduction efforts may lead to the relocation of economic activity to countries that do not have or have less stringent climate policies leading to limited reductions in global emissions—carbon leakage.

To prevent this and encourage decarbonization outside of its borders, on July 14, 2021, the European Commission (EC) released a regulatory proposal for a carbon border adjustment mechanism (CBAM) (European Commission, 2021d). The draft CBAM regulation proposes an emissions tax payable on aluminum, cement, electricity, fertilizer, and iron and steel imported by the European Union (EU).[1] In this chapter, we explore reactions to the draft CBAM regulation by public and private stakeholders within the EU and its main trading partners in the affected sectors (China, Russia, and Turkey) on the regulation's design, feasibility and fairness.

The CBAM would affect the EU's trading partners differently; the regulation will initially apply to a select number of emission-intensive industries at high risk of carbon leakage. Although the EU states the CBAM is a measure to prevent carbon leakage, the geopolitical implications of the CBAM for the EU may be significant since the EU is the main market for emission-intensive goods from major exporters like China and Russia. We rely on international trade statistics to identify the EU's trading partners that would be most affected by the CBAM and to guide the focus of our discussion on the geopolitical implications of the proposal.

The CBAM proposal is the EU's attempt to use its normative and regulatory power[2] to incentivize climate policy reforms in third countries.[3] However, we argue that the EU's normative and regulatory power is limited, particularly in China and Russia due to sensitive geopolitical relations which have been greatly affected following Russia's invasion of Ukraine on February 24, 2022. Furthermore, the EU faces internal frictions as individual member states and industry leaders aim to reformulate the CBAM proposal. We investigate how the draft CBAM regulation was received by public and private stakeholders in China, Russia and Turkey. We also discuss the internal conflict between the EU Commission and the member states before analyzing the potential resistance of China, Russia and Turkey against the CBAM proposal.

In the next section, we outline the specifics of border carbon adjustment (BCA) regulations before discussing the details of the EU's CBAM. We then present our conceptual framework. The framework relies on the concept of normative power (Manners, 2002) to explain the CBAM's potential role in incentivizing climate policy reforms in third countries. We proceed with discussing the geopolitical implications of the CBAM for the relationship between the EU with China, Russia, and Turkey while considering the role of the EU as a normative power in environmental world politics. We conclude that the EU needs to initiate bilateral conversations with its main trading partners on the framing and purpose of this regulation in order to prevent retaliatory actions and erosion of trust.

PURPOSE OF BORDER CARBON ADJUSTMENTS

Uncoordinated actions to reduce global emissions and the transboundary nature of greenhouse gas (GHG) emissions mean differences in environmental regulations may undermine achieving the Paris Agreement target. The outcome of these differences in regulations is of particular concern for the EU and other parties to the Paris Agreement implementing ambitious emissions-reduction policies. More strictly regulated firms in countries with stringent emissions-reduction regulations may decrease output as they lose competitiveness in domestic or global markets compared to less strictly regulated firms, or relocate to countries with weaker or no environmental standards. The resultant increase in emissions in part offsets the emissions reduction in strictly regulated countries, leading to cross-border carbon leakage. Leakage is central to the policy debate on unilateral emission-regulations; particularly for emissions-intensive and trade-exposed industries where emissions-intensive inputs represent a significant share of total production costs.

In response to such concerns, a BCA is a policy option to "level the playing field" in international trade. As a duty on emission-intensive goods, a BCA discourages imports. As an alternative to globally coordinated measures, a BCA, although complicated and costly to design and implement, limits carbon leakage by shifting part of the economic burden to countries with less stringent emission-regulations.[4] BCAs are also a coercive tool to incentivize or pressure trade partners to adopt more-stringent environmental policy.

The EU's main motivation in proposing the CBAM is to minimize the risk of carbon leakage by equalizing the cost of carbon between imported and domestically produced goods. The CBAM would cover mainly direct CO_2 emissions embedded in imported goods to make trading partners face an emissions price similar to what they would face if they produced the same goods in the EU. The EU is not the only jurisdiction considering a BCA. Notably, as Droege and Fischer (2020, p. 30) point out "nearly every example of draft climate legislation circulating in the US Congress includes BCA." The state of California has a BCA that applies to emissions from electricity imported from other U.S. states (McWilliams & Tagliapietra, 2021). In 2020, Canada also announced its intentions to explore a BCA and released an initial assessment report in August 2021 (Department of Finance, 2020). If the EU adopts the CBAM, it will apply to imports into the EU27, the European Economic Area (EEA) and Switzerland.[5]

CORNERSTONES OF THE EU'S DRAFT CBAM PROPOSAL

The CBAM is part of the broader "Fit for 55" climate plan which aims to reduce the EU's net emissions at least 55 % below 1990 levels by 2030 through a set of proposals that is supposed to deliver on the EU's climate goals from the 2019 European Green Deal (EC, 2019).[6] The EC, as the executive branch of the EU, pledged to achieve net-zero emissions by 2050 (European Commission, 2021c). The CBAM is one element among 13 policies presented in the "Fit for 55" plan. Details on many of these measures and policy objectives remain vague since the EC has not yet released the corresponding amendments. However, as highlighted in the documents issued by the EC, the CBAM would reduce the risk of carbon leakage and ensure a level playing field for select EU industries by equalizing the price of emissions between domestic products and imports.

Initially, the CBAM will have restricted coverage and apply to five industries with a relatively higher exposure to emissions pricing and international trade: aluminum, cement, fertilizer, iron and steel, and electricity generation. The emissions from these accounted for about 55 % of all industrial emissions in the EU27 in 2020 (EC, 2021b). Iron and steel production is the highest emitter at 30 % of industrial emissions. Aluminum emits the lowest amount of direct emissions due to its reliance on electricity. The EC (2021b, p. 43) states, "looking at total CO_2 equivalent emissions, CBAM sectors together with electricity generation accounted for nearly 40 % of emissions in 2020." Currently, there is no timeline for including indirect emissions as the EU Commission "will evaluate how the CBAM is working and whether to extend its scope to more products and services—including down the value chain, and whether to cover so-called 'indirect' emissions" (EC, 2021d, p. 41).[7] However, the European Parliament proposed an amendment that "by 31 December 2023 the Commission shall present a report to the European Parliament and the Council containing a calculation method to enable the extension of the scope of embedded emissions to indirect emissions and an impact assessment of that extension" (European Parliament, 2021, p. 37).

The Commission shall collect the information necessary with a view to extending the scope of the regulation to indirect emissions and goods other than those listed in Annex I, and develop methods of calculating embedded emissions based on environmental footprint methods. Since the CBAM would cover imports' direct emissions, it complements the internal emissions-pricing scheme of the EU, the EU ETS. For the industries subject to the EU ETS, total emissions are capped, and industrial facilities buy or receive allowances that cover their emissions. Although the allowances are in principle sold through competitive auctions, some industries receive free allowances to adjust for competitiveness pressures from non-EU producers; the number of free allocations is declining over time (Dobson & Winter, 2018). Under the draft CBAM proposal, the auction price of the ETS allowances determines CBAM certificates' price and when ETS free allowances are eliminated in 2035, the CBAM will apply to all the industries currently covered by the ETS.[8]

The EU envisions a transitional phase between 2023 and 2025 to navigate the trade-offs between the objectives and the proposal design. An outstanding question is to what extent the EU member states can come to an agreement during negotiations in the European Parliament (EP). Conflict and debates about the CBAM proposal are likely to emerge during the time-consuming negotiations between the EC and the EU member states (Imeri & Barzilska, 2021). This means that the EU's current proposed dates may not be realistic from an administrative and practical perspective given the lengthy legislative processes. This includes an assessment of including indirect emissions in the CBAM. Determining emissions embedded in imports will depend on the chosen mechanism. Under the EU ETS, the covered facilities are subject to a price based on their actual emissions and for fair treatment, the scope of the CBAM may be the same. However, this entails a significant administrative cost on both the importers and the implementing bodies in the EU. Establishing a default average emission-intensity value for each industry or product is another option considered by the EU, which would reduce the costs associated with the management of the system and the accuracy of the CBAM as a tool to level the playing field.[9]

During COP26, Frans Timmermans (the EC's Vice President) explained that the EU "will increasingly create a space across the planet where countries will take comparable measures to decarbonize their economies which will make the CBAM not necessary or only in a limited way" (Timmermans, 2021). This could imply the formation of a "climate club" whereby countries agree to cap emissions, or the EU could grant exemptions from the CBAM to countries that implement a national mechanism to price or cap emissions. The more countries adopt climate policies to limit emissions, the less likely a CBAM will be necessary to prevent carbon leakage (Burke, 2021). However, the reactions of industry proponents and third countries that we discuss in this chapter show the CBAM's implementation is uncertain.

THE NORMATIVE POWER OF THE EU AND ITS ROLE AS A "CLIMATE LEADER"

Manners' (2002) concept of normative power (Manners, 2002) illustrates the EU's external relations, which are influenced by a set of normative principles and shared beliefs that form the core of the EU's self-understanding and are codified in EU legislation and laws.[10] Wunderlich (2020, p. 1109) argues that the EU "aims to establish itself by differentiation, that is, as a different kind of power and a force for collective good." The EU achieves this through promotion of its universal values and shared interests, alongside the powers of attraction and persuasion of third countries (Manners, 2002). Based on the European Green Deal, Eckert (2021, p. 2) identifies several environmental and social norms that the EU aims to "diffuse" through policy reforms in third countries: climate neutrality, zero pollution, a circular economy and a "just transition both inside the EU and globally."

Pace (2007) presents several mechanisms the EU uses to exert political and economic pressure on third countries: dialogue, bilateral contractual relations (or politically binding agreements), and specific policy initiatives in key areas like energy. Several scholars discuss the role of the EU as a "global climate leader" in climate change mitigation policy (Parker et al., 2017; Parker & Karlsson, 2017;

Torney, 2019). Parker and Karlsson (2017) emphasize that throughout the last two decades, the EU spearheaded several initiatives (like the 20-20-20 targets[11]) and continues to be a main supporter of the Paris Agreement.

Lütz et al. (2021, p. 206) find that the EU "has been perceived as an environmental pioneer at the international level" and that the EU "has developed a leading position in the emergence of the climate regime and has provided significant impetus for further development." This is remarkable because climate policy is a shared competence between the EU Commission and the EU member states which means that the EU member states must unanimously agree on policies. However, the EU "is considered to be one of the most important actors in international climate policy" through its "professionalized negotiation structure" which places the EU in a strong negotiation position vis-a-vis its member states (Lütz et al., 2021, p. 206). Currently, the EP proposes that the EU "may conclude agreements with third countries with a view to take account of carbon pricing mechanisms and carbon reduction measures of equivalent efficiency other than carbon pricing mechanisms" (EP, 2021, p. 21).

In this chapter, we argue that, as reflected by reactions to draft proposal, while the CBAM may induce emissions-reduction strategies in third countries, its success in incentivizing climate policy adoption relies on the normative power of the EU. Figure 9.1 presents a timeline of the key events shaping reactions to the CBAM.

While the reactions expressed during these events imply the normative power of the EU, internal and external forces, manifested through the economic

Figure 9.1: Timeline of International Key Events related to the EU Commission's CBAM Proposal 2019–2021

Source: Authors' own elaboration.

interests of public and private stakeholders, compel the EU to deliver concessions to third countries. These concessions undermine the normative power of the EU and the multilateral participation necessary to achieve Paris Agreement targets. Next, we present the reactions to the draft CBAM proposal in the EU and by its main trading partners.

REACTIONS OF THE EU MEMBER STATES AND INDUSTRY LEADERS TO THE DRAFT CBAM PROPOSAL

Since the CBAM is a climate policy potentially affecting trade flows, it is likely to incite intense geopolitical debates among EU members, industry proponents, and the EU's main trading partners. All 27 EU member states are expected to defend their national interests during the negotiations, which will be influenced by the effects on their domestic industries. Several EU member states, like Finland (Kuusi et al., 2020) and France (Ministry for Europe and Foreign Affairs, n.d.), have already commissioned reports on the potential domestic effect of the CBAM, and these reports may indicate the direction of their vote on the proposal in the EC. Another example is the European Automobile Manufacturers' Association (ACEA), which announced its expectations for the regulation, including maintaining the industry's global competitiveness and avoiding retaliation from third countries (ACEA, 2021).

On March 23, 2021, several cabinet ministers from nine EU member states[12] co-authored an op-ed calling on the EC to develop a CBAM proposal that ensures non-discrimination and a "good articulation with the EU ETS which could mirror the European carbon market" (Blümel et al., 2021). On the same day, France held an international conference discussing design and implementation of a potential CBAM. France holds the Presidency of the Council of the European Union from January to June 2022 and has declared that a priority is developing a governance and implementation framework for the CBAM (Ministry for Europe and Foreign Affairs, n.d.). In April 2020, France proposed its own expectations for the CBAM (Table 9.1).

As a large economy within the union, Germany's reaction to the CBAM is important for the proposal's success. German industry proponents, like the Federation of German Industries (BDI), argue that central design and implementation questions remain unanswered in the CBAM proposal, such as exemption criteria. Similarly, Chief Executive Wolfgang Große Entrup of Germany's Chemical Association stated that "it is not enough [for the EU] just to be a role model for the world" but rather, the CBAM must uphold Germany's industrial competitiveness (Kurmayer, 2021). In general, German industry leaders expressed

Table 9.1: French CBAM Proposal Delivered to the European Commission in April 2020

French CBAM Proposal delivered to the European Commission in April 2020
• "Require those importing goods from outside the EU to acquire specific carbon quotas from a market mirroring the EU Emissions Trading System (EU ETS)."
• "Gradually replace the system of free allocation of ETS allowances following a transitional phase that would run until 2025."
• "Initially select a limited number of pilot sectors, including the highest-emitting activities and those most exposed to the risk of carbon leakage, such as steel and cement."
• "Consider the climate policies of third countries and their level of development in the design of the mechanism."
• "Provide a solution, in the form of compensation, to the issue of exporting sectors, to limit carbon leakage on other markets."

Source: Authors' own elaboration (data retrieved from Ministry for Europe and Foreign Affairs, n.d.)

concerns regarding the proposal and that they would prefer the status quo of the EU ETS. EU industry leaders claim that the CBAM "only protects companies within the EU and is associated with considerable legal and bureaucratic hurdles" (Kurmayer, 2021). There is strong internal resistance to the CBAM proposal among EU-based private stakeholders.

GLOBAL IMPLICATIONS OF THE CBAM: REACTIONS FROM THE EU'S MAIN TRADING PARTNERS

The draft CBAM proposal also sparked significant reactions from the EU's main trading partners. As shown in Table 9.2, China, Russia and Turkey are important trading partners in the five potentially affected sectors. These three countries are not the main trading partners in all five sectors, but are in the top three for at least two of the sectors.

The draft CBAM proposal lacks detail on crucial design elements, such as crediting trade partners' climate action. Nevertheless, the potential CBAM immediately prompted strong reactions from several third countries (Gläser & Caspar, 2021; see Table 9.3).

In a joint statement responding to the CBAM, China, South Africa, Brazil, and India expressed "grave concern" (Republic of South Africa, 2021). These four countries argue that BCAs are, in general, discriminatory according to the principles of Equity and Common but Differentiated Responsibilities and Respective

Table 9.2: Main Sources of Imports (Import Value [in million €] and Share of Total Industry Imports by Value, 2019)

	EU Imports' County of Origin for CBAM-affected Industries, 2019							
Aluminum	Norway 3,116 18 %	Russia 2,425 14 %	China 1,545 9 %	United Arab Emirates 1,206 7 %	Switzerland 1,170 7 %	UK 1,078 6 %	Turkey 1,059 6 %	Iceland 1,046 6 %
Cement	Turkey 106 35 %	Colombia 26 9 %	Ukraine 24 8 %	Belarus & Herzegovina 22 7 %	Bosnia 14 5 %	Morocco 10 4 %	China 2 1 % (18th)	Russia 0.7 <1 % (29th)
Electricity Generation	Switzerland 709 21 %	Russia 613 18 %	Norway 483 14 %	Serbia 478 14 %	Ukraine 323 10 %	Bosnia 242 7 %	Turkey 56 2 % (10th)	China n/a
Fertilizer	Russia 1,492 34 %	Egypt 451 10 %	Algeria 420 10 %	Morocco 355 8 %	Belarus & Herzegovina 209 5 %	Trinidad & Tobago 192 4 %	Turkey 89 2 % (11th)	China 67 2 % (15th)
Iron and Steel	China 4,876 14 %	Russia 4,740 14 %	Turkey 4,262 12 %	UK 3,674 10 %	Ukraine 2,726 8 %	South Korea 2,528 7 %	India 2,495 7 %	Switzerland 1,266 4 %

Source: Authors' own elaboration (Trade data for 2019 is retrieved from Eurostat Comext "EU trade since 1988 by HS2,4,6 and CN8" available from: https://ec.europa.eu/eurostat/web/international-trade-in-goods/data/focus-on-comext; Product codes from Annex I of https://eur-lex.europa.eu/legal-content/EN/TXT/?uri=celex:52021PC0564).

Note: We use 2019 data given the supply chain disruption from the COVID-19 pandemic may have affected more current trade statistics.

Table 9.3: Main Criticism of the CBAM by the EU's Main Trading Partners

CBAM Criticisms by the EU's Main Trading Partners		
Protectionism	Revenue Generator	Unilateral decision-making
• Allegedly protectionist and a trade barrier under a climate pretext. • Competitiveness of domestic industry.	• CBAM revenues could be seen as income for the overall EU budget. • Funds from less affluent countries redirected into the EU.	• The EU failed to consult with third-country trading partners. • Accusation of acting on a unilateral basis.

Source: Authors' own elaboration (data adapted from "Less confrontation, more cooperation." Gläser, A. and Caspar, O. (2021). *Germanwatch—Policy Brief.* Available from: https://germanwatch.org/en/20355).

Capabilities[13] (Republic of South Africa, 2021). Under these principles, industrialized countries should be championing emission reduction strategies by also supporting developing and least developed countries (LDCs).

Moreover, although the EU claims the CBAM was designed in compliance with WTO rules, scholars emphasize that a CBAM may be considered protectionist by the EU's trading partners and thus contradict WTO rules, in particular the General Agreement on Tariffs and Trade (Kolev et al., 2021). Therefore, EU trading partners may impose retaliatory measurements against the EU in order to express their discontent with such policies. This could also prompt judicial challenges, if third countries formally complain to the WTO against the CBAM (Mehling, 2019).

Before examining the individual reactions of China, Russia and Turkey to the EC's proposal, we discuss the countries' respective emissions-reduction policies. This provides important context for their current climate change mitigation objectives, which will form a basis for their negotiations with the EU (Table 9.4). China's national ETS differs significantly from the EU's in terms of implementation and sector applicability. Russia is developing a pilot ETS on the island of Sakhalin; however, it remains unclear if Russia will extend this pilot program nationally. Turkey is considering implementing an ETS; however, its proposal from December 2020 has yet to turn into legislation (ICAP, 2021). Although all three countries are at initial stages, China and Russia are among the largest global emitters of GHGs, in addition to the US, the EU and India (Friedrich et al., 2020). Thus, emissions-reducing efforts from these countries are particularly relevant for meeting Paris Agreement targets. The lack of consistency between national emissions-reduction policies also emphasizes the challenge for the EU to introduce a CBAM which would exempt third countries based on measures of "equivalent efficiency" (EP, 2021, p. 8).

Table 9.4: Status of Emissions Trading Systems in China, Russian Federation, and Turkey

Status of Emissions-Reduction Policies			
Jurisdiction	China (NATIONAL ETS)*	Russian Federation—Sakhalin	Turkey
Status	In force (since mid-2021)	Under development	Under consideration
Total GHG emissions	12,301 $MtCO_2e$ (2014)	2220.1 $MtCO_2e$ (2018)	520.9 $MtCO_2e$ (2018)
GHG Reduction Target	CO_2 peak before 2030; neutrality by 2060.	Emissions will not exceed 70 % of 1990s levels by 2030.	Up to 21 % reduction from 2021 levels by 2030.
GHG covered	CO_2	No information available.	No information available.
Sectors	Power sector. In the long-term, expected to cover nine industries: power, cement, aluminum, iron and steel, nonferrous metals, petroleum refining, chemicals, pulp and paper, and aviation. There is no specific timeline for this expansion.	No information available.	No information available.
Point of Regulation	Expected to cover both direct and indirect emissions from power generation.	No information available.	No information available.
Number of entities	The regional ETS pilot covered power sector entities, which may also fall under the national ETS. These entities are transitioning into the ETS national market.* Estimate: 2,225 facilities (2021).	No information available.	No information available.

(Continued)

Table 9.4: Continued

	Status of Emissions-Reduction Policies		
Cap	No absolute cap on emissions. The cap is adjusted ex post based on actual production levels. Monitors intensity, meaning a regulated plant receives more permits if it produces more output. The national ETS is estimated to have a cap of over 4,000 $MtCO_2$/year for 2021.	No information available.	No information available.
Permit Allocation	Free allocation based on four distinct fuel-based benchmarks: conventional coal plants below 300 MW; conventional coal plants above 300 MW; unconventional coal plants; and natural gas. Entities will receive allowances at 70 % of their 2018 output multiplied by the corresponding benchmark factor. Allocation will be adjusted later to reflect actual generation in 2019 and 2020. The National Measures clarify that auctioning may be introduced at a later point in time which has not been determined.	No information available.	No information available.

* China has the following regional ETS pilots: Beijing; Chongqing; Fujian, Guangdong, Hubei, Shanghai, Shenzhen, Tianjin.
Source: Authors' own elaboration (data retrieved from "Comparing ETS—China-Russia-Turkey." *International Carbon Action Partnership (ICAP)*, 2021. Available from: https://icapcarbonaction.com/en/ets-map).

China

China faces significant potential exposure to the CBAM, since the EU is China's biggest trading partner. In 2019, 13 % of China's total trade (imports and exports, in value) was with the EU (Table 9.5). The EU is China's largest source of imports and second-largest export market following the US, particularly for iron

Table 9.5: China's Total Trade (in million €) and Share of Total Industry Exports by value, 2019

	Exports		Imports		Total	
Global	2,231,223		1,847,573		4,078,795	
EU	308,843		225,590		534,433	
EU Share	13.8 %		12.2 %		13.1 %	
	Value of Exports	**Sector Share of Total Exports**	**Value of EU Exports**	**EU Share of Sector Exports**	**Sector's EU Exports as Share of EU Exports**	**Sector's EU Exports as Share of Total Exports**
Aluminum	13,627	0.61 %	1,483	10.88 %	0.48 %	0.0665 %
Cement	284	0.01 %	4	1.51 %	0.00 %	0.0002 %
Electricity	1,417	0.06 %	0	0.00 %	0.00 %	0.00 %
Fertilizer	5,809	0.26 %	50	0.87 %	0.02 %	0.0023 %
Iron and Steel	62,351	2.79 %	4,375	7.02 %	1.42 %	0.1961 %
Total	83,489	3.74 %	5,913	7.08 %	1.91 %	0.2650 %

Source: Authors' own elaboration (data retrieved from UN Comtrade Database "Trade Data" Available from: https://comtrade.un.org/. Product codes from Annex I of https://eur-lex.europa.eu/legal-content/EN/TXT/?uri=celex:52021PC0564).

Note: We use 2019 data given the supply chain disruption from the COVID-19 pandemic may have affected more current trade statistics.

and steel. In 2019, the EU was the destination of 13.8 % of China's total exports and the industries covered by the current CBAM proposal represent about 1.9 % of China's exports to Europe, in value. China's greatest exposure is in the aluminum and iron and steel sectors.

China's ETS may alleviate the CBAM's effect on Chinese exporters. The national ETS, which came into force in 2021, regulates more than 2,200 power facilities and covers around 40 % of China's CO_2 emissions (Kardish et al., 2021). China's 14th Five-Year Plan (2021–2025) is scheduled to expand the ETS to include iron, steel and aluminum production before 2025; however, a definitive implementation date is not set (Liu, 2021). This could mean that Chinese exporters may be exempt or face a lower EU border adjustment. Yet, a problem regarding the pricing persists. Average allowance prices in China ranged from USD 3.28 to USD 12.62 in 2020 while the EU ETS prices averaged USD 28.28. With this difference, the EU may not exempt China from a potential CBAM, unless the EU gives China special treatment based on its developing country status (González, 2019). According to WTO rules, countries can declare themselves as a "developing" or "developed" country; however, other WTO members can challenge this self-declaration (World Trade Organization, 2021). With the current amended CBAM proposal that was presented by the EP (2021, p. 21) in November 2021, it remains to be seen whether the EU considers the Chinese ETS as a system with "equivalent efficiency."

During the Leaders' Summit on Climate Change on April 22, 2021, Chinese President Xi Jinping delivered a speech outlining Chinese expectations on global actions against climate change. He reinforced that any action taken by individual countries must be based on multilateralism and comply with international law. Furthermore, he stated that "developed countries need to increase climate ambition and action, and at the same time help developing countries and support them in financing, technology, and capacity building" (Ministry of Foreign Affairs of the People's Republic of China, 2021). Accordingly, after the EU published its CBAM proposal, Liu Youbin, a spokesperson for the Chinese Ministry of Ecology and Environment, commented that the EU's CBAM is a unilateral measure and undermines WTO rules in addition to eroding trust in the global community (Reuters, 2021). This means that the EU can expect significant resistance from China to its proposal. China may reject the EU's CBAM proposal based on its potential non-compliance with WTO rules. This indicates resistance against the EU and may undermine its normative power to induce emissions-reduction measures in China.

However, Hubner (2021) surveying various public and private stakeholders, including academics and NGOs from China, finds the prevailing opinion among Chinese stakeholders is the CBAM will not significantly affect trade. The rationale is China's national ETS (see Table 9.4) would qualify as an equivalent emissions-reduction measure, allowing China to make a strong case at the WTO if CBAM disputes were to escalate. Hubner (2021) emphasizes that to avoid an escalation or retaliation against the EU, open communication and early bilateral engagement between the EU and China will be crucial for China to accept the CBAM.

When considering the geopolitical implications of the EU's CBAM proposal for China, it is important to note that China's key ambition is to maintain its trade relationship with the EU. However, Fouréa et al. (2016) predicted that a CBAM will generate export losses in the range of 0.4 to 1.4 billion USD for China, the US and India. In response to these losses, China could introduce retaliatory trade measures similar to those that affected the agricultural sector after the EU had announced to include aviation into the EU ETS in 2012 which resulted in a WTO dispute (Fouréa et al., 2016).

The EU has also been criticized for neglecting the impact of its CBAM on LDCs and developing countries as its proposal does not indicate use of the CBAM revenues. Brandi (2021, p. 3) argues that "a failure by the EU to invest in other countries would create the impression that it is generating an unfair competitive advantage for itself at the expense of other countries." Brandi recommends the EU exempt LDCs from the CBAM and China is likely to seek such an exemption, either based on its status as a developing country or based on its existing national ETS. As negotiations about the CBAM are still ongoing between the EC and the EP, the main challenge for the EU is to prevent the accusation that its proposed CBAM is a unilateral and protectionist trade measure which contradicts WTO rules. Under a CBAM the EU will have to consider its future trade relationship with third countries and it likely will have to deliver concessions to its domestic industry and prevent retaliatory trade measures from its main partners, including China.

Russia

The EU is Russia's biggest trading partner. In 2019, the EU accounted for about 39 % of Russia's total trade (Table 9.6). Like China, Russian exporters face substantial exposure to the CBAM since the EU is also Russia's largest export market. In 2019, 41 % of Russian exports went to the EU. The EU sources most of

Table 9.6. Russia's Total Trade (in million €) and Share of Total Industry Exports by Value, 2019

	Exports		Imports		Total	
Global	381,061		220,715		601,776	
EU	157,489		75,441		232,930	
EU Share	41.3 %		34.2 %		38.7 %	
	Value of Exports	**Sector Share of Total Exports**	**Value of EU Exports**	**EU Share of Sector Exports**	**Sector's EU Exports as Share of EU Exports**	**Sector's EU Exports as Share of Total Exports**
Aluminum	5,024	1.32 %	1,802	35.88 %	1.14 %	0.4730 %
Cement	60	0.02 %	2	3.92 %	0.00 %	0.0006 %
Electricity	814	0.21 %	565	69.44 %	0.36 %	0.1483 %
Fertilizer	6,415	1.68 %	2,007	31.28 %	1.27 %	0.5267 %
Iron and Steel	16,777	4.40 %	4,184	24.94 %	2.66 %	1.0979 %
Total	29,090	7.63 %	8,560	29.43 %	5.44 %	2.2465 %

Source: Authors' own elaboration (data retrieved from UN Comtrade Database "Trade Data" Available from: https://comtrade.un.org/. Product codes from Annex I of https://eur-lex.europa.eu/legal-content/EN/TXT/?uri=celex:52021PC0564).

Note: We use 2019 data given the supply chain disruption from the COVID-19 pandemic may have affected more current trade statistics.

its iron and steel and fertilizers from Russia and also represents the largest export market for Russia in these industries. Different from China and Turkey, Russia also has significant exposure to the CBAM through its electricity exports to the EU (Makarov, 2021). However, the industries covered by the CBAM comprise a relatively small share (7.6 % in 2019) of Russia's exports to the EU by value (Kardish et al., 2021) which is predominantly oil and natural gas. In 2019, Russia was the origin of 27 % of the EU's crude oil imports and 41 % of natural gas imports.

The CBAM proposal has provoked a discussion in the Russian government about carbon reduction measurements. According to Bank of Russia economists Morozov et al. (2020), Russia is one of the countries greatly affected by the full CBAM implementation. Unlike China, Russia's national emissions-reduction strategy is underdeveloped, providing it no leverage in negotiations with the EU over an exemption from the CBAM. However, although the details remain obscure, there are plans to expand the efforts to monitor emissions (Climate Action Tracker, 2021).

Prior to COP26, Russian government officials signed a document that allowed President Vladimir Putin to announce that Russia aims to reach net-zero carbon emissions by 2060 but with no details on a specific timeline (The Moscow Times, 2021). In response to the EU's CBAM proposal, Maxim Reshetnikov, Russia's Minister of Economic Development, criticized the lack of clarity in August 2021. He also stated "at present, there are a number of contradictions with the rules of the WTO and international climate change agreements" (Karpukhin, 2021). Reshetnikov also claimed that the CBAM would "perpetuate the gap between industrialized and developing nations. That is, those that have already achieved peak energy consumption and possess energy-effective technologies, and the others, which have not achieved this level yet" (Karpukhin, 2021).

The 13th BRICS[14] summit on September 9, 2021, led to the New Delhi Declaration whereby state leaders, including Vladimir Putin, declared that "it is critical that all WTO members avoid unilateral and protectionist measures that run counter to the spirit and rules of the WTO" (BRICS, 2021). Opposing the CBAM, Russia condemned the proposal as a unilateral measure that should be considered protectionist. Reshetnikov stated "if we take a close look at the WTO agreements, we will see that, according to our estimates, the EU's CBAM contradicts them, in particular, such basic principles as 'national treatment' and 'most-favored nation status,' the introduction of import restrictions and many other things. In other words, we have solid grounds to put forward grievances. It is hoped that these disagreements will be settled and major disputes will be avoided" (Karpukhin, 2021).

As of January 2022, diplomatic relationship between most western democracies and Russia had significantly deteriorated and tensions escalated when Russia invaded Ukraine on February 24, 2022. The invasion follows a long territorial dispute, exacerbated since the Russian annexation of the Crimean Peninsula in 2014. A UN General Assembly resolution condemned the Russian attack as it violates Ukrainian "sovereignty, independence, and territorial integrity" (United Nations, 2022). In response to the war countries such as the US and Canada, as well as the member states of the EU, imposed new economic sanctions against Russian banks, oligarchs, and other key economic entities (previous sanctions were in place following the Crimea annexation.) The results are internationally strained or entirely disrupted economic and political relationships with Russia. Notably, the EU's and particularly Germany's dependency on Russian oil and gas (Brauers et al., 2021; Paillard, 2010) is a key concern for western states. Notably, Germany placed the regulatory approve for Nord Stream 2 on hold in late February 2022 (Marsh & Chambers, 2022). This decision is considered the beginning of a new era for German foreign policy with significant "implications for energy security and Berlin's broader position towards Moscow" (Dirsus cited in Marsh & Chambers, 2022).

The change in the pipeline's regulatory approval is widely considered a critical move in reaction to the war in Ukraine as reduced fossil fuel imports from Russia will likely exacerbate the EU's current energy crisis. Several member states, including Germany, face severe gas shortages, inflation, and high energy prices since mid-2021 (Blair, 2022). The EU's dependency on Russian oil and gas is a key factor in the broader geopolitical crisis between East and West. Even though fossil fuels are not included in the CBAM proposal, energy resources and related infrastructure, such as Nord Stream 2, are currently politicized and considered to be political leverage against Russia (Gustafson, 2022). However, the Russian escalation of the Ukraine crisis into a war shows that President Vladimir Putin is not deterred from taking extreme measures if he perceives that Russia's sphere of influence is threatened through a potential territorial expansion of the EU and the military alliance of NATO to the East (Sauer, 2017).

Despite the deterioration between the EU and Russia, it is unlikely that the EU's CBAM proposal will be an escalating factor in the current trade relationship. Russia's reaction to the CBAM mirrors China's as it aims to prevent export losses through a carbon tax (Karpukhin, 2021). Similar to the protest against the EU's plans to include aviation in its ETS, Russia may form a coalition with China and other states to dispute the CBAM at the WTO (see Fouréa et al., 2016). Unlike China, however, Russia is a developed country and thus has fewer avenues to pursue an exemption. In addition, the international outrage against the invasion of Ukraine may leave Russia with fewer political allies. Russia will likely insist on the WTO principles that render protectionist trade measures illegal. In terms of the EU's normative and regulatory power to influence domestic policy reforms in third countries, Russia is unlikely to align its climate policy measures—unless it sees clear benefits to do so, such as in the form of CBAM exemptions.

However, before a rapprochement can happen between the EU and Russia, "peaceful relations and trust are a must, and these are presently sorely lacking" (Gustafson, 2022). Thus, Russia's reaction to the CBAM is unpredictable in the near future, especially as the war in Ukraine continues at the time of writing. From a normative perspective, it is unlikely that Russia will be pressured into adopting emissions-reduction measures that align with the EU's current ETS. Previous work has indicated that economic trade sanctions, imposed by both the EU and US, have not changed Russia's foreign policy approach (Michalski & Nilsson, 2019). In the same manner, it remains to be seen how negotiations between Russia and the EU will evolve over the CBAM and if the EU has the ability to leverage environmental policy reforms within Russia.

Turkey

In addition to the current policy discussion, historical political dynamics affect the CBAM's geopolitical implications for Turkey-EU relations. In 1987, Turkey formally applied to join the European Economic Community (now EU) and became eligible to join the EU in 1999 (Emerson, 2004). Accession negotiations, based on 35 negotiation chapters, began in 2005 (Directorate for EU Affairs, 2019). The unresolved Cyprus question—the ongoing dispute between Turkey and Cyprus after the Turkish military invasion and occupation of the northern third of Cyprus in 1974—has stalled negotiations since 2016. Furthermore, the EU often considers Turkey a "buffer" at its external border, and financially supports Turkey to prevent asylum-seekers from North Africa and the Middle East from entering the EU (Saatçioğlu, 2020).

The EU's CBAM proposal, which would affect Turkey most in the cement, iron and steel sectors (see Table 9.2), could further aggravate political tensions between both jurisdictions. Currently, Turkey does not have a domestic ETS in place.[15] However, since 2012, the country has been evaluating opportunities to achieve emissions mitigation targets (ICAP, 2021). The Turkish government is working closely with the EU on meeting EU accession requirements in the energy policy domain. Policy sectors under negotiations are also called "negotiation chapters." The negotiation chapter on EU energy policies includes three principles: competitiveness, security of supply, and sustainability (Directorate for EU Affairs, 2019). The negotiation chapter on energy has not yet been opened; however, Turkey perceives it as a policy domain where it can achieve a "high level of compliance" with EU regulations and directives (Directorate for EU Affairs, 2019).

With Turkey, the EU's normative power manifests itself through potential EU membership. However, negotiations have already taken more than a decade and accession requirements may change, especially in the face of accelerated climate change and corresponding EU environmental policy. Another factor to consider is the geopolitical situation in Europe since the Russian invasion in Ukraine which may influence EU accession negotiations for various candidate countries, including Turkey. At the same time, the EU's normative power to induce policy reforms in Turkey is greatly influenced by its dependency on Turkey preventing asylum-seekers from entering the EU in an irregular manner (Gürkan & Coman, 2021).

The CBAM could have a significant impact on EU-Turkey trade. Similar to China and Russia, the EU is by far Turkey's largest trading partner. In 2019, 32 % of Turkey's imports came from the EU and 37 % of the country's exports went to the EU (Table 9.7). Turkey supplies more than one-third of the EU's cement imports, and is the third-largest source of iron and steel for the EU after China and Russia (Table 9.2). The EU is a major market for Turkey's exports in all five CBAM industries, with electricity particularly exposed. Turkish public

Table 9.7: Turkey's Total Trade (in million €) and Share of Total Industry Exports by value, 2019

	Exports		Imports		Total	
Global	161,484		187,838		349,322	
EU	69,681		60,702		130,383	
EU Share	43.2 %		32.3 %		37.3 %	
	Value of Exports	**Sector Share of Total Exports**	**Value of EU Exports**	**EU Share of Sector Exports**	**Sector's EU Exports as Share of EU Exports**	**Sector's EU Exports as Share of Total Exports**
Aluminum	1,924	1.19 %	1,120	58.22 %	1.61 %	0.69 %
Cement	823	0.51 %	95	11.61 %	0.14 %	0.06 %
Electricity	93	0.06 %	92	98.90 %	0.13 %	0.06 %
Fertilizer	307	0.19 %	84	27.31 %	0.12 %	0.05 %
Iron and Steel	11,719	7.26 %	3,907	33.34 %	5.61 %	2.42 %
Total	14,866	9.21 %	5,299	35.65 %	7.60 %	3.28 %

Source: Authors' own elaboration (data retrieved from UN Comtrade Database "Trade Data" Available from: https://comtrade.un.org/. Product codes from Annex I of https://eur-lex.europa.eu/legal-content/EN/TXT/?uri=celex:52021PC0564).

Note: We use 2019 data given the supply chain disruption from the COVID-19 pandemic may have affected more current trade statistics.

and private sectors work closely with the European Bank for Reconstruction and Development (EBRD) to enable an environment for a "scaled-up domestic carbon market" (European Bank for Reconstruction and Development, 2021). For this, the EBRD has three instruments at its disposal: policy dialogue; support for Turkish banks to develop carbon market services; and carbon asset development processes. For example, through its Mid-size Sustainable Energy Financing Facility (MidSEFF) Carbon Market Development Support Programme, the EBRD supported the Sena run-of-river hydroelectric plant, expected to generate 68 GWh per year of renewable energy.

Similar to Russia, without an ETS in place, the CBAM could significantly affect Turkish producers exporting to the EU. During COP26, Turkey's chief negotiator evaluated the CBAM as a "very big threat" because of the high share of Turkish exports that go to the EU (Weise, 2021). In contrast, the general secretary of the Turkish Steel Producers Association noted, "as Turkish mills are already investing in green steel, I don't think that the CBAM will have a significant effect on our exports to the EU" (Can, 2020).

Timmerman (2021) argues that the potential launch of the CBAM encouraged Turkey to ratify the Paris Agreement on October 5, 2021, through a memorandum of understanding with the World Bank. Although it could be argued that the Turkish ratification is a result of the EU's normative power, other dynamics must also be considered. Because of this ratification, Turkey will receive $3.2 billion in loans from Germany and France for its domestic clean energy transition (Weise, 2021). Furthermore, Turkey unilaterally announced that it would implement the Paris Agreement as a developing country, despite its developed country status in the UN (Lo & Farand, 2021). Therefore, as Timmermans (2021) suggests, even though the CBAM is at a proposal stage, it has already delivered policy responses and reforms in third countries.

Nearly half of Turkey's total amount of exports are destined for the EU which underlines the significance of the trade relationship. In comparison with China and Russia, Turkey has an additional long-term interest in complying with EU environmental regulations that derives from its prospects as a potential EU member state. In general, Turkey is more likely to identify itself with western values as also indicated by its NATO membership. Turkey currently does not have an ETS despite its monitoring, reporting and verification system introduced in 2015 (ICAP, 2021). However, it launched its National Energy and Mining Policy in 2017 which "focuses on improving energy security of supply; increasing the use of domestic energy resources; and improving transparency in energy markets" (International Energy Agency, 2021).

Turkey may insist on a developing country status but at the same time, it may also extend its carbon reduction policies in order to avoid trade disadvantages. However, the EU relies on Turkey to maintain safety and security at its external border. This provides Turkey with a certain degree of political leverage; however, mainly in the policy domains of security and migration which are less relevant from an environmental and energy perspective (Jäntti & Klasche, 2021). At this stage, the CBAM is still in a negotiation phase and thus, Turkey's reaction remains cautious as it maintains a muted response, also due to the lack of clarity provided by the EU on its CBAM proposal.

CONCLUSION

The EU's CBAM proposal is a mechanism to help meet its climate goals in the "Fit-for-55" package. The EU's CBAM is likely an intentional strategy to initiate discussions about aligning emissions prices across the globe. The EU's CBAM could represent a first move toward a global "climate club" with exclusionary effects for third countries (Bierbrauer et al., 2021). One important—and outstanding—policy design question facing the EU is the grounds for exemptions from the CBAM. The EU has not released specific exemption criteria, and these criteria are likely to be part of ongoing negotiations.

The CBAM represents a collective effort of nine EU member states, who formally requested the EC deliver a proposal (Blümel et al., 2021). However, as this chapter discusses, while some individual EU member states and their governments are supportive, domestic industry leaders and some of the EU's main trading partners have expressed concerns. Industry leaders within the EU raised concerns that the CBAM may diminish their competitiveness and result in lost export sales. Our analysis focused on the reactions of China, Russia and Turkey—the EU's main trading partners in the five sectors (aluminum, cement, electricity, fertilizers, and iron and steel) initially covered by the CBAM. We outline industry and government reactions and show a general apprehension toward the EU's CBAM proposal due to the above-mentioned criticisms. All three countries raised three main concerns, arguing that the CBAM proposal is a protectionist measure; it is a revenue generator to enhance the EU's budget; and that the EU's decision-making process is unilateral, which goes against the WTO principles of multilateralism and international cooperation.

China and Russia could use these three key arguments to protest the CBAM proposal at the WTO if the EU does not present significant amendments that mitigate the impact on its main trading partners. Our analysis reveals that China and Russia, although having distinct self-interests, are likely to adopt a similar approach as they have formed coalitions in the past, for example in protesting the EU's inclusion of the aviation sector in its ETS (Fouréa et al., 2016). China and Russia may consider trade retaliation, such as restricting exports into the EU. However, Russia's geopolitical relations are already strained since its invasion of Ukraine and it is already limiting natural gas exports to the EU, possibly in response to the economic sanctions imposed by the West. As a result of the war, the trade relationship between the EU and Russia may diminish as economic sanctions persist. Furthermore, Ukrainian infrastructure has been targeted in the war, straining its export abilities for example in the agricultural sector. Consequently, trading relationships between the EU and other countries may shift as EU member states seek alternative suppliers. In terms of environmental policies, the EU may strengthen its relationship with western countries such as the US, contributing to the formation of a climate club which would further divide East and West.

Turkey has strong and intertwined political, economic and geographical relations with the EU. As a direct neighbor, Turkey has taken on the role as a "gatekeeper" between the EU and Middle Eastern countries, such as Syria. However, unlike Russia, Turkey does have a concrete interest in joining the EU which may indicate that the country may, for example, develop a national ETS which aligns with the EU's environmental policies. EC spokesperson Frans Timmermans claims that the CBAM incentivizes policy reforms in third countries (Timmermans, 2021). He uses the example of Turkey, which ratified the Paris Agreement in October 2021 in an effort to become exempt from a potential CBAM.

The CBAM proposal reflects the EU's normative and regulatory power: its ability to influence political reforms in third countries. At the same time, however, internal and external resistance against the EC's CBAM proposal remains and will force the EU to deliver concessions throughout negotiations which may weaken the EU's position as a global climate leader. Nevertheless, the EC's proposal is considered groundbreaking in the sense that it reflects the first international carbon levy, and currently spearheads international discourse on BCAs. Thus, the EU maintains its position as a normative power in matters of climate change and takes on the role of a climate leader (Torney, 2019).

The CBAM is simultaneously a domestic policy tool and a political tool for the EU to exert pressure on third countries to increase their emissions-reduction efforts. For the CBAM to be widely accepted by the international community, the EU needs to develop concrete action plans that reflect on the potential impact of a CBAM on LDCs and developing countries and offer corresponding mitigation strategies. For example, the EU has not yet clarified how it aims to avoid an unbalanced trade situation that disadvantages certain countries. This would help remedy the accusation that the CBAM is a unilateral measure. Furthermore, the CBAM may trigger trade retaliation especially from the EU's biggest trading partners in the affected sectors—China and Russia. Trade retaliation could take the form of individual import/export restrictions, for example of agricultural goods. Retaliation could also involve mobilizing the international community to consider punitive measures via the WTO, especially if components of the CBAM are considered inconsistent with WTO laws. From a global perspective, the EU is a major trading bloc which involves 27 EU member states and affiliated countries, such as Norway. If the CBAM does not comply with current WTO principles, for example of non-discrimination and open trade, the measure could erode trust in the global trade community and third countries will seek an appropriate response from the WTO which could force the EU to revise its CBAM proposal.

NOTES

1 Affected industries are aluminum, cement, energy, fertilizers, and iron and steel. A full list of emissions covered by the draft regulation for each individual industry is published by the EC (European Commission, 2021a). For all five industries, the focus is on carbon dioxide (CO_2) but fertilizers also include nitrous oxide and aluminum includes perfluorocarbon (PFC) emissions.

2 See Manners (2002) and Pace (2007).

3 "Third countries" are neither in the EU nor the European Economic Area which includes Iceland, Liechtenstein and Norway. Switzerland would also be exempt from a CBAM because it has a bilateral trade agreement with the EU.

4 Leakage-prevention is only partial, as a BCA protects domestic production's internal market share from lower-cost imports (where the cost difference is from less stringent environmental policy elsewhere). A complimentary tool that protects domestic firms' international and domestic competitiveness is an output-based pricing system, which provides an output subsidy to emissions-intensive and trade-exposed production, mitigating the costs of environmental policy. See Droege and Fischer (2020).

5 According to the draft proposal (European Commission, 2021d), the CBAM will apply to imports into EU27 (Austria, Belgium, Bulgaria, Croatia, Republic of Cyprus, Czech Republic, Denmark, Estonia, Finland, France, Germany, Greece, Hungary, Ireland, Italy, Latvia, Lithuania, Luxembourg, Malta, Netherlands, Poland, Portugal, Romania, Slovakia, Slovenia, Spain and Sweden), the members of the European Economic Area (EU27 plus Iceland, Norway and Liechtenstein) and Switzerland. Note that the UK is no longer part of the EU and there is no clear indication if the UK (plus Northern Ireland) will be exempt at this point.

6 According to the EC, the European Green Deal will "transform the EU into a fair and prosperous society, with a modern, resource-efficient and competitive economy where there are no net emissions of greenhouse gases in 2050 and where economic growth is decoupled from resource use" (European Commission, 2019, p. 2). The Green Deal is a holistic policy program focusing on areas including climate, energy, agriculture, industry, environment and oceans, transport, finance and regional development, and research and innovation.

7 Indirect emissions refer to "emissions from the production of electricity, heating and cooling, which is consumed during the production processes of goods" (European Commission, 2021d, p. 28).

8 The EU ETS covers emissions from the following industries: electricity and heat generation; energy-intensive sectors including oil refineries, steel works, and production of iron, metals, cement, lime, glass, ceramics, pulp, paper, cardboard, acids and bulk organic chemicals; and commercial aviation within the EEA. It also includes nitrous oxide (N_2O) from production of

nitric, adipic and glyoxylic acids and glyoxal; and PFCs from production of aluminum (European Commission, 2021a).

9 For a discussion of the challenges of implementing BCAs, see Böhringer et al. (2022).

10 The EU's "normative basis" builds on five core norms: peace, liberty, democracy, rule of law, and respect for human rights (Manners, 2002, p. 242).

11 In December 2008, the EU adopted a climate and energy package targeting GHG reductions of 20 % below 1990 levels, increasing EU energy efficiency by 20 %, and 20 % of energy consumption from renewable sources, was all by 2020 (Peña & Rodríguez, 2019).

12 Cabinet ministers from the following EU members authored the op-ed: Austria, Czech Republic, Denmark, France, Lithuania, Luxembourg, Slovakia, Spain, the Netherlands.

13 These principles are outlined in the 1992 United Nations Convention on Climate Change: "The Parties should protect the climate system for the benefit of present and future generations of humankind, on the basis of equity and in accordance with their common but differentiated responsibilities and respective capabilities. Accordingly, the developed country Parties should take the lead in combating climate change and the adverse effects thereof" (United Nations, 1992, p. 4).

14 BRICS is a consortium of five emerging economies—Brazil, Russia, India, China and South Africa—cooperating on matters of the economy, society, education and other policy domains.

15 Turkey has signed a bilateral customs union agreement with the EU. However, Turkey is still considered a "third country" and the CBAM would apply to its exports.

REFERENCES

ACEA. (2021). *Position paper—Carbon border adjustment mechanism.* https://www.acea.auto/publication/position-paper-carbon-border-adjustment-mechanism/

Bierbrauer, F., Felbermayr, G., Ockenfels, A., Schmidt, K. M., & Südekum, J. (2021). *A CO_2-border adjustment mechanism as a building block of a climate club.* https://www.econstor.eu/bitstream/10419/232523/1/1752576446.pdf

Blair, E. (2022). Why Russian gas puts Europe in a bind over Ukraine. *The Globe and Mail.*

Blümel, G., Gewessler, L., Schallenberg, A., Wammen, N., Le Drian, J.-Y., Le Maire, B., Pompili, B., & Gentvilas, S. (2021). To fight climate change, fight carbon leakage. *Politico.* https://www.politico.eu/article/europe-climate-change-carbon-leakage/

Böhringer, C., Fischer, C., Rosendahl, K. E., & Fox Rutherford, T. (2022). Potential impacts and challenges of border carbon adjustments. *Nature Climate Change, 12*, 22–29.

Brandi, C. (2021). *Priorities for a development-friendly EU Carbon Border Adjustment (CBAM)* (Briefing Paper Deutsches Institut Fuer Entwicklungspolitk (DIE), No. 20/2021). https://www.econstor.eu/bitstream/10419/242609/1/1770115099.pdf

Brauers, H., Braunger, I., & Jewell, J. (2021). Liquefied natural gas expansion plans in Germany: The risk of gas lock-in under energy transitions. *Energy Research & Social Science, 76*(102059). https://www.sciencedirect.com/science/article/pii/S2214629621001523

BRICS. (2021). *XIII BRICS Summit—New Delhi Declaration.* University of Toronto. http://www.brics.utoronto.ca/docs/2021-New-Delhi-Declaration.pdf

Burke, T. (2021, February 25). A carbon club? *E3G.* https://www.e3g.org/news/a-carbon-club/

Can, C. (2020, October 6). *A carbon border tax could be against the WTO rules: Dalbeler.* Eurometal. https://eurometal.net/a-carbon-border-tax-could-be-against-the-wto-rules-dalbeler/

Climate Action Tracker. (2021). *Russian Federation*. https://climateactiontracker.org/countries/russian-federation/

Department of Finance. (2020). *Exploring border carbon adjustments for Canada*. Government of Canada. https://www.canada.ca/en/department-finance/programs/consultations/2021/border-carbon-adjustments/exploring-border-carbon-adjustments-canada.html

Directorate for EU Affairs. (2019). *Negotiation chapters*. Republic of Turkey, Ministry of Foreign Affairs. https://www.ab.gov.tr/chapters_62_en.html

Dobson, S., & Winter, J. (2018). Assessing policy support for emissions-intensive and trade-exposed industries. *The School of Public Policy Publications*, *11*(28), 1–47.

Droege, S., & Fischer, C. (2020). Pricing carbon at the border: Key questions for the EU. *Ifo DICE Report*, *18*(1). https://www.ifo.de/en/publikationen/2020/article-journal/pricing-carbon-border-key-questions-eu

Eckert, S. (2021). The European green deal and the EU's regulatory power in times of crisis. *Journal of Common Market Studies*. https://onlinelibrary.wiley.com/doi/full/10.1111/jcms.13241

Emerson, M. (2004). Has Turkey fulfilled the Copenhagen Criteria? *Center for European Policy Studies*, *48*. http://aei.pitt.edu/6575/1/1104.pdf

European Bank for Reconstruction and Development. (2021, April 21). *Turkey and Europe's planned carbon border tax*.

European Commission. (2019). *The European green deal* (COM (2019) 640 final). https://eur-lex.europa.eu/resource.html?uri=cellar:b828d165-1c22-11ea-8c1f-01aa75ed71a1.0002.02/DOC_1&format=PDF

European Commission. (2021a). *Annexes to the Regulation of the European Parliament and of the Council establishing a carbon border adjustment mechanism* (COM (2021) 564 final). https://eur-lex.europa.eu/resource.html?uri=cellar:a95a4441-e558-11eb-a1a5-01aa75ed71a1.0001.02/DOC_2&format=PDF

European Commission. (2021b). *Commission Staff working document impact assessment report accompanying the document Proposal for a regulation of the European Parliament and of the Council establishing a carbon border adjustment mechanism*. https://eur-lex.europa.eu/resource.html?uri=cellar:be5a8c64-e558-11eb-a1a5-01aa75ed71a1.0001.02/DOC_1&format=PDF

European Commission. (2021c). *"Fit for 55": Delivering the EU's 2030 climate target on the way to climate neutrality* (COM (2021) 550 final). https://eur-lex.europa.eu/legal-content/EN/TXT/PDF/?uri=CELEX:52021DC0550&from=EN

European Commission. (2021d). *Proposal for a Regulation of the European Parliament and of the Council establishing a carbon border adjustment mechanism* (COM (2021) 564 final). https://eur-lex.europa.eu/resource.html?uri=cellar:a95a4441-e558-11eb-a1a5-01aa75ed71a1.0001.02/DOC_1&format=PDF

European Parliament. (2021). *DRAFT OPINION of the Committee on International Trade for the Committee on Environment, Public Health and Food Safety on the proposal for a regulation of the European Parliament and of the Council establishing a carbon border adjustment mechanism* (COM (2021) 0564). https://www.europarl.europa.eu/doceo/document/INTA-PA-699250_EN.pdf

Fouréa, J., Guimbarda, H., & Monjonab, S. (2016). Border carbon adjustment and trade retaliation: What would be the cost for the European Union? *Energy Economics*, *54*, 349–362. https://www.sciencedirect.com/science/article/pii/S0140988315003436

Friedrich, J., Ge, M., & Pickens, A. (2020). *This interactive chart shows changes in the world's top 10 emitters*. World Resources Institute. https://www.wri.org/insights/interactive-chart-shows-changes-worlds-top-10-emitters

Gläser, A., & Caspar, O. (2021). *Less confrontation, more cooperation: Increasing the acceptability of the EU Carbon Border Adjustment in key trading partner countries*. Germanwatch. https://germanwatch.org/sites/default/files/Less%20confrontation%2C%20more%20cooperation%20%28EN%29.pdf

González, A. (2019, March). *Bridging the divide between developed and developing countries in WTO negotiations*. Peterson Institute for International Economics.

Gürkan, S., & Coman, R. (2021). The EU-Turkey deal in the 2015 "refugee crisis": When intergovernmentalism cast a shadow on the EU's normative power. *Acta Politica*, *56*, 276–305. https://www.theglobeandmail.com/world/article-why-russian-gas-puts-europe-in-a-bind-over-ukraine/

Gustafson, T. (2022). *Russia can no longer ignore the threat posed by climate change*. Europp—London School of Economics and Political Science. https://blogs.lse.ac.uk/europpblog/

Hubner, C. (2021). *Perception of the planned EU carbon border adjustment mechanism in Asia Pacific—An expert survey*. Konrad Adenauer Stiftung. https://www.kas.de/documents/265079/265128/EU+Carbon+Border+Adjustment+Mechanism.pdf/fed1d5a4-4424-c450-a1b9-b7dbd3616179#page=22

ICAP. (2021). *Turkey*. https://icapcarbonaction.com/en/?option=com_etsmap&task=export&format=pdf&layout=list&systems%5B%5D=66

Imeri, D., & Barzilska, P. (2021, November 9). *Challenges for the planned carbon border tax measures in the EU*. IHS Markit. https://ihsmarkit.com/research-analysis/challenges-for-the-planned-carbon-border-tax-measures-in-the-eu.html

International Energy Agency. (2021). *Turkey 2021—Energy policy review*. https://iea.blob.core.windows.net/assets/cc499a7b-b72a-466c-88de-d792a9daff44/Turkey_2021_Energy_Policy_Review.pdf

Jäntti, J. J., & Klasche, B. (2021). "Losing Leverage" in the neighbourhood: A cognitive frame analysis of the European Union migration policy. *International Studies*. https://doi.org/10.1177/00208817211030643

Kardish, C., Mäder, M., Hellmich, M., & Hall, M. (2021, August 20). *Which countries are most exposed to the EU's proposed carbon tariffs?* Chatham House.

Karpukhin, S. (2021, August 24). *Maxim Reshetnikov: Nobody says CO_2 must be fought against at any cost*. TASS—Russian News Agency. https://tass.com/economy/1329635

Kolev, G., Kube, R., Schaefer, T., & Stolle, L. (2021). *Motivation, Ausgestaltung und wirtschaftliche Implikationen eines CO2-Grenzausgleichs in der EU* (IW-Policy Paper, 6). https://www.iwkoeln.de/studien/galina-kolev-roland-kube-thilo-schaefer-motivation-ausgestaltung-und-wirtschaftliche-implikationen-eines-co2-grenzausgleichs-in-der-eu.html

Kurmayer, N. J. (2021, July 15). *German industry worried about EU carbon market reform, sceptical of CBAM*. EurActiv.

Kuusi, T., Björklund, M., Kaitila, V., Kokko, K., Lehmus, M., Mehling, M., Oikarinen, T,, Pohjola, J., Soimakallio, S., & Wang, M. (2020). Carbon border adjustment mechanisms and their economic impact on Finland and the EU. *Prime Minister*. https://julkaisut.valtioneuvosto.fi/bitstream/handle/10024/162510/VNTEAS_2020_48.pdf

Liu, H. (2021, June 24). In-depth Q&A: Will China's emissions trading scheme help tackle climate change? *Carbon Brief*.

Lo, J., & Farand, C. (2021, October 6). *Turkey ratifies the Paris Agreement after approving a 2053 net zero goal*. Climate Home News. https://www.climatechangenews.com/2021/10/06/turkey-ratifies-paris-agreement-approving-2053-net-zero-goal/

Lütz, S., Leeg, T., Otto, D., & Woyames, V. W. (2021). *The European Union as a global actor: Trade, finance and climate policy* (Springer Texts in Political Science and International Relations). Springer.

Makarov, I. A. (2021). Less confrontation, more cooperation. In A. Gläser & O. Caspar (Eds.), *Germanwatch*. Germanwatch.

Manners, I. (2002). Normative power Europe: A contradiction in terms? *Journal of Common Market Studies*, *40*(2), 235–258. https://onlinelibrary.wiley.com/doi/10.1111/1468-5965.00353

Marsh, S., & Chambers, M. (2022). *Germany freezes Nord Stream 2 gas project as Ukraine crisis deepens*. Reuters. https://www.reuters.com/business/energy/germanys-scholz-halts-nord-stream-2-certification-2022-02-22/

McWilliams, B., & Tagliapietra, S. (2021, February 11). *Carbon border adjustment in the United States: Not easy, but not impossible either*. Bruegel. https://www.bruegel.org/2021/02/carbon-border-adjustment-in-the-united-states-not-easy-but-not-impossible-either/

Mehling, M. A. (2019). Designing border carbon adjustments for enhanced climate action. *American Journal of International Law*, *113*(3), 433–481.

Michalski, A., & Nilsson, N. (2019). Resistant to change? The EU as a normative power and its troubled relations with Russia and China. *Foreign Policy Analysis*, *15*(3), 432–449.

Ministry for Europe and Foreign Affairs. (n.d.). *Carbon border adjustment mechanism (CBAM): France hosts an international conference (March 23, 2021)*. France Diplomacy. Retrieved November 27, 2021, from https://www.diplomatie.gouv.fr/en/french-foreign-policy/europe/news/article/carbon-border-adjustment-mechanism-cbam-france-hosts-an-international

Ministry of Foreign Affairs of the People's Republic of China. (2021, October 30). *Xi Jinping attends session I of the 16th G20 leaders' summit and delivers an important speech*. https://www.fmprc.gov.cn/mfa_eng/topics_665678/kjgzbdfyyq/202111/t20211101_10435619.html

Morozov, M., Danilova, E., Loginova, V., & T. Yudina. (2020, December 21). *EU border carbon tax: A challenge for the Russian economy*. Economic Conversations. https://econs.online/en/articles/opinions/eu-border-carbon-tax-a-challenge-for-the-russian-economy/

Moscow Times, The. (2021, November 16). *What did Russia achieve at COP26?* https://www.themoscowtimes.com/2021/11/16/what-did-russia-achieve-at-cop26-a75562

Pace, M. (2007). The construction of EU normative power. *Journal of Common Market Studies*, *45*(5), 1041–1064. https://onlinelibrary.wiley.com/doi/full/10.1111/j.1468-5965.2007.00759.x

Paillard, C.-A. (2010). Russia's and Europe's mutual energy dependence. *Journal of International Affairs*, *63*(2), 65–84. https://www.jstor.org/stable/24384335?seq=1#metadata_info_tab_contents

Parker, C. F., & Karlsson, C. (2017). The European Union as a global climate leader: Confronting aspiration with evidence. *International Environmental Agreements: Politics, Law and Economics*, *17*, 445–461.

Parker, C. F., Karlsson, C., & Hjerpe, M. (2017). Assessing the European Union's global climate change leadership: From Copenhagen to the Paris agreement. *Journal of European Integration*, *39*(2), 239–252.

Peña, J. I., & Rodríguez, R. (2019). Are EU's Climate and Energy Package 20-20-20 targets achievable and compatible? Evidence from the impact of renewables on electricity prices. *Energy*, *183*, 477–486.

Republic of South Africa. (2021, April 8). *Joint statement issued at the conclusion of the 30th BASIC ministerial meeting on climate change hosted by India on 8th April 2021*. South African

Government. https://www.gov.za/nr/speeches/joint-statement-issued-conclusion-30th-basic-ministerial-meeting-climate-change-hosted

Reuters. (2021, July 25). *China says EU's planned carbon border tax violates trade principles.* Reuters. https://www.reuters.com/business/sustainable-business/china-says-ecs-carbon-border-tax-is-expanding-climate-issues-trade-2021-07-26/

Saatçioğlu, B. (2020). The European Union's refugee crisis and rising functionalism in EU-Turkey relations. *Turkish Studies*, *21*(2), 169–187.

Sauer, T. (2017). The origins of the Ukraine crisis and the need for collective security between Russia and the West. *Global Policy*, *8*(1), 82–91. https://onlinelibrary.wiley.com/doi/epdf/10.1111/1758-5899.12374

Timmermans, F. (2021, November 10). *European Parliament side event at COP26—Carbon pricing in the European Union: An invitation to the world.* European Parliament. https://multimedia.europarl.europa.eu/en/european-parliament-side-event-at-cop26-carbon-pricing-in-european-union-invitation-to-world_20211110-1130-SPECIAL-OTHER_vd

Torney, D. (2019). Follow the leader? Conceptualising the relationship between leaders and followers in polycentric climate governance. *Environmental Politics*, *28*(1), 167–186.

United Nations. (1992). *United Nations convention on climate change.* https://unfccc.int/process-and-meetings/the-paris-agreement/the-paris-agreement

United Nations. (2021). *The Paris agreement.* https://unfccc.int/process-and-meetings/the-paris-agreement/the-paris-agreement

United Nations. (2022). *General Assembly resolution demands end to Russian offensive in Ukraine.* https://news.un.org/en/story/2022/03/1113152

Weise, Z. (2021). EU's looming carbon tax nudged Turkey toward Paris climate accord, envoy says. *Politico.* https://www.politico.eu/article/eu-carbon-border-adjustment-mechanism-turkey-paris-accord-climate-change/

World Trade Organization. (2021). *Who are the developing countries in the WTO?* https://www.wto.org/english/tratop_e/devel_e/d1who_e.htm

Wunderlich, J.-U. (2020). Positioning as normative actors: China and the EU in climate change negotiations. *Journal of Common Market Studies*, *58*(5), 1107–1123. https://onlinelibrary.wiley.com/doi/full/10.1111/jcms.13019

CHAPTER 10

The European Union as a Military Green Player: Sustainability and Resilience in Security and Defense Actorness

ANA ISABEL XAVIER

INTRODUCTION

Although it was first coined back in 2012, it is only in 2014 that a Green Defence Framework was approved by the North Atlantic Council, including operational effectiveness, environmental protection, and energy efficiency. In 2018, linked to the smart energy concept, NATO boosted those three pillars and agreed to improve the energy efficiency of the military forces, comprising sustainable energy sources.

Within the European Union (EU), the concept was first recognized in 2012, when senior decision-makers and experts gathered in Brussels to discuss the role of defense and crisis management while enhancing the effectiveness of capabilities. The proceedings acknowledged that the concept of Military Green should be perceived both as an umbrella stretch fostering responsible and effective capabilities for the future, as well as the backbone of effective defense and crisis management.

In 2014, an Energy and Environment Working Group was shaped below the European Defence Agency's (EDA) Steering Board supervision to consider the crosswise and complex nature of energy and environmental actorness in the defense sector. In addition, the 2016 EU Global Strategy recognizes that "Climate change and environmental degradation exacerbate potential conflict, in light of their impact on desertification, land degradation, and water and food scarcity."

Within the EU's new priorities for 2019–2027—green, digital, resilient—more improvements in sustainability are expected, both within the investment in the capabilities and technology.

Bearing this framework in mind, this chapter aims to overview and map the concept and implementation of the EU as a military green player, defining the extent of its security and defense actorness. The academic literature reviewed anticipates that there are different criteria to assess, measure, and evaluate the EU's engagement toward a green military agenda. For that reason, the implementation of the concept and subsequent doctrines remains blurred.

Still, this chapter argues that military green is an important label to define the EU as a player. The strategic documents shaped since 2003 highlight the rationale security-sustainability, and EDA recognizes that going green teams up technology and allows new business models.

APPROACHING THE EU'S ACTORNESS

The EU's actorness has been widely explored in the academic literature, as this *sui generis* player is neither formally recognized as a regular State nor as a traditional international organization (Ginsberg, 1999). Rhinard and Sjöstedt (2019) evoked Jacques Delors' "unidentified political object" to attempt to understand the EU's position and role in the world. In fact, as the acceptance and recognition of International Organizations as "actorness owners" has been growing, an extensive controversy on identifying criteria to measure and evaluate the process and the nature of the player remains (Dryburgh, 2008).

However, as far as the EU is concerned, we must go back to 1977, when Gunnar Sjösted pioneered actorness as "the capacity to behave actively and deliberately in relation to other players in the international system" (Sjöstedt, 1999; Sjöstedt, in Niemann & Bretherton, 2013, p. 265). Sjöstedt's groundbreaking work recognized that the European Community embraces peculiarities typically acknowledged with state features (such as common interests and centralized structures) although the lack of clear-cut criteria made it impossible to judge the EU as a player (Niemann & Bretherton, 2013). Still, Sjöstedt's assessment opened a path for new debates and approaches in the academic field by claiming that the degree of actorness can oscillate depending on the ability to deliver in a given topic or issue (Pavese & Torney, 2012).

In turn, Jupille and Caporaso (1998) frame the legal basis of EU action and capabilities through recognition, authority, autonomy, and cohesion/coherence. The two scholars suggest a theoretical framework to measure the degree to which the EU can be considered a player (Pavese & Torney, 2012) converging on a "hybrid and ambiguous international entity, in a constant state of development" (Groen et al., 2012).

But what recognition, authority, autonomy, and cohesion/coherence means for Jupille and Caporaso (1998)? First, recognition, is perceived as a precondition for a player's existence and engagement in world politics. According to Ginsberg (1999), it is agreed among scholars that the EU possess an international presence because of its visibility in both regional and international systems. Also, Pavese and Torney (2012) claims that actorness does not always involve diplomatic or international law-based recognition by other players but can be acknowledged in practice.

Second, (formal) authority may be weighed by transference or delegation of the abilities to the EU to perform as a player in explicit and detailed political fields (Pavese & Torney, 2012) The authors admit that when operating below EU's legal competences, the more specific the stronger the EU's actorness will be. Therefore, the EU's authority depends on the nature and extent of the exclusive, shared, or lack of competence allocated by the treaty provisions (Heidener & Thomas, 2011).

Concerning autonomy, Jupille and Caporaso distinguish between institutional singularity and independence from other players (1998), acknowledging the ability of an entity's performance detached from its members. Also, as Heidener and Thomas (2011) argue, the conditions for EU actorness improves as the political position of the representatives (head of state of the country holding the presidency of the Council or the Commission President) the size of the delegations, or the decision-making authority also grows.

The fourth and last criteria leading to coherence is an entity's ability to formulate and convey coherent and consistent options to its member states (Pavese & Torney, 2012) assuring cohesion and avoiding discrepancies, among member states or EU and the member state level (Heidener & Thomas, 2011). For Jupille and Caporaso, coherence imply the similarity of values amid EU members and EU institutions, as well as a set of procedures and rules to solve any potential disagreement. That also requires an agreement on the ground rules based on which policies are made.

Coherence is also a key dimension for Bretherton and Vogler's (2005) definition of actorness, though capability is the dominant emphasis concerning the internal context of the EU's action or inaction, the availability of political instruments, and the ability to use them. The scholars argue that the EU cannot be fully understood only by studying its behavior: "Rather, actorness is constructed through the interplay of many players, both internal to the Union and in the external environment of ideas and events that permit or constrain EU action" (Bretherton & Vogler, 2005, p. 2).

This rational alludes to Hill (1993) when highlighting the required preconditions to agree on a joint position, the resources needed and the instruments available that the EU can display in its foreign policy. Rather than being a fixed and well-established feature (Pavese & Torney, 2012), the EU's actorness is therefore the result of the interaction of a complex assortment of internal and external circumstances, driven by three main principles—opportunity (external context); presence (employ influence beyond its borders); and capability (explore opportunities and benefit from the presence)—to measure the extent to which the EU has become a player in global politics (ibidem). This approach to "actorness" uncovers the EU's particularities, as well as its engagement in a multi-player global system in permanent progress and expansion (ibidem).

First, opportunity is needed for the background or organizational setting, as it covers, adjust, and regulate whether the EU will function as an international player in terms of action or inaction. In fact,

> While opportunity is a structural attribute it should not be seen as an "inert background"; rather it conceptualises a dynamic process where ideas are interpreted and events accorded meaning. (Jacobsen in Bretherton & Vogler, 2005, p. 25)

Within a constructivist perspective, the authors acknowledge that this dynamic process encourages the EU actorness as an opportunity to benefit from its external influence. According to Bretherton and Vogler (2005), the interaction of a complex combination of internal and external circumstances may lead to another important element—presence—pointing out that presence is the ability to apply external influence, thus changing perceptions, expectations, and behaviors (Bretherton & Vogler, 2005). However, this deployment of influence that follows an external action is not necessarily intentional but rather a consequence of simply "being" (ibidem), which converges to Ginsberg (1999), argument that the EU possesses an international presence just because of its visibility in regional and international settings.

Thus, presence implies two factors. The first refers to the character and identity of the EU. Bretherton and Vogler (2005) insist that character is related to the EU's political system and that it covers all Member States and their institutions. Identity, in its turn, "attempts to capture the fundamental nature of the EU; it refers to shared understandings that give meaning(s) to what the EU is and what it does" (Bretherton & Vogler, 2005, p. 27). In addition, Article 2 illustrates the values promoted by the EU:

> The Union is founded on the values of respect for human dignity, freedom, democracy, equality, the rule of law and respect for human rights, including the rights of persons belonging to minorities. These values are common to the Member States in a society in which pluralism, non-discrimination, tolerance, justice, solidarity and equality between women and men prevail. (European Union, 2012, p. 17)

The second factor of presence "refers to the external, often unanticipated, or unintended, consequences of the Union's internal priorities and policies" (Bretherton & Vogler, 2005, p. 27). One of the features that contributes significantly to this presence is the "appeal" of the EU, illustrated by the enlargements and growing membership applications (ibidem). Thus, the presence of the EU has been increasing because of its material expansion and policy extensiveness (ibidem).

The capability third criteria is, in turn, broadly grounded upon the work of Sjöstedt (1977). It "refers to the internal context of EU action or inaction—those aspects of the EU policy process which constrain or enable external action and govern the Union's ability to capitalize on presence or respond to opportunity" (Bretherton & Vogler, 2005).

On the other hand, Allen and Smith (1990) focus mostly on recognition and authority when discussing the structural presence of the EU within the global system. Authority is perceived as both the external influence and the capacity to shape the perceptions, expectations, and behaviors of others. Recognition is not an intentional action but rather a consequence of the identity of the EU, internal priorities, and policies.

In 2019, a new model was presented by Rhinard and Sjöstedt, dividing the traditional actorness variables identified by the previous authors between more general and more specific characteristics (2019). The model begins by assessing player capacity underneath general conditions (autonomy and coherence) and then moves on to specific settings (policy cohesion and capabilities). It follows the specific environment (which considers the geopolitical dynamics) in which these variables should be considered. Finally, the authors point out that evaluating the EU's performance and influence (the effect) will always be critical (Rhinard & Sjöstedt, 2019).

THE EU'S GREEN ROADMAP

Environmental issues, such as climate change, are "one of the most challenging and pressing issues that international institutions, national governments, and local communities face nowadays as a global phenomenon with strong transnational and cross border impact" (Xavier, 2019, p. 136).

Still, if we look back at the 1950s, when the European Economic Community was created, the environmental policies were not acknowledged as part of the founding treaties (Jordan et al., 2021). It was only in 1972 in Paris that the European Commission first recognized that an environmental strategy would benefit economic progress, urging the creation of an action programme after the first United Nations Conference on the Environment (European Parliament, 2021). This was a landmark occasion because it helped move the European Community toward environmental action. In fact, in 1973, an Environmental Action Programme was supplied, and "by 1987, some 200 items of environmental legislation had been agreed … but the lack of a clear legal base for the Community's environmental policy was criticised by several Member States" (Farmer, 2012, p. 2).

Indeed, in 1987, a new title, "Environment," was introduced by the Single European Act, which supplied a legal basis for the Community's environment policy, "providing the first legal basis of the community's policy on preserving the quality of the environment, protecting human health, and ensuring rational use of natural resources" (Xavier, 2019, p. 141). Also, this Treaty served as the initial legislative foundation for a shared environmental policy aimed at conserving environmental quality, safeguarding human health, and guaranteeing the efficient use of natural resources and attributed environmental competence for internal European environmental policy (Delreux, 2021).

Since then, over the last 50 years, the EU has gained internal competences, enabling it to act in the environmental arena (Delreux, 2021) embodying some of the most ambitious environmental laws of any region in the world (Jordan et al., 2021). In fact, according to Vogler (2005, p. 836), the emergence of the EU as a leading player in global environmental politics could hardly have been predicted. No common environmental policy was ever founded, and there was no formal treaty recognition of such activity until the 1987 Single European Act, although policymaking had been underway for some time under successive European Community Action Plans.

In 1990, the European Environment Agency, headquartered in Copenhagen, was founded to assist in the creation, implementation, and assessment of environmental policies, thus giving cohesion and coherence to the EU. In turn,

> The Maastricht Treaty also strengthened the role of the European Parliament in developing environmental policy, by establishing the co-decision procedure in which it has equal power to the Council and extending the number of policy areas where the Council could adopt environmental legislation using Qualified Majority Voting (QMV) rather than unanimity. (Farmer, 2012, p. 3)

In fact, the Maastricht Treaty (1993) established the environment as an official policy area of the EU, as well as the co-decision procedure and the wide-ranging norm of the qualified majority vote in the Council. To promote sustainable development, the Treaty of Amsterdam (1999) incorporated environmental protection in all sectorial EU policies, strengthening the need to establish the environment in multiple EU policy sectors and introduce new approaches. Like previous treaties, Amsterdam also moved the decision-making process to co-decision for environmental policy.

In 2000, the European Commission launched the European Climate Strategy and energy package to help identify the most environmentally and cost-effective policies at the European level to reduce greenhouse emissions. This was the first time that the European Commission started exploring an extensive range of policies and instruments (flexible mechanisms of emission trading, joint implementation, clean development mechanism, energy supply, energy demand, industrial processes, transport, research, agriculture, sinks in agriculture soils, and forest-related sinks) for reducing emissions based on cost-effectiveness. In 2005, they were called the second generation of the European Climate Change Program.

In 2001, the EU released its first Sustainable Development Strategy, revised in 2006, giving to the Lisbon Strategy an environmental component and providing "a framework for a long-term vision of sustainability in which economic growth, social cohesion and environmental protection go hand in hand and are mutually supporting" (European Commission, 2009). In the same year, the European Parliament and Council set eight basic requirements for (non-binding) environmental inspections to address the substantial variation in implementation across Member States (Kurrer, 2021).

In the Lisbon Treaty (2009), climate change was made an explicit goal for the EU. The Treaty focused on integrating the fight against climate change and the promotion of sustainable development in the EU's relations with third-party countries. Also, Article 191 of the Treaty on the Functioning of the European Union (TFEU) confirms the EU's capability by regarding multiple dimensions that should be considered while formulating environmental policies:

> In preparing its policy on the environment, the Union shall take account of available scientific and technical data; environmental conditions in the various regions of the Union; the potential benefits and costs of action or lack of action; the economic and social; development of the Union as a whole and the balanced development of its regions. (European Union, 2016, p. 133)

In turn, the European Green Deal, published in 2019, is "the most recent set of policy initiatives on sustainable development that represents an opportunity for the European Commission to explain sustainability practices and prioritise the issue of environmental protection" (Eckert & Kovalevska, 2021, p. 1). Also, overarches policy framework intended to achieve climate neutrality in Europe by 2050, and it can be regarded as a new venture in EU climate governance (Bloomfield & Steward, 2020; Dupont et al., 2020).

The European Green Deal is an ambitious package of policies promoting the reduction of greenhouse gas emissions and investing in cutting-edge research and innovation to protect Europe's natural environment. The Green Deal's first climate action measures include the European Climate Law, the European Climate Pact, the 2030 Climate Target Plan, and EU Strategy on Climate Adaptation.

In parallel to the recognition of climate action as part of the external dimension of the EU Green Deal, the EU as has also earnest to climate-mainstream its defense and security sectors with a Climate Change & Defence Roadmap, published in November 2020 (European External Action Service [EEAS], 12741/20). The document outlines the actions to be taken by the EU to address the links between climate change and defense, including in the context of the Common Security and Defence Policy (CSDP), contributing to the wider climate-security nexus. An intermediate review of the Climate Change and Defence Roadmap is foreseen by 2025, followed by a general review concerning the overall objectives by 2030 at the latest.

The document is divided into the operational dimension, capability development, and strengthening multilateralism and partnerships, suggesting ongoing approaches and new actions at the EU level—immediate/short-term impact (within 2020–2021); middle-term impact (within 2022–2024); and long-term impact (from 2025 onward)—and member state level.

Also, in 2020, the EC unveiled its Biodiversity Strategy 2030, a long-term plan to preserve the environment and reverse ecosystem deterioration. On February 24, 2021, the European Commission established a new EU strategy on climate change adaptation. The new policy lays out how the EU can adapt to climate change's unescapable effects and become climate resilient by 2050. This strategy's four main goals aim a smarter, faster, and more systemic adaptation, as well as to increase worldwide action on climate change.

The European Commission released a series of legislative initiatives on July 14, 2021, outlining how it plans to achieve climate neutrality in the EU by 2050 framed by the European green deal and "Fit for 55" package. These initiatives include the intermediate goal of a net reduction of at least 55 % in greenhouse gas emissions by 2030. The package seeks to update several pieces of EU climate law, including the Effort Sharing Regulation, and transportation and land use legislation, clearly stating how the Commission plans to meet EU climate targets under the European Green Deal. Massive investments, research, innovation, new ways of producing and consuming, as well as changes in the way we work, travel, and live together, will be required.

Despite all the efforts on the last few years regarding EU's green ambition, the fact is that the first semester of 2022 accelerated as never before the strategic autonomy of the member states. The aggression of the Russian Federation toward Ukraine since February 24, 2022, stepped up a plan to rapidly reduce dependence on Russian fossil fuels and fast forward the green transition named RePower EU. Presented in May, this plan intends to crosscut five main areas: (1) saving energy; (2) diversifying supplies and supporting our international partners; (4) accelerating the rollout of renewables; (5) reducing fossil fuel consumption in industry and transport; and (6) smart investment (European Commission, 2022).

WHEN SECURITY AND DEFENSE BECOME GREEN

As we previously argued, the EU has made significant progress in the global environmental arena and has established a strong global presence (Zito, 2005). Climate change has become a high priority and one of the most prominent topics of EU foreign and internal policy (Brosset & Maljean-Dubois, 2020), embracing an important role in promoting multilateral environmental agreements (Kelemen, 2010) in areas such as biodiversity, trade-in toxic wastes, or regulation of persistent organic pollutants. Supported by the European Parliament (2022), the EU can act in all areas of environmental policy, such as air and water pollution, waste management, and climate change.

Still, some questions remain: How can green policies and initiatives be applied to security and defense? How can the military field respond to the environmental challenges and provide support to the national and international goals addressed by the member states?

In 1991, NATO addressed the link between security and the environment in its Strategic Concept, but a green defense approach was only coined in the 2012 Chicago Summit. Conclusion 52 highlights that

> A stable and reliable energy supply, diversification of routes, suppliers and energy resources, and the interconnectivity of energy networks, remain of critical importance. ... We will continue to consult on energy security and further develop the capacity to contribute to energy security, concentrating on areas where NATO can add value. To this end, we will work towards significantly improving the energy efficiency of our military forces; develop our competence in supporting the protection of critical energy infrastructure; and further develop our outreach activities in consultation with partners, on a case-by-case basis. (NATO, 2012)

In addition, Conclusion 53 emphasizes that

> Key environmental and resource constraints, including health risks, climate change, water scarcity and increasing energy needs will further shape the future security environment in areas of concern to NATO and have the potential to significantly affect NATO planning and operations. (NATO, 2012)

In turn, at the 2014 Wales Summit, Allied leaders agreed in Conclusion 109 that NATO

> will enhance our awareness of energy developments with security implications for Allies and the Alliance; further develop NATO's competence in supporting the protection of critical energy infrastructure; and continue to work towards significantly improving the energy efficiency of our military forces, and in this regard, we note the Green Defence Framework. (NATO, 2014)

Also, according to Conclusion 110,

> Key environmental and resource constraints, including health risks, climate change, water scarcity, and increasing energy needs will further shape the future security environment in areas of concern to NATO and have the potential to significantly affect NATO planning and operations.

In 2014, a Green Defence Framework was approved by the North Atlantic Council, including operational effectiveness, environmental protection, and energy efficiency as the three main pillars for using fewer resources and enhancing sustainability. In practice, NATO foresees reducing the energy consumption of military vehicles and camps, minimizing the environmental footprint, saving energy in exercises and operations, and developing common energy efficiency standards and procedures.

A new strategic concept was presented in Madrid (June 2022) to drive NATO's strategic adaptation and guide its future political and military development (NATO, 2022). On what concerns this chapter's topic is worth to quote conclusion 46

> NATO should become the leading international organisation when it comes to understanding and adapting to the impact of climate change on security. The Alliance will lead efforts to assess the impact of climate change on defence and security and address those challenges. We will contribute to combatting climate change by reducing greenhouse gas emissions, improving energy efficiency, investing in the transition to clean energy sources and leveraging green technologies, while ensuring military effectiveness and a credible deterrence and defence posture.

In addition, conclusion 36 highlights the Alliance's role in preparing for the effects of climate change, food insecurity and health emergencies on allied security and 43 frames the NATO-EU strategic partnership also in terms of the impact of climate change on security.

Concerning the EU, references to green or military defense in strategic documents—such as the European Security Strategy (Council of the European Union, 2003), its implementation report (Council of the European Union, 2008),[1] or the European Union Global Strategy[2] (EEAS, 2016)—are not explicitly driven.

In fact, in 2003, the post-September 11 security environment showed more diverse, less visible, and less predictable (new) threats: terrorism, proliferation of weapons of mass destruction, regional conflicts, state failure, and organized crime (Council of the European Union, 2003). Still, no major references to green or military defense were highlighted aside from the acknowledgment that security is a precondition of development as conflict, insecurity, and poverty can be intensified by global warming and energy dependence. Regarding this strategy, Javier Solana cautions that Europe is the world's largest importer of oil and gas—about

50 % of energy consumption in 2003 came from the Gulf, Russia, and North Africa—but it could rise to 70 % in 2030.

In 2008, five years after the adoption of the European Security Strategy, the so-called "Report on the implementation of the European Security Strategy—providing security in a changing world" (Council of the European Union, 2008) broadened the threats catalogue to include energy security toward a more unified energy market, with greater interconnection. In addition, the report raised climate change to a new urgency path, assigning it as a threat multiplier that can lead to disputes over trade routes, maritime zones, and inaccessible resources. This is rather important, as the implementation report gives a step forward in acknowledging the relations between climate change, conflict prevention, and crisis management, as well as the need to improve analysis and early warning capabilities.

With no major progress on the strategic institutional catalogue, the trigger is displayed by the EDA as summed up in a 2012 publication entitled "Military Green - Energy & Environment at the European Defence Agency" (EDA, 2012). EDA was established on July 12, 2004, "to support the Member States and the Council in their effort to improve European defence capabilities in the crisis management field and to sustain the European Security and Defence Policy as it stands now and develops in the future." This Joint Action of the Council of Ministers was first replaced by a Council Decision on July 12, 2011, which was revised by Council decision 2015/1835 of October 12, 2015, on the statute, seat, and operational rules of EDA to implement the provisions of Art. 42 TEU of the Lisbon Treaty. For that purpose, EDA's mission is threefold: support the development of defense capabilities and military cooperation among the EU member states; stimulate defense research and technology and strengthen the European defense industry; and act as a military interface to EU policies.

Within its overall mission, Military Green is traded as EDA's strategic tool to make an environmental difference, supporting the mitigation of adverse effects to the climate and ecology while strengthening defense and crisis management capabilities. While boosting a defense and crisis management community, green or military defense may be operationalized in different ways—by tackling consumption when preparing for operations and conducting them; promoting environmental values and the development and implementation of environmentally responsible technologies; educating the local population for the benefits of taking environmental responsibility footprint; enabling post-conflict reconstruction to contribute to long-term stability and sustainable development; promoting cost efficiency and increased capabilities; enhancing the endurance, mobility, and autonomy of the capabilities; and reducing the likelihood of security crises. To illustrate this, the following Figure 10.1 shows how the life cycle of operations (from the ongoing planning to lessons learned) and the life cycle of material (from

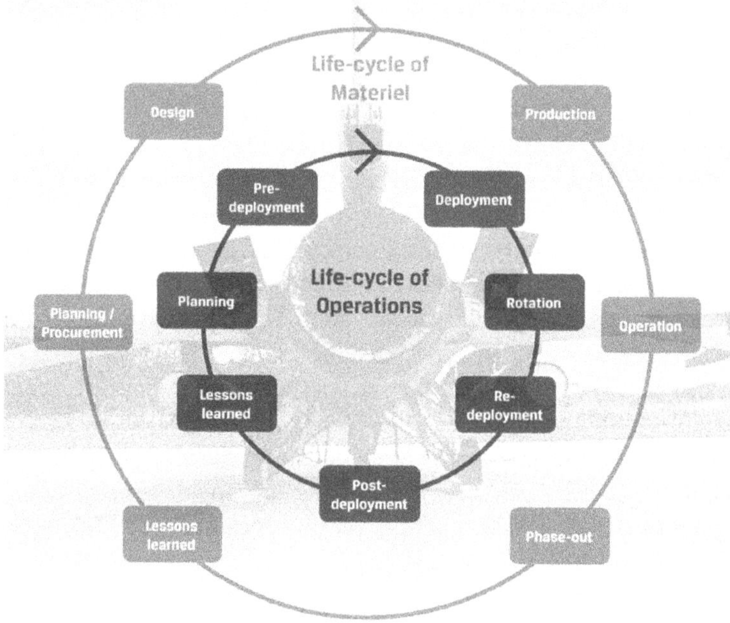

Figure 10.1: Life cycle of operations
Source: EDA (2012)

the ongoing planning/procurement to lessons learned) prospect a green ambition and an environmental footprint for all the phases of an operation.

In addition, EDA (2012) foresees five specific goals and focus areas for approaching the concept of military green:

1. Achieving energy efficiency by using energy supply technologies alongside conventional smart grids across all services (land, sea, and air), covering all systems down to the nano-level. The focus areas are fossil fuel dependencies, renewable/alternative energy sources, energy/power storage, efficient distribution and conversion, energy management, and efficient components.
2. Reducing the logistical footprints of waste and water. The focus areas are biomass and modular deployable water production systems.
3. Promoting smarter engagement through greener munitions. The focus areas are new propellants, scalable effects, precision, life cycle management, and insensitivity.
4. Minimizing through-life hazardous effects associated with materials. The focus areas are structural materials, smart materials, and surface protection.

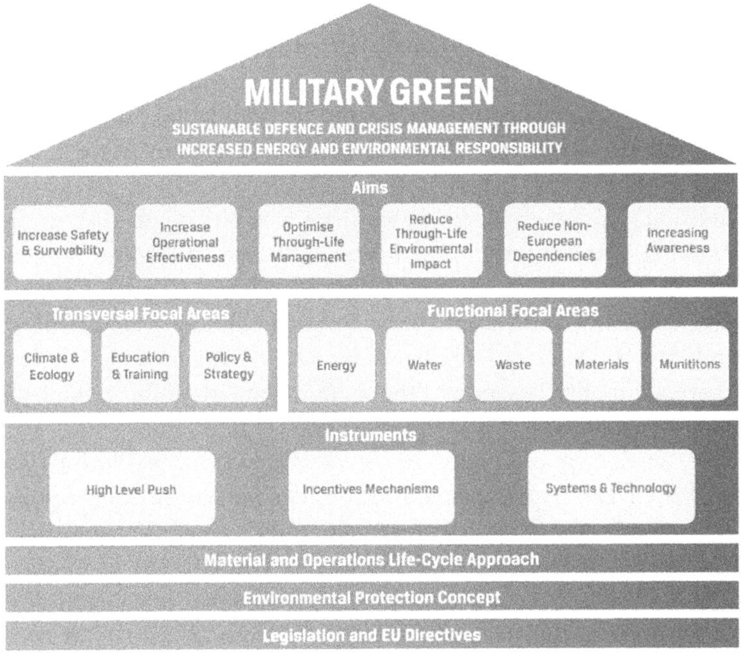

Figure 10.2: Military Green
Source: EDA (2012)

5. Studying the impact on climate and ecology, gathering statistical data on impacts, and providing guidance for eco-friendly design. The focus areas are the biological effects of exposure to acoustic and electromagnetic fields, statistics on energy consumption, and green design guidelines.

Barry (2022, p. 8) discusses how "central climate change is as a national-security issue, whether countries have developed specific defence climate change strategies, or undertaken assessments for individual branches/services," and identifies areas of opportunity for climate change adaptation and mitigation in defense: Sustainable mobility, energy storage, platforms, training, energy systems at installations, building offsets on the defense estate, improve emissions data collection, among other sustainability initiatives (Barry, 2022, p. 8). The same publication sums up the sustainable mobility options in detail (Barry, 2022, p. 17), highlighting the benefits and challenges.

In turn, Figure 10.2 illustrates how military green serves as the roof of a solid building for fostering responsible and effective capabilities for the future with an overall definition: sustainable defense and crisis management through increased energy and environmental responsibility. The five aims are identified, as are the transversal and functional areas of focus for each aim. The instruments—high-level push, incentives mechanisms, and systems and technology—frame the aims and areas. At the bottom, in addition to the material and operations life cycle approach (illustrated in Figure 10.1), are the environmental protection concept,[3] legislation, and EU directives, which complement the pillars of the EDA's institutional approach to military green.

In addition, EDA has launched a business model that cuts costs through the implementation of renewables in the homeland called "European Armed Forces GO GREEN." This project was established by Austria, Cyprus, Czech Republic, Greece, Germany, and Luxembourg, through public-private partnerships for investment, development, and suppliance in a win-win situation for all involved—namely, buyers, suppliers, users, and the environment—both in the homeland and in the field of operations.

In 2014, an Energy and Environment Working Group was formed under the direction of the EDA Steering Board to consider the nature of energy and environmental factors in the defense sector and to offer a structured approach.

This overview and mapping of EDA's role and concept of military green this concept and subsequent doctrines were implemented remains unclear at the European level. Nevertheless, the efficiency of a green or military defense is primarily decided by how it is implemented at the national, regional, and local levels. On that purpose, a reading of Barry (2022, p. 25) on a survey of defense strategies that address climate change and mitigation in each member state, comparing the national legislation of the 27 member states is worthwhile.

In addition, inadequate implementation and enforcement continue to be serious shortfalls. The EDA's progresses are important, but some shortages must be identified to critically assess the implementation in practice. The "fear that for the military climate-security is a topic to justify higher spending or even military intervention" (Van Schaik & Ramnath, 2021) is still controversial for member states, which are traditionally more skeptical about spending more on defense. Governmental and non-governmental authorities must be heard in green transitions in the sector.

More recently, in June 2016, "Shared Vision, Common Action: A Stronger Europe—Global Strategy for the European Union's Foreign and Security Policy" (EEAS, 2016) referred to the energy union and energy diplomacy, as well as to the implementation of EU's commitments on sustainable development and climate change. In addition, it was recognized that "Climate change and environmental degradation exacerbate potential conflict, in light of their impact on desertification, land degradation, and water and food scarcity."

On June 7, 2022, the European Parliament adopted with a large majority a report on the EEAS's Climate Change and Defence Roadmap (Council of the European Union & EEAS, 2020) that clearly assesses the defense sector as a key climate actor and for setting up the steps needed to restructure it in light of the 2050 European climate-neutral targets.

CONCLUSION

This chapter, entitled "The European Union as a military green player: Sustainability and resilience in security and defence actorness," aimed to explore the security and defense actorness of the EU and the extent of the institutional narrative of sustainability and resilience adapted to the military field. In the first section, the literature review confirmed that the EU's engagement and commitment have been assessed, measured, and evaluated to different degrees and in different forms. EU actorness cannot be articulated in a single, comprehensive definition; rather, it must be assessed on a case-by-case basis. Also, theoretical frameworks for defining actorness have evolved, and several scholars have upgraded the initial concept of actorness, although there is still no mutual agreement on this concept.

Section 2 clarified how the treaties framework links the EU's leading role in the green roadmap with the external environment that allows it, as well as to the set of tools it must affirm itself and the capability to put in practice concrete measures. However, since each Member State has its own preferences and viewpoints regarding foreign policy, this can sometimes hinder and constrain the type and effectiveness of the environmental policies that are disclosed or even erase the possibility that some of them will come to an end. Therefore, the role of international organizations is critical for tackling transnational cooperation and encourage member states to set realistic targets for optimal results.

For that purpose, in Section 3, by exploring the multilateral strategic acquis, we have identified 2012 as an important landmark, both for NATO and the EU, as the two organizations converged in an attempt to define "green or military defense." The definition of this term reaches far beyond classic environmental issues based on the reduction in fuel consumption and emissions and combines sustainability with effectiveness in crisis management and conflict prevention. We also acknowledged that within the EU, 27 different approaches can be framed in the EDA's role and capabilities, but the process is still ongoing.

We can conclude that the EU's capacity for action is limited by the involvement of the 27 member states in its security and defense policies, formulating policies that allow the EU to use these instruments and formulate a consistent and coherent green agenda. Although a lessons learned process has been clearly identified as an ongoing part of the EDA's leading role in the green or military agenda, the full potential of transforming the green into a military priority is still puzzling. The prospects for future research in this area, therefore, anticipate plenty of room for further discussion.

NOTES

1 Both presented by the EU High Representative for common foreign and security policy and secretary general of the Council Javier Solana (1999–2009).
2 Presented by High Representative of the Union for Foreign Affairs and Security Policy and Vice President of the European Commission Federica Mogherini (2014–2019).
3 This concept is being developed by the EU Military Staff and aims to establish the principles and responsibilities for meeting the requirements of environmental protection during EU-led military operations.

REFERENCES

Allen, D., & Smith, M. (1990). Western Europe's presence in the contemporary international arena. *Review of International Studies*, *16*(1), 19–37.

Barry, B. (2022). *Green Defence: The defence and military implications of climate change for Europe*. The International Institute for Strategic Studies.

Bloomfield, J., & Steward, F. (2020). The politics of the Green New Deal. *The Political Quarterly*, 91(4), 770–779.

Bretherton, C., & Vogler, J. (2005). *The European Union as a global player*. Routledge.

Brosset, E., & Maljean-Dubois, S. (2020). The Paris Agreement, EU Climate Law and the Energy Union. In Research Handbook on EU Environmental Law (pp. 412–427). Edward Elgar Publishing. https://doi.org/10.4337/9781788970679.00038

Council of the European Union. (2003). *European Security Strategy. A secure Europe in a better world.*

Council of the European Union. (2008). *Report on the implementation of the European Security Strategy—Providing security in a changing world.*

Council of the European Union & European External Action Service. (2020, November 9). *Climate change and defence roadmap* (12741/20 EN). Brussels. Retrieved from https://data.consilium.europa.eu/doc/document/ST12741-2020-INIT/en/pdf

Delreux, T. (2021). The EU in international environmental negotiations. In A. Jordan & V. Gravey (Eds.), *Environmental Policy in the EU* (4th ed.) (pp. 259–276). Routledge. https://doi.org/DOI:10.4324/9780429402333-1

Dryburgh, L. (2008). The EU as a global player? EU policy towards Iran. *European Security*, *17*(2–3), 253–271.

Dupont, C., Oberthür, S., & von Homeyer, I. (2020). The Covid-19 crisis: A critical juncture for EU climate policy development? *Journal of European Integration*, 42(8), 1095–1110.

Eckert, E. & Kovalevska, O. (2021), Sustainability in the European Union: Analyzing the Discourse of the European Green Deal, JRFM, 14, issue 2, p. 1-22, https://EconPapers.repec.org/RePEc:gam:jjrfmx:v:14:y:2021:i:2:p:80-:d:500748.

European Commission (2009), "Mainstreaming sustainable development into EU policies: 2009 review of the European Union strategy for sustainable development", https://eur-lex.europa.eu/LexUriServ/LexUriServ.do?uri=COM:2009:0400:FIN:EN:PDF.

European Commission. (2022, May 18). *REPowerEU: A plan to rapidly reduce dependence on Russian fossil fuels and fast forward the green transition*. https://ec.europa.eu/commission/presscorner/detail/en/IP_22_3131

European Defence Agency. (2012). *Military green: Energy & environment at the European Defence Agency*. https://eda.europa.eu/docs/default-source/news/military-green-leaflet.pdf

European External Action Service. (2016). *Shared vision, common action: A stronger Europe. A global strategy for the European Union's foreign and security policy.*

European Parliament. (2021). *Environment policy: General principles and basic framework*. https://www.europarl.europa.eu/ftu/pdf/en/FTU_2.5.1.pdf

Farmer, A. M. (2012). *Manual of European environmental policy*. Routledge.

Ginsberg, R. H. (1999). Conceptualizing the European Union as an International Actor: Narrowing the Theoretical Capability-Expectations Gap. In JCMS: *Journal of Common Market Studies* (Vol. 37, Issue 3, pp. 429–454). Wiley. https://doi.org/10.1111/1468-5965.00172

Groen, L., Niemann, A., & Oberthür, S. (2012). The EU as a global leader? The Copenhagen and Cancún UN climate change negotiations. *Journal of Contemporary European Research, 8*(2). https://doi.org/10.30950/jcer.v8i2.497

Heidener, U., & Thomas, J. (2011, September). *As time goes by: EU climate change actorness from Rio to Copenhagen* (Bruges Regional Integration & Global Governance Paper 3/2011; Working paper).

Hill, C. (1993). The capability-expectations gap, or conceptualizing Europe's international role. *Journal of Common Market Studies, 31*(3), 305–328.

Jordan, A., Gravey, V., & Adelle, C. (2021). EU environmental policy: Contexts, players and policy dynamics. In A. Jordan & V. Gravey (Eds.), *Environmental Policy in the EU* (4th ed., pp. 1–10). Routledge. https://doi.org/10.4324/9780429402333-1

Jupille, J., & Caporaso, J. (1998). States, agency and rules: The European union in global environmental politics. In C. Rhodes (Ed.), *The European Union in the world community* (pp. 213–229). Lynne Rienner.

Kelemen, R. D. (2010). Globalizing European Union environmental policy. *Journal of European Public Policy, 17*(3), 335–349.

Kurrer, C. (2021, May). Environment policy: general principles and basic framework, European Parliament, https://www.europarl.europa.eu/factsheets/en/sheet/71/environment-policy-general-principles-and-basicframework

NATO. (2012, May 20). *Chicago Summit Declaration*. https://www.nato.int/cps/en/natohq/official_texts_87593.htm

NATO. (2014, Sepember 5). *Wales Summit Declaration*. https://www.nato.int/cps/en/natohq/offici al_texts_112964.htm

NATO. (2022, June 29). *NATO 2022 Strategic Concept*. https://www.nato.int/nato_static_fl2014/assets/pdf/2022/6/pdf/290622-strategic-concept.pdf

Niemann, A., & Bretherton, C. (2013). EU external policy at the crossroads: The challenge of actorness and effectiveness. *International Relations, 27*(3), 261–275.

Pavese, C. B., & Torney, D. (2012). The contribution of the European Union to global climate change governance: Explaining the conditions for EU actorness. *Revista Brasileira de Política Internacional, 55*, 125–143.

Rhinard, M., & Sjöstedt, G. (2019). The EU as a global player: A new conceptualisation four decades after "actorness." *Swedish Institute for International Affairs, 6*.

Sjöstedt, G. (1977). *External role of the European community*. Lexington Books.

Van Schaik, L., & Ramnath, A. (2021). *Mission Probable: The EU's efforts to green security and defence* (Policy Brief). Planetary Security Initiative.

Vogler, J. (2005). The European contribution to global environmental governance. *International Affairs*, *81*(4).

Vogler, J. (2012). The European Union as a global environmental policy player: Climate change. In R. Wurzel & J. Connelly (Eds.), *The European Union as a Leader in International Climate Change Politics* (1st ed., pp. 21–37). Routledge.

Xavier, A. I. (2019). The European Union as a leading environmental player? A critical analysis on the policy and commitments towards global development and climate change. In T. Sequeira & L. Reis (Eds.), *Climate change and global development: Market, global players and empirical evidence* (pp. 135–151). Springer International Publishing.

Zito, A. R. (2005). The European Union as an environmental leader in a global environment. In Globalizations (Vol. 2, Issue 3, pp. 363–375). Informa UK Limited. https://doi.org/10.1080/14747730500377156

CHAPTER 11

The Energy Geopolitics of the European Green Deal: Two Case Studies of International Strategic Techno-Industrial Cooperation

ROBERTO ÁLVARO-HERMANA, JORGE FERNÁNDEZ-GÓMEZ, MACARENA LARREA-BASTERRA, AND JAIME MENÉNDEZ-SÁNCHEZ

INTRODUCTION

The renewable energy revolution and the necessity to respond with urgency to the climate change challenges and move away from conventional fossil fuels open the door to new approaches to global energy geopolitics based on a balance between competition and cooperation at various levels (technology, international markets, regulation, standards, etc.).

The European Union (EU) has recently taken steps to reposition itself in the global energy arena. The European Green Deal (EGD), a highly transformative process launched in December 2019 (European Commission, 2019a), includes a large set of strategies, action plans and legislative pieces that can be viewed, as a whole, as a wide-ranging, integral economic, industrial, energy and environmental strategy for the EU and its Member States, regions and cities.

The EGD attempts to tackle critical environmental and economic challenges, such as the need to comply with the 2015 Paris Agreement and the loss of industrial and technological competitiveness of the EU as a whole (Dennison et al., 2021), via an innovation-led medium-term growth and competitiveness strategy with a particular focus on developing a sustainable, competitive European industry that aims to position itself as a leader in world markets in the context of the global energy transition.

Recent events have led to the expectation that the EGD will play an even more relevant role in the EU and the world in the coming years. As a response to the coronavirus pandemic, most countries have put in place recovery strategies involving large sums of investments to tackle key social, economic and environmental challenges (OECD, 2020).

In this context, the EU has brought the so-called green, circular and digital transition, as defined by the EGD, to the forefront of the post-Covid economic recovery strategies. Thus, the NextGenerationEU financing package and the 2021–2027 EU budget will devote up to €750 billion—about one-third of the total recovery funds (European Council and Council of the EU, 2021a)—to green, sustainable projects and to foster innovation in low-carbon technologies. These include technologies ranging from energy storage (thermal, electrochemical or other forms of storing energy) to green gases and innovative generation technologies (e.g., tidal wave, offshore wind or hydrogen).

The "Fit-for-55" package, which is strongly linked to the EGD, includes several strategies and legislative pieces that aim to accelerate the decarbonization of the economy in light of the European Climate Law objectives of reducing greenhouse gas (GHG) emissions by 55 % relative to 1990 in 2030 and fully decarbonizing the economy by 2050 (European Council and Council of the EU, 2021b).

The mission-oriented innovation strategy of the EU in this area (Mazzucato, 2018) is expected not only to help it reach its highly ambitious energy and environmental goals (i.e., increasing the penetration of renewables to 40 % of gross final energy consumption and an energy efficiency target of 32.5 % relative to a 2007 reference in 2030, respectively, plus the above-stated emissions goals), but also to serve as a lever to create competitive value chains in different areas of the energy transition.

Additionally, the events in the world energy markets in the summer and fall of 2021, with record prices of natural gas, electricity, and GHG emissions allowances, clearly show the relevance of interregional cooperation in areas such as energy market rules or global infrastructure, especially in regions, such as Europe, with a high exposure to fossil fuel imports.

Although the EGD pays relatively little (explicit) attention to standard energy geopolitical issues, such as energy security and energy independence, it recognizes that "the ecological transition will reshape geopolitics, including global economic, trade and security interests" (European Commission, 2019a, p. 21).

In response to this challenge, the EGD pledges to convert the EU into a standard-setter, global leader in innovative climate change and environmental policies. Simultaneously, it will develop a "green deal and science diplomacy" focused on promoting sustainable development, forging green alliances, engaging with third parties in cross-cutting environment and climate policies, pursuing international cooperation and partnerships in climate change and strengthening its financial system to support the energy transition. This approach sets out the framework for a progressive reconfiguration of the European stance on global energy relations.

The EGD focus on international cooperation is clearly in line with the EU's general approach to international cooperation, most recently stated in a May 2021 Communication from the European Commission (2021a) that reaffirms the EU commitment to international openness and to strengthening the research and innovation ecosystem.

In short, the EU stance on international cooperation defines a playing field for the Member States and regions to partner with third parties concerning the technological, regulatory, market, and industrial issues related to climate change and sustainability. But it also paves the way for new forms of strategic, technological, and industrial cooperation at the firm level. EU companies now have strong incentives to explore partnerships and agreements with EU- and non-EU parties in order to develop new knowledge and technological expertise in low-carbon solutions, especially in hard-to-decarbonize sectors.

For instance, the focus of the EGD, the European Hydrogen Strategy and the "Fit-for-55" package on developing the hydrogen value chain opens the door to multilateral, international cooperation across energy and industrial companies, which will complement the various initiatives at the EU level to build a competitive hydrogen sector. Factors favoring cross-regional cooperation include the early stage of development of this industry, the uneven geographic distribution of wind and solar energy resources around the planet, and the fact that the solutions for decarbonizing fossil energy-intensive industries are required worldwide but may not be easily standardized.

The research question we address in this chapter is how techno-industrial collaboration agreements between EU and non-EU companies may jointly address (a) key EU sustainability objectives and (b) the challenges posed by energy geopolitics in the current context.

A case-study methodology is used to answer the above research question. According to Ridder (2017), one of the main strengths of this methodology is its capacity to create theory expanding constructs and relationships. In this particular case, following Yin (2003), case-study research can answer a "how" question when there is reduced control of the events and the target of study is a contemporary phenomenon. This article, written between July and November 2021, focuses on two (ongoing) case studies and qualitative data collection is carried out, mainly using public corporate documents as primary sources of information.

In order to answer the research question we first review the energy geopolitics of the EGD. We then explore the rationale for technological and industrial coopetition (i.e., cooperating in technological innovation while at the same time laying the ground for competition in world markets) in low-carbon technologies by EU companies within the EGD. Having established the case for technological coopetition, we analyze the opportunities and difficulties faced by companies in articulating research and development (R&D) and innovation agreements around new technologies, such as hydrogen, by focusing on two strategic collaboration agreements to develop hydrogen projects and technologies between Spanish oil and gas (O&G) company Repsol and oil major Saudi Aramco, on the one hand, and Spanish energy company Iberdrola and US technology developer Cummings, on the other hand. These case studies allow us to identify and delve into some of the reasons for strategic collaboration in innovative low-carbon technologies and the practical challenges faced by companies.

THE ENERGY GEOPOLITICS OF THE EUROPEAN GREEN DEAL

Rudolf Kjellén (1864–1922) first coined the term geopolitics to refer to the study of how geography affects international relations, power, and vulnerabilities, under the view that the spatial dimension creates different opportunities and limitations that shape societies and cultures (Gunnar Austvik, 2018).

Conant and Gold (2019) defined the geopolitics of energy as the study of the access to raw materials and, particularly, the access to energy. Energy security, a key element of energy geopolitics, gained influence since the 1970s and especially after 1990, in the face of a rapidly growing world demand for energy.

Since the end of the 1990s, climate and environmental concerns and awareness have been identified as key elements of energy policies around the world that have gradually shifted toward promoting energy efficiency, renewable energies and less dependence on fossil sources (in 2019, the EU energy import dependency rate was 60 %, with crude and LNG accounting for nearly 97 % of imports). This has led to an increasingly complex debate on global energy dynamics and relations between nations.

The New Global Geopolitics of Renewable Energies

The growth of renewable energy sources (RES) such as solar PV, wind, hydro, biofuels and geothermal energy, among others, and other clean energy technologies will eventually imply a profound shift in global energy geopolitics. RES differ from fossil fuels in aspects such as abundance, geographic spread, decentralization, lack of exhaustibility (Scholten et al., 2019) and their positive implications for international security and peace (Vakulchuk et al., 2020).

RES will also induce less oligopolistic global energy markets—strengthening regionalization according to Vakulchuk et al. (2020) and Franza et al. (2020), and foster electrification and more resilient energy systems. According to O'Sullivan et al. (2017), RES may induce the development of electric interconnections between nations and/or more widespread distributed energy generation. This will lead to increased cross-border electricity trade and growing interdependence among nations, and could even help to reduce political instability in energy-scarce regions. Decentralized renewable energy systems (based on hydro, solar, wind, and biomass, etc.) can also generate economic opportunities, especially in isolated rural areas or regions. Additional opportunities may be derived from the use of electricity to produce hydrogen and synthetic fuels (IRENA, 2022). According to Scholten et al. (2019), RES may help to solve the inconveniences of fossil fuels (i.e., import dependence, transport bottlenecks, impact on climate change and local pollution).

On the negative side, RES growth could create risks and geopolitical tensions linked to the demand for critical materials, cybersecurity, the uncertainty faced by key hydrocarbons exporters and the impact of rising energy prices and high fossil fuel dependence on developing countries. Also, the concentration of control over new clean energy technologies in a few players stresses the role of industrial policy in securing access to clean technologies (IRENA, 2019).

Nevertheless, there are discordant voices about the negative impact of RES growth. Authors such as Overland (2019) consider, for instance, that the risks of geopolitical competition over critical materials for RES deployment are limited and that cybersecurity risks will not necessarily increase as the RES grow. Independently of the evolution of these risks, the geopolitics of RES will differ from that of fossil fuels.

However, as fossil fuels will probably remain relevant in the foreseeable future (Lutz, 2021), energy geopolitics will be shaped by issues relevant to both RES and fossil energies, at least during a transition phase (Vakulchuk et al., 2020). In the particular case of the EU, this tension was underlying in the recent debate about whether the EU taxonomy for sustainable activities should include natural gas and nuclear energy (European Commission, 2022; Ohnesorge & Rogge, 2021). Eventually, the EU opted to include nuclear energy and natural gas in this taxonomy, under certain conditions.

Dependency and competition for access to critical minerals and metals, namely lithium, cobalt, nickel, copper, and rare-earth elements (Blakemore, 2021; IEA, 2021a) will lead to new supply chain risks.

Meanwhile, industrial rivalry over clean energy technologies and know-how will presumably intensify across regions around the globe. Although RES such as onshore wind or photovoltaic energy are technologically mature, there will be increasing uncertainty about which new technologies will be more viable and competitive in final uses (Criekemans, 2018) as well as about the prices of new technologies, materials and components (Franza et al. 2020).

The shift to renewable energy will likely alter the balance of power between states and regions and redraw the geopolitical map (Leonard et al., 2021). Also, RES may reconfigure economic and political connections and trade flows between countries, creating new interdependencies. New alliances and initiatives will foster multilateral cooperation in renewable technologies, such as the Oil and Gas Climate Initiative (OGCI), which brings together some of the main oil majors since 2014, or the Global Alliance for Sustainable Energy, an initiative launched in 2021 by 17 large industrial companies with interests in the renewable energy value chain (Bach, 2018; Politecnico di Torino, 2021).

Fossil fuel–producing countries will eventually see a gradual decline in their global influence, be exposed to a reduction in export revenues, and face the risk of destabilization, particularly those with more difficulties to adapt (Franza et al., 2020). Their main vulnerability is related to the complicated nature of their governance challenges. In the end, they probably should diversify their economies by increasing the share of RES in their energy mix and reorienting their national priorities (IRENA, 2019).

In contrast, fossil fuel importers could benefit from increased energy security as RES penetration grows. Also, suppliers of critical minerals and metals may find themselves in a privileged position, with the need to handle the new flows of revenues adequately, as Saudi Arabia or Russia have historically attempted to do with oil and natural gas revenues (Overland, 2019).

In this new global energy context, where renewable energies will grow in terms of both installed capacity and energy produced, three types of strategic leadership roles around RES can be identified: a) countries with high potential for renewable energy generation (e.g., Australia, USA, Chile, Morocco, Saudi Arabia or Spain), b) mineral-rich countries (e.g., China, Bolivia, Mongolia, Chile, Australia, Indonesia or the Democratic Republic of the Congo), and c) technological innovation leaders (e.g., China, Norway, Finland, Japan, Germany, India, Spain or South Korea). A number of factors will define the position of countries and regions from a geopolitical perspective, including endowment of critical materials, technology prowess, the control of knowledge (i.e., patents), the relative weight of capital investments in RES and the presence of leading companies in this new industry (Criekemans, 2018; IRENA, 2022; Lasheras Merino, 2021).

The Green Deal

The EGD aims to transform the EU into a fair and prosperous society, with a modern, resource-efficient and competitive economy with net-zero net GHG emissions by 2050 and in which economic growth will be decoupled from resource use (European Commission, 2019a). It is characterized by an ambitious industrial and global strategic vision and a robust external dimension (Franza et al., 2020).

Because EU environmental goals will not be achieved by European countries acting alone, as drivers of climate change and biodiversity loss are global (Franza et al., 2020; Grabbe, 2021), the EGD foresees that the EU will use its influence, technological expertise, and financial resources to mobilize its neighbors and strategic partners to join it on an environmentally sustainable path. The EU will need to become a standard-setter in GHG emissions reduction, sustainability and green, circular, digital and just growth, creating a level playing field in international markets and trade (Leonard et al., 2021).

The EU has progressively moved climate risks to the center of its security agenda in recent years (Johansson, 2013). In line with this, the EGD seeks to contribute to a leading role of the EU in international climate and biodiversity negotiations (i.e., defense of the Paris Agreement, a more straightforward commitment of the G20 with climate policies, development of international carbon markets, etc.). It also aims to strengthen the EU's so-called Green Deal Diplomacy through both multilateral and bilateral efforts by EU member states to induce partners to act in a way that is compatible with the EGD objectives (European Commission, 2019b) (i.e., the EU-China partnership on renewable energies and further engagement with African nations via green alliances (Franza et al., 2020)).

The Geopolitics of the EGD and the EU Green Diplomacy

One of the key EGD goals is for the EU to position itself globally as a sustainable industrial and technological leader, adding the climate and environmental dimensions to the Common Foreign and Security Policy and the Common Security and Defense Policy (Elkington & Evans, 2021). As the EGD Communication states in its third paragraph ("The EU as a global leader"), the EU will also need to develop an ecological (or green) foreign policy to push other states to do the same and support developing nations in the regeneration of their economies (Pastukhova et al., 2020; Youngs, 2021a), under the view that if the EU is successful in its sustainability transition, other regions may follow it (Grabbe, 2021). The EU geostrategy must therefore address the economic, social, technological and environmental gaps between North and South and also between East and West.

In this regard, although the EU has not fully developed a comprehensive foreign policy, international trade emerges as a second-best mechanism to address climate change (Goldthau, 2021) and an essential part of the EU's foreign policy (Youngs, 2021b).

The EGD will reshape the EU energy diplomacy policy (Pastukhova et al., 2020) designed in 2015 within the European Energy Diplomacy Action Plan framework, which targeted as key priorities the security of energy supply, fostering energy partnerships and dialogues and creating a multilateral energy governance (Council of the European Union, 2015). It will need to address the geo-economic and geopolitical challenges stemming from the global energy transition, and especially from the EU goal of becoming the first climate-neutral region by 2050.

The new EU diplomacy should consider the relevance of investments in adaptation, resilience and people (Franza et al., 2020) and also balance the O&G geopolitics of the past with sustainable energy development and the regional opportunities offered by the green recovery (Escribano & Lázaro, 2020).

In a nutshell, the EU green energy diplomacy, as devised by the EGD, will play a vital role in the maintenance and reinforcement of energy security of the EU and its partners, promoting the shift from fossil fuels to RES and energy efficiency, the development of low-carbon technologies, and the adoption of new environmental, nuclear safety and transparency standards, also deepening international cooperation on hydrogen (Council of the European Union, 2021).

New interdependencies across regions, countries and companies globally, where cooperation will be indispensable, are expected to grow in this scenario (Escribano, 2021; IDDRI, 2021). The global ramifications of climate change will perhaps lead to EU partnerships with the USA, China (a key player in critical raw materials), Saudi Arabia and Russia (relevant O&G producers and exporters) and the "Global South" (EsadeGeo, 2021).

One of the levers to achieve the EGD's stated environmental ambition is innovation in low-carbon technological and industrial solutions. A mixture of cooperation and competition is deemed necessary in order to advance toward a global, low-carbon economy (Leonard et al., 2021). As a consequence, the EU and other developed regions and nations are entering into a dynamic of cooperation in innovation, but also of competition to gain first-mover advantages and leading positions in key markets. Strategic autonomy, industrial and technological leadership, economic sovereignty and trade opportunities linked to sustainable development are some key factors that should be considered by decision-makers when designing international innovation policies (IDDRI, 2021).

To sum up, energy is a crucial geopolitical feature of the EGD and its goal to turn the EU into the world's sustainability leader (Kefferpütz, 2021) and achieve key energy, economic and geopolitical goals. The EU must be prepared to assume the repercussions and potential risks of its new stance (Figure 11.1) and to deal

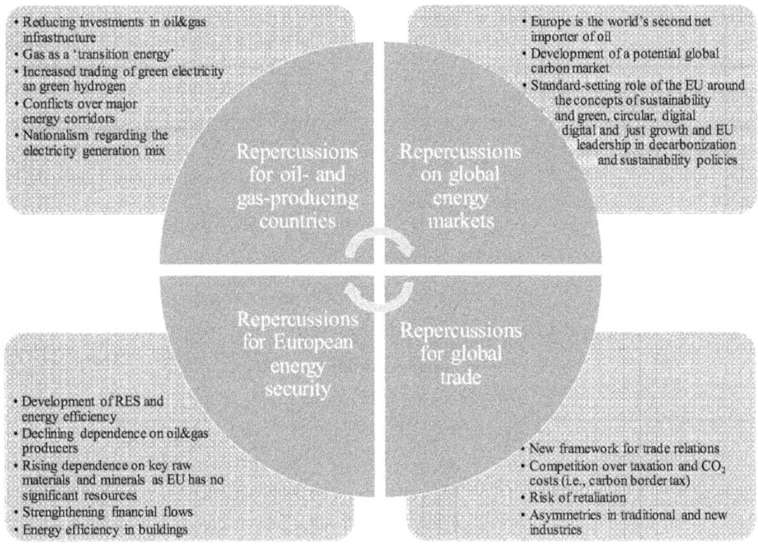

Figure 11.1: Geopolitical repercussions of the EGD

Source: Author's own elaboration.

with tensions stemming from its green leadership, including both those with internal and external impact (e.g., that the transition may not succeed because of geopolitical tensions) (Lasheras Merino, 2021).

TECHNOLOGICAL AND INDUSTRIAL COOPERATION AND CLIMATE CHANGE

The growing importance of sustainability and the diverse and asymmetric impacts of climate change are expected to transform the current relationships between countries (and companies in different countries), transitioning from a situation where technological competition is the norm (for instance, in telecoms, cybersecurity, defense, etc.) to a new paradigm with higher interdependency and need for cooperation across regional actors (both states and companies).

At the firm and industrial level, the need to reduce emissions across the entire economy, especially in hard-to-decarbonize sectors, is forcing many energy companies (mainly O&G companies) to redefine their overall business strategies, transforming them into all-around energy companies. This process is partly based on the forging of alliances with technological companies and former and future competitors and is being sped up by the growing political and social concern about climate change.

Climate Change, Public Goods, Externalities, Free Riding and Cooperation

The need to fight climate change, adapt to and mitigate its consequences has been seen in the past in many academic articles as a collective global problem about devising adequate mechanisms to cooperate in the face of strong incentives for free riding.

The atmosphere can be seen as a nearly pure public good (i.e., it is a non-excludable, non-rivalrous good, which means that benefiting from it is accessible to all and that enjoying it by one does not prevent usage or consumption by others).

Emitting GHG, a result of most human activities, imposes a cost on citizens, companies and societies worldwide. This cost is directly linked to climate change and its implications. Abatement costs are borne today and locally, whereas the benefits of emissions reductions (decarbonization) are reaped independently of the location of the emissions, and mainly in the distant future (Nordhaus, 2015).

Thus, there is room for free riding (i.e., countries and companies continue to emit GHG while avoiding the total cost of the externalities and not facing the need to abate the emissions). Although so-called climate clubs and international agreements such as the Kyoto Protocol or the Paris Agreement try to engage governments around the world to implement agreed decarbonization policies (or apply common policy guidelines), thus tackling free riding to some extent (Nordhaus, 2015), there do not exist to date effective mechanisms at the global level to assign the environmental costs of emissions.

This is an example of the "tragedy of the commons" (Lasheras Merino, 2021). Because there is no mechanism to limit the overuse of the atmosphere (in the form of GHG emissions) by firms and countries and because polluters do not face the direct consequences of their emissions, no company or country has incentives to unilaterally change their behavior.

Some recent studies challenge this view and suggest that conditional cooperation among countries, as reflected by the Kyoto Protocol or the Paris Agreement, is empirically unsubstantiated and that governments tend to implement climate policies regardless of what other countries do and irrespective of whether there is a global climate agreement in place or not (Aklin & Mildenberger, 2020). Under this view, countries do not care about reciprocal action and, instead, develop climate policies reflecting preferences from voters and interest groups.

A Global Challenge and Its Impact on International Relations

Whether the issue is analyzed from a game-theoretical or a political economy perspective, the growing relevance of climate change as a critical challenge for societies around the world is contributing to the need to shape new international relations and innovative firm strategies and business approaches.

Two additional factors, related to technological and non-technological innovation, also help to define the new context. First, the quest for sustainability is changing the nature of competition in most markets. The EGD, for example, is betting on developing a competitive green, digital and circular European industry. Many norms and strategies are being passed and approved to force European industrial (and services) companies to deliver goods and services with a low environmental footprint (i.e., low implicit emissions and no significant environmental impacts).

These policy-induced changes profoundly modify the playing field in all industrial sectors across Europe and force industrial companies to change their energy sources and technologies, become more efficient in the consumption and use of energy and materials, and implement new production and logistic processes. The EGD promise is that all markets will eventually evolve into sustainable markets where consumers only demand goods and services with low or zero environmental footprint. Companies that do not adapt to this new context through continuous innovation will eventually disappear. In this sense, sustainability is becoming a triple (social, economic and environmental) goal and a lever of competitiveness for companies and territories.

Secondly, there is a need to innovate on the technology side to tackle climate change and decarbonize all economic sectors successfully. While recent studies suggest that most of the decarbonization of the global economy could be based on existing technologies (DNV, 2021), the reality is that many of the technological solutions are still far from being economical and marketable (see the EIA's ETP Clean Energy Technology Guide; IEA, 2021b). Substantial research and innovation will be required to develop and deploy cost-efficient disruptive emissions-reducing (or removing) technologies, especially in hard-to-decarbonize sectors such as many industrial sectors or parts of the transport and mobility system.

Significant innovation will be required, for instance, and just to name a few, in areas ranging from renewable energies (e.g., marine wind energy or geothermal) to hydrogen, green gases, electricity and heat storage, CCUS (carbon capture, use and storage) or direct carbon removal technologies.

Cooperation or Competition in Innovation in Low-Carbon Technologies?

While the potential to develop groundbreaking energy technologies with impact on end-use markets has traditionally led to substantial amounts of competition across countries and regions and an attempt to protect intellectual and technological property, other factors, mostly related to energy security, have historically induced forced cooperation between countries on the energy front. The development in recent decades of natural gas pipelines from Russia to Central Europe that cross third countries (Belarus, Ukraine, Turkey) within a complex geopolitical context is a good example.

The global scale and the interconnected nature of the climate change challenge are leading most countries and regions, including the EU, to renew, in a positive way, their view about the benefits of technological coopetition (Amelang, 2021).

Coopetition allows companies and countries to reap the benefits from both cooperation (i.e., access to resources, talent, knowledge, know-how and capabilities at a lower cost; business opportunities; and, from the point of view of States, way to deploy diplomacy and external policy strategies) and competition (i.e., pressure to innovate and improve business outcomes). The positive impact of coopetition on innovation is well known: firms that cooperate with competitors internationally are more likely to show a higher propensity to introduce radical (new-to-market) innovations, although the magnitude of the effect depends on the size of the organizational adjustments (Vanyushyn et al., 2017). Thus, there is a positive link between international coopetition alliances and innovative performance.

A "coopetitive" approach to low-carbon technology can be found in the EGD. On the one hand, one of the key goals of the new energy-climate strategy of the EU is to become a global leader in developing a sustainable industry. This means adopting and creating best practices in manufacturing, circular economy, industrial logistics, transportation, but also developing sustainable competitive advantages throughout the entire industrial and R&D value chains in renewable energy and other relevant low-carbon technologies in different sectors (i.e., batteries, heat pumps, hydrogen technologies, smart power grids or carbon capture, use and storage) and also becoming a trend- and standard-setter globally in the area of environmental sustainability. It also means creating a technological and industrial field of play that allows European industrial companies to compete in international markets (thus the existence of certain "nationalistic" or protectionist features in the EGD toolbox; i.e., the carbon border tax).

On the other hand, there is a clear emphasis in the new energy-climate-sustainability strategy in the EU on enhancing technological cooperation to tackle the global climate challenge and, as a byproduct, to generate new opportunities for European companies. This is clearly in line with the EU R&D and innovation strategy and policies, which identify international cooperation in R&D as a strategic priority and encourage participation by third parties and countries in the Horizon 2020 program (European Commission, 2021b) and the development of "science diplomacy" (European Commission, 2019, 2021c) as a means to "project soft power and pursue [our] economic interests and values more effectively." This translates into a clear support for multilateral research and innovation partnerships that may take different forms, ranging from "informal arrangements between partners to coordinate their independent investments in key fields, through to partnerships providing for the pooling of resources in joint initiatives" (European Commission, 2021c).

To sum up, the EGD paves the way to new forms of technological and commercial cooperation between the EU, the EU member states and European companies with third parties as a way to (1) strengthen and implement its strategy to become a world leader in industrial sustainability; (2) create business opportunities and open new markets for European companies; and (3) contribute to other energy and sustainability geopolitical goals, such as energy or climate security.

TWO CASE STUDIES OF STRATEGIC R&D COLLABORATIONS IN HYDROGEN

Case Study #1: Collaboration Between Repsol-Petronor and Saudi Aramco

This case study addresses the collaboration between Spain's Repsol and Saudi Arabia's state-owned Aramco, announced in June 2020, which aims to develop clean energy and hydrogen-based decarbonization projects in the Basque Country, Northern Spain (Baratti, 2020; Brelsford, 2021; Repsol, 2021a, 2021b).

Aramco's activities are deeply linked to Saudi Arabia's policy and economy, which means that it will be a key actor in the fulfillment of "Vision 2030," Saudi Arabia's major strategy to diversify its economy and shift away from petroleum (Amran et al., 2020; Markarian & Stockhausen, 2018; Moshashai et al., 2018; Neal, 2019; Ramady, 2018; Woertz, 2019). This also applies to Saudi Arabia's announced net-zero emissions target for 2060 (Al-Atrush et al., 2021).

These ties may benefit from Aramco's ample experience in international cooperation in R&D and strategic projects. For example, with research institutions in Europe, the USA or South Korea, as well as joint ventures in the downstream business with companies like Shell, Total or ExxonMobil (Aramco, 2021a). These include green hydrogen, ammonia production and renewable energy (Aramco, 2018a, 2018b, 2021a, 2021b; Brown, 2021; Oommen, 2021).

Aramco's collaboration with Repsol can be included in this list. Repsol is considered an advanced player in clean energy development within the O&G sector, following a clear strategy of diversification away from fossil fuels by reconverting its industrial facilities into multi-energy hubs and pursuing collaboration with energy companies with similar interests, as part of its core business transformation.

An example of this is the agreement with EDP to develop green hydrogen projects in Portugal and other locations (Repsol, 2021c). This is also related to one of Repsol's flagship decarbonization projects: a profound transformation of its refinery in Bilbao (Spain), owned and operated by its subsidiary Petronor. According to Repsol's 2021–2025 Strategic Plan, Petronor is to become an R&D and innovation pole that will lead the multi-energy, decarbonization strategy of the whole group's industrial business, placing clean hydrogen at the forefront of its strategy (Repsol, 2020).

Aramco's historical willingness to engage in international cooperation is therefore aligned with Repsol's (and Petronor's) strategy, creating at the same time synergies between Saudi Arabia's strategic Vision 2030 and the EGD's energy and environmental goals.

The Repsol-Aramco agreement involves an €80 million investment in two projects. The first one involves the development of a synthetic fuels production process, while the second one consists of building a pyrolysis treatment plant to produce biogas from urban waste. Both projects are to be located in the port of Bilbao, near Petronor's refinery.

Aramco's interest is related to the technological collaboration in the strategic synthetic fuels project, which integrates several groundbreaking technologies and solutions: for example, the reverse water-gas shift (RWGS) reaction and Fischer-Tropsch process, the use of a 10 MW electrolyzer for green hydrogen production (fed with electricity from an on-site wind generation capacity) and the capture and use of some of the refinery's CO_2 emissions. This facility, scheduled to start operating in 2024, will initially produce 50 barrels (8,000–10,000 liters) per day of synthetic fuels to be supplied mainly for transport uses. Figure 11.2 shows the project's value chain.

According to the available information on the agreement, Petronor will host the projects and its parent company Repsol will participate in it through its main technological and scientific center, Repsol Technology Lab. Repsol-Petronor's interest in the collaboration stems from the need to urgently develop new decarbonization and diversification solutions to preserve the long-term competitiveness of its refinery and industrial businesses.

Several sources of synergies and value make this project strategic to both partners. First, synthetic hydrocarbon fuels are considered one of the key clean energy technologies needed for achieving net-zero emissions and their market potential is very high, although the current production pathways have low technological maturity (IEA, 2021b). R&D effort will be thus crucial to develop competitive synthetic fuels. The Petronor project may hence be viewed as a first phase of a broader process that, if successful, could lead to the creation of technological capacities that could be escalated and commercialized in a final stage, including their transfer to the rest of Repsol's refining facilities.

The installation of a 10 MW electrolyzer will create additional synergies, both in terms of know-how and local development. This represents a relevant

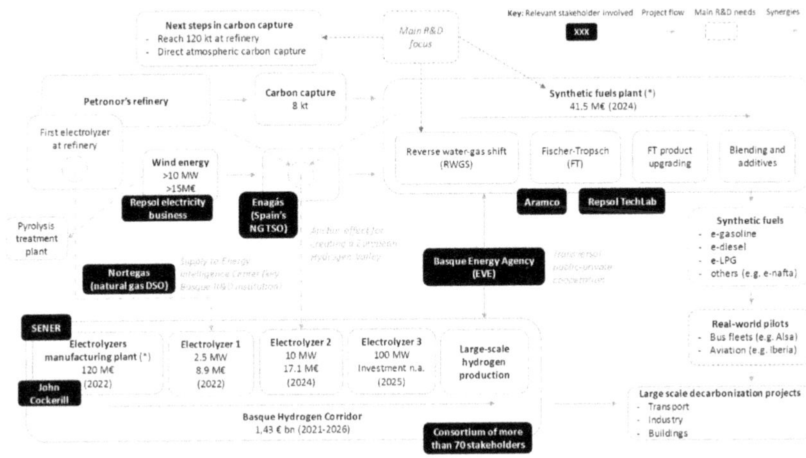

Figure 11.2: Value chain around the Repsol-Aramco collaboration

Note: (*) indicates activities covered by Petronor's new subsidiary Alba Free Energy. Source: own elaboration based on Petronor (2020, 2021a, 2021b, 2021c), BH2C (2020) and IEA (2021b).

Source: Author's own elaboration.

initial milestone in the Basque Hydrogen Corridor (BH_2C), a large consortium led by Petronor (BH_2C, 2021), with the participation of Aramco. It is also one of the so-called European Hydrogen Valleys (within the "local, medium-scale & industry-focused" archetype), which are key projects for hydrogen value chain development in the European Hydrogen Strategy (H2V Platform, 2021; Weichenhain, 2021; Weichenhain et al., 2021).

Petronor's refinery and its projected synthetic fuels plant would also act as a technological "anchor" for other clean energy and hydrogen-related projects in the Basque Country (including its use in transport). To top it all, green electricity production from the projected on-site wind park would also feed the pyrolysis treatment plant.

Geopolitical implications result from this kind multiple technology cooperation agreements signed by Aramco around the globe, with potential to create competitive advantages for Saudi Arabia to modernize and decarbonize its energy sector and innovation spillovers with a catalyst effect within the business ecosystem around Aramco. Furthermore, clean energy technologies could find additional diffusion streams into other oil-producing countries through Saudi Arabia's leading role within OPEC (Fattouh, 2021; Roth, 2020).

The connection between Repsol and Aramco on the basis of groundbreaking R&D activities and the potential for technology transference can also be seen as a way for the EU green diplomacy to contribute to the EGD goals. Firstly, because it is an example of how to "discreetly" persuade other nations to follow the ambitious energy transition path proposed by the EU around a coopetitive approach. Secondly, because it would allow balancing the past and present O&G geopolitics with sustainable development both inside and outside the EU.

International coopetition, as fostered by R&D collaborations similar to the Repsol-Aramco agreement, where cooperation in innovation will be coupled by competition in later stages in the commercialization of solutions, may positively introduce disruptive decarbonization technologies and solutions. The Repsol-Aramco agreement facilitates the pooling of technical expertise, financial resources and technology around strategic (and replicable) investments in key areas of the energy transition that, simultaneously, helps to align geopolitical strategies (i.e., the EU's EGD and Saudi Arabia's Vision 2030) with the global climate challenge and to generate new opportunities for companies in the EU and abroad conducive to sustainable growth (Escribano, 2017).

Case Study #2: Strategic Agreement Between Iberdrola and Cummins[1]

This case study reviews the agreement between Spanish global utility Iberdrola and technology developer and producer Cummins (US) to partner in large-scale hydrogen production projects in Spain and Portugal.

Iberdrola is one of the world-leading multinational energy companies, with presence in 18 countries, a global electricity production of 163 TWh and 34 million clients of electricity and gas in 2020. The company started its international expansion in 1992 by acquiring electric and gas companies in Latin America. In 2007, it acquired UK-based Scottish Power and created a vehicle for the deployment of renewable energy. Renewable power generation, primarily wind and hydropower generation, has been the main instrument for Iberdrola's worldwide expansion, reaching the USA, Brazil, Australia, Japan and multiple countries in Europe, and a key pillar of Iberdrola's corporate strategy.

Hydrogen has a great potential to redefine the energy sector and is thus viewed as a new field for expansion by Iberdrola and most major utilities. Green hydrogen, in particular, has a great synergy with renewable generation, representing an additional link in its current value chain, which can further be connected to other sectors: steel[2], ammonia, cement, etc. Therefore, alliances between agents from different sectors have been the norm in the promotion of hydrogen in recent times.

In July 2020, Iberdrola announced an agreement with Spanish fertilizer producer Fertiberia to provide green hydrogen to a Fertiberia ammonia production facility in Puertollano, Spain. The €150 million project would consist of a 20 MW electrolyzer plant fed by a 100 MW solar power plant and a 5 MW/20 MWh battery. In October 2020, the Spanish Government presented Spain's Hydrogen Strategy and Iberdrola and Fertiberia announced a substantial scale-up in their green hydrogen plans: 800 MW of electrolysis capacity in two ammonia plants, Puertollano and Palos de la Frontera (also in Spain), to start operations by 2027.

By 2021, when the NextGenerationEU program was launched, Iberdrola was already committed to hydrogen as a strategic growth vector. It applied for funding for 54 hydrogen-related projects, including those with Fertiberia, with a total electrolyzer capacity of more than 1 GW and €2,500 million worth of investments.

To support these projects, Iberdrola and Basque-based engineering company Ingeteam set up the joint venture Iberlyzer, for the production and installation of electrolyzers and the design and engineering of green hydrogen production plants. The location of the electrolyzer production facility was not decided yet, but the Basque Country was considered as a possibility, given the origin of the companies and the nascent and growing hydrogen value chain in this territory.

A missing piece in the creation of Iberlyzer was the absence of a technological partner: a company with previous experience in the production of electrolyzers. In order to close this technology gap, Iberdrola initially signed an agreement with Norway's Nel Hydrogen Electrolyzer, a division of Nel ASA and one of the most relevant electrolyzer producers in the world, to deploy electrolyzers and develop projects along the hydrogen value in Spain. To Nel, this agreement signified boosting its sales and contributing, via increased volume, to reduce the costs of their hydrogen technology. Under the agreement, Nel was the preferred supplier for the first electrolyzer for Fertiberia's Puertollano plant and was awarded the contract in January 2021. Iberlyzer would, later on, be supplying electrolyzers for 200 MW of capacity by 2023. Despite the interest by all parties, however, the negotiations between Iberdrola, Ingeteam, Nel and the Basque Government broke down in May 2021.

In a twist of events, in late May 2021, Iberdrola announced an agreement with US electrolyzer producer Cummins and the Castilla-La Mancha Government (a region in South Central Spain) to build the electrolyzer factory in the province of Guadalajara, in Castilla-La Mancha. It would require an initial investment of €50 million to reach an annual capacity of 500 MW by 2023, expandable to 1 GW. One of its initial customers would be the 230 MW green hydrogen electrolyzer for Fertiberia's plant near Palos de la Frontera. This new alliance between Iberdrola and Cummins would be continued in other projects in Spain, Portugal and additional "new markets, bringing new clean technology to customers, and supporting efforts to bring the European Union's Green Deal to fruition," in the words of Tom Linebarger, Chairman and CEO of Cummins.

This change, of course, can be associated with several reasons. Nel was reluctant to share its technology with Iberdrola and Ingeteam, already had an electrolyzer factory in Notodden, Norway, and was constructing a second one in Herøya, Norway.

For Cummins, the Guadalajara project made a lot of sense. First, Spain represents a great potential hydrogen market in Europe due to the availability of renewable energy, and Cummins could benefit from Iberdrola's strong presence in the Castilla-La Mancha region, where it operates 2,376 MW of renewable energy. Cummins already had plans for eight factories in Europe, focusing on different segments of the hydrogen value chain (i.e., assembly and integration of both polymer electrolyte membrane [PEM] and alkaline electrolyzers in Oevel, Belgium, and assembly of fuel cell systems for Alstom's hydrogen trains in Herten, Germany). Moreover, the company could benefit from higher tax credit in Castilla-La Mancha, as compared with the Basque Country, due to Guadalajara being qualified as a "depressed area" by the EU. Additionally, since Cummins intended to continue its electrolyzer R&D activities in its home country, it was not eligible for some of the Basque Country's tax benefits. A facility in Guadalajara would also be close to Cummins' distribution center in Madrid, inaugurated in 2018.

This agreement helps to materialize the synergies between Iberdrola's position in renewable energy in many markets and the hydrogen value chain on the back of a technological partner with presence on both sides of the Atlantic Ocean. The Iberdrola Group had begun to launch hydrogen projects in Spain (a hydrogen station in Barcelona, with Cummins); in the UK (an electrolyzer in Inverness, Scotland, by the end of 2021, via Scottish Power); in the US (with multiple project concepts related to hydrogen production and usage proposed by its US subsidiary, Avangrid); and in other countries (e.g., Italy or Germany).

As a collateral benefit, the agreement also transferred to Cummins the responsibility to scale up current state-of-the-art electrolyzer capability, which represents a major challenge (and risk) even for already existing electrolyzer-producing companies. Finally, it also alleviated the financing of the Iberdrola Group, whose investments in different areas of the energy transition (mainly power generation, storage and smart grids) are expected to amount to €150 billion worldwide between 2021 and 2030.

From a geopolitical perspective, the Iberdrola-Cummins accord is another example of how regional geostrategic interests in the energy sector can be aligned with the goals of private companies via (future) coopetition in clean, promising technologies, thus accelerating the investments and developments required for energy transition.

CONCLUSIONS

The EGD will affect global geopolitics through its impact on various dimensions. Indeed, the development of renewable energy and the need to curb GHG emissions and fight the consequences of climate change are reshaping the energy geopolitics landscape.

While the growth of renewable energy tends to increase energy independence (in the EU and elsewhere), thus changing the decades-long energy geopolitics map that evolved around O&G producers and importers, the common challenge of tackling the consequences of climate change opens the door to new relationships between companies, regions and nations.

New forms of international collaboration will emerge to materialize the energy transition opportunities and achieve the global goal of full decarbonization. The need to innovate in order to reduce emissions in hard-to-abate sectors will inevitably force companies, countries and regions to cooperate.

Decarbonizing the economy will imply vast amounts of investments and significant, groundbreaking innovation in clean energy technologies. Technological innovation (and cost reductions) will also have to be coupled by adequate market and regulatory contexts. For example, in the case of hydrogen, a massive scale-up of both the production (of electrolyzers) and the demand (for green hydrogen and green end products) will be required.

Regions and countries may foster the required investments and innovation activities via high-level institutional R&D agreements. These should be coupled with an environment that generates incentives for companies to seek alternative, less formal ways of cooperation in projects that align both the energy and geopolitical goals (of the EU, for instance) with their own profit-maximization and growth strategies.

Under adequate boundary conditions, coopetition between private companies is likely to be the norm in the new context, as they can benefit from sharing resources in the R&D phase of the projects and then materialize gains through the commercialization of much-needed solutions in high-growth markets, expanding both technologically (for instance, the market for industrial decarbonization solutions) and regionally (to countries in which companies previously had low or no previous presence).

The review of the Repsol-Aramco and Iberdrola-Cummins agreements provides some insights about the research question of how techno-industrial cooperation-competition agreements between EU and non-EU companies jointly address (a) key EU (and other regions) sustainability objectives and (b) the challenges posed by energy geopolitics in the current context (Figure 11.3).

In particular, these case studies show that cross-regional and cross-country cooperation may be used as a strategic instrument to achieve geopolitical, economic and sustainability goals. From the point of view of the EU, these agreements (1) are clearly aligned with the grand objective of the EGD to transform the EU into a sustainable and competitive economy and society; (2) achieve conventional geopolitical goals such as energy security; (3) attract foreign and

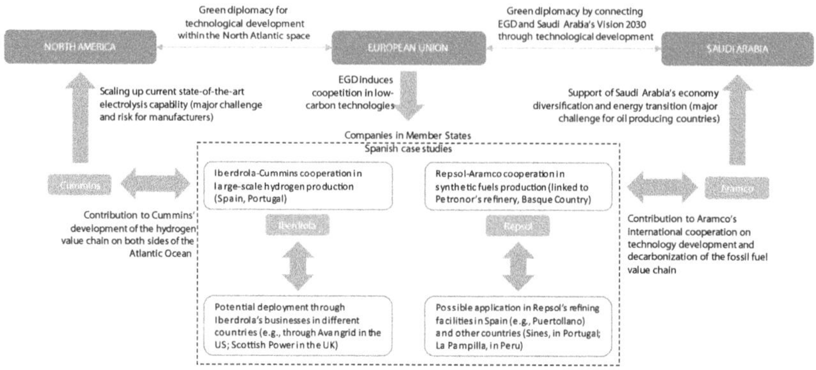

Figure 11.3: Geopolitical implications of the Repsol-Aramco and Iberdrola-Cummins case agreements

Source: Authors' own elaboration.

local investment that helps to create value around strengths in the energy and industrial sectors (e.g., renewable energy, hydrogen or advanced and digitalized industries); (4) open the way to technological innovations and solutions that may facilitate the decarbonization of hard-to-abate sectors; (5) have a solid technological and industrial basis that helps to create macro and microeconomic value locally; (6) strengthen the ties between EU and strategic third parties—i.e., O&G-producing nations—via soft persuasion (the so-called green diplomacy); and (7) generate incentives for private companies to engage in disruptive innovation and R&D cooperation-competition schemes.

Future research on this topic may focus on analyzing additional case studies involving different energy technologies, actors and regions in order to gain insights about how technological cooperation and competition may help to achieve the zero-net global emissions goal. Analyzing to what extent non-EU countries are adapting their legislation and regulatory frameworks in line with the EGD sustainability framework may also shed light on the issue of how global regulatory and technological leadership evolve in a changing, interconnected world. The development of a structured analytical framework could also be useful in providing adequate theoretical and conceptual bases for research lines related to international industrial, R&D and technological cooperation and competition on the road to an environmentally sustainable global economy.

NOTES

1. Except where explicitly noted, all the data and information in this section come from Iberdrola's, Cummins', Iberlyzer's and Nel's webpages.

2. In December 2021, Iberdrola and Swedish company H2 Green Steel announced an agreement to establish a green hydrogen production facility with 1 GW electrolysis capacity and a DRI process capable of producing approximately 2 million tons of direct reduced green iron per year (H2 Green Steel, 2021). The electrolyzer will be jointly owned and operated by Iberdrola and H2 Green Steel. Iberdrola will supply renewable energy to the plant, while the DRI and green steel production processes will be operated H2 Green Steel.

REFERENCES

Aklin, M., & Mildenberger, M. (2020). Prisoners of the wrong dilemma: Why distributive conflict, not collective action, characterizes the politics of climate change. *Global Environmental Politics*, *20*(4), 4–27.

Al-Atrush, S., Sheppard, D., Hook, L., & Wilson, T. (2021, October 23). Saudi Arabia 2060 net zero target keeps crude in the picture. *Financial Times*. https://www.ft.com/content/399f3cb5-2256-4f3c-9443-48ee18263d41

Amelang, S. (2021, February 3). Cooperation vs. competition: How EU-China relations shape fight against climate change. *Clean Energy Wire*. https://www.cleanenergywire.org/dossiers/cooperation-vs-competition-how-eu-china-relations-shape-fight-against-climate-change

Amran, Y. H. A., Amran, Y. H. M., Alyousef, R., & Alabduljabbar, H. (2020). Renewable and sustainable energy production in Saudi Arabia according to Saudi Vision 2030; Current status and future prospects. *Journal of Cleaner Production*, *247*, 119602. https://doi.org/10.1016/j.jclepro.2019.119602

Aramco. (2018a). *Saudi Aramco highlights its contributions to the realization of Saudi Vision 2030 at future investment initiative, signs 15 MOUs with business partners worth US$ 34 billion*. https://www.aramco.com/en/news-media/news/2018/saudi-aramco-highlights-contributions-to-vision-2030-at-fii

Aramco. (2018b). *Saudi Aramco signs 15 memoranda of understanding (MoUs) at the Future Investment Initiative (FII) forum worth $34 billion*. https://www.aramco.com/en/news-media/news/2018/saudi-aramco-signs-15-mous-at-the-fii-2018

Aramco. (2021a). *Global research centers*. https://www.aramco.com/en/creating-value/technology-development/globalresearchcenters

Aramco (2021b). *Strategic investments*. https://www.aramco.com/en/creating-value/technology-development/strategic-investments

Bach, M. (2018). The oil and gas sector: From climate laggard to climate leader? *Environmental Politics*, *28*(1), 87–103. https://doi.org/10.1080/09644016.2019.1521911

Baratti, G. (2020). *Spain's Repsol to develop hydrogen-fed synthetic fuel plant at Bilbao*. S&P Global Platts. https://www.spglobal.com/platts/es/market-insights/latest-news/coal/061520-spains-repsol-to-develop-hydrogen-fed-synthetic-fuel-plant-at-bilbao

BH2C. (2020). *El corredor vasco del hidrógeno. Presentación de la iniciativa*. Unpublished manuscript.

BH2C. (2021). *About us: BH2C members*. https://185.118.57.121/en/bh2c-members/

Blakemore, R. (2021). *Biden's major report on critical minerals supply: Domestic mining + processing, innovation, EVs, global allies + more.* Energypost.eu. https://energypost.eu/bidens-major-report-on-critical-minerals-supply-domestic-mining-processing-innovation-evs-global-allies-more/

Brelsford, R. (2021). Spain's Repsol adding renewable hydrogen production at Petronor refinery. *Oil & Gas Journal.* https://www.ogj.com/refining-processing/refining/article/14210749/spains-repsol-adding-renewable-hydrogen-production-at-petronor-refinery

Brown, T. (2021). *Aramco plans Saudi green hydrogen, ammonia project.* ICIS. https://www.icis.com/explore/resources/news/2021/10/27/10699127/aramco-plans-saudi-green-hydrogen-ammonia-project

Conant, M. A., & Gold, F. R. (2019). *The geopolitics of energy.* Routledge. https://doi.org/10.4324/9780429311246

Council of the European Union. (2015). *Council conclusions on Energy Diplomacy.* https://data.consilium.europa.eu/doc/document/ST-10995-2015-INIT/en/pdf

Council of the European Union. (2021). *Council conclusions on Climate and Energy Diplomacy. Delivering on the external dimension of the European Green Deal.* General Secretariat of the Council. https://www.consilium.europa.eu/en/press/press-releases/2021/01/25/council-adopts-conclusions-on-climate-and-energy-diplomacy/#

Criekemans, D. (2018). Geopolitics of the Renewable Energy Game and Its Potential Impact upon Global Power Relations. In Scholten D. (eds) *The geopolitics of renewables.* Lecture Notes in Energy, 61. Springer. https://doi.org/10.1007/978-3-319-67855-9_2

Dennison, S., Loss, R., & Söderström, J. (2021). *Europe's green moment: How to meet the climate challenge* (Policy Brief). European Council on Foreign Relations. https://ecfr.eu/publication/europes-green-moment-how-to-meet-the-climate-challenge/

DNV. (2021). *Pathway to net zero emissions. Energy Transition Outlook 2021.* https://download.dnv.com/eto-2021-download?&_ga=2.241298753.2121137416.1637598287-886903620.1637598287

Elkington, J., & Evans, T. (2021). Economic regeneration as a vehicle for system resilience. In O. Lazard & R. Young (Eds.), *The EU and climate security: Toward ecological diplomacy.* Carnegie Europe. https://carnegieeurope.eu/2021/07/12/economic-regeneration-as-vehicle-for-system-resilience-pub-84880

EsadeGeo. (2021). *The geopolitics of the Green Deal.* https://dobetter.esade.edu/en/geopolitics-green-deal

Escribano, G. (2017). *El nuevo contexto de la relación económica entre España y Arabia Saudí.* Real Instituto Elcano. http://www.realinstitutoelcano.org/wps/portal/rielcano_es/contenido?WCM_GLOBAL_CONTEXT=/elcano/elcano_es/zonas_es/politicaexteriorespanola/ari3-2017-escribano-nuevo-contexto-relacion-economica-espana-arabia-saudi

Escribano, G. (2021). *Las geopolíticas de la transición energética y su gobernanza.* Agenda Pública. https://agendapublica.es/las-geopoliticas-de-la-transicion-energetica-y-su-gobernanza/

Escribano, G., & Lázaro, L. (2020). *Balancing geopolitics with the Green Deal recovery: In search of a comprehensive Euro-Mediterranean energy script.* Real Instituto Elcano. http://www.realinstitutoelcano.org/wps/portal/rielcano_en/contenido?WCM_GLOBAL_CONTEXT=/elcano/elcano_in/zonas_in/ari95-2020-escribano-lazaro-balancing-geopolitics-with-green-deal-recovery

European Commission. (2019a). *Communication from the Commission to the European Parliament, the European Council, the Council, the European Economic and Social Committee of the Regions. The European Green Deal.* https://eur-lex.europa.eu/legal-content/EN/TXT/?uri=CELEX%3A52019DC0640

European Commission. (2019b). *Annex to the communication from the Commission to the European Parliament, the European Council, the Council, the European Economic and Social Committee of the Regions. The European Green Deal.* https://ec.europa.eu/info/strategy/priorities-2019-2024/european-green-deal_en

European Commission. (2021a). *Communication from the Commission to the European Parliament, the European Council, the Council, the European Economic and Social Committee of the Regions on the global approach to research and innovation. Europe's strategy for international cooperation in a changing world.* https://eur-lex.europa.eu/legal-content/EN/TXT/?uri=COM:2021:252:FIN

European Commission. (2021b). *International cooperation.* https://ec.europa.eu/info/research-and-innovation/strategy/strategy-2020-2024/europe-world/international-cooperation_en

European Commission. (2021c). *Europe's strategy for international cooperation in a changing world. Communication from the Commission to the European Parliament, the European Economic and Social Committee and the Committee of the Regions on the global approach to research and innovation* (18.5.2021 COM (2021) 252 final). https://eur-lex.europa.eu/legal-content/EN/TXT/?uri=COM:2021:252:FIN

European Commission. (2022). *EU taxonomy: Commission begins expert consultations on Complementary Delegated Act covering certain nuclear and gas activities.* https://ec.europa.eu/commission/presscorner/detail/en/ip_22_2

European Council and Council of the European Union. (2021a). *Long-term EU budget 2021–2027 and recovery package.* https://www.consilium.europa.eu/en/policies/the-eu-budget/long-term-eu-budget-2021-2027/

European Council and Council of the European Union. (2021b). *Fit for 55.* https://www.consilium.europa.eu/en/policies/green-deal/eu-plan-for-a-green-transition/#

Fattouh, B. (2021). *Saudi oil policy: Continuity and change in the era of the energy transition* (OIES Paper WPM 81). https://www.oxfordenergy.org/publications/saudi-oil-policy-continuity-and-change-in-the-era-of-the-energy-transition/

Franza, L., Bianchi, M., & Bergamaschi, L. (2020). *Geopolitics and Italian foreign policy in the age of renewable energy* (IAI Papers). https://www.iai.it/sites/default/files/iaip2013.pdf

Goldthau, A. (2021). Widening the EU's geoeconomic and regulatory approach to climate policy. In O. Lazard & R. Young (Eds.), *The EU and climate security: Toward ecological diplomacy.* Carnegie Europe. https://carnegieeurope.eu/2021/07/12/widening-eu-s-geoeconomic-and-regulatory-approach-to-climate-policy-pub-84877

Grabbe, H. (2021). Conclusion. In O. Lazard & R. Young (Eds.), *The EU and climate security: Toward ecological diplomacy.* Carnegie Europe. https://carnegieeurope.eu/2021/07/12/conclusion-pub-84881

Gunnar Austvik, O. (2018). *Concepts of geopolitics and energy security.* IAEE Energy Forum. https://www.researchgate.net/publication/323990484_Concepts_of_Geopolitics_and_Energy_Security

H2 Green Steel. (2021). *H2 Green Steel and Iberdrola announce €2.3 billion Green hydrogen venture.* https://www.h2greensteel.com/h2-green-steel-and-iberdrola-announce-23-billion-green-hydrogen-venture

H2V Platform. (2021). *Hydrogen valley map.* https://www.h2v.eu/hydrogen-valleys

IDDRI. (2021, January 6). *2021, a crucial geopolitical year for the European Green Deal* [Blog post]. https://www.iddri.org/en/publications-and-events/blog-post/2021-crucial-geopolitical-year-european-green-deal

IEA. (2021a). *The role of critical minerals in clean energy transitions*. http://www.iea.org

IEA (2021b, November 4). *ETP clean energy technology guide*. https://www.iea.org/articles/etp-clean-energy-technology-guide

IRENA. (2019). *A new world. The geopolitics of the energy transformation*. https://www.irena.org/publications/2019/Jan/A-New-World-The-Geopolitics-of-the-Energy-Transformation

IRENA (2022). *Geopolitics of the energy transformation: The hydrogen factor*. https://www.irena.org/publications/2022/Jan/Geopolitics-of-the-Energy-Transformation-Hydrogen

Johansson, B. (2013). Security aspects of future renewable energy systems. A short overview. *Energy*, *61*, 598–605. https://doi.org/10.1016/j.energy.2013.09.023

Kefferpütz, R. (2021, March 11). A green deal for a geopolitical age. *Green European Journal*. https://www.greeneuropeanjournal.eu/a-green-deal-for-a-geopolitical-age/

Lasheras Merino, M. A. (2021). Geopolitics under the green deal: A challenge for the EU. In Spanish Ministry of Defense (Ed.), *Energy and geostrategy 2021* (pp. 107–183). ISSN 2697–2204. https://publicaciones.defensa.gob.es/media/downloadable/files/links/e/n/energy_and_geostrategy_2021.pdf

Leonard, M., Pisani-Ferry, J., Shapiro, J., Tagliapietra, S., & Wolf, G. B. (2021). *The geopolitics of the European Green Deal*. Policy Contribution, 4. https://www.bruegel.org/2021/02/the-geopolitics-of-the-european-green-deal/

Lutz, J. (2021, February 10). *EIA says natural gas and oil will remain integral, but where will they come from?* American Petroleum Institute. https://www.api.org/news-policy-and-issues/blog/2021/02/10/eia-says-natural-gas-and-oil-will-remain-integral-but-where-will-it-come-from

Markarian, G., & Stockhausen, T. (2018). Quo vadis: Politics, uncertainty and Saudi Aramco. *The Journal of World Energy Law & Business*, *11*(6), 487–505. https://doi.org/10.1093/jwelb/jwy027

Mazzucato, M. (2018). *Mission-oriented research & innovation in the European Union. missions. A problem-solving approach to fuel innovation-led growth*. European Commission. https://op.europa.eu/es/publication-detail/-/publication/5b2811d1-16be-11e8-9253-01aa75ed71a1

Moshashai, D., Leber, A. M., & Savage, J. D. (2018). Saudi Arabia plans for its economic future: Vision 2030, the national transformation plan and Saudi fiscal reform. *British Journal of Middle Eastern Studies*, *47*(3), 381–401. https://doi.org/10.1080/13530194.2018.1500269

Neal, M. (2019). *A dictionary of business and management in the Middle East and North Africa*. https://www.oxfordreference.com/view/10.1093/acref/9780191843266.001.0001/acref-9780191843266

Nordhaus, W. (2015). Climate clubs: Overcoming free-riding in international climate policy. *American Economic Review*, *105*(4), 1339–1370. http://dx.doi.org/10.1257/aer.15000001

OECD. (2020). *Building back better: A sustainable, resilient recovery after COVID-19*. https://www.oecd.org/coronavirus/policy-responses/building-back-better-a-sustainable-resilient-recovery-after-covid-19-52b869f5/

Ohnesorge, L., & Rogge, E. (2021). Europe's green policy: Towards a climate neutral economy by way of investors' choice. *European Company Law*, *18*(1), 34–39. https://kluwerlawonline.com/journalarticle/European+Company+Law/18.1/EUCL2021005

Oommen, A. (2021, October 27). *Aramco inks MoUs for green hydrogen, sustainable tech.* Mechanical Electrical & Plumbing. https://www.mepmiddleeast.com/business/aramco-inks-mous-for-green-hydrogen-sustainable-tech-projects

O'Sullivan, M., Overland, I., & Sandalow, D. (2017). *The geopolitics of renewable energy.* SIPA, Harvard Kennedy School, Norwegian Institute of International Affairs. https://energypolicy.columbia.edu/sites/default/files/CGEPTheGeopoliticsOfRenewables.pdf

Overland, I. (2019). The geopolitics of renewable energy: Debunking four emerging myths. *Energy Research & Social Sciences*, *49*, 36–40. https://doi.org/10.1016/j.erss.2018.10.018

Pastukhova, M., Pepe, J., & Westphal, K. (2020). *Beyond the green deal: Upgrading the EU's energy diplomacy for a new era* (SWP Comment, No. 31). https://www.swp-berlin.org/10.18449/2020C31/

Petronor. (2020). *Petronor avanza el futuro con la producción de combustibles sintéticos.* https://petronor.eus/es/2020/06/petronor-avanza-el-futuro-con-la-produccion-de-combustibles-sinteticos/

Petronor. (2021a). *Petronor crea Alba, una nueva empresa que aglutinará todas sus actividades de descarbonización.* https://petronor.eus/es/2021/09/67084/

Petronor. (2021b). *Petronor instala un electrolizador de 2,5 MW como primer paso del corredor vasco del hidrógeno.* https://petronor.eus/es/2021/09/petronor-instala-un-electrolizador-de-25-mw-como-primer-paso-del-corredor-vasco-del-hidrogeno-2/

Petronor. (2021c). *Petronor instala un electrolizador de 2,5 MW como primer paso del corredor vasco del hidrógeno.* https://petronor.eus/es/2021/09/petronor-instala-un-electrolizador-de-25-mw-como-primer-paso-del-corredor-vasco-del-hidrogeno/

Politecnico di Torino. (2021). *The sustainability mission of the energy transition: Presenting the global alliance for sustainable energy.* https://www.politocomunica.polito.it/events/appuntamenti/(idnews)/17293

Ramady, M. (2018). *Saudi Aramco 2030. Post IPO challenges.* Springer. https://doi.org/10.1007/978-3-319-67750-7

Repsol. (2020). *2021–2025 strategic plan.* https://www.repsol.com/en/about-us/2025-strategy/index.cshtml

Repsol. (2021a). *Repsol to start up the first electrolyzer at its Petronor refinery.* https://www.repsol.com/en/press-room/press-releases/2021/repsol-to-start-up-the-first-electrolyzer-at-its-petronor-refinery/index.cshtml

Repsol. (2021b). *Repsol will invest €2.549 billion to boost renewable hydrogen.* https://www.repsol.com/en/press-room/press-releases/2021/repsol-will-invest-2.549-billion-to-boost-renewable-hydrogen/index.cshtml

Repsol. (2021c). *Repsol and EDP enter an agreement to implement renewable hydrogen projects in the Iberian peninsula.* https://www.repsol.com/en/press-room/press-releases/2021/repsol-and-edp-agreement-to-implement-renewable-hydrogen-projects-in-iberian-peninsula/index.cshtml

Ridder, H.-G. (2017). The theory contribution of case study research designs. *Business Research*, *10*(2), 281–305. https://doi.org/10.1007/s40685-017-0045-z

Roth, V. (2020). Incorporating unconventional and renewable energy into the international energy framework: The diminution of OPEC in a new energy world order. *Journal of World Energy Law & Business*, *13*(1), 68–80. https://doi.org/10.1093/jwelb/jwaa008

Scholten, D., Bazilian, M., Overland, I., & Westphal, K. (2020). The geopolitics of renewables: New board, new game. *Energy Policy*, *138*, 111059. https://doi.org/10.1016/j.enpol.2019.111059

Vakulchuk, R., Overland, I., & Scholten, D. (2020). Renewable energy and geopolitics: A review. *Renewable and Sustainable Energy Reviews*, *122*, 109547. https://doi.org/10.1016/j.rser.2019.109547

Vanyushyn, V., Bengtsson, M., Näsholm, M. H., & Boter, H. (2017). International coopetition for innovation: Are the benefits worth the challenges? *Review of Managerial Science*, *12*(2), 535–557. https://doi.org/10.1007/s11846-017-0272-x

Weichenhain, U. (2021, June 2). *Hydrogen valleys: First elements of the new hydrogen economy.* https://www.rolandberger.com/en/Insights/Publications/Hydrogen-Valleys-first-elements-of-the-new-hydrogen-economy.html

Weichenhain, U., Kaufmann, M., Benz, A., & Matute, G. (2021). *Hydrogen valleys. Insights into the emerging hydrogen economies around the world.* https://www.fch.europa.eu/sites/default/files/documents/20210527_Hydrogen_Valleys_final_ONLINE.pdf

Woertz, E. (2019). *Aramco goes public: The Saudi diversification conundrum.* German Institute of Global and Area Studies (GIGA). http://www.jstor.org/stable/resrep21206

Yin, R. K. (2003). *Case study research. Design and methods* (Applied Social Research Methods Series, Vol. 5, 3rd ed.). Sage.

Youngs, R. (2021a, October 26). *COP26 and the foreign policy blind spot in Europe's climate action.* In Judy Dempsey's *Strategic Europe*. Carnegie Europe. https://carnegieeurope.eu/strategiceurope/85648

Youngs, R. (2021b). The EU's indirect and defensive approach to climate security. In O. Lazard & R. Young (Eds.), *The EU and climate security: Toward ecological diplomacy.* Carnegie Europe. https://carnegieeurope.eu/2021/07/12/eu-and-climate-security-toward-ecological-diplomacy-pub-84873

CHAPTER 12

The Chinese Energy Rush in Pakistan as a Regional Geopolitical Game-Changer

JORGE TAVARES DA SILVA

INTRODUCTION

For more than 60 years, China and Pakistan have maintained a relatively consistent diplomatic relationship based on bilateral interests and mutual trust, despite times of greater strategic cooperation and others of dullness (Silva, 2019, p. 120). In 1950, Islamabad was one of the main international actors to recognize the People's Republic of China (PRC), and Beijing was among the first actors to recognize the new Islamic Republic. Islamabad supported China's seat in the United Nations (UN) in 1961 and Beijing's "One-China Policy," and it gave political support after the 1989 crackdown on the Tiananmen protests (Wolf, 2020, pp. 7–8). The Chinese also assisted Pakistan in its effort to develop a nuclear program, even though Beijing often rejected this accusation.

Bilateral relations have intensified since the beginning of this new millennium, marked by evident reciprocal geopolitical interests. Both countries describe their special combined relations using melodious words, including the expression "sweeter than honey" (Ali, 2017, p. 1). An example is the expansion of the deep-water port in Gwadar since 2002, developed in several phases (Ahmad, 2016, p. 161). More recently, in 2013, both countries established the China-Pakistan Economic Corridor (CPEC), a group of infrastructure projects that includes railway tracks, energy pipelines, and optical fiber to connect China's Kashgar with Pakistan's Gwadar Port (Ali, 2017, p. 203). All these initiatives are integrated into the vast plan of the Belt and Road Initiative (BRI), which involves the development of joint projects, both public and private, making connections from South Asia to the Indian Ocean through Central Asia to Europe (Leandro, 2018). Frequent shortages due to low power capacity have led the PRC to invest billions in the Pakistani energy sector. In 2015, during the visit of the Chinese President Xi Jinping to Pakistan, Beijing promised more than 46 billion U.S. dollars for a variety of energy and infrastructure projects, which pretends to enhance trade and economic activities to further integrate the countries of the region (Kashmeri, 2019, p. 44).

The massive mutual plans and programs to improve infrastructure and increase power generation capacity in Pakistan are not consensual, as they have implications for the country's ethnical divisions. For instance, Balochistan is one of the poorest in the country despite a quantity of development projects organized by the central government in cooperation with Beijing. Rebel groups have organized revolt against the exploitation of province by dominant ethnic groups such as Punjabis or Pashtuns, associated with foreign interests. On the other hand, some investments have coal and other polluted solutions as their primary energy source. Carbon is a basic element of organic chemistry, being present in both human life and fuels, in multiple aspects of private life, as well as in the industrial world. Due to its characteristics, which contribute to global warming, it has become one of the great enemies of environmentalists. One of the fuels targeted by these groups is coal, as it is the most carbon intensive and therefore the most polluting. According to the International Energy Agency (2021b), Pakistan is very dependent on oil and natural gas: "more than 40 million people remain without access to electricity and half the population lack access to clean cooking facilities." There is a strong difference between green energies and polluting energies: 64 % fossil fuels, 27 % hydropower, and 9 % other renewables and nuclear power (International Trade Administration [ITA], 2021). It is not surprising that the projects have received strong criticism by environmental organizations and opened a new conflict in the traditional stalemate between the center and provinces in the country.

This chapter analyzes Pakistan's vulnerabilities in terms of energy, which leads the country to accept investment and installation of Chinese companies to explore coal sites, adding around 10,000 MW to the national grid (Kashmeri, 2019, p. 45). In spite of solving the problem of energy shortages, the use of dirty power has provoked in public opinion a negative impression of the Chinese presence. However, China is committed to the goals outlined at the United Nations Conference on Climate Change (COP26) and intends to promote a positive image in the world. The main objective of this article is to determine the impacts of this energy transition on bilateral relations, but also the economic and geopolitical challenges in a world of increasing competition. Primary sources were used in the research, particularly IEA energy reports, but also secondary sources such as books and journal articles.

In this chapter, we first examine Sino-Pakistani reciprocal relations from their initial political dimension to the security and economic contexts, including the many Chinese investment projects in Pakistani territory. Then, we explore Pakistan's energy problems, a structural weakness that led the country to accept strong investment from China anchored on the BRI. Finally, following previous analyses, we look at the geopolitical effects of the Chinese investments on energy in Pakistan, particularly the transition to a greener solution and the impacts of this strategy. We conclude that the energy transition in Pakistan brings good news for the environment in the medium/long term and the overloaded national energy capacity, but it creates new problems. Among these problems are the gradual dependence on China and the incapacity of people to pay the high costs of green energy, creating new animosities in the regional game of interests.

THE *CURIOUS* CASE OF SINO–PAKISTAN BILATERAL RELATIONS

The collaborative affairs between China and Pakistan, a kind of "entente cordiale" according to John W. Garver (2001), are probably "the most stable and durable element of China's foreign relations" (p. 187). Official rhetoric considers that this relationship is "higher than mountains, deeper than oceans, sweeter than honey, and stronger than steel" (Wolf, 2020, p. 9). Although China and Pakistan did not have the same ideologies, cultures, or political systems, they shared many interests, including reduction of Indian influence on Central Asia and the Indian Ocean. The Sino-Indian border conflict of 1962 is one of the reasons to promote bilateral cooperation between the countries (Small, 2015), a region that has returned to new episodes of confrontation in 2021. In 1965, a military confrontation between India and Pakistan opened a corridor of cooperation with the Islamic state beyond the sphere of relations in the communist world. Since then, the PRC has been one of Pakistan's main suppliers of military equipment, including fighter aircrafts (JF-17), *Hangor* submarines (Type 042 Yuan-class), frigates (Type 054A/P), guided missiles, and light weapons. The ties with Beijing avoided international isolation perpetrated by Washington. The future collaboration of the Pakistani regime in the "War on Terror" after September 11, 2001, improved combined cooperation. In 2006, both countries signed a Free Trade Agreement (FTA), activating the banking sector to facilitate business and introducing the currency swap. Since then, Beijing assisted Pakistan in many domains, including construction of infrastructure, financial support, opening lines of credit, military training exercises, space technology, and the energy sector (Ali, 2017, p. 188).

China also gives assistance to Pakistan in its nuclear program, even though Beijing refuses to confirm this collaboration in such a sensitive area. Apparently, Abdul Qadeer Khan, the father of Pakistan's nuclear program, revealed this connection in a letter referring that "a C-130 Pakistani left the Chinese city Urumqi with a sufficient level of uranium for two atomic bombs" (Ramana, 2011). As stated by the Stockholm International Peace Research Institute (2013), the Islamic country is precisely the international actor that buy most weapons to China. The good bilateral relation would be proved by the support that Beijing gave to Islamabad after the military operation that killed Bin Laden in 2011 (Siddique, 2014). Besides that, both countries support each other in the voting processes in the UN and Pakistan has supported the "One-China Policy." For example, in the Security Council, China used its veto power on behalf of Pakistan to prevent Bangladesh's membership, while demanding first the release of Pakistani prisoners of war (Siddique, 2014). Pakistan supported China's membership in the South Asian Association for Regional Cooperation (SAARC), while China supported the participation of Pakistan in the Shanghai Cooperation Organization (SCO) in 2017. Beijing support to Pakistan is challenging, in the sense that the Islamic Republic is linked to countries that are often seen negatively by the international community, such as North Korea, Myanmar, Zimbabwe, or Sudan. Pakistan is a country plagued by Islamic radicalism, putting China in a delicate position. It would affect Uighur separatist groups in Xinjiang province, and China is not interested in getting involved in religious radicalism and ethnic conflicts. Transactions of goods through the Karakoram Highway are always under pressure due to attacks by radical and terrorist groups against Chinese interests (Silva, 2009, p. 234).

In 2000, then-president of Pakistan Pervez Musharraf suggested that his country could serve as a "conduit for China," accepting investments in port infrastructures in order to facilitate easier access to energy sources and proposed transit facilities between both territories (Ali, 2017, p. 203). In November 2014, the governments of Pakistan and China signed an agreement "[f]ollowing market-based principles of openness, equality and mutual benefit to develop related energy projects," under which 14 projects were listed as "prioritized" and another seven as "actively promoted" (Husain, 2021). Pakistan's infrastructural situation is critical and needs investment in many domains, including the water, irrigation, power, and transport sectors (Wolf, 2020, p. 76; World Bank, 2007). On April 20 and 21, 2015, Xi Jinping visited Pakistan to strengthen ties with his neighboring country, which resulted in the signature of 51 memoranda of understanding and the promise to invest 46 billion dollars in structural infrastructure. Pakistan has a trade deficit with China at a ratio of 1 to 5. Xi Jinping has highlighted in his speeches the bilateral political complicity, and Prime Minister Nawaz Sharif referred that China and Pakistan are "true iron brothers" and that the security worries of China are also a concern to Islamabad (Small, 2015). In 2017, both heads of state announced an investment of more than U.S. $56 billion to the CPEC at the Beijing and Belt Road Summit that was attended by 29 heads of state (Sender & Stacey, 2017). The corridor aims to connect Kashgar, in China's northwest Xinjiang Uygur Autonomous Province, and the deep-sea Gwadar Port on the Baloch coast in southwest Pakistan (and partly the city of Karachi) (Wolf, 2020, p. 125). The Gwadar Port and the adjacent Special Economic Zone are a neuralgic point, a privileged facility near the Persian Gulf and Middle East. This represents a deep strategic target and economic bonds between both states. The ports of Karachi (Karachi Port and Port Qasim) and Gwadar will both serve as the main transit points for the southern corridor, relevant not only in terms of security energy, but also for tourism, shipping, and fisheries (Wolf, 2020, p. 128). One important mention is that is always the interests that justify the advance of countries in collective projects. The main objective is to try to understand the motivations behind each country's actions.

THE DILEMMAS OF CHINA'S NEW POWER GENERATION IN PAKISTAN

Since gaining independence, Pakistan has shown a structural weakness in its national energy panorama: the frequent shortages and a subsequent necessity to import fossil fuels. Sixty-five percent of its electricity has been generated by this source of energy, dependent on international demand and price fluctuations. The installed capacity of power generation is 22,000 MW, but 25,000 MW are needed, which represents a shortfall of around 3,000 MW. One of the problems is that electricity consumption was always higher than economic growth, exacerbated by a huge concentration of people in cities (Irman, 2020). However, the main difficulty does not come from the lack of capacity, but from economic feasibilities, started by the process of privatization in the energy sector. Since the beginning of the 1990s, the national market of energy opened to independent power producers (IPPs). Some national indicators of energy in the country changed dramatically. Thus, while in 1980 60 % of energy generation was hydro and 40 % thermal (cheaper but coming from fossil fuels, such as coal and oil, which are highly polluting and harmful to the planet) in 2010, privatization resulted in a 70 % change to thermal energy and only 30 % in hydro (Irman, 2020).

The case is particularly serious in Karachi, a city of more than 20 million people and one of the main industrial centers in the country. Between the last decade of the twentieth century and the first of the current century, a huge number of 91 million people had access to grid electricity for the first time, while about

50 million Pakistanis still lack access to energy, which represents 26 % of the total population (World Bank, 2021).

Since 2017, following the Chinese investments, Pakistan substantially reduced imports of oil, while coal persists as a relevant source of energy in the country. China has transformed a "nation plagued by power shortages" into a country with a surplus power generation capacity (Husain, 2021; Mangi, 2021). The country has not invested in the grid as equally as it has financed power plants, which resulted in new problems. The new Chinese plants brought energy, but the capacity to acquire it remains low, not only by the government through subsidies but especially by citizens. The costs are included in the individual invoices to consumers, which are not supported by the government budget, which results in the rise of power tariffs (Husain, 2021).

It turns out that there are difficulties provoked by the singular system of "circular debts." This consists in public debt that works on a continuous flow of unpaid government subsidies, resulting in accumulation of debt provoked by the shortfall of payments at the Central Power Purchasing Agency (CPPA). The lack of payments by public and private energy institutions, such as the Pakistan Water & Power Development Authority (WAPDA), Private Power and Infrastructure Board (PPIB), Generation Company (GENCO), K-Electric, and Pakistan Electric Power Company (PEPCO), results in the absence of payments to other companies and shortages of energy in the supply chain (Malik, 2020). Furthermore, energy theft from informal groups and organized crime is frequent, which increases difficulties in the supply lines. As mentioned by Safiya Aftab (2014), "the energy crisis [significant restriction in the supply of energy resources] is the largest single drain on Pakistan's economy," in this case responsible for about 2 % to 4 % of the GDP (Patel & Zhao, 2014). This vulnerable situation has negative effects on socioeconomic development, particularly for industrial attractiveness. According to a recent analysis, the dramatic gap between the demand and production of electricity in the country is around 5,000–8,000 MW, with a constant increase of 6 %–8 % per annum (Raheem et al., 2016, pp. 1–14).

Pakistan's energy needs led the country to internal reforms and, above all, to look for investment abroad, with China at the forefront of its external relations. Beijing is making substantial investments in the Pakistan energy sector under the CPEC, integrated into the extensive project of the BRI. However, some of these initiatives are under criticism because they are essentially based on coal rather than cleaner energies such as hydropower. Chinese investment in coal projects abroad avoids using non-green industries in its own territory, or, in another version, permits cutting back on pollution at home while cheering on deeply polluting projects abroad. It is important to remember that China is the world's biggest public financier of coal. It has struggled against the idea that it should be subject to the same constraints as rich countries that started the process of global warming at a much earlier stage. Defending the legitimacy of polluting, as it is at a late stage of development, China argues that a substantial part of its industry is destined for exports to the West (Jacques, 2009, p. 171).

Pakistan has one of the largest coal reserves in the world (particularly in the Thar Desert) sufficient to solve national needs for more than 300 years (Patel & Zhao, 2014). The problem is that most of its power plants are not operational. China offered to dig and convert coal to help Pakistan cover its electricity shortfall of 25,000 MW (Hoodbhoy, 2017). We may include the Port Qasim Coal-fired Power Plant, the Huaneng Shandong Ruyi-Sahiwal Coal Power Plant, the HubCo Coal-fired Power Plant, and the Sindh-Engro Thar Coal Power Plant. This includes excavations in the desert of Tharparkar in Sindh province, an ambitious Sino-Pakistani project linking the western provinces of China to Karachi and other ports on the Arabian Sea. In 2016, a Sino-Pakistani agreement established that 3.8 million tons of coal will be excavated each year, to fuel a 660 MW power plant (Cooke, 2016). While the rest of the world is turning away from this source of energy, Chinese and Pakistani companies are cooperating to increase production of coal. The coal from Tharparkar is mainly lignite, which is considered by scientists one of the most polluting types of coal. Fatih Birol (2021), executive director of the International Energy Agency, explained in an interview that:

> Coal is the single largest source of global carbon emissions, and this year's historically high level of coal power generation is a worrying sign of how far off track the world is in its efforts to put emissions into decline towards net-zero. (IEA, 2021a)

The plants have boosted coal generation to a high level of production, but Pakistan needs to increase other energy sources in the power mix, particularly wind and solar energy to 30 %, and another 30 % to hydro (Mangi, 2021). One of the major problems in Pakistan is the high risk of natural disasters provoked by climate change. In recent years, it has endured a significant number of floods and droughts and many deaths as a consequence of heatwaves (Cooke, 2016). Coal-powered plants promise to worsen the quality of the air, national health, and quality of the water, with clear consequences for the national economy. In order to provoke less discontent among local populations, investors have implemented promotion of employment, particularly for the younger generation and women. The Sindh-Engro Coal Mining Company (SECMC) is one of the Pakistani companies working with Chinese partners to find a more social and environmental equilibrium. This company wants to compensate and relocate local inhabitants in modern homes, beyond schools and hospitals (Hoodbhoy, 2017). There is a general desire to increase the use of renewable energy and progressively reduce fossil fuel imports and carbon emissions.

THE CHINESE ENERGY TRANSITION IN PAKISTAN AND ITS GEOPOLITICAL IMPACTS

The Chinese polluting industries in Pakistan included in the BRI have raised a wave of protests by local inhabitants, particularly in Balochistan (Meer, 2021). The negative impact of this kind of social unrest in the international public opinion motivated a new Chinese strategy for investment in foreign countries, with clear effects on investment in Pakistan. Xi Jinping said in April that the country will reduce coal use beginning in 2026, and Beijing has set climate targets, pledging to bring its emissions to a peak before 2030 and to make the country carbon-neutral by 2060 (Ember, 2021). After the participation in the COP26, held between November 1 and 12, 2021, in the city of Glasgow, Scotland, China decided to end investments in coal plans abroad. The COP26 follows the Paris climate accords, adopted in 2015, which suggested countries reduce emissions in order to keep global temperatures at less than 2°C above pre-industrial levels. Many countries have made commitments to move to a net-zero emissions economy. Net-zero means cutting indirect carbon emissions from upstream suppliers to end users, a complex feat in a world where companies do not control their entire value chain. At this moment, China is one of the countries in the world that invests most in clean energy, including overseas low-carbon energy projects. The Chinese president announced at that event that China will no longer finance overseas coal projects: "China will step up support for other developing countries in developing green and low carbon energy and will not build new coal-fired power projects abroad" (Xinhua, 2021). For many analysts, this intention proclaimed by the Chinese president could mean a substantial contribution to the end of coal as a primary source for the world (Gunia, 2021).

There is a substantial change in the Chinese posture in its investment strategy for the world, assuming a role of responsibility. Since 2021, China has not funded any more coal projects around the world, particularly in Pakistan. According to Muyi Yang, senior electricity policy analyst at Ember:

> The transition towards a low-carbon electricity system is a mainstay of China's bid to become carbon neutral by the mid-century. Making the country's growth of electricity demand more sustainable is critical for facilitating this transition. For this, China needs to drive electricity consumption to be more efficient, to further promote "high-quality" economic growth, and to deepen electricity pricing reform, aimed at making electricity prices more cost-reflective. (Ember, 2021)

Primarily, the carbon decoupling is part of the Chinese soft power strategy to create a positive image in the world when looking to use green energies (i.e., wind, solar, and, in some conditions, hydrogen). In fact, the Asian Giant, which is the world's biggest emitter of greenhouse gases, has pledged to cut back on the use of coal for power generation (Cooke, 2016). Climate change is not only a great threat to the economic sustainability of China but also a global hazard. It is particularly important when the world is living in a phase of tensions between China and the United States, which is not positive for progress in the global struggle to curb global warming and climate change. Beijing is using "the second face of power," an indirect way to get what it wants, by promoting its image and showing the superiority of its economic system in relation to the United States, a country worried about social and environmental problems (Nye, 2004, p. 5). China intends to ward off critical voices regarding its economic ascent. The theory of China as a threat persists in some parts of the world, partially derived from its great size as a country. Napoleon's old pronunciation that "Let her sleep, for when she wakes she will shake" shows this entire sensible dimension (Peyrefitte, 1976). In fact, a good image usually generates trust and opens windows of opportunity to cooperation between actors. On the 50th anniversary of Sino–French diplomatic relations in 2014, Chinese President Xi Jinping claimed that China is in fact now awake but is not a danger; it is "peaceful, pleasant and civilized" (Lee, 2018, p. 1). On the contrary, negative images provoke negative reactions and create an unstable atmosphere. Beijing defends the UN system for the resolution of international conflicts, openly condemning unilateralism. In many ways, it condemns the American foreign policy of interfering in the internal affairs of other states. Beijing defends and promotes its political and economic model as superior, and it intends that other countries follow its values.

The change in the energy paradigm has vital importance in the international power game for the coming decades, forcing the powers to look for new sources of raw materials. Clean energy technologies oblige looking for critical minerals—i.e., those metals and non-metal minerals that are considered essential for welfare in emerging economies—whose supply may be at threat due to geopolitical pressure from international competition. Many of these minerals are used in technological equipment. China's control of the world's access to raw materials is vital to the digital economy, particularly 5G technology (Foreign Policy, 2019). China is a renewable energy leader, gaining in the international race in the installation of solar panels, wind turbines, batteries, and electric vehicles (GCGET, 2019). More than half of the global electric vehicles are produced in China. Every year thousands of new patents are registered, and Chinese citizens are motivated to buy electric vehicles from state-owned companies (Kerry & Khanna, 2019). In 2019, John Kerry and Ro Khanna warned that "it would be folly to replace a world order too dependent on Middle Eastern oil with one that's too dependent on Chinese technology." One of the risks for Pakistan is that the Chinese-backed energy transition could increase India's and the United States' distrust of the Islamic Republic. Furthermore, China has developed some projects near the delicate Indian border region. The Gujarat border is a very sensitive point, and there are plenty of Indian watchtowers to avoid possible territorial intrusions. In 1965, Pakistan made an incursion on those lands, and India does not want an identical scenario. Since 2000, Islamabad has been building transport infrastructures on the same area and maintains restricted control over the movements of people (Hoodbhoy, 2017). The energy transition taken on by China especially since the beginning of 2021 will have important regional geopolitical effects. Relations with the Middle East could be less decisive for China's foreign relations, and even Pakistan's potential as a guarantor of oil flows could diminish in importance. One of China's goals is to reduce the Malacca Strait's reliance on water supplies. Eighty percent of the energy import to China takes place through the Malacca Strait.

The price of oil in international markets could also decline. Russian gas could gain greater importance, strengthening relations with Moscow. Strategic partners could also change: the changing views of "energy security" in China as the energy transition unfolds and the implications for China's outbound economic diplomacy and security policy. Throughout history, the demand for natural resources has always been a factor at the "heart of geopolitics" (Crow & Saran, 2021, p. 5). Examples are the asymmetries created between actors in the international system, between those who achieve a quick, successful transformation and those who are more rigid. The great concern is to verify whether the energy transition in Pakistan will alter the game of forces with India, a traditional competitor with China. In this part of the world there are many political sensitivities that involve energy security dynamics. India and Pakistan are both nuclear powers. Pakistan, within the framework of the BRI's investment, has functioned as a policy laboratory for China's energy transition. The dilemma of managing the social upheavals deriving from the traditional polluting Chinese investment and the risk of opting for an energy transition led Beijing to choose this latter solution.

The energy transition carried out in Pakistan from fossil fuels to low carbon will be challenging for the weak political situation in the Islamic country. The strategic industry related to renewables offers simultaneously opportunities and risks (Goldthau, 2019). The Pakistani government has also advanced to a green energy transition and approved the Renewable Energy Policy 2019 that intends to increase the share of electricity from 5 % to 30 % until 2030 (Government of Pakistan, 2019). This process is accompanied by public policies and incentives that benefit investors that adopt new forms of energy. If the transition does not have adequate public investment, it could be in an even more vulnerable situation. The decoupling from carbon and the new race for renewable energies open a new opportunity for corruption, which forces the Chinese government to be vigilant. Decarbonization is a time-consuming and risky process that involves many security challenges in a context of competition with the United States. The path to net-zero emissions could bring social instability by the fact that some communities and sectors have economic activities centered on the use of fossil fuels. Renewable energy is more expensive, and many citizens do not have the capacity to acquire it. Frustration with socioeconomic and welfare expectations is an engine for uprisings. Chinese production of energy in Pakistan has fueled inflation. Pakistan's exports are in jeopardy due to the increase of prices affecting national production, particularly the textile industry (Husain, 2021). If the use of coal is a factor in Pakistan's discontent on the part of the population, its replacement will also be a source of conflict. Countries with a longer tradition in the use of renewable energies will benefit from the new effort by the Chinese government in the renewal of energies, not particularly Pakistan, which has high production costs, a weak fiscal regime, and frequent political instability.

The truth is that hydrocarbons continue to underpin the global energy infrastructure (Sharan & Saran, 2021). Despite the positive trend in China's posture, it produced more than 53 % of the world's total coal-fired power in 2020, growing from 44 % in 2015 (Ember, 2021). In China, there is always a gap between political rhetoric and effective results. Pakistan remains wedded to previous China-backed coal power projects and previous investment agreements, particularly fossil fuel investments, including mining, drilling, and power generation. The BRI has financed hundreds of coal projects in countries from Egypt to the Philippines, many of them trying to solve electricity scarcity (Gunia, 2021).

The search for alternative energy sources has geopolitical implications, forcing a new assessment of traditional relationships of interdependence. Pakistan may lose strategic importance to China as Beijing reduces the importance of the Middle East in its strategic orientations. It is true that the energy transition process is slow, but in the short term, Chinese investment in Pakistan could lose significance. In this process, countries with natural gas like Russia or Australia will gain geopolitical relevance. In 2021, Australia exported a record volume of natural gas to China, similar to the previous year (Crow & Saran, 2021; Morrison, 2021). The transition to greater use of electric vehicles will lead to a reduction in oil imports, protecting the transport sector and opening new business opportunities (Qasim, 2020). This reduction of oil imports leads to a reduction of foreign dependency and improves self-sufficiency and energy security. Changing a national economy to a green model is always a profound and time-consuming process, greatly hampered by years of wrong investment in infrastructure. For instance, Chinese investments in Pakistan for decades were focused on polluting industries, and it was not until the beginning of 2021 that Beijing developed the will to change its strategy abroad. The widespread and rushed demand for natural gas makes the price of this resource soar, accompanied by inadequate infrastructure, reversing the process and returning to the previous model. This phenomenon has been called "the revenge of the old economy" (Currie, 2021).

CONCLUSION

Relations between China and Pakistan are historic, reinforced at the turning point of the new millennium. Since then, China has increased its projection on the international scene, its naval presence in the surrounding areas and the security of its maritime communication lines, the development of projects such as the New Silk Road, and security in access to natural resources (energy security). Since Pakistan has a structural weakness in its energy supply, China has also been investing over the years in setting up coal-mining companies. Because China is promoting the use of unclean energy in its neighboring countries, it has led to discontent among some local populations.

With involvement in the Glasgow agreements, China has been changing its strategy in Pakistan, betting on an energy transition. Xi Jinping's international commitments in defense of the environment are a very important factor for change. But this process is not simple, cheap, or quick, and it promises to bring a risky picture due to changes in the geopolitical dimension. From the outset, there is a possibility of social unrest, which, on the one hand, results from the use of dirty energy, but the change in energy can bring new sources of discontent. Pakistan is a country with very sensitive ethnic tensions, so any structural economic or strategic change is always a factor of unrest. The search for new sources of clean energy could force a strengthening of cooperation with other international actors, and even Pakistan could lose with this change. On the other hand, the Chinese-supported energy transition could be a factor of instability with India, which could be challenged by being inferior in this equation. The energy transition proposed by China and Pakistan governments are until now more political and rhetorical than real, as it involves strong and costly structural commitments. The change in strategy is not without risks in the regional security framework, representing a shakeup of the regional geopolitical framework. In spite of changes that are good for the environment, it can be challenging for people's serenity.

REFERENCES

Aftab, S. (2014). Pakistan's energy crisis: Causes, consequences and possible remedies. *Expert Analysis*, NOREF—The Norwegian Peacebuilding Resource Centre. Retrieved January 6, 2022, from https://www.files.ethz.ch/isn/177484/ade59fba5daf67a11a1c217434abf440.pdf

Ahmad, A. (2016). Gwadar: A Historical Kaleidoscope. In Policy Perspectives: The Journal of the Institute of Policy Studies (Vol. 13, Issue 2). Pluto Journals. https://doi.org/10.13169/polipers.13.2.0149.

Ali, G. (2017). *China-Pakistan relations*. Oxford University Press.

Cooke, K. (2016). *Pakistan signs coal mining deals with China*. Climate Home News. https://www.climatechangenews.com/2016/01/19/pakistan-signs-coal-mining-deals-china/.

Crow, A., & Saran, S. (2021). The geopolitics of energy transition: A guide for policymakers, executives, and investors [Special report]. *Observer Research Foundation*, *174*, 1–19.

Currie, J. (2021, October 21). The revenge of the old economy. *Financial Times*. Retrieved January 3, 2022, from https://www.ft.com/content/c7732d53-2e34-4fde-b5fb-6f45f114111f

Ember—Coal to Clean Energy Policy. (2021). Global electricity review—Global trends. Retrieved December 28, 2021, from https://ember-climate.org/wp-content/uploads/2021/03/Global-Electricity-Review-2021.pdf

Foreign Policy. (2019). *Mining the future—How China is set to dominate the next industrial revolution* (pp. 1–14). Analytics, the Research Division of the FP Group.

Garver, J. W. (2001). *Protracted contest—Sino-Indian rivalry in the twentieth century*. University of Washington Press.

Goldthau, A. (2019). *Global energy in transition—How the EU should navigate new realities and risks* (Policy Brief, No. 4, pp. 1–8). The German Council on Foreign Relations (DGAP).

Government of Pakistan. (2019). *Alternative and Renewable Energy Policy*. https://www.aedb.org/images/Draft_ARE_Policy_2019_-_Version_2_July_21_2019.pdf

Hoodbhoy, N. (2017, November 18). Coal project is latest sign of growing Pakistan-China relationship. *East-Asia*. Retrieved January 7, 2022, from https://www.voanews.com/a/coal-project-is-latest-sign-of-growing-pakistan-china-relationship/4125106.html

Husain, K. (2021, March 21). *Pakistan's surplus power generation capacity has come at a price. The country confronts steep electricity payments amidst persistent blackouts*. Scroll.in. Retrieved January 8, 2022, from https://scroll.in/article/989919/pakistans-surplus-power-generation-capacity-has-come-at-a-price

International Energy Agency. (2021a). Coal power's sharp rebound is taking it to a new record in 2021, threatening net zero goals. Retrieved January 6, 2022, from https://www.iea.org/news/coal-power-s-sharp-rebound-is-taking-it-to-a-new-record-in-2021-threatening-net-zero-goals

International Energy Agency. (2021b). *Pakistan*. Retrieved December 29, 2021, from https://www.iea.org/countries/pakistan

International Trade Administration. (2021). *Pakistan—Country commercial guide*. Retrieved December 29, 2021, from https://www.trade.gov/country-commercial-guides/pakistan-market-overview?section-nav=3640

Irman, A. (2020, August 21). *Pakistan's energy crisis*. Pamir Times. Retrieved January 6, 2022, from https://pamirtimes.net/2020/08/21/pakistans-energy-crisis

Jacques, M. (2009). *When China rules the world—The rise of the middle kingdom and the end of the western world*. Allen Lane.

Kashmeri, S. (2019). *Grand strategy—Weaving a new Silk Road to global primacy*. Praeger.

Kerry, J., & Khanna, R. (2019, December 9). Don't let China win the green race. *The New York Times*. Retrieved January 23, 2022, from https://www.nytimes.com/2019/12/09/opinion/china-renewable-energy.html

Leandro, F. J. (2018). *Steps of greatness: The geopolitics of OBOR*. University of Macau.

Lee, C. S. (2018). *Soft power made in China: The dilemmas of online, offline media, and transnational audiences*. Palgrave Macmillan.

Malik, A. (2020). *Circular debt—An unfortunate misnomer* (PIDE Working Paper, No. 2020:20, pp. 1–35). Pakistan Institute of Development Economics.

Mangi, F. (2021, January 27). *Nation plagued by power shortages suddenly has too much electricity*. Bloomberg. Retrieved January 8, 2022, from https://www.bloomberg.com/news/articles/2021-01-27/pakistan-struggles-to-tackle-an-unfamiliar-glut-of-electricity

Meer, S. (2021, August 20). Protests in Pakistan erupt against China's belt and road plan. *The Guardian*. Retrieved January 3, 2022, from https://www.theguardian.com/environment/2021/aug/20/water-protests-in-pakistan-erupt-against-chinas-belt-and-road-plan

Morrison, K. (2021, December 2). *Australian LNG exports hit record high in October*. Argus. https://www.argusmedia.com/en/news/2279279-australian-lng-exports-hit-record-high-in-october

Nye, J. S. (2004). *Soft power—The means to success in world politics*. Public Affairs.

Patel, R., & Zhao, N. (2014a). Keeping the lights on: Fixing Pakistan's energy crisis. *Public Interest Report*, *67*(2).

Patel, R., & Zhao, N. (2014b, June 5). *Keeping the lights on: Fixing Pakistan's energy crisis*. Federation of American Scientists. Retrieved January 6, 2022, from https://fas.org/pir-pubs/keeping-lights-fixing-pakistans-energy-crisis/

Peyrefitte, Al. (1976). *Quand la Chine S'Éveillera...le Monde Tremblera* [Portugese ed.]. Parceria.

Qasim, M. (2020). *Pakistan leapfrogging to a green energy future*. EastAsia Forum. Retrieved December 31, 2021, from https://www.eastasiaforum.org/2020/09/18/pakistan-leapfrogging-to-a-green-energy-future/

Raheem, A., Abbasi, S. A., Memon, A., Samo, S. R., Taufiq-Yap, Y. H., Danquah, M. K., & Harun, R. (2016). Renewable energy deployment to combat energy crisis in Pakistan. *Energy, Sustainability and Society*, *6*(1). https://doi.org/10.1186/s13705-016-0082-z

Ramana, S. (2011). *China-Pakistan nuclear alliance* [Special report]. Institute of Peace and Conflict Studies.

Sharan, V., & Saran, S. (2021, November). *India's coal transition: A market case for decarbonisation* (ORF Issue Brief No. 505), pp. 1–19.

Siddique, Q. (2014). *Deeper than the Indian Ocean? An analysis of Pakistan-China relations*. SISA.

Silva, J. T. (2019). Sino-Pakistani axis of cooperation in China's new Silk Road. In C. A. Mendes (Ed.), *China's New Silk Road—An emerging world order* (pp. 120–132). Routledge.

Silva, J. T. (2009). O Porto Paquistanês de Gwadar no Enquadramento Geopolítico da República Popular da China. *Geopolítica*, *3*, 221–251.

Small, A. (2015). *The China-Pakistan axis—Asia's new geopolitical*. Oxford University Press.

Wolf, S. O. (2020). The China-Pakistan economic corridor of the Belt and Road Initiative. Springer.

World Bank. (2021). *Access to electricity (% of population)*. Retrieved December 23, 2021, from https://data.worldbank.org/indicator/EG.ELC.ACCS.ZS

Xinhua (2021, September 2). *Xi Focus: China to stop building new coal-fired power projects abroad*. http://www.news.cn/english/2021-09/22/c_1310201218.htm

Zhang, F. (2019). *In the dark—How much do power sector distortions cost South Asia*? World Bank Group.

CHAPTER 13

Transition to Low-Carbon Energy Resources in India: Issues and Challenges

VENKATESH DUTTA AND ROOPINDER OBEROI

INTRODUCTION

> Decarbonization of the global energy systems is the greatest challenges facing man in the 21st Century. The energy sector is critical for tacking the climate change as it accounts for approximately two thirds of global carbon dioxide. (Quitzow, 2021)

"Since 1970s, the global gross domestic product (GDP) has increased by around 4.5 times, while the consumption of primary energy has grown from 155.22 EJ in 1965 to 556.63 EJ in the year 2020. The total proved energy reserves of the dominant fuels, that is, oil, natural gas, and coal at the end of 2020 could last just 53.5 years for oil, 48.8 years for natural gas, and 139 years for coal" (BP, 2021). Fossil fuels continue to dominate the global energy basket, accounting for more than 80 % of total energy production. International Energy Agency (IEA) statistics study indicates that the "global energy supply in 2018 reached 14,279,569 Ktoe, with coal, oil and natural gas accounting for 26.88 %, 31.49 % and 22.84 %, respectively" (IEA, 2020). In the face of climate change, it is vital "to synergize the economy, energy consumption, and climate change so as to achieve sustainable development and carbon neutrality" (Howard et al., 2020). The widespread use of fossil fuels and energy poverty has resulted in a complex web of conflicts for human society, including a rising supply-demand mismatch in the global energy market, the risk of oil resource depletion, increase in GHG emissions, and so on. Furthermore, because of the massive amount of carbon dioxide released by burning fossil fuels, the global temperature has risen by around 1.0°C above pre-industrial levels. According to the emissions gap report, "the total greenhouse gas emissions in 2018 was about 55.3 GtCO2e of which 37.5 GtCO2 were on account of fossil fuels combustion in various operations and activities including electricity generation" (UNEP, 2019). Between 2030 and 2052, if carbon emissions continue to rise at their current rate, the temperature is expected to rise by 1.5°C. Meanwhile, global warming's harmful and spillover impacts, such as rising sea levels and increasing heat waves, could endanger people's lives and disrupt economic activity.

Climate change impacts are intensifying, emphasizing the significance of a worldwide shift to a "low-carbon economy" with decreased fossil fuel usage and greenhouse gas emissions. Globally, steady progress has already been made in the energy transition, and many countries are expanding their renewable energy baskets. Global renewable energy installation capacity, for example, grew by about 200 billion kilowatts in 2019. Concerns have been voiced throughout the world regarding the overemphasis on economic recovery at the expense of energy transition progress (Tian et al., 2022). Governments and businesses are pushing for a sustainable recovery plan that would help the economy while also protecting the environment. Government backing, fossil fuel divestment, inadequate renewable energy production capacity, global supply chain disruptions, and energy poverty might all impede low-carbon technology adoption.

Globally, technology and innovation landscape has pushed renewable energy in the world economy as a result of rising concerns about climate change impacts. During the current fourth industrial revolution, a green energy transformation is silently taking place. The goal of the green energy transition is to shift away from carbon-intensive fossil fuels toward low-carbon clean energy sources. Solar, wind, hydro, bioenergy, geothermal, and other low-carbon renewable energy sources make up the majority of clean energy basket.

In response to growing anxieties about high carbon-intensity of traditional energy usage, countries throughout the world have enacted legislation and put restrictions on fossil fuels. In dealing with fossil fuel divestment challenges, more voices are pushing for greater international cooperation and meaningful partnership. Climate governance aims to decarbonize the economy by converting non-renewable energy use to clean and renewable energy sources. Global demand for renewable energy is expanding, as evidenced by international climate agreements and Sustainable Development Goals (SDGs). In its Emissions Gap Report 2019, the United Nations Environment Programme (UNEP) cites that overall GHG emissions from energy production and industrial activities reached 37.5 Gt in 2018, with total carbon dioxide emissions increasing by as much as 2 % (Olhoff

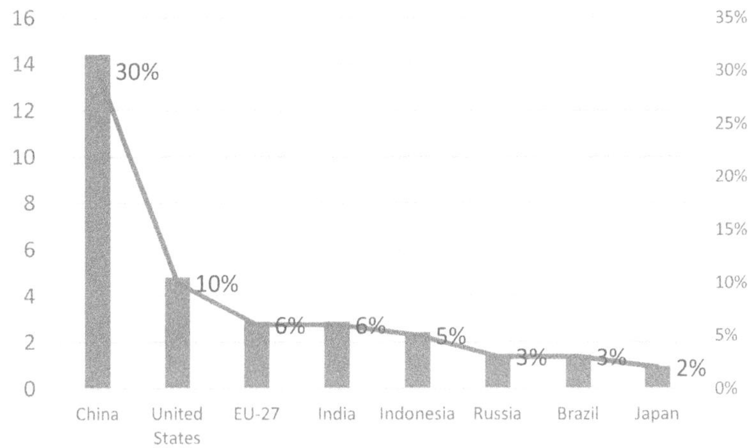

Figure 13.1: Share of net GHG emissions in 2020 from the world's largest emitters (in billion metric tons of CO2e, including LULUCF, and share of global total in %)

Source: Authors' own elaboration (data retrieved from Rhodium Group, 2021).

and Christensen, 2019). To achieve SDGs and carbon neutrality, it is critical to synergize the economy, energy consumption, and climate change. India is the world's third-largest carbon emitter, behind China and the US, although its per capita emissions are around seven times lower than the US (Figure 13.1).

INDIA'S DEVELOPMENT ASPIRATIONS

India just makes up 2.4 % of the world's land mass, yet it is home to 17.5 % of the world's population. Climatic change is a big concern for emerging economies such as India, which experience large-scale climate variability, where droughts are ever more recurrent and are more vulnerable to catastrophic weather events in the future. Few nations in the world are as sensitive to the consequences of climate change as India, with its massive population mostly dependent on the rainfed agriculture. There are also long coastline, the Himalayan fronts, and islands that are vulnerable to extreme weather events. Appropriate trade-offs between economic growth and societal development must be made in improving the quality of life of its vast disadvantaged communities. This aspect should be taken into account in the policy matrix, as poverty eradication and inclusive growth are two of the government's top concerns (Dubash & Rajamani, 2021).

India's footprint in the global economy is significant and expanding. Many sectors and services are performing well. The central government has introduced several social welfare policy measures and plans to launch more. The modification of price subsidies has improved the fairness of household assistance to basic services especially in housing provisions, energy access and health infrastructure. It has improved the well-being and productivity. After tariff barriers were reduced in the early 1990s, trade exposure increased dramatically. India's export market share in the information and technology (IT) sector has increased dramatically, producing numerous skilled job opportunities and drawing significant global investment. India is also doing well in several complicated, skill- and capital-intensive commodities, such as pharmaceuticals, automobiles, agri-foods and fertilizers.

In recent years, per capita income has risen rapidly, lifting millions of Indians out of poverty. The GDP per capita is still 86 % lower than OECD best performers (Figure 13.2). Each year, India adds a metropolitan the size of London to its urban populace, involving massive construction of whole infrastructure networks. A younger population, in combination with a move away from the agricultural sector, has reasonably led to a surge in India's urbanization rate. India's urban population is anticipated to more than double by 2030, and "[i]ts cities will be asked to hold more than 300 million more people, which will hasten the usage of modern fuels, lead to a rise in appliance and vehicle ownership, and provide an uptick in demand for construction materials, all of which are expected to increase greenhouse gas (GHG) emissions" (Pandey, 2017, p. 2). Fossil fuels have been India's bedrocks for industrial development and modernization which includes providing citizens an access to modern energy amenities. This means providing basic amenities like electricity connections for 50 million citizens every year over the past decade. The fast rise in consumption of fossil energy means that India's

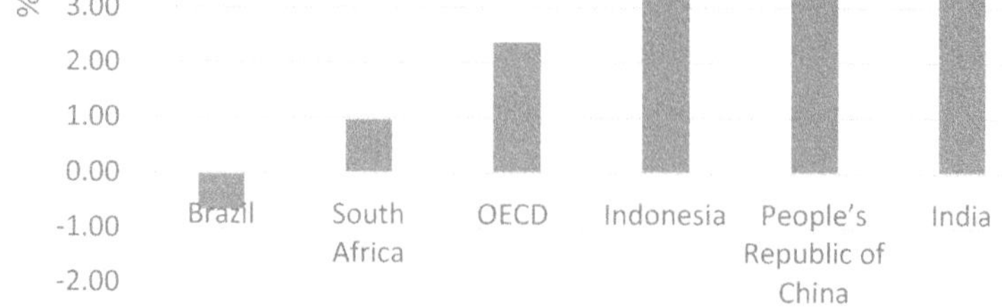

Figure 13.2: Annualized GDP growth rates (2014 to 2019Q2)

Source: Authors' own elaboration (data retrieved from OECD Economic Surveys: India 2019 © OECD 2019, available from: https://www.oecd-ilibrary.org/economics/oecd-economic-surveys-india-2019_554c1c22-en).

annual CO_2 emissions has mounted to third highest in the world. But, India's CO_2 emissions per person is still lowest of the world's emitters if considered from historical emissions per person perspective. Similarly, the energy consumption of the average Indian household is one tenth as compared to the average household in the United States.

The execution of a comprehensive set of reforms has boosted economic activity and slowed inflation while also reducing fiscal and current account imbalances. The economy is picking up steam after the second infection wave crested in May 2021, with GDP expected to increase at 9.4 % in the fiscal year 2021–2022, before reversing to 8.1 % in FY 2022–2023 and 5.5 % in FY 2023–2024. Inflation has stayed close to the Reserve Bank of India's (RBI) upper band, although it could ease once supply chain disruptions are resolved. Financial markets are showing signs of improved health, and capital inflows are helping to boost reserves, even though the global economic and financial environment is less supportive. The pandemic hit the informal sector particularly hard, where a large portion of the Indian population works, reinforcing the need for job growth in the formal sector, health care reforms, and the protection of vulnerable individuals, households, and communities.

Access to public services is improving, but there is still room for improvement in terms of quality and delivery outcomes. Quality job creation, underemployment, skill-building and income inequality are all issues that need to be addressed along with bridging the development divide between rich and the poor. The employment rate has fallen and is now at an all-time low. Public funds allocated to healthcare and education is insufficient. Despite the implementation of several social housing projects, a sizable population is still without standard housing, and it is expected that growing urbanization will exacerbate the problem particularly in metropolitan areas. According to official estimates, nearly 40 million families experienced housing shortages in 2015. As most of the upcoming cities and towns have a high population density, housing prices are relatively higher, pushed up by expensive construction industry, as well as strict zoning rules. The government's "Homes for All" initiative intends to give housing to everyone by 2022. How to provide shelter for the poorest of the poor is a major challenge. Since October 2014, about 100 million toilets have been built to eradicate open defecation, and to improve health and hygiene practices in rural areas. In 2018, electricity reached all villages, but not all homes, and power outages continue to be common in many regions. The government has pledged to supply piped drinking water to every household by 2024, as well as to speed the rural connectivity to better link the impoverished in remote areas. The government has also promised expanded hospital and retirement insurance programmes for informal employees, as well as the establishment of primary health care centers in all the states. There is significant scope to improve the targeting of subsidies through direct cash transfers, as access to finance is difficult, especially for low-income people.

Labor regulations are complicated; some are particularly onerous for industrial businesses, and the majority of them kick in when businesses expand, preventing formal job creation. Most workers are not covered by core labor regulations and social security in practice. Efforts to modernize labor legislation should continue in order to encourage job growth and thereby enhance fairness. Firms will be able to develop and take advantage of economies of scale if labor standards are modernized further.

India has preferential trade agreements; however, they are restricted in scope. Restrictions on services, which are critical inputs for other sectors, have a detrimental impact on manufacturing and, more broadly, on income. India has made it easier to do business and is easing international investment restrictions. Extending state and special economic zone success stories to the rest of the country will boost India's competitiveness and encourage investment.

The concentration of GHGs is showing a rising trend and the majority of Indians are exposed to high levels of air pollution. Air pollution is already high and will only get worse unless drastic measures are taken. Nine of the top 10 cities in the world with the worst air pollution, as measured by fine particulate matter, are in India. Poor people frequently cook with wood biomass, dung, and agricultural wastes, adding to indoor and outdoor air pollution (Shukla & Dutta, 2022), which is a leading cause of early mortality and harms infant development. Power plants, industry, transportation, and agriculture are major sources of carbon emissions. By 2040, energy consumption may have more than doubled, and the government has promised to using 40 % renewable energy by then.

THE EVOLVING INTERNATIONAL CLIMATE POLICY ARCHITECTURE

The energy transition has emerged as a new front in the fight against climate change. The Kyoto Protocol and the Paris Agreement are the major climate governance milestones that provided the groundwork for a worldwide low-carbon energy transition (Grasso & Dutta, 2018). The Pairs Pact was signed by 196 participating parties in 2015 to accomplish a decarbonization agreement. The accord aspires to keep global warming well below 2°C, ideally 1.5°C, over pre-industrial levels. Many regions of the world are working hard to reach the stated objects. Many countries have made deliberate attempts to reorganize their energy systems in order to reach this ambitious target. For example, the European Union (EU) issued a 20–20–20 objective, which calls for a 20 % improvement in energy efficiency, a 20 % reduction in carbon emissions, and a 20 % increase in renewable energy by 2020. China established a "30.60" plan, vowing to reach carbon neutrality by 2060 and peak carbon dioxide emissions by 2030. A growing number of countries are committing to net-zero emissions to be reached by the middle of the century. From a global viewpoint, the tipping point for net-zero targets has been reached, since more than 110 nations have stated such promises. Indian critics, on the other hand, differ regarding the need for achieving net-zero targets (Dubash, 2021; Nordenstam, 2021). The Biden administration has re-entered the Paris Climate Accord, and announced intentions to invest over $400 billion in renewable energy over the next 10 years as part of a wide mobilization. Biden intends to put the US on track to reach net-zero emissions by 2050, which is an ambitious goal. During the CoP 26 at Glasgow after failing to agree on a promise to "phase-out" coal, India and China instead debated over "phasing down" coal, raising dismay and concern about the world's ability to keep average global temperature rise below 1.5°C. Many analysts now believe that China and India will be forced to defend their actions to nations that are vulnerable to climate change.

INDIA'S CLIMATE POLICY LANDSCAPE

International agreements, objectives and commitments have motivated adoption of many domestic climate measures and the formulation of national and state action plans to minimize the negative effects of climate change in India. Even though climate action was not a domestic priority until the 1990s, international agreements prompted the framing of national action plans. Since 2008, India's climate policy has evolved significantly (see Table 13.1). The 2008 National Action Plan on Climate Change (NAPCC), which came up in the run-up to COP 15 in Copenhagen, and the 2015 Nationally Determined Contributions (NDCs) are the two major policy strands that explain India's national climate policy priorities. The NAPCC integrated climate policy to many sectors such as transport, housing, energy efficiency, water supply, and solar energy. The NAPCC also initiated several missions within the domestic climate policy and many states evolved their own climate policy and action plans.

Specific missions, which were first included in the NAPCC, are an important part of India's climate policy implementation phase. These missions institutionalize Indian climate policy on a variety of subjects as aspirational document and policy guidelines. Five missions can be broadly included in the *adaptation* category: The National Water Mission, the National Mission for Sustaining the Himalayan Ecosystem, the National Mission for a "Green India," the National Mission for Sustainable Agriculture, and the National Mission on Strategic Knowledge for Climate Change. While three missions, the National Solar

Table 13.1: Important Events That Shaped India's Climate Policy Architecture

Year	Events
1989	The Ministry of Environment and Forests (MoEF) formed a group of experts on "Global Climate Change"
1991	Anil Agarwal and Sunita Narain from Centre for Science and Environment in New Delhi published an important paper titled "Global Warming in an Unequal World: A Case of Environment Colonialism"
1992	India signs the United Nation Framework Convention on Climate Change (UNFCC)
1997	Launching of "Indian Hydrocarbon Vision"
2002	India ratifies the Kyoto Protocol as well as hosted United Nations climate conference (CoP-8) in New Delhi
2006	India joins the Asia-Pacific partnership on "Clean Development and Climate." Formulation of "National Environment Policy" and "Integrated Energy Policy"
2007	Set up of "Prime Minister Council on Climate Change" by the scientific experts
2008	"National Action Plan on Climate Change" framework was published with eight national missions to solve climate change
2009	India's voluntary announcement reduced the CO_2 emission by 30–35 % of its GDP intensity within 2025, considering 2005 as the base year. Formation of "Indian Network on Climate Change Assessment"
2010	The Expert Group on "Low-Carbon Strategies for Inclusive Growth" was set up by the Planning Commission to suggest low-carbon pathways consistent with inclusive growth
2015	India declared its NDCs two months before CoP21, the Paris Agreement aims to keep global average temperature rises well below 2°C this century, and to push for further reductions to 1.5°C over pre-industrial levels. As a result of India's argument, the term *climate justice* has been included in the UNFCCC constitution
2016	121 Countries joined the International Solar Alliance headed by India, launched in Paris climate meet. United Nations as a collaborator institution
2018	16th International Energy Forum Ministerial Meet at New Delhi
2019	PM Modi made a commitment to ramp up climate action at the UN Climate Action Summit in 2019 by increasing the installed renewable energy capacity to 450 GW by 2030
2020	Comprehensive National Hydrogen Energy Mission is launched
2021	CoP 26 at Glasgow, PM Modi pledged to cut emissions to net zero by 2070, reduce carbon emissions by one billion tons by 2030, and raise the share of renewable in the energy mix to 50 %, however, opposed a commitment to "phase-out" coal and instead, agreed to "phase-down" coal while negotiating the final agreement

Source: Authors' own elaboration

Mission, the National Mission for Enhanced Energy Efficiency, and the National Mission for Sustainable Habitat involve *mitigation* components.

Prime Minister Manmohan Singh established the PM Council on Climate Change and named the first Indian Envoy on Climate Change. While the office of Envoy was only temporary, the Council continues to function even today. The intensity of India's global leadership aspirations has risen substantially since 2010, particularly after the strengthening of International Solar Alliance (ISA) and the G20, and active contribution in the IPCC's assessment report.

In the run-up to COP 21 in Paris in 2015, India's climate policy evolved once again. Rather than refusing to join a global agreement, as many observers had predicted, India declared its NDCs two months before COP21. The NDCs outlined India's climate policies for the global climate framework prior to COP21 (Dubash & Ghosh, 2019). The 2015 NDCs should be evaluated largely in the context of global climate agreements. Additional missions on wind energy, health, waste to energy, and coastal regions was highlighted in the NDCs, which also asked for the national water mission and the national mission on sustainable agriculture to be improved. When the NDCs were first announced, some observers saw them as a "new climate strategy" for India, while others saw them as a "lost opportunity." India ratified the Paris Agreement in 2016 in order to "present itself as a country eager to be part of the solution, rather than a part of the problem."

Later, Prime Minister Modi made a commitment to ramp up climate action at the UN Climate Action Summit in 2019 by increasing the installed renewable energy capacity to 450 GW by 2030. He also launched a new Comprehensive National Hydrogen Energy Mission in November 2020 that provided political momentum for the building of green hydrogen reactors. At the 2021 CoP 26, India's Prime Minister Narendra Modi announced a five-point plan dubbed as the *panchamrita* to attain the goal of carbon neutrality. The five points:

- India's non-fossil energy capacity will reach 500 gigawatts (GW) by 2030.
- By 2030, India will meet 50 % of its energy needs using renewable energy.
- From now until 2030, India will lower overall estimated carbon emissions by one billion tonnes.
- By 2030, India's economy will have reduced its carbon intensity by less than 45 %.
- As a result, India will attain Net Zero by the year 2070.

However, the commitment over pashing out coal was opposed raising disappointment and concern. These targets are no doubt daunting, but the clean energy changeover is already well underway in India. India demonstrated that it over-achieved its pledge made at COP 21—Paris Summit by meeting 40 % of its power capacity from non-fossil fuels- nearly 9 years in advance of its obligation and the portion of solar and wind in India's energy combination has risen extraordinarily.

The climate diplomacy became an important part of the foreign policy. Recently, climate policy and cooperation became a key component of deliberations at the regional forums such as the South Asian Association for Regional Cooperation, EU and many bilateral agreements. In recent years, the renewable energy sector has gained a significant momentum at the global scale, and India became one of the frontrunners in adopting renewable in a big way.

While there is general consensus in India and abroad about the urgent need for climate action, questions have been expressed concerning the US's and EU's long-term aspiration of achieving carbon neutrality by 2050. India has also established itself as a major player in the climate negotiations while putting forward strong case for climate justice based on carbon space. India's declaration that it intends to reach net-zero emissions by 2070 and to cater to 50 % of its electricity supplies from renewable energy sources by 2030 is an enormously noteworthy moment for the international fight against climate change. India is pioneering a new model of economic development that could avoid the carbon-intensive approaches that many countries have pursued in the past—and provide a blueprint for other developing economies. Even China's commitment for carbon neutrality by 2060 is much further away due to large dependency on coal and other fossil fuels. At all climate discussions, India has maintained its stance of equality and historical carbon load. Climate-sensitive industries such as agriculture, water, energy, and health will confront several issues as a result of extreme weather events.

However, many scholars believe that the net-zero target in India combined with state's action plan could be a potential job generator and contributor to the mitigation of climate impacts. The co-benefit potential offers the implementation of India's climate policy by combining domestic growth and development with climate change mitigation. According to the researchers, implementation of climate policy is hampered by a lack of institutional capability and a fragmented coordination strategy. India's NDCs are consistent with keeping global warming below 2°C. In comparison, the EU's climate action efforts are deemed insufficient, with a temperature rise of up to 3°C on the horizon, while China is on path to contribute to global warming of 3°C–4°C.

India is making strides on many fronts to create a safe energy future for its citizens, drawing on its deeply embedded development values and implementing a broad range of policy initiatives under the legal framework of the Energy Conservation Act, which covers 15 energy-intensive industries, and the Energy Conservation Building Code, which covers all new urban infrastructures. Many state governments have developed and started implementing their respective State Action Plans on Climate Change (SAPCC).

RISE OF THE RENEWABLE AND INDIA'S POSITION

Renewable power generation, mostly solar and wind, has surpassed fossil fuel-fired generation in terms of investment, and the government has pledged to increase it further. The government has launched a biofuel initiative and updated technical regulations for thermal power plants and cars. It also helps the under-privileged get clean gas connections.

The International Energy Agency estimates that $48 trillion will be required to fulfill global energy demands by 2035, with at least half of that investment going toward renewable energy and energy efficiency projects. Owing to scientific progresses, firm policy backing and a vibrant private sector solar power plants are more economical to build than coal ones. Renewable electricity is rising at a quicker pace in India than in other economies with additional capacity to rise two-fold by 2026. India is likewise one of the world's major manufacturers of contemporary bioenergy and has ambition to scale up its usage in economy. The IEA assumes India to surpass China in the next few years to become the third largest ethanol market globally after the United States and Brazil. Not just public money, but also commercial banks, state investment banks, and even multilateral development banks are increasingly guiding such investments (Sovacool, 2021). As a result, estimated adoption and diffusion rates for renewables and other climate mitigation solutions are likely to increase at an exponential rate.

Renewable energy is thought to be critical for limiting global warming to 1.5–2°C. However, for the Indian situation, the influence of renewable energy capacity increase on sustainability parameters has not been well examined. Laha and Chakraborty (2021) analyzed the ideal renewable capacity installation and

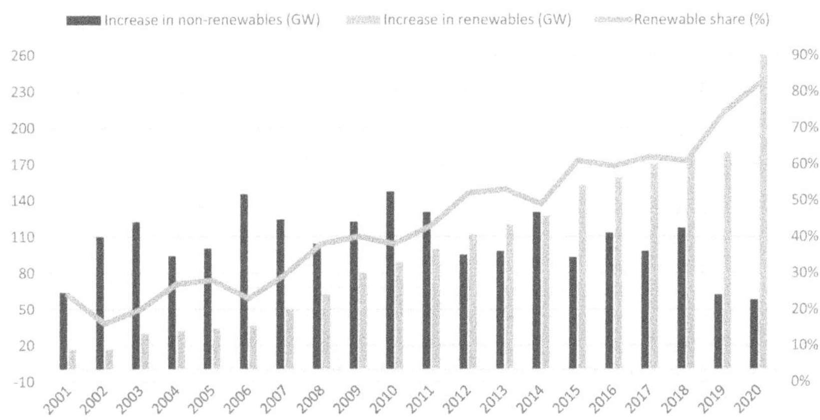

Figure 13.3: Global share of renewable in the annual power capacity expansion

Source: Authors' own elaboration (data retrieved from IRENA, 2021)

indicated that renewable uptake might range from 25.5 % to 41.2 % by 2030. Onshore wind, utility solar PV, and hydropower dams are among the top-ranked solutions on the Pareto frontiers. High river hydropower combined with high offshore wind can provide a large contribution to low-carbon power without going over budget. Overall, the energy mix with the least amount of coal power generation (1,175 TWh/yr) is predicted to be the most sustainable.

India has an excellent track record with renewables; its goal was 20 gigawatts (GW) by 2010, and by 2016, it was on its way to 175 gigawatts. Renewables may develop tremendously if India can strengthen the manufacturing base and provide the right incentives. Globally, 260 GW of renewable energy capacity were installed in 2020, surpassing increase in 2019 by close to 50 %—and breaking all prior records. According to the International Renewable Energy Agency (IRENA) Renewable Capacity Statistics 2021, renewables accounted for more than 80 % of all *new electrical capacity* installed in 2020, with solar and wind accounting for 91 % of new renewable (IRENA, 2021). Over the same time span, total fossil fuel additions decreased from 64 GW to 60 GW. In 2050, solar, wind, and coal together will account for 90 % of India's energy generating mix (Figure 13.4).

India's Central Electricity Authority has made an energy mix estimate for 2030. According to this estimate, India's non-fossil energy installed capacity for power generation—solar, wind, hydro, and nuclear—was 134 GW in 2019, and will reach 522 GW by 2030. Solar energy installed capacity must increase to 280 GW, while wind energy capacity must increase to 140 GW. In 2030, total

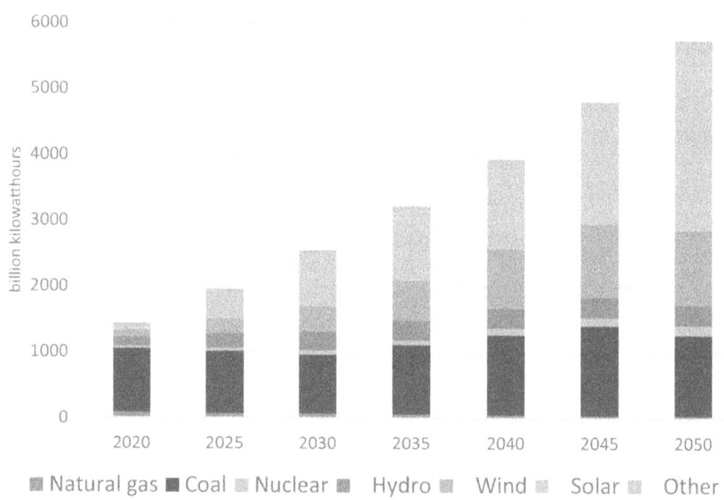

Figure 13.4: India's net electricity generation by fuel, reference case 2010–2050

Source: Authors' own elaboration (data retrieved from US Energy Information Administration, International Energy Outlook, 2019, available from: https://www.eia.gov/outlooks/ieo/tables_side_xls.php)

installed capacity will be 817 GW, with electricity generation totaling 2,518 billion units, according to this projection.

Renewables will account for around half of global electricity use by 2050, according to the US Energy Information Administration (International Energy Outlook, 2019). By the same period, green hydrogen may provide up to 24 % of global energy needs, reducing emissions by around a third. As a result, the shift to green hydrogen may provide $11 trillion in infrastructure investment possibilities over the next 30 years, as well as $2.5 trillion in direct yearly revenue.

According to the US Energy Information Administration (EIA), total global power generation will reach about 45 trillion kilowatthours (kWh) by 2050, an increase of nearly 20 trillion kWh from 2018 (Figure 13.4). During the forecast period (2018–2050), global renewable energy generation will rise by more than 20 %, accounting for nearly half of all global electricity output by 2050. Global coal-fired generation will fall by 13 % during the same time span, accounting for only 22 % of total generation in 2050. Global power generation is expected to expand at a rate of 1.8 % per year through 2050. Despite the fact that India has set targets for solar and wind capacity, the country lacks a strong emissions-reduction programme, therefore it is expected that coal-fired production will rise alongside solar and wind.

POLITICAL ECOLOGY OF LOW-CARBON TRANSITIONS

Developing nations, such as India, claim that they are being pressured to switch from fossil fuels to renewables, while wealthier countries refuse to assist them financially or technologically. Several authors have cautioned about inequity and injustice implications of climate change mitigation which adds to worsening of inequality or vulnerability. Many researchers point out that the climate action narrative ignores structural inequities, since affluent countries such as the United States, Europe, and China envision a low-carbon global economy as "fixing the problem," but impoverished people will continue to live in poverty. Power conflicts and worsening vulnerability are evident in low-carbon transitions and climate mitigation projects. Many developing regions of the world have taken up a wide variety of mitigation activities, including building nuclear power plants, augmenting fossil fuels by biofuels, changes in land use, and adoption of energy-efficient devices like electric vehicles, fuel cells, in addition to renewable energy sources like wind, solar, and hydropower. Enclosure (land or resource grab), exclusion (unfair planning), invasion (environmental degradation), and entrenchment are four separate processes in the political ecology of low-carbon transitions (Sovacool, 2021). It also adds to destruction of pristine ecosystems in the long run. Low-carbon transitions and climate action can sometimes prioritize degradation above sustainability, resulting in enraged communities, disillusioned labor, spurned corporate partners, and ruined ecosystems. Nonetheless, there are several possibilities for a future low-carbon society to be more diverse, egalitarian, and just.

> It can be concluded that both renewable and non-renewable sources of energy will have a leading role to play in the short and long-term energy transition. They comprise energy sources like solar, wind, hydro, hydrogen, bioresources, marine energy, nuclear, natural gas substitute of other fossil fuels and application of clean and efficient technologies for existing fossil fuel and non-renewable systems. More research and development into efficient, environmentally friendly, and competitive technology is needed to facilitate innovation and diffusion of sustainable energy technologies.

CONCLUSION

Energy transitions is gaining impetus globally, and India is no exception. The nation has accomplished the noteworthy double leapfrog of linking approximately all homes to power while also generating one of the world's major markets for renewable energy. India's per capita emissions are well below the global average, but they are likely to rise in the future as the country's economy expands to meet the expectation of a rising population. Despite facing large development divide and being badly impacted by climate variability due to its natural resource base, large coastlines and significant reliance on climate-sensitive sectors such as agriculture, India has been a prominent actor in global efforts to build a cohesive climate response as a conscientious international stakeholder. Adaptation, mitigation, funding, technology transfer, and capacity building are all included in various policy texts as well as national and state action plans. Simultaneously, legitimate development demands for an equal carbon space in order to promote inclusive sustainable development must be protected. India has said in a number of international forums that, while pursuing social and economic development goals, it will not allow its per capita emissions to exceed those of industrialized nations. In India's climate diplomacy, ideas such as climate justice and the *Common but Differentiated Responsibility and Respective Capabilities* principle (CBDR-RC) are still championed. It indicates that nations who have signed the UN climate pact share a shared responsibility to combat climate change, but they have differing capacity to do so due to their economic growth phases. Equity might be considered a key concept as well, although it is not pushed strongly.

The NAPCC lays out India's climate action plan, with detailed suggestions under each mission, with the twin goal of environmentally sustainable development as well as adaptation and mitigation against climate change. There are several constraints that restrict the capacity of national action plans to provide the intended results in the desired timeframe. Lack of political will, knowledge gaps in crucial scientific domains, a lack of observational and scientific data, and a fragmented knowledge base in terms of people, organizations, and skills are just a few examples (Sinha et al., 2018). The political leadership cannot be overlooked and has a significant impact on India's climate policies. Along with the action plans, adequate institutional capacity for research infrastructure, such as access to essential data sets, modeling and computing capabilities, and awareness to enhance the quality of sector-specific climate change scenarios, is necessary (Dutta et al., 2016). Despite its aspirations to be a global leader, India's domestic climate change plan has not received significant funding, and the lack of a national budget for climate action could constrain the ambitious climate agenda.

Climate change is a big threat to development aspiration of India. As a large developing economy with around 1.4 billion citizens, India's climate adaptation and mitigation goals are not just imperative for India but for the whole world. There is still a lot of work to be done at home. As India strives to reconcile its developmental goals along with mitigating climate impacts, the transition to a low-carbon economy is considered both as a challenge and as key strategic aspiration. The road ahead is fraught with predicament as well as possibilities, however, building climate-resilient infrastructure, formulating coherent state policies with intersectoral linkages, and resource planning that take climate risks into account are considered significant steps. Taking adequate action on climate change can also have significant economic and political benefits. It has the potential to enable India to pool resources with its allies and develop effective partnership in the global renewable energy transition, as well as offer up opportunities for political leadership, particularly among developing and vulnerable countries. A people-centric egalitarian approach, supported by efficient policy design, will benefit India shape a clean and inclusive energy future, but also provide a prototypical for other nations and societies worldwide.

REFERENCES

BP. (2021). *Statistical review of world energy*. https://www.bp.com/en/global/corporate/energy-economics/statistical-review-of-world-energy.html

Dubash, N. K., & Ghosh, S. (2019). National climate policies and institutions. In *India in a warming world* (pp. 329–348). Oxford University Press. https://doi.org/10.1093/oso/9780199498734.003.0019

Dubash, N. K. (2021). *Should India consider a net-zero pledge?* Centre for Policy Research, https://environmentality.cprindia.org/netzero/should-india-consider-a-net-zero-pledge

Dubash, N. K., & Rajamani, L. (2021). New imperatives for international and domestic climate policy: Rethinking India's approach. In *The crisis of climate change* (pp. 9–18). Routledge India.

Dutta, V., Dasgupta, P., Hultman, N., & Gadag, G. (2016). Evaluating expert opinion on India's climate policy: Opportunities and barriers to low-carbon inclusive growth. *Climate and Development*, *8*(4), 336–350.

Grasso, M., & Dutta, V. (2018). A comparative assessment of climate policies of top emitters: Towards strengthening climate diplomacy and action. In *Revisiting Globalization* (pp. 69–89). Springer.

IEA. (2020). *World Energy Outlook*. https://www.iea.org/reports/world-energy-outlook-2020

IRENA. (2021, March). *Renewable Capacity Statistics 2021*. https://irena.org/publications/2021/March/Renewable-Capacity-Statistics-2021

Howard, D. B., Soria, R., Thé, J., Schaeffer, R., & Saphores, J.-D. (2020). The energy-climate-health nexus in energy planning: A case study in Brazil. *Renewable and Sustainable Energy Reviews*, *132*, 110016. https://doi.org/10.1016/j.rser.2020.110016

Laha, P., & Chakraborty, B. (2021). Low carbon electricity system for India in 2030 based on multi-objective multi-criteria assessment. *Renewable and Sustainable Energy Reviews*, *135*, 110356.

Nordenstam, A. (2021). *A shared understanding of India's climate policy? Insights from a survey of Indian climate experts* (UI Paper, 5). The Swedish Institute of International Affairs.

Olhoff, A., & Christensen, J. M. (2019). *Emissions Gap Report 2019*. UNEP. https://www.unep.org/resources/emissions-gap-report-2019

Pandey, A. (2017). *India's low carbon transition*. Issue Briefs and Special Reports Observer Research Foundation (ORF). https://www.orfonline.org/wp-content/uploads/2017/12/ORF_Issue-Brief_51_Low-Carbon.pdf

Quitzow, R. (2021). *Energy transitions and societal change*. Institute of Advanced Sustainability Studies. https://www.iass-potsdam.de/en/research-area/energy-systems-and-societal-change

Rhodium Group. (2021). *Preliminary 2020 global greenhouse gas emissions estimates*. https://rhg.com/research/preliminary-2020-global-greenhouse-gas-emissions-estimates/

Sinha, S. K., Subramanian, K. A., & Dutta, V. (2018). India's progress and plan of action in addressing climate change and its role in setting an effective, cooperative and equitable climate policy architecture. *Climate Change and Environmental Sustainability*, *6*(1), 1–15.

Sovacool, B. K. (2021). Who are the victims of low-carbon transitions? Towards a political ecology of climate change mitigation. *Energy Research & Social Science*, *73*, 101916.

Tian, J., Yu, L., Xue, R., Zhuang, S., & Shan, Y. (2022). Global low-carbon energy transition in the post-COVID-19 era. *Applied Energy*, *307*, 118205.

United Nations Environmental Program. (2019). *Emissions Gap Report 2019*. https://wedocs.unep.org/bitstream/handle/20.500.11822/30797/EGR2019.pdf?sequence=1&isAllowed=y

CHAPTER 14

The Role of Angola and Mozambique in the New Global Energy Trend

PAULO ZAGALO

"With its young and dynamic population, Africa has an increasingly important role in the world's energy future." (International Energy Agency [IEA], 2020a)

Dr. Fatih Birol, IEA's Executive Director

INTRODUCTION

After more than four centuries of European rule, in different levels, Africa has begun to write its own indelible and increasingly firm history.

African decolonization was one of the most significant political phenomena of the last century. It represented an adjustment in the international system, either by rescuing the historical and cultural trajectory of the peoples of the continent or based on the need to establish cultural unity among the inhabitants of the new "national units." However, some of these units did not have the necessary preparation to constitute themselves as political structures or support autonomous economic and social events because, before the time of decolonization (and, consequently, independence), these countries had always been governed by their conquerors.

In addition to these factors, which enhance instability, the fact that these newly independent states were obliged or invited to believe in the current social and political organization, in which the European-type economic model is the only one to be applied in governance. The created states had mostly fragile bonds of cultural unity among their inhabitants due to the diversity of tribes and the amalgam of nationalism (Nationalism, n.d.). The only point of union between the inhabitants was the recent end of decolonization, which had not always been friendly, often achieved only after several years of war. Furthermore, these inhabitants did not always fight side by side despite the existence of a common enemy. We were, at that time, before nations (Nation, n.d.) and not states (State, n.d.), although this is the internationally accepted way to consider them as partners, particularly at the United Nations (UN). The adoption of a capitalist or socialist governmental and their administrative theories is most often different from the one until then in use, sponsored by several international institutions. This process created ruptures in the existing historical-cultural content.

The dimension of geopolitics (Geopolitics, n.d.) in economic development depends on the political strategies of states. However, they are heavily dependent on the existing internal power hierarchies and the external relationships and balances intended to maintain the supposedly harmonic linear and dynamic progress of regional and global markets, as well as energy generation, distribution, and consumption.

Sub-Saharan Africa (SSA) has 13 % of the world's population but consumes only 4 % of global energy. The inhabitants of this area mostly live in rural areas (although this is changing as population densities in large urban centers continue to increase) (International Energy Agency, 2014). Another factor worth considering is that the primary energy sources are forms of solid biomass (wood and charcoal). These energy sources have natural environmental impacts via the emission of carbon dioxide (CO_2) into the atmosphere (BP, 2021). They also comprise about three-quarters of the energy mix of SSA, and two out of three houses in Africa are not linked to an electrical distribution system (International Energy Agency, 2014).

Nearly half of Sub-Saharan Africans (47.9 %) have no access to electricity in their homes. Therefore, a massive investment is needed to achieve widespread access to affordable, reliable, and sustainable electricity. Meanwhile, other African countries have inadequate grid infrastructures for accommodating conventional energy sources, resulting in high electricity losses and low supply quality, among other issues. The number of people without access to electricity in SSA has steadily declined since 2013, pushing many countries away from achieving the goal of universal access to electricity by 2030.

The health crisis and economic downturn caused by COVID-19 have compounded the difficulties faced by governments as they look to alleviate energy poverty and expand access. Shifting government priorities, supply chain disruptions, and social distancing measures have slowed access programs and hindered activities in the decentralized energy access area. SSA has been particularly affected, and the effects of the pandemic are reversing recent progress achieved in the region; our initial estimates indicate that the number of people without access to electricity dropped from almost 860 million in 2018 to 770 million in 2019, a record low in recent years (International Energy Agency, 2019).

The countries in SSA are diverse and range from energy-resource rich countries (e.g., Nigeria and South Africa) to countries that are among the world's most energy-poor (e.g., Mozambique). This in-depth study analyzes and discusses Angola and Mozambique in particular.

Like other African countries, the Republic of Angola (Angola) and the Republic of Mozambique (Mozambique) suffer from the historical, social, and cultural rupture after a long period of colonization and the very short time since the conquest of independence to put into practice, in the correct way, the model of a modern nation-state. Meanwhile, northern African countries have already had several centuries to define and revise the model with a completely different cultural and historical framework.

Immediately after Mozambique attained its independence, the new republic experienced a 16-year civil war that killed or uprooted many people, caused extensive damage to the nation's social and economic infrastructure, and harmed its economic development. These factors reflect the difficulties Mozambique has experienced since gaining its independence. Furthermore, the country's energy sector is illustrative of many of the specific difficulties that it has suffered, as the underdevelopment of this sector has delayed Mozambique's economic development.

As with the Mozambican Civil War, The Angolan Civil War started immediately following the county's official independence from Portugal on November 11, 1975. The war was a direct consequence of ethnic tensions and international pressures, and it served as a proxy war on behalf of Cold War rival states such as the Soviet Union, the United States, Cuba, and South Africa. This war was characterized by extreme violence and destruction, as it was responsible for the displacement of one-third of the population. According to the UN, by the end of the war in 2002, roughly 80 % of Angolans lacked access to basic care. Furthermore, an exodus was registered from rural areas to urban centers, where people live with no basic accommodation conditions, such as electricity or paved roads.

Ecological challenges are relevant but also paradoxical in that they go beyond the limits of discussions within nations, states, movements, and even science. Currently, ecology is a fundamental theme of relations between states and cannot be overlooked in national agendas or discussions within organizations, including the UN, the European Union (EU), and the Southern Africa Development Community (SADC)—of which Angola and Mozambique are part—and their founding members in the context of the implementation of industrialization projects and economic development. This is because such relations are crucial to achieving these organizations' goals, including the SADC's goal of "achieving sustainable utilization of natural resources and effective protection of the environment" (SADC, 2012). Adding to this point, "energy security is vital for the socio-economic development of the African continent. Africa cannot deliver meaningful development to its growing population unless there is an adequate, available, and sustainable energy to meet the pressing energy needs of the continent" (Alemzero et al., 2021).

This chapter assesses the energy trends of Angola and Mozambique, considering that renewable energy sources make sustainable development possible through economic development, social equity, and environmental protection. This chapter is intended to answer the following question: What is the role of these two countries in the new global energy trends, and what strategy will be followed to decarbonize and use this energy for the overall progress of humanity, considering that both countries signed the Paris Agreement and considering the ability to obtain energy and the energy security element? This chapter is organized as follows. The current section introduced the scope. The section The Geopolitics of Oil and Gas on the African Continent presents an overview of the geopolitics of oil and gas in Africa, focusing on Angola and Mozambique. In the subsequent sections, the implications of the Paris Agreement in Angola and Mozambique are explained, the ecological challenges related to decarbonization are briefly presented, and the relationship between energy resources and sustained development is discussed. Later, energy security is explored as a development issue, and a discussion on how energy can turn into power instruments in Angola and Mozambique is presented. Finally, the conclusion is provided in the last section.

THE GEOPOLITICS OF OIL AND GAS ON THE AFRICAN CONTINENT

The demand for and dependence on fossil fuels have always influenced global geopolitics and geostrategies disputes over these vital natural resources. It is assumed that the geopolitics of oil and gas is part of the geopolitics of energy. To speak of oil and gas geopolitics is to speak of global dynamics, which have particular economic, environmental, and social impacts on critical resources. The importance of these resources is evident, as they are highly coveted and sometimes disputed by nations. They also represent power, wealth, or, at the very least, the capacity to generate sustained development (especially when referring to countries like Angola or Mozambique). The importance of these two energy sources is linked to the fact that the functioning of society depends on them, especially since they are used extensively in everyday life, not only as fuel but also in the production of plastics, mattresses, paints, lubricants, and many other items.

The unequal distribution of oil and gas reserves, mostly in Middle Eastern and African regions, where existing or latent conflicts occur and the people p experience difficulties accessing vital resources such as water, food, and energy. In countries like Angola and Mozambique, such difficulties have become sources of conflict and disputes.

According to the International Energy Agency (IEA), oil was responsible for 31.9 % of energy generation in the world in 2019, with gas accounting for 22.1 %. Such data cannot be overlooked when discussing renewable energy use and decarbonization agendas. Oil is the most widely used energy source in the world, with the Middle East having the world's largest reserves, representing about 65 % of the world's oil. However, this resource is also present in Africa, particularly on the western coast (mainly in Angola). Thus, these resources are of great importance to the international economy and are particularly affected by issues of safety, extraction, refining, transport, storage, and distribution. All these factors are greatly influenced by the dynamics of the actors involved and their abilities to control all stages of the process. Natural gas is the cleanest and fastest-growing fossil fuel in the world, contributing almost one-third of global total energy demand throughout the last decade. Today it accounts for 23 % of total energy demand and nearly a quarter of electricity generation, which is more than any other fuel.

The transition to renewable energy sources with less (or no) CO_2 emissions is urgently needed, but it will be difficult to implement the changes needed to meet the targets set, approved, and accepted at the Paris Agreement. IEA data indicate that technological developments allow oil and gas to be exploited more efficiently than in the past, thus reducing CO_2 emissions. Such developments, combined with the use of non-polluting energy sources (e.g., wind, solar or geothermal), provide moderate optimism that people's reliance on the above-mentioned products will decrease. Furthermore, the oil sector (oil and gas) has a significant influence on local economies, providing direct and indirect employment for thousands of workers, with the obvious socioeconomic impact associated with and therefore, a source of power. The concrete case of Mozambique, located in the province of Cabo Delgado, is described below.

Concerning the exploration of natural gas in Mozambique, a total investment of around $23 billion is expected, making this liquefied natural gas (LNG) project by far the largest investment in Mozambican history. It will make Mozambique the largest producer and exporter of gas in Africa. Other projects include a floating LNG project of the Italian energy company ENI in Area Four of the Rovuma Basin, and another project headed by ExxonMobil, for further onshore trains. The total investment envisaged soars to over $50 billion, with a total production of LNG of over 30 million tonnes a year. These investments benefit the country and its inhabitants by creating jobs, diversifying the economy, and providing widespread access to energy. These investments also lead to the creation of businesses in domestic terms, which will reduce poverty. The geopolitics of oil and gas stems from the great importance of these natural resources. Thus, they are a reason for greed and disputes among several nations of the globalized world in which we live.

THE PARIS AGREEMENT FROM THE PERSPECTIVES OF ANGOLA AND MOZAMBIQUE

Climate change is the most significant ecological challenge facing the world today, and social concern in this regard increases annually. Access to energy is a precondition for economic development and social progress, especially in peri-urban and rural areas. Renewable natural resources can contribute to economic diversification and improve the well-being and livelihoods of people living in developing countries, such as Angola and Mozambique, which are among the poorest in the world.

Following the signing of the Paris Agreement in December 2015, leading countries and companies announced down to net-zero plans to reduce carbon gas emissions by the middle of the twenty-first century. However, the need to use non-renewable fuels such as oil, coal, and natural gas must be reduced or eliminated to achieve this goal. Furthermore, sources of renewable and unlimited energy, made available by the sun, wind, or tides, must be used.

The Paris Agreement contains the very succinct objectives of "holding the increase in the global average temperature to below 2°C above pre-industrial levels" and "limit[ing] the temperature increase to 1.5°C" in this century. Energy production and use are prominent sources of global greenhouse gas (GHG) emissions, meaning that the energy sector is crucial to achieving these objectives.

Among the various African countries that ratified the agreement, we analyzed the cases of Angola and Mozambique. In both cases, it is stated that there are problems with these countries' contributions, as they lack precision in the objectives of adaptation and mitigation, as well as cost estimates. Also, sources of funding are not identified, and the objectives are quite ambitious. Furthermore, these countries are not equipped with qualified human resources to conduct the required processes and lack the installed capacity to achieve them (Phiri, 2016).

Angola has initially agreed to participate actively in the international fight against climate change as part of the solution by contributing to global efforts to reduce GHG emissions. As a statement of this commitment, it elaborated the

Intended Nationally Determined Contribution (INDC) (Republic of Angola, 2015), which includes, for mitigation purposes, specific, conditional, and unconditional measures. Its analysis includes the Angolan commitment to stabilize its emissions and contribute to climate change mitigation by 2030. Furthermore, two areas of activity are defined: the generation of energy from renewable sources and reforestation.

About 80 % of Angola's population uses biomass (wood energy and agricultural waste) to produce energy for daily use (e.g., for heating water, cooking, and lighting) at the domestic level and in small commercial sectors. Therefore, the use of wood is a factor in forest destruction and GHG emissions. Thus, the intense cutting of trees to supply coal to urban and suburban areas puts extreme pressure on local resources (two-thirds of Luanda's population live on the periphery and use about 270,000 tons of coal annually). Biomass consumption can be reduced in the agricultural sector by using biofuels to produce ethanol and sugar (as is already done in Brazil), which will reduce CO_2 emissions.

Also, according to the INDC, Angola intends, unconditionally, to reduce GHG emissions by at least 35 % by 2030 compared to 2005 emission levels. In addition, it is expected that, through conditional mitigation, the country will be able to reduce its emissions by more than 15 % compared to the levels recorded in 2005. In the end and achieved the objectives, Angola intends to reduce its GHG emissions by 50 % by 2030 per the Paris Agreement.

Knowing that nations have accepted to report their commitments to the Paris Agreement through nationally determined contributions (NDCs), the Government of Mozambique has implemented a long-term plan known as the 2020–2025 NDC Roadmap. Mozambique was engaged in climate action before the Paris Agreement and has based its current NDC implementation on its previous National Climate Change Adaptation and Mitigation Strategy (2013–2030). This strategy aims "to increase resilience in communities and the national economy, including the reduction of climate risks and promotion of low-carbon development and the green economy through the integration of adaptation and mitigation in sectoral and local planning" (Ministério da Coordenação da Acção Ambiental, 2012).

The document specifies that "Mozambique is particularly vulnerable to CC due to its location in the zone of inter-tropical convergence, downstream of shared watersheds; its long shoreline and the existence of extensive lowlands below sea level. The country's vulnerability is also increased by its low adaptive capacity, poverty, limited investment in modern technology, and weaknesses in its infrastructure and social services, especially those related to health and sanitation" (Ministério da Coordenação da Acção Ambiental, 2012).

Mozambique has considerable energy resources, with an estimated hydropower potential of 12,000 MW, gas reserves of as much as 700 billion cubic meters, and vast coal reserves (estimated to reach 140 million terajoules).

THE ECOLOGICAL CHALLENGES OF DECARBONIZATION

Decarbonization is the process of reducing carbon emissions (especially CO_2) into the atmosphere by using low-carbon power sources. The goal of decarbonization is to lower the output of GHGs into the atmosphere and improve the global economy by reducing emissions, thus achieving climate neutrality through the energy transition. The term "decarbonization" is often used to refer to the process of reducing "carbon intensity" to lower the amount of GHG emissions produced by burning fossil fuels.

Decarbonization involves increasing the prominence of low-carbon power generation, thereby reducing the use of fossil fuels. This process includes using renewable energy sources like wind power, solar power, and biomass. The use of carbon power can also be reduced through the large-scale use of electric vehicles and other clean technologies. Decreasing the power and transport sectors' reliance on carbon will contribute to the early achievement of net-zero emission targets consistent with government standards and the standards set by the Paris Agreement.

More energy-efficient and less carbon-intense energy sources are among the most prominent ways to achieve decarbonization (TWI, n.d.). By burning fossil fuels to develop the economy, humans have increased CO_2 emissions, which lead to the greenhouse effect and, therefore, global warming and climate change. Decarbonization involves an energy transition process (i.e., a structural change that eliminates carbon from energy generation). It consists of boosting the economy by using clean alternative energies that emit only what the planet can absorb.

Natural gas influence on reducing CO_2 emissions is significant, as natural gas has a relatively low standard carbon content (15.3 kg/GJ), making it a cleaner option than coal (25.8 kg/GJ) or crude oil (20 kg/GJ). Therefore, natural gas could be utilized to meet industrial emissions targets. That is, although natural gas is not a clean energy source, it is considered a transitional fuel because it provides a low-carbon energy alternative to other fossil fuels. It is also more cost-effective than other fuels. Studies have indicated that by 2035, the share of natural gas in the global energy mix will be higher than that of coal and oil. Studies have also reported that global electricity consumption will increase by 70 % by 2035; as part of this change, gas-based electricity generation is expected to almost double.

Societies must ensure that projections of the energy sector's growth consider concerns about climate change, particularly those outlined in the Paris Agreement. However, the fight against climate change should not conflict with human progress and poverty reduction, particularly in developing countries, such as Angola and Mozambique.

The International Renewable Energy Agency notes in its Africa 2030 report that renewable energy may provide up to one-quarter of electricity in Africa by 2040 (Africa Energy Portal, 2021). The IEA states that "the transition to a low-carbon economy leads to a more efficient energy system that relies less on fuel combustion; this plays a major role in improving air quality, reducing both outdoor and household air pollution" (IEA, 2020b). Furthermore, according to Deloitte Africa energy and resources leader Andrew Lane, "the complete decarbonization of Africa will not occur in the short or medium term, although some progress will be made in the long term."

Although natural gas is a fossil fuel, it generates up to 50 % fewer emissions than coal. Therefore, it is relatively clean but not entirely decarbonized. One of the major reasons is that the rest of the world is increasingly moving away from energy generated by fossil fuels while Africa continues to make large investments in oil and gas infrastructures and engages in exploitation on a massive scale.

The greatest challenge preventing further decarbonization in Africa is that the continent remains dependent on fossil fuels for power because "although there is massive potential in Africa for renewables, ineffective governments and a lack of economic headroom prevent it from being implemented at the pace that is needed" (Delloite, 2020). Delloite (2020) further states that "there is a cognitive dissonance between the drive to decarbonize while further industrializing Africa" and that "the growth imperative in Africa, which depends on increased industrialization for socio-economic upliftment, is going to make rapid decarbonization very difficult."

Before Islamic radicals attacked the northeast region of Mozambique, Cabo Delgado, numerous large-scale LNG projects were underway along the country's coast. Massive investments were pouring in from major oil and gas companies such as Total, Exxon Mobil, and Eni, as well as from financial institutions and consortiums worldwide.

ENERGY RESOURCES VS. SUSTAINABLE DEVELOPMENT

Energy is an integral component of the development of any economy. As such, an adequate and reliable supply of energy is essential to all industrial and familiar systems. Energy efficiency is based on the goal of obtaining as much output or service as possible from each unit of energy (Murray-Leach, 2019). In this way, each unit of energy is thought of as a means to an end, such as environmental or economic gains. Thus, energy is considered a development resource and is recognized as the "first fuel," considering that it increases competitiveness, generates employment, secures energy, reduces poverty,[1] and potentially boosts development.

Sustainable development has been described as a type of development that aims for current generation without depleting resources for future generation. As such, sustainable development involves a balance between the development of economic and social activities and the protection of the environment. In other words, development is sustainable when it encompasses economic development, social inclusiveness, and environmental sustainability. To be deemed green, an economic growth strategy must involve these three crucial dimensions. An economy that intends to grow in a sustainable manner must be based on a new economic model that enhances development, alleviates poverty, and improves people's overall quality of life.

These goals are best achieved through green growth. Green growth essentially seeks to promote the efficient utilization of resources, ensure equity, and consider the environment in all production techniques. It represents an attempt to add growth and the environment. Green growth is an inevitable aspect of protecting the global environment, raising living standards, and ensuring reliable energy supplies (Akinyemi, 2015). The first challenge that must be overcome to achieve these goals is to give people access to enough electricity to meet their daily living needs, no matter where they live. This must be done while considering the decarbonization challenge and, thus, promoting private-sector investments while strengthening and modernizing the grid, thereby supporting a systemic innovation.

In Africa, the number of people with access to electricity doubled from 9 million between 2000 and 2013 to 20 million people between 2014 and 2019, which outpaced population growth. As a result, the number of people without access to electricity, which peaked at 610 million in 2013, declined progressively to around 580 million in 2019 (IEA, 2020c). In Angola and Mozambique, access to electricity increased by 17.2 % and 4.2 %, respectively, between 2005 and 2019, ultimately reaching rates of 42.5 % and 34.9 % (IEA, 2020c).

To ensure that energy access progress continues is a critical mobilization of the development finance institutions and donors, in addition to adequate internal and national energy investment on sustainable renewable, especially hydropower and solar electricity generation (IEA, 2020c).

Angola is expected to become the largest producer of crude oil in southern Africa. However, it also has a foundation in place for the sustainable development of renewable energy through investments and supportive measures (IEA, 2021a). The main reason behind the decision of increasing the renewable energy investments is to ensure that basic human needs are met, as only 45.67 % of Angola's population had access to electricity in 2019 (The World Bank, 2022).

Moreover, those living in cities such as Luanda who have access to electricity experience frequent blackouts, forcing wealthy families to use their own power generators, which consume large amounts of fossil hydrocarbons. Meanwhile, people living in rural areas have no access to a grid and, thus, have no electricity at all.

During the 2021 Angola+Green virtual seminar (organized by the Portuguese presidency of the Council of the EU, Minister of Energy and Water of Angola, João Baptista Borges), the diversification of the energy mix and universal access to electricity were identified as priorities in Angola. By fulfilling these priorities, the country could give all its citizens—including those living in rural areas—access to electricity. Furthermore, Power Africa and the African Development Bank are working with the Government of Angola to develop and expand infrastructure and facilitate new electricity connections to attain a universal electrification rate of 60 % by 2025. This collaboration will also evaluate 1,000 MW of potential energy throughout the country to improve access to electricity and strengthen the energy's sector financial viability" (Energy Capital & Power, 2021).

For developing countries in SSA, including Angola and Mozambique, improved energy efficiency could lead to needed economic growth. However, many barriers contribute to the currently limited uptake of energy efficiency opportunities. An especially prominent obstacle is the lack of attention paid to energy efficiency investment opportunities by stakeholders in private and government sectors.

Access to clean, modern, and reliable energy in Angola remains low at 33 % countrywide (69 % in urban areas and only 6 % in rural areas) (African Development Bank [AfDB], 2020). The use of renewable energy sources is highly relevant to environmental sustainability and will help reduce production costs and oil consumption associated with energy use. As a result, the electrical grid could be expanded to give more Angolan citizens access to electricity.

As part of its long-term development strategy, the Government of Angola aims to provide electricity access to 60 % of the population by 2025. Furthermore, renewable energy will constitute 70 % of the country's installed capacity.

Angola intends to reduce its GHG emissions as stated in its INDC, thus covering various conditional measures and unconditional measures. In terms of conditional measures, the country intends to reduce GHG emissions by 15 % or more by 2030 (in comparison to 2005 levels). Meanwhile, regarding unconditional measures, the country intends to reduce emissions by at least 35 % by 2030, considering the same base year. Therefore, the defined objectives are planned to be achieved by 2030 by promoting renewable energy use and reforestation (Barros, 2019).

According to the IEA (2018), “Angola has set the foundation for the sustainable development of renewables through investments and supportive measures and has particularly strong hydropower generation potential that remains underutilized.” Angola is now exploring renewable energy opportunities through diversification, predominantly consisting of solar, wind, and hydropower, with the potential for further expansion throughout the country. The country is estimated to have a capacity of 55 GW of solar energy, 3 GW of wind energy, and 18 GW of hydropower (Schyff, 2020).

Hydropower is the government’s top priority (as evidenced by the construction of the Caculo Cabaça Hydroelectric Project, the Laúca Hydroelectric Plant, the Balalunga Project, and several others throughout the southern region of the country), and so, Angola has launched a major energy project that could save the country 1.4 million liters of fossil fuel per day in power generation.

Paul Ghiotto, the deputy political-economic chief/energy officer of the United States (U.S.) Embassy in Luanda, stated that “Angola, through the development of hydropower, particularly from the Cuanza Basin, has a very strong base concerning generation, potentially sufficient to meet future demand.” Accordingly, the benefits of such resources justify the government’s focus on renewables (Schyff, 2020).

Furthermore, it is estimated that more than 1.2 million families could benefit from the solar project, whose construction is planned to be completed in 2025, as described in the Evolution Plan for the Electrical Sector until 2025, following the process of identification of the projects and feasibility studies, aiming for their integration in the National Electrical Grid; a demand forecast, along with the generation and transmission lines reassessment (including generation from new renewable energy sources identified in the project) and tentative redesign; new electrification scenarios and rural electrification alternatives.

As a clear commitment to that purpose João Baptista Borges, Minister of Energy and Water of Angola, stated, as part of the “Angola power sector long term vision,” that “the global objectives of the long-term strategy Angola 2025, for promoting human development and the well-being of Angolan citizens, promoting a fair and sustainable development, ensuring a high rhythm of economic development and a fair and well-balanced development of the national territory, can only be achieved by means of an adequate response by the electricity sector” (Gesto Energy Consulting, 2014).

In recent years, Mozambique has experienced both impressive economic growth and persistent poverty. While it has benefitted from the discovery of new large coal and natural gas reserves, its natural resource base is declining. Furthermore, it has increasingly faced the energy challenge posed by climate change (AfDB, 2015). Mozambique has substantial energy resources, ranging from fossil fuels (natural gas and coal) to renewables (solar, hydro, wind, geothermal and tidal power). However, the exploitation of these resources for national use is limited. In fact, most of Mozambique's primary energy consumption is met by traditional biofuels such as wood, charcoal, and agro or animal waste.

Mozambique's population has grown at an impressive rate of 7.2 % during the last decade. Since the discovery of new world-class coal reserves in 2009 and the later discovery of natural gas reserves, Mozambique's attractiveness to foreign investors increased significantly. This situation generated several billions of dollars of foreign direct investment from the world's largest mining and oil companies from South Africa, Australia, Brazil, the U.S., Italy, France, and (more recently) China. According to some estimates, the overall investment in such projects was expected to reach up to US$200 billion over the next 20 years, which has led to the use of the term "the African Qatar."

At the 2019 Africa Oil and Gas Conference, Angolan President João Lourenço said that "Africa has great unexplored hydrocarbon potential," adding that "Angola occupies one of the top spots on the continent. The Angolan government is aware of its reality and its potential [and] considers petroleum and gas as catalyzers for a new dynamic, renewable and self-sustainable dynamic economy" (Africa.com, 2019). Nevertheless, it is important to remember that "global energy is increasing at a steady pace. To meet that demand and sustain economic development, trillions of dollars will be invested over the coming decades" (Singh, 2018).

That unexplored hydrocarbon potential can be an opportunity for countries like Angola and Mozambique. Regarding Mozambique and sustainable development, Florival Mucave, executive president of the Oil and Gas Mozambique Chamber, stated on the 21st October, 2020, that "to have sustainable economic development through industrialization, Mozambique needs to expand access to electricity." Furthermore, Mozambican Petroleum Law 21/2014 states that "Petroleum resources are assets whose proper exploitation can contribute significantly to national development." This position is echoed in the Mozambique Gas Master Plan (Republic of Mozambique Cabinet Council, 2014), which suggests that the Government of Mozambique should develop natural resources to maximize their benefits to Mozambican society and improve the quality of life of the Mozambican people while minimizing adverse social and environmental impacts.

Many difficulties in Mozambique are rooted in the chronic lack of reliable access to electricity. Only 29 % of the population has access to energy. The Petroleum Law 21/2014 incorporates a clause on domestic gas to help the country cope with this limited access to energy. According to this law, 25 % of the natural gas produced in Mozambique should be used in the domestic market. As a result of domestic gas obligations, considerable new investments have been observed in gas-to-power projects in Mozambique, such as the Ressano Garcia CTRG Project, the Kuvaninga project, and the Temane Regional Electricity project, which is expected to begin soon and which will include a 400 MW gas power plant, and the planned 250 MW power plant for the Nacala district, which will run on gas from the Rovuma Basin in Mozambique" (Mucave, 2020). Adding to that, Florival Mucave has stated the following:

> In its five-year economic plan, the Government of Mozambique has indicated agriculture as its top priority. Currently, almost 80% of our population works in the agricultural sector, which generates about 25% of our GDP. However, due to low levels of productivity, many of our farmers still live in extreme poverty. But this could change. Simply by using fertilizers, farmers can increase their income by almost 40%. Although imported fertilizers are very expensive for most of our farmers, Mozambique can create a more affordable option. By building infrastructure to transform natural gas into nitrogen-based fertilizers, Mozambique would not only help its farmers but also create local employment opportunities. Mozambique can significantly reduce its imports of agricultural products from South Africa and become an affordable source of food for domestic consumption. (Mucave, 2020)

Green growth and energy security are closely related. Sustainable development comprises social inclusiveness, economic development, and environmental sustainability, all of which are objectives pursued by Angolan and Mozambican leaders. However, these objectives will require help from international organizations and donor countries.

THE "SECURITY OF THE ENERGY" AS A DEVELOPMENT ISSUE

For a long time, energy security has focused on issues such as the reliability of energy supply, the high concentration of energy sources in specific areas, and whether these factors influence the destabilization and implementation of political energy management tools. Energy is an integral part of any form of economic activity (Chalaris, 2021). Improved energy security[2] is one of the main targets of energy policy, particularly when development is the only purpose. Generally, energy security can be characterized by multiple factors, like the sources of risk; the scope of impacts; and the severity filters in the form of the speed, size, sustention, spread, singularity, and sureness of impacts. Given the importance of energy, energy security is an important objective related to achieving a green economy. Energy security, defined as the availability of energy resources at an affordable price, continues to be a key component of energy policies in many countries of the world (Akinyemi et al., 2015). "You cannot expand the industrialization of the country without secure power throughout" (Schyff, 2020).

Being the situation on its way to be fully implemented in Angola under the Angola Renewable Energy Strategy, which contributes to the National Energy Security Policy and Strategy of Angola (Gesto Energy Consulting, 2015), let us pay attention to the situation in Mozambique.

According to multiple sources (and in military terms), morale in a large number of regular units (not counting special troops) is anemic in Mozambique despite a comprehensive territorial distribution. A probable cause for this is the priority placed on economic development and the lack of support given to security and defense issues. Religious violence is another factor in this issue, with the "Salafist" faction more "jihadist," having a steady increase from the 2000s, also in Christianized areas, and the violent action of armed extremist groups.

This situation may have induced attacks by Islamist radicals in the northern part of the country (i.e., in the Cabo Delgado area), where jihadist acts have occurred since 2018. More specifically, Islamic state elements have been reported since autumn 2017. This movement takes advantage of social factors—specifically, the large number of young people without jobs and the fact that about 20 % of the Mozambican population (representing more than 50 % of the population of the North) is of a Muslim orientation. This makes the north part of the country a fertile ground for radicalization.

The most significant problem with the radicals' actions is that they occur in locations central to natural gas exploration. The gas-producing companies located here—particularly in the Rovuma basin in the Cabo Delgado region—are a source of income for Mozambique, as they send gas, by concession, to Total and Exon Mobile. The gas produced in these areas represents a total investment of 20 billion euros and is considered the largest private investment in Africa. These factors make this area a high-value military target with international repercussions at the level of domestic policy.

From an economic and development point of view, some decisions made by Total were of particular concern. These included the decisions to withdraw all personnel, suspend the activity indefinitely, and abandon the gas project site in the Peninsula of Afungi (6 km south of the village). These decisions were made a week after an attack was launched against the head office of Palma district on March 24, 2021. Because of the consequent drastic reduction in income to be collected from the export of natural gas, regional and national development objectives have been compromised or, at the very least, are now more time-consuming.

As a national response to this threat, the Mozambican government has requested international assistance. Rwandan and SADC forces are now carrying out executive missions, as well as a non-executive mission to strengthen training, support, and advice to the EU and Security Forces of Mozambique (the European Union Training Mission-EUTM).

ENERGY AS A POWER INSTRUMENT FOR ANGOLA AND MOZAMBIQUE

Mozambique affirms in its Constitution Chart that "the State shall promote initiatives to ensure ecological balance and the conservation of the environment, in order to improve the quality of life of its citizens."[3] Green growth in support of sustainable, long-term development has been promoted since the beginning of Mozambique's existence as a state. Furthermore, the National Development Strategy 2015–2035 (dated July 2014) recognizes the fundamental role of increasing revenue flows from the extraction of Mozambique's significant natural resources. Such revenue enables the country to give its citizens a better standard of living, and the management of sustainable natural resources benefits present and future generations (CABRI, 2015).

Meanwhile, the Angolan National Constitution states that one of the country's fundamental tasks is "to promote harmonious and sustainable development throughout national territory, protecting the environment, natural resources and the historic, cultural and artistic heritage of the nation."[4] Furthermore, regarding environmental rights, the constitution defines that "the State shall take the requisite measures to protect the environment and species of flora and fauna throughout national territory, maintain the ecological balance, ensure the correct location of economic activities and the rational development and use of all natural resources, within the context of sustainable development, respect for the rights of future generations and the preservation of species."[5]

According to Jas Singh, senior energy efficiency specialist with the World Bank's Europe & Central Asia Energy Unit, "energy efficiency is among the cheapest and cleanest energy resources available." Thus, the World Bank, together with its development partners and client governments, is committed to ensuring that energy efficiency becomes the "first fuel" of energy policymakers and governments around the world (Singh, 2018).

Studies suggest that oil and (especially) natural gas will boost the economy of Angola and Mozambique. Natural gas is a potent instrument of power—as stated by Barak Obama, former president of the United States, "the potential for natural gas is enormous" (The White House, 2011).

Under specific circumstances, cutting the oil supply would have devastating effects on the economies of producers and consumers. It is easy to see why natural gas is considered more potent than oil as an instrument of development and coercion. For example, natural is the cleanest-burning hydrocarbon with the lowest carbon emissions, and it is odorless, colorless, and non-toxic. Owing to such factors, using more natural gas and less oil can help countries meet energy demands and move toward the use of renewable energy sources. Furthermore, natural gas is versatile and abundant. The IEA assesses that if consumption remains at its present level, recoverable resources will last for around 230 years. The IEA also reported that Mozambique is currently the third-largest exporter of LNG (Ichumile, 2013). Another advantage of natural gas is that it can be shipped efficiently. It can easily be cooled down to a liquid (which reduces its volume by 600 times) before being transported via pipelines or LNG carriers.

Angola needs to diversify its oil-dependent economy by capitalizing on other energy sources such as natural gas to prevent future financial crises. It has been reported that "the decline in the price of crude oil badly hit Angola. The national currency kwanza nearly crashed, and imports have drastically reduced. Food is scarce and more expensive. Supermarkets have to ration it" (Deutsche Welle, 2016).

Per the commitment to support decarbonization, Ernesto Max Tonela (the minister of Mineral Resources and Energy of Mozambique) and Claudio Descalzi (Eni's chief executive officer) signed a memorandum of understanding for the definition of sustainable development and decarbonization projects. This act was intended to ensure ongoing cooperation between Eni and the Government of Mozambique regarding the definition of joint initiatives to support the country's National and Local Economic and Social Development Agenda.

These initiatives are defined under the framework of the UN's Sustainable Development Goals (SDGs),[6] as well as the NDCs' aim to reduce national emissions and adapt to the impacts of climate change as part of the Paris Agreement. The areas of cooperation include reducing emissions, fostering conservation, sustainably managing forests, and enhancing forest carbon stocks per the framework of Reducing Emissions from Deforestation and Forest Degradation (UN, n.d.b). The primary objective is to protect 1 million hectares of forests, which will all counteract the CO_2 produced by Eni's projects in the country. Other initiatives are intended to promote access to energy (SDG 7); industry, innovation, and infrastructure development (SDG 9); sustainably managed forests (SDG 15); action on climate change and environmental impacts (SDG 13); access to education and training (SDG 4, 8); economic diversification (SDG 8); access to water (SDG 6); and access to health (SDG 3) (Eni, 2019).

CONCLUSION

"We have no other planet. We share this fragile globe of ours with several species indispensable to the survival of humanity." This certainty forces us to "move to an economy that is able to re-put on and sustain what is necessary for the survival of these species" (Pedro Siza Vieira, Minister of Economy, Portugal, 2009, June 5). A green growth model implies an all-embracing, "holistic" approach to economic development that maximizes synergies between economic, social, and environmental objectives while minimizing conflicts and contradictions (AfDB, 2015).

Given the discussion put forth in this document and in response to the research question (i.e., What is the role of these two countries in the new global energy trends, and what strategy will be followed to decarbonize and use this energy for the overall progress of humanity, considering that both countries signed the Paris Agreement and considering the ability to obtain energy and the energy security element?), it can be said that while environmental, climatic, and technological issues can influence the transition of the energy matrix, they certainly do not determine it. One reason is that its determinants are political and economic—or, more precisely, geopolitical (the long term of energy security) and financial (the short term of shareholder gain).

Thus, it can also be claimed that the problem is not when we will reach the "peak" of oil demand, but when it will reach the "valley" of new investments in oil and gas exploration and production and at what point these large companies will take the lead in the development of other energy sources. These elements are likely to indicate the speed and feasibility with which the transition of the energy matrix can be operationalized. Even more important are the commitments of Angola and Mozambique to promote decarbonization despite their social, cultural, and economic weaknesses by using energy sources other than hydrocarbons. As mentioned throughout this discussion, such alternative energy sources include hydropower, solar power, and wind power, all of which could feasibly augment the wealth these countries gain from natural production.

As stated above, energy security is vital for the socioeconomic development of Angola and Mozambique. Therefore, the ruling powers are focused on providing their citizens with access to electricity, running water, and environmental protection by following a sustainable development path per the Paris compromises and guides. As part of these goals, these countries will reduce their dependence on coal usage. It remains unknown whether this set of geopolitical, national, and business changes will take place in the long-term temporality of geology or in the short-term speed of finance. Nevertheless, "it is certain that the configuration of new oil and gas geopolitics is underway," as Professor William Nozaki says (Nozaki, 2018).

According to the above discussion and despite the obstacles that have been identified (mainly in terms of infrastructure investment), the advantages achieved by following renewable energies should contribute to sustained development. Furthermore, it is essential that energy policies and implementation approaches are based on the security of extraction and supply, wide distribution, competitiveness between stakeholders, and energy efficiency. Angola and Mozambique have renewable resources, which can be used internally and improve these countries' positions in the international market, thus reinforcing its economic competitiveness and fostering much-needed sustainable development.

Angola is devoted to addressing the global fight against climate change and has articulated its intention to reduce GHG emissions as defined in its INDC within the framework of the Paris Agreement. Similarly, the Mozambican government is committed to increasing community and economic resilience to climate risks and promoting low-carbon development and a green economy, and it has started to work toward fulfilling these outcomes per the terms outlined in the Paris Agreement.

In Angola and Mozambique, energy efficiency should cover different scales and levels of intervention in urban and rural areas, from its extraction to its use, through its distribution to the entire network of national users in the housing, agriculture, industry, and public buildings sectors. Energy efficiency activities should reduce the pressure imposed on natural resources and the climate while fostering the much-needed social and economic growth of these two African countries.

As a broad conclusion, we state that the green growth model used by Angola and Mozambique implies an all-encompassing holistic approach to economic development. This model maximizes the synergy between economic, social, and environmental objectives while minimizing conflicts and contradictions. Applying this model means addressing existing and emerging development challenges in a way that does not deplete national natural capital but also reduces the vulnerability of the economy and people's livelihoods to climate change and other environmental, social, and economic risks. The green growth model also protects the country against unruled access to oil and natural gas extraction operations.

To summarize this chapter, we use a quotation from the "World Bank": "Transitioning to a low-carbon economy can unlock more and better jobs that young Africans urgently need. Therefore, financing for climate change adaptation is critical, and policymakers need to mobilize resources both domestically and internationally to deliver more and greener jobs. Linking climate-related finance with critical governance reforms and conservation of natural capital as foundational assets may serve as an entry point. Ultimately, climate change adaption must be at the top of the policy agenda of African countries to address increasing climate impacts and achieve a green, resilient economic transformation" (The World Bank, 2021).

NOTES

1 According to the UN "Poverty entails more than the lack of income and productive resources to ensure sustainable livelihoods. Its manifestations include hunger and malnutrition, limited

access to education and other basic services, social discrimination and exclusion, as well as the lack of participation in decision-making. In 2015, more than 736 million people lived below the international poverty line. Around 10 per cent of the world population (pre-pandemic) was living in extreme poverty and struggling to fulfill the most basic needs like health, education, and access to water and sanitation, to name a few. There were 122 women aged 25 to 34 living in poverty for every 100 men of the same age group, and more than 160 million children were at risk of continuing to live in extreme poverty by 2030." Peace, dignity and equality on a healthy planet (UN, n.d.a).

2 The IEA defines energy security as the uninterrupted availability of energy sources at an affordable price. Energy security has many aspects: long-term energy security mainly deals with timely investments to supply energy in line with economic developments and environmental needs. On the other hand, short-term energy security focuses on the ability of the energy system to react promptly to sudden changes in the supply-demand balance. (IEA, 2021b)

3 Art° 117° (Environment and quality of life) of the Constitution of the Republic of Mozambique (revised 2018) (Republic of Mozambique, 2018)

4 Art° 21° (Fundamental tasks of the state) of the Constitution of the Republic of Angola (revised 2010) (Republic of Angola, 2010)

5 Art° 39° (Environmental rights) of the Constitution of the Republic of Angola (revised 2010) (Republic of Angola, 2010)

6 The United Nations' 17 Sustainable Development Goals (SDGs) aim to achieve decent lives for all on a healthy planet by 2030. As things stand, most of them are likely to be missed. This is partly because they fail to address human population growth. Positive, empowering population solutions are key to meeting the SDGs. Read on to learn about the links between population and each of the 17 goals (UN, 2015).

REFERENCES

Africa.com. (2019). *President of Angola's statement on Angola oil & gas conference and exhibition.* Retrieved June 30, 2021, from https://www.africa.com/president-of-angolas-statement-on-angola-oil-gas-2019-conference-and-exhibition/

Africa Energy Portal. (2021). *The renewable energy transition in Africa, powering access, resilience and prosperity.* https://africa-energy-portal.org/sites/default/files/2021-05/The%20Renewable%20Energy%20Transtion%20in%20Africa.pdf

African Development Bank. (2015). *Transition towards green growth in Mozambique—Green growth Mozambique.* https://www.afdb.org/fileadmin/uploads/afdb/Documents/Generic-Documents/Transition_Towards_Green_Growth_in_Mozambique_-_Policy_Review_and_Recommendations_for_Action.pdf

African Development Bank. (2020). Angola—Angola Renewable Energy Program—Enabling environment—SEFA appraisal report. Retrieved September 22, 2021, from https://www.afdb.org/en/documents/angola-angola-renewable-energy-program-enabling-environment-sefa-appraisal-report

Akinyemi, O., Alege, P., Ogundipe, A., & Osabuohien, E. (2015). *Energy security and the green growth agenda in Africa: Exploring trade-offs and synergies.* Retrieved February 25, 2021, from https://papers.ssrn.com/sol3/papers.cfm?abstract_id=2587287

Alemzero, D. A., Sun, H., Mohsin, M., Iqbal, N., Nadeem, M., & Vo, X. V. (2020). Assessing energy security in Africa based on multi-dimensional approach of principal composite analysis. *Environmental Science and Pollution Research*, *28*(2), 2158–2171. https://doi.org/10.1007/s11356-020-10554-0

Barros, H. (2019). *A Energia solar é uma nova luz nos espaços públicos urbanos*. Água & Ambiente. Retrieved April 24, 2021, from https://ambienteonline.pt/canal/detalhe/opiniao-helena-leitao-de-barros-angola-a-energia-solar-e-uma-nova-luz-nos-espacos-publicos-urbanos

BP. (2021). Statistical review of world energy. Retrieved September 17, 2021, from https://www.bp.com/en/global/corporate/energy-economics/statistical-review-of-world-energy.html

CABRI. (2015). National Development Strategy (2015–2035). Retrieved September 21, 2021, from https://www.cabri-sbo.org/en/documents/national-development-strategy-2015-2035

Chalaris, M. (2021). *Security of energy infrastructure*. Academia Letters. Academia.edu. https://doi.org/10.20935/al1116

Deutsche Welle. (2016). Oil crisis leads to food rationing in Angola. Retrieved August 12, 2021, from https://www.dw.com/en/oil-crisis-leads-to-food-rationing-in-angola/a-19051909

Energy Capital & Power. (2021). Renewable developments accelerate Angola's energy transition. Retrieved September 23, 2021, from https://energycapitalpower.com/renewable-developments-accelerate-angolas-energy-transition/

Eni. (2019). *Eni and the Government of Mozambique strengthen cooperation for sustainable development and decarbonization*. Retrieved September 1, 2021, from https://www.eni.com/en-IT/media/press-release/2019/10/eni-and-the-government-of-mozambique-strengthen-cooperation-for-sustainable-development-and-decarbonisation.html

Geopolitics. (n.d.). Retrieved September 21, 2021, from https://dictionary.cambridge.org/pt/dicionario/ingles/geopolitics

Gesto Energy Consulting. (2014). *Angola Energy 2025—Power sector long term vision*. Retrieved August 28, 2021, from https://gestoenergy.com/project/angola-energy-2025-power-sector-long-term-vision/

Gesto Energy Consulting. (2015). *Angola new renewable energy strategy*. Retrieved September 2, 2021, from https://gestoenergy.com/project/angola-new-renewable-energy-strategy/

Ichumile, G. (2013, August). *A boom for whom? Mozambique's natural gas and the new development opportunity*. South African Institute of International Affairs (SAIIA). African perspectives. Globais insights (Occasional Paper Nº 151). Retrieved September 2, 2021, from https://saiia.org.za/research/a-boom-for-whom-mozambiques-natural-gas-and-the-new-development-opportunity/

International Energy Agency. (2014). *World Energy Investment Outlook: World energy outlook special report*. OECD/IEA.

International Energy Agency. (2018). *Country profile, Angola*. Retrieved August 18, 2021, from https://www.iea.org/countries/angola

International Energy Agency. (2019). *Access to electricity*. Retrieved September 17, 2021, from https://www.iea.org/reports/sdg7-data-and-projections/access-to-electricity

International Energy Agency. (2020a). *African ministerial roundtable highlights energy's vital role in response to the Covid-19 crisis*. Retrieved September 2, 2021, from https://www.iea.org/news/african-ministerial-roundtable-highlights-energy-s-vital-role-in-response-to-the-covid-19-crisis

International Energy Agency. (2020b). *World energy model*. Retrieved August 26, 2021, from https://www.iea.org/reports/world-energy-model

International Energy Agency. (2020c). *SDG7: Data and projections.* Retrieved September 2, 2021, from https://www.iea.org/reports/sdg7-data-and-projections/access-to-electricity
International Energy Agency. (2021a) *World Energy Outlook 2021.* Retrieved September 21, 2021, from https://www.iea.org/countries/angola
International Energy Agency. (2021b). *Energy security. Reliable, affordable access to all fuels and energy sources.* Retrieved August 30, 2021, from https://www.iea.org/topics/energy-security
Ministério da Coordenação da Acção Ambiental. (2012). *National climate change adaptation and mitigation strategy.* https://www.ctc-n.org/sites/www.ctc-n.org/files/resources/mozambique_national_climate_change_strategy.pdf
Mucave, F. (2020). *How Mozambique can guarantee all the benefits of natural gas production.* Retrieved September 5, 2021, from https://cartamz.com/index.php/carta-do-fim-do-mundo/item/6386-como-mocambique-pode-garantir-todos-os-beneficios-da-producao-de-gas-natural-por-florival-mucave
Murray-Leach, R. (2019). *The World's First Fuel: How energy efficiency is reshaping global energy systems.* Energy Efficiency Council. https://www.productivity.nsw.gov.au/sites/default/files/2020-01/Green%20Building%20Council%20of%20Australia_Redacted.pdf
Nation. (n.d.). Retrieved September 2, 2021. from https://www.oxfordlearnersdictionaries.com/definition/english/nation?q=nation
Nationalism. (n.d.). Retrieved September 2, 2021. from https://dictionary.cambridge.org/dictionary/english/nationalism
Nozaki, W. (2018). *The new oil geopolitics in the 21st century.* Retrieved September 15, 2021, from https://diplomatique.org.br/a-nova-geopolitica-do-petroleo-no-seculo-xxi/
Phiri, F. (2016). *Desafios do Acordo de Paris na África.* Retrieved March 1, 2021, from https://envolverde.com.br/desafios-do-acordo-de-paris-na-africa/
Republic of Angola. (2010). *Constitution of the Republic of Angola* (revised 2010). Retrieved September 2, 2021, from https://aceproject.org/ero-en/regions/africa/AO/constitution-of-the-republic-of-angola-2010/view
Republic of Angola. (2015). *Intended nationally determined contribution for the Republic of Angola.* http://www.ungsp.org/sites/default/files/documents/indc_angola_deposito.pdf
Republic of Mozambique. (2018). *Constitution of the Republic of Mozambique* (revised 2018). Retrieved September 2, 2021, from https://www.informea.org/en/legislation/constitution-republic-mozambique-revised-2018
Republic of Mozambique, Cabinet Council. (2014). *Mozambique gas master plan.* http://www.inp.gov.mz/en/content/download/1075/8445/version/5/file/NATURAL%2BGAS%2BMASTER%2BPLAN%2B2014.pdf
Southern African Development Community. (2012). *Objectives.* Retrieved September 10, 2021, from https://www.sadc.int/about-sadc/overview/sadc-objectiv/
Schyff, S. (2020). *Angola explores renewable energy opportunities through diversification.* Retrieved September 1, 2021, from https://energycapitalpower.com/angola_explores-renewable-energy-opportunities-through-diversification/
Singh, J. (2018). *Energy efficiency in the public sector.* In *Live Wire.* World Bank. Retrieved June 30, 2021, from https://openknowledge.worldbank.org/handle/10986/31023
State. (n.d.). Retrieved September 2, 2021, from https://www.oxfordlearnersdictionaries.com/definition/english/state_1?q=state
United Nations. (n.d.-a). *Ending poverty.* Retrieved August 24, 2021, from https://www.un.org/en/global-issues/ending-poverty

United Nations. (n.d.-b). *What is REDD+?* Retrieved September 5, 2021, from https://unfccc.int/topics/land-use/workstreams/redd/what-is-redd~

United Nations. (2015). *2030 Agenda for sustainable development.* Retrieved September 1, 2021, from https://www.un.org/development/desa/disabilities/envision2030.html

Welding Institute, The. (n.d.). What is decarbonization? Retrieved June 24, 2021, from https://www.twi-global.com/technical-knowledge/faqs/what-is-decarbonisation

White House, The. (2011, March 30). *Remarks by the President on America's Energy Security*, Georgetown University. https://obamawhitehouse.archives.gov/the-press-office/2011/03/30/remarks-president-americas-energy-security

World Bank, The. (2021). *Africa's Pulse: Climate Change Adaptation and Economic Transformation in Sub-Saharan Africa.* Retrieved October 2, 2021, from https://www.worldbank.org/en/publication/africa-pulse

World Bank, The. (2022). *Access to electricity (% of population)—Angola.* Retrieved January 5, 2022, from https://data.worldbank.org/indicator/EG.ELC.ACCS.ZS?locations=AO

CHAPTER 15

The Implications of Energy Transitions in Argentina

GERARDO RABINOVICH

INTRODUCTION

Argentina is a middle-income country located in the extreme south of South America that has formed an economic bloc (MERCOSUR) with Brazil, Uruguay, and Paraguay. It also has strong connections with Chile in terms of gas trade.

In 2018, natural gas and oil made up 53 % and 34 % of Argentina's total primary energy supply (TPES). It ranks second in the world in shale gas resources and fourth in shale oil. It also has substantial wind and solar resources. At the beginning of this century, Argentina was self-sufficient and even exported some oil and gas. However, during the 2010s, it began to import natural gas, diesel, and gasoline, which has significantly impacted its energy trade balance and led to severe macroeconomic imbalances. The energy transition requires decarbonizing electricity production, electrifying all possible consumptions, incorporating hydrogen, and improving efficiency, thus leading to substantial technological changes in all business models. This is a condition of the fulfillment of Argentina's emission reduction obligations (per the framework of the Paris Agreement) that it has assumed in its National Determined Contribution (NDC) and its commitment to reach the net-zero emission goal by 2050.

This chapter reviews Argentina's commitments related to decarbonizing the energy sector and the economic, technical, and geopolitical barriers it will have to overcome to achieve its objectives related to the national energy transition.

The economic reports of various multilateral organizations are analyzed, as are the official presentations made by Argentina to the United Nations Framework for Climate Change. Further, the compatibility between the available resources and the commitments assumed are evaluated to determine Argentina's potential geopolitical positioning as it relates to its national policies

Energy integration in the Southern Cone of America, access to technology, and financing for the energy transition will be difficult but inevitable (Ferre et al., 2019). These factors will also require strong internal and external support, as well as favorable geopolitical positioning. This chapter explores these factors. Specifically, Section 1 presents the influence of the current economic situation of Argentina in their evolution to the energy transition. Section 2 describes the behavior of the energy sector, the main trends toward the growth of energy sources that do not emit greenhouse gases, and the geopolitical restrictions that arise from these changes. Finally, conclusions are presented based on the most probable scenarios and decisions regarding geopolitical matters that should be arbitrated for Argentina to achieve its decarbonization objectives by 2050.

THE CURRENT SITUATION OF THE ECONOMY OF ARGENTINA AND ENERGY CHOICES

Argentina is the third-largest economy in Latin America and the Caribbean and the 24th largest in the world. Its population is 44 million, and its gross domestic product (GDP) per capita is US$11,562, making it an upper-middle-income country. It is a member country of the G20 and, before the COVID-19 pandemic, was considered an emerging economy in the FTSE Global Equity Index (based on World Bank development indicators); recently, Argentina's country classification changed from "secondary emerging" to "frontier"[1] (Banco Interamericano de Desarrollo, 2019).

Concerning the economic performance of Argentina, the Economic Commission for Latin America and Caribbean Countries (2021) states that:

> In 2020, the Argentine economy shrank for the third consecutive year, this time owing to the impact of the crisis caused by the coronavirus disease (COVID-19) pandemic, which hit private consumption, investment, and exports hard. By the end of the year 2020, GDP has fallen by 10.5%—more than the 2.1% contraction recorded in 2019. With this backdrop and based on a smaller depreciation of the official exchange rate and a freeze on a set of regulated prices, inflation eased to 43.5% year-on-year cumulatively to October 2021, compared to the previous year's average of 53.5%. In 2021, the economy is expected to recover by 10%, thanks to the gradual reopening of the sectors affected by the pandemic. This is expected to generate an improvement in labour incomes and boost private consumption, while also increasing international export demand. This estimate

is contingent on the spread of the pandemic, which in turn depends largely on the widespread availability of the COVID-19 vaccine.

Argentina sends exports mainly to Brazil, the European Union, China, and the United States. According to the country's export profiles, diversification has been observed since 1990, when the country began exporting to new markets in Asia—such as India, Indonesia, South Korea, and Vietnam—and Africa. Argentina's main partners in South America are Brazil, Chile, Peru, and Uruguay. In 2020, Argentina's exports were worth US$55 billion. Of these exports, 29 % were primary goods, 39 % were agricultural manufactures, and 7 % were fuels and other energy resources. By 2020, the value of Argentina's imports had decreased to US$42.3 billion, owing to a 4.2 % reduction in prices and an 8.2 % reduction in volume. Consequently, the country's trade balance had a surplus of US$12.5 billion in 2020. The country's main import items are intermediate goods, which make up 40 % of all imports. Other significant imports are capital goods (17 %), parts and accessories (14 %), consumer goods (6 %), fuels and natural gas (5 %), and cars (National Institute of Statistics and Censuses INDEC, 2020, 2021).

Figure 15.1 depicts the areas that received the most exports from Argentina between 2016 and 2020. Brazil is the most common destination in all years, followed by the European Union, China, and the United States. These four destinations received 43 % of Argentina's exports in 2020. This is less than the nearly 50 % in 2016.

These four destinations also account for 67 % of Argentina's total imports (Figure 15.2). Throughout the study period, this share decreased, indicating

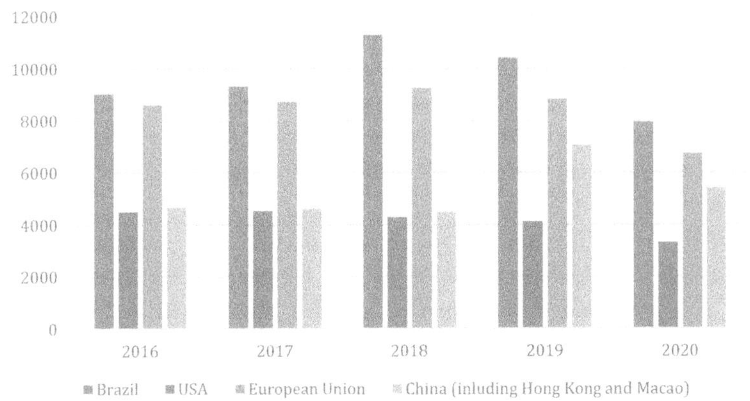

Figure 15.1: Argentina's Exports (million US$) 2016–2020

Source: Author's own elaboration (data retrieved from National Institute of Statistics and Censuses INDEC, 2016, 2017, 2018, 2019, 2020).

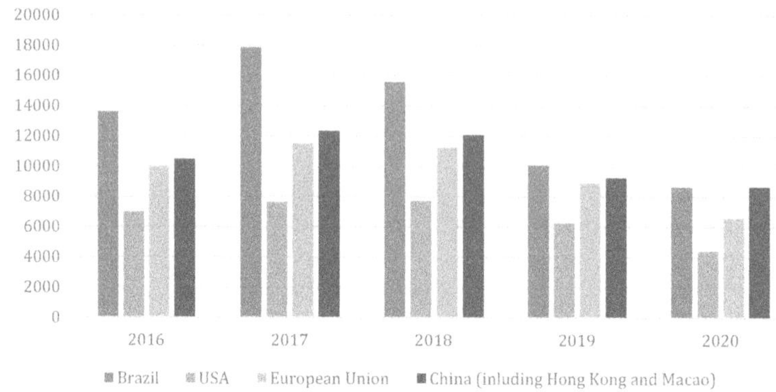

Figure 15.2: Argentina's Imports (million US$) 2016–2020

Source: Author's own elaboration (data retrieved from National Institute of Statistics and Censuses INDEC, 2016, 2017, 2018, 2019, 2020).

increased diversification in Argentina's imports. However, this matter should be analyzed in greater depth, as the COVID-19 pandemic has significantly affected the terms of international trade.

Table 15.1 shows the commercial outcomes in the first nine months of 2021, with strong growth observed in exports and imports compared to the same period in 2020. This growth indicates an increase in post-pandemic economic activity. The significant decreases in trade with China, Brazil, and the United States have been offset by enhanced trade with other regions. This implies a need to balance trade relations, especially between Argentina and China.

These data indicate that Argentina's main areas of geopolitical interest are Brazil, the other countries of MERCOSUR and Chile. Due to its strong trade deficit, China has gained substantial attention in the evolution of international relations. The European Union is another important commercial partner of the country. A special reference to international financial markets because of the high external debt, which has a short-term profile, increasing the value of the country's relations with the United States.

In 2018, Argentina signed an agreement with the International Monetary Fund and obtained US$42.285 billion, the largest loan that this institution had ever approved. This loan came with a short-term maturity profile as follows: US$3.172 billion in December 2021, US$13.42 billion in 2022 and 2023, US$3.42 billion in 2024, and the rest over the next 12 years (International Monetary Fund [IMF], 2019).

This situation has sparked an intense political debate, as the current government wants to renegotiate the terms and interest rate of the loan, while the creditors have requested a consistent economic plan that should be approved by all

Table 15.1: Argentina: Trade Balance in the First Three-Quarters of 2021 vs. 2020

	Export		Import		Balance	
Continents and countries	Jan-Sep 2021	Jan-Sep 2020	Jan-Sep 2021	Jan-Sep 2020	Ene-Sep 2021	Ene-Sep 2020
Total Africa	4,651,467	3,434,028	871,669	459,914	3,779,798	2,974,114
Total America (excluding Brazil and United States)	10,137,612	7,202,549	6,283,678	4,796,452	3,853,934	2,406,097
Brazil	8,387,556	5,494,591	9,088,121	6,061,363	-700,565	-566,772
United States	3,482,179	2,509,331	4,348,767	3,166,996	-866,587	-657,665
Total de Asia (excluding China)	15,429,555	10,712,767	6,787,582	3,798,243	8,641,973	6,914,524
China	5,002,615	4,218,939	9,514,328	5,934,405	-4,511,714	-1,715,466
Total Europa	9,990,083	7,384,566	8,372,306	5,677,246	1,617,777	1,707,320
Total	57,081,067	40,956,771	45,266,451	29,894,619	11,814,616	11,062,152

Source: Author's own elaboration (data retrieved from National Institute of Statistics and Censuses INDEC, 2020, 2021).

political sectors, which is still far from happening. From these perspectives, the threat of default is unavoidable (Einstoss, 2021; Einstoss & Rojo, 2020).

The weakness of the Argentine economy—due to a long recession, double-digit inflation, high indebtedness, and increased poverty and unemployment—prevents the country from undergoing the energy transition and fulfilling the commitments signed in the Paris Agreement in 2015 and the Determined National Commitments[2] (Einstoss, 2021; Einstoss & Rojo, 2020).

ENERGY TRANSITION IN ARGENTINA

This section discusses energy transition as the passage from a starting point (E_0) that must be substantially modified to a final point (E_f). Ultimately, net carbon emissions from the energy and transport sector must be zero. In each case, the trajectory responds to the conditions of the starting point, the availability of natural resources, the main socioeconomic variables, the population density, and the main commercial partners that make this trajectory feasible.

Energy Transition: A Starting Point (E_0)

The starting point is the national energy balance (Secretaría de Energía, 2019) which indicates that Argentina depends on oil and natural gas for 85 % of its TPES. Figure 15.3 shows the share of each primary energy source according to the country's energy balance in 2018.

Argentina's heavy dependence on oil and natural gas is present in all economic sectors. For example, in the residential sector, natural gas has a share of 60 % of final consumption (e.g., for cooking, heating, and hot water). In the transportation sector, oil products have a share of 90 %. Moreover, in the industrial sector, natural gas represents 57 % of the total energy consumption. Natural gas also predominates in the electric power generation matrix. Figure 15.4 shows that the power capacity in August 2021 was 42,064 MW, of which almost 60 % corresponds to thermoelectric plants (fueled by 90 % natural gas), 25 % to hydroelectricity, 11 % to non-conventional renewables (mainly wind and solar photovoltaic energy), and 4 % nuclear.

Argentina presents specific characteristics, both in its final energy consumption and its production of electricity. For one, the country produces and consumes

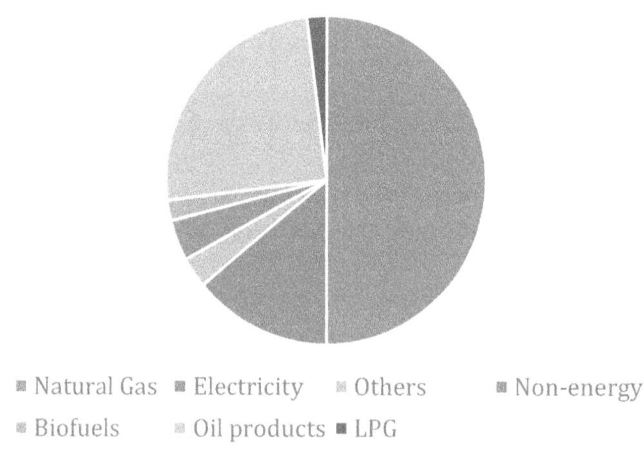

Figure 15.3: Argentina National Energy Balance 2018—Share of primary energy sources

Source: Author's own elaboration (data retrieved from Secretaría de Energía, 2019).

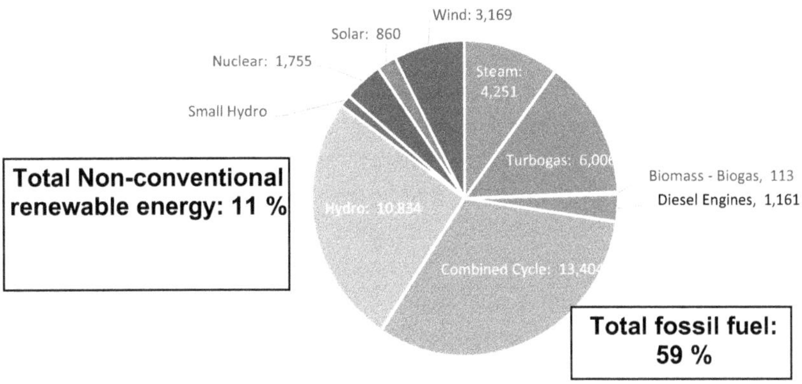

Figure 15.4: Installed power generation capacity 2021 (MW)

Source: Author's own elaboration (data retrieved from CAMMESA Argentine Wholesale Electricity Market Clearing Company, 2022).

almost no coal. Moreover, it has developed an advanced knowledge of nuclear technology, as it is perhaps the Latin American country with the most developed nuclear industry for civil uses. The country exports nuclear reactors for research purposes.[3]

Since 2016, the number of wind and solar power plants in the country has increased according to public policy. Furthermore, a successful auction system (Plan Renov.ar) was implemented, enabling the construction and commissioning of 3,200 MW of wind energy and 860 MW of photovoltaic solar energy. In 2015, the Law of Non-Conventional Renewable Energies (NCRE)[4] was established. According to this law, by 2025, 20 % of all electricity consumed in the country should come from these energy sources.

In August 2021, NCRE penetration was only 12 %, meaning it will be difficult to reach 20 % by 2025. In 2019, the auction program was interrupted due to a decision made by the government that took office in December of that year. The situation has worsened since the outbreak of COVID-19 in 2020. A contract market called the long-term market for renewable energies was enabled to accelerate the use of NCRE. It is currently proposed to resume.

The initial state (E_0) from which Argentina must begin its energy transition process to meet its goal of net-zero emissions by 2050 was defined simply. The actions that need to be carried out are difficult, especially considering that natural gas does not appear to be a source of transitional energy, the small margin to substitute liquid fuels, and the inability to substitute coal. Therefore, Argentina's trajectory consists of substituting natural gas for electricity produced by NCRE.

A description of the starting point would be incomplete without mentioning that Argentina is an oil- and gas-producing country with modest reserves but great potential to utilize unconventional hydrocarbons, namely shale oil and shale gas. This helps to explain the ambiguous public policies in response to the uncertainty in the promotion of upstream activities, the required investments in natural gas transportation infrastructure, and even the ambitious projections of Argentina's status as a future liquefied natural gas exporter within a few years if the net-zero emissions commitment is to be met by 2050.

Indeed, information from the US Energy Information Administration (2015) highlights the significant potential of oil and natural gas from shales in the geological formation known as Vaca Muerta ("Dead Cow" in English), which has created great expectations for and great hope in Argentina. As a result, Argentina ranked second in the world in terms of its technically recoverable resources of natural gas, with more than 1,000 trillion cubic feet (Tcf). Furthermore, it ranks fourth in the case of oil, with 27 Giga barrels (Gb).

This could translate into multiplying the current gas proven reserves by almost 100 and the current oil proven reserves by 10. However, 15 billion US$ per year is required to obtain some of these resources. Investments and production would be competitive when the price of oil in international markets exceeds US$80 per barrel; the same can be said of natural gas when the prices in the main regional markets exceed US$8/MMBtu (Rabinovich, 2020, p. 54).

The development of Vaca Muerta fields, where the investments cannot be recovered for at least 15 years, must be very fast. The political decision to accelerate the development of Vaca Muerta is hindered by the country's lack of capital, combined with the progressive decrease in international financing for oil and gas development projects.

The discussion now turns to the different positions of this dichotomy. These positions—and how they are expressed in a contradictory way in the national plans—will be explained. The discussion will also include the determined national contributions and the difficulties associated with presenting a long-term strategy per the mechanisms established in the Paris Agreement.

The Difficulties of Reaching Net-Zero Emissions in the Energy Sector (E_f)

The path that Argentina must follow to achieve its commitments and climate objectives is difficult. It also contains contradictions owing to the starting point described above. Furthermore, the fragile economic situation limits the adoption of the measures proposed in the plans and scenarios.

In December 2020, Argentina presented its second NDC in the United Nations Framework for Climate Change. Argentina expressed its intentions to increase its ambition and its willingness to achieve zero net emissions by 2050. In 2016, according to the National Inventory of Greenhouse Gases, the country's emissions were 364 million tons of CO_2e ($MtCO_2e$).

Argentina is a highly vulnerable country that needs to adapt due to its great diversity of climatic areas. The absolute, comprehensive, and unconditional commitment not to exceed net emissions of 359 $MtCO_2e$ in 2030 stated in the new NDC is very ambitious. Per this commitment, the country will have to lower its energy consumption by 19 % by 2030 as the population grows and while its gross domestic product (GDP) grows by less than 3 %/year. Achieving this goal would represent a total emissions reduction of 19 % by 2030 (compared to peak emission rate in 2007) and a reduction of 25.7 % compared to the first NDC introduced in 2016.

The Guidelines for an Energy Transition Plan to 2030 (Secretaría de Energía, 2021) recognizes that Argentina faces a complex social and financial situation because of the global transition process. It defines two scenarios regarding electricity generation. The first is REN 20, according to which NCRE will represent 20 % of electricity consumption in 2030. The second is REN 30, which states that 30 % of all electricity consumed will be powered by NCRE (Figure 15.5).

For gas and oil, there is a scenario in which natural gas production grows from 124 million m^3/day in 2020 to 186 million m^3/day in 2030; this translates to an increase of 50 %. Meanwhile, oil production will increase from 486 thousand barrels/day in 2020 to 969 thousand barrels/day in 2030. In both cases, the increase is due almost entirely to the unconventional oil and gas field of Vaca Muerta. Furthermore, total CO_2 emissions will grow compared to 2016, which does not comply with the most recent NDC from the supply side. Such an increase in CO_2 emissions would mean that an incredible effort would be required to meet the NDC from the demand side and ensure efficient energy consumption.[5]

Investments of US$9.924 billion (REN 20) or US$13.970 billion (REN 30) would be required to achieve these results in the electricity subsector. These investments do not include those for new nuclear power plants, which would cost another approximately US$8 billion. The US$3.371 billion investment in a new gas pipeline and gas transportation infrastructure between Buenos Aires and Vaca Muerta must also be added to this. Finally, we must consider investments in the development of unconventional hydrocarbon production in the Vaca Muerta field over the next 10 years, which are estimated to be approximately US$100 billion.

The Argentine government, alongside the Ministry of the Environment and Sustainable Development, also prepared a document called the "Long-Term Development Strategy, Low in Emissions and Resilient." This strategy was not presented at COP 26 in Glasgow in compliance with the requirement for countries to provide documentation related to the Paris Agreement.

In 2021, Argentina established an absolute emission goal of 349.16 $MtCO_2e$ by 2030. This goal relates to all sectors of the economy and strengthens the actions of adaptation. The new commitment raises the ambition of the Nationally Determined Contribution by 27.7 % compared to that presented in 2016 and by 2 %

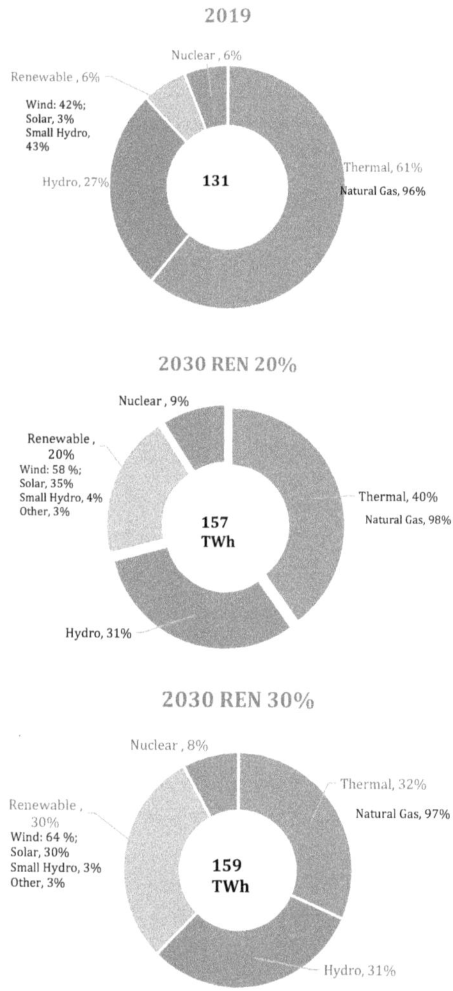

Figure 15.5: Generation of Electricity Balance in 2019 and 2030 per REN 20 and REN 30
Source: Author's own elaboration (data retrieved from Secretaría de Energía, 2021).

compared to that presented in 2020. The actions to do this are: (i) a commitment to reach 30 % of renewable energies in the electrical matrix; (ii) the plan of efficiency measures for industry, transport, and construction; (iii) adopt cutting-edge technologies to reduce methane emissions and (iv) promote the country's status as a complex producer and exporter of hydrogen.

A sustained growth of electricity generation from renewable sources is expected by 2050 in solar photovoltaic energy, wind power plants, electrical bioenergy from different biomass, and small hydroelectric plants.[6] The incorporation of new nuclear or large hydroelectric plants is not foreseen beyond those that are already planned or at construction stage. This additional electrical energy will be produced from solar photovoltaic and wind energy, requiring capacities close to 30 GW and 40 GW, respectively, by 2050. This should be compatible with the demands of other economic sectors.

The transformation of the energy system will require time to design, agree on, and develop specific policies and measures that allow each of the lines of action to be carried out. The energy resources used today, as well as infrastructure and transformation technologies, will continue to be part of the system for more than a decade. Among these resources are natural gas, which has multiple uses, such as generating electrical energy for use in the industrial, residential, commercial, and public sectors. Furthermore, oil and derived fuels are resources used for transportation, industrial, and other non-energy uses. It will be critical to evaluate and avoid the expansion of infrastructures related to the exploitation, transportation, and the use of these hydrocarbons that imply long repayment periods because they could result in stranded assets in the medium term as the transformation of the sector advances.

The production of biofuels for use mainly in long-distance passenger transport, rail freight transport, and agricultural machinery will be promoted, as will the production of biofuels suitable for use in commercial aviation. This will require increasing production by almost five times by 2050. Reducing the impact of this production on land use will require efficiency improvements to be encouraged during the production of first-, second-, and third-generation biofuels (Caratori & Magnasco, 2021).

The generation of photovoltaic electricity in residential rooftops, close to the consumption offers great opportunities to diversify the resources used, decentralize production, reduce losses due to the transport of electrical energy over long distances, and increase the system's resilience against the impacts of climate change. Distributed generation in the residential sector will be improved until an installed power of close to 50 GW is reached in 2050. Among commercial, public, and small and medium-sized companies' the installed power will be close to 20 GW by 2050. This development will promote entrepreneurship, enhance local value chains, and create jobs.

Long-term strategies include the development of electric vehicles and a corresponding charging infrastructure, as well as various advancements in the field of energy efficiency. Medium-term objectives (i.e., those to be met by 2030), as defined by the Secretary of Energy, must still be reconciled with the long-term objectives that the Ministry of Environment and Sustainable Development is drawing up, the most recent NDC, and the engagement to be carbon-neutral by 2050. The greatest inconsistency can be found in the oil and gas policy that the energy sector wants to be carried out, as it involves significant increases in production until 2030 that would be possible only with high economic returns that are not possible given the country's economy.

CONCLUSION

Argentina depends heavily on natural gas and oil, which represent 53 % and 35 % of its TPES, respectively. This situation will make it difficult for Argentina to achieve its planned net-zero emissions goal through an energy transition process by 2050. This difficulty is even more severe considering that the economy has been in recession since 2018, annual inflation exceeds 40 %, unemployment is close to 12 %, and the poverty rate is over 40 %. Furthermore, the country has a debt maturity profile with institutions such as the IMF that is impossible to comply with and is being renegotiated. In addition, the COVID-19 pandemic has had a tremendous impact on all activity indicators.

The main areas of geopolitical interest in Argentina are MERCOSUR countries, especially Brazil, which is Argentina's largest trading partner in terms of the quantity and quality of exchanges. European Union, and the United States, are other high-priority areas. Regarding China specifically, important cooperation agreements have been signed in recent decades that have increased the importance of Argentina's relations with China. These agreements have also balanced the pressures exerted from financial markets, which are referenced in the institutions of Bretton Woods based in the United States. Meanwhile, the large Spanish and Italian communities in Argentina strengthen its ties with the European Union. Moreover, many Argentines live in the United States, which reinforces the link between both countries.

European, American, and Chinese companies have important assets in Argentina, particularly in the electricity, oil and gas, and energy sectors. These assets will be essential to Argentina's planned energy transition process and, thus, its compliance with its international commitments regarding change climate and decarbonization. Large sums of capital are required for this, and, in that sense, political and institutional stability is a priority. The signals sent to investors must be clear, and current inconsistencies must be overcome. Otherwise, the energy transition process—and, hence, Argentina's progress—will be in danger.

NOTES

1 FTSE v11. 1 Global Equity Index, accessed on December 2021 from https://research.ftserussell.com

2 Gross domestic product fell by 2.6 % in 2018; 2/1 % in 2019, and 10.5 % in 2020 (estimated); Consumer Prices Index growth was 47.1 % in 2018; 52.9 % in 2019 and 35.1 % in 2020; open urban unemployment rate was 9.2 in 2018; 9.8 in 2019 and 11.8 in 2020 (Economic Commission for Latin America and Caribbean Countries, 2020).

3 With 66 years of history, the National Atomic Energy Commission (CNEA) placed Argentina at the head of technological development of nuclear power plants in Latin American, and occupies an important role worldwide, exporting reactors to more developed countries like Australia, and others like Peru, Egypt, and Algeria, and with projects to commercialize reactors to Brazil, Arabia, India, Netherlands, South Africa, and the United States (Argentine Center of Engineers, 2016).

4 National Promotion Regime for the use of Renewable Sources of Energy to produce Electric Power (Law 27191, October 2015).

5 The emission of CO_2e will be 201.4 $MtCO_2e$ in 2030 in REN 20 Scenario, and 193.7 $MtCO_2e$ in the same year in REN 30 Scenario, vs. 193.4 MtCO2 eq in 2016.

6 The solar photovoltaic capacity will increase to 40 GW from its current value of 0.8 GW; wind plants will total 100 GW (up from the current value of 3.8 GW), according to the LTS of the Ministry of Environment and Social Development.

REFERENCES

Argentine Center of Engineers. (2016, September). *Reactores nucleares para el mundo* (No. 1121). https://www.cai.org.ar/wp-content/uploads/2018/09/CAI1121.pdf

Banco Interamericano de Desarrollo. (2019). *Documento de Enfoque Argentina 2016–2019*. Oficina de Evaluación y Supervisión. https://publications.iadb.org/publications/spanish/document/Documento_de_enfoque_Evaluaci%C3%B3n_del_Programa_de_Pa%C3%ADs_Argentina_2016-2019_es.pdf

CAMMESA Argentine Wholesale Electricity Market Clearing Company. (2022, May). *Informe Anual 2021*. https://microfe.cammesa.com/static-content/CammesaWeb/download-manager-files/Informe%20Anual/2022/Inf%20Anual%202021.pdf

Caratori, L., & Magnasco, E. (2021, October 6). *La nueva ley de biocombustibles: un paso atrás en materia ambiental*. https://www.crea.org.ar/la-nueva-ley-de-biocombustibles-un-paso-atras-en-materia-ambiental/

Economic Commission for Latin America and Caribbean Countries. (2021, February). *Preliminary overview of the economies of Latin America and Caribbean Countries, 2020*. https://www.cepal.org/en/publications/46504-preliminary-overview-economies-latin-america-and-caribbean-2020

Einstoss, A. (2021, November). *La encrucijada energética*. Econometrica. https://www.econometrica.com.ar/attachments/article/428/Econom%C3%A9trica_Informe_Macro_La_encrucijada_energ%C3%A9tica_Por_Einstoss_Nov21.pdf

Einstoss, A., & Rojo, J. (2020, December). *La energía a la deriva: ¿tres restricciones al populismo energético?* Econometrica. https://www.iae.org.ar/wp-content/uploads/2020/12/Econometrica-Informe-Especial-La-energia-a-la-deriva-Einstoss-Rojo-Dic-2020-1.pdf

Ferre, A. L., Tejeda, J. A., & Di Chiara, L. (2019). *Integración Eléctrica Regional Oportunidades y Retos que enfrentan los países de América Latina* (IDB MG 742). Inter-American Development Bank (IADB).

International Monetary Fund. (2019, July 15). *Fourth review under the standby arrangement, request for waivers of applicability and modification of performance criteria, and financing assurances review* (Country Report No. 19/232). https://www.imf.org/-/media/Files/Publications/CR/2019/1ARGEA2019004.ashx

National Institute of Statistics and Censuses INDEC. (2016, November 16). *Argentine foreign trade statistics, January–September 2016*. https://www.indec.gob.ar/uploads/informesdeprensa/i_argent_11_16.pdf

National Institute of Statistics and Censuses INDEC. (2017, November). *Argentine foreign trade statistics, January–September 2017*. https://www.indec.gob.ar/uploads/informesdeprensa/i_argent_11_17.pdf

National Institute of Statistics and Censuses INDEC. (2018, November). *Argentine foreign trade statistics, January–September 2018*. https://www.indec.gob.ar/uploads/informesdeprensa/i_argent_11_18.pdf

National Institute of Statistics and Censuses INDEC. (2019, November). *Argentine foreign trade statistics, January–September 2019*. https://www.indec.gob.ar/uploads/informesdeprensa/i_argent_11_1956C228DA82.pdf

National Institute of Statistics and Censuses INDEC. (2020, November). *Argentine foreign trade statistics, January–September 2020*. https://www.indec.gob.ar/uploads/informesdeprensa/i_argent_11_205EA93F6C2E.pdf

National Institute of Statistics and Censuses INDEC. (2021, November). *Argentine foreign trade statistics, January–September 2021*. https://www.indec.gob.ar/uploads/informesdeprensa/i_argent_11_21331342A8AD.pdf

Rabinovich, G. (2020, November–December). *Shale oil and gas in Argentina: The case of Vaca Muerta* (No. 653). La Revue de l'Energie. https://www.larevuedelenergie.com/petrole-et-gaz-de-schiste-en-argentine-le-cas-de-vaca-muerta/

Secretaría de Energía. (2019, November). *Balance Energético Nacional*. http://www.energia.gob.ar/contenidos/archivos/Reorganizacion/informacion_del_mercado/publicaciones/energia_en_gral/balances_provinciales/2019_11_10_sintesis_balances_energeticos_2018_pub.pdf

Secretaría de Energía. (2021, October 28). *Lineamientos para un Plan de Transición Energética*. http://servicios.infoleg.gob.ar/infolegInternet/anexos/355000-359999/356100/res1036.pdf

US Energy Information Administration. (2015). *World Shale Resource Assessments*. https://www.eia.gov/analysis/studies/worldshalegas/

Part III

CHAPTER 16

Energy Issues in EU Agreements, Between Supply Security, Solidarity, and Sustainability, Before and After the Russian-Ukrainian Conflict: Can the EU Become a Leader in Global Energy Relationships?

SARA PUGLIESE

INTRODUCTION

Energy has always been a key issue in the European integration process. Suffice it to recall the 1951 treaty establishing the European Coal and Steel Community (ECSC),[1] seeking to create a common market for coal, the most important energy source in the fifties, or the 1957 Treaty establishing the European Atomic Energy Community (EAEC/Euratom)[2] to foster research on nuclear power and manage the supply of nuclear components.

As the ECSC and Euratom focused on specific energy sources, since the Treaty establishing the European Economic Community (TEEC) did not contain a specific legal basis for the energy sector, energy was considered a "good," subject to general common market rules.[3]

From the late sixties, the shortage of oil, which had substituted coal as a principal energy source, and its significant socioeconomic effects highlighted the special nature of energy and energy services, as well as the need to adopt a specific discipline in this field. During the eighties, it was acknowledged that energy was not a traditional "good" but a "commodity": it had intrinsic value as it was indispensable for producing other goods, and energy infrastructures came to be seen as "essential facilities."[4] Far from representing mere "trading" terminology,[5] considering energy as a commodity implies assuring continuity and sufficiency of supply, price stability and predictability, as well as open, transparent, and fair infrastructure accessibility. Nevertheless, some structural issues, such as the difficulty of transporting and storing some types of energy (such as electricity), which causes a high degree of volatility of prices, undermined the market efficiency essential for commodities (Berrie & Hoyle, 1985, p. 508 ff.). To correct the limitations of the energy market, from the nineties the European Community (EC) made significant efforts to liberalize it through privatization and by ending State monopolies, also fostering fair international trade.

After the Treaty of Lisbon introduced a specific legal basis for energy policy, the urgency of reducing the impact of energy consumption on climate change and dependency on third countries, as well as ensuring an energy supply to all the Member States led the European Union (EU) Institutions, in particular the European Commission, to promote a new development model. This model should reduce emissions and fostered a sustainable way of life and production (the so-called European Green Deal; see *infra*, paragraph 2). In an effort to promote new systems of production and consumption at EU and global levels, the European Commission insisted on adding provisions on cooperation for energy security, solidarity, and sustainability in bilateral, macro-regional, and multilateral agreements.

During the 2021 Conference of Parties of the United Nations Climate Change Conference (or COP 26),[6] the EU aimed to play the role of change-driver in international relations to promote a global sustainable energy transition. Nevertheless, the most important EU contribution to formulating new rules in the energy sector is the regulation it applies at the internal and external level.

The present chapter aims to verify if the EU efforts to affirm, both in the internal and external regulation, principles of security, sustainability, and solidarity of energy market could contribute to assure it a role of leader in creating an effective and equitable energy regulation at international level. Framing the EU energy regulation in a multilevel perspective, the Chapter presents an innovative approach aimed to verify if the EU is becoming a significant player in the elaboration of effective regulatory solutions to the exigencies of States, citizens, and businesses of obtaining, suitable, prompt, and not expensive energy sources necessary for their activities, without forgetting the needs of the future generations.

To this extent, after having recalled the principal steps of the energy policy evolution, an analysis of chapters on energy in EU bilateral agreements is proposed aimed to verify if they contribute to reinforce the EU accountability in the Energy regulation. In the same perspective, the effects of Brexit on the EU energy policy are investigated to verify if the 2020 Trade and Cooperation Agreement (TCA) has been able to create a balance between energy security and market effectiveness. Furthermore, an analysis of the macro-regional and multilateral energy treaties where the EU is part is offered aimed to verify if the EU is contributing to elaborate a set of multilateral rules able to realize a balance between public and private interests in the energy sector. At the end, the Chapter proposes an "in-depth" analysis of the choices made by the EU to contrast the effects of the Russia-Ukraine conflict aimed to put a definitive end to the EU dependency from energy sources coming from third countries.

EUROPEAN ENERGY POLICY AS A MEANS OF STRENGTHENING THE EU POSITION IN GLOBAL ENERGY MARKET

As already underlined, the TEEC did not contain any specific provision concerning energy. Nevertheless, at the end of sixties, the oil and petroleum shortage led to the adoption of sectorial legislation[7] under Article 103 TEC concerning economic crises. After the Treaty of Maastricht explicitly featured energy among the EC's objectives (Article 3, letter t TEC),[8] common rules for the electricity and gas sector were established, based on the provisions concerning the free movement of services, the right of establishment, and legislative rapprochement.[9] At the same time, the EC acted to strengthen the energy multilateral cooperation culminating in the 1994 Energy Charter Treaty (ECT) (see paragraph 5 for more details).

After September 11, 2001, growing instability in the Arab countries and on the Eastern European borders caused reductions in the energy supply and rising prices. In response to these events, as well as to the growing attention to the environmental concerns, the European Institutions created the Emission Trading System (ETS)[10] and adopted laws to bolster energy security and mutual solidarity between the Member States.[11] In parallel, a new package of rules pursued the liberalization of the energy sector.[12] In the same year, Regulation 713/2009 established the Agency for the Cooperation of Energy Regulators (ACER) to assist the national regulatory authorities and, where necessary, coordinate their action, also adopting binding individual acts.[13]

In Article 194 of the Treaty on the Functioning of the European Union (TFEU), the Treaty of Lisbon established a specific legal basis regarding the energy sector. According to Article 194 TFEU, "in the context of the establishment and functioning of the internal market and with regard for the need to preserve and improve the environment, Union policy on energy shall aim, in a spirit of solidarity between the Member States, to ensure the functioning of the energy market; ensure the security of energy supply in the Union; promote energy efficiency and energy saving and the development of new and renewable forms of energy; and promote the interconnection of energy networks."[14]

As underlined in the scholarship, this provision is important because it allows the Institutions to draw up an "overall" energy policy, creating uniform measures rather than the previous unconnected and disaggregated ones (Marletta, 2014, p. 1654). At the same time, the need to consider issues concerning the environment and solidarity, and to conceive energy as a commodity (paragraph 1 above) highlighted the need to work together, maintaining a network of interconnections and being ready to provide institutional and interstate assistance in the event of an energy shortage due to economic crisis. From this perspective, Article 194 TFEU should be read in connection with Article 122, § 1 TFEU, which states that "Without prejudice to any other procedures provided for in the Treaties, the Council, on a proposal from the Commission, may decide, in a spirit of solidarity between the Member States, upon the measures appropriate to the economic situation, in particular, if severe difficulties arise in the supply of certain products, notably in the area of energy" (Sciaudone, 2014, p. 1312).[15]

Following the Paris Agreement,[16] the most urgent issues were the adoption by the European Council of the 2030 Energy and climate policy framework[17] fixing the target of a 40 % emissions reduction by 2030, and the subsequent reform of the EU ETS,[18] together with the need for a radical reform of European energy regulation (Quadri, 2016, p. 1 ff.). Consequently, the "Clean Energy Package" (or "fourth energy package") was adopted, including eight legislative texts on the electricity market and consumers, energy efficiency, renewables, and bioenergy sustainability.[19] The main goals of the package were to establish governance for European Energy focusing on environmental sustainability and to develop energy relationships between the Member States according to a logic of solidarity.[20]

The General Court explained the scope of the solidarity in the energy sector—and EU in general—in the 2019 *Republic of Poland v. Commission* judgment. According to the General Court, "the 'spirit of solidarity' referred to in Article 194(1) TFEU is the specific expression in this field of the general principle of solidarity between the Member States, mentioned, among other things, in Article 2 TEU, Article 3(3) TEU, Article 24(2) and (3) TEU, Article 122(1) TFEU, and Article 222 TFEU. This principle lies at the heart of the whole Union system, in line with the undertaking set out in Article 4(3) TEU."[21] In the context of energy policy, the principle of solidarity, read in connection with the principle of sincere cooperation, entails both specific obligations in extraordinary situations falling under EU competence, according to Article 194, § 2 TFUE and implemented by secondary law, and general obligations that EU and the member states have to consider when exercising their respective competencies to protect the interests of other stakeholders.[22] The Court of Justice (ECJ) confirmed the General Court's arguments in the 2021 *Republic of Germany v. European Commission* judgment. It explicitly affirmed that "the spirit of solidarity between Member States (…) constitutes a specific expression, in the field of energy, of the principle of solidarity, which is itself one of the fundamental principles of EU law."[23]

The two judgments underline the connection between energy solidarity and the energy security arising from the physical integration of gas systems and the harmonization of market rules through the interdependence of Member States in the natural gas sector. They call both Member States and the EU to consider the impact of strategic energy policy decisions on neighboring Member States. At the same time, concerning the EU interest project Nord Stream, as already underlined, these decisions underscore the geopolitical implications of energy projects and the challenges of applying EU law to projects with external implications (Boute, 2020, p. 898 ff.).

After the outbreak of the COVID-19 emergency, the structure of the energy sector has seen rapid change. Firstly, after lockdown, which brought about a period of deflation period due to difficulties in transporting energy sources and decreased demand, a new surge in demand took place, driven by economic recovery (Olubusoye et al., 2021, p. 10235 ff.; Salisua et al., 2020, p. 1 ff.). Nevertheless, the supply of energy has not responded to the increasing demand, and prices are soaring, creating many challenges for businesses and people.

To react to this situation, the European Commission, on July 14, 2021, proposed the package "Delivering the European Green Deal" ("Fit for 55"),[24] aimed not only to align energy policy to the EU objectives to fight climate change but also to reduce EU dependence on third-country suppliers through a radical transformation of the EU economy and society, innovating production methods and lifestyles following a development model based on economic, environmental, and social sustainability (the "Green Deal"; Tufano, forthcoming).[25]

In the same perspective, strongly desiring to bring the energy sector to a sustainable turning point, during COP 26 the European Union has incentivized actions to reduce dependence on polluting and scarce resources and to carry out research to implement new energy sources.[26] At the same time, the European Commission is reassessing old energy sources from a "green" perspective (such as nuclear power or liquefied natural gas[27]). It is also taking measures to stop price increases[28] and create initiatives to make energy consumption in European buildings more efficient,[29] this too in a bid to counteract energy poverty and support citizens and businesses. In parallel, the Next Generation Programme[30] and the 2021–2026 structural funds programming cycle[31] are expected to provide substantial support in accelerating the green transition in the coming years. All these regulatory and funding initiatives represent a particularly innovative pattern in the energy sector, and it could also become a model for other countries.

It is also necessary to consider the significant impact of energy law on private interests. From this perspective, it may be interesting to consider the recent Opinion of General Advocate General Bobek in the Nord Stream 2 AG case. Bobek stated that Nord Stream 2 AG could challenge the Directive extending the scope of the Gas Directive to pipelines connecting the EU with third countries before the EU Courts, as it is capable of producing legal effects by extending the scope of the Gas Directive to situations such as those concerning Nord Stream, which were not previously covered by that legislation.[32] In the July 12, 2022 judgment, the Court declared the Nord Stream 2 AG action for annulment admissible and referred the case back to the General Court.[33]

Due to the need to balance diverse interests, the internal provisions to increase EU autonomy may not be sufficient to ensure the EU can be a global change-driver. In an effort to strengthen its relationship with energy exporters while stimulating international cooperation, the EU introduced energy chapters to the bilateral agreements and strengthened macro-regional and multilateral cooperation.

CHAPTERS ON ENERGY IN EU BILATERAL AGREEMENTS, BETWEEN SECURITY, SUSTAINABILITY, AND SOLIDARITY

Article 194 TFEU contains no reference to the EU's external competence in the energy sector. Nevertheless, some considerations on the matter may be inferred from TFEU provisions relating to competencies. More specifically, Article 3, § 2, TFEU specifies that the Union has exclusive competence to conclude international agreements when "conclusion is provided for in a legislative act of the Union or is necessary to enable the Union to exercise its internal competence, or in so far as its conclusion may affect common rules or alter their scope." This implies that, while the EU always has external competence, as far as shared competencies are concerned, the perimeter of external action must be established by EU institutions through secondary acts (among others; Baratta, 2014, p. 380 ff.).[34]

As energy is mentioned in Article 4, § 2, letter i), to conclude international treaties in the energy sector between subjects of shared competence, it would be necessary to wait for secondary acts based on Article 194 TFEU to be adopted or to apply the flexibility clause envisaged by Article 352 TFEU (Marletta, 2014, p. 1659).

Nevertheless, based on the above-mentioned ECJ case law, which considers energy as a good, and energy provision a service subject to internal market regulations, the European Commission, deeming energy issues to be part of European Commercial Policy, added chapters concerning energy to its bilateral free trade agreements, in the agreement on partnership and cooperation, and in the more recent "comprehensive" agreements.[35]

The provisions concerning energy contained in the bilateral agreements can be classed in three categories:

A. Provisions aiming to stimulate cooperation with energy exporters (e.g., agreements with Eastern countries or Gulf Council);
B. Provisions aiming to strengthen energy-sector cooperation with developed countries (e.g., with Canada or Japan);
C. Provisions aiming to stimulate cooperation with emerging countries in the energy sector.

The following sections examine these three categories to identify the different strategies pursued by the European Union to stimulate new patterns of cooperation and shared management in the energy sector.

A. Provisions to Stimulate Cooperation with Energy Exporters

Russia is the main EU supplier of crude oil, natural gas and solid fossil fuels (source Eurostat; Bruegel). The largest share of gas is delivered from Russia via four distinct corridors Nord Stream (via Baltic Sea), Yamal (via Poland), Ukraine, and Turkstream (via Turkey). For this reason, starting from the EC-Russian Federation Agreement of 1997,[36] the EC-Russia cooperation in the energy field has been really intense. Article 65 establishes that cooperation in energy sector shall take place within the principles of the market economy and the European Energy Charter, against a background of the progressive integration of the energy markets in Europe. It is mainly focused on assuring the quality and security of energy supply and the improvement in management and regulation of the energy sector in line with a market economy, as well as the introduction of a range of institutional, legal, fiscal, and other conditions necessary to encourage increased energy trade and investment. Issues concerning the energy saving and efficiency, modernization of energy infrastructure and improvement of energy, and the environmental impact of energy production, supply and consumption are not specifically addressed.

Differently, these problems were particularly relevant in the agreements stipulated by the EC/EU with the other Eastern countries, which are strategic for energy transit but often are dependent from their own by Russian resources. The

EC intensified the relationship with these countries in the early nineties in the ambit of the "European Neighbourhood Policy" and in 2008 the Eastern Partnership (EaP) was launched with Armenia, Azerbaijan, Belarus, Georgia, Moldova, and Ukraine, specifically "to strengthen energy security through cooperation with regard to long-term stable and secure energy supply and transit, including through better regulation, energy efficiency and more use of renewable energy sources."[37]

Within the EaP framework, the EU and Ukraine concluded an Association Agreement in March 2014. It established a Deep and Comprehensive Free Trade Area (DCFTA)[38] whose trade-related energy chapter establishes rules concerning pricing,[39] customs duties, quantitative restrictions,[40] cooperation on infrastructure (Article 274), interruptions (Articles 275–276)[41] and specific provisions concerning hydrocarbons.[42] Speedier procedures of dispute settlement resolution were established to manage urgent energy disputes caused by "an interruption, in full or in part, of any transport of natural gas, oil, or electricity."[43] Regarding energy cooperation, including nuclear issues,[44] an "Early Warning Mechanism" was established, setting out practical measures to prevent and rapidly react to an emergency or threat of one.[45]

While the Association Agreement between EU and Moldova, with its DCFTA, signed on June 16, 2014,[46] has a similar structure to the EU-Ukraine Association Agreement, the EU and Georgia Association Agreement, concluded on the same day,[47] appears more concise as the Parties merely assumed some specific commitments regarding transit and secure, sustainable, and open markets, in addition to access to energy facilities.[48] In this case, too, speedier dispute settlement resolution procedures were established for urgent energy disputes.[49] Specific provisions were established regarding energy cooperation to create energy infrastructures of common interest and enhance the security of energy supplies, trade, transit, and transport.[50] Clearly, despite mentioning environmental issues, the energy provisions in the Agreements with Eastern countries focus on the security of energy supply and aim to avert energy shortages in the EU member states.

More recently, greater attention has also been paid to sustainability issues in the context of the Eastern Partnership. At the December 15, 2021 EaP summit—strongly influenced by increasing tensions between Ukraine and Russia (Hart, 2021)—partners expressed their intention to accelerate the energy transition process to reduce the carbon footprint and further strengthen inclusive sustainable development in the energy sector in line with European Energy Union strategy.[51] It is hoped that, by also offering Eastern countries financial support, the EU can encourage them to modify their energy systems in a logic of sustainability and security.

As for cooperation between the EU and the Gulf States, Article 6 of the 1989 Cooperation Agreement between the European Community and the Gulf

Cooperation Council[52] establishes (very weak) cooperation in the energy sector.[53] In the years following September 11, relations between the EU and the Gulf States became increasingly complex and fraught (Cristiani, 2021, p. 321 ff.). At the same time, an attempt to gradually reduce EU dependence on oil and petroleum, in conjunction with the willingness of EU member states (United Kingdom/UK, France and Germany) to maintain bilateral relationships with the principal oil-producing countries (Saudi Arabia, Yemen, and the United Arab Emirates), which depend on EU countries' supply of weapons and military technologies, weakened EU interest in strengthening energy cooperation in the Gulf area.

B. Provisions to Strengthen Cooperation with Developed Countries in the Energy Sector

As the Treaty of Lisbon extended the scope of EU commercial policy,[54] the European Commission began negotiations with numerous trading powers (Canada, US, Japan, China), taking European Commercial Policy in new directions. The goal was to lower or eliminate tariff barriers and draw up better rules in sectors already covered by World Trade Organization agreements[55] and in sectors not governed by other multilateral agreements (competition, State-owned enterprises, investments, sustainable development, regulatory cooperation). Given their overall approach, they are referred to as "comprehensive." These too contain provisions concerning energy.

The energy provisions are set out in chapter 24, "Trade and environment," of the EU-Canada Comprehensive Economic and Trade Agreement (CETA), signed in 2016 and provisionally in force.[56] More specifically, Article 24.9 requires the Parties to facilitate the removal of obstacles to trade or investment in goods and services of particular relevance for mitigating climate change and, in particular, trade or investment in renewable energy goods and related services. In Article 24.12, the Parties commit to cooperate on trade-related environmental issues of common interest in areas such as "trade-related aspects of (…) carbon markets, (…) as well as means to promote energy efficiency and the development and deployment of low-carbon and other climate-friendly technologies" and "trade and investment in environmental goods and services, including (…) renewable energy (and) energy efficiency." In synergy with the CETA perspective, where energy issues are part of a broader environmental protection framework, at COP 26 in Glasgow, both the EU and Canada strongly committed to the Paris agreement reform of November 13, 2021.[57]

In the EU-Japan Economic Partnership of 2018,[58] references to the energy sector are principally found in the provisions concerning sustainable development.[59] Nevertheless, "energy security" is mentioned in the areas where the Parties' "right to regulate" is safeguarded.[60] In reality, Japan has gradually reduced its sensitivity to sustainable energy issues. Indeed, although it led the negotiations for reducing greenhouse gas emissions, ending with the signing of the Kyoto Protocol in 1997,[61] it became coal-dependent after the 2011 Fukushima disaster and is now less engaged in sustainable energy. Indeed, during COP 26, it refused to sign the "Global Coal to Clean Power Transition Statement,"[62] which calls for advanced economies to end the use of coal-fired plants by the 2030s and the rest of the world to do so by the 2040s. It is hoped that the EU can convince Japan to redirect its energy system toward renewable sources.[63]

Commitment to promoting and facilitating investment to mitigate climate change and promote renewable energy, low-carbon technologies, and energy-efficient products and services also features in the EU-China Comprehensive Agreement on Investment (CAI) signed on December 30, 2020.[64] In light of China's unexpected commitment to fighting climate change during COP 26,[65] it may be hoped that it is working hard to modernize its energy system.

Lastly, regarding the EU's relationship with the US, after the Transatlantic Trade and Investment Partnership (TTIP) negotiations floundered,[66] energy cooperation has continued thanks to the US-EU Energy Council, established in 2009, mainly in the context of de-carbonizing the energy sector, energy security, and sustainable energy supply chains.[67]

C. Provisions to Stimulate Cooperation with Emerging Countries in the Energy Sector

After the Treaty of Lisbon came into force, the EU began negotiations with several emerging countries and stipulated agreements with South Korea (KOREU)[68] (2011), the Philippines[69] (2012), and, more recently, Singapore[70] (2018) and Vietnam[71] (2019).[72] Even if the consumption of traditional energy sources (in particular coal, petroleum, oil, and natural gas) continues to be exceptionally high in these countries and, especially in southern Asia, coal-fired production has been expanding, several countries have opened up their systems to renewable sources of energy (International Energy Agency, 2020). The EU tries to help these countries make their energy systems sustainable through energy cooperation.

Little attention was paid to the energy sector in the earliest agreements. More specifically, "sustainable renewable energy" and "energy-efficient products and services" are mentioned in Article 13, KOREU § 2, concerning "Trade favouring sustainable development."[73] Under Article 33 of the Agreement with the Philippines, the Parties endeavor to enhance cooperation in the energy sector, promoting sustainability, efficiency, and security in particular.

In the more recent agreements, however, provisions regarding energy have become more specific and far-reaching. Indeed, in the 2018 EU-Singapore and the 2019 EU-Vietnam FTAs, a specific chapter (Chapter 7) is devoted to "Non-Tariff

Barriers to Trade and Investment in Renewable Energy Generation," aiming to promote, develop, and increase energy production from renewable and sustainable non-fossil sources by facilitating trade and investment in particular (Cima, 2018, p. 672).[74] The "right to regulate" or "the measures necessary for the safe operation of the energy networks concerned, or the safety of the energy supply" is assured as long as these measures are "subject to the requirement that those measures are not applied in a manner which would constitute a means of arbitrary or unjustifiable discrimination between the Parties' products, service suppliers or investors under like circumstances, or a disguised restriction on trade and investment between the Parties."[75] In the chapter concerning the "Trade and sustainable development,"[76] the Parties commit above all to facilitating "climate-friendly goods and services," such as "sustainable renewable energy goods and related services," in addition to "energy-efficient products and services."

Despite these commitments, during COP 26, many emerging countries (such as Vietnam) claimed that the more prosperous countries ought to complete their de-carbonization process during the coming decade to allow emerging economies (whose impact on climate change is said to be limited) to carry out their energy transition more slowly in a logic of "solidarity." This means that the EU member states need to accelerate the Green Deal reforming their domestic energy production, storage, and consumption methods. This would compensate for the delay with which emerging countries can achieve their sustainability objectives.

It may be concluded from the proposed analysis that bilateral agreements complement the EU's internal regulation in pursuing the objectives of energy security, sustainability, and solidarity and in bringing about the European energy transition. The EU uses its bilateral instruments in an attempt to export its energy regulation pattern beyond its borders to create a model of energy sector discipline that could act as an example for shared rules at the multilateral level.

EU ENERGY POLICY AND BREXIT, BETWEEN ENERGY SECURITY AND MARKET EFFECTIVENESS

Regarding its energy requirements, the United Kingdom (UK) has always depended on the gas supply coming from the Eastern countries and passing through continental Europe.[77] This means that Brexit has exposed the UK to more significant energy-security risks than the EU. Nevertheless, thanks to the UK's prominent position in the Gulf due to its historical role in the area and its solid mutual economic and financial relationships (Cristiani, 2021, p. 327 ff.), an independent UK could significantly undermine the EU's contractual power in the area.

Given the shared interest in maintaining cooperation in the energy sector, the EU-UK TCA signed on December 30, 2021[78] includes a Title VIII ("Energy") "to facilitate trade and investment between the Parties in the areas of energy and raw materials, and to support the security of supply and environmental sustainability, notably in contributing to the fight against climate change in those areas." More specifically, regarding electricity and gas, each Party will ensure that its regulatory framework is non-discriminatory and that prices reflect actual supply and demand, prohibiting market abuse (Articles 305–308). Furthermore, each Party is required to ensure the designation and maintenance of an "operationally independent regulatory authority or authorities for electricity and gas" to fix or approve tariffs, charges, and conditions for access to networks.

As for trading over interconnectors, each Party will ensure that their management is "market-based, transparent, and non-discriminatory" to ensure their efficient use and reduce barriers to trade between the EU and the UK.[79]

To guarantee the security of supplies, the Parties "will cooperate to facilitate the timely development and interoperability of energy infrastructure connecting their territories" and will draw up plans for risk assessment, management, and mitigation (Article 316), by promoting the energy efficiency, the use of energy from renewable sources, and offshore renewable energy, by sharing best practices and, where appropriate, by facilitating the development of specific projects. Lastly, specific rules for export pricing, regulated pricing, and the exploration and production of hydrocarbons have been established.

Highly detailed provisions on energy are devoted explicitly to guaranteeing an energy supply sufficient to adequately satisfy the needs of the UK's people and farms. Even if the Parties maintain the right to autonomously regulate the energy sector (Article 302) as far as their strategic choices relating to energy production and consumption are concerned, they still appear to be highly interdependent and interconnected and can undoubtedly exert mutual influence.

Due to growing demand and difficulties, including interrupted supplies following the COVID-19 emergency and of the Russia-Ukraine conflict, both the EU and the UK are experiencing significant increases in energy prices, causing severe problems for citizens and businesses. Consequently, cooperation and risk-preparedness are vital to avoid the UK system collapsing. From this perspective, energy could become the principal field for testing the effectiveness and good-functioning of TCA and its specialized committee network.[80]

MACRO-REGIONAL AND MULTILATERAL ENERGY TREATIES: TOWARD INTERNATIONAL ENERGY REGULATION?

As already mentioned, the EC has always played an important role in driving elaboration of multilateral energy treaties at the regional and global levels.

At the regional level, the Treaty establishing Euratom sought to tackle the general shortage of "conventional" energy (coal) in the fifties, to achieve energy independence and share the costs of investing in nuclear energy. Euratom aimed to raise the standard of living in the Member States and develop relations with other countries by creating the conditions necessary for the speedy establishment and growth of nuclear industries. It works to promote research and disseminate technical information, set uniform safety standards to protect the public and industry workers, facilitate investment, and establish the basic installations necessary for developing nuclear energy in the EU (Cenevska, 2012; Mathijsen, 1966). The Treaty established an Agency with an exclusive right to conclude contracts relating to the supply of ores, source materials, and fissile materials originating inside or outside the Community. Euratom's importance emerged specifically in the context of 2004 enlargement. As nuclear power was an important energy source for many eastern European countries, but their safety standards were much lower, the EC pursued a harmonized Community approach to nuclear energy, with which candidate countries must comply. In this context, the Commission has supported them through the PHARE programme.[81] Since the collapse of the Soviet Union, many of the Newly Independent States (NIS) have received aid from the Commission to modernize their nuclear systems. More recently, due to renewed interest in nuclear energy, boosted by concerns over supply security and climate change, Euratom's role in guiding the development of EU nuclear industries and establishing safety and security standards is expected to become crucial once more (Engstedt, 2021; Södersten, 2018).

Among the regional initiatives, mention should also be made of the European Energy Community (EnC),[82] an international organization established in 2005 between the EU and several Southeast European States[83] to create an integrated pan-European energy market. The EnC's most important activities involve implementing the *acquis communautaire* on energy, environment, competition, and renewable energies in all the States Parties, as well as compliance with specific general European standards relating to technical systems. In addition, the Treaty sets up a mechanism to react to any sudden crisis on the network energy market in the territory of an EnC Member. Furthermore, the Treaty creates an energy market without internal borders between the Parties. Parties my not apply customs duties, quantitative energy import and export restrictions, or any measures with an equivalent effect. The Treaty also contains provisions on relations with third countries and mutual assistance in the event of disturbance.[84] The Treaty envisages a political/diplomatic dispute settlement mechanism in which the final decision is the prerogative of the Ministerial Council. However, its effectiveness is undermined by the absence of sanctions, except for the freezing of voting rights (Verhagen, 2019, p. 156 ff.).

Whereas Euratom is a regional organization, open to the EU member states and aimed at complementing EU energy competencies with specific interventions in the atomic sector, the EnC is a "macro-regional" body, extending EU energy regulation to southeastern non-EU neighbors. Through its EnC initiative, the EU is trying to extend "general integration dynamics beyond its borders" (Göler & Kurze, 2020, p. 321 ff.) and gain leadership of the European energy macro-region in an effort not only to strengthen energy security but also to affirm the principle of energy solidarity on the European continent.

On the multinational plane, the EC was the first promoter of the ECT. The process leading to this Treaty began with the European Energy Charter, signed in December 1991 by 50 States, including most of the newly independent Republics born from the dissolution of the USSR, for which it was the first independent act on the international stage. It was essentially an instrument to promote openness and the liberalization of the previous Soviet Bloc (Jones, 1992). The Charter was not legally binding, being essentially a political commitment and a declaration of intent. However, the establishment of the European Energy Charter Conference and the organization of regular negotiation sessions favored adhesion, in December 1994, to the European Energy Charter Treaty ("the Treaty"),[85] a legal framework aiming to promote long-term cooperation in the field of energy, grounded in complementarities and mutual benefits. It pursued two objectives: to develop an open and competitive market for energy materials and products and to promote and protect investments. This Treaty too paid only scarce attention to sustainable development and the environment (Layard, 1995, p. 151 ff.; Mauro, 2021, p. 309), but it focused in particular on protecting investments, establishing specific treatment standards[86] and offering a mechanism of State-investor dispute settlement resolution (ISDS) based on ICSID rules and devoted to protecting investors' interests (Article 26 ECT). In reality, in the first years that the ECT was in force, very few disputes were submitted to the ECTS ISDS mechanism. This was essentially due to the structure of the energy sector at the time, characterized as it was by state-owned monopolies regularly conducting businesses with each other and, consequently, more likely to manage disputes without recourse to litigation (Wälde & Hobér, 2005, p. 83 ff.).

Nevertheless, given the high number of Western States adhering to the Treaty, from a merely West-Eastern investment treaty, it gradually became even a "West-West common investment regime" (Wälde, 1995, p. 6). At that time, the ECT signatories were growing,[87] and the 2015 International Energy Charter, a declaration of political intent also involving non-ECT Parties such as the US and China (but not Russia),[88] gave new life to the ECT process. At the same time, the proliferation of investments in the energy sector increased the number of disputes and the interventions of the ISDS mechanism, also in connection with intra-EU investments. More recently, the EU has been incentivizing the modernization of the ECT in order to better balance the interests of investors and protect the States' right to regulation, also strengthening sustainability to contrast climate change, excluding investment in fossil sources from the application of the ECT investment protection rules[89] (Mauro, 2021, p. 322 ff.). The *Moldova v. Komstroy* judgment,[90] handed down by the ECJ on September 2, 2021, excluding the possibility to submit intra-EU disputes to the ECT ISDS mechanism, did not reduce EU interest in ECT reform.[91] On June 30, 2022, the negotiation was concluded with the adoption of the "Agreement in principle reached on Modernised Energy Charter Treaty." The final text will be released in August 2022, and the proposal will be voted on by the Conference in November 2022.

As the ECT represents the most important locus of multilateral energy cooperation up to now and constitutes the most important forum of dialogue between both West-West and West-Eastern countries regarding the energy sector, the EU has to continue to play a pivotal role in its own modernization and effectiveness.

THE EU REACTION TO THE RUSSIA-UKRAINE CRISIS EFFECT ON ENERGY SECTOR: TOWARD A MORE INDEPENDENT AND RESILIENT EU ENERGY SYSTEM

After that, on February 24, 2022, Russia attacked Ukraine, the EU member states' necessity of overcoming the dependence from Russian energy sources, especially gas, became compelling. In this perspective, on March 8, 2022 the European Commission adopted the Communication "REPowerEU: Joint European Action for more affordable, secure and sustainable energy."[92] Noticing that, "after the invasion of Ukraine by Russia, the case for a rapid clean energy transition has never been stronger and clearer," the Commission is pursuing the objective of reaching independence from Russian gas well before the end of the decade. To this aim, the EU has to become able "to diversify its supply, accelerate the roll out of green energy technologies, and reduce its demand of energy."

In this perspective, on March 23 the European Commission adopted the Communication "Security of supply and affordable energy prices: Options for immediate measures and preparing for next winter"[93] that, beside presenting some short-term options to temper price spikes,[94] proposes collective European actions "to address the root causes of the problem in the gas market with a view to ensure security of supply at reasonable prices for next winter and beyond." More specifically, putting in evidence that the price dynamics are strongly conditioned by the interconnections between the energy sources,[95] the European Commission proposes a common strategy based on two instruments: Task Force for common gas purchasing and the proposal of regulation on energy storage.

As it concerns the Task Force, it has the aim to pull the demand, facilitating and strengthening EU's international outreach to suppliers of liquified natural gas (LNG) and of natural gas in order to secure well-priced LNG and gas imports ahead of next winter. The principal aim of the Task Force is managing energy long-term partnerships with key suppliers of LNG, gas and hydrogen in the Mediterranean region, with EU partners in Africa, but also the Middle East and USA as a means to obtain better prices also in short term. The Task Force is also charged with promoting the efficient usage of EU's gas infrastructure, notably LNG terminals, storage facilities and pipelines. The Task Force would be supported by Member States representatives in a Steering Board. A joint negotiation team led by the Commission would hold talks with gas suppliers.

As it concerns gas storage, taking into account its relevance of the gas storage for security of supply,[96] the Regulation 2022/1032[97] has been adopted amending Regulation (EU) 2017/1938 concerning measures to safeguard the security of gas supply[98] and Regulation (EU) 715/2009 on conditions for access to natural gas transmission networks,[99] establishing a mandatory minimum level of gas in storage facilities reinforcing the security of supply ahead of the winter 2022/2023 and for the following winter periods. More specifically, the existing storage infrastructure will be filled up to at least 90 % of their capacity by November of each year (so-called filling target) and a "filling trajectory" system shall enable continuous monitoring throughout the filling season (from April 1 to September 30). The regulation describes a very articulated mechanism aimed to assure that the European Commission could be constantly informed on deviations from the national filling trajectories and could take measures to avoid problems coming from unfilled storage.[100]

To comply with the principle of energy solidarity, the proposal establishes burden sharing mechanism where a Member States without storage should contribute to the storage filling levels in other Member States and in exchange benefit from enhanced security of supply. The mechanism is aimed to ensure a fair allocation of security of supply costs among all Member States as they all benefit, thanks to the EU energy market, from lowering the risks of supply disruption regardless of where storage is located in the EU. This mechanism builds on the solidarity agreements which should be concluded without delay to allow that gas be shared effectively in case of an emergency. Equally important is transparency and monitoring of the progress toward reaching the filling target. The Gas Coordination group is charged with applying the mechanism.[101]

Finally, in the RePower EU strategy a relevant role is played by the mechanisms of investment screening. Indeed, as storage facilities are considered critical infrastructure within the meaning of Council Directive 2008/114/EC on the identification and designation of European critical infrastructures,[102] a specific mechanism of investment screening is established. More specifically, Member

States should ensure that each storage system operator, including such operators controlled by transmission system operators, is certified by the regulatory authority or another competent authority designated by the Member State to ensure that the influence over storage system operators does not put at risk the security of energy supply or any other essential security interest in the Union or any Member State.

Regulatory authorities should refuse the certification if a person who directly or indirectly controls or exercises any right over the storage system operator may put at risk the security of energy supply or any other essential security interest Member State, regional or Union level. In this assessment the regulatory authorities should take into account commercial relationships that could negatively affect the incentives and ability of the storage operator to fill the storage facility, as well as the international obligations of the Union and any other specific facts and circumstances of the case. To ensure the consistent application of those rules across the Union, respect for the international obligations of the Union, and solidarity and energy security within the Union, the regulatory authorities should take into utmost account the Commission's opinion when they take decisions on certification. Where a regulatory authority refuses the certification, it should have the power to require any person to dispose of the shareholding or rights they have over the storage system operator and to set a time limit for such disposal, to order any other appropriate measure to ensure that that person or those persons cannot exercise any control or right over that storage system operator, and to decide on appropriate compensatory measures. Any measure taken in the certification decision to address security of supply risks or other essential security interests should be necessary, clearly defined, transparent, proportionate and non-discriminatory.

To further strengthen the relevance of foreign investment screening as an important tool in the EU strategy to react to the effects of Russia-Ukraine crisis, on April 6, 2022 the European Commission adopted the Communication from the Guidance to the Member States concerning foreign direct investment from Russia and Belarus in view of the military aggression against Ukraine,[103] where it put in evidence that Russia's military aggression against Ukraine calls for greater vigilance toward Russian and Belarusian direct investments within the Single Market. Indeed, there is a heightened risk that any investment directly or indirectly related to a person or entity associated with, controlled by or subject to influence by the Russian or Belarusian government into critical assets in the EU may give reasonable grounds to conclude that the investment may pose a threat to security or public order in Member States. To this end, the European Commission calls upon Member States to systematically use their screening mechanisms to assess and prevent the threats related to Russian and Belarusian investments on grounds of security and public order; ensure close cooperation between national authorities competent for sanctions ("NCAs") and those competent for the screening of investments in the context of implementing EU sanctions, as well as to identify breaches and imposing penalties; implement fully the FDI Screening Regulation.[104]

On May 18, 2022, the European Commission has presented the REPowerEU Plan, establishing measures of energy savings,[105] accelerating the rollout of renewables[106] and diversifying supplies through the EU Energy Platform, enabling voluntary common purchases of gas, LNG and hydrogen by pooling demand, optimizing infrastructure use and coordinating outreach to suppliers, as well as through the development of a "joint purchasing mechanism" which will negotiate and contract gas purchases on behalf of participating Member States. At the same time, the European Commission launches the EU External Energy Strategy, aimed at facilitating energy diversification and building long-term partnerships with suppliers, including cooperation on hydrogen or other green technologies. More specifically, in the Mediterranean and North Sea, major hydrogen corridors will be developed. In the face of Russia's aggression, the EU will support Moldova, the Western Balkans, the Eastern Partnership countries, and especially the Ukraine, with which the EU will continue to work together to ensure security of supply and a functioning energy sector, while paving the way for future electricity and renewable hydrogen trade, as well as rebuilding the energy system under the REPower Ukraine initiative.[107] Finally, amendments to the Recovery and Resilience Facility Regulation are proposed to sustain smart investments in the energy sector.[108] On May 18, 2022, the Commission adopted the RePower Plan that "puts forward an additional set of actions to: save energy; ·diversify supplies; ·quickly substitute fossil fuels by accelerating Europe's clean energy transition; ·smartly combine investments and reforms."[109]

As already happened in reaction to the pandemic, EU institutions and member states, putting aside unilateral initiatives and interests, are working jointly to overcome the energy crisis with a common strategy, common instruments, and also common sacrifices and renounces, toward the creation of an effective and cohesive Energy Union (Pugliese, 2022).

CONCLUSION

Although the EU efforts to strengthen its role within the international regulatory energy sector, some issues concerning its institutional and regulatory framework could undermine its ability to play a pivotal role in stimulating the elaboration of multilateral treaties on energy. Firstly, the energy sector is a shared competence, where Member States' unilateral choices maintain a significant weight. Secondly, even if the Article 194 TFEU establishes that decisions should be taken according to ordinary legislative procedure, in the Article 218 TFEU, disciplining the procedure of stipulation of agreements with third States, the European Parliament plays a secondary role. Indeed, it is fully excluded from the decisions authorizing to starting negotiations and from the decision to sign the agreements, intervening only in the phase of conclusions. This asset of competences limits the legitimacy, transparency, and democracy of negotiations, often making the reached agreements very distant from the exigencies of families and businesses. Thirdly, European Commission independence in pursuing the EU interest is often restrained by the Council, conditioned by the contingent needs of the Member States.

The COVID-19 crisis and the Russia-Ukraine conflict urged to rethink the European energy system toward a more consistent and effective governance model. During the pandemic, overpassing unilateralism and unifying the efforts revealed itself a very effective method to collect prompt and proper the material and financial resources necessary to exit the emergency.[110] The efforts of RePower EU to coordinate the decisions both in terms of producing, purchasing, storing, and sharing the energy resources at regional and macro-regional level go in the same direction and it is hoping that they could gain the same results. In the same perspective, strengthening the control on foreign investments pursues the objective not only to protect the EU infrastructures ownership and management from foreign interferences, but also to maintain a strict control on supply chain and avoid distortions coming from unilateral choices that Member States could make for mere national contingent interest, that could appear desegregating and not farsighted also from a geopolitical point of view.

Nevertheless, all these efforts could be not sufficient to reinforce the EU energy role at regional, macro-regional, and multilateral level without a deep reform of the institutional framework and decision—making in a perspective of legitimacy, transparency, and democracy. Only reinforcing the accountability of the European Commission as a reform driver and the power of the European Parliament, it will be possible to make the EU action really incisive inside and outside its border. At the same time, it is necessary to strengthen the action at multilateral level. From this point of view, the EU should assume a pivotal role in realizing the ECT reform and to avoid the EnC paralysis due to the Russia-Ukraine conflict. In this perspective, the effect of the reflection and proposals emerged during the Conference on the Future of Europe, which closed its work on May 9, 2022, on the creation of a Union of energy could be the interesting objective of further analysis.

NOTES

1 The Treaty was signed in Paris on April 18, 1951 and came into force on July 23, 1952. It had a fifty-year duration. Upon expiration in 2002, the Member States opted to transfer ECSC competencies to the EC.

2 The Treaty was signed on March 25, 1957 together with the Treaty establishing the European Economic Community (TEEC), entering into force on January 1, 1958.

3 Articles 9–37 TEEC. On the acknowledgment of energy as a good, see ECJ judgment of July 15, 1964, case 6/64, *Costa v. Enel*; July 10, 1984, case 72/83, *Campus Oil Limited and others v Minister for Industry and Energy and others*, point 12 ff.; April 27, 1994, case C-393/92, *Municipality of Almelo and others v NV Energiebedrijf Ijsselmij*, point 27 ff.

4 Commodities are basic goods with standard characteristics; they are exactly the same, regardless of where they are bought. Consequently, their price is determined essentially on the basis of their availability (the greater their scarcity, the more value they acquire). They differ from other rare goods (e.g., luxury goods such as diamonds or works of art) as they are indispensable for the production of other goods. Furthermore, it becomes problematic to separate goods and services when commodities are intangible, like energy. Infrastructures that produce, transport, store, and use intangible commodities are therefore considered essential facilities, access to which is indispensable to all the operators that need them for their activities. Commodities and their infrastructures thus need specific regulation to ensure availability, access, and price control.

5 "Trading" is the activity of selling and buying stocks and shares on the financial market.

6 Signed on June 4, 1992 and in force from March 21, 1994, the Convention sought to stabilize the concentration of greenhouse gases in the atmosphere. The treaty called for ongoing scientific negotiations and future policy agreements to enable sustainable economic development. It was implemented through the Kyoto Protocol, signed on December 11, 1997, coming into force on February 16, 2005. The Parties committed to reducing greenhouse gas emissions by at least 5 % from 1990 levels between 2008 and 2012. The Kyoto Protocol was initially scheduled to expire on December 31, 2012, but it was amended to extend to December 31, 2020. The amendments came into force in the same day as the original expiration date, but the Paris Agreement then replaced the Kyoto Protocol. Signed on December 12, 2015 and coming into force on November 4, 2016, the Paris Agreement aimed to reduce global greenhouse gas emissions to limit the global temperature increase this century to 2°C while pursuing efforts to limit the increase even further to 1.5 degrees. All Parties were to submit their plans for climate action known as nationally determined contributions (NDCs) by 2020, substituting the Kyoto engagements.

7 See Council Directive 68/414/EEC of December 20, 1968 imposing an obligation on Member States of the EEC to maintain minimum stocks of crude oil and/or petroleum products and Council Directive 72/425/EEC of December 19, 1972 amending the Council Directive of December 20, 1968 imposing an obligation on Member States of the EEC to maintain minimum stocks of crude oil and/or petroleum products.

8 The question of energy also featured in Title XVII concerning Trans-European Networks (Article 129 B) and Title XVI "Environment" (Article 130S, § 2).

9 Directive 96/92/EC of the European Parliament and of the Council of December 19, 1996 concerning common rules for the internal market in electricity, and Directive 98/30/EC of the European Parliament and of the Council of June 22, 1998 concerning common rules for the internal natural gas market ("first energy package") based on articles 57, § 2 (free movement of services), 66 (right of establishment) and 100 A (legislative rapprochement) TEC; Directive 2003/54/EC of the European Parliament and of the Council of June 26, 2003 concerning common rules for the internal market in electricity, repealing Directive 96/92/EC and Directive 2003/55/EC of the European Parliament and of the Council of June 26, 2003 concerning

common rules for the internal market in natural gas, repealing Directive 98/30/EC ("second energy package"), based on articles 47,§ 2, (free movement of services), 55 (right of establishment) and 95 TEC (legislative rapprochement) according to the 1996 Treaty of Amsterdam.

10 The EU ETS was established by Directive 2003/87/EC of the European Parliament and of the Council of October 13, 2003 establishing a scheme for greenhouse gas emission allowance trading within the Community. It is based on a "cap-and-trade" approach: the EU sets a cap on how much greenhouse gas pollution can be emitted each year, and companies need to hold a European Emission Allowance (EUA) for every metric ton of CO_2 they emit within one calendar year. They receive or buy these permits—and can trade them. The EU ETS is for CO_2 emissions from power stations, energy-intensive industries (e.g., oil refineries, steelworks, and producers of iron, aluminum, cement, paper, and glass) and civil aviation. Companies face a fine of 100 euro if they emit more CO_2 than their emission allowances permit. Conversely, they have an incentive to reduce emissions by investing in energy efficiency because they can then sell excess allowance.

11 More specifically, with Council Directive 2004/67/EC of April 26, 2004 concerning measures to safeguard the security of the natural gas supply, the European Community sought to establish genuine solidarity between the Member States in the event of major emergency supply emergencies, all the more so as Member States became increasingly interdependent in terms of supply security and ensuring an adequate level gas supply, in particular in the event of a major supply disruption. The Directive was based on Article 100 TEC, which established that the Council can decide on the measures best suited to the economic situation, in particular if severe difficulties arise in supplying of specific products. See also Directive 2005/89/EC of the European Parliament and of the Council of January 18, 2006 concerning measures to safeguard the security of electricity supply and infrastructure investment, based on the Article 95 TEC.

12 Directive 2009/72/EC of the European Parliament and of the Council of July 13, 2009 concerning common rules for the internal electricity market and repealing Directive 2003/54/EC; Directive 2009/73/EC of the European Parliament and of the Council of July 13, 2009 concerning common rules for the internal natural gas market and repealing Directive 2003/55/EC. See also Regulation (EC) No 714/2009 of the European Parliament and of the Council of July 13, 2009 on conditions for access to the network for cross-border exchanges in electricity and repealing Regulation (EC) No 1228/2003 and Regulation (EC) N. 715/2009 of the European Parliament and of the Council of July 13, 2009 on conditions for access to the natural gas transmission networks, based on Article 95 TEC and modified by Commission Decision 2012/490/EU of August 24, 2012 ("third energy package").

13 Regulation (EC) No 713/2009 of the European Parliament and of the Council of July 13, 2009 establishing an Agency for the Cooperation of Energy Regulators (based on 95 TEC), Articles 7, 8, and 9.

14 The European Parliament and the Council, acting in accordance with ordinary legislative procedure and after consulting the Economic and Social Committee and the Committee of the Regions, must take measures to achieve these objectives. These must not affect a Member State's right to determine how it employs its energy resources, its choice of energy sources, and the overall structure of its energy supply. When these measures are primarily of a fiscal nature, the Council has to reach a unanimous decision after consulting the European Parliament. These provisions, clearly aiming to respect the Member States' autonomy regarding strategic decisions concerning the energy sector, must be read in parallel with Article 192, § 2 letter c), which states that environmental measures significantly affecting a Member State's choice

between different energy sources and the overall structure of its energy supply have to be taken unanimously (Amadeo, 2014, p. 1639).

15 Article 122 TFUE modified Article 100 TEC mentioned in note 6.

16 See *supra*, note 6.

17 European Council, *Conclusions*, October 23 and 24, 2014, p. 2 ff.

18 Decision (EU) 2015/1814 of the European Parliament and of the Council of October 6, 2015 concerning the establishment and operation of a market stability reserve for the Union greenhouse gas emission trading scheme and amending Directive 2003/87/EC established a market stability reserve to enhance synergies between the ETS and other climate and energy actions (see recital 5). Both acts were further emended by Directive (EU) 2018/410 of the European Parliament and of the Council of March 14, 2018.

19 Directive (EU) 2018/844 of the European Parliament and of the Council of May 30, 2018 amending Directive 2010/31/EU on the energy performance of buildings and Directive 2012/27/EU on energy efficiency; Directive (EU) 2018/2001 of the European Parliament and of the Council of December 11, 2018 on the promotion of the use of energy from renewable sources; Directive (EU) 2018/2002 of the European Parliament and of the Council of December 11, 2018 amending Directive 2012/27/EU on energy efficiency; Regulation (EU) 2018/1999 of the European Parliament and of the Council of December 11, 2018 on the Governance of the Energy Union and Climate Action; Regulation (EU) 2019/941 of the European Parliament and of the Council of June 5, 2019 on risk-preparedness in the electricity sector and repealing Directive 2005/89/EC; Regulation (EU) 2019/942 of the European Parliament and of the Council of June 5, 2019 establishing a European Union Agency for the Cooperation of Energy Regulators; Regulation (EU) 2019/943 of the European Parliament and of the Council of June 5, 2019 on the internal market for electricity; Directive (EU) 2019/944 of the European Parliament and of the Council of June 5, 2019 on common rules for the internal market for electricity. The package reflected the "European Climate Law," Regulation (EU) 2021/1119 of the European Parliament and of the Council of June 30, 2021 establishing the framework for achieving climate neutrality and amending Regulations (EC) No 401/2009 and (EU) 2018/1999 ("European Climate Law"), aiming to set out a binding objective of climate neutrality in the Union by 2050 in pursuit of the long-term temperature goal established by the Paris Agreement.

20 See Directive 2018/1999, Article 43,§ 2, letter a).

21 See General Court judgment of September 10, 2019, T-883/16, *Republic of Poland v. Commission*, point 69. According to point 70, due its linkage with the principle of sincere cooperation, the General Court argues that the principle of solidarity "entails rights and obligations both for the European Union and for the Member States. On the one hand, the European Union is bound by an obligation of solidarity towards the Member States and, on the other hand, the Member States are bound by an obligation of solidarity between themselves and with regard to the common interest of the European Union and the policies pursued by it." The judgment is particularly important in the energy sector as it concerns the action presented by Poland for the annulment of Decision C(2016) 6950 final of the Commission adopted, on the basis of Article 36(9) of Directive 2009/73, on review of the exemption of the Ostseepipeline-Anbindungsleitung (OPAL) pipeline from the requirements on third-party access and tariff regulation granted under Directive 2003/55, addressed to the BNetzA, the German national regulatory authority. OPAL is the terrestrial section, to the west, of the Nord Stream 1 gas pipeline, whose point of entry is located close to Lubmin, near Greifswald in Germany, but the

point of exit is in Brandov in the Czech Republic. The two decisions concerned the respective shares held by the two owners of the OPAL pipeline. The Opal pipeline is owned by WIGA Transport Beteiligungs-GmbH & Co. ("WIGA," previously W & G Beteiligungs-GmbH & Co. KG, previously Wingas GmbH & Co. KG), which holds an 80 % share of the pipeline, and E.ON Ruhrgas AG, which owns a 20 % share. WIGA is jointly controlled by OAO Gazprom and BASF SE. The company operating the share of the OPAL pipeline belonging to WIGA is OPAL Gastransport GmbH & Co. KG ("OGT"). Nord Stream is a twin pipeline system running, through the Baltic Sea, from Vyborg, Russia to Lubmin near Greifswald, Germany. The pipelines were built and are operated by Nord Stream AG. The Nord Stream route crosses the Exclusive Economic Zones of Russia, Finland, Sweden, Denmark and Germany, as well as the territorial waters of Russia, Denmark, and Germany. The two 1,224-kilometre offshore pipelines are the most direct connection between the vast gas reserves in Russia and energy markets in the European Union. As the project strengthens the EU energy market and reinforces supply security, the project has been designated as being of "European interest" by the European Parliament and Council.

22 According to points 71–72 these are "obligations of mutual assistance in the event that, following for example natural disasters or acts of terrorism, a Member State is in a critical or emergency situation as regards its gas supply." The reference is to the Regulation No 994/2010 (replaced by Regulation (EU) 2017/1938 of the European Parliament and of the Council of October 25, 2017 concerning measures to safeguard the security of gas supply and repealing Regulation No. 994/2010. More specifically, the energy policy "requires the European Union and the Member States to endeavour, in the exercise of their powers in the field of energy policy, to avoid adopting measures liable to affect the interests of the European Union and the other Member States, as regards security of supply, its economic and political viability, the diversification of supply or of sources of supply, and to do so in order to take account of their interdependence and de facto solidarity" (point 73).

23 Court of Justice judgment of July 15, 2021, C-848/19, *Federal Republic of Germany v. European Commission*, points 38 ff.

24 The package is composed of COM (2021) "Fit for 55": delivering the EU's 2030 Climate Target on the way to climate neutrality COM (2021) 550 final and 16 proposals. See https://ec.europa.eu/info/strategy/priorities-2019-2024/european-green-deal/delivering-european-green-deal_en (Hancher & Talus, 2022; Huhta, 2022; Jones & Piebalgs, 2022; Penttinen et al., 2022). The most innovative proposal concerns the introduction of the "carbon border adjustment mechanism," introducing a levy on imports of certain basic materials, based on the CO_2 emissions embedded in these materials. The measure seeks to disincentivize carbon and compensate for the ETS (Schippers & De Wit, 2022, p. 10 ff.).

25 The reference is to the "just transition" promoted by President of the European Commission Ursula von der Leyen to achieve the European energy, environmental, and digital transition without unduly damaging undertakings and weak social groups. See Ursula von der Leyen, *A Union that strives for more. My agenda for Europe, Political Guidelines for the Next European Commission 2019–2024*, July 16, 2019; *Speech in the European Parliament Plenary Session as delivered Ursula von der Leyen President-elect of the European Commission Strasbourg*, November 27, 2019; Brussels, COM(2019) 640 final of December 11, 2019, *The European Green Deal.*

26 See the Global Methane Pledge, an initiative launched by the US and EU to reduce global methane emissions. See the EU Catalyst partnership, launched with the European Investment Bank and the Breakthrough Energy Association to accelerate deployment and rapidly commercialize innovative technologies mainly in the clean hydrogen sector.

27 See the Reuters news coverage in early 2022, when energy prices soared: Abnett, J. (2022, January 1). *EU drafts plan to label gas and nuclear investments as green*. Reuters; De Luna, C. (2022, January 6). *Gas gap in Europe drives U.S. LNG exports to record high*. Reuters.

28 COM (2021) 660 final of October 13, 2021, *Tackling rising energy prices: A toolbox for action and support*, where the European Commission envisaged several immediate measures to protect consumers and businesses (such as providing emergency income support for energy-deprived consumers; authorizing temporary deferrals of bill payments and temporary reductions in taxation rates for vulnerable households; providing aid to companies or industries, in line with EU state aid rules; facilitating wider access to renewable power purchase agreements, supporting them via flanking measures) and some medium-term measures for a decarbonized and resilient energy system (such as stepping up investments in renewables, renovations and energy efficiency and speeding up renewables auctions and permit processes, develop energy storage capacity to support the evolving renewables share, including batteries and hydrogen).

29 See COM (2020) 662 final of October 14, 2020, *A renovation wave for Europe—greening our buildings, creating jobs, improving lives*, to launch several initiatives, such as the "New European Bauhaus," an interdisciplinary project co-steered by an advisory board of external experts including scientists, architects, designers, artists, planners and civil society, whose first results were published in COM (2021) 573 final of September 15, 2021, *New European Bauhaus Beautiful, Sustainable, Together*, and the "Affordable Housing Initiative," aiming to revitalize 100 neighborhoods as lighthouse projects across the EU in the coming years.

30 The Next Generation Programme has been launched by the EU institutions to support Member States and undertakings to exit from the economic crisis caused by the COVID-19 emergency. See Regulation (EU) 2021/241 of the European Parliament and of the Council of February 12, 2021 establishing the Recovery and Resilience Facility, Article 17,§ 3; Annex VI, field of interventions 024–033; Regulation (EU) 2021/523 of the European Parliament and of the Council of March 24, 2021 establishing the Invest EU Programme and amending Regulation (EU) 2015/1017, Article 8, § 1, letter a).

31 See Regulation (EU) 2021/1060 of the European Parliament and of the Council of June 24, 2021 laying down common provisions on the European Regional Development Fund, the European Social Fund Plus, the Cohesion Fund, the Just Transition Fund and the European Maritime, Fisheries and Aquaculture Fund and financial rules for those and for the Asylum, Migration and Integration Fund, the Internal Security Fund and the Instrument for Financial Support for Border Management and Visa Policy, Article 5, § 1, letter b); Regulation (EU) 2021/1058 of the European Parliament and of the Council of June 24, 2021 on the European Regional Development Fund and on the Cohesion Fund, Articles 3§ 1 letter b); Regulation (EU) 2021/1056 of the European Parliament and of the Council of June 24, 2021 establishing the Just Transition Fund, Article 8, § 2, letters d)-g).

32 See Opinion of Advocate General Bobek delivered on October 6, 2021, Case C-348/20 P, *Nord Stream 2 AG v. European Parliament and Council of the European Union*. In this Opinion, the AG Bobek proposes to set aside the order of May 20, 2020, *Nord Stream 2* v *Parliament and Council* (T-526/19, EU:T:220:210) and declare Nord Stream 2 AG's action for annulment admissible. For an analysis of the Nord Stream 2 "saga," see Himmelreich, 2020, p. 206 ff. On February 22, 2022, in the light of the growing tensions that led, on February 24, to the Russia-Ukraine conflict outbreak, Germany decided to suspend the certification of Nord Stream 2, already built and waiting for approval for the taps to be turned on.

33 Judgment of the Court (Grand Chamber) of July 12, 2022, C-348/20, *Nord Stream 2 AG v European Parliament and Council of the European Union*, point 151 ff., 163.

34 As is well known, the Treaty of Lisbon put an end on the difficult interpretation of ECJ case law on the "principle of parallelism," See Judgment of the Court of March 31, 1971, *Commission of the European Communities v. Council of the European Communities (European Agreement on Road Transport)*, point 12 ff., Opinion of the Court of April 26, 1977, Opinion 1/76, *Draft Agreement establishing a European laying-up fund for inland waterway vessels*, points 3 ff.; Opinion of the Court of March 19, 1993, Opinion 2/91, *Convention N° 170 of the International Labour Organization concerning safety in the use of chemicals at work*, point 3; Opinion of the Court of March 24, 1995, Opinion 2/92, *Competence of the Community or one of its institutions to participate in the Third Revised Decision of the OECD on national treatment*, point 6; Opinion of the Court of November 15, 1994, Opinion 1/94, *Competence of the Community to conclude international agreements concerning services and the protection of intellectual property*, point 36 ff., 54 ff.; Opinion of the Court of March 28, 1996, Opinion 2/94, *Accession by the Community to the European Convention for the Protection of Human Rights and Fundamental* Freedoms, point 23 ff.; Opinion of the Court of February 7, 2006, Opinion 1/03, *Competence of the Community to conclude the new Lugano Convention on jurisdiction and the recognition and enforcement of judgments in civil and commercial matters*, point 133 "(…) a comprehensive and detailed analysis must be carried out to determine whether the Community has the competence to conclude an international agreement and whether that competence is exclusive. In doing so, account must be taken not only of the area covered by the Community rules and by the provisions of the agreement envisaged, insofar as the latter are known, but also of the nature and content of those rules and those provisions, to ensure that the agreement is not capable of undermining the uniform and consistent application of the Community rules and the proper functioning of the system which they establish."

35 These agreements differ from the traditional free trade agreements as they contain not only provisions concerning trade of goods and services, but also a chapter on competition, investments, public procurement, public-owned enterprises, intellectual property, and sustainability.

36 Agreement of November 28, 1997 on partnership and cooperation establishing a partnership between the European Communities and their Member States, of one part, and the Russian Federation.

37 See the *Joint Declaration of the Prague Eastern Partnership Summit*, Prague, May 7, 2009. According to the Declaration (p. 8), "Provisions on energy interdependence could be included in the new Association Agreements or other bilateral arrangements between the EU and the partner countries. Energy cooperation should take into account the EU's Second Strategic Energy Review and each partner country's energy policy."

38 Council Decision 2014/295/EU of March 17, 2014 on the signing on behalf of the European Union and provisional application of the Association Agreement between the European Union and the European Atomic Energy Community and their Member States, on one side, and Ukraine on the other, as regards the Preamble, Article 1, and Titles I, II and VII. The agreement came into force on October 1, 2017, after being provisionally applied from January 1, 2016.

39 See Article 269 "The price for the supply of gas and electricity to industrial consumers shall be determined solely by supply and demand. By way of derogation from paragraph 1 of this Article, the Parties may impose in the general economic interest an obligation on undertakings

which relates to the price of supply of gas and electricity, (hereinafter referred to as "regulated price"). The Parties shall ensure that this obligation is clearly defined, transparent, proportionate, non-discriminatory, verifiable and of limited duration. In applying this obligation, the Parties shall also guarantee equality of access to consumers for other undertakings. Where the price, at which gas and electricity are sold on the domestic market, is regulated, the Party concerned shall ensure that the methodology underlying the calculation of the regulated price is published prior to the entry into force of the regulated price." See also Article 270 "…neither Party or a regulatory authority thereof, shall adopt or maintain a measure resulting in a higher price for exports of energy goods to the other Party than the price charged for such goods when intended for domestic consumption. The exporting Party shall at the request of the other Party provide evidence that a different price for the same energy goods sold on the domestic market and for export does not result from a measure prohibited by paragraph 1 of this Article."

40 Article 271 "Customs duties and quantitative restrictions on the import and export of energy goods and all measures having equivalent effect shall be prohibited between the Parties. This prohibition shall also apply to customs duties of a fiscal nature. Paragraph 1 shall not preclude quantitative restrictions or measures having equivalent effect, justified on grounds of public policy or public security; protection of human, animal or plant life or health, or the protection of industrial and commercial property. Such restrictions or measures shall not, however, constitute a means of arbitrary discrimination or a disguised restriction on trade between the Parties. The provision is based on the well-consolidated ECJ jurisprudence on "mandatory requirements" as justification for obstacles to movements. See Judgment of the Court of February 20, 1979, case 120/78, *Rewe-Zentral AG v Bundesmonopolverwaltung für Branntwein*, point 8.

41 In particular, according to Article 276 "Each Party shall ensure that transmission system operators take the necessary measures to: (a) minimise the risk of accidental interruption, reduction or stoppage of transit and transport; (b) expeditiously restore the normal operation of such transit or transport, which has been accidentally interrupted, reduced or stopped. A Party through whose territory energy goods transit or are transported shall not, in the event of a dispute over any matter involving the Parties or one or more entities subject to the control or jurisdiction of one of the Parties, interrupt or reduce, permit any entity subject to its control or jurisdiction, including a state trading enterprise, to interrupt or reduce, or require any entity subject to its jurisdiction to interrupt or reduce the existing transport or transit of energy goods, except where this is specifically provided for in a contract or other agreement governing such transit or transport, prior to the conclusion of a dispute resolution procedure under the relevant contract. The Parties agree that a Party shall not be held liable for an interruption or reduction pursuant to this Article where that Party is in an impossibility to supply, transit or transport energy goods as a result of actions attributable to a third country or an entity under the control or jurisdiction of a third country."

42 Article 279 "Each Party (1) has, in accordance with international law including the United Nations Convention on the Law of the Sea of 1982, full sovereignty over hydrocarbon resources located in its territory as well as in its archipelagic and territorial waters in addition to sovereign rights for the purposes of exploring and exploiting hydrocarbon resources located in its exclusive economic zone and continental shelf. Each Party retains the right to determine the areas within its territory as well as in its archipelagic and territorial waters, exclusive economic zone and continental shelf to be made available for the exercise of the activities of prospecting, exploring for and producing hydrocarbons. Whenever an area is made available for the exercise of these activities, each Party shall ensure that entities, as regards access to and exercise

of these activities, are treated on an equal basis. For the purpose of this Article, 'Party' is to be understood as a Member State with reference to its territory or as Ukraine with reference to its territory. Each Party may require an entity, which has been granted an authorisation for the exercise of the activities of prospecting, exploring for and producing hydrocarbons, to pay a financial contribution or a contribution in hydrocarbons. The detailed arrangements of such contribution shall be fixed in such a way so as not to interfere in the management process and decision-making of entities." See also Article 280 "Parties shall take the necessary measures to ensure that licences, through which an entity is entitled to exercise, on its own behalf and at its own risk, the right to prospect or explore for or produce hydrocarbons in a geographical area, are granted following a published procedure and invite potentially interested applicants to submit applications by means of a notice."

43 See Article 307, § 8; 308, § 4; Article 309, Article 310, § 3; Article 314.

44 See Articles 337 ff., Articles 342 ff.

45 See Annex XXVI to Chapter 1. The mechanism establishes an early evaluation of potential risks and problems relating to supply and demand for natural gas, oil, or electricity and prevention and rapid reaction in an emergency.

46 Council Decision 2014/492/EU of June 16, 2014 on the signing, on behalf of, the European Union and provisional application of the Association Agreement between the European Union and the European Atomic Energy Community and their Member States on one side, and the Republic of Moldova on the other. The Treaty came into force on July 1, 2016.

47 Council Decision 2014/494/EU of June 16, 2014 on the signing on behalf of the European Union and provisional application of the Association Agreement between the European Union and the European Atomic Energy Community and their Member States, on one side and Georgia on the other. The Treaty came into force on July 1, 2016.

48 See Title I, Chapter 11 "Trade-related energy provisions," Articles 210 ff.

49 Article 249, § 7; 251,§ 5; Article 252; Article 253, § 3; Article 258.

50 See Title VI, Chapter 2, Articles 297 ff. Regarding the relationship between EU and other Eastern countries: the 1999 EU-Azerbaijan Partnership and Cooperation Agreement contains an article on energy (Article 55); the 2017 EU-Armenia Comprehensive and Enhanced Partnership Agreement (CEPA) contains a chapter on energy cooperation (Title V, Chapter 2). No agreements between Belarus and the EU have been signed.

51 See Joint Declaration of the Eastern Partnership Summit, Brussels, December 15, 2021, point 16. See also points 20 and 26.

52 The Cooperation Council for the Arab States of the Gulf (GCC) is a regional organization set up in 1981. It has six members: the Kingdom of Bahrain, the State of Kuwait, the Sultanate of Oman, the State of Qatar, the Kingdom of Saudi Arabia, and the United Arab Emirates.

53 Council Decision 89/147/EEC of February 20, 1989 concerning the conclusion of a Cooperation Agreement between the European Economic Community, of the one part, and the countries parties to the Charter of the Cooperation Council for the Arab States of the Gulf of the other part.

54 See Article 208 TFEU "The common commercial policy shall be based on uniform principles, particularly with regard to changes in tariff rates, the conclusion of tariff and trade agreements relating to trade in goods and services, and the commercial aspects of intellectual property, foreign direct investment, the achievement of uniformity in measures of liberalisation, export policy and measures to protect trade such as those to be taken in the event of dumping or subsidies."

55 Provisions implementing WTO agreements on sanitary and phytosanitary measures, technical barriers to trade, subsidies, intellectual properties, public procurements, customs, and trade facilitation are defined "WTO-plus."

56 Council Decision (EU) 2017/37 of October 28, 2016 on the signing on behalf of the European Union of the Comprehensive Economic and Trade Agreement (CETA) between Canada, on one side, and the European Union and its Member States, of the other; Council Decision (EU) 2017/38 of October 28, 2016 on the provisional application of the Comprehensive Economic and Trade Agreement (CETA) between Canada, of the one part, and the European Union and its Member States, of the other part.

57 Between the EU-Canada common efforts to contrast climate change, see the Ministerial on Climate Action, co-convened together with China (the fifth edition took place on March 23, 2021).

58 Council Decision (EU) 2018/1907 of December 20, 2018 on the conclusion of the Agreement between the European Union and Japan for an Economic Partnership, entered into force on February 1, 2019.

59 See Article 16.5 "Trade and investment favouring sustainable development" according to which the Parties "shall strive to facilitate trade and investment in goods and services of particular relevance to climate change mitigation, such as those related to sustainable renewable energy and energy efficient goods and services, in a manner consistent with this Agreement." See also Annex 2-C, Motor Vehicles and Parts, Article 3 letter a).

60 See Article 18.1, § 2. Provisions concerning "Right to regulate" allow the State to maintain their autonomy in assuming their public decisions without risking to be involved in disputes by the counterpart of an agreement or, in the International Investment Agreements, by an investor (Levashova, 2019; Titi, 2014).

61 See *supra*, note 6.

62 See *Global Coal to Clean Power Transition Statement*, signed by 46 States on November 4, 2021 during the 2021 COP 26.

63 In this perspective, see the EU-Japan Green Alliance.

64 *EU-China Comprehensive Agreement on Investment the Agreement in Principle*, December 30, 2020. On May 20, 2021 the European Parliament adopted the *Resolution 2021/2644 on Chinese countersanctions on EU entities and MEPs and MPs* to freeze ratification of the EU-China Comprehensive Agreement on Investment (CAI) in response to Chinese sanctions on European human rights advocates.

65 See *U.S.-China Joint Glasgow Declaration on Enhancing Climate Action in the 2020s*, November 10, 2021.

66 The TTIP negotiations were launched in 2013 and ended without conclusion at the end of 2016. In the Decision of April 15, 2019 authorizing the opening of negotiations with the United States of America for an agreement on the elimination of tariffs for industrial goods, recital 3, Council acknowledged that "The negotiating directives for the Transatlantic Trade and Investment Partnership must be considered obsolete and no longer relevant."

67 U.S.-EU Summit Statement, *Statements and Releases*, June 15, 2021.

68 Council Decision 2011/265/EU of September 16, 2010 on the signing, on behalf of the European Union, and provisional application of the Free Trade Agreement between the European Union and its Member States, of the one part, and the Republic of Korea, of the other part; Council Decision (EU) 2015/2169 of October 1, 2015 on the conclusion of the Free Trade

Agreement between the European Union and its Member States, of the one part, and the Republic of Korea, of the other part. The Agreement entered into force on December 13, 2015.

69 Council Decision 2012/272/EU of May 14, 2012 on the signing, on behalf of the Union, of the Framework Agreement on Partnership and Cooperation between the European Union and its Member States, of the one part, and the Republic of the Philippines, of the other part; Council Decision (EU) 2017/2414 of September 25, 2017 on the conclusion, on behalf of the Union, of the Framework Agreement on Partnership and Cooperation between the European Union and its Member States, of the one part, and the Republic of the Philippines, of the other part. The Agreement entered into force on March 1, 2018.

70 Council Decision (EU) 2018/1599 of October 15, 2018 on the signing, on behalf of the European Union, of the Free Trade Agreement between the European Union and the Republic of Singapore; Council Decision (EU) 2019/1875 of November 8, 2019 on the conclusion of the Free Trade Agreement between the European Union and the Republic of Singapore. The Agreement entered into force on November 21, 2019.

71 Council Decision (EU) 2019/1121 of June 25, 2019 on the signing on behalf of the European Union of the Free Trade Agreement between the European Union and the Socialist Republic of Vietnam; Council Decision (EU) 2019/753 of March 30, 2020 on the conclusion of the Free Trade Agreement between the European Union and the Socialist Republic of Vietnam. The Agreement entered into force on July 31, 2020.

72 Negotiations for a Free Trade Agreement (FTA) between the EU and Malaysia were launched in 2010 and put on hold after seven rounds in 2012 at the request of Malaysia. Negotiations between EU and India started in 2007 and were suspended in 2013. On May 8, 2021, EU and India announced their decision to resume negotiations for a balanced and comprehensive trade agreement after a gap of eight years and unveiled an ambitious connectivity partnership. See Report of the 1st round, July 1, 2022. As it concerns Indonesia, the negotiation rounds stopped in November 2021.

73 See also Annex 13 "Cooperation on Trade and Sustainable Development," paragraph 1, letter f).

74 To this effect, the Parties commit to cooperate toward removing or reducing tariffs as well as nontariff barriers (Article 7.4 "Principles"), and cooperate on fostering regulatory convergence with or toward regional and international standards (Article 7.5 "Standards, Technical Regulations and Conformity Assessment" and Article 7.7 "Implementation and Cooperation").

75 Article 7.6, § 2.

76 Chapter 12. See, in particular, Article 12.11.

77 UK Department for Business, Energy & Industrial Strategy (2021, p. 9). Even if UK significantly increased its renewable source production recently, it is not yet able to meet the gas demand.

78 Council Decision (EU) 2020/2252 of December 29, 2020 on the signing on behalf of the Union and on provisional application of the Trade and Cooperation Agreement between the European Union and the European Atomic Energy Community, of the one part, and the United Kingdom of Great Britain and Northern Ireland, of the other part; Council Decision (EU) 2021/689 of April 29, 2021 on the conclusion on behalf of the Union of the Trade and Cooperation Agreement between the European Union and the European Atomic Energy Community, of the one part, and the United Kingdom of Great Britain and Northern Ireland, of the other part.

79 According to Article 312, the charge to assure the arrangement between transmission system operators is attributed to the Specialized Committee on Energy.
80 See Article 8 EU-UK TCA, establishing 19 specialized committees.
81 Council Regulation (EEC) No 3906/89 of December 18, 1989 on economic aid to the Republic of Hungary and the Polish People's Republic replaced by Council Regulation (EC) No 1085/2006 of July 17, 2006 establishing an Instrument for Pre-Accession Assistance (IPA).
82 The Treaty establishing the Energy Community was signed in Athens, Greece, on October 25, 2005 and came into force on July 1, 2006. See Council Decision 2006/500/EC of May 29, 2006 on the conclusion by the European Community of the Energy Community Treaty.
83 Albania, Bosnia and Herzegovina, North Macedonia, Montenegro, Serbia and Kosovo, Moldova, Georgia, and Ukraine.
84 The institutional framework comprises a Ministerial Council, provided with binding powers and assisted by a Permanent High-Level Group, by the Regulatory Board, with advising functions, and by the Secretariat. The Ministerial Council, made up of one representative for each party to the Treaty, provides general policy guidelines, takes measures to meet the Treaty's objectives and adopts procedural acts such as the allocation of tasks, powers or obligations. The key mission of the Permanent High-Level Group is to prepare the work of the Ministerial Council. It consists of one representative of each party to the Treaty. The Regulatory Board's primary role is to advise the other institutions and issue recommendations in the event of cross-border disputes. It is composed of one representative of the energy regulator from each party to the Treaty, with the EU being represented by the European Commission, assisted by one regulator from each participating Member State, and one representative of the European Regulators Group for Electricity and Gas (ERGEG). The permanent Secretariat, based in Vienna, provides, among other things, administrative support to the other institutions of the Energy Community and reviews proper fulfillment by the parties of their obligations. The Energy Community makes decisions (binding) and recommendations (non-binding). In the event of serious and persistent breach by a party of its obligations, the Ministerial Council may, acting unanimously, suspend certain rights granted to this party by the Treaty.
85 The Energy Charter Treaty was signed in December 1994 and came into force in April 1998.
86 In reality, consistently with the 1990s' BIT models, ECT presents few pre-establishment standards and more specific post-establishment standards (Wälde, 1995, p. 21 f., p. 30 ff.).
87 The ECT has 51 signatories, including the EU and all its Member States—apart from Italy which denounced it in 2016 due to the high number of Investor-State disputes it was involved in—and Euratom. Many others have observer status, including the US, Canada, China, and Russian Federation, which notified its intention to cease provisional application of the Treaty in 2009.
88 International Energy Charter, signed on May 20, 2015.
89 European Commission, *EU text proposal for the modernization of the Energy Charter Treaty (ECT)*, June 20, 2020.
90 Judgment of the Court (Grand Chamber) of September 2, 2021, case C-741/19, *République de Moldavie v Komstroy LLC*.
91 The documents from the negotiation rounds are available at https://www.energychartertreaty.org/modernisation-of-the-treaty/.
92 COM (2022) 230 final 18.03.2022, *REPowerEU Plan. Joint European Action for more affordable, secure and sustainable energy.*

93 COM (2022) 138 final, 23.03.2022, *Security of supply and affordable energy prices: Options for immediate measures and preparing for next winter.*

94 To lower electricity prices intervention options including or excluding financial compensation are envisaged. Between the first ones, the Communication proposes: (a) Retail side, aimed at cushioning the effects of the high prices on end-consumers while letting the European electricity and gas markets set the price at wholesale level. All the options on the retail side aim at providing direct relief to citizens and businesses struggling with excessive energy prices. (b) Wholesale side, where Member States can consider setting up an aggregator model under which an entity would buy electricity on favorable commercial terms and make it available to certain consumer categories below market price passing onwards the advantages to the consumers, essentially subsidizing the difference between lower retail prices and higher wholesale ones. Other options would involve intervening directly in the functioning of the wholesale electricity markets, consisting in either compensating financially fossil-based electricity generators for part of their extraordinary high fuel costs so that they reduce their offered price in the wholesale market or in directly capping the electricity price in the wholesale market by establishing a reference benchmark and compensating the difference with the offered price. Between the second ones, the Communication proposes: (a) regulatory options without fiscal compensation, consisting in establishing a regulatory cap for the maximum price that certain baseload generators can charge. While this option would bring the costs down in the longer term, its added value in the short term is to address the excessive profits of certain technologies. See also Council Regulation (EU) 2022/1854 of October 6, 2022 on an emergency intervention to address high energy prices.

95 More specifically, the Commission puts in evidence that "high electricity price is driven by the high gas price, as gas-based generators are still often the energy providers coming last into the electricity market to close on actual demand. In the gas spot market, volatility is high and not fully linked to fundamentals." In reaction to these problems, see Council Regulation (EU) 2022/1854 of October 6, 2022 on an emergency intervention to address high energy prices.

96 According to the European Commission data, "storage supplies 25–30 % of gas consumed in winter. During the heating season, storage reduces the need to import additional gas. Storage contributes to absorbing supply shocks. Over the last six months, an unbalanced gas market has led to a sharp increase in gas prices (…). As prices may be higher in summer than in winter, this is expected to lead to a situation in which storage is not attractive to market participants and filling needs to be ensured by public interventions, including financial support to incentivize the use of storage. According to the Commission and the Gas Coordination Group risk-preparedness analysis in February 2022, while the winter 2021/2022 was eventually safe, there could be risk of insufficient gas in storage ahead of the next winter 2022/2023. Optimizing the storage capacities over the filling season would require immediate injection as from the start of the filling season." It has also to taken into account that "gas storage levels in 2021/2022 have proven to be particularly low at sites owned by third-country entities. This has contributed to nearly half of the unusually low storage level this year."

97 Regulation (EU) 2022/1032 of the European Parliament and of the Council of June 29, 2022 amending Regulations (EU) 2017/1938 and (EC) No 715/2009 with regard to gas storage.

98 Regulation (EU) 2017/1938 of the European Parliament and of the Council of October 25, 2017 concerning measures to safeguard the security of gas supply and repealing Regulation (EU) No 994/2010.

99 Regulation (EC) No 715/2009 of the European Parliament and of the Council of July 13, 2009 on conditions for access to the natural gas transmission networks and repealing Regulation (EC) No 1775/2005.

100 "From the year 2023 onwards storage shall also be specifically monitored in February (the 'February control point') to avoid sudden withdrawal of gas from storage in the middle of the winter, which could cause security of supply challenges before the end of winter. The filling target and the filling trajectory can be adjusted by the Commission from 2023 onwards, by means of a delegated act." It is necessary to ensure the Member States flexibility in case that should not "be able to meet the filling targets on time due to technical issues such as problems related to the pipelines feeding the storage site or with the injection facilities. However, the filling target should be met as soon as technically possible and no later than on the 1 December in order to ensure the security of supply for the winter period. Competent authorities shall continuously monitor the filling of the underground storage facilities in order to ensure that their national filling trajectories are met. The national filling trajectories are defined considering a bandwidth of two percentage points. If the filling level of a given Member State is more than 2 percentage points below the targets of the filling trajectory, the competent authorities shall immediately take effective measures to increase the filling level. Member States shall inform of such measures the Commission and the Gas Coordination Group, created in 2006 according to Directive 2004/67, chaired by the European Commission and composed of gas competent representatives of Member States, the European organisations of the gas sector, and consumers. In case of such substantial and sustained deviations, the Commission should therefore be empowered to take effective measures to avoid security of supply problems resulting from unfilled storages. When deciding upon the adequate measures, the Commission shall take into account the specific situation of the respective Member State, such as the size of the storage facilities in relation to the domestic gas consumption or the importance of the storage facilities for security of supply in the region. In case of such substantial and sustained deviations, the Commission should therefore be empowered to take effective measures to avoid security of supply problems resulting from unfilled storages. When deciding upon the adequate measures, the Commission shall take into account the specific situation of the respective Member State, such as the size of the storage facilities in relation to the domestic gas consumption or the importance of the storage facilities for security of supply in the region. Member States should take all necessary measures to ensure that the mandatory filling targets are met but, due to the different regulatory regimes already in place in many Member States to support storage filling, no specific instrument to meet the filling trajectory and reach the filling target is prescribed, and Member State enjoy freedom to choose the instrument which is most appropriate in their national system. Member States therefore have the freedom to choose which market participants to oblige to ensure the filling of the storages. They can also decide whether regulatory means, such as measures to oblige capacity holders to free up unused capacity which are possible under existing EU market rules, may be sufficient to meet the filling targets, or if financial incentives, which might constitute State aid, are necessary. They should use coordinated instruments, such as platforms for the purchase of LNG, with other Member States to maximize the utilisation of LNG to fill storages, and reduce infrastructure and regulatory barriers to the shared use of LNG to fill storages. Any measure taken to ensure the filling of gas storage should be necessary, clearly defined, transparent, proportionate, non-discriminatory and verifiable, and should not unduly distort competition or the effective functioning of the internal market in gas or endanger the security of gas supply

of other Member States or of the Union. In particular, such measures taken should not lead to strengthening a dominant position or windfall gains for undertakings controlling storage facilities or having booked but not used storage capacity. Moreover, any measure taken to ensure the filling of gas storage should not block or restrict cross-border capacities."

101 The Gas Coordination Group will monitor the progress in filling toward the target and consider appropriate actions to sustain the storage filling effort if necessary. "In case there is no interconnection with other Member States, or limited cross-border transmission capacity or other technical reasons make it impossible to use storage facilities in other Member States, the obligation should be reduced accordingly." In every case, "Member States should not be subject to such an obligation if they jointly develop an alternative burden sharing mechanism with one or more Member States with storage facilities. Such alternative mechanism can take into consideration, among others, already existing equivalent legal obligations to store alternative fuels. Member States should notify such alternative burden sharing mechanisms to the Commission. Member States without storage facilities may therefore provide financial incentives or compensation to market participants for the shortfall of revenues or for costs incurred by obligations imposed on them which cannot be covered by revenue. If the measure is financed through a levy, that levy shall not be allocated to cross-border interconnection points. If enterprises are due to purchase more gas when such gas is expensive, this could further drive up prices. Therefore, this Regulation is accompanied by the removal of entry and exit tariffs for transmission capacity to and from storage, making storage more attractive for market participants. Regulatory and competition authorities should also use their competences to effectively exclude undue increases of storage tariffs."

102 Council Directive 2008/114/EC of December 8, 2008 on the identification and designation of European critical infrastructures and the assessment of the need to improve their protection

103 Communication from the Commission (2022/C 151 I/01), April 6, 2022, *Guidance to the Member States concerning foreign direct investment from Russia and Belarus in view of the military aggression against Ukraine and the restrictive measures laid down in recent Council Regulations on sanctions.*

104 Regulation (EU) 2019/452 of the European Parliament and of the Council of March 19, 2019 establishing a framework for the screening of foreign direct investments into the Union.

105 COM (2022) 240 final, 18.5.2022, *EU "Save Energy."*

106 COM (2022) 221 final, 18.5.2022, *EU Solar Energy Strategy*; COM (2022) 222 final, 18.5.2022, *Proposal for a Directive of the European Parliament and of the Council amending Directive (EU) 2018/2001 on the promotion of the use of energy from renewable sources, Directive 2010/31/EU on the energy performance of buildings and Directive 2012/27/EU on energy efficiency*; Commission Recommendation C/2022/3219 final of May 18, 2022 on speeding up permit-granting procedures for renewable energy projects and facilitating Power Purchase Agreements and related guidance.

107 JOINT (2022) 23 final, 18.05.2022, *EU external energy engagement in a changing world.*

108 COM (2022) 231 final 2022/0164, 18.5.2022, *Proposal for a Regulation of the European Parliament and of the Council Amending Regulation (EU) 2021/241 as Regards RepowerEU Chapters in Recovery and Resilience Plans and Amending Regulation (EU) 2021/1060, Regulation (EU) 2021/2115, Directive 2003/87/EC and Decision (EU) 2015/1814.*

109 COM (2022) 230, 18.05.2022, RePower Plan.

110 The reference is to the Joint Procurement for medical devices and medicines managed by the European Commission on behalf of the Member States and to the Advance Purchase Agreements stipulated by the European Commission with the big pharm to stimulate the fast vaccine development (D'Arienzo & Pugliese, 2021; Pugliese, 2021).

REFERENCES

Amadeo, S. (2014). Articolo 192 TFUE [English translation]. In A. Tizzano (Ed.), *Trattati dell'Unione europea* (pp. 376–386). Giuffré.

Baratta, R. (2014). Articolo 3 TFUE. In A. Tizzano (Ed.), *Trattati dell'Unione europea* (pp. 1650–1659). Giuffré.

Berrie, T. W., & Hoyle, M. (1985). Treating energy as a commodity. *Energy Policy, 13*(6), 506–510. https://doi.org/10.1016/0301-4215(85)90001-1

Boute, A. (2020). The principle of solidarity and the geopolitics of energy: Poland v. Commission (OPAL pipeline). *Common Market Law Review, 57*(3), 889–914.

Cenevska, I. (2012). Protection of the health of workers and the general public under the Euratom Treaty and the EU Environmental Policy—The ratio between human health protection and environmental protection. *European Energy and Environmental Law Review, 21*(4), 176–187.

Cima, E. (2018). Promoting renewable energy through FTAs? The legal implications of a new generation of trade agreements. *Journal of World Trade, 52*(4), 663–695.

Cristiani, D. (2021). The evolution of EU-GCC relations between Brexit and the active Gulf. *European Foreign Affairs Review, 26*(2), 309–330.

D'Arienzo, M., & Pugliese, S. (2021). Health services after COVID-19 emergency: Toward a multilevel system? *Amministrativamente, 2*, 228–252.

Engstedt, R. (2021). *Handbook on European nuclear law: Competences of the Euratom Community under the Euratom Treaty*. Kluwer Law International.

Göler, D., & Kurze, K. (2020). Extending the logic of integration beyond EU borders: External differentiated integration in the case of the energy community. *European Foreign Affairs Review, 25*(3), 321–338.

Hancher, L., & Talus, K. (2022). "Fit for 55"—Europe's man on the moon moment? *Oil, Gas & Energy Law*, 20(1).

Hart, E. (2021, December 14). *Tensions between Russia and Ukraine: How likely is another war?* Foreign Policy Research Institute. https://www.fpri.org/article/2021/12/tensions-between-russia-and-ukraine-how-likely-is-another-war/

Himmelreich, J. (2020). Nord Stream 2: A political economic crime novel and its EU legal consequences. *European Energy and Environmental Law Review, 29*(5), 206–215.

Huhta, K. (2022). The "Fit for 55"-package in the context of EU energy law and policy. *Oil, Gas & Energy Law*, 20(1).

International Energy Agency. (2020). *Electricity market report—December 2020*. https://www.iea.org/reports/electricity-market-report-december-2020

Jones, C. (1992). The European Energy Charter. *Review of European Community & International Environmental Law, 1*, 154–157.

Jones, C., & Piebalgs, A. (2022). The Commission's proposal of a "Fit for 55" legislative package—What impact could it have? *Oil, Gas & Energy Law*, 20(1).

Layard, A. (1995). The European Energy Charter Treaty: Tipping the balance between energy and the environment. *European Environmental Law Review*, *4*(5), 150–156.

Levashova, Y. (2019). *The right of states to regulate in international investment law: The search for balance between public interest and fair and equitable treatment*. Wolters Kluwer.

Marletta, M. (2014). Articolo 194 TFUE [English translation]. In A. Tizzano (Ed.), *Trattati dell'Unione europea* (pp. 1650–1659). Giuffré.

Mathijsen, P. (1966). Some legal aspects of Euratom. *Common Market Law Review*, *3*(3), 326–343.

Mauro, M. R. (2021). Il Trattato sulla Carta dell'energia: conflittualità e sinergie tra la protezione degli investimenti e la lotta ai cambiamenti climatici. In *Studi sull'integrazione europea* (pp. 299–332). Cacucci.

Olubusoye, O. E., Ogbonna, A. E., Yaya, O. S., & Umolo, D. (2021). An information-based index of uncertainty and the predictability of energy prices. *International Journal of Energy Research*, *45*(7), 10235–10249. https://doi.org/10.1002/er.6512

Penttinen, S.-L., Nippala, E. K., & Kallioharju, K. A. (2022). Energy efficiency in the "Fit for 55" framework: Increasingly ambitious targets coupled with hardening governance. *Oil, Gas & Energy Law*. 20(1).

Pugliese, S. (2021). Appalti di aggiudicazione congiunta nell'emergenza COVID-19 e sistema Omc: un esperimento regionale per una risposta globale. *Quaderni di SIDIBlog*, *7*, 251–281.

Pugliese, S. (2022). Toward a new EU strategic dimension: Common purchase and investment screening mechanisms as a means of crisis preparedness and management. *Il Diritto dell'Unione europea*, *2*, pp. 391-424.

Quadri, S. (2016). EU energy market integration through Energy Union: A new holistic approach. *Bocconi Legal Papers*, *7*, 1–16.

Salisua, A. A., Akanni, L., & Raheem, I. (2020). The COVID-19 global fear index and the predictability of commodity price returns. *Journal of Behavioral and Experimental Finance*, *27*, Article 100383. https://doi.org/10.1016/j.jbef.2020.100383

Schippers, M. L., & De Wit, W. (2022). Proposal for a carbon border adjustment mechanism. *Global Trade and Customs Journal*, *17*(1), 10–18.

Sciaudone, F. (2014). Articolo 122 TFUE. In A. Tizzano (Ed.), *Trattati dell'Unione europea* (pp. 1311–1316). Giuffré.

Södersten, A. (2018). *Euratom at the crossroads*. Edward Elgar. https://kluwerlawonline.com/JournalArticle/Common+Market+Law+Review/56.1/COLA2019024

Titi, C. (2014). *The right to regulate in international investment law*. Hart Publishing.

Tufano, M. L. (forthcoming). *Lo sviluppo sostenibile in tempo di COVID-19 tra uso efficiente delle risorse, innovazione, equità sociale e Stato di diritto*, in Aa.Vv., *Scritti in onore di Gianluigi Cecchini*. Giuffré.

UK Department for Business, Energy & Industrial Strategy. (2021). *Energy trends: UK, July to September 2021*.

Verhagen, G. (2019). The compliance and dispute settlement system of the European Energy Community. *Legal Issues of Economic Integration*, *46*(2), 149–160.

Wälde, T. W. (1995). International investment under the 1994 Energy Charter Treaty. *Journal of World Trade*, *29*(5), 5–72.

Wälde, T. W., & Hobér, K. (2005). The First Energy Charter Treaty Arbitral Award. *Journal of International Arbitration*, *22*(2), 83–104.

CHAPTER 17

Critical Legal Insight into the EU's Hydrogen Strategy

JAVAD KEYPOUR, TANEL KERIKMÄE, AND ARCHIL CHOCHIA

INTRODUCTION

Hydrogen is not an energy source in itself, but it has been introduced as a new energy carrier that, if it replaces fossil fuels, can facilitate carbon reduction in the future (Rosen & Koohi-Fayegh, 2016). Since hydrogen does not have carbon atoms in its structure, its combustion does not emit carbon. Thus, hydrogen can provide energy in two pollutant energy sectors where decarbonization is challenging, that is, transportation and power (and heat) generation (Edwards et al., 2007). Additionally, hydrogen offers other benefits, including its effective energy conversion and the possibility of zero-carbon production (if produced from renewable energy sources), making it suitable for establishing a circular economy and higher electrification (Ishaq & Dincer 2020). Hydrogen can also be used for storing electricity in combination with renewable energy generation methods, for example, solar and wind power production. This increases the performance of renewable power generation and covers their intermittency problems (Maleki et al., 2017). Additionally, hydrogen may be integrated into traditionally independent sectors, namely electricity, heat, and transport, resulting in sector coupling (Parra et al., 2019). This is beneficial for establishing an integrated energy market, among other things, in the EU.

Despite the potential of hydrogen to reduce carbon emissions, up to 96 % of the hydrogen currently produced in Europe originates from natural gas, which is a source of CO_2 emissions. Hydrogen accounts for less than 2 % of Europe's present energy consumption and is primarily used to produce chemical products, such as plastics and fertilizers, instead of acting as an energy carrier. The EU has addressed hydrogen in Directive 2018/2001, the so-called Renewable Directive (RED), as a green energy carrier if it originates from renewable sources. To enhance the share of renewable hydrogen, the EU Commission has developed "A hydrogen strategy for a climate-neutral Europe" or the EU hydrogen strategy, as it is called (European Commission, 2020b). Moreover, due to the role of hydrogen in linking the electricity and gas sectors, it has also been addressed by the "EU strategy for energy system integration" (European Commission, 2020a). It is expected that these two documents will pave the way for achieving the EU's climate targets in 2050 (European Commission, 2021, November 11).

The EU hydrogen strategy classifies hydrogen into different types, including renewable/clean hydrogen, that is, hydrogen generated via electrolysis using renewable electricity. It envisages raising the clean hydrogen production level rapidly to one Mt (million tons) and the installed capacity of electrolyzer to six gigawatts by 2024, reaching 10 Mt and 40 gigawatts (GW) in 2030. Despite the reduction in the cost of hydrogen production thanks to technological developments, these targets still look ambitious; the current EU electrolyzer capacity is well under one GW, and the largest electrolyzer under construction in Europe has a capacity of 10 MW. Thus, a more significant role for low-carbon hydrogen seems inevitable to form a smooth transition to renewable hydrogen in the perspective of 2050 (Lambert, 2020). Similarly, a smooth transition and the gradual decarbonization of natural gas look more realistic in achieving the EU Green Deal goals, in a broader perspective (Belyi, 2021; Piebalgs & Olczak, 2018). This means greater attention to low-carbon hydrogen[1] is needed than the extent to which the EU hydrogen strategy is achieved.

A gradual transition to pure hydrogen has implications for its transmission. The EU hydrogen strategy assumes that hydrogen demand is initially met through on-site production, so the demand for new hydrogen-specific networks will remain limited. Even if transmission of pure hydrogen is needed, the current 1,600 km of hydrogen pipelines will not be sufficient as they cover only some parts of Germany, France, Belgium, and the Netherlands (Steen, 2016, p. 271). This network should expand to 11,600 km by 2030, and then to the pan-European network with a length of 39,700 km by 2040, which shows a lot has yet to be done. Establishing such a network is capital intensive and time-consuming, estimated to cost $43–81 billion, especially for the optimizing compressors (Jens et al., 2021). As a result, injecting hydrogen into the available natural gas network, which results in a natural gas-hydrogen mixture (NGH2), has been proposed as a beneficial solution in the transitional phase to create the demand and pave the way for establishing the final EU hydrogen market (Kleperis et al., 2021).

The above-mentioned transition to the hydrogen economy and the establishment of the pan-European hydrogen market where hydrogen can flow freely across the EU (and certain neighbors) requires legal prerequisites. This is critical since the current EU legal frameworks should be assessed if they are to be applicable during the transition time and in the final EU hydrogen market. Thus, the main aim of this chapter is to talk about these legal prerequisites, posing the question: What main regulations are required on the way to achieving the EU hydrogen strategy goals? To this end, we discuss to what extent the current EU energy acquis is generally applicable to the hydrogen development plan's segments. Then, we discuss the more environmental aspects of the energy transition, such as the guarantee of origin and, finally, state aid. The latter issue will also be addressed beyond the EU legal frameworks, that is, in terms of the World Trade Organization outlines. The legal challenges of hydrogen promotion have been discussed earlier, mainly from a technical perspective concerning the technical regulations needed for hydrogen transportation or production. However, this chapter looks at the topic from a more macro perspective to discuss what the EU and the member states should do. Each section will approach the topic critically and will end with recommendations. Finally, the conclusion will address the main areas of legal requirements. These prerequisites include the need for clearer Gas and Electricity Directives, reforming the guarantee of origin and state aid regulations. The writing of this chapter was concluded in January 2022.

HYDROGEN AND THE CURRENT EU ENERGY ACQUIS

The Applicability of the Gas Directive to NGH2 and Hydrogen

Although the Lisbon Treaty of 2009 was the first treaty that explicitly addressed energy as a shared competence, the Commission had started to restructure the EU's natural gas market in the late 1990s when it ratified the First Energy Package. Functional unbundling and third-party access (TPA) to electricity and gas networks were among the critical issues included in Directives 96/92/EC and 98/30/EC (Talus & Aalto, 2017, p. 16). The EU energy acquis then evolved into the Third Energy Package, encompassing Directive 2009/73/EC, the so-called Gas Directive. With the advent of hydrogen and consideration being given to using the existing natural gas network for its transmission, the question arises if the current EU legal framework applies to NGH2, and even pure hydrogen, systems in the future.

The Gas Directive explicitly talks about its conditional applicability to other gases under Article 1(2):

> The rules established by this Directive for natural gas, including LNG [liquified natural gas], shall also apply in a non-discriminatory way to biogas and gas from biomass or other types of gas in so far as such gases can technically and safely be injected into, and transported through, the natural gas system.

Accordingly, NGH2 is treated differently from pure hydrogen. Since NGH2 is obtained when hydrogen is safely injected into the operating natural gas pipeline and in compliance with the (harmonized) standards, the Gas Directive applies to it. In other words, a safe composition of NGH2 can be transmitted through the natural gas system and, therefore, it can be regulated by the Gas Directive. However, it is tricky to treat pure hydrogen legally, and even scholars are not unanimous about this. While Lengyel (2021) and Fleming and Fershee (2018) believe that the current directive should regulate pure hydrogen, Benrath (2020) limits the Gas Directive jurisdiction to those hydrogen pipelines integrated into natural gas systems. Conversely, a report by GEODE[2] (2020) believes these EU rules only refer to natural gas networks but not to other gases, in practice. Similarly, Tarkowski et al. (2021) recognized an existing loophole preventing underground hydrogen storage as the Gas Directive does not apply to pure hydrogen gas systems.

The legal complexity of the hydrogen systems lies in the fact that a hydrogen system can be established in two forms: first, a natural gas system converted and optimized to handle pure hydrogen (for instance, following a modification of the compressors and pipelines), and second, a system designed and constructed from scratch to transmit pure hydrogen. In the first scenario, if hydrogen is safely injected into a system used to transport natural gas, the first condition enshrined in Article 1(2) is fulfilled. However, it is problematic when claiming that the requirements of Article 1(2) are met entirely for application to pure hydrogen. The directive stipulates its jurisdiction over other gases injected safely into the natural gas system, meaning that natural gas should be still there to essentially act as the carrier gas, considering the definition of the system rendered by Article 2(13).[3] Otherwise, it is doubtful if a system handling pure hydrogen can still be considered a natural gas system (even if it is used as one). As a result, Article 1(2) will not be entirely applicable to hydrogen passing through a reformed natural gas system as the Directive has been drafted to regulate natural gas exclusively.

Nevertheless, the possible counterargument seems viable as well as there is no rigid criterion nor a clear threshold to distinguish a natural gas system against Article 2(13). It seems the current wording of Article 1(2) causes a Paradox of the Heap as the line of distinction is not evident in the transition from a natural gas network to a hydrogen one. It seems the current wording of Article 1(2) causes a *sorites paradox* as the line of distinction is not evident in the transition from a natural gas network to a hydrogen one. For instance, should we consider a system carrying a natural gas (1 %) + hydrogen (99 %) composition as a natural gas system? As it handles natural gas and another gas supposedly injected safely into the system, nothing hinders us from considering it to be a natural gas system from a legal perspective. Considering such a case as a natural gas system and rejecting a pure hydrogen transmission system just because it does not contain (the trace content of) natural gas will not make sense, mainly as safety considerations are at the same level. To prevent such confusion in our legal perception, one can argue that once a natural gas system is converted to another gas system, the last part of Article 2(1) becomes a negative proposition because of its subject being *non-existing ab initio* and, therefore, there is no further need to fulfill it. As a result, a natural gas system will remain under the jurisdiction of the Gas Directive even if its functionality changes to handling hydrogen. Thus, one can conclude the Directive is often overridden in relation to such a system.

Thinking about the second form, that is, a system designed originally to handle hydrogen, the issue is still legally complicated. At first glance, the Gas Directive does not apply to such a system, mainly because the primary purpose of the Gas Directive was exclusively to regulate the natural gas market (or systems). However, one can argue that the lack of other gas markets at the time of ratification of the Gas Directive does not prevent it from being applied to them, primarily as Article 2(1) was intended to recognize the possibility of such markets existing (Fleming & Kreeft, 2020, p. 110). Thus, the Commission may render a new extensive interpretation of the Directive to include hydrogen or other gases in the Gas Directive, arguing that they have taken some share of the energy market previously met by natural gas, and this should be now treated similarly. This extensive interpretation assumes that the capability of a gaseous energy carrier, for example, hydrogen, to be safely injected into and transported through the natural gas system makes it eligible to become a matter for the Gas Directive universally (i.e., even if it passes through an independent system).

Nevertheless, even if we accept such an extensive interpretation, it might violate the non-retroactivity principle, making it problematic to apply the Gas Directive to a pure hydrogen system. Moreover, it is not expected that the Commission will initially render a new interpretation of an ongoing law on its own behalf as this procedure needs to commence by one Member State, and this has not occurred yet. Thus, it is most probably not applicable to such a newly established system. The different interpretations discussed above are summarized in Table 17.1.

The Gas and Electricity Directive and Hydrogen Storage

Hydrogen can be stored using diverse physical forms (compressed or liquid state) or chemical methods (Niaz et al., 2015). However, underground hydrogen storage (UHS) looks to be the most promising method, both economically and

Table 17.1: The Applicability of the Gas Directive to Different Types of Hydrogen Systems

Case	NGH2	Converted NG system	Newly constructed H_2 system
Applicability of the Gas Directive	Yes	More often than not	Most probably not

Source: Authors' own elaboration.

technically. Hydrogen is injected and stored in depleted reservoirs or salt caverns (Zivar et al., 2021). The UHS capacity of Europe is estimated at 84.8 PWh[4] with Germany having the highest potential of 11.1 % of total capacity (Caglayan et al., 2020).

On the one hand, hydrogen storage can be perceived as gas storage, especially if hydrogen is obtained from fossil fuels. The same argument in Section 1 can be used to investigate if the Gas Directive applies to storing NGH2 or pure hydrogen. The applicability of the Gas Directive to hydrogen storage means TPA obligations (according to Recitals 23 and 24 and Article 33) and unbundled principles (addressed particularly in Article 15) should rule hydrogen storage. This can be especially the case for low-carbon hydrogen as it is produced from fossil fuels.

On the other hand, hydrogen can be stored as a method for electricity storage, especially when integrated into a renewable, particularly solar electricity production system. The former Directive 2009/72/EC on the internal electricity market did not address electricity storage using hydrogen or batteries as storage was mainly limited to mechanical means, that is, pumped-storage hydroelectricity. Thus, some member states, like Germany, Italy, Spain and the UK, adopted their own approach to approving battery pilots in motivated cases where transmission system operators (TSOs) and distribution system operators (DSOs) were involved (Meeus & Bhagwat, 2018). However, the Commission has since recast it to the new Electricity Directive 2019/944.

Article 2(59) of the Electricity Directive defines energy storage in the electricity system as "[...] the conversion of electrical energy into a form of energy which can be stored, the storing of such energy, and the subsequent reconversion of such energy into electrical energy or use as another energy carrier." According to Article 2(60), the device where the storage happens is known as an *energy storage facility*. This means the act of storing hydrogen produced from the electrolysis process is classified as energy storage. The Directive articulates energy storage in an electricity system instead of defining electricity storage, and it does not provide a clear definition of a system. Moreover, the definition includes three inextricably linked segments; conversion, storing and reconversion to energy. This implies that if the electrical hydrogen is used for non-energy application (for instance, as feedstock), it will not be considered as storage even if it was stored in the meantime.

The current approach of the EU energy acquis on hydrogen raises questions about the legal situation of some hypothetical cases. For example, which directive covers electrical hydrogen stored in a UHS facility part of the natural gas system, especially if it is stored for electricity network congestion management? One can argue that the Gas Directive applies since it is stored in the natural gas system. The counterargument recognizes it as electricity, converted to another form of energy and, therefore, should be ruled by the Electricity Directive. Under the second scenario, the legal situation of the UHS system after depleting hydrogen remains vague about whether such a storage facility remains an electricity system or not. It is especially the case because conversely to the Gas Directive, the Electricity Directive does not clearly define a *system*.

What if the reservoir was not previously part of the natural gas system and was initially prepared for hydrogen storage? While some electricity system operators can own the storage facility, could gas undertakings be prevented from owning or operating such a reservoir just because the stored hydrogen is a form of electricity? Moreover, since salt caverns can be used for hydrogen, natural gas, and carbon dioxide storage, this may set up a conflict of interest between gas and electricity operators. It is not entirely clear how these conflicts should be managed under current legal frameworks. This case can become more complicated because the efficiency of salt cavern UHS facilities is increased by injecting a cushion gas, such as methane, before injecting the main gas (here, hydrogen) (Zivar et al., 2021). One can question whether the injection of methane (the main component of natural gas) has any legal consequences and whether it turns a UHS facility into a part of the gas system. Such an argument becomes even more vital if a gas undertaking performs the injection process.

Finally, we can talk about the direct conversion of solar energy to hydrogen. While the technology has only been developed at the pilot scale, it will likely be industrialized by 2030 (Radowitz, 2021). In this method, solar energy is transferred directly to water to produce hydrogen without generating electricity. Regarding Article 2(59), storing such hydrogen cannot be considered electricity storage and, if it is stored in pressure vessels but not UHS, the Gas Directive will not apply either.

The above-mentioned cases indicate scenarios in which hydrogen is either under the concurrent jurisdiction of two directives or of none. The former is more complicated because the two directives have different approaches, although amended simultaneously most recently. The Gas Directive amendment was aimed at solidifying the unbundling outlines of the new gas pipelines coming from third countries to the EU (like the Nord Stream 2). Conversely, recasting the Electricity Directive was a part of the clean energy for all Europeans package. Thus, recasting aligned it with EU environmental targets to integrate renewables more and, therefore, it elaborated explicitly on hydrogen storage. The concurrent jurisdiction is especially problematic as the Electricity Directive bans generators, and the distributors, in particular, from owning storage facilities (Fleming & Fershee, 2018; Fleming & Kreeft, 2020), while the Gas Directive allows this: however, only under certain circumstances. Additionally, the compliance of a gas undertaking handling hydrogen storage facilities with the Electricity Directive remains questionable and needs to become transparent.

This conclusion necessitates revising the Directives in line with the hydrogen development targets. While the Commission is reviewing the hydrogen and decarbonized gas market package to "ensure that the gas market framework is in line with our Fit for 55 ambition" (European Commission, 2021, September 01), the new provisions should be outlined based on the gradual transition from the current gas network system to the desired hydrogen one. It should also clarify the legal status of a network handling NGH2 and pure hydrogen to safeguard the security of supply. Furthermore, the applicability of unbundling outlines and network operators' roles in hydrogen system development should become clear, as will be discussed next. However, without prejudice to the ongoing reform of the Gas or Electricity Directive, nothing will diminish the need for clarification of the legal status of hydrogen concerning the current energy acquis, a revision procedure that is expected to be time-consuming.

HYDROGEN NETWORK DEVELOPMENT IN THE EU ENERGY ACQUIS

Legal Challenges of Hydrogen Transmission System Development

Assuming the necessity of NGH2 as a part of the transition phase on the way to establishing the EU (pure) hydrogen market, two actions seem necessary to be implemented simultaneously: the optimization of the existing natural gas network for NGH2 and the creation of a hydrogen transmission network (which can be the existing network, but adapted to handle pure hydrogen, partially or entirely). However, such a twofold strategy requires revisions in the current legal frameworks. To understand the aimed revisions, the existing legal outlines of the energy transmission sector needs to be examined first.

Before the restructuring of the EU energy market and during the monopoly era, the producers, merchant gas transmission companies (MGTCs) and local distribution companies cooperated in a vertically integrated structure to meet the demand. With privatization, liberalization and unbundling, the EU natural gas market has been fundamentally reshaped. Most importantly, the MGTCs have been replaced by the following:

(a) Utilities: the gas (and power) assets owners, like gas-fired power stations and regasification terminals;
(b) Mid-stream energy traders of gas and power;
(c) Network companies, including DSOs and TSOs;
(d) LDCs, which serve smaller customers in competition with a range of other suppliers, and
(e) Storage owners and operators, some of which are owned by TSOs, and some are in independent ownership.

The Gas Directive unbundled the network; it turned the TSOs and DSOs into pure gas (and power) network companies, preventing them from engaging in energy supply (Stern, 2017).

Despite the unbundling, the energy acquis kept the TSOs/DSOs responsible for developing the network to meet the demand and safeguard a secure and reliable energy supply. According to Article 22(1) of the Gas Directive, TSOs should draft a network development plan (NDP or NEP) in a ten-year horizon for their affiliated state and submit it to the national regulatory authority (NRA) after consulting all the relevant stakeholders. The plan should contain efficient measures to safeguard the system's adequacy to preserve the security of supply. Since cross-border trading is essential for the EU natural gas market to function, an EU-wide plan is also needed to harmonize the NDPs. Therefore, the European Network of Transmission System Operators for Gas (ENTSO-G) has adopted a non-binding community-wide ten-year NDP (TYNDP) according to Article 8(3)(b) Regulation 715/2009. The TYNDP includes a European supply adequacy outlook and should be updated every two years. It also must be consistent with the NDPs.

Forecasting supply and demand and needed investment for developing the network, especially for building interconnections, is an intrinsic task of the TSOs, along with the help of the NRAs. While the ENTSO-G is a platform to facilitate cooperation between gas TSOs, the Agency for Cooperation of Energy Regulators (ACER) is a forum for coordination between the NRAs. This means that the NDPs, including the TYNDP, are formed and monitored based on close cooperation between ENTSO-G and ACER, and are reported to the European Commission (Hancher & Salerno, 2017).

Additionally, to establish closer links between national and EU-wide markets and to accelerate the development of strategically important cross-border energy transmission projects, the EU parliament has ratified Regulation 347/2013 on guidelines for a trans-European energy infrastructure (TEN-E). It has defined eight priority energy corridors labeled projects of common interest (PCIs) (Melgar, 2017). The PCIs will deliver positive net welfare benefits for the EU member states as a subset of the projects listed in the TYNDPs. ACER has a central role in providing essential and comprehensive information for defining PCI lists and reviewing national, regional, and European network development plans (ACER, 2021). Figure 17.1 demonstrates a brief scheme of natural gas development planning in the EU.

Such a legal structure has been formed gradually over time. The European gas network was first formed based on a monopoly structure. Then, the above-mentioned legal framework was implemented on the pre-existing natural gas network over time to make it a competitive market where non-discriminatory access was granted to third parties. However, the EU Green Plan now targets decarbonization, which is not necessarily in line with the competition. In other words, regardless of whether the current energy acquis is applicable for establishing a new hydrogen network, it is more probable that it does not assure the decarbonization aims as it was designed to guarantee other targets.

Despite the inconsistencies, the principle of structural cooperation for harmonic network development is still needed for hydrogen networks. Thus, the fundamental question of who should bear the costs or plan the development remains open. This is important because network development plans for alternative gases, such as hydrogen, are not enshrined in the TYNDP or the NEP. Natural gas TSOs may be equally accused of breaching the law if they become involved in hydrogen network development. Additionally, developing a hydrogen network requires massive investment, while the law prohibits the provision of this through natural gas network fees (GEODE, 2020). This indicates the existence of a legal

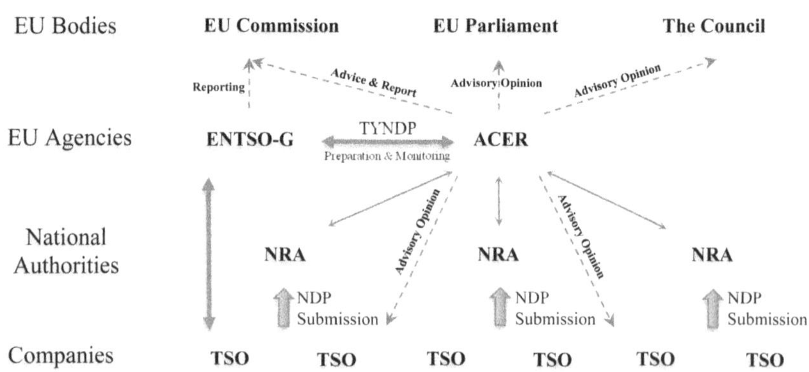

Figure 17.1: A brief scheme of natural gas development planning in the EU.
Source: Authors' own elaboration

void and the need to design a planning structure for the hydrogen network expansion.

In addition to pure hydrogen network development, financing the existing natural gas network optimization for NGH2 transmission is not without its challenges. Studies have shown that the addition of hydrogen to the gas composition requires increasing the flow rate to conserve energy per unit volume of the transported natural gas. This is costly since some of the network rotating equipment might need to be redesigned or reinforced. As depicted in Table 17.1, we assume that the Gas Directive applies to the NGH2 transmission network, meaning that the TYNDP and NEP can sketch the main outlines. However, it might be problematic for the DSOs. For instance, Italian DSOs counteract municipalities that do not currently account for hydrogen transportation (Saccani et al., 2020), and it should become clear how and who should afford the machinery adapted for handling NGH2.

Cross-Border Hydrogen Transportation: The Gas Quality Standard Issue

The technical assessment shows that injecting up to 15 % vol hydrogen into the existing EU natural gas network may require only modest technical modifications to the pipelines (Melaina et al., 2013). The obtained NGH2 is also compatible with standard metering instruments (Jaworski et al., 2020) and has been assessed safe and compatible with the EU's home appliances (Isaac & Lewis, 2021; European Commission, 2017). However, blending can change the natural gas Wobbe Index[5] (Fleming & Fershee, 2018). As the member states have different thresholds for the Wobbe Index in their gas standards, this may hinder the cross-border movement of NGH2, the central element of the EU hydrogen market, between them.

Even in the early attempts to design the internal gas market, the European Parliament recognized unharmonized gas quality standards as a barrier causing uncertainty for companies who wanted access to the different national networks (Stiphout, 2021). To address these concerns, the EU Commission issued mandate M/400 to the European Committee for Standardization (CEN) in 2007 to analyze the effects of changes in gas quality on consumer appliances. A later report (GL Noble Denton; Pöyry Management Consulting, 2012) prepared for the Commission provided insights into the costs and benefits of gas quality harmonization, highlighting the vast array of issues and interests in gas quality specifications among the member states. The report reflected no consensus on how harmonization could be achieved, or even if it should be at all. Contrary to these efforts, the rejection of cross-border gas movement due to the incompatibility of gas quality between the two sides has rarely happened. Moreover, the proposed mandate was non-binding for the member states and, as a result, unifying gas quality standards has not been strictly pursued nor has it occurred.

In the absence of an EU-wide gas specification standard, Article 15(1) of the Commission Regulation 2015/703 considers TSOs responsible for reaching a joint proposal for solving the issues that may arise due to the gas quality differences in cross-border movement in cooperation with NRAs. Such a procedure has never been triggered as issues have been solved by cooperation between TSOs (Piebalgs & Olczak, 2018). While the Commission previously pointed out the importance of "interoperability" under Article 6 of the Directive 2003/55/EC[6] to issue the mandate M/400, harmonization of standards will become more of an energy security matter in the EU hydrogen market as time goes by. This is notably because Article 7(4)(b) of Regulation (EU) 2017/1938 classifies safety and gas quality considerations as the risks that affect the security of the gas supply and makes the member states responsible for taking necessary action to eliminate them. This implies that in a pan-European hydrogen market, cross-border gas movement may become a daily need that requires a more proactive ex ante regulation instead of the current ex post approach of Article 15 (1) Regulation 2015/703.

The current challenges of the transmission network in meeting the objectives of the EU hydrogen strategy require some legal reforms. This could include but is not limited to:

(1) A comprehensive network development plan which encompasses and meets the demands of natural gas, NGH2 and hydrogen together is needed to safeguard the security of the gas supply in the transition era. Such a plan should find a balance between the fundamental rights of the member states to determine "their choice between different energy sources and the general structure of its energy supply," according to Article 194(2) of the Treaty of Functioning European Union (TFEU), and to promote hydrogen in line with the climate-neutrality general goals of the EU. The EU should meticulously manage this balance since the legal framework of TFEU does not allow for the compelling of a member state to give up a specific energy source due only to environmental considerations (Talus & Aalto, 2017).

Additionally, affirmative and preventive measures and policies should guide investments to support the gradual shift to hydrogen. In other words, the existing gas network should not become a stranded asset unless the market is assured of the proper functionality of the new hydrogen network. For instance, the Belgian NRA has mandated the depreciation of the pipeline networks by 2050, and Austria has taken a similar approach, using weighted average cost of capital (WACC) as a lever (FSR, 2021).

Member states can also allocate their state aid to accelerating the hydrogen market establishment as a complementary measure (see Section 6). The EU should also outline TEN-E to support hydrogen more than fossil fuel projects; however, the considerations regarding the gradual shift to hydrogen must be observed.

(2) The current gas network and its corresponding energy acquis has developed gradually. Even Poland and the Baltic states were given a moratorium to comply with the EU energy regulations to protect their markets from uninhibited seizure by Russian companies upon entry into the Union (Talus & Aalto, 2017). Thus, it is not logical to expect the under-construction hydrogen network to comply with the same legal outline from the beginning, especially the strict TPA or unbundling obligations. Instead, it is conducive to allowing TSOs/DSOs to contribute to constructing the new network. Such policy is beneficial for both sides from a financial perspective; while it gives the grounds for the above-mentioned idea of gradual depreciation of gas facilities, it allows the EU to preserve a financial channel for running hydrogen development plans (Barnes & Yafimava, 2020; GEODE, 2020).

(3) Although a unified gas specification standard is critical for the pan-European hydrogen network establishment, it may not be needed from the early stages significantly because not all the member states benefit from the same level of preparedness of using hydrogen. For instance, while the high capillarity of the natural gas network in Italy or Germany makes it ready to step into the hydrogen economy (Saccani et al., 2020), the island states of Malta and Cyprus do not yet benefit from an extended gas network in their territory (Papsch, 2021, p. 584). Moreover, not all the member states have the same plans for utilizing hydrogen in the future as their energy demand and market volumes are not the same. For instance, Finland seems to see limited potential for the deployment of hydrogen, instead favoring nuclear electricity to decarbonize the energy sector (Costescu et al., 2021). Thus, it is reasonable to assume that the regional gas exchanges between neighbors will soon look more realistic than EU-wide transportation.

Limitation of the movement of hydrogen to the local markets makes harmonization of standards simpler as, instead of targeting an EU-wide standard, one can focus on regional ones. This means that the harmonization of gas standards should first be implemented in areas where regional NGH2 exchanges are expected to be higher. This is important because the EU hydrogen strategy pays special attention to the production of hydrogen electrolysis in neighboring countries and its import into the EU, including through Ukraine. Therefore, it is necessary to remove technical barriers to the transfer of hydrogen production from priority routes, that is, between the main production sites to important consumption centers.

GUARANTEE OF ORIGIN (GO)

In recent years, growing attention to climate change has necessitated the compliance of power generation with the carbon abatement goals and higher facilitation of renewables. However, it is still difficult to guarantee the carbon neutrality of the electricity delivered to a specific consumer since a liberalized market aims at providing the cheapest electricity, not the greenest. In other words, a liberalized market is characterized by the availability of competing electricity suppliers fed by diversified primary resources. Thus, it is problematic to identify where the electrons flowing to each consumer come from (renewable, nuclear, or fossil-based origins).

To solve this issue, Directive 2001/77/EC, drafted to promote electricity produced from renewable energy sources in the internal electricity market, addresses the question of guarantee of origin (GO). While Recital 10 introduced the idea, Article 5 defined a GO as a certificate issued upon a producer's request and confirms the content of the source and the time and place of power generation (and, if hydroelectric power, the plant's capacity). Shortly after, Directive 2003/54/EC attempted to outline "disclosure" of the electricity generation source; however, it did not refer to GO explicitly (Evercooren, 2020, p. 203). The issuance of GO for eligible renewable energy sources was then reaffirmed in Article 15 of the Directive 2009/28/EC (the first Renewable Directive, RED I). Then, Recital 59 of the Directive (EU) 2018/2001 (RED II) extended the coverage of GO to gaseous renewable energy forms, including hydrogen, and even non-renewables. Moreover, Article 19 of RED II stipulates what information the GO should contain, including but not limited to the place of power generation, any dedicated investment support or national support scheme, facility commissioning time, and a unique identification number. Accordingly, the GOs "have the sole function of showing to a final customer that a given share or quantity of energy was produced from renewable sources."

There have been critiques on the efficiency of the GO system, primarily to attract additional investment, claiming that GO has failed to bring any additional investment for the European electricity system but has just added to the bureaucratic complexity of the market. The low price of the GO, as a result of its oversupply in the European market, is attributed mainly to Norwegian producers. Therefore, it has even been proposed to limit the access of Norwegian GOs to the EU market (Hamburger, 2019).

Contrary to such claims, one can attribute the GO market oversupply to its developing status, which has changed in recent years for a better supply-demand balance. For instance, the Association of Issuing Bodies, as the most prominent and longest operating GO issuer, has reported the growth of market activity regarding GOs over time. By the end of 2019, 79 % of GOs issued for electricity produced during 2018 and 49 % of GOs issued for electricity produced in 2019 were reported as having been canceled. 6 % of GOs issued for electricity produced in 2018 have expired, up from 3 % the previous year (Pototschnig & Conti, 2021). These statistics indicate how the GO is drawing more attention.

It is expected that the GO market will become more mature in the years to come due to consumers' more significant attention to the environmental footprint of power generation. This is expected to balance the market and solidify the GO system in the future. When writing this chapter, the Commission is reviewing RED II, including the certification mechanism that the "Member States will no longer be allowed to exempt GOs for supported electricity" (European Commission, 2021, July 14). It is essential to regulate the GO market, along with the developing hydrogen market, by relying on complementary measures, as below, to avoid the adverse influences of market failure.

First, Article 19 of RED II simultaneously authorizes the states to issue GOs for non-renewable sources in addition to renewable gases, including hydrogen. As a result, both renewable and low-carbon hydrogen (derived from fossil fuels) can receive GOs. Such GOs must display the carbon footprint for the different types of hydrogen, including non-renewable ones. However, an important question will still be how to calculate the carbon footprint of fossil-based hydrogen, to include the carbon emission of the natural gas extraction step, as a source of non-renewable hydrogen production. This is even more difficult for the imported natural gas from non-EU sources.

One suggestion is to consider statistics declared by the producer or monitoring systems embedded in the European methane strategy (Piebalgs & Jones, 2020). However, the reliability of self-declared data can be controversial. The efficiency of the proposed monitoring systems for imported gas is questionable as the emission level of major gas exporters, for example, Russia, Norway, or the United States, are not the same. Russia has the highest associated natural gas flaring volume globally, making its emission per unit of produced gas the highest. Moreover, there are occasional disparities between the data provided by two sources, the Russian government and global authorities, such as the Global Gas Flaring Reduction Partnership (GGFR), using satellite monitoring methods (Taherifard et al., 2019, p. 211). The emission of shale gas production in different regions of the United States is not the same, and different estimations with a significant range between high and low are available (Stern, 2017). This makes taking such measurements more complex.

Additionally, how to verify if a non-EU gas exporter claims it recycles the released emission of natural gas extraction (for instance, via carbon capture units)? The same situation may arise if the exporter claims a certain carbon emission level of its fossil-based produced hydrogen. Although Article 19 (11) of the RED II has discussed the conditions of third-country GO recognition, due to the complexities of hydrogen GO issuance, the EU should elaborate on a fully-fledged verification mechanism for hydrogen produced in third countries. This is particularly important since Russia, the leading gas exporter to Europe, has planned to export 0.2 Mt of hydrogen by 2024 and 2 Mt by 2035 (Zabanova & Westphal, 2021). Verifying hydrogen GOs from Norway could be included, given the current Norwegian GOs circulating in the European market and the transparency of Norwegian emissions data. Ultimately, the designed mechanisms must adhere to the principle of non-discrimination, which is mandatory for GO market expansion in the future (Abad & Dodds, 2020).

Third, since GO does not have a fixed price, its value being determined by the law of supply and demand, customers should be stimulated to buy renewable electricity proofed by GOs to retain market balance. While in some countries, suppliers still have a monopoly position on GO, some other states have made it possible for consumers to buy GO directly from manufacturers. This has helped with attracting new customers, especially corporations (Evercooren, 2020). Nevertheless, it is still necessary that the information provided in the GOs remains clear, reliable, efficient and, at the same time, easily understood by all customers; complicated or untrustworthy information will not create new GO demand. The implication of this requirement for hydrogen GO means the hydrogen taxonomy enshrined in the EU hydrogen strategy should be simply reflected in the GO, somehow understandable for (non-professional) customers, from the carbon emission perspective. Evidence from studies shows that a lack of understanding of the disclosure mechanisms in the Netherlands in 2019 has led to a lack of public trust in the "existence of green electricity," which may adversely impact GO performance (klimaatstichting HIER, 2019).

Finally, expanding the GO market could become possible by facilitating cross-border exchanges. However, the current certificates are not the same content-wise, partly because the member states still have a significant role in regulating the content of GOs, and a standard form of GO is needed. While the RED II has underpinned the standardization basis, including setting the minimum required level of 1 MWh, expiration and validation time, it is still not enough. GO Standardization is especially vital for hydrogen as it is produced using different methods and from different sources, in which case certificates can differ and, therefore, be confusing. Therefore, it seems logical to design a standard certificate for the different specific steps in the production procedure, based on the applied technology and source of production. In a similar proposal, White et al. (2021) proposed the design of modular certificates based on the various components and technologies used in the hydrogen production process, considering the emission level of each step. Such modular certificates can harmonize the exchanges of hydrogen-based certificates and, thus, retain the market supply and demand balance.

STATE AID

State aid is known to be a conducive measure for developing new technologies, including renewables. The TFEU prohibits the competition-distorting state aid, particularly, Articles 107–109, which were elaborated in Commission Regulation 651/2014. These state that the member states have to inform the EU Commission of their decision to support firms in specific circumstances, defined in the mentioned frameworks, to assure the EU that their actions are not in breach of the fair competition rules. Additionally, as an external factor, the non-discriminative trade provisions of the World Trade Organization (WTO) curtail (but not entirely prohibit) state aid. Since both the EU and the member states are members of the WTO, the latter find themselves complying with the WTO rules per se and the EU's interpretation of them. Moreover, since the eligibility criteria of state aid support are complicated, it is up to the court to decide its legality in a disputed situation, if the case does not end in the hands of the Commission. As a result, state aid is classified as part of the field of case law, which is overwhelmed with documented cases. This limits the scope of our study to specific (hypothetical) situations of devoting state aid for the promotion of hydrogen.

State Investment in Infrastructures Development

The first question is whether state aid can be allocated to hydrogen infrastructure development. According to the provisions of the TFEU and section 7 of Regulation 651/2014, it is possible to do so, contingent on the necessity of infrastructure to prevent market failure. The Commission has rendered three criteria for distinguishing the necessity: (i) the absence of such infrastructure should be detrimental for achieving the development plans, (ii) TPA is guaranteed, and (iii) the project will contribute to the security of the supply in the Union (Hancher & Salerno, 2019, p. 857).

Achieving the ambitious goals of Europe's hydrogen strategy requires massive infrastructure development, including a significant leap in renewable electricity production, and gas and electricity network development and optimization. Given the recent analysis results by Belmans et al. (2021), there is little room for supplying the additional renewable electricity demand by 2030. Therefore, state aid is *necessary* to attain hydrogen strategy goals and preserve the EU security of the supply in the future. It means the EU Commission's criteria for state aid allocation will be met if the TPA is guaranteed in hydrogen infrastructures. Such development plans can be realized under PCIs and within the framework of the TEN-E regulations. This confirms the need to revise the TEN-E legal framework favoring renewables development, including hydrogen targets, as has already been discussed above (see section "Cross-Border Hydrogen Transportation: The Gas Quality Standard Issue").

While the three criteria seem helpful for understanding a case's legality, a lasting hydrogen development plan needs more straightforward solutions. The EU regulations should clearly outline the exemption circumstances regarding state aid so that the member states can implement their plans without following intensive bureaucracy, specifically for hydrogen development. This can be achieved, for instance, by granting a mid-term exemption for allocating state aid to these development plans. Such solutions will also enhance the certainty of investment. This would also lift the burden of proof from the member states' shoulders. Current regulations require them to demonstrate their compliance with the triple criteria. However, this can be assigned to the EU Commission to assess if there is a violation of competition or it can become the responsibility of the complainant, exclusively for renewable development plans.

Since renewable hydrogen costs more than fossil-based hydrogen, one may suggest subsidizing the electricity used by the electrolyzers to reduce the cost and make it more competitive. However, different aspects of competition regulations preclude this. Within the WTO, supportive measures for renewables, that is, subsidies, might be justified under Article XX(b) of the General Agreement on Tariffs and Trade (GATT)[7] in addition to the Agreement on Subsidies and Countervailing Measures (ASCM). These provisions are not easy to fulfill in this case. First, Article XX(b) of GATT has put the burden of proof of "necessity" on the party invoking it, which is practically impossible, more often than not.

Additionally, it is difficult to prove that renewable development is in line with environmental protection under the conventional jurisprudence of the WTO and, therefore, it is challenging to invoke Article XX exceptions in this case (Cottier et al., 2011, p. 226). Even if proved, the applicability of the exceptions allowed by Article XX of GATT to the ASCM subsidies remains questionable to many trade lawyers (Rubini, 2009, p. 195). Finally, such subsidization of the electricity delivered to electrolyzers would fall under the definition of specific subsidies, that is, those explicitly dedicated "to an enterprise or industry or group of enterprises or industries," and it would be prohibited according to ASCM, Article 2. As a result, exclusive renewable electricity subsidies would be discriminatory and non-necessary and, therefore, prohibited.

Alternatively, the Emission Trading System (ETS) can be applied to incentivize the production of renewables and low-carbon hydrogen. The Commission aims to revise the ETS and prepare it for the fourth round of implementation, 2021–2030. The revised ETS scheme could include the dedication of free allowances to these two hydrogen types, or to other hydrogen types (Barnes & Yafimava, 2020). Nevertheless, some European energy firms, like EnBW, have filed cases against the European Court of Justice, objecting to the allowance allocation system being a form of competitive distortive subsidies.[8] While the Court of First Instance has treated the case cautiously so as not to challenge the whole scheme, such firms may find a way out of the stalemate by availing themselves of the rules of the ASCM. This is because the free allocation of allowance can be perceived as a form of subsidy. Therefore, some temporary exemptions should also be comprised in the ASCM, in addition to the ETS revision. For instance, it is proposed to implement a temporary exemption grandfathering of up to 20 % of the distributed allowances for industry sectors exposed to fierce international competition from regions that are not subject to an equivalent regulation of their carbon emissions (Cottier et al., 2011).

Preferential Taxation

If renewable hydrogen cannot be subsidized, can fossil-based hydrogen be taxed on its non-renewable electricity consumption base and carbon emissions (i.e., a carbon tax)? Such an idea may look destructive for developing hydrogen competing fossil fuels in the early years; however, it may look reasonable in the long term when empowering renewable hydrogen against other sorts of gases becomes logical. While the EU is reviewing the energy taxation law, imposing a tax, in this case, depends on other field facts. Particularly, if one of the two hydrogens is imported, it may potentially violate WTO regulations banning the imposition of different taxes on "like" products. The four criteria of the "likeness test" states that two goods are the same if they share (i) physical characteristics, (ii) end-uses of products, (iii) consumers' tastes and (iv) preferences and tariff classification (Selivanova, 2014, p. 282). One can argue that imposing different taxes, in this case, is only justifiable by citing differences in customer tastes. Accordingly, if some goods pose a higher risk to human health than others, the government may perceive and tax them differently.[9] While this argument sounds logical, the Appellate Body and the Panel of the WTO are the final decision-makers who evaluate the solidity of the government's argument for proving the necessity of such policy for achieving the desired goal: that is, health protection. This is mainly clarified on a case-by-case basis and, thus, it is difficult to be judged beforehand. However, if similar solutions, like the standardization of state aid allocation for renewables discussed above, are designed and adopted within WTO rules and regulations, they can facilitate the renewable development needless of time-consuming litigation processes.

Market Expansion and the Local Content

The expansion of the hydrogen market requires new production capacity and expansion of the transmission networks. Since the network development will probably need more time, the EU hydrogen strategy foresees that most hydrogen production will be quickly consumed locally. However, if the local demand is not big enough, the production cost may rise due to the economies of scale. Can the government adopt policies to create additional local demand, for instance, by persuading some consumers to buy hydrogen from such producers, under national hydrogen policies?

Any enforcement of an undertaking to conclude such an agreement is in breach of Article 101 (e) of the TFEU, which prohibits "the conclusion of contracts subject to acceptance by the other parties of supplementary obligations." Nevertheless, using incentives can be assessed separately. For example, if such concessions include waiving the government's revenues, subsidization provisions can be applied. Additionally, the enjoyment of such a conditional concession may be restricted to the subject matter of local content regulations stated within Article III of the GATT. The implication of Article III means that no discrimination can be made between two enterprises on the pretext that one of them uses a locally produced product, even if it is for the better of renewable energy promotion. Such a situation has been experienced in the Canada Feed-In Tariff (FIT) Program case.[10] Therefore, in this scenario, the government must consider any concession to any customer who consumes hydrogen, not just those who buy it from a local producer.

CONCLUSION

In this chapter, the main outlines of the EU hydrogen strategy have been discussed from a legal perspective. Given the assumption that a gradual transition to pure hydrogen is the only sustainable strategy to safeguard the security of the energy supply in the EU, using a hydrogen and natural gas mixture, NGH2 as a transition fuel is justified in the transition era. While the Gas Directive is currently under review to include hydrogen, the current legal situation of hydrogen and NGH2 should also be clarified. This must be realized if the TPA and unbundling regulations should rule the hydrogen networks and how the EU-wide hydrogen network development plans, and the unification of gas quality standards, should be implemented currently.

New regulations are also needed to ensure there is enough financial support to run development plans in the transition phase. The current legal frameworks of state aid as part of the EU competition law and WTO look too strict and bureaucratic to facilitate the achievement of the hydrogen development goals. Resolving this complexity necessitates designing a legal framework that assigns the burden of proof of competition violation on the complainant, with a clear framework to facilitate hydrogen infrastructure development by granting a mid-term exemption for allocating state aid, for instance. Such a framework should also eliminate any potential legal dilemma that may arise due to both the EU and the member states' membership in the WTO.

The results of this chapter show that in addition to the general outlines of the EU energy acquis' applicability to the transiting energy market, other environmental measures, like the GO scheme, need to be revised to hasten the EU hydrogen strategy, considering the elaborated taxonomy of hydrogen in the strategy that has been published. The necessity of this can also be proved when one considers the importance of low-carbon hydrogen usage in the transition era. While these documents should indicate the total released emission of fossil fuel-based hydrogen, such guarantees of origin should be standardized to make trade possible and to facilitate the mutual recognition of third state certificates.

NOTES

1 "Low-carbon hydrogen" encompasses fossil-based hydrogen with carbon capture and electricity-based hydrogen, with significantly reduced full life cycle greenhouse gas emissions than existing hydrogen production (European Commission, 2020b).

2 Founded in 1991, GEODE is made up of European independent distribution companies of gas and electricity. The association represents more than 1,200 companies in 15 countries, both private & public owned. For further information, look at www.geode-eu.org.

3 According to Article 2 (13), "system" means any transmission networks, distribution networks, LNG facilities and/or storage facilities owned and/or operated by a natural gas undertaking, including linepack and its facilities supplying ancillary services and those of related undertakings necessary for providing access to transmission, distribution and LNG.

4 Considering each kg of hydrogen equals to 33.33 kWh, it will be 2,500 Mt hydrogen.

5 The Wobbe Index is an indicator used to compare the combustion energy output of different composition fuel gases.

6 Article 8 in the current Gas Directive declares, "technical rules shall ensure the interoperability of systems and shall be objective and non-discriminatory." Moreover, a year earlier, the High-Level Group on Competitiveness noted in its report: "The interoperability of gas systems requires greater harmonization including coordination of the gas quality specifications at the EU entry points and within the EU to facilitate the development of a liberalized and competitive European gas market" (Stiphout, 2021). The group consisted of Energy and the Environment representatives, in which Commissioners Verheugen (Enterprise and Industry),

Dimas (Environment), Kroes (Competition) and Piebalgs (Energy), as well as the member states and industry representatives. The report is available at https://www.epsu.org/sites/default/files/article/files/HLG_energy_JM_statement_2_June_06.pdf

7 Article XX of GATT states: "Subject to the requirement that such measures are not applied in a manner which would constitute a means of arbitrary or unjustifiable discrimination between countries where the same conditions prevail, or a disguised restriction on international trade, nothing in this Agreement shall be construed to prevent the adoption or enforcement by any contracting party of measures:
(a) [...]
(b) necessary to protect human, animal or plant life or health."

8 CFI Case T-387/04, EnBW Energie Baden-Württemberg AG v. Commission, 30.4.2007 para 41 ff.

9 The complexity of the case also comes from the fact that even if the effect of carbon emissions on human health is scientifically questionable, the government can impose different taxes here. According to the Appellate Body in Case European Communities—Hormones (DS26), "responsible and representative governments may act in good faith based on what, at a given time, may be a divergent opinion coming from qualified and respected sources." See Appellate Body report, para. 194 available at: https://docs.wto.org/dol2fe/Pages/SS/directdoc.aspx?filename=q:/WT/DS/26ABR-01.pdf&Open=True

10 In the Canada Feed-In Tariff (FIT) Program case, the Ontario local government linked the eligibility for its FIT scheme to a local content requirement. Japan and the EU submitted that the FIT programme was not compatible with Canada's obligations, including Article III (4) of the GATT 1994, and requested the elimination of the domestic content requirement, which was recognized as the same by both the Panel and the Appellate Body (Rutherford, 2020).

REFERENCES

Abad, A. V., & Dodds, P. E. (2020). Green hydrogen characterisation initiatives: Definitions, standards, guarantees of origin, and challenges. *Energy Policy*, *138*, 111300.

ACER. (2021, October 31). *Network Development Plans*. https://www.acer.europa.eu/gas/infrastructure/network-development-plans

Barnes, A., & Yafimava, K. (2020). *EU Hydrogen Vision: Regulatory opportunities and challenges*. Oxford Institute for Energy Studies.

Belmans, R., Reis, P. C., & Vingerhoets, P. (2021). *Electrification and sustainable fuels: Competing for wind and sun*. Florence School of Regulation.

Belyi, A. (2021, May 23). *Choosing between decarbonisation options for European gas*. https://www.naturalgasworld.com/european-commission-discusses-scenarios-for-gas-79057

Benrath, D. (2020). Applicable law to hydrogen pipelines for energy purposes in Germany. *Journal of Energy & Natural Resources Law*, *38*(1), 65–89.

Caglayan, D. G., Weber, N., Heinrichs, H. U., Linßen, J., Robinius, M., Kukla, P. A., & Stolten, D. (2020). Technical potential of salt caverns for hydrogen storage in Europe. *International Journal of Hydrogen Energy*, *45*(11), 6793–6805.

Costescu, A., Eisaks, J., Hansen, N., Rodriguez-Gomez, N., Miranda, A., Hemptinne, B., Maduka, E. D., Vohra, C., Fischer, G., Vegere, K., Kovacovska, L., Kiecis, O., Orglerova, P., Strahovnik, T., Rudnytska, U., Zabanova, Y., & Bezerra, J. (2021). *Comparison of the German national hydrogen strategy to the Norwegian, Finnish and Australian strategies*. Florence School of Regulation.

Cottier, T., Malumfashi, G., Matteotti-Berkutova, S., Nartova, O., Sepibus, J. D., & Bigdeli, S. Z. (2011). Energy in WTO law and policy. In T. Cottier & P. Delimatsis (Eds.), *The prospects of international trade regulation. From fragmentation to coherence* (pp. 211–244). Cambridge University Press.

Edwards, P., Kuznetsov, V., & David, W. (2007). Hydrogen energy. *Philosophical Transactions of the Royal Society A: Mathematical, Physical and Engineering Sciences*, *365*(1853), 1043–1056.

European Commission. (2017). *Energy storage—The role of electricity*.

European Commission. (2020a, July 8). *An EU strategy for energy system integration*. https://eur-lex.europa.eu/legal-content/EN/ALL/?uri=COM:2020:299:FIN

European Commission. (2020b, July 8). *A hydrogen strategy for a climate-neutral Europe*. Retrieved from European Commission. https://ec.europa.eu/energy/sites/ener/files/hydrogen_strategy.pdf

European Commission. (2021, July 14). *Commission presents Renewable Energy Directive revision*. https://ec.europa.eu/info/news/commission-presents-renewable-energy-directive-revision-2021-jul-14_en

European Commission. (2021, September 1). *Hydrogen*. https://ec.europa.eu/energy/topics/energy-system-integration/hydrogen_en

European Commission. (2021, November 11). *Hydrogen and decarbonised gas market package*. https://ec.europa.eu/energy/topics/markets-and-consumers/market-legislation/hydrogen-and-decarbonised-gas-market-package_en

Evercooren, D. V. (2020). The EU approach to the regulation of guarantees of origin. In M. M. Roggenkamp & C. Banet (Eds.), *European Energy Law report XIII* (pp. 197–218). Intersentia.

Fleming, R., & Fershee, J. P. (2018). The "hydrogen economy" in the United States and the European Union. In D. Zillman, L. Godden, L. Paddock, & M. Roggenkamp (Eds.), *Innovation in energy law and technology: Dynamic Solutions for Energy Transitions* (pp. 137–153). Oxford University Press.

Fleming, R., & Kreeft, G. (2020). Power-to-gas and hydrogen for energy storage under EU energy law. In M. M. Roggenkamp & C. Banet (Eds.), *European Energy Law report XIII* (pp. 101–123). Intersentia.

FSR. (2021, May 5). *Stranded gas assets: The dilemma of the energy transition costs*. https://fsr.eui.eu/stranded-gas-assets-the-dilemma-of-the-energy-transition-costs/

GEODE. (2020). *Towards the New Age of Gas Networks*.

GL Noble Denton; Pöyry Management Consulting. (2012). *Gas quality harmonisation cost benefit analysis final report*. GL Industrial Services.

Hamburger, Á. (2019). Is guarantee of origin really an effective energy policy tool in Europe? A critical approach. *Society and Economy*, *41*(4), 487–507.

Hancher, L., & Salerno, F. (2019). State aid for environmental protection. In L. Hancher, A. d. Hauteclocque, C. Jones, L. Kjølbye, V. Landes, F. Salerno, & L. Sandberg (Eds.), *EU energy law. Volume II: EU competition law and energy markets* (pp. 819–860). Claeys & Casteels.

Hancher, L., & Salerno, F. M. (2017). EU energy and competition: Analysis of current trends and a first assessment of the new package. In R. Leal-Arcas & J. Wouters (Eds.), *Research handbook on EU energy law and policy* (pp. 48–66). Edward Elgar.

Isaac, T., & Lewis, A. (2021). *hydrogen blending—Lessons from HyDeploy*. Oxford Institute for Energy Studies.

Ishaq, H., & Dincer, I. (2020). The role of hydrogen in global transition to 100% renewable energy. In T. S. Uyar (Ed.), *Accelerating the transition to a 100% renewable energy era* (pp. 275–307). Springer.

Jaworski, J., Kułaga, P., & Blacharski, T. (2020). Study of the effect of addition of hydrogen to natural gas on diaphragm gas meters. *Energies*, *13*(11), 3006.

Jens, J., Wang, A., van-der-Leun, K., Peters, D., & Buseman, M. (2021, April). *Extending the European hydrogen backbone.* https://gasforclimate2050.eu/wp-content/uploads/2021/06/European-Hydrogen-Backbone_April-2021_V3.pdf

Kleperis, J., Boss, D., Mezulis, A., Zemite, L., Lesnicenoks, P., Knoks, A., & Dimanta, I. (2021). Analysis of the role of the Latvian natural gas network for the use of future energy systems: Hydrogen from Res. *Latvian Journal of Physics and Technical Sciences*, *58*(3), 214–226.

klimaatstichting HIER. (2019, June 21). *Een op de vijf Nederlanders gelooft niet dat groene stroom bestaat.* https://www.nu.nl/economie/5946804/een-op-de-vijf-nederlanders-gelooft-niet-dat-groene-stroom-bestaat.html

Lambert, M. (2020). *EU hydrogen strategy—A case for urgent action towards implementation.* Oxford Institute for Energy Studies.

Lengyel, A. (2021). EU and domestic regulation on the production of renewable hydrogen, constitutional issues related to the domestic regulation. *Journal of Agricultural and Environmental Law*, *16*(30), 123–154.

Maleki, A., Hafeznia, H., Rosen, M. A., & Pourfayaz, F. (2017). Optimization of a grid-connected hybrid solar-wind-hydrogen CHP system for residential applications by efficient metaheuristic approaches. *Applied Thermal Engineering*, *123*, 1263–1277.

Meeus, L., & Bhagwat, P. (2018). Classical grey areas since the start of the internal market. In L. Meeus & J. Glachant (Eds.), *Electricity network regulation in the EU: The challenges ahead for transmission and distribution* (pp. 105–129). Edward Elgar.

Melaina, M. W., Antonia, O., & Penev, M. (2013). *Blending hydrogen into natural gas pipeline networks: A review of key issues.* National Renewable Energy Lab. (NREL).

Melgar, B. H. (2017). EU energy law in the maritime sector. In L. Hancher & F. M. Salerno (Eds.), *Research handbook on EU energy law and policy* (pp. 335–352). Edward Elgar.

Niaz, S., Manzoor, T., & Pandith, A. H. (2015). Hydrogen storage: Materials, methods and perspectives. *Renewable and Sustainable Energy Reviews*, *50*, 457–469.

Papsch, J. (2021). Derogations and exemptions. In C. Jones & W.-J. Kettlewell (Eds.), *EU energy law. Volume I: The internal energy market* (p. 584). Claeys & Casteels Law Publishing.

Parra, D., Valverde, L., Pino, F. J., & Patel, M. K. (2019). A review on the role, cost and value of hydrogen energy systems for deep decarbonisation. *Renewable and Sustainable Energy Reviews*, *101*, 279–294.

Piebalgs, A., & Jones, C. (2020). *A proposal for a regulatory framework for hydrogen guarantees of origin.* Florence School of Regulation.

Piebalgs, A., & Olczak, M. (2018). *Decarbonising the gas sector: Is renewable gas a serious option?* Florence School of Regulation.

Pototschnig, A., & Conti, I. (2021). *Upgrading guarantees of origin to promote the achievement of the EU renewable energy target at least cost.* European University Institute, Florence School of Regulation. https://doi.org/10.2870/848062

Radowitz, B. (2021, August 24). *"Very disruptive" direct solar-to-hydrogen commercially viable by 2030, says oil group Repsol.* https://www.rechargenews.com/energy-transition/very-disruptive-direct-solar-to-hydrogen-commercially-viable-by-2030-says-oil-group-repsol/2-1-1056771

Rosen, M. A., & Koohi-Fayegh, S. (2016). The prospects for hydrogen as an energy carrier: An overview of hydrogen energy and hydrogen energy systems. *Energy, Ecology and Environment*, *1*(1), 10–29.

Rubini, L. (2009). *The definition of subsidy and state aid: WTO and EC Law in comparative perspective*. Oxford University Press.

Rutherford, A. (2020). The applicability of the law of the WTO to green energy security. In *Energy security and green energy. International law and economics* (pp. 103–139). Springer.

Saccani, C., Pellegrini, M., & Guzzini, A. (2020). Analysis of the existing barriers for the market development of power to hydrogen (P2H) in Italy. *Energies*, *13*, 4835.

Selivanova, Y. (2014). The WTO agreements and energy. In K. Talus (Ed.), *Research handbook on international energy law* (pp. 275–307). Edward Elgar.

Steen, M. (2016). Building a hydrogen infrastructure in the EU. In M. Ball, A. Basile, & T. N. Veziroğlu (Eds.), *Compendium of hydrogen energy* (pp. 267–292). Woodhead Publishing.

Stern, J. (2017). *The future of gas in decarbonising European energy markets: The need for a new approach*. Oxford Institute for Energy Studies.

Stiphout, M. v. (2021, September 10). *Gas quality standards in the European Union*. http://members.igu.org/html/wgc2009/papers/docs/wgcFinal00785.pdf

Taherifard, A., Mahdavi, R., Sahebhonar, H., Keypour, J., & Kamali, M. J. (2019). *Associated petroleum gase flaring reduction in Iran*. Talab.

Talus, K., & Aalto, P. (2017). Competences in EU energy policy. In R. Leal-Arcas & J. Wouters (Eds.), *Research handbook on EU energy law and policy* (pp. 15–29). Edward Elgar.

Tarkowski, R., Uliasz-Misiak, B., & Tarkowski, P. (2021). Storage of hydrogen, natural gas, and carbon dioxide—Geological and legal conditions. *International Journal of Hydrogen Energy*, *46*(38), 20010–20022.

White, L. V., Fazeli, R., Cheng, W., Aisbett, E., Beck, F. J., Baldwin, K. G., Howarth, P., & O'Neill, L. (2021). Towards emissions certification systems for international trade in hydrogen: The policy challenge of defining boundaries for emissions accounting. *Energy*, *215*, 119139.

Zabanova, Y., & Westphal, K. (2021). *Russia in the global hydrogen race; advancing German-Russian hydrogen cooperation in a strained political climate*. German Institute for International and Security Affairs. https://doi.org/10.18449/2021C34

Zivar, D., Kumar, S., & Foroozesh, J. (2021). Underground hydrogen storage: A comprehensive review. *International Journal of Hydrogen Energy*, *46*(45), 23436–23462.

CHAPTER 18

New Patterns of Resource Management for the Circular Economy: A Chinese-European Comparative Outlook on the Evolution of Circular Economy Law

GIANMATTEO SABATINO

INTRODUCTION: THE CONCEPT OF CIRCULAR ECONOMY AND ITS RELATION TO LEGAL THINKING

The concept of circular economy has experienced some success among policymakers and legislatures in recent decades. It was initially linked mainly to environmental protection, following the economic analysis of the relation between industrial development and resource consumption (Bermejo, 2014; Mathis & Huber, 2017, pp. 3–42). Of similar economic origin was the theory that compared an open economy and a closed economy, which stressed the durability of resources and promoted their reuse (Alwood, 2014, pp. 445–477; Boulding, 1966). Therefore, the notion of a closed economy reflects that of circular economy (Bovino, 2014).

For economists, the main issues are financing the circular economy (Benetto et al., 2018, pp. 427–432) and activating incentives that may render the circular production rationally advantageous. At the same time, the economic perspective is integrated by a political-cultural awareness that strives to overcome a purely market-oriented development model in light of the purpose of ensuring the preservation of natural resources.[1] Such an objective is also channeled by the 2030 United Nations Agenda with its sustainable development goals, as well as by the Paris Agreements of 2015.[2] From such a perspective, a circular economy can be identified through a broad model of socioeconomic development that can affect and orient the interpretation and application of rules pertaining to both vertical relations (state-private subjects) and horizontal relations (among private subjects).

Therefore, it is interesting to assess how different legal systems deal with such instances, especially in a time like during the pandemic crisis, which ultimately emphasized the issues concerning the rationalization of consumption, including with regard to environmental protection. On account of its comprehensiveness, circular economy, as a regulatory paradigm, indeed looks at the whole life cycle of a product—comprising its production, consumption, and waste management.

As a consequence, issues concerning the management of such a cycle are also regulatory (Mathis & Huber, 2017, pp. 305 ff.). However, they must balance a coercive and a promotional character (Mathis & Huber, 2017, pp. 313 ff.) to induce economic operators to comply with the circularity of new productive processes.

In this chapter, I have decided to carry out a comparison between the systems of circular economy law in the European Union and the People's Republic of China. The choice is motivated by different reasons. First, in both the EU and China, the paradigm of circular economy is contained within a development theory. On the one hand, that of the Social Market Economy in the EU (Art. 3 TEU), which is now fully displaying an ecological dimension (Mureşan, 2014, pp. 150 ff.); on the other hand, that of the Socialist Market Economy in China, whose latest orientations point toward the achievement of an ecological civilization (Tao, 2020). Such an integrated perspective favors a comprehensive approach to the issue, as highlighted by the EU Commission's definition of a European plan for the circular economy (2015) and the Opinions of the State Council of the People's Republic of China on accelerating the development of a circular economy (2005).[3]

Second, both the EU and China have achieved a high degree of complexity in their legislation concerning circular economy, and today, their models display a deep network of legal interactions among socioeconomic players. The comparative analysis, therefore, also aims to detect the critical inter-institutional relations underlying the transition toward a sustainable society.

SUSTAINABLE DEVELOPMENT AND CIRCULAR ECONOMY IN CHINA AND THE EU

Since the beginning of the economic reforms in 1978, China has experienced a steady decline in its environmental conditions, together with rapid economic growth (Qi et al., 2016, pp. 10 ff). China's environmental legislation originated in the 1980s, but since the beginning of the new millennium, environmental issues have become a topic of political analysis and public debate. In terms of political legitimacy, this means that the evaluation of the performance of public officials and party officials is increasingly based on criteria that take into account the impact of environmental policies. At the same time, national and local development plans include the reduction of polluting emissions as binding objectives (Castellucci, 2019, pp. 33–78).

At the normative level, in 2008, China enacted the Law for the Promotion of the Circular Economy (henceforth, also the Law on Circular Economy). This law displays a promotional legislative style, although it does not lack rules directly aimed at regulating the relations between economic operators. The most important of all is the one that prohibits credit institutions from granting loans to companies that produce, distribute, or use materials and techniques classified as prohibited by law (Art. 45 § 3).

More recently, the Chinese legislator has included instances of the circular economy in the process of codification of civil law, establishing in Art. 9 of the General Provisions of Civil Law (民法总则, *minfa zongze*), which is now Art. 9 of the Chinese Civil Code, the so-called green principle (绿色原则, *luse yuanze*). According to this principle, any activity of the subjects of the legal system must lead to saving resources and protecting the environment. This provision brings two cornerstones of economic circularity (i.e., saving resources and environmental protection) into the domain of the general principles of Chinese civil law, thus imposing the adherence to such rules on all private subjects. In doing so, Art. 9 mirrors the aspiration to achieve an ecological civilization into civil law as an integral part of the "Chinese dream" (Xi Jinping, 2014, pp. 229–234; 2017, pp. 419–432).

The correlation between a public law approach based on programming and an approach based on regulating private relations interpreted in the context of a multilevel system is an element that characterizes, *mutatis mutandis*, even the recent evolutions of European circular economy law. The attention to environmental issues by EU institutions dates back to the 1970s. However, in the last 15 years, and in particular after the Lisbon Treaty, the Union has addressed the issue of which market economy model is more functional to circularity. Above all, the reference to the "social market economy" (Art. 3 § 3 of the TFEU) has piqued the attention of the scholars who have incorporated a strong "ecological" character into this notion (Mureşan, 2014, p. 166). The ecological dimension was then viewed as one of the pillars of the development model reflected by the notion of social market economy (Mureşan, 2014, p. 166). Such a stance is worth reflecting upon, especially if one considers that the social market economy is a concept that draws its content from the historical experience of post-war West Germany, where the sensitivity toward the social value of ecology was certainly not on the agenda (Müller-Armack, 1978; Van Hook, 2004; Watrin, 1979). Other scholars have emphasized that, first in Germany and then in the European Community, the adjective "social" did not (and does not) indicate a preference for market rebalancing measures to protect disadvantaged groups or extra-economic interests. Instead, more simply, it emphasizes the idea that the market is a social institution (Somma, 2016). Consequently, the rebalancing activity toward the economy should play an ancillary role in competition law. The very same provision is referred to in Art. 3 § 3 TFEU and almost seems to be a mere wish for a market that takes into account the social dimension without introducing a legal basis for specific commands or actions of the Union going in that direction (Šmejkal & Šaroch, 2014).

Based on these premises, even the introduction of Art. 37 of the Charter of Fundamental Rights of the European Union was judged as insufficient to establish a true ecological vocation of the internal market (Somma, 2016).

However, the post-Lisbon European legal system at least allows the verification of the existence of the potential for the ecological declination of the social market economy (Šmejkal & Šaroch, 2014). A specific EU action in environmental matters provides that the Council, unanimously (after consulting the Parliament, the Economic and Social Committee, and the Committee of the Regions) may adopt fiscal measures, measures related to urban and rural planning and the management of water and land resources, as well as more general measures that address the choice between different sources of energy at the member states' level (Art. 192 TFEU).

Art. 192 § 5 TFEU indicates that the measures adopted, where they impose disproportionate costs on the recipients, may include both derogation clauses and, above all, access to the Cohesion Fund pursuant to Art. 177. The reference to European structural funds to support projects for the promotion of the circular economy constitutes a significant incentive reservoir and connects the European environmental policy to the economic and social planning of the Union. The theoretical basis of such connection is represented by the principle of cohesion (Art. 174 TFEU), interpreted in light of a notion of welfare based not only on economic growth but also on social and environmental criteria (Vettori, 2012).

The social market economy, therefore, has been burdened with implications related to the promotion of a circular economy. On a practical level, the construction of a social and ecological market economy has been associated with the modulation, in terms of regulation, of three fundamental variables: (i) the influence of public powers on the economy, (ii) the role of civil society, and (iii) the responsibility of the subjects of the legal system (Benecke, 2008). Among these elements, the second evokes a principle of inclusiveness of decision-making procedures. Such inclusiveness, however, must address not only the relationship between institutions and social bodies but also the inter-institutional relations between the various levels—European, national, regional—in light of the broad competencies that, depending on the member states, can be entrusted to local authorities in terms of circular economy (Magri, 2018).

In Europe, great attention has also been paid to the definition of the rules of responsibility in the cycle of the use of resources and to the contractual declination of the ecological need, especially in the sector of public contracts (Sabatino, 2020a). In hindsight, the problem that European law poses is that of overcoming the idea that the control over the life cycle of resources is satisfied by introducing the responsibility of the producer of the waste, which is a typical solution of so-called linear economies (Magri, 2018). The goal of the European legislator is to create a legal regime focused on the concept of sustainable products. Therefore, the legislator looks first and foremost to the responsibility of the product manufacturer and to the choices of the buyers, among which are public administrations. As a consequence, the legislation also takes into account tenders and public procurement of goods.

With the spread of the COVID-19 pandemic and the subsequent initiative to foster post-pandemic development, European law has further emphasized the significance of the ecological transition, as indicated not only by the first emergency regulatory documents issued in the fields of state aid but also by the legal framework for the Next Generation EU program (Sabatino, 2020b). For instance, Art. 18 § 3(d) of Reg. 241/2021 states that EU member states, in preparing the recovery plans to submit to the Commission to obtain funds (in terms of both subsidies and loans) have to explain how the envisaged recovery measures do not cause harm to the environmental objectives set in Art. 17 of Reg. 852/2020 on the facilitation of sustainable investments. Such objectives are defined with regard to different areas (e.g., climate change, circular economy, pollution control) and outline some general examples of activities that are considered to be detrimental.

On the one hand, the approach recently chosen by European legislation, especially concerning the displacement of investment and recovery funds, displays the promotion of a new theory of economic development transposed into promotional measures aimed at fostering sustainable transition. On the other hand, it outlines a complex network of legal interactions among regulatory sources, which increasingly reflect a certain fascination with comprehensive and highly technical planning instruments.

CHINA'S CIRCULAR ECONOMY LAW

Chinese law incorporates the correlations between public intervention, civil society, and individual responsibility. Art. 3 of Law on Circular Economy seeks to harmonize the diversity in the application purposes of the legislation by defining specific tasks that target at least three major players. First, the government's role is one of promotion. Second, the market forces (i.e., enterprises, both public and private) must implement, in concrete, the objectives of circular economy. Third, the public opinion is encouraged to participate, in terms of opinion-gathering and discussion, in the evaluation of existing instruments and in the elaboration of further ones. The same principle emerged clearly from the Regulations of the Shenzhen Special Economic Zone for the Promotion of the Circular Economy of 2006,[4] a sort of "rehearsal" of the national law of 2008. Both documents are structured based on the Opinions of the State Council of 2005 on the same theme (Qi et al., 2016, pp. 34 ff.).

Beyond the general provisions, however, the Chinese legislature has emphasized the organizational nature of the legislation on the circular economy, thus focusing on the prominence of its planning-related features. At the same time that the Circular Economy Law was enacted, a ministry for environmental protection was set up within the State Council (Qi et al., 2016).

The promotional nature of the legal framework for circular economy revolves around three connected main normative groups:

(a) an administrative reorganization functional to the promotion of the circular economy and the definition of national and local plans for the implementation of the objectives (Art. 6–7 and 12–13–14 of the Circular Economy Law);
(b) the definition of objectives, standards, and restrictive measures or sanctions against economic operators who do not respect these objectives and standards;
(c) the establishment of a system of incentives and benefits for virtuous operators.

Such an approach has been judged by some scholars as incompatible with the fundamental role of the market in allocating resources and determining the economic model pursued (Guo, 2017).

This argument is not convincing. It seems to ignore the theoretical foundations of the socialist market economy, which sees the market as the main force in determining the allocation of resources, but under the coordination and control of the state. In addition, in the past two decades, environmental protection has been promoted and implemented through the use of binding plan indicators (Zhang et al., 2012).

According to the law, the enforcement of the plans (Art. 6–7) should be ensured by local governments through the establishment of an objective system of liability (目标责任制, *mubiao zerenzhi*). In practice, such an expression means determining standards for assessing the work of public officials as well as investments by local governments (Lu & Song, 2010). From this perspective, enforcement is carried out in practice through the prior approval of local or national investment projects by the State Council. The economic operator (public or private) in charge of carrying out the project must present a prior assessment of energy costs that certifies its compatibility with the objectives set by laws or regulations.[5]

Industrial associations and other social organizations may also be mandated by governments to conduct initiatives aimed at promoting the circular economy, as well as to deal with advertising and technical advice in this regard (Art. 11).

The participation of social bodies such as associations, universities, or, more generally, public opinion in the evaluation procedures of economic initiatives with a potentially high environmental impact appears to be a constant in Chinese legislation on the subject. This is envisaged, for example, by Art. 16 of the Measures for the Administration of Energy Conservation of High Energy Consumption Entities and by Art. 5 of the Law on Environmental Impact Assessment.[6]

Art. 11 of the law further indicates that when defining the environmental impact assessment programs, competent authorities (i.e., the departments for the environment at the national and local level) must collect the opinions of the relevant authorities, experts, and the public. Evidently, such provision deals with the issue of participation of civil society mediated by the intervention of the authorities. A participation which, in the culture of Chinese decision-making, is also aimed at giving the public as much information as possible and then summarizing the most suitable position to incorporate the requests of each social actor in the definition of final plans (Wang & Yan, 2016).

On a practical level, this translates into the determination of targets and objectives whose satisfaction affects the evaluation of the performance of public officials and party officials.[7] In principle, this mechanism is inherent in the incorporation of the objectives of the circular economy into the system of economic and social planning. In some cases, however, the legislator has found it necessary to be explicit, as in the Law on Energy Saving. This law requires the elaboration of targets not only with the state (Art. 6) and public institutions (Art. 49) but also with some "key" economic operators selected on the basis of the annual consumption of coal, regardless of whether such operators are public or private (Section 6).[8]

Compared to more comprehensive pieces of legislation (such as the Circular Economy Law), the provisions on energy saving appear to be more focused on outlining specific obligations, in addition to incentives, for public and private economic operators. Indeed, in a country where most of the industrial activity is still fueled by coal, the energy sector is a reasonable starting point for the circularity of the economy.

The Circular Economy Law also outlines the incentive tools that can be implemented in order to promote a circular economy:

(a) the establishment—at the central and provincial level—of funds for the development of the circular economy, research, the promotion of new technologies, the implementation of specific projects, and information services (Art. 42);
(b) the incorporation of strategic projects for the development of the circular economy into scientific and technological development plans, ensuring access to specific funds and subsidies (Art. 43) (Castellucci, 2019, pp. 33–78);
(c) the implementation (Art. 44) of tax regimes that favor industrial activities that promote the development of a circular economy. Such provision is connected to Art. 27 (3) of the Enterprise Income Tax Law of 2008, which provides for the application of lower tax rates on income from projects for environmental protection and energy and water saving (Zhang, 2017);
(d) the integration of a price policy functional to the development of a circular economy (Art. 46) (Qi et al., 2016, p. 40);
(e) the determination of a procurement policy that is also functional to the development of a circular economy (Art. 47).

In relation to these incentive measures, Art. 45 states that no credit institution may grant loans to companies that produce, distribute, or use materials and techniques classified as prohibited by the Circular Economy Law. The concrete implementation of this article is still unclear. It is well known that, pursuant to Art. 34 of the Law on Commercial Banks, Chinese financial institutions are required to comply with national development and industrial policies. At the same time, however, that obligation is often interpreted as a kind of mild suggestion (Xi, 2018). The practical value of Art. 45 of the Circular Economy Law is upheld by that view which argues that the legal provision introduces a specific duty of care borne by the lender (i.e., an obligation to thoroughly assess the position of the potential borrowers to verify whether they are currently subjected to prohibitions from carrying out specific activities) (Feng, 2019).

If the lender fails to comply, and if the borrower uses the funds loaned to carry out those activities as a consequence, the lender will be held liable.

The system designed by the Circular Economy Law also seems to be in line with Chinese antitrust legislation. Firstly, the legislation restricts competition for purposes of public interest such as energy saving or environmental protection.[9] Secondly, the functionalization of market regulation for social purposes is accepted among Chinese scholars (Jiao, 2017). Furthermore, the 2016 *Opinions of the State Council on Establishing A Fair Competition Examination System in the Building of the Market System*[10] legitimized the implementation of policies that restrict competition when they intend to promote energy saving and environmental protection (Point 3).

In the ideal scheme pursued by the Chinese legislator, the legal connection between the state and the market is complemented by the participation of civil society and associates in the implementation of a circular economy system. Conserving resources, protecting the environment, and consuming resources reasonably (Art. 10 of the Circular Economy Law) are conceived as logically necessary consequences of the right to the health of the environment attributed to the community and to sustainable development (Li, 2011). Furthermore, citizens have the right to report acts of waste of resources, access information available to the public administration regarding the state of development of the circular economy, and issue opinions or suggestions.[11]

Therefore, an ethical-behavioral guideline is codified in both vertical and horizontal relationships. In the Chinese context, this generic responsibility implies a pedagogical component of the law, implemented not only by the authorities through their policy documents and their actions but also by private subjects, primarily by social organizations, especially through informative and promotional campaigns (Fang & Tan, 2014).

The trend of increasing ethically oriented accountability of social relationships pushed Han (2018) to advocate adding the codification of consumers' responsibility to society regarding the correct use of products to the already existing rules of producer responsibility regarding, for example, waste disposal. The proposal is based on the idea that the promotion of a circular economy has become a constitutional foundation of the Chinese economic system and, as such, is capable of orienting the act of consumption similarly to what happens with the general clauses of public order and good customs.

Chinese consumer law, to date, does not accept the notion of a comprehensive consumer responsibility concerning the environment. However, in its General Provisions, the Civil Code lays out a general clause that directs civil relations to save resources and protect the environment. This is Art. 9, also known as 绿色原则 (*lüse yuanze*) or the green principle.

This principle, by virtue of its location and its scope, may act as a regulatory axis of the whole system of circular economy law (Cai & Zhang, 2018). At the same time, it constitutes a limit to the exercise of property rights and contractual freedoms and a general interpretative criterion to define the civil relations between the subjects of the legal system. The green principle has constitutional significance to the doctrine, as it transposes the aspiration to ecological civilization already inherent in the development of the theory of market socialism in the Chinese civil law system (Zhang & Zhang, 2019).

As He (2019) pointed out, the green principle has been unpredictable so far, as it has been treated by judges in very different situations and for very different purposes.

For instance, the People's Court of Guanyang Country (Guanxi Province)[12] had to decide on the compatibility with the legal system of a customary rule that requires all brothers to contribute to the costs of the reconstruction of their ancestors' graves after a certain period of time from a funeral. The court assessed whether this custom could give rise to an obligation for one of the brothers to pay the other half of the expenses incurred for this reconstruction. The court noted how, despite the existence of a value such as filial piety, the reconstruction of a family tomb subsequent to a funeral may constitute a waste of resources that does not comply with the provisions of Art. 9 of the (then) General Provisions of Civil Law.

Therefore, the court ruled that the defendant—in this case, the brother who did not want to contribute to the expenses—was at fault. In doing so, the court used Art. 9 as an interpretative criterion to assess the compliance with the legal system of a lower-ranking legal rule (in this case, a custom).

Another court, perhaps more incisively, relied on Art. 9 to intervene in the dynamics of contractual relations. Based on the principle set out in Art. 9, the Intermediate People's Court of Zhengzhou (Henan Province) assessed the justifiability of a delay in a contractual performance consisting of the suspension of construction work on some premises for a period of time characterized by heavy pollution in the area.[13]

Finally, even when it has not been used in the solution of a specific case, Art. 9 has been applied on a pedagogical level. In a dispute in which the plaintiff complained that the defendant (his neighbor) accumulated litter in a section of his housing complex, the Chongqing Intermediate People's Court found there was insufficient evidence to ascertain who had accumulated the litter. However, it still considered it appropriate to reflect on the ethical wrongfulness and legal illegitimacy of any behavior that is not respectful of the environment and that wastes resources.[14]

From the overview of such judicial decisions, it may be argued that, so far, Art. 9 of the Chinese Civil Code has acted as an interpretative tool applicable to the whole range of legal relations that it covers. Even from a relatively small amount of cases, it can be noted how Chinese judges, though often not relying solely on Art. 9 but instead using it as a complementary basis for the judgment, displayed a certain degree of creativity in assessing the impact of concrete situations on environmental quality and resources in the light of the general green principle.

Such a trend, if confirmed in the future, will inevitably strengthen the hermeneutic relevance of Art. 9, making it a cornerstone of Chinese civil law. This is a significant occurrence from a comparative perspective.

CIRCULAR ECONOMY IN EUROPEAN UNION LAW

Compared to the Chinese experience, the cultural foundations of circular economy law in Europe have two differences with very significant systemic consequences. The first, as already mentioned, is the emphasis placed on the product and its life cycle.[15] The second concerns the interpretation of economic relations functional to circularity in terms of exchanges among producers and consumers (Somma, 2013). The doctrine of the social market economy links circularity to market efficiency. However, it is a political stance compared to what happens in China. It is less linked to ideology and, above all, more attentive to a bottom-up implementation of the cultural paradigm of circularity.

The first relevant feature is the absence of a comprehensive regulation on circular economy in European law, meaning that the notion of circularity is not transfused into a framework source; instead, it underlies various sectoral regulations, some of which inspired the Chinese legislative innovations (Peng & Chen, 2017).

A more comprehensive, albeit largely programmatic approach, is contained in the policy documents that deal with the issue. Even before the 2020 action plan, the Commission Communication of December 2, 2015 recognized the relationship between circular economy and efficiency in the production and consumption processes of resources.[16] The Communication of June 18, 2003 on the Integrated Product Policy is even older. There, the concept of "environmental life cycle" was developed in connection with a series of needs that were subsequently reaffirmed in European and national legislation, such as the integration of environmental needs in public procurement and in the purchasing policy of companies.[17]

However, it was in the sectorial regulations that the organizational and programmatic nature of European rules took shape. Among the first important sectors involved was that of waste management, in particular with the EU Directive No. 2008/98 (relating to waste) amended by EU Directive No. 2018/851. Specifically, Chapter V of Dir. 2008/98 requires member states to adopt waste management (Art. 28) and prevention (Art. 29) plans to promote reuse and recycling. Furthermore, the directive in Art. 11, goes so far as to set two real numerical indicators to represent the objectives that the member states must achieve by 2020: i) a 50 % increase in the weight of all household products prepared for reuse and recycling and ii) a 70 % increase in the weight of some construction and demolition products prepared for reuse and recycling. The actual effectiveness of these provisions was also questioned as to the national (and regional) implementation plans of the generic provisions of the directive often display just as much genericity and vagueness (Muratori, 2013).

Much more structured than Dir. 2008/98 is the EU Regulation 2018/1999, nicknamed the European law on climate. In Reg. 2018/1999, programming is the central aspect of the discipline. Firstly, the regulation makes extensive and explicit references to international and European agreements and strategies for sustainable development as real "guiding" principles.[18] In addition, the regulation requires member states to adopt integrated national energy and climate plans every ten years (Art. 3). It should be noted that the regulation, by defining these plans, intends to intervene in "five dimensions" of the Energy Union, namely decarbonization, energy efficiency, energy security, internal energy market and research, and innovation and competitiveness (Art. 4).

For each general policy area, the regulation sets both numerical targets and policy directives to reduce reliance on fossil energy and ensure a deeper diversification of energy sources. The objectives are closely connected to the objectives outlined by the Paris Agreement and the Union's strategies. By refining the model proposed by Dir. 2008/98, Reg. 2018/1999 provides an inclusive procedure for preparing the energy plans. The plans' proposals must be sent by the member states to the Commission, which can then formulate specific recommendations both on the objectives set and about the implementation tools envisaged (Art. 9). There is also a phase of public consultation (Art. 10) and a "multilevel dialogue" that involves not only local authorities but also "stakeholders" (e.g., civil society organizations, business organizations) (Art. 11). The implementation of the plans is subsequently monitored at the European level through periodic reports sent by the member states (Art. 13–14 and Chapter 4, Section I).

From the analysis of the national plans, it is also possible to identify the specific tools employed to implement the European objectives, namely (to a large extent) fiscal incentives, administrative simplification measures, reorganization measures, and promotional funds.

With the outbreak of the COVID-19 pandemic, the EU legislature (i.e., Council and Parliament), under pressure from the Commission, rapidly adapted its traditional cohesion policy instruments to further enhance its promotional stance toward a green transition. In particular, with Reg. 2021/1056, the Union established a new structural fund (i.e., the Just Transition Fund) with the clear goal of ensuring a transition toward an environmentally sustainable, climate-neutral, and circular economy (Recitals nn. 1–2 and 12). As laid out in Art. 2, the regulation is specifically aimed at achieving the Union's 2030 targets on energy and climate, also in the light of the Paris Agreement. As a consequence of such a close link, the Just Transition Fund functions according to a specific conditionality, which connects full access to resources with a policy commitment to climate neutrality to be achieved by 2050. If a member state does not make such a commitment, only 50 % of the annual allocations for that member state are made available (Art. 7). This point is particularly significant since it shows how the fund employs a traditional notion of EU law (i.e., that of conditionality (Baraggia, 2017)) but interprets it not in light of economic and financial stability, as happened with the aids disbursed after the 2008–2009 debt crisis, but in light of an ecological commitment.

Furthermore, the Just Transition Fund revolves around two lists of economic activities, which define its scope of application. The "positive list" (Art. 8) describes the activities and investments supported by the fund; the "negative list" (Art. 9) excludes certain activities from the scope of the fund.[19]

Another instrument that is obviously strategically relevant to the ecological transition is Reg. 2021/241, which establishes the Recovery and Resilience Facility within the context of the Next Generation EU initiative. Like the aforementioned policy instruments, this one also refers to broad European and international strategies on climate change and ecological transition (see Recitals nn. 4 and 23, as well as Art. 4). From the operative point of view, the regulation requires the European Commission to indicate in its review report on the implementation of the recovery plans their impact on climate targets (Art. 16). Furthermore, national recovery plans must comply with climate and energy plans elaborated pursuant to Reg. 2018/1999 and must include an explanation of the impact of the measure on climate transition (Art. 18 § 4(e)).

The regulation relies on already known legal forms, such as non-repayable financial support and loans. Its comprehensive nature and wide scope, however, display far-reaching potential, especially in terms of alignment between national and supranational industrial policy strategies to promote ecological advancements.

THE CIRCULARITY OF THE PRODUCT: SUSTAINABILITY AND DURABILITY

The notion of product sustainability was referred to in Dir. 2008/98 through an expansion of producer responsibility, re-adapting legal concepts initially developed for the purpose of protecting the consumer or, in any case, the user of defective products (Benacchio, 2016, pp. 317 ff.).

Art. 8 of Dir. 2008/98 allows member states to adopt extended producer responsibility regimes, which include: (a) the collection of products at the end of their period of use and waste, (b) management—also in terms of costs—of the waste material received, and (c) information to the public about the possibilities and limits of reuse and recycling of the product.

In any case, the application of the producer responsibility rules must take into account the social and environmental impacts of the related activities, their technical feasibility and economic convenience, as well as the possible impact on the functioning of the internal market (Art. 8 § 3). In other words, a balance is required. The principle of extended producer responsibility must also be coordinated with that of shared responsibility (Röttgen, 2016) of all subjects (i.e., producers and holders of waste) "involved" in waste management (Art. 15).

The variety of liability regimes, therefore, involves a significant shift of the focus of the discipline from "waste" to "product," as subsequently confirmed by Dir. 2009/125 on the eco-design of energy-related products. The directive refers, among the specifications of the notion of eco-compatible design functional to the issue of the European Union's declaration of conformity, not only to the environmental impact of the product but also to the possibilities of reuse and recycling (Annex I). Significantly, if the manufacturer of the product is not established within the EU and in the absence of an authorized representative, the directive obliges the importer to ensure that the product complies with the legislative provisions (Art. 4).

Specific marking requirements and extended producer responsibility schemes are also provided for by the recent EU Directive No. 2019/904 on the reduction of the incidence of certain plastic products on the environment. The directive, in addition to recalling the regime, referred to in Dir. 2008/98, subjects the manufacturer to the extended responsibility for the construction characteristics of single-use plastic products and, for some products, their design (Muratori, 2019).

In the European context, the sustainability of the product has been implemented with special emphasis on market relations in terms of the sale and purchase of sustainable goods. One of the main areas displaying such an approach is that of sustainable procurement of goods by public administrations (Clarich, 2007; Dell'Anno & Picozza, 2012, p. 487 ff.). In defining the criteria governing tender procedures, Art. 67 of Directive n. 2014/24 mentions that the most economically advantageous offers may also be selected on the basis of social and environmental considerations. When transposing the directive, member states have introduced a series of criteria and targets that may be taken into account by public administrations and included in calls for procurement contracts. For instance, the Italian government introduced the CAM (Minimum Environmental Criteria), which may be considered during procurement procedures and may adjust the evaluation of proposals presented by enterprises participating in the procedure.[20]

Indeed, even before Directive 24/2014, in 2008, the Italian government issued an action plan for the environmental sustainability of public administrations' consumption (Interministerial decree of April 11, 2008). The action plan sets targets and standards for the ecological transition of consumption (Point 4.2) and delegates the competent ministry (usually the Ministry of the Environment) to issue specific decrees setting environmental considerations, which must be taken into account by administrations when managing tender procedures for the procurement of goods (3.6).

The same approach is upheld by the legislative decree no. 102/2014, which requires public administrations to respect targets of energy efficiency when stipulating contracts for the purchase or the lease of premises, as well as for the purchase of goods and services.

In the recent years, however, the notion of product sustainability has also been interpreted in light of another important dimension—namely, that of the durability of the product itself in the context of consumer sales (Alpa, 2019; Faccioli, 2020; Pagliantini, 2020; Simonini, 2019). The EU Directive n. 2019/771 relating to certain aspects of contracts for the sale of goods defines durability as the ability of the goods to maintain their required functions and performance through normal use (Art. 2 n. 13). It also advocates the use of durability as an objective criterion for assessing the conformity of goods (Recital 32). The regulatory framework of this durability represents the cultural heritage of the Draft Uniform Discipline of the Sales Contract, which was aborted in 2014 due to the opposition of some member states (Alpa, 2019). Dir. 2019/771 adopts a more restricted approach than the Draft Uniform Discipline, but it functions as a reference point for the harmonization of European private law, in whose domain, therefore, the concept of durability enters as an objective component of product compliance. The point is confirmed by Art. 7 § 1 lett. d) of the directive, pursuant to which durability must be determined according to the normal characteristics in a good of the same type and that the consumer can reasonably expect, taking into account the nature of the good and the public declarations made by or on behalf of the seller or by other persons in the previous phases of the commercial process.

On the one hand, there is a seller's guarantee, regulated by the traditional remedies of the restoration of conformity (i.e., repair or replacement), price reduction, and termination of the contract (Art. 13). Furthermore, the directive establishes a regime of protection particularly favorable to the consumer with regard to the burden of proof: indeed, it burdens the seller with the proof of the defect (also if its entity is small), such as not to justify the termination of the contract (Art. 13) (Pagliantini, 2020).

Therefore, if the durability of the good had been upheld by means of public declarations made by other subjects in the commercial chain (above all, the manufacturer), the seller, to be exempted from the guarantee, must demonstrate that they could not have reasonably known such declarations or that such declarations had been subsequently corrected or even that they had been irrelevant for the choice to purchase the good (Art. 7 § 2).

On the other hand, the directive provides a double guarantee between the seller and the producer of the goods, where the latter issues commercial guarantees concerning the durability of certain goods over a certain period of time (Art. 17 § 1). In this case, the manufacturer is liable for the entire duration of the warranty for the repair and replacement of the goods. The double level of protection, which connects the position of the manufacturer to the issue of the commercial guarantee for a duration determined by the manufacturer itself, partially disappoints expectations (Simonini, 2019). Above all, the provision clashes with the reality of the facts, as information on the durability of the asset, which must necessarily originate in the manufacturer, is often lacking and uncertain. In some cases, such as in devices that use software (e.g., smartphones and laptops), it is the manufacturers' policy to frequently release updates that affect the regular and fast operation of the device in the long run to incentivize the consumer to buy new versions of the device (Simonini, 2019). This practice is clearly incompatible with the objectives of circularity.

Related to this point, a certain degree of protection can be recovered by applying the rules on unfair commercial practices. For instance, this was the stance taken by the competition authorities in both France and Italy with regard to the sale of electronic devices (i.e., smartphones) that required frequent updates of their software systems. The authorities, in particular, focused on electronic products sold by Apple and ascertained that frequent and mandatory updates of smartphone software imposed an increasing burden on the hardware, decreasing the speed of the operation of the devices, thus reducing their performance and ultimately shortening the life-span of the products themselves. The competition authorities stated that the failure to inform the consumer about not only the mandatory updates but also the consequences of such updates on the performances of the devices amounted to an unfair commercial practice.[21] As can be easily noted, the core of the examined decisions is not environmental protection nor the product life cycle from a circular economy perspective. However, in assessing the unfairness of the commercial practice in light of the potential and actual durability of products sold to consumers, the competition authorities stressed the importance of informing the public about the products' life-span, as well as the factors that may affect it. The ultimate aim of such information is that of giving consumers the chance to make choices according to the products' durability.

On a more general level, unfair commercial practices can be a channel for conveying into the field of consumer protection considerations pertaining to corporate social responsibility, such as the environment-friendly production policies of companies as advertised in public statements or in ethical codes (Conte, 2009; Magli, 2019; Massimino & Prati, 1999). In such cases, the unfairness of the practice would lie in the difference between what is declared to the consumers and what is actually implemented. From the perspective of the contract itself, some arguments even call for the nullity of the contract (Seminara, 2018).

The reference to the communicative dimension of the corporate social responsibility (declarations made public, ethical codes, etc.) inevitably raises an issue, namely the fact that the manufacturing company would be bound only within the limits of what it decides to declare. Thus, one would face the same problem that emerges from Dir. 2019/771 and that was subjected to criticism by Simonini

(2019), who advocates the legislative affirmation of a legal guarantee of the manufacturer legally equivalent to that of the seller.

The conclusions of the competition authorities against Apple instead show that the public enforcement of competition law, starting from the notion of unfairness and pondering the alteration of the consumer's full awareness, manages to enhance, albeit indirectly, the protection of the durability of the product.

CONCLUSION

This chapter offered a brief comparative overview of the main regulatory instruments provided by the Chinese and the European Union legal system in order to promote the transition toward a circular economy. The choice of the systems was motivated by the emergence of complex cultures of circular economy embedded into comprehensive development models, as well as by the relatively high degree of complexity reached by specific legislation concerning circular economy.

A first conclusion that may be drawn is that both systems have incorporated an increasingly stronger environmental character into their own doctrine of development, albeit from very different perspectives, supporting a transition toward a circular economy.

The concrete instruments adopted by each system to pursue such goals, however, are different. In Chinese law, the emphasis seems to be placed on planning so that the transition is guided by promotional policies enacted by authorities on the basis of specific development plans, making full use of instruments such as funds and subsidies.

Planning, however, is complemented by the affirmation of a general ecological responsibility, which encompasses all the subjects of the legal system. It is a responsibility that judges tend to use as a supporting argument in order to interpret citizens' conduct in light of resource-saving purposes. At the same time, it implies a strong pedagogical element to guide and educate citizens about a new environmental culture.

European law, on the other hand, relies on a much less strict planning process and displays a clear preference for project financing, channeled through the development and structural funds. The complementary instrument is instead an increasingly complex private law regulatory framework aimed at promoting circularity through the diversification of liabilities and guarantees among the subjects involved in the production chain. From this perspective, however, it should be noted that the legal regime of antitrust enforcement, especially with regard to unfair practices, represents an additional instrument that has been dynamic in addressing environmentally unfit conduct.

The general impression is that of global regulatory models that are in a state of constant evolution. While the reinforcement of planning systems and funding systems seems to be a constant element that is emphasized occasionally, the integration of environmental considerations into the regulation of private relations is a real challenge, which stimulates original solutions while also leaving much space for future research.

NOTES

1 European Commission, *Circular Economy Action Plan—For a cleaner and more competitive Europe*, 4–5.
2 See Art. 2.
3 *Guowuyuan guanyu jiakuai fazhan xunhuan jingji de ruogan yijian.*
4 *Shenzhen jingji tequ xunhuan jingji cujin tiaoli*
5 See, for instance, the *Measures for the Energy Conservation Examination of Fixed-Asset Investment Projects*» (固定资产投资项目节能审查办法) of 2016.
6 *The state encourages relevant entities, experts and the general public to participate in the appraisal of the environmental impacts in appropriate ways.*
7 See Art. 6 of the Law on Energy Saving (中华人民共和国节约能源法).
8 In particular, Art. 52 defines as "key" companies those that consume more than ten thousand tons of coal per year; companies that consume between five thousand and ten thousand tons of coal can instead be designated as "key companies" by the competent energy departments at national and local level.
9 Art. 15 of the Anti-Monopoly Law (反垄断法, *fan longduan fa*).
10 *Guowuyuan guanyu zai shichang tixi jianshe zhong jianli gongping jingzheng shencha zhidu de yijian*
11 Art. 10 co. 3 of the Circular Economy Law.
12 Decision of September 28, 2018 n. 473.
13 Decision of December 12, 2018, n. 14963.
14 Decision of March 17, 2020, n. 233.
15 Communication of the Commission of March 11, 2020—COM (2020) 98 final—*A new circular economy action plan. For a cleaner and more competitive Europe.*
16 Communication on the Action Plan for Circular Economy, 2.
17 Point 5.3 of the Communication.
18 For instance, there are references to the Paris Agreement as well as the EU 2030 climate and energy framework. See Recitals no. 1, 6, 7, 8, and 9.
19 These activities are, in particular: (a) the decommissioning or the construction of nuclear power stations; (b) the manufacturing, processing, and marketing of tobacco and tobacco products; (c) an undertaking in difficulty, as defined in point (18) of Art. 2 of Commission Regulation (EU) No. 651/2014 (18), unless authorized under temporary state aid rules established to address exceptional circumstances or under de minimis aid to support investments reducing energy costs in the context of the energy transition process; and (d) investment related to the production, processing, transport, distribution, storage, or combustion of fossil fuels.
20 Decree of the Ministry of the Environment, October 11, 2017.

21 Italian Competition Authority (AGCM), decision of September 25, 2018; French Competition Authority (DGCCRF), Communiqué de presse, February 7, 2020. In the French case, Apple agreed to pay a fine so to reach an early closure.

REFERENCES

Alpa, G. (2019). Aspetti della nuova disciplina delle vendite nell'Unione Europea. *Contratto e impresa*, *3*, 825 ff.

Alwood, J. (2014). *Squaring the circular economy: The role of recycling within a hierarchy of material management strategies*. In *Handbook of recycling* (pp. 445–477). Elsevier.

Baraggia, A. (2017). *Ordinamenti giuridici a confronto nell'era della crisi: la condizionalità economica in Europa e negli Stati nazionali*. Giappichelli.

Benacchio, G. (2016). *Diritto privato della Unione Europea*. Cedam.

Benecke, D. W. (2008). *Social and ecological market economy. A general overview. The social and ecological market economy—A model for Asia?* Deutsche Gesellschaft für Technische Zusammenarbeit (GTZ) GmbH.

Benetto, E., Gericke, K., & Guiton, M. (Eds.). (2018). *Designing sustainable technologies, products and policies*. Springer International Publishing. https://doi.org/10.1007/978-3-319-66981-6

Bermejo, R. (2014). *Handbook for a sustainable economy*. Springer.

Boulding, K. (1966). *The economics of the coming spaceship earth*. In H. Jarret (Ed.), *Environmental quality in a growing economy* (pp. 3–14). John Hopkins University Press.

Bovino, C. (2014). Verso un'economia circolare: la revisione delle direttive sui rifiuti. *Ambiente e Sviluppo*, 10, 682 ff.

Cai, S., & Zhang Y. (2018). 绿色原则之文义解释与体系解读 [Cultural interpretation and systemic interpretation of the "Green Principle"]. *甘肃政法学院学报* [*Gansu zhengfa xueyuan xuebao*], *5*, 1–8.

Castellucci, I. (Ed.). (2019). *Saggi di diritto economico e commerciale cinese*. Editoriale Scientifica.

Clarich, M. (2007). La tutela dell'ambiente attraverso il mercato. *Diritto pubblico*, *1*, 219–239.

Conte, G. (2009). Vincoli Giuridici, Principi Economici e Valori Etici nello Svolgimento dell'Attività d'Impresa. *Contratto e impresa*, *3*, 679 ff.

Dell'Anno P., & Picozza, E. (2012). *Trattato di diritto dell'ambiente* (pp. 487 ff). Cedam.

Faccioli, M. (2020). La nuova disciplina europea della vendita di beni ai consumatori (Dir. UE 2019/771): Prospettive di attuazione delle disposizioni sui termini. *Nuove Leggi Civili Commentate*, *1*, 250 ff.

Fang, S., & Tan B. (2014). 论促进公民低碳行动的行政指导 [On administrative guide for promoting citizen's low-carbon action]. *faxue*, *2*, 20–29.

Feng, R. (2019). 贷款人生态环境损害赔偿责任的认定及立法完善—种法解释学路径的分析 [On the determination and legislative perfection of the lender's liability for ecological environmental damage—An analysis from the perspective of legal interpretation methods]. *Hebei faxue*, *4*, 97 ff.

Guo, Y. (2017). 立法是促进循环经济还是规范物质资源综合利用 [Whether the legislative aim is promoting circular economy or regulating comprehensive utilization of material resources]. *Zhengzhi yu falu*, *8*, 130–141.

Han, Z. (2018). 循环经济法中消费者责任之规制解构 [Deconstructing the regulation of consumer responsibility in the recycling economy law]. *Hebei Law Science*, *36*(11), 145–157.

He, J. (2019). 绿色原则与法经济学 [The green principle and law and economics]. *Zhongguo faxue*, *2*.

Jiao, H. (2017). 社会政策目标的反垄断法豁免标准 [Anti-monopoly law exemption criteria for social policy objectives]. *Faxue pinglun*, *4*, 124–138.

Li, Y. (2011). 论构建我国循环经济法律体系 [On the construction of China's circulative economic legal framework]. *Faxue zazhi*, *4*, 37–41.

Lu, K., & Song M. (2010). 我国农村实施《循环经济促进法》的问题及对策 [Problems and solutions of the implementation of the law for the promotion of a circular economy in Chinese countryside]. *Tianjin Legal Science*, *104*(2), 61–66.

Magli, C. (2019). Pratiche Commerciali Scorrette e Rimedi Civilistici nel Contesto della Responsabilità Sociale d'Impresa. *Contratto e impresa*, *2*, 716.

Magri, M. (2018). Regioni ed "Economia Circolare." *Giornale di diritto amministrativo*, *6*, 706 ff.

Massimino, F., & Prati L. (1999). La politica ambientale delle imprese tra globalizzazione e tutela dei consumatori. *Ambiente e sviluppo*, *11*, 1063 ff.

Mathis K., & Huber B. (Eds.). (2017). *Environmental law and economics*. Springer.

Muratori, A. (2013). Programma Nazionale Prevenzione Rifiuti: La montagna ha partorito il topolino? *Ambiente e Sviluppo*, *12*, 980 ff.

Mureşan, S. (2014). *Social market economy*. Springer.

Müller-Armack, A. (1978). *The social market economy as an economic and social order. Review of Social Economy*, *36*(3), 330 ff.

Pagliantini, S. (2020). *Contratti di vendita di beni: armonizzazione massima, parziale e temperata della dir. UE 2019/771*. Giurisprudenza italiana.

Peng, F., & Chen, S. (2017). 欧 盟 «循环经济» 立法：起源、概念与演进 [EU legislation on circular economy: Origin, concepts and evolution]. *Shanghai zhengfa xueyuan xuebao*, *6*, 21–28.

Qi, J., Zhao, J., Li, W., Peng, X., Wu, B., & Wang, H. (2016). *Development of circular economy in China*. Springer.

Röttgen, D. (2016). Rifiuti: tra corresponsabilità, responsabilità estesa del produttore e responsabilità condivisa. *Ambiente e Sviluppo*, *6*, 415 ff.

Sabatino, G. (2020a). Il diritto dell'economia circolare tra programmazione, contratto e responsabilità. Profili teorici ed applicativi in dialogo tra Repubblica Popolare Cinese ed Unione Europea. *Il diritto dell'economia*, *103*(3), 379–418.

Sabatino, G. (2020b). COVID-19, European law and the geo-policy of aids. The incomplete structures of European development planning. *Concorrenza e Mercato*, *26–27*, 65–91.

Seminara, A. (2018). La tutela civilistica del consumatore di fronte alle pratiche commerciali scorrette. *Contratti*, *6*, 689 ff.

Simonini, G. F. (2019). Verso una nozione allargata di difetto di conformità: sarà rilevante anche la «durabilità» del bene? *Danno e Responsabilità*, *4*, 47 ff.

Somma, A. (2013). Private law as biopolitics: Ordoliberalism, social market economy, and the public dimension of the contract. *Law and Contemporary Problems*, *76*(2), 105–116.

Somma, A. (2016). Il diritto privato europeo e il suo quadro costituzionale di riferimento nel prisma dell'economia del debito. *Contratto e Impresa*, *1*, 124 ff.

Šmejkal, V., & Šaroch, S. (2014). EU as a highly competitive social market economy—Goal, options, and reality. *Review of Economic Perspectives*, *14*(4), 393–410.

Tao, K. (2020). 以习近平生态文明思想为指引切实贯彻实施《民法典》绿色条款 [The effective implementation of the green clauses in the "Civil Code" with Xi Jinping though on ecological civilization as guidance]. *Falü shiyong*, *23*, 3 ff.

Van Hook, J. (2004). *Rebuilding Germany: The creation of the social market economy*. Cambridge University Press.

Vettori, G. (2012). Diritti e coesione sociale. *Obbligazioni e contratti*, 7.

Wang, S., & Yan, Y. (2016). *A democratic way of decision-making: Five year plan process in China*. Renmin University Press.

Watrin, C. (1979). *The principles of the social market economy—Its origins and early history*. *Journal of Institutional and Theoretical Economics*, *135*, 405 ff.

Xi Jinping. (2014). *The Governance of China*. Foreign Language Press.

Xi Jinping. (2017). *The Governance of China—II*. Foreign Language Press.

Xi, T. (2018). (席涛), 市场准入负面清单与产业政策、相关法律的修订与衔接 [The negative list of access to market and the review and connection of industrial policies and relevant laws]. *Zhongguo zhengfa daxue xuebao*, *65*(3), 47–60.

Zhang, C. (2017). 财政补贴的税法评价: 基于 税法文本与法理的分析 [Tax law evaluation of financial subsidies: An analysis on the basis of tax laws and jurisprudence]. *Jingji fa lun cong*, *29*(1), 277–298.

Zhang, D., Aunan, K., Martin Seip, H., Larssen, T., Vennemo, H., Larssen, S., Feng, L., Wu, C., & Xie, R. (2012). Air pollution reduction during China's 11th Five-Year Plan period. *Environmental Development*, *4*, 36–53.

Zhang, Z., & Zhang, Y. (2019). «民 法总则»中 "绿色原则"的宪法依据及其展开 [The constitutional basis and development of the green principle in the General Provisions of Civil Law]. *Fazhi xiandaihua yanjiu*, *4*, 99–110.

CHAPTER 19

The Politics of Biodiesel and the Structuring of a New Market for Brazilian Agribusiness

GABRIELA BENATTI, ANTÔNIO BUAINAIN, MARCELO PEREIRA DA CUNHA, AND PEDRO CAVALCANTE FILHO

INTRODUCTION

In Brazil, bioenergy policies have been driven and conditioned by macroeconomic factors, pressures from civil society, and diplomacy. In the 1970s, the economic policy agenda was dominated by the impacts of oil shocks on Brazilian macroeconomic conditions, particularly regarding the trade balance and inflation rate. Brazil was then heavily dependent on fossil fuel imports. Therefore, the upsurge of oil prices directly and severely impacted the structural deficit of the balance of trade and initiated price increase. Ultimately, these conditions undermined political support for the military government that had ruled the country since the 1964 coup d'état.

As we will explain, to curtail the growing trade deficit, the federal government launched a strategy to promote import substitutions and reduce Brazil's dependency on imported energy. The National Alcohol Program (*Proálcool*) was launched in 1975 in response to the deteriorating macroeconomic conditions in the country. Furthermore, until the United Nations Conference on Environment and Development (UNCED), also known as the Rio de Janeiro Earth Summit, the political economy of energy was primarily driven by economic concerns and rarely by environmental issues. The debates held at the Rio Earth Summit echoed on the Brazilian civil society, which was then emerging from 25 years of military rule.[1] Environmental concerns and issues were upgraded both in the official policy agenda and in the struggles of civil society organizations whose importance was increasingly acknowledged in the aftermath of the 1988 Federal Constitution, which sealed the democratization of the country. After the 1990s, energy policies became more concerned with and incorporated more measures related to climate change and the environment (Brinkman et al., 2018; Cunha & Scaramucci, 2006). In addition to economic signals and determinants, the energy policy has also responded to civil society pressures and the international agenda.

In many countries, there has been a sharp increase in renewable energy sources[2] and the adoption of programs to foster the use of alternative energy sources and accelerate the replacement of fossil energy with renewable energy. Brazil was a forerunner in this effort, and by the end of the second decade of the twenty-first century, it was the second-largest producer and consumer of biofuels in the world (United States Department of Agriculture, F. A. S. (2019). Specifically, Brazil has emphasized the production of alcohol for automotive use (i.e., biodiesel) since the first decade of the twentieth century.

The state and the public policies were decisive in promoting renewable energy sources, especially bioenergy (Costa, 2017; Garcia, 2007; Sampaio, 2017). The energy sector was dynamized via financing under favorable conditions, consumer subsidy, technological support, regulation throughout the supply chain, and economic incentives in combination with compulsory measures in some aspects (e.g., the mandatory mixture of ethanol and biodiesel into gasoline and mineral diesel) and facilities in others (e.g., environmental rules that facilitate the expansion of sugar cane production). Since the 1970s, biofuels have gradually been included in the Brazilian energy matrix (Costa, 2017). In 2021, a law was passed stating that automotive gasoline and diesel must contain 27 % anhydrous ethanol and 10 % biodiesel, with these percentages adjusted according to relative prices and availability of biofuels. The target is the addition of 15 % biodiesel by 2023.

The first biofuel production experiments in Brazil date back to the 1930s, with the production and mixture of ethanol into gasoline at a minimum proportion of 5 %. However, public policies and regulations did not begin to support technological research, commercial-scale biofuel production, or the structuring of the biofuel market (most notably in the context of the automotive and agricultural industries) until the 1970s (Garcia, 2007).

As mentioned above, the first oil shock, which occurred in 1973, represented a true milestone in the global energy history. During this time, the price of oil skyrocketed from US$2.90 to US$11.65 per barrel. With the second crisis (in 1979), the trade balance situation of countries such as Brazil became unsustainable as the average price of oil rose 10-fold, from US$3.88 per barrel in 1973 to US$36.59 when prices peaked in 1981 (Távora, 2011).

In response to the structural problems revealed by the oil crisis, the Brazilian government launched the 2nd National Development Plan (NDP). This plan contained ambitious goals in industry, infrastructure, and energy to reduce the country's dependence on imports of oil and industrial inputs. Proálcool was announced in 1975 with the objective of promoting the partial replacement of automotive gasoline with ethanol produced in Brazil and reducing oil imports (Fishlow, 2011; Macarini, 2011).

Proálcool was the first of a set of initiatives focused on the biofuel sector. Other initiatives include the Plan for Vegetable Oil Production for Energy Purposes (Proóleo) in 1975, the National Energy Forest Program in 1980, the Incentive Program for Alternative Energy Sources (Proinfa) and the Brazilian Biodiesel Technological Development Program (ProBiodiesel) in 2002, the National Biodiesel Production and Use Program (PNPB) in 2004, the National Energy Policy (Law No. 11,097) in 2005, the National Agroenergy Plan in 2006, and the National Biofuels Policy (RenovaBio) in 2017. They all incorporated the goals of reducing dependence on fossil fuels, reducing greenhouse gas (GHG) emissions, promoting technological development, and creating employment opportunities and income in industrial and rural sectors (Bosi, 2015).

There are many advantages to using biofuels instead of mineral sources, mainly regarding the decreased impact on the environment (Dufey, 2006; Lapuerta et al., 2008; Pousa et al., 2007). However, the diffusion of bioenergy—especially if implemented at the scale needed to meet demand and replace fossil fuels—involves several contradictions. Concerns related to food security, deforestation, social exclusion, and the sustainability of bioenergy production chains have been raised (Ewing & Msangi, 2009; McNeely et al., 2009; Molony & Smith, 2010; Pingali et al., 2008; Silva, 2014).

These concerns have fueled debates regarding bioenergy policy, which have seen vivid participation from civil society organizations and institutions that hold differentiated, contradictory, and even conflicting views. Mandates regarding energy alternatives, priorities for public policies, and the mechanisms needed to promote the energy transition and the suitable agents for the process have also been debated (Biber-Freudenberger et al., 2020; De Oliveira & Coelho, 2017; Tiburcio, 2011). These controversies suggest that bioenergy needs to be promoted and adopted responsibly (Favareto & Moralez, 2014). Various dimensions should be considered as opposed to the mere replacement of dirty energy sources with clean ones. To many authors (Abramovay & Magalhães, 2007; César & Batalha, 2013; Garcia, 2007; Gonçalves et al., 2014; Leite et al., 2013a; Ribeiro et al., 2018), biofuels present an opportunity to drive deeper transformations and induce a virtuous cycle of social, economic, and environmental sustainability. As will be shown in this chapter, the PNPB of 2004 followed this path and attempted to develop a more inclusive and sustainable productive chain based on the supply of non-food products from small farmers rather than the supply of raw materials from large-scale producers such as in the sugar cane-ethanol chain. Whether it attained such a goal is indirectly discussed in the chapter.

The history of the implementation of several programs aimed at introducing biofuels into the national energy matrix has been shaped by the intense and active participation of organized civil society by increasing awareness about climate and environmental threats and the risks to food security. Democratization, civil society participation, and environmental awareness have all contributed to the design and implementation of a new generation of biofuel programs whose objectives and governance are not defined as much by macroeconomic issues (e.g., trade deficit, import substitution, and inflation rate) as by the promotion of sectoral and regional development, the use of clean energy per the global climate agenda (Sampaio, 2017), and the need to foster the inclusion of thus far marginalized sectors and population groups in the dynamic value chains leading the Brazilian economy. The strengthening of the ethanol production during the 1990s and the PNPB in 2004 have partially incorporated these concerns.

The PNPB has innovated by associating bioenergy production with the goal of promoting the development of historically underdeveloped and poor regions of Brazil.[3] It was also innovated by including family farming[4]—which was until then marginalized—as a supplier of raw materials. Finally, it incorporated the goals to reduce Brazil's dependence on fossil fuels and GHG emissions. The ambitious goals to achieve and reconcile were attempted to be met by implementing a program devised based on particular governance, which included market incentives with compulsory measures such as adding an increasing percentage of biodiesel to mineral diesel. This ensured an increasing market for biodiesel production and resulted in the rapid expansion and consolidation of a vigorous biodiesel production chain in Brazil.

In this chapter, we broadly reflect on the institutional dynamics and results of the National Program for the Production and Use of Biofuels, which was launched in 2004 as part of the Brazilian strategy to increase the use of green fuels and promote the productive inclusion of small farmers in the country's modern agribusiness. We also develop the hypothesis that the PNPB successfully created the biodiesel sector in Brazil, with positive impacts on the economy in terms of income generation and occupation. However, we also indicate that the results were less clear in relation to the objectives of developing the poorest regions of the country, using new sources of raw materials, and including small farmers and family farmers in the program.

THE NATIONAL BIODIESEL PRODUCTION AND USE PROGRAM

Background and Creation

The use of biofuel (biodiesel and ethanol) in Brazil dates to the first half of the twentieth century. Cunha et al. (2019) briefly described the use of biofuels from

1925 when "Ford tested a vehicle that travelled around Brazil on pure ethanol trying to encourage the substitution of gasoline derived from petrol" (p. 124). There are reports of the extensive use of biodiesel in rural areas (Hémery et al., 1993). Furthermore, during World War II, the addition of biodiesel to mineral diesel was legalized and became a common method for curtailing the short supply of imported oil. However, only in 1975, with the institution of Proóleo, did the state begin to foster technological development to promote the production of vegetable oils in the country. Support was provided to research and investments to reduce production costs throughout the chain, thus improving biodiesel's competitiveness against diesel oil. This situation was perceived as a necessary step to introduce the addition of vegetable oil into diesel without causing the final prices to have significant impacts on fiscal expenditures due to subsidies as had happened during the initial phase of Proalcohol in the 1970s and 1980s (Cunha et al., 2019). *Proóleo* proposed a mixture of 30 % vegetable oil at the initial stage, which is rather unrealistic. The strategic objective—which is equally unrealistic—was the total replacement of fossil fuels in the long term. Soybean was the main raw material used, but experiments were also done with peanuts, rapeseed, sunflower, and palm oil (Homem de Mello, 1983; Pousa et al., 2007; Sá Parente, 2003). As mentioned, none of these crops were diffused in Brazil—not even soybeans, which were then cultivated basically in the southern part of the country (see Shurtleff & Aoyagi, 2009).

In the context described above (and as an offshoot of the National Program for Plant-based Renewable Energy Alternatives), the Vegetable Oils Program was launched in 1983. This program sought technical feasibility by using different mixtures in diesel engines while involving agents such as automakers, vegetable oil processors, federal agency technicians, research organizations, and transporters. However, the uncertainty regarding the economic viability of biodiesel and the recovery of oil price stability from the mid-1980s to the end of the 1990s weakened further initiatives to foster vegetable oil-based biofuel production—especially biodiesel (Bosi, 2015; Brum, 2014; Sampaio, 2017).

In the early 2000s, international oil prices rose again, which had an immediate impact on fuel prices in Brazil, which still had a strong dependence on diesel oil imports.[5] This context renewed the search for alternative sources of imported diesel oil, and biodiesel extracted from transesterification was once again considered an alternative to promote this replacement. In 2002, ProBiodiesel was instigated under the management of the Ministry of Science and Technology. ProBiodiesel involved specialists, technology and research institutions, and public and private companies aiming (among other objectives) to structure the Brazilian Biodiesel Network are considered strategic to achieving the specific objectives of the program. Specifically, these objectives are to reduce Brazil's dependence on petroleum products, reduce GHG emissions, form new markets for oilseeds (especially soybeans), and create the global market for renewable fuels.

ProBiodiesel presented a plan for including biodiesel in the Brazilian energy matrix that would have positive impacts throughout the production chain. The program proposed an initial mixture of 5 % (B5)[6] biodiesel in diesel oil, which was valid in 2005, which would be gradually increased to 10 % (B10) in 2010 and 20 % in 2020 (B20). However, a change of the federal government interrupted the program's operation before it was started. The new administration decided to create an Interministerial Working Group, which is directly linked to the Presidency of the Republic and involves the broad participation of corporate segments and rural and urban workers to reevaluate ProBiodiesel. The Interministerial Working Group's report reaffirmed the validity of the objective to promote biodiesel as a complementary fuel source and recommended redesigning the program to include feasible objectives of social inclusion and regional development (Garcia, 2007; Pedroti, 2013; Sampaio, 2017). Among other recommendations, the report indicated the importance of including family farming in biodiesel production chains in a sustainable manner, thereby providing full financial support and adequate technical assistance to ensure their participation.[7]

The IWG report was endorsed by the federal government, which promulgated, through Provisional Measure[8] No. 214 of September 13, 2004, the regulatory framework to promote the production and use of biodiesel. The National Petroleum Agency[9] (ANP—*Agência Nacional do Petróleo*) was empowered to regulate, contract, inspect, and authorize the production and marketing of biodiesel in the domestic market (Brasil, 2004).

Conception and History of the PNPB

In December 2004, the federal government officially launched the PNPB following the recommendations of the Interministerial Working Group. The implementation of the PNPB involved several ministries, led by the Ministry of Agrarian Development, reporting directly to the Presidency of the Republic. The program involved sustainability precepts,[10] goals, and guidelines aligned with sustainable development.[11] From an environmental aspect, the program associated the introduction of biodiesel with GHG emission reductions and the country's commitments as put forth in international forums. From an economic perspective, the program's goals are to reduce Brazil's dependence on diesel oil imports, enable tax incentives, ensure flexibility in the regulation of production to condition the use of different raw materials (oilseeds), and define the technology used for production. In the social sphere, the PNPB prioritized the creation of employment and income and the inclusion of family farming in the value chain of biofuels. It also included goals related to regional development—specifically, it aimed to foster the development of the North and Northeast regions, where raw materials for biodiesel were expected to be produced (Costa, 2017; Cunha, 2011; Garcia, 2007; Sampaio, 2017).

The sanction of Law No. 11,097, which came into effect in 2005, represented the beginning of the actions established by the PNPB and officially—through legislation—introduced biodiesel in the national energy matrix. The ANP was maintained as a regulatory body with comprehensive regulatory and supervisory powers covering the entire production chain, as well as research, production, and marketing. The law expressed a recommended (but optional) minimum percentage of biodiesel to be added to diesel oil. In 2008, adding 2 % biodiesel (B2) to mineral diesel became compulsory nationwide. Furthermore, pre-defined increases were applied, with the minimum percentage reaching 5 % (B5) in 2013.[12] The National Council for Energy Policies (CNPE—*Conselho Nacional de Políticas Energéticas*) enforced the mixture levels and biofuel quality (Brasil, 2005).

Soybean was the main raw material used for biofuel production for at least five reasons: (i) it can be produced on a large-scale production, (ii) it has high productivity and technical efficiency, (iii) it can be obtained in several states and regions, (iv) it makes production could be expanded in the future, and (v) it has competitive advantages over alternatives (Souza et al., 2017). However, soybeans were not traditionally farmed by Brazilian family farmers, except for those in southern Brazil. Nevertheless, the inclusion of these farmers was one of the fundamental objectives of the PNPB (Bergmann et al., 2013; Ramos et al., 2017). This posed a significant challenge to the program; specifically, it was unclear how to ensure the production of enough biodiesel meeting the legal 2 % level while relying on raw materials supplied by family farming (Cunha et al., 2019; Sampaio, 2017).

The agents involved in the soybean chain recognized the opportunities created by the Program and quickly adhered to it, seeking to adjust the rules to suit their interests. Owing to the political importance of maintaining the official discourse favoring family farming and regional development, the viability of the Program required flexibility regarding the importance attributed to alternative sources of raw materials and the inclusion of family farming (Buainain et al., 2021; Flexor et al., 2011). The program's goal of diversifying raw materials was clearly unfeasible in the short- and medium-term and, thus, was established as a long-term goal (Ramos et al., 2017; Souza & Seabra, 2014).

The Social Fuel Seal and the Productive and Social Inclusion

The main mechanism used by the PNPB to promote the productive and social inclusion of family farmers was the Social Fuel Seal (SFS). The SFS established incentives to purchase oilseeds produced by family farmers. According to an assessment carried out by Cavalcante Filho et al. (2021), in 2018, the PNPB contributed R$10.3 billion to the Brazilian economy and created 193,000 jobs in rural and urban areas. Thus, the program positively impacted development in some regions.

The SFS is a certificate showing that a biodiesel-producing company has purchased the minimum percentage of raw material from the formally classified farmers per the National Program for Strengthening Family Farming (PRONAF)—as family farmers. The conception of the SFS incorporated the widely accepted diagnosis that family farmers face serious difficulties accessing dynamic markets due to lack of technical capacity and financial support (see Buainain et al., 2007; Fialho et al., 2021).

Accordingly, in addition to ensuring a share of the growing market of raw materials supplies to biodiesel production, the rules of the seal include the following: (i) the establishment of formal contracts for the purchase of raw materials from rural family farmers, which are agreed by the producers directly or by representative associations or cooperatives; (ii) the provision of technical assistance; and (iii) the promotion of capacity building for family farmers with whom they maintain a supply contract. The seal is granted by the Ministry of Agrarian Development[13] according to a detailed examination of the contract signed by the companies and the farmers and endorsed by the union of rural workers of the municipality where production occurs (Abramovay & Magalhães, 2007). SFS-certified biodiesel plants obtain access to financial incentives and different tax rates according to the raw material and region, as well as preferential participation in purchase auctions, among other benefits.[14]

Governance and Marketing Model[15]

The biodiesel marketing model is a highly regulated market instituted by Resolution No. 5 of October 3, 2007. The market operates through public auctions organized by the ANP, by which diesel oil refineries and importers purchase biodiesel from producers in compliance with legislation establishing the minimum percentage of biodiesel to be added to mineral diesel. Biodiesel purchases are mediated by Petrobras,[16] with distributors having the right to choose lots while considering various parameters, including the price of products. Regular auctions are held bimonthly, and additional auctions can be held to meet unforeseen market fuel requirements or fulfill the supply of *default* producers, that is, those which did not deliver the fuel contracted in the regular auctions (ANP, 2019; Prado & Vieira, 2010).

The auction model is flexible to accommodate variance in structural condition, which differentiates the costs that characterize biodiesel production as determined by various technological routes, the possibility of reusing chemical reagents, and the destination of co-products, such as bran and glycerin. The auction model also fosters the formation/development of the domestic biodiesel market, the structuring of the entire production chain, reductions in the asymmetry of information concerning prices and costs in an emerging market, and increased opportunities for social inclusion. One of the basic prerequisites for participation in an auction is SFS accreditation (i.e., the acquisition of a minimum portion of raw materials from family farmers) (Rodrigues, 2006).

The operational rules of the auctions have evolved over time, but generally speaking, they are divided into six steps. The first step involves qualifying suppliers who attend the auction if they have provided the required documents.[17] The second step is for companies to submit their offers by determining the prices and volumes of the offered biodiesels. In the third step, buyers select offers of SFS-certified producers.[18] The fourth step is the resubmission of offers by suppliers—according to Biodieselbr (2012), this step represents the primary novelty of the process, as it enables suppliers to reduce their prices between the first and second rounds of purchases. In the fifth step, buyers select additional offers, both from SFS-certified and uncertified suppliers. The sixth and final step is the consolidation and disclosure of the final results by the ANP (Brasil, 2012).

Sometimes, the need arises to meet demands higher than agreed upon during the public auctions. Therefore, Ordinance No. 116 of April 4, 2013, established directives for forming stocks in the country (informally referred to as stock auctions). In this case, only biodiesel producers accredited with the SFS can supply their products to purchasers. Distributors, in turn, can purchase biodiesel by acquiring the product to be stored in the distributor's facility or under their direct responsibility and contracting the purchase option, with the product being stored in the producer's facility and under their full responsibility (Brasil, 2013). The rules of the auctions emphasize the value of the SFS, which contradicts the hypothesis that the objectives of social inclusion are being relegated throughout the operation of the supply chain.

THE EVOLUTION OF THE BIODIESEL SUPPLY CHAIN IN BRAZIL

At the end of 2020, 50 biodiesel-producing plants were operating in Brazil, representing an installed biodiesel production capacity of 11.2 million m^3/year (Table 19.1). In 2017, 50 % of the plants were located in the Midwest region, (representing 46.8 % of the country's soybean production), and 25 % were located in the South region (representing 33.4 % of the country's soybean production). These

Table 19.1: Production Capacities of Authorized Biodiesel Plants in Different Brazilian Regions in 2020

Region	Productive Cap. (m³/ year)	Plants	SFS (%)
North	320,400	2	2.0
Northeast	880,200	4	6.0
Southeast	824,040	6	12.0
South	4,497,480	12	24.0
Midwest	4,670,280	26	40.0
Brazil	11,192,400	50	84.0

Source: Authors' own elaboration using data from the ANP (2021) and MAPA (2021b).

two regions represent more than 75 % of Brazil's biodiesel production capacity; when the Southeast region is included, this percentage rises to 90 %. The North and Northeast regions have a low share in the biodiesel production chain. Both regions combined contain six plants and provide 10 % of Brazil's total production capacity. The inclusion of family farming is certified by the SFS; in 2021, more than 80 % of the plants were accredited with the SFS (ANP, 2021; MAPA, 2021a).

Biodiesel production has grown significantly (Figure 19.1) since the PNPB was initiated in 2005. At this time, the national production of biofuel was 4,600 barrels of oil equivalent; by 2008, it had exceeded 7.3 million barrels of oil equivalent (ANP, 2021). This substantial and continued growth results from policies designed to foster the use of biodiesel, such as the legal requirement for a certain percentage of biofuel to be included in diesel oil. There was a slight decrease in

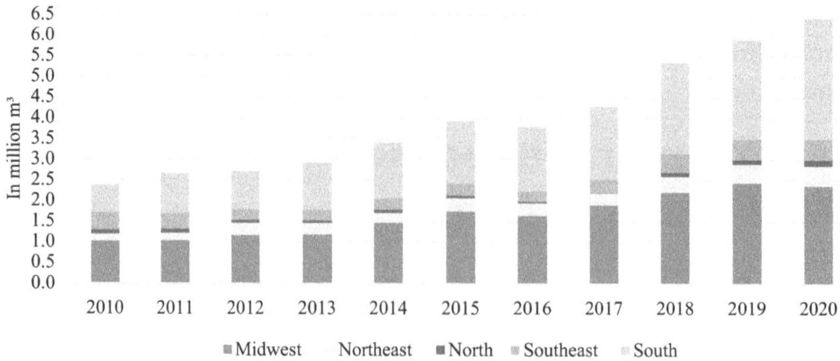

Figure 19.1: Biodiesel production (B100) in Brazil by Region (in million m³) between 2010 and 2020

Source: Authors' own elaboration using data from the ANP (2021).

growth only in one year—2016—which was a direct result of the downturn in overall economic activity in Brazil.

The production structure involves a high level of idleness in the industry (Figure 19.2). In 2005, the level of idleness was 99 %. Meanwhile, from 2005–2020, the plants operated with 65 % idleness on average. This decrease indicates that the incentive for expanding the agro-industrial capacity purchase machinery and equipment—mainly through the National Bank for Economic and Social Development (BNDES)—ensured that a significant supply structure was in place to introduce biodiesel into the energy matrix. The aforementioned bank made resources available to finance all segments of biodiesel production, including the production of raw material (agricultural) and biodiesel, storage, logistics, the acquisition of machinery and equipment, and the processing of biodiesel byproducts (Pedroti, 2013).

At least three factors determine the idle capacity of a company. The first is whether the percentage of biodiesel used (as defined by the ANP) increased at a slower pace than the industry had expected based on vigorous advocacy in favor of biofuels carried out by the most prominent authorities of the federal government. President Lula mentioned multiple times that Brazil would "become the Saudi Arabia of the biofuels" (Jornal de Brasília, 2007). This perception was shared by many international consultancy firms and multilateral organizations, thus providing a solid basis for the optimistic expectations of the industry. The second factor is whether the productive capacity was dimensioned according to market growth expectations that did not materialize (mostly due to the slowdown of the economy following the 2008 international crisis). The third factor is whether diesel consumption was lower than the figures used by the biofuel sector. In short,

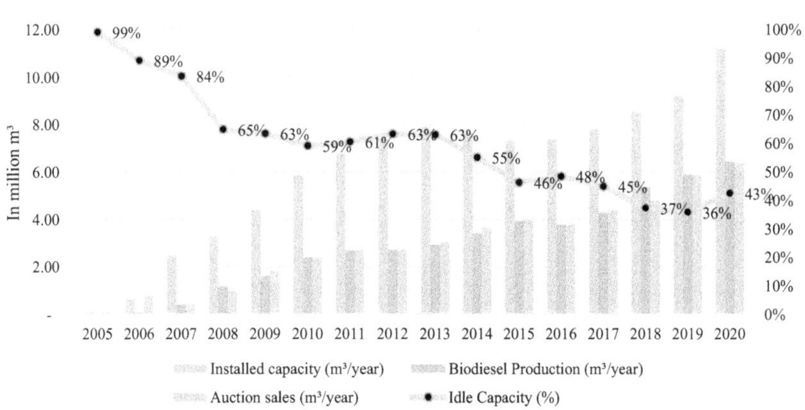

Figure 19.2: Installed Capacity and Biodiesel Production (in million m³) and Idle Capacity (in percentage) in Brazil between 2005 and 2020

Source: Authors' own elaboration using data from the ANP (2021).

according to Buainain et al. (2021), the overcapacity can be attributed to planning failure, the uncertainty of the economy, and to the political use of biofuels by politicians and government officials campaigning in the political arena.

The Association of Biofuel Producers of Brazil (APROBIO) indicates that an idle capacity of around 15 %–20 % is healthy for the sector, provides security for supply, and is supported by the Brazilian territorial extension and the many climatic variations between regions (APROBIO, 2019). However, the actual levels have been much higher, reaching 90 % in some cases, with activities having even stopped for a few months when companies could not make viable offers in auctions. As biodiesel is perishable, it makes no sense to reduce the idle capacity in unfavorable market conjunctures, such as those that have prevailed since 2017. The installed capacity at the end of 2019 is sufficient to meet the projected demand growth until 2023 (ANP, 2021; APROBIO, 2019).

From 2006–2020, there was plenty of biodiesel to supply the market according to the regulatory parameters defined by the ANP, which it adjusts according to the dynamics of supply and demand. However, in July 2020, considering signs of possible difficulties supplying the market, the ANP reduced the mandatory percentage of biodiesel from 12 % to 10 % to preserve companies and the sector during the global crisis (APROBIO, 2021).

The advances were significant regarding the inclusion and use of biodiesel in the Brazilian energy matrix, which increased from the minimum of 2 % compulsorily in 2008 to 11 % in 2019. The viability and functioning of this chain are associated with governance, organization, and its institutionality as defined by the State and within the scope of the PNPB. They are also associated with the market strategies defined by stakeholders. Next, we examine the structure of the biodiesel production chain in Brazil and some elements of governance that have regulated the sector.

The growth and dynamics of the biodiesel production chain are strongly characterized by the rules, incentives, and actions stipulated and implemented by the PNPB. They are also affected by specific rules associated with the design and governance of the biodiesel market. This sector has been gaining strength in regions with more dynamic agricultural production and which have the highest levels of development (Barros Ribeiro et al., 2018; De Oliveira & Coelho, 2017).

Progress and Limits of the Social Fuel Seal

In 2021, it was already possible to observe the effects of the SFS on social inclusion. For instance, the number of supplying families increased in the initial years of the Program between 2009 and 2011, reflecting the engagement of the institutions responsible for the program and the interest of plants and families in leveraging the benefits of the SFS. Buainain and Batalha (2007) observed that approximately 20,000 family units in the North and Northeast regions were already participating in the program in the first year of its operation (2005). They estimated that this number would reach 250,000 in 2007. However, this expected growth did not occur—in 2008, the program registered only 17,400 families in these two regions (MAPA, 2019).

Furthermore, the number of supplying families began to fall in 2012. This decline was partly due to the stricter process of selecting family farmers by plants as various constraints—such as logistics and the poverty and organizational weakness of producers—proved stronger than the voluntarism of agents and the benefits of inclusion (Leite et al., 2013b). Meanwhile, more flexible rules facilitated the selection of family farmers in the South region, primarily regarding soybean producers, thus enticing them to move from the North and Northeast regions[19] to engage primarily in extractive activities focusing on castor bean and *dendê* palm oil. The number of supplying families increased again in 2018; between 2017 and 2019, almost 60,000 producers (1.2 % of all family farmers in Brazil) signed supply contracts. In 2017, the participation of the North and Northeast regions was practically nonexistent, indicating the failure of the PNPB to accomplish the objective of leveraging the development of these relatively poor areas. The result is generally considered unsurprising (César et al., 2019; Silva et al., 2017).

Garcia (2007) and Monteiro (2007) pointed out that the configuration of family farming in these regions—which are characterized by poverty, technological lag, low organizational level, and environmental and logistical conditions—created substantial barriers preventing the inclusion of family farming in a chain that required dynamism and transactions mediated by contracts. In practice, the incentives provided by the SFS aimed to provide short-term benefits. Furthermore, they did not sufficiently encourage biodiesel plants to engage with this segment of producers in the North and Northeast regions, whose participation required structural interventions with a long maturation period. For instance, the tax and credit incentives that were adopted to encourage biodiesel producers to use other oilseeds[20] and enable the diversification of raw materials were not sufficient to replace soybeans, given the low competitiveness of these alternative raw materials (César et al., 2019; Freitas & Lucon, 2011).

To meet the minimum quotas determined by the legislation, agroindustry began to purchase the agricultural production of oilseeds from family farmers in states in regions other than those where the plants are installed. The program requires that the raw materials must be purchased from family farmers but not that the purchased raw materials must be used to produce biodiesel. Thus, companies located in the Midwest region—characterized by large-scale oilseed and livestock production and low presence of family farmers—purchase soybeans from family farmers in the south[21] to obtain the SFS. They use the SFS for other purposes[22] but process the purchased raw material in areas near the processing plant (César & Batalha, 2013; Freitas & Lucon, 2011). This accounting practice is carried out to maintain the advantages of the SFS and has positively impacted family farmers in the South region[23] (Frozza & Tatsch, 2014).

Soybean purchases from farmers in the South region have contributed to revitalizing a segment of family farming that was becoming excluded, as soybeans are typically characteristic of non-family farming. Through the instruments established by the program, which conditioned the production infrastructure in conjunction with market induction, other oilseeds[24] produced by family farmers were included in the production process, albeit to a low extent (Abramovay & Magalhães, 2007; Campos & Carmélio, 2009).

Some studies consider this procedure inadequate. Biodiesel producers in the south also have reservations. They claim that the demand from other regions raises the prices of the raw material and makes it difficult to purchase for the companies that have invested in the area (Frozza & Tatsch, 2014). However, the increased competition is advantageous for producers because it allows them to charge higher prices and provides them with technical assistance contracts and bonus payments that are not imposed by the rules of the SFS. However, this flexibility compromises the development of other regions and the strengthening of family farming in general. The benefits are strongest in already well-developed regions where family farming is well-structured and often included in markets in general (Barros Ribeiro et al., 2018).

The volume and value of the raw material sold by family farmers saw considerable growth between 2008 and 2018, when it increased by more than R$4.6 billion. The increase in the production value of raw materials between 2010 and 2019 was concentrated in the South and Midwest regions. These results are inconsistent with the social objectives established by the PNPB, as the North and Northeast regions did not include a significant number of families, nor did they generate significant production values (Isolani & Tonin, 2013).

The objective of productive and social inclusion through the diversification of raw materials was not achieved. On the one hand, technical difficulties have severely hindered the production of the oilseeds chosen as alternatives, including castor beans, the flagship of government projects within the PNPB. Limited scientific and technological developments intended to promote the large-scale commercial production of castor beans in the North region and to ensure supply to the biodiesel market were only some of the limitations. Regarding economic viability, small-scale production and high production costs, logistical difficulties, and high price volatility were determined as additional limitations (Flexor et al., 2011). Meanwhile, due to the competitiveness and advantages of soybeans, they were the main oilseed crop marketed by small family farmers.

The supply of bovine tallow among family farmers seems to clash with the production capability and dominant profile of family farming, which, in general,

Table 19.2: Number of Registered Families, Volume in Thousand Tons, and Value in Million Reais of Raw Materials Supplied in the Social Fuel Seal Between 2010 and 2019

Region	Variable	2010	2011	2012	2013	2014	2015	2016	2017	2018	2019
North	Families	246	56	60	327	313	304	260	255	326	325
	Thousand tons	16.9	8.9	8.7	9.0	8.3	11.0	3.3	2.4	27.4	21.5
	Million BRL	3.6	5.6	7.4	8.3	7.8	10.9	3.9	6.4	27.3	39.4
Northeast	Families	41,253	37,226	25,210	12,949	4,757	3,926	1,923	485	556	883
	Thousand tons	33.4	7.0	0.5	0.7	2.6	9.5	31.9	53.5	52.8	63.2
	Million BRL	46.6	7.4	0.6	1.2	4.3	13.6	49.0	72.3	83.5	109.5
Midwest	Families	3,388	3,533	4,513	5,133	4,757	4,548	4,109	3,266	2,773	2,388
	Thousand tons	441.8	429.1	560.4	603.2	543.1	530.9	480.2	373.0	383.5	308.7
	Million BRL	243.2	295.0	434.0	526.4	527.5	521.1	545.6	407.2	436.7	367.1
Southeast	Families	3,297	2,486	2,378	2,287	1,837	1,818	1,040	474	433	384
	Thousand tons	66.2	68.7	101.4	129.5	94.2	129.7	85.1	42.1	43.7	35.0
	Million BRL	42.1	54.1	92.6	129.8	97.8	136.8	98.4	46.7	48.4	42.6
South	Families	52,187	60,994	60,512	63,058	61,815	61,889	62,923	55,429	57,895	55,285
	Thousand tons	1,094	1,398	1,534	2,051	2,385	2,801	2,717	2,585	3,400	3,090
	Million BRL	723.2	1,157	1,576	2,190	2,615	3,260	3,577	2,970	4,581	4,038

Source: Authors' own elaboration using data from MAPA (2021a).

practices poor, atomized, and markedly informal livestock farming, unsuitable to meet the demand from the biodiesel production chain. It should be noted that cattle ranching is mostly a large-scale economic activity in Brazil, and there are several meat processing plants throughout the country. However, the breeding and raising of large animals are incompatible with the agrarian structure of family farming, which is characterized by small properties, thus restricting the contracting of bovine tallow (Martins et al., 2011).

Tiburcio (2011) and Barros Ribeiro et al. (2018) found that the PNPB was the result of broader political dynamics and consequences and was intended to meet the demands of the oil sector, diesel vehicle manufacturers, and the soybean production chain, where opportunities for family farming arise. However, the market established for biodiesel was subordinated to the soybean sector and, therefore, the participation of family farmers is limited to producers specialized in soybean production. Thus, the production of raw materials for biodiesel favors economic aspects, to the detriment of social and environmental aspects, which compromises the sustainable development of rural territories.

CONCLUSION

The implementation of the PNPB was fundamental for the creation and consolidation of the biodiesel production chain in Brazil, contributing to the exponential growth of production capacity and production until 2018. The geographical distribution of the plants, concentrated in the soybean producing regions, was mainly guided by market forces and not by the rules and objectives of the PNPB, which projected greater participation of the North and (especially) the Northeast region, where differentiated and productive tax incentives were implemented. Legislation was introduced that reduced or removed taxes for plants that acquired specific raw materials (e.g., castor beans and jatropha) for family farms in the northeast. Furthermore, not even the installation of three Petrobras Biocombustível units could make this region stand out among the leading producers. Farmers in the North were faced with obstacles related to weakened collective actions, low access to inputs, and limitations of the market and production factors (capital, land, and labor) and, thus, could not enter the biodiesel production chain, resulting in low participation in the PNPB (Leite et al., 2013a; Silva, Fernandes, et al., 2014; Silva, Teixeira, et al., 2014).

The actions of the PNPB to promote the inclusion of family farmers present varying results in different Brazilian regions and states. The concentration of biodiesel production is itself evidence of such differences. The evaluation carried out by Cavalcante Filho et al. (2020) shows the ambiguity of the state concerning the program's initial objectives. They argue that, on the one hand, the evolution of the SFS, one of the pillars of the Program—in particular regarding the changes in the regulations—indicates genuine attempts to improve its effectiveness and promote the inclusion of family farmers. On the other hand, the program may have neglected alternative sources of raw materials for biodiesel production and their regional distribution. According to the authors, the PNPB has accommodated the advantages provided by soybeans and bovine tallow as priority sources of raw materials, along with the geography of biodiesel production, which was gradually configured under market forces, whose outcomes are inconsistent with the objectives of promoting regional development and productive and social inclusion.

Regarding the objective of diversifying raw material sources, the incentives for purchasing alternative raw materials were not sufficient to replace soybean as the main oilseed used in production in plants. Mendes and Costa (2010) expressed the need for innovations[25] to enable the reformulation of some dominant paradigms that restrict the expansion of new energy sources, such as biodiesel itself. In this case, the medium-term viability, sustainability, and relevance of the biodiesel production chain are associated with the replacement of soybeans—an essential product for the global agri-food chain—as the main source of raw material for biodiesel production with alternative sources, including raw materials that do not compete with food demand.

The high regional concentration of productive capacity is not consistent with the program's objective of promoting regional development, especially in the North and Northeast regions. On the one hand, the agricultural base and the organizational, technical, and productive experiences of the agro-industrial chains already installed in traditionally agricultural regions (the Midwest and South) and industrialized regions (the Southeast) have shaped the setup and expansion of the biodiesel production chain. On the other hand, the instruments used by the PNPB, despite maintaining the original objectives of the program, were used with the primary concern of ensuring the supply of biodiesel. Meanwhile, the objectives of regional development and productive inclusion were given secondary importance.

Available evidence indicates that the program's evolution was clearly guided by market coordination rather than public policies that formally include objectives of regional development and productive inclusion. The market promoted the most developed regions, which already had abundant sources of raw materials such as soybeans and animal fat. This situation provided short-term competitive advantages for entrepreneurs in these segments. Moreover, the policies strengthened market coordination without seeking to use incentives to foster alternative and competitive arrangements. Therefore, the concentration of plants in highly developed regions distorted the program's objectives, which had small impacts in less-developed regions.

The experiments analyzed in this chapter, such as that of the PNPB, contribute to creating state capacities. Several instruments combining incentives and rules for production and marketing were created to achieve the objectives. The increased ability to build coalitions and consensuses among different stakeholders (who often have opposite interests) represents an important development. The operation of the program—specifically of the SFS—was challenging and required some adjustments. Large projects were developed and received substantial capital contributions and national recognition. However, many mistakes were made, resulting in institutional learning and development processes and—in some cases—negative impacts for the farmers involved.

NOTES

1 The redemocratization process comprised a series of measures that progressively expanded individual guarantees and freedom of the press until the election of the first civilian president after 21 years of military dictatorship.

2 According to IEA (2021), the overall capacity for generation of renewable energy increased by 45 % in 2020.

3 Brazil is marked by strong regional inequalities. The Northeast and North, which corresponds to 63.74 % of the national territory and 9 % and 28 % of the population, respectively, in 2020, are the poorest regions of the country. Since the end of the 1950s, governments have been implementing programs to promote the development of these regions. Despite economic growth, both regions continued to register social and economic indicators well below the national average. In 2020, life expectancy at birth was 76.8 years for the country and ranged from 71.4–74.8 in states located in the Northeast and North regions (see IBGE, 2021)

4 Agrarian structure in Brazil is marked by the steep skewed distribution of landownership and strong structural heterogeneity encompassing regions, farmers, crops, and productive systems (Vieira Filho & Fishlow, 2017). According to the 2017 agricultural census (IBGE), agricultural farmers make up 76.8 % of rural establishments in the country, occupy 23.03 % of arable land, and are responsible for 23 % of the total gross production in terms of value. Despite marked differentiation within the group, agricultural farmers have been neglected by public policies and largely excluded from the benefits of innovation and the success of Brazilian agribusiness (Buainain et al., 2007; Guanziroli et al., 2013). The launch of Pronaf in 1996 recognized the marginalization and of this group and the need for intervention to revert the increasing expulsion of family farmers to already overpopulated urban areas, as well as to strengthen family farming throughout the country.

5 Fuel prices are especially sensitive in Brazil, as the country's economy has been substantially affected by skyrocketing inflation rates since the late 1970s and several unsuccessful attempts to control inflation through the so-called heterodox measures, from general prices freezing in the 1980s (Cruzado Plan and others) to the massive confiscation of savings and financial assets in early 1990 (Collor Plan). The Real Plan stopped the steady increase in inflation and brought relative price stabilization. Nevertheless, the inflationary memory persisted and, even in 2020, economic policies and the general attitudes of society are influenced by inflationary risk. Fuel prices are the most politically sensitive and, therefore, are closely monitored by the authorities. In general, the population feels that any increase in fuel prices is equivalent to inflation. The popular saying, *subiu o petróleo sobe tudo* (when the oil price goes up, everything else goes up), reflects this popular wisdom (Carneiro & Modiano, 2014; R. Carneiro, 2002).

6 Represents the percentage quantity of biodiesel added to mineral diesel oil.

7 The report included a detailed set of recommendations, such as immediately adopting the mixture of 5 % biodiesel (B5) in mineral diesel; fostering partnerships with countries producing this biofuel; conducting technical studies to identify, qualify, and quantify potential raw materials; preparing evaluations of the impact of biodiesel production and use on the agricultural sector; evaluating the technical feasibility of using fresh vegetable oil in engines; improving the biodiesel production process with various oilseeds; establishing a special tax standard to be applied in marketing; determining standards, regulations, and quality models for biodiesel, especially regarding GHG emissions; introducing public policies for funding and rural extension in conjunction with technical assistance and incentive to research; defining, mapping,

structuring, and developing national competence in research and development; and preparing a Permanent Interministerial Commission to oversee the establishment of public policies and directives determined by the federal government (Brasil, 2003).

8 Provisional measures are rules with the force of the law issued by the president of the republic in relevant and urgent situations. Despite producing immediate legal effects, these measures need further consideration by the National Congress of Brazil to become law (Chamber of Deputies and Federal Senate).

9 Thereafter, the ANP was assigned the designation of National Agency of Petroleum, Natural Gas and Biofuels as the regulatory body for the activities of the industries of these sectors in Brazil.

10 Socially fair, environmentally responsible, and economically efficient.

11 The report prepared by the World Commission on Environment and Development, called *Our Common Future* states that "Sustainable development is development that meets the needs of the present without compromising the ability of future generations to meet their own needs."

12 The initial projections for the percentages of addition were brought forward, and, in 2008, the mixture of 2 % (B2) became mandatory. In 2009, the added level increased to 4 % (B4) and, in 2010, it increased again to 5 % (B5). Continuing the advances in fostering the production and use of biodiesel, in the following years, several changes increased the mandatory level of mixture. In the legislation that has been in effect since 2018, the mandatory mixture is 11 % and allows a voluntary mixture of up to 15 %, considering the technical specifications (Ministério de Minas e Energia, 2015, 2016, 2018).

13 Currently, the coordination is conducted by the Department of Family Farming and Cooperativism (SAF) within the Ministry of Agriculture, Livestock and Supply (MAPA).

14 Public auctions are the biodiesel marketing model; details of their operation and governance will be presented below.

15 In January 2022, the auction marketing model was replaced by the direct acquisition of biodiesel by distributors without the intermediation of Petrobras or the ANP.

16 Petrobras is a publicly traded company, the main shareholder of which is the Government of Brazil. In the biodiesel marketing model, Petrobras acts only as an organizer of auctions.

17 In the old auction system, the documents were analyzed only after the sale of all biodiesels, which led to several problems for the ANP and the plants involved.

18 On the first day of the auction, 80 % of the volume of biodiesel provided for in the tender document is purchased only from producers accredited with the SFS. On the following days, the auction is open to the other producers.

19 These were the priority regions for the actions of the PNPB.

20 Some examples are castor bean, coconut, and *dendê* palm oil.

21 The South region has the most cooperatives of family farmers and the highest level of technological development.

22 Some mills purchase raw materials from family farms simply to meet the requirements of the SFS; they then sell them in the conventional soybean market.

23 Since 2017, the South region has included more than 90 % of all families supplying raw materials to produce biodiesel.

24 Some examples are cottonseed oil, beef tallow, castor oil, *macaúba*, and jatropha.

25 The inclusion of new raw materials that are competitive in relation to soy.

REFERENCES

Abramovay, R., & Magalhães, R. (2007). *O Acesso dos Agricultores Familiares aos Mercados de Biodiesel: Parcerias entre Grandes Empresas e Movimentos Sociais* (p. 36). Fundação Instituto de Pesquisas Econômicas.

Agência Nacional do Petróleo, G. N. e B. (2019). *Anuário estatístico brasileiro do petróleo, gás natural e biocombustíveis 2019.*

Agência Nacional do Petróleo, G. N. e B. (2021). *Painel Dinâmico de Produtores de Biodiesel.*

Associação dos Produtores de Biocombustíveis do Brasil. (2019, August 26). *Indústria do biodiesel celebra entrada do B11.*

Associação dos Produtores de Biocombustíveis do Brasil. (2021, April 9). *Setor aponta impactos que a redução da mistura de biodiesel representa para toda a cadeia produtiva.*

Barros Ribeiro, E. C., Moreira, A. C., Ferreira, L. M. D. F., & da Silva César, A. (2018). Biodiesel and social inclusion: An analysis of institutional pressures between biodiesel plants and family farmers in southern Brazil. *Journal of Cleaner Production, 204*, 726–734. https://doi.org/10.1016/j.jclepro.2018.09.085

Bergmann, J. C., Tupinamba, D. D., Costa, O. Y. A., Almeida, J. R. M., Barreto, C. C., & Quirino, B. F. (2013). Biodiesel production in Brazil and alternative biomass feedstocks. *Renewable and Sustainable Energy Reviews, 21*, 411–420. https://doi.org/dx.doi.org/10.1016/j.rser.2012.12.058

Biber-Freudenberger, L., Ergeneman, C., Förster, J. J., Dietz, T., & Börner, J. (2020). Bioeconomy futures: Expectation patterns of scientists and practitioners on the sustainability of bio-based transformation. *Sustainable Development, 28*(5), 1220–1235. https://doi.org/10.1002/sd.2072

Bosi, J. A. (2015). *O Programa Nacional de Produção e Uso de Biodiesel e a Agricultura Familiar* (Vol. 1). Universidade de São Paulo. http://ir.obihiro.ac.jp/dspace/handle/10322/3933

Brasil. (2003). *Relatório Final do Grupo de Trabalho Interministerial encarregado de apresentar estudos sobre a viabilidade de utilização de óleo vegetal—Biodiesel como fonte alternativa de energia.* Brasília.

Brasil. (2004, September 13). Medida Provisória nº 214. Pub. L. No. 214, Altera dispositivos das Leis nos 9.478, de 6 de agosto de 1997, e 9.847, de 26 de outubro de 1999.

Brasil. (2005, January 13). Lei nº 11.097. Pub. L. No. 11.097, Dispõe sobre a introdução do biodiesel na matriz energética brasileira; altera as Leis nos 9.478, de 6 de agosto de 1997, 9.847, de 26 de outubro de 1999 e 10.636, de 30 de dezembro de 2002; e dá outras providências.

Brasil. (2012, August 15). Portaria nº 476. Pub. L. No. 476, Ministério de Minas e Energia.

Brasil. (2013, April 4). Portaria nº 116. Pub. L. No. 116, Ministério de Minas e Energia.

Brinkman, M. L. J., da Cunha, M. P., Heijnen, S., Wicke, B., Guilhoto, J. J. M., Walter, A., Faaij, A. P. C., & van der Hilst, F. (2018). Interregional assessment of socio-economic effects of sugarcane ethanol production in Brazil. *Renewable and Sustainable Energy Reviews, 88*, 347–362. https://doi.org/10.1016/j.rser.2018.02.014

Brum, A., Lucca, E., & Wildner, M. (2014). O mercado de biodiesel no Brasil. In *52° Congresso Da Sociedade Brasileira de Economia, Administração e Sociologia Rural (SOBER)*, 20. SOBER.

Buainain, A. M., & Batalha, M. O. (2007). *Cadeia Produtiva da Agroenergia* (3rd ed.). http://www.agricultura.gov.br

Buainain, A. M., Silveira, J. M. F. J. da, Cunha, M. P. da, Bueno, C. da S., Ribeiro, C. H., Benatti, G. S. de S., Jardim da Silveira, J. M. F., Pereira da Cunha, M., & Cavalcante Filho, P. G. (2021). *Cadeias de Valor em Bioeconomia Maduras e Inovadoras: Avaliando a Maturidade e*

Estudando Meios de Melhorar seu Desempenho: O Caso do Brasil. Instituto de Economia, Universidade Estadual de Campinas.

Buainain, A. M., Wilkinson, J., Alves, E., Di Sabbato, A., Souza, A. C. de, Guanziroli, C. E., Souza Filho, H. M., Silveira, J. M., Batalha, M., & Salles Filho, S. (2007). *Agricultura familiar e inovação tecnológica no Brasil: características, desafios e obstáculos* (1st ed., A. M. Buainain, Ed.). UNICAMP.

Campos, A. de A., & Carmélio, E. de C. (2009). Construir a diversidade da matriz energética: o biodiesel no Brasil. In R. Abramovay (Ed.), *Biocombustíveis: a energia da controvérsia* (1st ed., Vol. 1, pp. 59–97). Senac.

Carneiro, D. D., & Modiano, E. M. (2014). Ajuste externo e desequilíbrio interno, 1980–1984. In M. de P. Abreu (Ed.), *A ordem do progresso: dois séculos de política econômica no Brasil* (2nd ed., Vol. 1, pp. 263–280). Elsevier.

Carneiro, R. (2002). *Desenvolvimento em crise: a economia brasileira no último quarto do século XX* (1st ed., Vol. 1). UNESP, IE—Unicamp.

Cavalcante Filho, P. G., Buainain, A. M., & Cunha, M. P. da. (2020). Avaliação do Programa Nacional de Produção e Uso de Biodiesel no Contexto do Desenvolvimento Regional e Inclusão Social. *Desenvolvimento Em Debate*, *8*(2), 11–39.

Cavalcante Filho, P. G., Buainain, A. M., & Cunha, M. P. da. (2021). Avaliação dos impactos socioeconômicos da cadeia produtiva do Biodiesel na agricultura familiar brasileira. *Estudos Econômicos (São Paulo)*, *51*(3), 493–527. https://doi.org/10.1590/0101-41615133pam

César, A. da S., & Batalha, M. O. (2013). Brazilian biodiesel: The case of the palm's social projects. *Energy Policy*, *56*, 165–174. https://doi.org/10.1016/j.enpol.2012.12.014

César, A. da S., Conejero, M. A., Ribeiro, E. C. B., & Batalha, M. O. (2019). Competitiveness analysis of "social soybeans" in biodiesel production in Brazil. *Renewable Energy*, *133*. https://doi.org/10.1016/j.renene.2018.08.108

Costa, A. O. da. (2017). *A Inserção do Biodiesel na Matriz Energética Nacional: Aspectos Socioeconômicos, Ambientais e Institucionais*. Universidade Federal do Rio de Janeiro.

Cunha, M. P. da. (2011). *Avaliação socioeconômica e ambiental de rotas de produção de biodiesel no Brasil, baseada em análise de insumo-produto*. Universidade Estadual de Campinas.

Cunha, M. P. da, & Scaramucci, J. A. (2006). Bioethanol as basis for regional development in Brazil: An input-output model with mixed technologies. In *46th Congress of the European Regional Science Association: "Enlargement, Southern Europe and the Mediterranean."* Volos: 46th Congress of the European Regional Science Association: "Enlargement, Southern Europe and the Mediterranean," August 30–September 3, 2006, Volos, Greece Provided in Cooperation with: E.

Cunha, M. P., Ribeiro, C. H., & Guarengui, M. M. (2019). Bioenergy and biofuels in Brazil. In A. M. Buainain, R. Lanna, & Z. Navarro (Eds.), *Agricultural development in Brazil—The rise of a global agro-food power* (1st ed., Vol. 1, p. 16). Routledge.

De Oliveira, F. C., & Coelho, S. T. (2017). History, evolution, and environmental impact of biodiesel in Brazil: A review. *Renewable and Sustainable Energy Reviews*, *75*, 168–179. https://doi.org/10.1016/j.rser.2016.10.060

Dufey, A. (2006). *Biofuels production, trade and sustainable development: Emerging issues* (p. 2). International Institute for Environment and Development.

Ewing, M., & Msangi, S. (2009). Biofuels production in developing countries: Assessing tradeoffs in welfare and food security. *Environmental Science and Policy*, *12*(1), 520–528.

Favareto, A., & Moralez, R. (2014). *Energia, Desenvolvimento e Sustentabilidade* (1st ed., Vol. 1). Editora Zouk.

Fialho, M. F., Ferreira Neto, J. A., & Reis, J. D. dos. (2021). A evolução do Pronaf nas Regiões de Desenvolvimento (RD) de Pernambuco. *Research, Society and Development*, *10*(10), Article e59101018466. https://doi.org/10.33448/rsd-v10i10.18466

Fishlow, A. (2011). *Starting over: Brazil Since 1985* (1st ed., Vol. 1). Brookings Institution Press.

Flexor, G., Kato, K. Y. M., Lima, M. do S., & Rocha, B. N. (2011). Dilemas Institucionais Na Promoção Dos Biocombustíveis . *Cadernos Do Desenvolvimento*, *6*(8), 329–354.

Freitas, S. M., & Lucon, O. (2011). Programa Nacional de produção e Uso de Biodiesel: a transição para um estilo de desenvolvimento sustentável. In Instituto de Economia Agrícola (Ed.), *Texto para Discussão* (27th ed., Vol. 27). Instituto de Economia Agrícola.

Frozza, M. S., & Tatsch, A. L. (2014). Sistema setorial do biodiesel no Rio Grande do Sul: caracterização e oportunidades para a consolidação de um sistema inovativo em agroenergia. *Ciência Rural*, *44*(12), 2286–2292. https://doi.org/10.1590/0103-8478cr20130756

Garcia, J. R. (2007). *O Programa Nacional de Produção e Uso de Biodiesel Brasileiro e a Agricultura Familiar na Região Nordeste*. Universidade Estadual de Campinas.

Gonçalves, K. Y., Favareto, A., & Abramovay, R. (2014). As estruturas sociais do mercado de matérias-primas para o biodiesel no Semiárido brasileiro e os bloqueios à inserção dos agricultores pobres do Nordeste. In A. Favareto & R. Moralez (Eds.), *Energia, desenvolvimento e sustentabilidade* (pp. 245–262). Editora Zouk.

Guanziroli, C., Buainain, A., & Sabbato, A. (2013). Family farming in Brazil: Evolution between the 1996 and 2006 agricultural censuses. *Journal of Peasant Studies*, *40*(5), 817–843. https://doi.org/10.1080/03066150.2013.857179

Hémery, D., Debier, J., & Deleáge, J. (1993). *Uma história da energia* (1st ed., Vol. 1). Editora Universidade de Brasília.

Homem de Mello, F. B. (1983). *O Problema Alimentar no Brasil: A Importância dos Desequilíbrios Tecnológicos* (1st ed., Vol. 1). Paz e Terra.

Instituto Brasileiro de Geografia e Estatística. (2021). *Tábuas Completas da Mortalidade*. Retrieved February 8, 2022, from https://www.ibge.gov.br/estatisticas/sociais/populacao/9126-tabuas-completas-de-mortalidade.html?=&t=o-que-e

International Energy Agency. (2021). *Renewables 2021—Analysis and forecast to 2026*.

Isolani, K. A., & Tonin, J. M. (2013). Produção de biodiesel no Brasil com o advento do Selo Combustível Social e os impactos na agricultura familiar Biodiesel. *Desenvolvimento e Meio Ambiente*, *28*, 157–171.

Jornal de Brasília. (2007, March 25). *Lula diz que Brasil será a Arábia Saudita do biocombustível*. Retrieved February 10, 2022, from https://jornaldebrasilia.com.br/noticias/brasil/lula-diz-que-brasil-sera-a-arabia-saudita-do-biocombustivel/

Lapuerta, M., Armas, O., & Rodríguez-Fernández, J. (2008). Effect of biodiesel fuels on diesel engine emissions. *Progress in Energy and Combustion Science*, *34*(2), 198–223. https://doi.org/10.1016/j.pecs.2007.07.001

Leite, J. G. D. B., Bijman, J., Giller, K., & Slingerland, M. (2013a). Biodiesel policy for family farms in Brazil : One-size-fits-all ? Joa. *Environmental Sciense & Policy*, *27*, 195–205. https://doi.org/10.1016/j.envsci.2013.01.004

Leite, J. G. D. B., Bijman, J., Giller, K., & Slingerland, M. (2013b). Biodiesel policy for family farms in Brazil: One-size-fits-all? *Environmental Science & Policy*, *27*. https://doi.org/10.1016/j.envsci.2013.01.004

Macarini, J. P. (2011). Governo Geisel: transição político-econômica? Um ensaio de revisão. *Revista de Economia Contemporânea*, *15*(1), 30–61. https://doi.org/10.1590/S1415-98482011000100002

Ministério da Agricultura Pecuária e Abastecimento. (2019). *Balanço do Selo Combustível Social.* Retrieved June 16, 2021, from http://www.mda.gov.br/sitemda/sites/sitemda/files/user_img_1754/SCS-Balanço_2017_Publicação_20-11-18.pdf

Ministério da Agricultura, P. e A. (2021a). *Balanço do Selo Combustível Social.*

Ministério da Agricultura, P. e A. (2021b). *Empresas com Selo Combustível Social—Atualizado em 1° de março de 2021.*

Martins, R., Nachiluk, K., Bueno, C. R. F., & Freitas, S. M. (2011). O Biodiesel de Sebo Bovino no Brasil. *Revista de Informações Econômicas*, *41*(5).

McNeely, J. A., Solh, M., Hiremath, R. B., Kumar, B., Suarez, P. A. Z., Uprety, K., Abdulrahim, M. A., Ruf, F. O., & Legoupil, J. C. (2009). Experts address the question: Can the growing demand for biofuels be met without threatening food security? *Natural Resources Forum*, *33*(1), 171–173.

Ministério de Minas e Energia.. (2015, September 21). Resolução CNPE n° 03. Pub. L. No. 03, Autoriza e define diretrizes para comercialização e uso voluntário de biodiesel.

Ministério de Minas e Energia. (2016, December 14). Resolução CNPE no 11. Pub. L. No. 11, Dispõe sobre adição obrigatória de biodiesel ao óleo diesel vendido ao consumidor final, em qualquer parte do território nacional.

Ministério de Minas e Energia.. (2018, October 29). Resolução CNPE n° 16. Pub. L. No. 16, Dispõe sobre a evolução da adição obrigatória de biodiesel ao óleo diesel vendido ao consumidor final, em qualquer parte do território nacional.

Molony, T., & Smith, J. (2010). Biofuels: Food security, and Africa. *African Affairs*, *109*(1), 489–498.

Monteiro, J. M. G. (2007). *Plantio de Oleaginosas por Agricultores Familiares do Semi-Árido Nordestino para Produção de Biodiesel como uma Estratégia de Mitigação e Adaptação às Mudanças Climáticas* (Vol. 53). Universidade Federal do Rio de Janeiro.

Pedroti, P. M. (2013). Os Desafios do Desenvolvimento e inclusão social: o caso do arranjo político-institucional do Programa Nacional de Produção e uso do Biodísel. In Instituto de Pesquisa Econômica Aplicada (Ed.), *Capacidades estatais e democracia: arranjos institucionais de políticas públicas* (Texto para, Vol. 1858, p. 66). https://www.ipea.gov.br/portal/index.php?option=com_content&view=article&id= 19498

Pingali, P., Raney, T., & Wiebe, K. (2008). Biofuels and food security missing the point. *Review on Agricultural Economics*, *30*(1), 506–516.

Pousa, G. P. A. G., Santos, A. L. F., & Suarez, P. A. Z. (2007). History and policy of biodiesel in Brazil. *Energy Policy*, *35*(11), 5393–5398. https://doi.org/10.1016/j.enpol.2007.05.010

Prado, J. N., & Vieira, W. C. (2010). Leilões de Biodiesel Conduzidos pela ANP: Uma Avaliação Preliminar. *Nexus Econômicos*, *4*(6), 67–88.

Ramos, L. P., Kothe, V., César-Oliveira, M. A. F., Muniz-Wypych, A. S., Nakagaki, S., Krieger, N., Wypych, F., & Cordeiro, C. S. (2017). Biodiesel: Matéria-Primas, Tecnologias de Produção e Propriedades Combustíveis. *Revista Virtual de Quimica*, *9*(1), 317–369. https://doi.org/10.21577/1984-6835.20170020

Ribeiro, E. C. B., Moreira, A. C., Ferreira, L. M., & César, A. da S. (2018). Biodiesel and social inclusion : An analysis of institutional pressures between biodiesel plants and family farmers in southern Brazil. *Journal of Cleaner Production Journal*, *204*, 726–734. https://doi.org/10.1016/j.jclepro.2018.09.085

Rodrigues, R. (2006). Biodiesel no Brasil: diversificação energética e inclusão social com sustentabilidade. In J. R. Ferreira & C. M. P. N. Cristo (Eds.), *O futuro da indústria: biodiesel—coletânea de artigos* (1st ed., Vol. 1, pp. 15–25). MDIC-STI/IEL.

Sá Parente, E. J. (2003). *BIODIESEL: Uma Aventura Tecnológica num País Engraçado*. http://www.xitizap.com/Livro-Biodiesel.pdf

Sampaio, R. M. (2017). *Biodiesel no Brasil: Capacidades Estatais, P&D e Inovação na Petrobras Biocombustíveis* (Vol. 1). Universidade Estadual de Campinas.

Shurtleff, W., & Aoyagi, A. (2009). *History of soybeans and soyfoods in South America (1882–2009): Extensively annotated bibliography and sourcebook*. Soyinfo Center.

Silva, A. N. da. (2014). *Os biocombustíveis afetam a segurança alimentar no Brasil? Discussão e abordagem quantitativa*. Universidade Federal de Viçosa.

Silva, F. D. S., Grasel, D., & Mertens, F. (2017). Participação da agricultura familiar no Programa Nacional de Biodiesel. *Revista de Política Agrícola*, *26*(1), 65–80. Retrieved from https://seer.sede.embrapa.br/index.php/RPA/article/view/1250/1040

Silva, M. S., Fernandes, F. M., Lima, F., Teixeira, C., & Torres, E. A. (2014). Biodiesel and the "Social Fuel Seal" in Brazil: Fuel of Social Inclusion? *Journal of Agricultural Science*, *6*(11), 212–228. https://doi.org/10.5539/jas.v6n11p212

Silva, M. S., Teixeira, F. L. C., Torres, E. A., Fernandes, F. M., & Rocha, A. M. (2014). Family farming and biodiesel: The difficulties of socioeconomic inclusion in the northeast of Brazil. *Journal of Agricultural Science*, *6*(7), 231–252.

Souza, S. P., & Seabra, J. E. A. (2014). Integrated production of sugarcane ethanol and soybean biodiesel: Environmental and economic implications of fossil diesel displacement. *Energy Conversion and Management*, *87*, 1170–1179. https://doi.org/10.1016/j.enconman.2014.06.015

Souza, S. P., Seabra, J. E. A., & Nogueira, L. A. H. (2017). Feedstocks for biodiesel production: Brazilian and global perspectives. *Biofuels*, *9*(4), 455–478. https://doi.org/10.1080/17597269.2017.1278931

Távora, F. L. (2011). *História e Economia dos Biocombustíveis no Brasil*. Brasília.

Tiburcio, B. A. (2011). *Atores sociais, agricultura familiar e desenvolvimento territorial: uma análise do Programa Nacional de Produção e Uso de Biodiesel*. Rio de Janeiro, Brazil: Universidade Federal do Rio de Janeiro.

United States Department of Agriculture, F. A. S. (2019). *Biofuels annual: Indonesia*.

Vieira Filho, J. E. R., & Fishlow, A. (2017). Agricultura e Indústria no Brasil: Inovação e Competitividade. In *IPEA*. http://www.ipea.gov.br/portal/index.php?option=com_content&view=article&id=29768

CHAPTER 20

Scaling Up Renewable Energy Technologies in Bangladesh: Prospects and Challenges

DIPTA MAJUMDER AND FERDOUS RAHMAN

INTRODUCTION

Bangladesh is an emerging economy in Asia that is expecting to graduate from the list of the Least Developed Countries (LDCs) of the United Nations by 2023 (UNDESA, 2018). It has also set an ambitious goal of becoming a developed country by 2041 (GED, 2021, p. i). Uninterrupted access to electricity will play a vital role in achieving this target, not only for business and economic activities but also for the improved quality of life. Electricity demands will continue to rise along with economic development. Bangladesh endeavored to ensure access to electricity to 100 % of the nation's population by 2021. The country was among the top 20 with the largest access deficits in 2010. However, in the last ten years, Bangladesh has made significant improvements and is now ranked fourth out of 20 countries with the highest level of off-grid access (International Energy Agency, 2020). It had already provided access to electricity to 97 % of its population by 2020 (USAID, 2021, p. 1).

The contribution of renewable energy (RE) behind this success of providing access to high-quality electricity at a low cost cannot be denied. The development of the RE sector in Bangladesh can be traced back to the 1970s, when biogas technology was launched (Alauddin, 2014). Nevertheless, RE technologies took off with the solar home system (SHS) program in 2003, funded by the World

Bank, Asian Development Bank, and other development partners. Through this program, 4.1 million SHSs were installed, providing access to electricity to the population living in off-grid areas (Cabraal et al., 2021). In addition to the RE technologies in off-grid areas, Bangladesh has recently started implementing a net metering policy for rooftop solar photovoltaic (PV) systems connected to the main grid (Nguyen, 2020).

According to the data published by the World Bank, more than 5 % of the population with access to off-grid electricity are supplied by SHSs, although the SHS program ended in 2018. The remaining few parts of off-grid electricity have been taken from solar mini-grids. Twenty-one solar mini-grids were installed in Bangladesh with financial assistance from the development partners in the form of soft loans and grants (Aziz & Chowdhury, 2021). Data published by the Sustainable and Renewable Energy Development Authority (SREDA) (2021) shows that the total RE installed capacity is 777.24 MW, of which 69.9 % is sourced from solar energy, 29.6 % is from hydro energy, and 0.4 % is from wind energy.

In 2020, the Bangladesh government published its development strategy to achieve its vision for economic prosperity in the Perspective Plan of 2041 (PP2041). The PP2041 aims to bring the energy sector on a sustainable path, ensuring consistent production without interrupting environmental protection by 2041 (PP2041, 2021, p. xii and pp. 133–134). Hence, the RE sector has received special focus. The PP2041 identified the unfinished electricity reforms in Bangladesh, namely energy mix, energy pricing and financing, and energy efficiency (PP2041, 2021, p. 131). It has also set some future initiatives to promote RE that have been mentioned, such as incentives for private investment in the RE sector and for households to adopt clean energy technologies, and the sale of electricity by private producers to the grid and consumers (PP2041, 2021, pp. 137–138).

This chapter assesses the policy-level readiness of Bangladesh to complete these unfinished plans and to achieve the proposed initiatives in the PP2041 by 2041. This chapter has four major parts in addition to the introduction and conclusion. It starts by putting the international best practices forward, followed by the present status of RE policies and projects in Bangladesh. The next part analyzes the financial, technical, and regulatory gaps in the current policy framework. This section will identify the gaps and scope of improvement from these three perspectives. Finally, recommendations have been formulated that are expected to enable the current framework to be more private-investment-friendly, considering the aspects of financial and technical risk-management vis-a-vis the regulatory assistance. These recommendations are in line with the country's 2041 vision and will assist in scaling it up in both the short and mid-term.

INTERNATIONAL BEST PRACTICES

The International Energy Agency (2018) suggests some best practices at the policy level for RE. The most relevant suggestions in the context of Bangladesh are challenges in the availability of data, cross-sectoral energy planning and higher RE-based electricity integration.

A good RE policy can reflect the available resources, current deployment state, regulatory framework, governmental priorities, and fiscal constraints. For example, targets could be incorporated into legislation, as this would provide some certainty to potential investors. Alongside the policy, a detailed strategic and action plan will also be needed. This will help to develop a clear trajectory and guide the sector in the required direction. Furthermore, the RE policy should be aligned with the energy efficiency policy.

From the public sector, reliable data on the resource potential, information on identified lands for RE-based projects, and integration points in the grid network should be made available. Wherever possible, data based on a geographic information system (GIS) should be made available to generate interest among potential investors. Data flow in the other direction is also needed to monitor the implementation progress and the effectiveness of the policies and measures.

The government should take measures to ensure that there is a level playing field for all energy sources. Not all the benefits of RE adoption can be transferred into monetary benefits (e.g., reduced air pollution and carbon dioxide emissions). Coupling between different sectors such as the transportation, electricity, and heating/cooling sectors could also help, although heating/cooling does not broadly apply to Bangladesh. Nevertheless, there are some possibilities of cross-linkages between the electricity and transportation sectors. Achieving this will require the gradual electrification of the transportation sector, which requires integrated energy planning. Another sector coupling possibility is with the agriculture and food supply chain.

Financial support will be needed to support a greater share of RE-based electricity due to the significant initial capital needed. Moreover, new installers may face high costs when connecting to transmission or distribution lines, which may impact the competitiveness and the outcome of the project. The government can establish clear grid connection rules, allowing private operators to prepare. At high levels of RE integration, policymakers need to introduce measures for variable energy sources with the possibility of incorporating energy storage. For this purpose, the government should recognize the different locational, time, and technological values of renewable power plants. This may require the electricity market to be reformed to provide accurate pricing of high RE shares, flexible system designing, and a good mix of sources.

The government should also adopt policies and adjust frameworks to remove non-economic barriers (e.g., skill shortages, licenses). Public funding schemes should be introduced to reduce the cost of financing. Possible strategies to accomplish this include power purchase agreements, debt programs at low interest rates in partnership with international financial organizations, and public funding programs to leverage private investment.

Bangladesh's RE resource data suggests that there is considerable potential for solar PV Power with 3.68–4.23 kWh/kWp/day, while neighboring India and Myanmar have 3.63–4.85 and 3.67–4.44 kWh/kWp/day, respectively. Solar potential in this range can be considered moderate since some countries enjoy more than 4.5 kWh/kWp/day, such as Pakistan (the World Bank, 2020, p. 32). The government aims to have 40 GW installed based on Solar PV technology by 2041, 40 % of which will come from rooftop solar energy. Other sources like wind, hydro, and biogas show little potential to impact the grid level soon. Although, the U.S. National Renewable Energy Laboratory (NREL) recently reported that Bangladesh has more wind potential than previously thought, which is 30 GW (Tachev, 2021). Another report from the Institute for Sustainable Futures indicated that Bangladesh could deploy up to 156 GW of utility-scale solar energy and 150 GW of wind power (Teskem et al., 2019, pp. 3–4). Such ambitious scaling will require a robust but flexible policy and regulatory framework that can support the sector.

PRESENT STATUS OF THE POLICIES FOR THE RENEWABLE ENERGY SECTOR IN BANGLADESH

The Bangladesh government has signed and ratified the United Framework Convention on Climate Change (UNFCCC) as well as the Kyoto Protocol (UNFCCC, 2021). Under these international legal instruments, the government has the positive obligation to promote environmentally friendly energy sources. Bangladesh is also a recipient of the Green Climate Fund (GCF) to emphasize clean energy sectors (GCF, 2021). The geographical position of Bangladesh also makes the RE sources an efficient energy production opportunity for the country (Karim et al., 2019, p. 6).

The literature emphasized three areas for governmental awareness to promote the RE sectors: introducing RE technologies instead of conventional energy sources, building the capabilities of stakeholders in this sector, and developing networks of stakeholders for further promotion (Islam & Ferdousi, 2007, p. 425). Currently, Bangladesh uses multiple types of RE technologies, including SHSs, solar-powered irrigation, solar mini-grids, biogas-based household energy, biomass-based energy generation, wind, and hydropower.

According to International Renewable Energy Agency (2021), Bangladesh heavily relies on non-RE sources for electricity generation. Specifically, according to data from 2020, 98 % of the total capacity (i.e., 23,100 MW) is fossil fuel based, whereas only 515 MW comes from renewable sources like hydropower and solar power. Even though the per capita generation reached ~500 kWh in 2019, as a consequence of relying on non-renewable sources, at the end of 2019, the CO_2 emission factor for electricity and heat generation reached 599 tCO_2/GWh, which is higher than the global average.

Seven indicators of the Sustainable Development Goals based on 2018 data show that 92 % of the population has access to electricity, whereas RE contributes 30.7 % of the total final energy consumption of the country. The most recent national RE target was renewable sources to contribute 10 % of the electricity capacity by 2021, which could not be fulfilled.

An efficient administrative and regulatory framework is essential to increase capacity building. It was emphasized that Bangladesh had no umbrella institution for regulating, facilitating, and promoting clean energy and energy efficiency (Islam & Ferdousi, 2007, p. 429). Hence, the SREDA was established under the Sustainable and Renewable Energy Development Authority Act of 2012 to create a comprehensive and coherent framework. The SREDA was formed to increase the use of RE as part of Bangladesh's pledge to reduce global warming while ensuring the country's energy security. One of the SREDA's primary focuses has been RE development alongside energy efficiency and conservation.

A non-exhaustive list of the key stakeholders, particularly the relevant ministries and public agencies, includes the Ministry of Power, Energy and Mineral Resources, the Bangladesh Power Development Board (BPDB), the Bangladesh Rural Electrification Board (BREB), a generation, transmission, and distribution company, the Bangladesh Standards and Testing Institution (BSTI), the Local Government Engineering Department (LGED), and the Bangladesh Energy Regulatory Commission (BERC). The BPDB acts as the core governmental body for the electricity reform in Bangladesh. The BREB is exclusively assigned for the expansion of access to electricity in rural underserved or unserved areas. According to the Standards of Weights and Measures Act 2018 (Act no. 56 of 2018), the BSTI is the national standard body responsible for ensuring the quality of energy efficiency products.

The SREDA has two mandates related to climate change issues, namely, the promotion of RE and the adoption of energy efficiency measures to ensure the energy security of the nation (the SREDA Act, 2012, preambular paragraphs 1 and 2 and section 6). The BERC, constituted under the Bangladesh Energy Regulatory Commission Act of 2003, works with the mandate of promotion of RE. Its objectives comprise the creation of an investor-friendly environment for private sectors in electricity generation and a competitive market ensuring consumer protection (the BERC Act, 2003, the preamble and section 22). Any person engaged in power generation, energy transmission, distribution and marketing, or supply and storage from any energy sources, including RE, is required to obtain a license from the BERC (the BERC Act, 2003, section 27).

Whereas the United Nations Development Programme addressed the lack of involvement of financial sectors in the RE sector as a pitfall for Bangladesh in 2004 (Islam & Ferdousi, 2007, p. 429), the present challenge has become finding motivated and compliant private investors in these sectors. Motivating private investors has been a real challenge for this sector for several reasons. This chapter endeavored to discuss these challenges. One of the objectives of PP2041 is to incentivize private investment. The literature identified the unavailability of financing as a common challenge for investors (Karim et al., 2019, p. 11). Currently, several Bangladesh government agencies are working as implementing agencies to fulfill the governmental mandate, the funds generated from the development partners, and the private investors in RE sectors. The Infrastructure Development Company Limited (IDCOL) acts as one of the government agencies that implement the RE-related mandate of the government. The IDCOL performs the role of the national designated authority for the GCF in Bangladesh (GCF, 2021). In addition, Bangladesh Bank (BB), the central bank of Bangladesh and the regulatory body for the financial sectors, has published green financing policies and circulars for the banks and non-bank financing institutions (NBFIs) since 2011.[1]

The majority of RE projects operate based on soft loans and grants from development partners. Extensive reliance on financial support may affect the growth of the sector. The outcomes of these projects might be uncertain without this foreign development assistance. Nevertheless, Bangladesh has sourced some dedicated funds for financing RE projects, such as BB's revolving funds, the Bangladesh Climate Change Trust Fund, the Bangladesh Climate Change Resilience Fund, half of the allocation from the Taka for Work (KABITA), and test relief (TR) (Alauddin, 2020, p. 9). Several incentives have been offered in the Income Tax Ordinance of 1984 (the Ordinance no. 36 of 1984) to attract more entrepreneurs for RE projects. For example, section 46C of this ordinance provides corporate tax holidays for up to 15 years and income from capital gain by transfer of shares in these companies. Foreign employees can be recruited for technological capacity building with income tax exemptions for three years to make their jobs in the RE projects in Bangladesh more lucrative. Moreover, tax exemptions are also provided on royalties, technical know-how, and technical assistance fees, and interest on foreign loans under various Statutory Regulatory Orders (SROs) of the National Board of Revenues (NBR) of Bangladesh. For instance, import tax, value added tax, and supplementary duties are also exempted for the import of solar panels following SRO No. 155-Law/2004/2047/Duty (dated June 10, 2004) to facilitate the import of advanced technologies in Bangladesh.

Despite having a regulatory framework, available funds, and fiscal incentives, policy-level preparation and effective methodology are necessary for the study of project viability, efficient assessment of risk, mitigation and management of risks, disbursement of funds, and implementation of the projects. The following section analyzes the gap in the financial, technical, and regulatory aspects for the smooth operation of the RE projects in Bangladesh.

GAP ANALYSIS

The level of readiness at the policy and regulatory level, as well as the administrative framework, impacts the quick adoption of RE technologies. The World Bank Group developed a set of indicators known as Regulatory Indicators for Sustainable Energy (RISE) to compare national policies and regulatory frameworks for sustainable energy. The RISE cover four areas: access to electricity, access to clean cooking, energy efficiency, and RE. Bangladesh's overall score in 2019 was 58. Even though this was higher than the global average (48), it was still far behind countries like Germany (95), the United Kingdom (95), Denmark (94), and India (86) (RISE, 2019).

Bangladesh has made significant progress in electricity access, scoring 81, but it still has much catching up to do in other areas (i.e., clean cooking (61), RE (44), and energy efficiency (44)). In line with the scope of this chapter, only the gaps in electricity access and RE are listed in Table 20.1.

For the RE indicator alone, Bangladesh performs poorly in planning for RE expansion, incentives and regulatory support for RE, attributes of financial and regulatory service, network connections and use, counterparty risk, and carbon pricing. However, Bangladesh scored comparatively high regarding the legal framework for RE. Even with a legal framework in place, there is room for improvement in planning and execution.

Recently, the USAID published a report in 2020 on the "Challenges in the Development of Variable Renewable Energy in Bangladesh" under their Scaling Up Renewable Energy (SURE) program. This report investigated the challenges and identified some gaps from policy to implementation. The key gaps identified are as follows (SURE, 2020, pp. XV–XVI):

- Bangladesh needs to reevaluate and set new targets for the immediate future as the previously set targets for RE integration have not been achieved. The current set target for 2041 is quite some time away and does not encourage immediate action.
- Integrated planning should be done that considers not only the lowest-cost options but also considers emissions and the energy security of the country.

Table 20.1: Identified Gaps in Bangladesh's Sustainable Energy Regulatory Framework

Indicator	Gap
Electrification Planning	• No concrete electricity access target in the national electrisfication plan
Scope of officially approved electrification plan	• The electrification plan does not include off-grid solutions • The national plan does not specifically address the electricity access of female-headed households • The plan does not include areas with informally settled people/groups
Framework for grid electrification	• No consumer financing mechanisms to support consumers in paying the connection fee • No consumer financing mechanism specifically for female-headed households • No consumer financing mechanisms targeting low-income households • No periodic reporting system to ensure standards compliance
Framework for mini-grids	• Lack of clear licensing procedures for mini-grid operators and consumers
Framework for stand-alone systems	• No legal restrictions on how much the stand-alone home system or retailer can charge • No technical standards are publicly available • No safety standards are publicly available
Utility creditworthiness	• Low debt service coverage ratio

Source: Authors' own elaboration (data compiled from RISE, 2019).

- the available RE policy needs to be updated so that it is linked to the short-term, mid-term, and long-term targets of the 2041 master plan.
- The development of a separate procurement agency for the independent power producers is suggested that can handle all the procurement activities, related planning, and communication.
- A review of roles, responsibilities, and activities to be undertaken by different stakeholders.
- It is important to ensure that the changes in policies or new policies are implementable and practical. A designated agency should monitor the progress made and identify any challenges or barriers to adopting/implementing the policies.
- Proper demand-side management needs to be done so that the Bangladesh government does not have to make capacity payments due to unused electricity plants.

- For utility-scale integration of varying RE sources, Bangladesh should engage with donors and developers so that international best practices and lessons learned can be implemented.

Other key areas that need immediate action are the provision of land for RE deployment and adjustments to the grid network. This chapter further investigates the challenges from the perspective of an investor under three distinct heads: financial, technical, and regulatory.

Financial

Similar to any other commercial project, the investors bear the risks in RE projects and share them with financiers and insurers. The current model for financing RE projects in Bangladesh involves loans at a low interest rates (Zheng et al., 2021, p. 795) and, in some cases, combinations of grants (IDCOL, 2021). The common pitfall faced by private investors is providing security for their loans. More private small and medium entrepreneurs (SMEs) and local investors should be engaged in investing to scale up RE projects. Assessments of the profitability of the RE projects at the same scale as other commercial projects act as a bottleneck for entrepreneurs. Risks particular to the RE projects and their assessments are vital for the successful operation of a project. A lack of skills and experience of banks and NBFIs to conduct due diligence on a RE project is a major challenge (Hossain, 2019).

Such traditional assessments require entrepreneurs to secure full loans by providing enforceable securities such as land mortgages, bank guarantees, hypothecations, and personal guarantees. Local SMEs may not have the capacity to provide mortgages securing the full amount of the loan depending on their business portfolio (Hossain, 2018, p. 13). Nevertheless, banks and NBFIs need to secure their credit finances (Zheng et al., p. 14.). Given that project lands are situated in off-grid or underserved areas, their value does not cover the loan value to be secured. Hence, additional securities become a burden for entrepreneurs.

Similarly, the insurance sector is not ready to perceive the shifting paradigm of the energy sector. Entrepreneurs also require insurance coverage to protect their project assets from natural and artificial perils. Perils prone to the RE technologies are not commonly covered in offered insurance packages. In some cases, additional perils need to be covered, which ultimately increases the premium rate and, in turn, raises the costs for the entrepreneurs. In many cases, full insurance coverage is a requirement for the disbursement of loans. The financing institutions or banks require insurance as a condition precedent to disburse the funds. Even before getting any finances from banks and/or NBFIs, entrepreneurs need to arrange the credit report of their business, land valuation report, due-diligence costs, documentation costs, and other documents. These increase the transaction costs for entrepreneurs (Zheng et al., p. 14).

In some cases, a grant portion is provided by an NBFI, such as IDCOL, to reduce the costs for entrepreneurs. However, empirical research shows a moral hazard problem in the loan repayment stage (Hossain et al., 2021). Experts advise using market-based approaches to solve the moral hazard problem and suggest removing the grant portion to make RE markets more competitive (Hossain et al., 2021). Nevertheless, after the construction of the project, price instability acts as another barrier to the commercial feasibility of RE projects (Eleftheriadis & Anagnostopoulou, 2015). The collection of electricity prices (e.g., for solar mini-grid projects) and installments of SHS prices from consumers are significant challenges (Zheng et al., 2021, p. 15). Defaults of the consumers eventually result in defaults of local SMEs. The absence of efficient corporate governance increases entrepreneurs' operational risks of RE projects and causes poor financial performance.

Technical

Bangladesh has achieved a deep rural penetration of stand-alone SHSs. However, this can be a stopgap solution only until the main grid reaches these areas and people get access to a better quality of power. Bangladesh will move from small SHSs to more utility-scale solar power plants that can supply electricity to the main grid.

Due to the varying nature of RE sources, electricity is not always available. Over a certain limit, it can cause stability issues in the grid. This risk is mitigated by tying energy storage or keeping the penetration to a level that the grid can handle. To date, seven utility-scale solar power plants with a total capacity of approximately 175 MW have been operational and have provided electricity to the main grid. Another 1,700 MW has been approved by the Government through independent power producers, while an additional 712 MW is in the process of being approved. In addition to this, small rooftop solar systems, solar irrigation systems, and solar streetlights are gaining traction, though they are not likely to substantially impact the whole energy mix. The key technical challenges are the scarcity of land; complex legal administration; a lack of data on available land, resources, and grids; grid stability; and energy storage integration. These technical challenges are vastly connected with the gaps in the regulatory framework.

Regulatory

The current model of encouraging private investment in the RE sector requires the private investor to arrange the land for the project. However, land management in Bangladesh still follows the laws and rules from the pre-independence era.[2] The laws related to land management and titles are fragmented and complex. Documents are still managed manually, although the government has taken some initiative to digitize this process. The proposed Bangladesh Land Act of 2020 codifying all the land-related matters in a single law has not been passed yet (Ahmed, 2020). Therefore, the scarcity of land and the need to ensure the legal title and possession of land are substantial challenges for private investors.

Moreover, RE entrepreneurs, financiers, and regulatory authorities have expressed similar concerns about the absence of conceptual clarity among the stakeholders. Bank officials assess the RE projects like any other conventional commercial projects financed by the banks which are detrimental to scale up. The RE project-financing needs special understanding to study the project's feasibility, determine financial terms, repayment schedule etc. (Rahman, 2021). Despite the loan disbursement quota given by BB, the lack of any guidelines for checking the feasibility of RE projects at the proposal stage compels the front officers of banks and NBFIs to appraise RE projects similarly to any other commercial projects. Therefore, despite having the proposals from the local SMEs, few projects qualify for financing. This obstructs green financing for entrepreneurs, banks, and NBFIs (Hossain, 2018, p. 13). The regulatory environment is still not ready for the green bond market in Bangladesh. Hence, the unprepared capital market acts as an impediment to RE projects in Bangladesh (Hossain, 2018, p. 12).

Obtaining licensing and permissions is another challenge for entrepreneurs. It is also a precondition for the disbursement of loans and grants (if any). Entrepreneurs are required to receive approvals from about 30 different offices (Rahman, 2021), such as the local government, the Department of Environment under section 12 of the Environmental Conservation Act of 1995 and rule 7 of the Environmental Conservation Rules of 1997, a license from the BERC under section 27 of the BERC Act 2003, and a certificate from the NBR for tax incentives under section 46C of the Income Tax Ordinance of 1984. The cost and time employed for procuring each license and approval increase transaction costs and reduce the time efficiency of the project.

SUGGESTIONS FOR MOTIVATING PRIVATE INVESTORS TO SCALE UP RE PROJECTS

Creating a One-Stop Solution for Registration, Licensing, and Approvals

Even though the SREDA is increasing its capacity to advocate for RE projects, implement RE policies, coordinate public and private stakeholders, and provide necessary information, there is still a need for a one-stop service, particularly if

Bangladesh wants to attract foreign investment into the sector and scale up the intervention. The SREDA has the potential to become such a service point for the project developers by continuing the role of a coordinator on the government side; taking care of the necessary registration, licensing, and approval process; and essentially becoming the single point of contact for the project developers. This will help reduce the delays that occur when several stakeholders are involved. A working group of high-level officials from the relevant public stakeholders could be formed. This working group's role would be to strategize and coordinate different ministries and agencies. The project developer would not need to run to multiple organizations, which sometimes is a barrier to speeding up the administrative processes. Once such an organization has been properly set up, the costs of project development and financing will also drop.

Single regulatory authority publishing information on available lands, grid connection.

Taking the one-stop service discussed in the previous point further, the same designated agency could publish detailed information on the countrywide potential for different forms of RE, the possibility of selecting technology, grid connection points or network routes, and available demarcated lands for project development.

An increasing number of countries and organizations are utilizing geospatial data science and GISs to map out potential project sites and resources, model them for different applications, and visualize the best possible scenarios. Such transparent information sharing not only saves time for the project development but also allows the government to take an integrated approach and prioritize the intervention points. Such a bottom-up methodology is likely to lead to sustainable development in this sector compared to an ad-hoc basis or a first come, first serve basis. Examples of such practices are available from the NREL (U.S.), South Korea, Nigeria, and other countries.

There are some studies and reports available on the SREDA website. However, they do not provide clarity that the government is taking a logical approach in transitioning from fossil fuel sources to renewable ones. There are some basic tools available (for rooftop solar systems) to assess the viability of a project. The information available is still quite limited, however, and there are indications that there is a continual improvement on this part.

Bangladesh faces another problem in finding the appropriate land for such project development, particularly utility-scale solar projects or solar parks. This can be improved by having a public agency perform countrywide GIS mapping and identify which lands are suitable and/or available as non-agricultural land for developing RE plants.

Solar resource potential alone is not enough; combined with available land, rooftop, and other available and suitable spaces and the solar radiation and other meteorological data, potential investors will be able to scale up their portfolios. Alternatively, the government can invite bids (in auction format) from interested investors once the lands are identified. There are wind energy resources available, although the available information does not readily aid decision-making.

Developing Guidelines/Templates for the Appraisal of RE Projects and Securitization

The requirements of documentation and security, which are needed by government agencies for approval before going into a contract or public-private partnership, are daunting. The situation is similar for financiers, as they have a separate appraisal process of their own. The same argument can be made for other regulatory agencies like the BERC and LGED. This calls for significant effort and delays the process, ultimately increasing project costs.

Standardized templates or guidelines must be developed by government agencies and possibly financiers as well so that such efforts can be optimized. Data and documents can be shared in a single digital platform by the developer/applicant, which can be accessed in real-time by all stakeholders. This will reduce the working hours spent reviewing and approving these documents. Such digital tools can either be developed or adopted from the available tools. The key recommendations are as follows:

- Decide on standardized data/document sharing, reporting, templates, and contracts among the stakeholders so that the developer does not need to produce separate documentation for each of them.
- Develop or adopt a digital tool with which the applicant or project developer can upload necessary documents and with which the stakeholders can access the documents in real-time and review them immediately.

Capacity Building for Bankers, Insurers, and Entrepreneurs Specializing in RE Projects

Even though Bangladesh has succeeded in off-grid rural electrification programs, it is still in a nascent stage of the large-scale integration of RE. The private and public sectors need the capacity to minimize risks and gain momentum to achieve the targets and increase the use of RE. Therefore, capacity building is required across the sector, starting with public agencies, financing organizations, and development partners to the project developers and operators. The international best practices can be transferred through donor-funded projects. If assessed as not risky, Bangladesh may encourage more foreign investment for large RE projects. The key recommendations for improving capacity are listed below.

- RE-based research needs to be diversified, and more human-centric design should be done that fits the local context. The local industry and academia should continue to lead this effort by cooperating with other leading research organizations.
- Course or degree programs should be introduced so that more skilled people will enter the market ready for jobs and already aware of the challenges.
- General public engagement to increase awareness with the use of different accessible media (including social media).
- Requiring or encouraging foreign companies to employ more local personnel who can learn on the job or introduce internship programs to build capacity.

CONCLUSION

Bangladesh had experienced the benefits of RE technologies even before setting the legal and regulatory framework. The success of the SHS program of IDCOL between 2003 and 2018 and long-term funding from the development partners for this program showed the potential of the RE sector in Bangladesh. The first policy, namely the Renewable Energy Policy, was implemented in 2008. Since then, it has been a steppingstone of the legal framework for the development, research, and investment in the RE sectors (Karim et al., 2019, p. 14). The aim of generating 10 % of all electricity from RE sources by 2020 was set in section 2 (xi) of this policy. Such an approach leads to the need to review the policy after the expected timeline has passed. A new goal has been set in the PP2041, although the revision of the policy has not yet been released. Since the enactment of the Renewable Energy Policy in 2008, policy and legal frameworks have been adopted on a piecemeal basis, which has not helped scale up the RE contribution or fully implement the policies.

Bangladesh is currently standing at its no return position from its LDC graduation. Given the size of the country's population, once it graduates from the list of LDCs in 2023, it cannot be reverted to an LDC according to the rules of the UN (UN-OHRLLS, 2022). After graduation, Bangladesh will not be entitled to the exemptions it is currently enjoying as an LDC (Bose, 2018). Hence, the achievement of the goal of energy efficiency is necessary to keep the momentum of the targeted LDC graduation in 2023 to reduce the cost of fuels and stay competitive in the market (Akiwumi, 2019). Such an ambitious target can be reached only by scaling up RE technologies through private investments or public-private partnerships. RE projects are still facing challenges from their project initiation stage to their commercial operation, though the stakeholders have brought about several positive policies to encourage more engagement from the private sector. Several fiscal incentives have been offered for SMEs, and mandatory disbursement targets have been set for banks and NBFIs to ensure that RE projects receive financing. However, a comprehensive and integrated approach is still missing.

Many development partners have come forward with suggestions and best practice guidelines to improve the legal and regulatory conditions in Bangladesh to advance RE technologies. The literature shows the gap between the current policy status of Bangladesh considering international best practices (Karim et al., 2019). This chapter scrutinized the policy-level preparation of Bangladesh to implement its energy strategy stated in PP2041. It concluded that inviting private investment is the inevitable way to scale up the RE technologies. Nevertheless, this chapter also identified certain financial, technical, and regulatory challenges for encouraging private investment in this sector. Given the constraints, this chapter discussed the proposal of developing a one-stop service point for entrepreneurs to reduce transaction costs and increase the time efficiency of the projects. Similarly, a single regulatory authority can bear the responsibilities of publishing necessary information on available lands and grid interconnection points to ease the project development process. These two proposals cannot flourish unless comprehensive customized guidelines are prepared for the appraisal of RE projects and securitization. Finally, all the relevant stakeholders will be able to take advantage of the available funds, adopted guidelines, and publicly circulated information, by which they could receive necessary training regarding the technicalities and distinctiveness of the RE projects.

NOTES

1 The Green Banking Policy Guidelines (2011), Policy Guidelines for Green Banking for Financial Institutions and Banks (2013), the Sustainable Finance Policy for Banks and Financial Institutions (2020), the minimum target for direct green finance from the total loan disbursed (GBCSRD Circular no. 04/2014, 05/2020), the allocation for the Climate Risk Fund (GBCSRD Circular no. 04/2015), the constitution of Sustainable Finance Unit and Sustainable Finance Committee (GBCSRD Circular no. 02/2016), quarterly reports to be submitted by the banks and financing institutions for their green banking initiatives (GBCSRD Circular no. 01/2018), the recognition of renewable energy sectors as green financing (GBCSRD Circular no. 01/2019), and the sustainability rating methodology for the banks and financing institutions (GBCSRD Circular no. 03/2021 and 05/2021). (Bangladesh Bank, n.d., 2020a, 2020b)

2 The Transfer of Property Act (1882), the Land Survey Act (1875), the Bengal Tenancy Act (1885), the Registration Act (1908), the Public Demands Recovery Act (1913), the Non-Agricultural Tenancy Act (1949), the State Acquisition and Tenancy Act (1950), the Land Law

Development Tax Ordinance (1976), the Land Reform Ordinance (1984), the Land Reform Board Ordinance (1989), the Land Appeal Board Ordinance (1989), the Land Management Manual (1990) etc.

REFERENCES

Ahmed, N. (2020, September 15). *Proposed Bangladesh Land Act 2020: What legal experts say*, Law & Our Rights, the Daily Star. Retrieved January 4, 2022, from https://www.thedailystar.net/law-our-rights/news/special-supplement-draft-bangladesh-land-act-2020-1961561

Akiwumi, P. (2019). *Green transition: Least developed countries cannot afford to Strand their assets, given their development challenges, OECD development matters.* UNCTAD.

Alauddin, M. (2014, November 11). *Development of Renewable Energy in Bangladesh*, the Daily Star. Retrieved December 19, 2021, from https://www.thedailystar.net/development-of-renewable-energy-in-bangladesh-49670

Alauddin, M. (2020, January 28). *Bangladesh Legal Framework and Current solar PV development*, Ministry of Power, Energy and Mineral Resources. Retrieved December 24, 2021, from https://www.german-energy-solutions.de/GES/Redaktion/DE/Publikationen/Praesentationen/2020/200128-iv-pep-bangladesch-pakistan-praes2.pdf?__blob=publicationFile&v=3

Aziz, S., & Chowdhury, S. A. (2021). Performance evaluation of solar mini grids in Bangladesh: A two-stage data envelopment analysis. *Cleaner Environmental Systems*, *2*, 1–12.

Bangladesh Bank. (n.d.). *Investment Facility.* Retrieved January 4, 2022, from https://www.bb.org.bd/investfacility/invesfac.php

Bangladesh Bank. (2020a). *The sustainable finance policy for banks and financial institutions.* Retrieved February 14, 2022, from https://www.bb.org.bd/mediaroom/circulars/gbcrd/dec312020sfd05.pdf

Bangladesh Bank. (2020b). *The green banking policy guidelines 2011.* Retrieved February 14, 2022, from https://www.bb.org.bd/mediaroom/circulars/brpd/feb272011brpd02e.pdf

Bose, S. (2018). International trade negotiations: Bangladesh perspective. Lecture given in training on the LDC Graduation: Challenges and Prospects for Bangladesh, organized by the WTO Cell under the Ministry of Commerce, Bangladesh and University of Dhaka on March 21–24, 2018.

Cabraal, A., Ward, W. A., Bogach, V. S., & Jain, A. (2021). *Living in the light: The Bangladesh solar home systems story.* World Bank. Retrieved December 19, 2021, from https://openknowledge.worldbank.org/handle/10986/35311

Eleftheriadis, I. M., & Anagnostopoulou, E. G. (2015). *Identifying barriers in the diffusion of renewable energy sources. Energy Policy, 80*, 153–164.

General Economics Division. (2021, May). *Making vision 2041 a reality: Perspective plan of Bangladesh (2021–2041).* Ministry of Planning, Government of People's Republic of Bangladesh, p. i. Retrieved December 20, 2021, from http://oldweb.lged.gov.bd/UploadedDocument/UnitPublication/1/1049/vision%202021-2041.pdf

Government of Bangladesh, The. (1984). *The Income Tax Ordinance 1984* (Ordinance No. 36 of 1984). http://bdlaws.minlaw.gov.bd/act-672.html

Government of Bangladesh, The. (2003). *The Bangladesh Energy Regulatory Commission Act 2003* (Act No. 13 of 2003). http://extwprlegs1.fao.org/docs/pdf/bgd65122.pdf

Government of Bangladesh, The. (2008). *The Renewable Energy Policy of Bangladesh 2008*. https://policy.asiapacificenergy.org/sites/default/files/REP_English.pdf

Government of Bangladesh, The. (2012). *The Sustainable and Renewable Energy Development Authority Act, 2012* (Act No. 48 of 2012). http://bdlaws.minlaw.gov.bd/act-1107.html

Government of Bangladesh, The. (2018). *The Standards of Weights and Measures Act 2018*, (Act No. 56 of 2018). http://bdlaws.minlaw.gov.bd/act-1270.html

Green Climate Fund. (2021). *Bangladesh*. Retrieved December 24, 2021, from https://www.greenclimate.fund/countries/bangladesh

Hossain, M. (2018). *Green financing in Bangladesh: Policies, institutions and challenges* (ADBI Working Paper No. 892). Asian Development Bank Institution (ADBI).

Hossain, M. (2019). Green finance in Bangladesh. In *Handbook of green finance* (pp. 513–537). Springer. https://doi.org/10.1007/978-981-13-0227-5_2

Hossain, M., Yoshino, M., & Taghizadeh-Hesary, F. (2021, February). Default risks, moral hazard and market-based solution: Evidence from renewable energy market in Bangladesh. *Economic Modeling*, *95*, 489–499.

International Energy Agency. (2018). *20 renewable energy policy recommendations*. Retrieved December 30, 2021, from https://www.iea.org/reports/20-renewable-energy-policy-recommendations

Infrastructure Development Company Limited. (n.d.). *Lending terms of renewable energy*. Retrieved December 27, 2021, from https://idcol.org/home/r_lending_terms

International Energy Agency, World Bank; World Health Organization, International Renewable Energy Agency, United Nations Statistics Division. (2020). *Tracking SDG 7: The energy progress report 2020*. World Bank. https://openknowledge.worldbank.org/handle/10986/33822

International Renewable Energy Agency. (2021). *Energy profile: Bangladesh*. Retrieved February 10, 2022, from https://www.irena.org/IRENADocuments/Statistical_Profiles/Asia/Bangladesh_Asia_RE_SP.pdf

Islam, M. T., & Ferdousi, S. (2007). Renewable energy development: Challenges for Bangladesh. *Energy and Environment*, *18*(3–4), 421–430.

Karim, M. E., Karim, R., Islam, M. T., Sukki, F. M., Bani, N. A., & Muhtazaruddin, M. N. (2019). Renewable energy for sustainable growth and development: An evaluation of law and policy of Bangladesh. *Sustainability*, *11*(20), 5774.

Nguyen, T. (2020, January 28). *Bangladesh: Financing options for rooftop solar PV projects*. Federal Ministry for Economic Affairs and Energy. Retrieved December 24, 2021, from https://www.german-energy-solutions.de/GES/Redaktion/DE/Publikationen/Praesentationen/2020/200128-iv-pep-bangladesch-pakistan-praes4.pdf?__blob=publicationFile&v=2

Rahman, M. (2021, August 22). Renewable energy development and sustainable project financing. *The Financial Express*. Retrieved January 4, 2022, from https://thefinancialexpress.com.bd/views/views/renewable-energy-development-and-sustainable-project-financing-1628869121

Regulatory Indicators for Sustainable Energy. (2019). *Country profile: Bangladesh*. Retrieved December 28, 2021, from https://rise.esmap.org/country/bangladesh

Scaling Up Renewable Energy. (2020, June). *Challenges in the development of variable renewable energy in Bangladesh*. USAID. Retrieved January 5, 2022, from https://pdf.usaid.gov/pdf_docs/PA00WPXQ.pdf

Sustainable and Renewable Energy Development Authority. (2021). *National database of renewable energy*. Retrieved December 24, 2021, from http://www.renewableenergy.gov.bd/index.php

Tachev, V. (2021, July 21). *Solar and wind power potential in Bangladesh.* Energy Tracker Asia, Retrieved January 4, 2022, from https://energytracker.asia/solar-and-wind-power-potential-in-bangladesh/

Teskem, S., Morris, T., & Nagrath, K. (2019). *100% renewable energy for Bangladesh: Access to renewable energy for all within one generation.* Institute for Sustainable Future. https://www.worldfuturecouncil.org/wp-content/uploads/2019/10/100-Renewable-Energy-for-Bangladesh.pdf

United Nations Department of Economic and Social Affairs. (2018, March 13). *Leaving the LDC category: Booming Bangladesh prepares to graduate.* Retrieved March 4, 2020, from https://www.un.org/development/desa/en/news/policy/leaving-the-ldcs-category-booming-bangladesh-prepares-to-graduate.html

UNFCCC. (n.d.). *Bangladesh.* Retrieved December 24, 2021, from https://unfccc.int/node/61013

UN-OHRLLS. (2022). *Criteria for Identification and Graduation of LDCs.* Retrieved January 10, 2022, from http://unohrlls.org/about-ldcs/criteria-for-ldcs/

USAID. (2021, May). *Power Sector Reforms in Bangladesh.* https://pdf.usaid.gov/pdf_docs/PA00XR95.pdf

World Bank, The. (2020, June). *Global photovoltaic power potential by country.* Energy Sector Management Assistance Program. https://documents1.worldbank.org/curated/en/466331592817725242/pdf/Global-Photovoltaic-Power-Potential-by-Country.pdf

Zheng, G. W., Siddik, A. B., Masukujjaman M., Fatema, N., & Alam, S. S. (2021). *Green financing development in Bangladesh: The role of private commercial banks (PCBs). Sustainability, 13*, 795.

CHAPTER 21

At the Forefront of Change: The Environment and Social Innovations by Generation Z in Russia

LISHA FU, CHONG MIN FUI NICOLE, AND FU FAUSTINA YIP

INTRODUCTION

American culture defines four main generations of today: the silent generation, the Baby Boomers, Generation X, and the Millennials (Taylor & Keeter, 2010). The Pew Study (Pew Research Center, 2015) specifies these four generations as (1) the traditionalist (born from 1928 through 1945), also known as the silent generation, as kids born in this era were children of World War II (WWII), who were mainly conservatives and conformists, thus earning them the "silent" label; (2) the Baby Boomers (born from about 1946–1964), with the name derived from a phenomenon known as the baby boom, which saw spurge in childbirth that took place after WWII when soldiers returned home to start families; (3) Generation X (born between 1965–1980), also known as "post-boomers," spanning a unique time in history defined by such things as the development of modern computers; and (4) the Millennials (born between 1981 and 1996), also known as Generation Y, said to be more educated than any of their prior generations. For the last decade, scholars have primarily studied the Millennials.

However, by 2018, it had become apparent that the cutoff point between Millennials and the next generation had already passed. The new generation was definable and marked by demographic changes and changes in attitude. Establishing this new generation by researchers and sociologists was necessary for the study of the generation of Millennials to remain relevant (Dimock, 2019). This post-Millennial generation—known as Generation Z (born between 1997 and 2012)—is also the focus of this chapter.

Members of Generation Z are also called digital natives and are also collectively known by other names, such as the iGeneration, Net Gen, and more. Gen Z (short of "Generation Z") now refers to young individuals born between the mid-1990s and the late 2010s (Turner, 2015). There is no scientific process to define this particular age range, as some researchers use other ranges. For example, the Pew Research Center uses 1996 to mark the last birth year for the Millennials (LeDuc, 2019). One big distinction for Gen Z is that technology has been integral to their upbringing (LeDuc, 2019). Unlike the previous generations, Gen Z has never experienced life without the Internet. Technology has always been readily available for this generation of contemporary youth, as they have been exposed to mobile phones, social media, and the Internet from a tender age. Members of Gen Z are, therefore, true digital natives. For many of today's children, smartphones and tablets—albeit more entertainment and pastimes than necessity—and digital interactions and connectivity are inseparable parts of their lives; the alternative is not something to which they are accustomed.

Different generations also adapt to technology differently, and technological advancement influences how people from each generation communicate and interact with each other. It is a generation-shaping factor, as Baby Boomers grew up in an era of the dissemination and proliferation of television and radio, significantly changing their way of life and how they connect with the world (Dimock, 2019). Gen X was raised during the computer revolution, and Millennials were raised amid the Internet revolution. Gen Z is unique in that all of the above technological revolutions have already been absorbed into their lives since birth (Dimock, 2019). The digital natives have evolved beyond traditional PCs—mobile devices with built-in WiFi and high-speed cellular connectivity are not optional but fundamental (Gentina, 2020). Unlike their predecessors, Gen Z needs minimal instructions to pick up new technologies.

As Gen Z becomes more digitalized, a sense of social innovation has also been awoken, spearheading organizational, communal, and society-wide changes. For example, their widespread, effective use of cross-platform media to raise awareness of environmental-induced social inequity has given much momentum to current global rhetoric on environmentalism and decarbonization. This chapter will explore how Gen Z has become instigators of social innovations that bridge inequity and inequality gaps between communities and populations. Using Russia as a case study, we attempt to delineate the perspectives that Gen Z adopts toward the environment through activism driven by social media and other digital social innovation platforms. Finally, we examine how the generation has transformed the social landscape of environmentalism by using education as a medium for digitalization methodologies. We will also see how this generation has become the forefront of change and how Gen Z activism has impacted reshaping and redeveloping social attitudes and policies.

LITERATURE REVIEW

Paradigm Shift: The Environment and Geopolitics

Geopolitics is inextricably interwoven with the environment and environmental issues, including its changes and transformations. By analyzing environmental issues, scientists and politicians can better understand the trends, state, structure, and prospects of developing modern geopolitics and vice versa. In turn, geopolitics itself "occupies an important place in political science, the subject of which is the study of the determination of politics by geography, the dependence of the power and influence of the state on its position on the earth's surface, and the various relations between the states as a whole" (Ignatyeva & Isaev, 2019).

The father of geopolitics, the German geographer Friedrich Ratzel (1844–1904), treated it as a (new) science as he developed it, as evidenced by the logic of presentation, connection, and order of elements in Ratzel's work. More importantly, he suggests that geographical conditions do not only shape human societies but that society creates its own cultural patterns and its artificial habitat identifiable from its history of development. Therefore, to study and understand society, it is necessary to consider its "soil," "blood," geographical data, history, anthropology, ethnography, and cultural aspects.

The concept of geostrategy is the "implementation" of geopolitics, and such implementation can be undertaken multi-directionally. For example, Peter the Great's attempt to gain Russia access to the sea took several directions: toward the Black Sea and Baltic Sea, and despite falling short in the first, he succeeded in the latter two. Such geopolitical differences and further changes determined the differentiation of the geopolitical structure to accommodate the further differentiation of the world, gaining new opportunities to study new realities and adapt to them. In the mesospheric structure of modern geopolitics, Ratzel's classical geopolitics was constructed upon three natural environments: the geosphere (i.e., the terrestrial environment), the hydrosphere (i.e., the marine environment), and the atmosphere. Modern geopolitics has been extended to include the underwater environment (e.g., submarine communications cables), the Internet and cyberspace, radio, television, printed matter (including electronic publications), space and satellite communication, and the virtual world. As such, modern geopolitics can be said to form a structure of intermediate spheres, upon which geopolitical phenomena and processes occurring in different natural and virtual spheres may be discerned, and ensuing fragmentation and redistribution of these environments may be observed. This echoes what Ratzel explains in the article "On the Laws of Spatial Growth of the State," that the state, in its spatial expansion, seeks to cover the most important areas of development: coasts, river basins, valleys, and, in general, all areas of affluence (Ratzel, 1901).

Today, environmental and energy paradigm changes are the main factors influencing geopolitics (Farinelli, 2000). Still, different changes in different environments have disproportionate impacts, especially on communities whose livelihoods and lifestyles depend heavily on the environment. Bennett and Friel (2014) have investigated the adverse effects of environmental change on the health of particularly vulnerable children. Although improvements have been made to educate the public on such health disparities, certain populations and communities that are socially and economically disadvantaged and vulnerable to the environment continue to require attention. Therefore, it is essential to have adaptation and mitigation strategies to respond to environmental changes. Randell and Gray (2019) offer various examples of tropical countries to show how drastic environmental changes may induce shock and negatively impact health, nutrition, and education, particularly how exposures to extreme temperatures and precipitations can impact childhood development. Impairments in children's cognitive and physical development can, in turn, contribute to the retention of poverty, especially knowing that formal education is integral to economic development.

A study by Parzonko et al. (2021) on Gen Z in Poland suggests that this generation is more engaged with pro-environmental behavior than other generations. Moreover, such behavior can very much be associated with the everyday household (e.g., sorting waste, switching off lights, using eco-friendly shopping bags), and the costs for performing them habitually are lower inside the household than outside, where additional costs may incur. The paper concludes that state-sanctioned policies like legal regulations and financial incentives tend to motivate Gen Z to engage in pro-environmental behavior and that there are long-term economic benefits such as those associated with costs for energy and other resources (e.g., water). More importantly, social media helps shape Gen Z's individual and collective behavior, beliefs, attitudes, and decision-making.

Environmental Policies and Strategies

Approximately one billion young people are extremely vulnerable to the negative impacts induced by climate change and other environmental changes. A recent UNICEF (2021) report suggested that the consequences have been extreme inequities and inequalities in food security, health, and education. For example, 9 % of the global carbon emissions come from 33 countries at "extremely high risk," while the top 10 emitting countries produce 70 % of the share. To alleviate such severe disparity and to promote sustainable development, educational programmes and strategies, such as the Principles of Responsible Management Education and the UNESCO Global Action Programme on Education for Sustainable Development, have been developed in conjunction with the United Nations (UN). In 2015, the United Nations Sustainable Development Goals (UNSDGs) launched as a global initiative, and all 193 UN member states pledged to cooperate on the agenda. The UNSDGs cover a wide range of issues ranging from environmentalism, sustainable consumption, innovation, and peace and justice, and all countries, including highly developed members, are required to act on them (Montiel et al., 2020, p. 245). These UNSDGs may provide the needed mitigation strategy (as mentioned above) to remedy the inequality induced by environmental changes and to transition various economies toward being more sustainable, fairer, more inclusive, and more low-carbon or even carbon-neutral. The global community needs these aspects as the world becomes more socially, health-wise, economically, and politically interconnected and intertwined (Markkanen & Anger-Kraavi, 2019, pp. 2–3).

Second-generation immigrants, marginalized communities, and family members who are committed to the environmental agenda often exhibit varied adaptability toward environmental changes (Walker, 2020, p. 2). For environmental initiatives, strategies, and adaptations to succeed, a community must be inclusive of such diverse adaptability (Parzonko et al., 2021, p. 15). A report conducted by the Pew Research Center found that Gen Z is much more active and adaptable than the older generations in engaging with environmental issues, both offline and on various social media platforms, disseminating a great deal more environmental-related posts on these online platforms (2021, p. 21). This adoption of digital technologies allows the old and new generations to explore and better understand the complexity of such issues and possible solutions. The extensive use of social media has also paved the way for the democratization of education, changing how different generations view the environment. It has also influenced the adoption of technologies to advance their perspectives and narratives on environmental issues (Montiel et al., 2019, p. 245). The authors will apply various secondary sources to a Russian case study to shed light on how Gen Z has continued to use pedagogy to transform their environmental views.

Digitalization of Education

Like every other aspect of life today, technology has dramatically impacted education (Purdue Online, 2021). First, technological advancement has significantly increased access to education. In medieval times, books were scarce, and only the elites had access to education. Students would have to commute to a physical classroom to receive an education. Today, abundant sources of information (e.g., videos, images, articles, news) are available, all at one's fingertips, the vast majority of which are accessible via the Internet (Purdue Online, 2021). As a result, even access to formal education is now becoming a mainstay with the availability of online degree courses and programmes (Cahn, 2020).

Technology plays a central role in the education of Gen Z. There has been an increase in Gen Z enrollment in higher education (Chunta et al., 2021). Most Gen Z also prefers online learning for its flexibility: it eliminates the time needed to commute to a physical classroom and allows students to access learning materials online at their own pace, anytime, anywhere. It is reported that Gen Z also prefers visual learning through instructional videos and using virtual reality as a platform (Acer Inc., 2019). Despite its benefits, e-learning demands a high level of computer and technology literacy from the users—both students and teachers. Barnes and Noble College (2018) has found that Gen Z has come to expect their educational experience to incorporate technology for more engaging and interactive lessons. This should hardly come as a surprise, as, having grown up in an era saturated with digital and other technologies, these true digital natives can engage with any online environment effortlessly.

COVID-19 and the Educational Crisis of Our Generation

The COVID-19 pandemic has disrupted the lives of countless people around the world. Education has faced unprecedented challenges. School closures worldwide and other secondary consequences of the COVID-19 pandemic are expected to have extensive implications for children, their families, and their communities. School environments could pose a high risk for COVID-19 transmission, and many countries closed schools and educational institutions to contain the spread of the virus (ACAPS, 2020). According to a UNESCO press release, school closures have impacted 1.5 billion students in 165 nations (Tan, 2020), with 24 million children projected to drop out of school, running the risk of sinking deeper into a cycle of poverty and passing the disadvantaged conditions on to future generations (Reliefweb, 2020). The World Bank predicts that if countries cannot find an effective solution, five months of school closures will cost students $10 trillion in lifetime earnings (Azevedo et al., 2021).

According to the World Bank, students in Russia missed roughly 55 days of school during the 2019–2020 school year; some students would go on to miss another 46 days in 2020–2021 (Tigran, 2021). Many educational institutions in Russia turned to remote learning to adjust to the situation and minimize the number of lessons canceled due to school closures. They also did so to help them transition to distance learning, with the Russian government offering operational support to educational groups, students, and teachers (World Bank Group, 2021).

The COVID-19 pandemic has, therefore, given rise to an unprecedented shift toward e-learning. The shift initiated a new era in education where there has been an acceleration in the integration of technology and overall digitalization.

Educators now use technology to teach, collaborate, and connect with students, parents, and various stakeholders, as face-to-face lessons have been severely restricted or outright suspended (Egan, 2020).

However, it is crucial to be mindful that online learning "works" because there are no alternatives, and it is neither the best nor a sustainable solution. From a pedagogical standpoint, it is imperative to ensure that e-learning is utilized to improve student learning outcomes rather than to replace conventional face-to-face teaching and learning (Ng, 2020). During the COVID-19 pandemic, many school systems worldwide switched to online learning mode. Countless educators have had no choice but to adapt to the changes brought by that switch, learning to adopt technological tools with varying degrees of success and certain individuals becoming more skillful than others. Such acquired technological skills may well be here to stay, opening the door for new research on the pedagogical use of technology in education, with educators now having a better understanding of what technology tools can do for them.

Nevertheless, the COVID-19 pandemic has exacerbated the inequality in education between advanced economies and middle- and lower-income countries that cannot provide an online learning alternative for their students (Kodachi, 2020). For less technologically advanced societies, school closures have a particularly detrimental impact on education. According to statistics from the UN's education and culture agency UNESCO and its partners, the epidemic has unveiled significant inequality in digitally based remote learning (UNESCO, 2020). The report states that an estimated 830 million (half of all out-of-school students) did not have a computer in their household, and an additional 43 % had no Internet access at home. Especially in austere times, when much of the population has had to resort to digitally based remote learning to maintain educational continuity, such disparity is particularly pronounced between high- and low-income nations: close to 90 % of students in Sub-Saharan Africa did not have a computing device. In addition, about 80 % did not have access to the Internet (UNESCO, 2020).

Compared to the global digital divide, Russia has had a high to medium digital divide, according to the E-Government Development Index (United Nations E-Government Survey, 2018). This indicates that inequality exists in Russia and would have been magnified by the COVID-19 pandemic.

EDUCATION AND EDUCATING: GENERATION Z AT THE FOREFRONT

As much as environmental effects are intertwined with our communities and our lives, and despite clear signs of human-induced physical disasters, there is still a detachment and lack of awareness of the possible environment-induced predicament in different communities and countries. The fully digitalized Gen Z is motivated by the inaction (including lack of appropriate policy changes) in the face of what has been recently coined as the "environmental crisis." Global campaigns have been initiated by young Gen Z activists to further instill and spread the spirit of activism among the younger generation. For example, #FridaysForFuture is a youth-led global campaign at the forefront of environmental activism (Walker, 2020, p. 2). In such campaigns, there has been a focus on sustainability and to incite a general sense of urgency among the different generations toward the environmental crisis. Such activism has been more prevalent in the Global North, where most environmental education agendas are shaped, than in the South.

As environmental issues are intertwined with our communities and our lives, environmental challenges are also social challenges. For green activism to be successful, education must be transformed into something sustainable and ethical. It must also be made equally accessible to both low- and higher-income groups (Friel et al., 2011, p. 890). For example, migrants who leave lower-income countries to live in more advanced economies may need better access to education on sustainable practices (Walker, 2020, p. 3).

Emerging technologies, such as mobile apps, Web 2.0 platforms, virtual and augmented reality, and simulations, can create new opportunities to improve education sustainability for students and the general public (Montiel et al., 2019, p. 244). As such digital platforms and media can spread and reach targeted audiences quickly, they are particularly effective where traditional environmental initiatives would otherwise require substantial capital but offer slow payback (Friel et al., 2011, p. 15). In fact, on an individual level, using online platforms and apps has become so widespread that these devices are almost natural extensions of people's daily activities. On a social level, they can help to democratize education and ethics and help corporations become more socially responsible, contributing to building a more inclusive and equal society. Therefore, part of the effort to adopt digital technologies is to ensure that communities are given fair access to quality education and learning opportunities. Doing so can be particularly effective for lower-middle-income countries, where the use of mobile resources can make a very significant difference in disseminating education (Montiel et al., 2019, p. 245).

Furthermore, in an age dominated by big data analytics, incorporating different digitalization methodologies helps to understand the magnitude of these social challenges. This is especially true in an era where information is very complex and false information abounds, causing young people to become disempowered and disengaged with societal issues (Montiel et al., 2019, p. 245). For Gen Z, a generation becoming increasingly visible, their role becomes pivotal in shaping an appropriate narrative toward promoting and integrating pro-environmental behavior at every level of the educational system, both inside and outside the curriculum (Parzonko et al., 2021, p. 15).

Generation Z in Russia

Approximately 63 million (or 43 %) of Russia's 146 million residents (including in Crimea) are under age 34. Thirty million of them belong to Generation Y (millennials in their 20s and early 30s), 15 million to Generation Z (teenagers), and 18 million to the youngest generation (those under the age of ten) (Laruelle, 2019). Russia's Gen Z is more politically influential than any other time in its history. They are more confident and less afraid of being heard, are committed to a real fight against corruption, and are (more) willing to participate in social activism (Miroshkina, 2015, p. 16). To them, individual rights and freedoms are crucial, and they are less willing to tolerate police coercion and government threats than citizens of the Soviet era. This generation aspires to a respectable standard of living, and unlike previous generations, Gen Z is less affected by the financial crisis of the 1990s (Gavrilova, 2016). At the same time, because fragmented virtual communication ignores any spiritual connections between individuals, the prevalence of social networks and the proliferation of technological gadgets, modern teenagers are more inclined to live in the moment, have fun, and do work that brings pleasure, joy, and a reasonable income while taking up little time (Young space, 2017).

Young Russians account for a sizable portion of the social media audience. The most active social network users are between the ages of 25 and 34 (about 27 % of Internet users). Facebook differs from other social networks because it targets a more mature audience, while Twitter and VKontakte attract a younger audience. According to Kibakin and Korablev (2020), digital services for teenagers are seen as critical in addressing individual, collective, and social needs. Young people take an active role in political debates, critically assess current events, and exhibit real concern for their own nation's future; their political consciousness is growing daily. As a result, many public organizations, social initiatives, and activities are developed, as well as creative endeavors, such as music, songwriting, poetry, and art. Considering that Gen Z is an active, adaptable, and large segment of society, their position dictates the course of Russia and its civil society's growth (Kulakova, 2018).

Additionally, this generation is well known for their concern for the state's future, increasing political engagement. As a result, more people now dare to voice up and defend their views, opinions, and interests that appeal to a diverse range of political leaders and parties (Grishaeva & Lebedeva, 2021). Various political forces will compete for the support of young people, including using electronic platforms. According to Vasilenko and Zotov, "electronic platforms are becoming the technological foundation of the emerging model of public administration-open and technically neutral means that provide conditions for the free exchange of resources" (2020, p. 6).

Social Innovation Projects in the Russian Regions

Social innovation takes into account the laws of natural development, according to which a person achieves their sustainable development goal by improving the labor process itself. The social essence of innovative activity lies in its creative beginnings. Separating social innovation as a separate category allows for linking the issues of economic development and social transformation (Kondrashova & Kolontayevskaya, 2013, p. 84). Economic innovation is measured by increasing the efficiency and competitiveness of the national economy, and improved quality of life characterizes social innovation. The positive social impact of innovation is reflected in the creation of new jobs, increased income, and self-fulfillment of skilled workers, ensuring their decent working conditions, recreation, health care, and improved quality of education. In addition, factors related to housing and road construction, preventing brain drain, increasing employment in the most efficient sectors of the national economy, and improving quality of life are also considered (Solov'eva et al., 2018, p. 54).

Currently, Russia is trying to create a friendly environment for social innovation. Some achievements have been made in establishing various institutions that support the implementation of social innovations, and the relevant infrastructure is being developed. In Russia, the most important is the Our Future Foundation (founded by V. Alikperov), providing financial and consulting assistance to social entrepreneurs and organizes project competitions. In addition, "Armor LLC" in Moscow, "Elfo Scientific and Social Center" in Ekaterinburg, "Nadezhda Foundation" in St. Petersburg, "Development School" in Novosibirsk, "Care Public Association" in Nizhny Novgorod, etc. (Mityakov et al., 2018, p. 56).

The author lists social activity projects in various regions of Russia (2021).

1. "Helping Hands" (Voronezh region). The public organization "Dawn" has opened a shelter for the homeless where people can get all possible help, including accommodation, food, clothes, medical care, and other assistance.
2. "Food for Life Charity Foundation" provides food to socially unprotected categories of people affected by natural and manmade disasters and travels to the site in time.
3. "Caring Citizen" (Primorsky Territory). The A. Monastyrev Charitable Foundation actively promotes the spiritual development of individuals,

supports socially significant projects in science, education, culture, and art, and provides charitable assistance to citizens in difficult situations.

4. "With Mom" (Volgograd region). The project aims to reduce the number of children placed in orphanages at their request: children from 2 months to 2 years of age should be placed in a day-care group, where a team of specialists works with children.
5. "Mothers of the World" (Khabarovsk Territory). The project aims to create conditions for young families' active lives. Free courses are organized for parents, including seminars and master classes on various topics.

Social innovations play an increasingly important role in the sustainable development of the country and the region, creating a favorable environment for improving the quality of human capital and eliminating various social policy failures. Social innovation in Russia is associated with public-private partnerships, corporate social responsibility, and philanthropy. Recently, social innovation has been actively promoted in many regions of the country, and legislative frameworks are being established.

Innovative Environmental Practices in Russia

For a long time, the international community has recognized the threat of ecological crisis. However, despite the numerous conferences devoted to environmental issues and the adoption of various legal acts, it is not yet possible to say that humanity has made significant progress on the road to peaceful coexistence with nature. As a result of the world's rapid economic development and exponential growth in production, there are signs of an ecological crisis today: climate change, the depletion of non-renewable natural resources, and environmental pollution. In turn, environmental challenges impede global economic development and the normal functioning of societies, manifesting themselves in the deterioration of human health, increased costs of environmental protection, and increased competition for natural resources (including armed conflicts). At the same time, several countries stand out as successfully embarking on the path of sustainable development, successfully minimizing sustained rates of economic growth and high living standards for their people with minimal environment impact (Bondarevaa & Kirsanova, 2017, p. 57).

More higher education institutions in Russia are trying to put into practice the concept of "green universities," which means "greening" universities and creating "green" campuses. This effort improves the environmental culture of students and teachers, introduces sustainability courses as mandatory subjects, and organizes ecological festivals and other environmental events. Russian universities are gradually taking similar initiatives. For example, a network of "green" universities has been established in St. Petersburg, uniting 11 educational institutions to organize student life according to ecological principles. In addition, St. Petersburg State University has established separate waste collection and paper recycling in the Botanical Garden. At the same time, ITMO organizes bicycle rides that can change the image of the city; students have proposed the creation of infrastructure for bicycle lanes on Vasilievsky Island and Sredny Street. If cafeteria customers refuse to use disposable cups and bring their own, they will receive a discount on coffee. This year, the annual interuniversity festival on sustainable development, "Вуз Эко фест" was held in St. Petersburg with the participation of students from 11 cities in Germany, Poland, and Russia, and the main purpose of the event was to exchange experiences and practices in environmental protection (Menshikova, 2017).

"Ecological patriotic education of Russian youth"

According to some scientists, "Russia is one of the countries with the worst environmental situation in the world" (Mosin, 2011). While European countries are abandoning harmful energy sources and introducing separate waste collection everywhere, landfills in our country are growing, and waste incineration plants are being built. This problem seems farfetched in the vast territory of Russia, where landfills are not conspicuous and cause real inconvenience. As a result, it is now necessary to fight the deterioration of the country's ecological situation at the national, family, and school levels, where the younger generation learns the norms of attitudes toward the space around them, forming a personal ecological culture. The importance of the greening country's citizens' awareness and behavior depends on the need to shift to the strategy of sustainable development, which Russia nominally chose decades ago. Authors like Monakhova and Agalarova (2007) and others wrote about the need for greening education and forming an ecological culture of sustainable development (Vorobyeva, 2010; Zakharov, 2008).

The following projects and forms of educational work are part of the many integrated ecological-patriotic educational activities (Kukushkina, 2017, p. 69):

- Festivals for improvement of courtyards and school grounds: tree planting, creation of flower beds, art objects made of recycled materials
- Organization of individual waste collections in schools/yards/neighborhoods
- Create information and awareness booths
- Develop greening projects for schools or neighborhoods
- Create virtual journeys around their native land, photo archives, etc.
- Environmental Marathon-Competition between schools
- Create eco-cafes based on schools or universities, using local products

- Cleanup campaign followed by outdoor activities/creating artwork/landscaping/installing information stations
- Design and implement excursions and adventures for peers and adults

All these activities aim to develop a sense of responsibility for the environment among youth and their awareness of their abilities. They combine various practical, research, and creative activities of the participants. Some of the above-mentioned forms of work have been tested in Veliky Novgorod with the participation of students at Novgorod State University.

The creation of a geo-detection guide for the UNESCO World Heritage Site in Veliky Novgorod is aimed at fostering respect among young people for their homeland and promoting Veliky Novgorod as a tourist destination. Throughout two and a half months, students and schoolchildren worked in small groups, first finding already existing geocaches and learning how to use the navigator, and then creating their own geocaches dedicated to the UNESCO sites in Veliky Novgorod (Ryurik settlement, Detinets, Antoniev Monastery, etc.). Each group had to create a geocache, place it, and prepare an information block with interesting facts about where the geocache was placed. During the project, the participants also participated in ecological activities of cleaning the UNESCO sites—the territory of Yuriyev Monastery and the walls of Okrnoegori. The organizers of the project introduced an environmental element, as participants of geocaching communities around the world often organize similar actions under the slogan "Тайникам—да! Мусору—нет!" With the support of Novgorod State University, the work resulted in the publication of a geocaching guide, which contains descriptions of more than 30 historical sites in the city and guidance for novices. Currently, the electronic version of the guide is available on the city's tourism portal, and the printed version is distributed in hotels and hostels in Veliky Novgorod to popularize active recreation (Geocaching, 2021).

The idea of "No Subbotnik" was to ensure the cleanliness of the area around St. George's Monastery and eliminate the concept of traditional subbotniks. Teams of participants collected different categories of garbage, and each bag of garbage earned points. In the end, the winners received their prizes from the sponsor Novgorod chain. After the cleanup, the participants held a master class for the children of the Yuriyev Center to make Christmas decorations from plastic bottles. As for the participants, the organizers of "Ne Subbotnik" held a master class on making magnets from corks, thus promoting the idea of recycling raw materials and the possibility of creative use of "trash."

In May 2017, the first urban environmental festival, "Good Sunday," was held in Kremlin Park. The park's summer stage featured recyclable-materials workshops, separate waste collection, family explorations of environmental issues, and a concert program. The money raised at the bazaar was donated to the "Save" fund for stray animals. Students who attended could see firsthand how much their hometown and the nonprofit could help together. Other activities designed to raise environmental awareness among students include free markets (where owners distribute useful but unused items) and book exchanges at each college, where students share their books and borrow others' books. Eventually, there are plans to establish independent institution-based paper and plastic collections.

In conclusion, it should be noted that ecological-patriotic education is a promising vehicle for solving various social and spiritual-moral problems in Russian society in the modern era. A deep sense of patriotism begins with knowledge of native nature, love, and care for it. This care should be translated into responsible and informed actions to protect their families and small and large homelands. Care for the environment becomes the basis for uniting all the citizens of the country and the inhabitants of the planet. Introducing patriotic feelings into environmental activities can make these activities more spiritual and creative.

CONCLUSION

As demonstrated in this chapter, the consequences of different environmental changes have increased inequities and inequality between different demographic groups. Our chapter shows that the Russian Generation Z's social innovation is social activism driven by the wide usage of technologies and their adaptability to technologies through digitalizing education. It has proven that the Russians have taken charge of a social movement to reverse the adverse effects of environmental changes, and they are now at the forefront of pushing forth their agendas. Digitalization has also induced democratization even in autocratic societies, as digital platforms have provided the means to bring changes and bridge information gaps between various sectors and communities. Through the dissemination of information via online platforms, there is huge potential for any developments to reach larger parts of the population. These platforms have allowed information to spread to and become more visible in vulnerable, poor rural communities and undemocratic societies.

As the COVID-19 pandemic entailed significant de-globalization, we must stay connected to raise awareness and improve our understanding of environmental-related issues. The pandemic has shown the human population's resilience and creativity in using technology to democratize our education, as shown by the case study of Russia. Beyond Russia, the extension of education through incorporating technologies has brought about global awareness and changing attitudes toward the importance of our relationship with the environment, giving us a fresh look at how we interact with our habitats. Even in societies closed off, digitalization has brought ways for messages to reach them. The patriotism and nationalism behind these messages are shaping the Russian Gen Z's focus on social issues, particularly the environment, and, more broadly, how they are exploring the impact of shifts and changes in the world today on people's lives to help them make decisions. They analyze how global macro forces and micro trends are reshaping the planet. They also explore the past, the present, and the projected future. Finally, Generation Z connects seemingly unrelated processes and shows how everything is intertwined.

REFERENCES

ACAPS. (2020). *Global analysis covid-19: Impact on education.* https://reliefweb.int/sites/reliefweb.int/files/resources/20201102_acaps_thematic_series_review_of_covid-19_impacts_on_global_education.pdf

Acer Inc. (2019). *Millennials vs Generation Z: How education is evolving.* Education Technology. https://acerforeducation.acer.com/education-trends/education-technology/infographic-millennials-vs-generation-z-how-education-is-evolving/

Azevedo, J. P., Hasan, A., Goldemberg, D., Iqbal, S. A., & Geven, K. (2021). Simulating the potential impacts of COVID-19 school closures on schooling and learning outcomes: A set of global estimates. *The World Bank Research Observer, 36*(1), 1–40. https://doi.org/10.1093/wbro/lkab003

Barnes & Noble College. (2018). *Getting to know Gen Z.* https://www.bncollege.com/wp-content/uploads/2018/09/Gen-Z-Report.pdf

Bennett, C. M., & Friel, S. (2014). Impacts of climate change on inequities in child health. *Children (Basel), 1*(3), 461–473. https://doi.org/10.3390/children1030461

Bondarevaa, G., & Kirsanova, G. (2017). The use of ecological innovations as a factor in solving environmental problems: Domestic and foreign experience. *Russkaya politologiya, 3*(4), 57–64. (in Russian)

Cahn, D. J. A. (2020). *Why online learning is here to stay.* https://www.ecampusnews.com/2020/05/28/why-online-learning-is-here-to-stay/

Chunta, K., Shellenbarger, T., & Chicca, J. (2021). Generation Z students in the online environment: Strategies for nurse educators. *Nurse Educ, 46*(2), 87–91. https://doi.org/10.1097/nne.0000000000000872

Dimock, M. (2019). *Defining generations: Where millennials end and Generation Z begins.* https://www.pewresearch.org/fact-tank/2019/01/17/where-millennials-end-and-generation-z-begins/

Egan, A. (2020). *Technology & education in a post-Covid era.* https://www.ei-ie.org/en/item/23569:technology-education-in-a-post-covid-era-by-alison-egan

Farinelli, F. (2000). Friedrich Ratzel and the nature of (political) geography. *Political Geography, 19*(8), 943–955.

Gavrilova, A. V. (2016). Socio-psychological features of the mentality of the new generation. *Philosophy, Psychology, Pedagogy, 26*(2), 58–63. (in Russian)

Gentina, E. (2020). Generation Z in Asia: A research agenda. In E. Gentina & E. Parry (Eds.), *The new generation Z in Asia: Dynamics, differences, digitalisation* (pp. 3–19). Bingley, UK: Emerald Publishing.

Geocaching. (2021). https://www.geocaching.com/cito/

Grishaeva, S. A., & Lebedeva, A. A. (2021). Prospects for the development of digital forms of political participation of generation Z in modern Russia. *Digital Sociology*, *3*(4), 12–18. https://doi.org/10.26425/2658-347x-2020-3-4-12-18 (in Russian)

Isaev, B. A., & Ignatyeva, I. F. (2019). Structure of geopolitics. In Vestnik Tomskogo gosudarstvennogo universiteta. *Istoriya*, *59*, 66–74. https://doi.org/10.17223/19988613/59/9 (in Russian)

Kibakin, M. V., & Korablev, G. G. (2020). Social mechanisms to counteract corruption in the youth of digital society. *Digital Sociology*, *3*(2), 27–34. (in Russian)

Kodachi, H. (2020). *COVID-19 worsens education inequality between rich and poor.* DATAWATCH. https://asia.nikkei.com/Spotlight/Datawatch/COVID-19-worsens-education-inequality-between-rich-and-poor

Kondrashova, O. I., & Kolontayevskaya, I. F. (2013). Social innovations in business: prospects for development in Russia. *Materialovedenie. Power Engineering*, *4–2*(183), 83–88. (in Russian)

Kukushkina, A. G. (2017). Ecological-patriotic education of university students. *Bulletin of Yaroslav the Wise Novgorod State University*, *4*(102), 68–71. (in Russian)

Kulakova, A. (2018). Generation Z: Theoretical aspect. *Territorial Development Issues / Вопросы территориального развития*, *2*(42). https://doi.org/10.15838/tdi.2018.2.42.6 (In Russian)

Laruelle, M. (2019, March 7). *Beyond Putin: Russia's Generations Y and Z*. PONARS Eurasia. https://www.ponarseurasia.org/beyond-putin-russia-s-generations-y-and-z/

LeDuc, D. (2019). Who is Generation Z. *Trust Magazine*.

Markkanen, S., & Anger-Kraavi, A. (2019). Social impacts of climate change mitigation policies and their implications for inequality. *Climate Policy*, *19*(7), 827–844. https://doi.org/10.1080/14693062.2019.1596873

Menshikova, E. (2017). *Solar panels, CupChange and own garden: How green universities are arranged in Germany and Russia*. ITMO.NEWS. http://itmo.news/ru/education/trend/news/6578. (in Russian)

Miroshkina, M. R. (2015). The digital generation. A portrait in the context of education. An interdisciplinary study. *Personality Education*, *2*, 16–21. (in Russian)

Mityakov, S. N., Mityakova, O. I., Mityakov, E. S., & Egorova, N. A. (2018). Innovative development of Russian regions: social innovations. *Innovations*, *4*(234), 56–62. (in Russian)

Monakhova, G. A., & Agalarova, P. I. (2007). Conception of sustainable development and tasks of ecological education of students at school and university. *South of Russia: Ecology, Development*, *1*(C), 113–116. (in Russian)

Montiel, I., Delgado-Ceballos, J., Ortiz-de-Mandojana, N., & Antolin-Lopez, R. (2019). New ways of teaching: Using technology and mobile apps to educate on societal grand challenges. *Journal of Business Ethics*, *161*(2), 243–251. https://doi.org/10.1007/s10551-019-04184-x

Mosin, O. V. (2011, October 13). *Ecological situation in Russia*. http://ecologysite.ru/public/item/418-экологическая-ситуация (In Russian)

Ng, P. T. (2020). Timely change and timeless constants: COVID-19 and educational change in Singapore. *Educational Research for Policy and Practice*, *20*(1), 19–27. https://doi.org/10.1007/s10671-020-09285-3

Parzonko, A. J., Balińska, A., & Sieczko, A. (2021). Pro-environmental behaviors of Generation Z in the context of the concept of homo socio-oeconomicus. *Energies*, *14*(6), 1597. https://www.mdpi.com/1996-1073/14/6/1597

Pew Research Center. (2015, September 3). *The whys and hows of generations research*. https://www.pewresearch.org/politics/2015/09/03/the-whys-and-hows-of-generations-research/

Pew Research Center. (2021). *Gen Z, millennials stand out for climate change activism, social media engagement with issue.* https://www.pewresearch.org/science/wp-content/uploads/sites/16/2021/05/PS_2021.05.26_climate-and-generations_REPORT.pdf

Purdue Online. (2021). *How has technology changed education?* https://online.purdue.edu/blog/education/how-has-technology-changed-education

Randell, H., & Gray, C. (2019). Climate change and educational attainment in the global tropics. *Proceedings of the National Academy of Sciences, 116*(18), 8840–8845. https://doi.org/10.1073/pnas.1817480116

Ratzel, F. (1901). *Der lebensraum: Eine biogeographische studie.* H. Laupp.

Reliefweb. (2020, November). *Global Analysis COVID-19: Impact on education.* https://reliefweb.int/sites/reliefweb.int/files/resources/20201102_acaps_thematic_series_review_of_covid-19_impacts_on_global_education.pdf

Shamis, E., & Antipov, A. (2018). *Theory of generations.* https://www.psycho.ru/library/2581

Solov'eva, T., Popov, A., Caro-Gonzalez, A., & Hua, L. (2018). Social innovation in Spain, China and Russia: Key aspects of development. *Economic and Social Changes: Facts, Trends, Forecast / Экономические и социальные перемены: факты, тенденции, прогноз, 2*(56). https://doi.org/10.15838/esc.2018.2.56.4

Tan, J. (2020). *Commentary: Teachers now have new jobs. Schools will never be normal again after COVID-19* [Commentary]. https://www.channelnewsasia.com/news/commentary/teachers-coping-covid-19-coronavirus-new-roles-challenges-13055482

Taylor, P., & Keeter, S. (Eds.). (2010). *The millennial count.* Pew Research Center. http://www.pewsocialtrends.org/2010,02/24/millennials-confident-connectedopen-to-change/

Tigran, S. (2021, May 10). *The pandemic poses a threat to academic progress of Russian school students.* World Bank. https://www.worldbank.org/en/news/opinion/2021/05/10/the-pandemic-poses-a-threat-to-academic-progress-of-russian-school-students

Turner, A. (2015). Generation Z: Technology and social interest. *The Journal of Individual Psychology, 71*(2), 103–113. https://doi.org/10.1353/jip.2015.0021

UNESCO. (2020). *Startling digital divides in distance learning emerge* [Press release]. https://en.unesco.org/news/startling-digital-divides-distance-learning-emerge

UNICEF. (2021). *One billion children at "extremely high risk" of the impacts of the climate crisis* [Press release]. https://www.unicef.org/press-releases/one-billion-children-extremely-high-risk-impacts-climate-crisis-unicef

United Nations E-Government Survey. (2018). *Gearing E-government to support transformation towards sustainable and resilient societies.* United Nations. https://www.unescap.org/resources/e-government-survey-2018-gearing-e-government-support-transformation-towards-sustainable

Vasilenko, L. A., & Zotov, V. V. (2020). Digitalization of public administration in Russia: Risks, casuses, problems. *Digital Sociology, 3*(2), 4–16. https://doi.org/10.26425/2658-347x-2020-2-4-16 (in Russian)

VI Forum of Social Innovations of Regions. (2021). https://social-forum.ru/

Vorobyeva, V. V. (2010). Ecological-patriotic education of cadets in the socio-natural conditions of the Far East region. *Higher Education Today, 4*(C), 62–66.

Walker, C. (2020). "Generation Z" and "second generation": An agenda for learning from cross-cultural negotiations of the climate crisis in the lives of second-generation immigrants. *Children's Geographies, 19*(3), 267–274. https://doi.org/10.1080/14733285.2020.1817334

World Bank Group. (2021, October 21). *Covid-19 (coronavirus) policy response to addressing learning gaps and inequalities in Russia*. Retrieved December 26, 2021, from https://www.worldbank.org/en/country/russia/brief/covid-19-response-learning-gaps-inequalities-russia#russia

Young Space. (2017). *30 facts about modern youth: A study of Sberbank and Validata Young space*. http://youngspace.ru/faq/sberbank-issledovanie-molodezhi

Zakharov, V. M. (2008). *Formation of ecological culture and development of youth movement*. Center for Ecological Policy and Culture, Center for Ecological Policy of Russia, 340 c. (in Russian)

Conclusion: Energy Geopolitics—A Changing Paradigm

JOÃO SIMÕES, FRANCISCO JOSÉ LEANDRO, EDUARDO CAETANO DE SOUSA, AND ROOPINDER OBEROI

This chapter recapitulates in a broader context of the changing world the paradigm shifts in energy geopolitics outlined throughout this book, as well as offers some concluding remarks and suggests questions to stimulate future research. The world today is to varying degrees and scales undergoing transformations on multiple, inter-related, and intertwined fronts. Such transformations include digitalization, social transformations, and energy transitions, in addition to experiencing and counteracting climate change. In turn, these transformations induce new scientific, technological, and industrial capabilities, influence societal models and organization, as well as impact the way global states will interact with each other.

Geopolitics traces and analyzes every detail of these transformations within the context of the international system—histories, causes, developments, variables and parameters, risks, conditions, dynamics, scenarios, and outcomes. In particular, it seeks to understand issues relating to state sovereignty and national interests, regardless of whether a state has a collaborative or confrontational approach. Under the umbrella of geopolitics, contemporary energy geopolitics focuses not only on energy security but also on how energy resources are utilized both locally and globally, sorting through the labyrinth of energy-induced power relations between states, international organizations, NGOs, large multinational companies, and non-state actors whose interests are directly or indirectly at stake.

Meanwhile, as we face our current challenges, the future is also at stake, and we cannot afford to put all of our eggs into one basket at the expense of the other—neither our common future nor common home can be compromised. In his visionary book *Dark Skies*, Deudney (2020) suggests that space exploration and the subsequent emergence of geopolitics there will dependent heavily on not only technological evolution but also whether or not human society can put forth, agree upon, and share a peaceful and cooperative vision; he points out that humankind is still a long way from undertaking the enterprise of space expansion, as we still need to develop immensely in multiple aspects. Embedded at the heart of Deudney's discussions is, of course, the question of energy—energy is as much a common interest and fundamental resource to humankind in outer space as it is down on Planet Earth, be it for our advancement or collective survival into the future: we must find and/or produce enough energy to sustain and ensure our existence. Such is one of the most challenging tasks of our generation—to lay the foundation for a future of clean and sustainable energy.

A RAPIDLY CHANGING WORLD

Globalization has been dealt an unprecedented double blow in the past two years by the COVID-19 pandemic and the ongoing Russian invasion of Ukraine. Prior to the pandemic, globalization had been witnessing both ebb and flow of protectionist policies, the rise of identity politics, trade wars between China and the U.S., and the retaliatory increases of tariffs. The COVID-19 pandemic has further strained the global order and put supply chains in deep distress, jeopardizing the financial model that the world has been relying on for over three decades—one where manufacturing became increasingly delocalized while the global order became hyper-integrated, and one which, despite having removed trade barriers, has driven nations toward becoming too dependent on and intertwined with each other. The Washington Consensus was supposed to have lifted all boats, but, in retrospect, we now know that globalization has inherent propensity to exacerbate existing fissures and increase inequalities. There is another dimension to the de-globalization debate: the role and significance of a state's own decision-making amid a wave of states withdrawing from a global order struggling to keep the world permeable to goods, services, and people. What we have actually witnessed is: during the COVID-19 pandemic, national interests and public health concerns not only led to the closing of borders but also gave justifications for states to impose trade barriers. Disputes over distributions of vaccines were also a particularly vivid case in point.

Businesses all over the world are fraught with the need to cope with major bottlenecks in the global supply chain. Russia's war in Ukraine has caused more uncertainty to shroud over commodities—energy, exports of food grains, and raw materials. Energy security has now joined the energy transition as a top global priority. The world is being hit by inflation and economic contraction immediately after pandemic, and the most challenging task ahead is likely to dampen that inflation which is rapidly spreading from one nation to another in a global economy that remains tightly coupled. Some experts even suggest that the Russian invasion of Ukraine has effectively put an end to the era of globalization (Fink, 2022). It has also put a spotlight on the global order and its institutions, as well as its vulnerabilities. French President Emmanuel Macron has echoed that COVID-19 has "change[d] the nature of globalization, with which we have lived for the past 40 years," adding that it was "clear that this kind of globalization was reaching the end of its cycle" (Financial Times, 2020).

The global order has been unwinding and fragmenting. The U.S. and European Union have imposed punishing sanctions on the Russian economy (11th largest in the world), severing it from global commerce, and hundreds of Western companies have voluntarily ceased operations in Russia. Amid these geopolitical, public health, and economic crises, countries are reconfiguring their strategies and corporations are restructuring how they can keep themselves afloat as soaring costs and unpredictable delays in the global supply chains cause profits to dwindle. These changes run contrary to the central doctrines of post–Cold War financial policies and world order, one that was forged by the United States and its Western allies and adopted by emerging economies. Other scholars like Edward Alden, a senior fellow at the Council on Foreign Relations, fear that we could be moving toward a more divided world (Wong & Swanson, 2022), and economic integration cannot and will not survive the global order being subjected to a prolonged period of partisan fragmentation and polarization. In fact, even during the Trump administration, "America First" trade policies were already giving impetus to the de-globalization; the COVID-19 pandemic and Putin's onslaught on Ukraine only brought to the foreground the serious uncertainties facing the existing economic order, the consequence of which can be that the world's countries split into economic blocs as they did for much of the twentieth century. The conflicts and disruptions could trigger further tides of de-globalization, with deep, long-lasting impact.

In the near term, coal consumption may surge in the next few years, as Europe and Asia try to move away from their dependence on Russian oil and gas, and the soaring energy bills will make renewable energy sources more competitive, catalyzing many countries to transition toward greener energy sources in the long run. Bordoff and O'Sullivan believe that:

> ... energy security has returned to the fore, joining climate change as a top concern for policymakers. Together, these dual priorities are poised to reshape national energy planning, energy trade flows, and the broader global economy. Countries will increasingly look inward, prioritizing domestic energy production and regional cooperation even as they seek to transition to net-zero carbon emissions. If countries retreat into strategic

> energy blocs, a multidecade trend toward more energy interconnectedness risks giving way to an age of energy fragmentation. (2022b)

The world is at a critical juncture: worries about dependence on others are mounting, and even though an inward turn may not spell the absolute end of globalization, partial setbacks and potential restructuring of the global system are almost unavoidable. Reflecting on and writing about such turmoil and uncertainties (such as those induced in Europe by the war in Ukraine) is akin to observing a hurricane from the eye of the storm, forcing us to revisit and reassess the different scenarios that might play out, especially regarding whether, going forward, we will gravitate further toward globalization, or regress from it.

NEW ENERGY, OLD GEOPOLITICS?

The world has previously witnessed three major energy transformations, characterizable as transitioning from biomass to fossil fuels—from coal to oil and later natural gas (Smil, 2017). The latest transitions are the rapid deployment of renewable technologies driving the decarbonization of the global economy, in turn driven by a combination of factors, among which are the aforementioned global turmoils, together with climate change and other environmental concerns, and ensuing social, economic, and geopolitical changes.

Amid the oil crises of 1973 and 1979, which caused major disruptions to oil supply, soaring inflation and energy prices leading to further global energy woes, Conant and Gold published the seminal work *The Geopolitics of Energy* (1978) which provided a comprehensive analysis of the interactions between the locational and geographical factors that influence energy supply and demand. One of the focuses of the analysis was on such sensitive choke points as the Strait of Hormuz or the Suez Canal, both critical to the supply and transportation of oil around the world. Conant and Gold anticipated a "profound revolution" in the early decades of the twenty-first century comparable to the one that "followed the use of coal and oil" which "could free many states from most geographic restraints" (1978, pp. 5–7). Geopolitics of energy generates multiple security perceptions based on technology, cooperative spaces, and expectations on the availability of energy at affordable prices. Later, in the 2000s, the recurrent Russian-Ukrainian conflict has renewed academic interest in energy geopolitics, in particular regarding the use of energy and manipulation of energy supply as tools of foreign policy.

More recently, declining costs and the rapid deployment of renewable energy technologies have led to a new round of discussion, often called the geopolitics of renewables, the geopolitics of decarbonization, or the geopolitics of the energy transition or transformation (Hafner & Tagliapietra, 2017; Ivleva & Tänzler, 2019; O'Sullivan et al., 2017; Scholten, 2018; Scholten et al., 2020). In

2019, the International Renewable Energy Agency (IRENA, 2019) released a groundbreaking report entitled "A New World: The Geopolitics of the Energy Transformation" discussing the geopolitical implications of an accelerated global shift toward renewables. This report would become the flag-bearer of this new green-focused energy geopolitics. In short, the report argues that the energy transitions have the potential to be "one of the major elements that reshape geopolitics in the 21st century, alongside trends in demography, inequality, urbanization, technology, environmental sustainability, military capability, and domestic politics in major states." The report puts forward four main reasons to support the potential of using renewables to transform geopolitics: first, unlike fossil fuels, different renewable energy resources are available across the world, thereby alleviating the significance of current choke points; second, most renewables do not exhaust themselves and for this reason are less likely to lead to disruptions of supply; third, renewable energy sources democratize the access to energy, facilitating cost-effective decentralization of energy production and consumption; fourth, renewable sources have near-zero marginal costs of production (IRENA, 2019, pp. 23–24).

The "New World" report became a landmark study which has been widely cited, and has also sparked lively debate among scholars. Goldthau et al. (2019) recognize that the report "puts the geopolitics of the energy transformation on the political map," but they challenge some of the report's key premises. For instance, the authors suggest that the report falls into the trap of assuming that the decrease of renewable technology costs, combined with market mechanisms, will promote the use of renewable energy and lead to the decline of fossil fuels. According to these authors, in some contexts, fossil fuel systems are extremely resilient and that the political economy might play a more important role than the costs of technology alone. In addition, the authors suggest that the IRENA's report has underestimated the risks of the "Global South" countries "getting stuck in a fossil economic pathway," since economic nationalism and other protectionism measures from developers of clean technology may exclude those countries from receiving clean technologies. In response to the report, Akchurina (2019) questions "whether the transformation to renewables will make oil irrelevant for geopolitics" and suggests that it may "be more realistic to talk about the shift to mixed types of energy, rather than purely to renewables in the foreseeable future." In line with this view, Braun and Scholten (2019) argue that the report "owes an explanation on how and to what extent 'the geopolitics of conventional energy' could challenge, influence, and (possibly) undermine the energy transformation."

From a critical geopolitics perspective, Overland (2019, pp. 36–38) challenges the recent growing body of literature on the geopolitics of renewables, targeting particularly arguments that tend to "involve the transposition of the geopolitical logic of oil and gas onto renewables" and narratives that revolve around "resource-rich locations, key infrastructure, transportation routes, control over energy supplies, and the potential for supply disruptions" where there is an underlying assumption that "control over resources and their distribution endows states with power in the international system." In particular, Overland challenges: a) the frequent claims that there should be more competition for materials that are critical to electronics and renewable energy technologies; b) the assumption that new resources will follow a course dictated by countries with access to the critical materials—in the same manner that oil producers dictated markets in the past; c) the exploitation of disruptions to energy supply as a foreign policy tool and/or geopolitical weapon; and d) the risks posed by further digitalization of pertinent electrical systems.

On a different tone, Bordoff and O'Sullivan (2022a) argue that the "[t]alk of a smooth transition to clean energy is fanciful" and warn against putting too much hope on any promises that clean energy will help relieve tensions over energy resources. The authors encourage policymakers to appreciate the new risks and dangers that the energy transitions will bring in the coming decades "as the new geopolitics of clean energy combines with the old geopolitics of oil and gas"—a failure to do so "will not only have security and economic implications; it will also undermine the energy transition itself."

Transitioning into renewable energy sources presents a great deal of challenges not only to individual states but also to relations between states. Scholten (2018, pp. 5–17) puts forward an analytical framework to analyze how the geographical and technical specificities of renewable technologies shape such interstate energy relations: the geotechnical features of renewable energy systems (i.e., sources, generation, distribution) can be expected to reshape business models, energy markets, trade patterns, and social welfare, which will in turn affect interstate energy relations (strategic realities faced by producers, consumers, and transit countries, policy considerations to safeguard energy security and effects on the patterns of cooperation and conflict). The relationships between the renewables and the interstate energy relations are studied on three levels: (1) the global level—emerging global energy game among great powers, winners, and losers; (2) regional and bilateral energy relations of established and rising powers; and (3) infrastructure developments and government responses. Ivleva and Tänzler (2019) similarly attempt to define geopolitics of decarbonization as a field of inquiry by establishing links between how decarbonization processes are embedded in global dynamics, and how they change the geographies and geopolitics of resources. The authors build on existing literature to suggest a framework for researching the geopolitics of decarbonization with these conceptual dimensions: the structure of the socio-technological systems (institutions, actors, ideas, individual values, power), the systemic mechanisms (feedback loops, windows of opportunity, tipping points), and the resources and catalysts of change (know-how, investment, new technologies). The empirical focuses of the framework are the geographies, sectors, and actors. The authors pinpoint how the geopolitics of decarbonization is relevant to policymaking, from climate and economic policies to foreign policies. In terms of development and cooperation, the authors see a pressing need for "strategies that bring decarbonization trends in line with the pursuit of equality, economic development and peace."

Overland (2021, pp. 7–9) reminds us that "existing projections of the consequences of the energy transition are more uncertain than they appear," questioning the suitability of analytical frameworks that are based on "assumptions about the global energy system of the past," since the past is "open to conflicting interpretations." Overland further argues that it is necessary to pay more attention to "how interpretations of the past and present shape our predictions of the future."

Keohane and Victor (2013, p. 97) argue that "[f]or countries to deal successfully with energy issues they must engage in international cooperation [...], but the structure of international cooperation on some energy problems, such as climate change, is prone to deadlock." They further explain how state interest has jeopardized efforts to build a coherent international regime for energy and climate change. Nevertheless, despite enormous volatility across the world, complexity in the global energy landscape, and uncertainties on the road to decarbonization, there are voices of hope and informed optimism. Crow and Saran (2021) suggest that energy transitions can be a "geopolitical salve" rather than a "source of discord" by "underpinning ties of trade, development, and civic diplomacy." Per Högselius (2019, pp. 155–156) revisits the concept of "energy transnationalism," drawing on a philosophical tradition inspired by the French philosopher Claude-Henri de Saint Simon, who on the occasion of the Vienna Congress in 1814–1815 pointed to transnational infrastructures as a means of promoting peace and harmony. Energy transnationalism envisages energy as "a 'soft' foreign policy tool" that can be mobilized "for the purpose of strengthening international cooperation, fostering global political stability and economic prosperity." IRENA's "New World" report suggests that renewable energy "can be applied to promote social justice and human welfare, encourage local empowerment and local wealth generation, contribute to safer climate, improve public health, and advance gender equality and educational opportunities" (2019, p. 69). Miller et al. (2013) also point out that "[r]e-envisioning energy is a potentially powerful contributor to improving human well-being around the globe through the creation of thriving, innovative, sustainable communities," and "could generate a very different policy conversation about the future of energy."

***

Chapter 1 of this volume opened the discussion about the changing paradigms of energy geopolitics by identifying the logics that drive conventional energy biopolitics across space and time. It not only argued that the contemporary paradigm of energy geopolitics is evolving toward global neomercantilism, but also flagged some of the promising sustainable alternatives offered by regenerative energy movements. Chapter 2 picked up this inspiring conversation by providing an original overview of energy geopolitics research over the past two decades and a concise summary of the field's key trends. This review may serve as a solid foundation not only for new researchers in energy geopolitics, but also for interested scholars who seek to broaden their collaborative networks and diversify their research perspectives.

Though energy focuses, perspectives, and scenarios may abound, no energy policies can be truly global. In fact, energy geopolitics is a matrix of interests and realities that motivate how interdependent actors (e.g., states) to conduct themselves inside a particular regional space, seeking to influence, even impose themselves on each other in complex scenarios. These realities, perspectives, scenarios, as well as matrices of actors and their specific energy interests and developments may change course constantly as they are impacted by global developments. The COVID-19 pandemic has, for example, elucidated how energy scenarios can change and the progress of many climate-related goals can be derailed, which has been detailed in Chapter 8 through examining energy policies laid down by the U.S. administration, as well as the country's economic recovery and efforts to mitigate the climate crisis.

Moreover, no energy-based narrative of the twenty-first century can have removed from it the reality of China's powerful regional influence on energy and its global geopolitical implications. As discussed over several topics in this volume, the momentous geo-economic and geopolitical project of the Belt and Road Initiative (BRI) has important energy implications on multiple domains and models, and reinforces the Chinese state's commitment to energy and programmes to transition toward renewable energy sources (Chapter 3). In addition, China's announced goal of achieving carbon neutrality by 2060 reinforces to the entire international community the importance and seriousness of its commitment. It is in this context that Chapter 12 outlines China's agreement and broader objectives with Pakistan, as well as the strategic importance of the Port of Gwadar to not only the Pakistan-China Economic Corridor but also the overall region. The 2022 Beijing Winter Olympics' "Sustainability for the Future" vision further demonstrated China's strong determination as well as the innovative aspect of its environmental projects and use of sustainable energy.

Chapters 4, 5, 6, and 16 dissected the direct impact that recent energy issues have had on the economic policies of major powers such as China, Russia, the U.S., and the European Union in various scenarios of energy transition, and now, emerging major powers of great regional relevance such as India are seeking to take on more significant roles toward the environment and environmental issues

(Chapter 13). What has been made plain throughout this book is that the course of most energy transitions and environmental sustainability policies are as much conditioned by individual states' planned strategic objectives as they are affected by unforeseen events occurring unannounced, such as the war in Ukraine, which is putting not only the European Union and Russia but all other pertinent actors' strategies, alliances, economic influence, relations and correlations, as well as different outcome scenarios to the test. In light of this, it is imperative that this book explains the controversial Nord Stream 2 pipeline in the Baltic region (Chapter 7), as Nord Stream 2 and energy security will be, for some time to come, a substantial subject of study for many politicians and observers of energy geopolitics and economics.

The European Union will continue to use regulatory mechanisms to direct its Green Deal. In this way, Russian and Chinese trade actions as well as other players in the European energy market can be conditioned more easily, as Chapter 9—"Carbon Border Adjustment Mechanism"—rightly points out. Further, the role of the European Union to inspire energy transitions is analyzed in Chapters 10 and 11: Chapter 10 discusses the European Union as a green military player, while Chapter 11 looks at the energy geopolitics relating to the European Green Deal, and presents through case studies new possibilities for strategic international techno-industrial cooperation.

Energy transitions and environmental sustainability will likely play out in similar scenarios in Africa (Chapter 14) and on other continents (Chapters 15 and 20), inducing comparable challenges for the coming decades. For many fossil fuel–producing states such as Argentina, Angola, and Mozambique, this will be an equation to resolve, given the current energy reality.

The chapters that have been referred to in the previous paragraphs fit into the global, regional, and bilateral levels of analysis proposed in Scholten's framework to explore the relationship between renewable energy sources and interstate energy relations (2018, pp. 5–17). Likewise, those chapters fit into Ivleva and Tänzler (2019)'s framework: the socio-technological structure of the international systems, with empirical focus on the actors, in the context of transitioning systems in different geographies—states, regions, and joint areas of geopolitical interest. Chapters 17 to 21 of this volume offer different insights into government responses, legal issues, reshaping of markets, patterns of resource management, and social innovation. These chapters belong to the dimensions of "resources and catalysts of change" proposed by Ivleva and Tänzler (2019) and "government responses" proposed in Scholten's analytical framework (2018, pp. 5–17). Collectively, these chapters offer perspectives that expand and complement our understanding on the geopolitics of decarbonization.

***

The geopolitics of energy transitions is a field in the making: Major actors such as the European Union, China, Japan, and others have announced ambitious roadmaps and strategies toward achieving carbon neutrality by mid-century, and other countries and regions are expected to follow suit. Yet, the related body of literature has only limited scope, with most research focusing on each state's roadmap and strategies toward transitioning to low-carbon energy systems, neglecting the more global perspectives, such as how the states' individual transitions will impact global dynamics and interstate relations.

As regards what has been researched in the field of geopolitics of energy transitions, some scholars foresee greater government intervention in the energy sector, as "[m]arket forces alone cannot deliver a sufficiently low-carbon economy" (Bordoff & O'Sullivan, 2022b). Bordoff and O'Sullivan specifically suggest that greater government intervention needs to be imposed on producers and consumers to make them bear ("internalize") the full cost of the carbon and other pollutants that they emit, while the private sector can be further incentivized to invest in infrastructure required by countries seeking to ensure both their energy security and climate goals. These will necessitate that the study of the geopolitics of energy transitions be further developed and expanded: first, its literature needs to address and recognize the speculative nature and uncertainties pertaining to the global energy future; second, policymaking needs to be examined more closely.

Therefore, this book has far from ended the debate around the geopolitical ramifications of the ongoing energy transitions and decarbonization of the planet; it has only inspired and induced more discussions. Energy geopolitics will continue to draw tremendous public interest and concern, and further literature on this topic must address topics ranging from the challenges facing the architecture of global energy governance and the institutional design of a possible hydrogen economy, new interdependencies arising from the energy transformations and from programmes underlying major global infrastructure development, the role of energy diplomacy in a time of transitions, the role of citizens in transforming the energy paradigm, energy poverty, to energy as an enabler of sustainable development in a broader sense.

As much as the notion that energy is a powerful contributor that fosters development and improves human well-being is adequately reinforced in the literature, current narratives revolving around energy transitions often fail to recognize the paradox that exists between the sustainable future promised by adopting clean technologies, and the damages that extracting critical minerals required to build those technologies will bring us now and in the future. What these discourses on energy transitions tend to overlook is the interconnectedness between the finitude of the global ecosystem and past human choices and behavior. In a recent interview on the 50th anniversary of his pathbreaking book (co-authored) The *Limits to Growth*, Meadows reminds us that we live in a world with finite resources:

> Our ecological footprint is too high: we're consuming more resources than the Earth can regenerate, whether it be fossil fuels, fertile soil, clean water, etc. [...] But for 50 years, we have not acted. As a result, we've passed beyond the Earth's capacity to support us. [...] Renewable energy is terrific, but there's no way it will give us as much energy as we currently get from fossils. There is no solution without a drastic reduction in our energy needs. (Garric, 2022)

Indeed, without changing our energy paradigms, sustainability is but a hollow word.

Technical challenges facing decarbonization of the world's energy systems will continue to revolve around issues of efficiency, decentralization, and storage. Fair, general access to energy for all should also be the core consideration of every energy paradigm, and equitable low-carbon transitions must be more than a political slogan. As such, the energy horizon that we will have for the next decades will likely be heavily based on renewable energy sources: solar, wind, ocean, and nuclear fusion—the holy grail of renewable energy, whose exact timeline and outcome continue to be elusive. One thing, however, is certain: stigmas, misrepresentations, and distortions associated with energy and interstate relations will always be alive and present; however, as we confront them, we should not underestimate the transformative power of education, but that is a story to tell in another book.

REFERENCES

Akchurina, V. (2019, February 19). The geopolitics of energy transformation on practicalities of the big shift. *Trends Research.*

Bordoff, J., & O'Sullivan, M. L. (2022a). *Green upheaval: The new geopolitics of energy.* Foreign Affairs. https://www.foreignaffairs.com/articles/world/2021-11-30/geopolitics-energy-green-upheaval

Bordoff, J., & O'Sullivan, M. L. (2022b). *The new energy order: How governments will transform energy markets.* Foreign Affairs. https://www.foreignaffairs.com/articles/energy/2022-06-07/markets-new-energy-order

Braun, J., & Scholten, D. (2019, March 25). What's next for the geopolitics of energy transformation? *Energy Post.*

Conant, M., & Gold, F. R. (1978). *The geopolitics of energy.* Westview Press.

Crow, A., & Saran, S. (2021). *The geopolitics of energy transition: A guide for policymakers, executives, and investors.* https://www.eia.gov/todayinenergy/detail.php?id=49996#:~:text=October%2018%2C%202021-,Annual%20U.S.%20coal%2Dfired%20

Deudney, D. (2020). *Dark skies: Space expansionism, planetary geopolitics, and the ends of humanity.* Oxford University Press.

Fink, L. (2022, March 24). *Larry Fink's 2022 chairman's letter.* BlackRock. https://www.blackrock.com/corporate/investor-relations/larry-fink-chairmans-letter

Garric, A. (2022, April 15). *Dennis Meadows: "Uncontrolled growth, the cancer of society, must be stopped."* Le Monde. https://www.lemonde.fr/en/opinion/article/2022/04/15/dennis-meadows-uncontrolled-growth-the-cancer-of-society-must-be-stopped_5980644_23.html

Goldthau, A., Eicke, L., & Weko, S. (2019, January 2). *The geopolitics of renewables. A new but messy energy world.* Institute for Advanced Sustainability Studies, Potsdam. https://www.iass-potsdam.de/en/output/publications/2019/geopolitics-renewables-new-messy-energy-world

Hafner, M., & Tagliapietra, S. (2017). *The geopolitics of the global energy transition.* http://www.springer.com/series/8874

IRENA. (2019). *A new world: The geopolitics of the energy transformation.*

Ivleva, D., & Tänzler, D. (2019). *Geopolitics of decarbonisation: Towards an analytical framework.* https://climate-diplomacy.org/sites/default/files/2020-10/Geopolitics-of-decarbonisation_Towards-an-analytical-framework.pdf

Keohane, R. O., & Victor, D. G. (2013). The transnational politics of energy. *Daedalus*, *142*(1). https://doi.org/10.1162/DAED_a_00196

Mallet, V., & Khalaf, R. (2020, April 17). Emmanuel Macron says it is time to think the unthinkable. *Financial Times.*

Miller, C. A., Iles, A., & Jones, C. F. (2013). The social dimensions of energy transitions. *Science as Culture*, *22*(2). https://doi.org/10.1080/09505431.2013.786989

O'Sullivan, M., Overland, I., & Sandalow, D. (2017). The geopolitics of renewable energy. *SSRN Electronic Journal.* https://doi.org/10.2139/ssrn.2998305

Overland, I. (2019). The geopolitics of renewable energy: Debunking four emerging myths. *Energy Research & Social Science*, *49*, 36–40. https://doi.org/10.1016/j.erss.2018.10.018

Overland, I. (2021). Uncertain past, uncertain future: How assumptions about the past shape energy transition expectations. *Oxford Energy Forum*, *126*.

Per Högselius. (2019). *Energy and geopolitics.* Routledge.

Scholten, D. (Ed.). (2018). *The geopolitics of renewables* (Vol. 61). Springer International Publishing. https://doi.org/10.1007/978-3-319-67855-9

Scholten, D., Bazilian, M., Overland, I., & Westphal, K. (2020). The geopolitics of renewables: New board, new game. *Energy Policy*, *138*, 111059. https://doi.org/10.1016/J.ENPOL.2019.111059

Smil, V. (2017). *Energy and civilization.* The MIT Press. https://doi.org/ 10.7551/mitpress/9780262035774.001.0001

Wong, E., & Swanson, A. (2022, March 22). Ukraine war and pandemic force nations to retreat from globalization. *The New York Times.* https://www.nytimes.com/2022/03/22/us/politics/russia-china-global-economy.html

Notes on Contributors

Roberto Álvaro-Hermana is an industrial engineer and holds a Ph.D. in industrial engineering from the Technical University of Madrid (UPM). He is a researcher at the Energy Lab at Orkestra–Basque Institute of Competitiveness (University of Deusto), where he works in energy transition, energy policy, sustainable mobility, power grids, and the circular economy. His previous publications include articles on electric vehicle integration, renewable generation testing with electric machines, the evolution of smart grids, and circular economy issues.
roberto.alvaro@orkestra.deusto.es
https://orcid.org/0000-0002-3691-4627

Alexandros Bakos is a Ph.D. candidate in international investment law and arbitration at City, University of London. His thesis focuses on the impact of economic sanctions on international investment arbitration. Before beginning his Ph.D. studies, Alexandros worked as a research analyst, focusing on the legal and geopolitical aspects of certain sanctions regimes, especially in North America. Alexandros's research interests include international investment law, public international law, international human rights, international sanctions law, and geopolitics.
a.c.bakos@gmail.com

Gabriela Benatti is a Ph.D. student in the Economic Development Program at the Institute of Economics at the University of Campinas (IE/Unicamp) and Delft University of Technology (Delft TU). She is also a researcher at the Center for Applied, Agricultural and Environmental Economics (NEA+).
gssbenatti@gmail.com
https://orcid.org/0000-0002-1594-9919

Antônio Buainain is a professor of economics at the Institute of Economics of the University of Campinas–Unicamp in Campinas, Brazil. He is also a senior researcher at the National Institute of Science and Technology in Public Policy, Strategy and Development (INCT/PPED) and a permanent researcher at the Center for Applied Economics, Agricultural and Environmental Research (NEA+) at the Institute of Economics/Unicamp. He obtained his degree in economics and law in 1977 from the State University of Rio de Janeiro and his Doctorate in Economics from the Institute of Economics at Unicamp in 1998. In addition to his academic work, his professional experience includes serving as an economist at the Food and Agriculture Organization (FAO) in Rome. He has also served as an advisor to several Brazilian ministries, including the Ministry of Agriculture, Ministry of Rural and Agrarian Development, and the Ministry of Science, Technology and Innovation. In addition, he has acted as a consultant for international and national institutions that primarily deal with innovation policies, intellectual property issues, agricultural policy, rural development, poverty alleviation programs, agrarian reform, and family farms. Since 1989, he has co-edited and co-authored 47 books and published 87 book chapters and 99 papers in academic journals. Most of his academic work deals with development issues, ranging from agriculture to innovation and sectoral public policies.
buainain@gmail.com
https://orcid.org/0000-0002-1779-5589

Eduardo Caetano de Sousa is a retired full colonel of the Portuguese Army. He is qualified by the Portuguese Military Academy Artillery Course, the Artillery School Captain Promotion Course, the General Staff Course, and the Promotion Course to General Officer, all from the War College. He holds a Master of International Relations (Political-Diplomatic) from Lusíada University. He has authored several articles and reports on energy geopolitics and energy security. He has recently been invited by universities, the Order of Engineers, and other groups to hold public conferences and debates in energy geopolitics. He wrote the article "The Natural Gas in the Confrontations of Global Geopolitics," which was published in the magazine *Nação e Defesa* (2019) (IDN) in 2020 as part of the weekly online chronicle "The geopolitics of things." Another of

his articles, "O Conceito, a Estratégia e a Defesa Nacional," was published in *«Segurança e Defesa»—Diário de Bordo* in 2021. Furthermore, he has published the following books: *The WEU at the crossroads of European Security* (2001), *How Gas Moves the International System—Natural Gas in the New Disputes of Global Geopolitics* (2018), and *Chronicle by Streets and Squares of Power—from Lisbon to Hong Kong* (2020/2021). He participated in the EuroDefense Reflection Group in 2020 as an author of work on the theme Security and Defense in the Energy and Environmental Field—A Strategic Matrix. He was a member of the Board of EuroDefense—Portugal Study Centre and coordinator for the Working Group on Energy, Climate, Security and Defence of the European network EuroDefense.
edumanuel2001@yahoo.com

Pedro Cavalcante Filho is a Ph.D. student in the Economic Development Program at the Institute of Economics at the University of Campinas (IE/Unicamp) and a researcher at the Center for Applied, Agricultural and Environmental Economics (NEA+).
pedro.gilberto@hotmail.com
https://orcid.org/0000-0003-1776-0295

Archil Chochia is a Senior Researcher at Tallinn University of Technology (TalTech) Law School. Dr. Chochia obtained his doctoral degree from TalTech in 2013 and had previously studied at Tbilisi State Medical University. He also completed short study programs at the University of Scranton, University of California, Pepperdine University, and Harvard University. He has more than 90 academic publications to his name and is a co-editor of three books: *Political and Legal Perspectives of the EU Eastern Partnership Policy* (Springer, 2016), *Brexit: History, Reasoning and Perspectives* (Springer, 2018), and *Russian Federation in the Global Knowledge Warfare—Influence Operations in Europe and Its Neighborhood* (Springer, 2021). Archil is a managing editor of the TalTech Journal of European Studies. His research fields of interest are law and technology, the ethical aspects of digitalization, alternative dispute resolution, EU integration, and the EU Neighbourhood Policy. Archil is a senior fellow of the Weinstein International Foundation.
archil.chochia@taltech.ee
https://orcid.org/0000-0003-4821-297X

Nicole Minfui Chong is a registered special education teacher in Singapore who teaches kids with mild intellectual disabilities and autism spectrum disorder. She believes that every child is unique and deserving of a loving, nurturing, and safe environment to grow in. She is passionate about empowering kids with disabilities

and improving their quality of life through education. She received her training as a special education teacher at the National Institute of Education, Singapore. She also holds a bachelor's degree in international hotel and tourism management.
chongminfui@gmail.com
https://orcid.org/0000-0001-5117-6987

Cátia Miriam Costa is a guest professor at ISCTE–IUL and a researcher at the Centre for International Studies–Instituto Universitário de Lisboa. She is the director of the Chair Global Ibero-America of the European Institute of International Studies (Stockholm). Her research focuses on international communication and discourse analysis, specifically concerning the cases of Macau, Hong Kong, and China. She is also developing her academic work on China's international relations and Macau's public diplomacy in Eurasia, Portuguese-speaking Countries, and Latin America.
catia.miriam.costa@iscte-iul.pt
https://orcid.org/0000-0002-7666-5661

Fernanda Delgado is the corporate executive director at the Brazilian Petroleum and Gas Institute (IBP) and a professor at the Getúlio Vargas Foundation (FGV). She holds a doctoral degree in energy planning from the Federal University of Rio de Janeiro (UFRJ).
fernanda.delgado@ibp.org.br
https://orcid.org/0000-0003-1177-5664

Venkatesh Dutta is a professor of environmental sciences at the School of Earth and Environmental Science (SEES), Babasaheb Bhimrao Ambedkar University, Lucknow. He is a sustainability practitioner and a thought leader specializing in Natural resource management, environmental flows, catchment planning, and river restoration. He has contributed to significant changes in public discourse, law, and policy for environmental sustainability and natural resource management in India. He is a Fulbright-Nehru fellow (2011–2012) and a British Chevening scholar (2006). He served as a member of the drafting committee of the State Water Policy of Uttar Pradesh and the Technology-led Innovation Policy Framework of the Department of Science and Technology, Govt of India. He also sits on the state-level committee for the restoration of small rivers and tributaries of the Ganga. He has mentored several doctoral scholars and contributed to more than 80 research papers, policy drafts, and op-ed articles. He is the recipient of the Global Development Research Medal, Nadi Mitra Samman, Springer-Society

Award (2020), and the Rajat Ki Boonden National Water Award (2021). He is also a Gomti River Waterkeeper.
dvenks@gmail.com
https://orcid.org/0000-0003-4925-7432

Carla Fernandes is a visiting assistant professor at the Faculty of Social Sciences and Humanities of Universidade NOVA de Lisboa. She is also an integrated researcher at the Portuguese Institute for International Relations (IPRI–NOVA) and an auditor of National Defense of the Portuguese Ministry of National Defence. She received a degree in history and social sciences from the University of Minho. She also holds a Master of Chinese Studies (from the University of Aveiro) and a Doctorate of International Relations (from the NOVA University). Her thesis was titled "China Today—Energy needs and International Relations. The relations with Portuguese Speaking Countries." Her latest published book is *The Future of Energy: Prospective Scenarios on EU-Russia Relations* (Nova Science Publishers Inc). She is also the author of the article "China's Energy Security and Portugal in the BRI."
carlafer@fcsh.unl.pt
https://orcid.org/0000-0003-3834-4055

Jorge Fernández-Gómez received a Ph.D. in economics from Georgetown University (Washington, DC). He is a senior researcher and coordinator of the Energy Lab at the Orkestra–Basque Institute of Competitiveness (University of Deusto). His research focuses on energy transition processes, smart grids, green financing, new business models in sustainable mobility, energy markets, and the relationship between environmental sustainability and industrial competitiveness. He has published articles on issues such as electricity market design, green finance, and new mobility business models and the sustainability strategies of companies.
jorge.fernandez@orkestra.deusto.es
https://orcid.org/0000-0003-3357-8338

Lisha Fu is a Ph.D. candidate at the School of Journalism and Mass Communication at Saint Petersburg State University. Her doctoral research investigates the leisure practice of Generation Z and their interrelations with mass media between 2019 and 2022; she is also examining de-Westernization in media studies. She takes a multidisciplinary approach that encompasses the fields of media, sociology, culture, and generation analysis theories. She holds a master's degree in international journalism from the University of Saint Petersburg, Russia, and has investigated geopolitics and media reflection in Russia.
fu.lisha@bk.ru
https://orcid.org/0000-0001-5628-985X

Victor Gaspar Filho is a researcher at the Brazilian Naval War College (EGN). He holds an MA degree in maritime studies from the Brazilian Naval War College and an undergraduate degree in international relations from Pontifical Catholic University.
v_gasparfilho@uol.com.br
https://orcid.org/0000-0002-2491-3811

Susann Handke received a Ph.D. in international law from the Erasmus School of Law, Rotterdam, in 2020. The topic of her Ph.D. dissertation was the evolution of the UN climate regime. She has been conducting research on issues of energy and climate governance for over 15 years. Her research covers a broad range of legal and political aspects of the energy transition and international climate cooperation. She is currently writing and lecturing on international and European energy and climate governance as she prepares for further academic research projects. Recent publications that she has authored include the book chapter "Renewables and the Core of the Energy Union: How the Pentalateral Forum Facilitates the Energy Transition in Western Europe" (D. Scholten, ed. The Geopolitics of Renewables, 2018), the policy paper "Regulating Post-Paris Climate Cooperation: The Geopolitics of Transparency, Flexibility, and Common Timeframes" (Clingendael International Energy Programme Paper, May 2021), and a brief reflection on the Glasgow climate summit in 2021: "Asia's Contribution to Post-Paris Climate Action: Putting Equity, Transparency, and the 'Phasedown' of Coal Use into Perspective" (IIAS—The Newsletter, no. 93, pp. 12–13, March 8, 2022).
susannhandke@yahoo.de

Jennifer Keahey is an assistant professor at Arizona State University. She is interested in food, energy, and water sovereignty. Her work examines alternatives to development that support socially just transitions to sustainability and participatory democracy. As an emancipatory sociologist, Jennifer utilizes feminist, antiracist, and decolonial approaches that challenge conventional theory and practice. She is currently writing a comparative historical book on food, heritage, and trade movements in post-authoritarian environments.
jennifer.keahey@asu.edu
https://orcid.org/0000-0001-8874-4618

Tanel Kerikmäe is a tenured professor of European legal policy and law and technology at TalTech. He also serves as the head of the university's department of law and is a chief strategist of its legal lab. Tanel has also been invited to speak and lecture at several universities in Japan, Switzerland, China, and elsewhere. In addition to being a principal investigator and researcher for EU-funded research

grants, Tanel has been active with capacity-building projects and fieldwork, such as working in Central Asia and Southeast Asia. In the last five years, he has been an invited expert by the European Parliament, the European Commission, and other international institutions, as well as several law firms. He has helped design a new type of tech-minded, cosmopolitan, and interdisciplinary legal education. Currently, his research activities are related to law, technology issues, and new challenges to the rule of law in the digital market and AI. Tanel is a member of an excellent academic network in the field and has completed many research projects with top universities.
tanel.kerikmae@taltech.ee
https://orcid.org/0000-0002-5972-827X

Javad Keypour is an early stage researcher and Ph.D. candidate at the Law Department, School of Business and Governance, Tallinn University of Technology (Taltech). He has worked for the Iranian Vice Presidency for Science and Technology office for five years as an energy markets expert and at a private think tank, ATEF, in Tehran. He is also the chief editor of the Energy Diplomacy journal, published in Iran. Javad gained his MA in 2019 in international relations and his MSc in chemical engineering in 2011. His research focuses on EU energy law, energy security, and EU-Russia energy relations. He has published more than 16 papers and has presented his research results in more than 10 scientific events.
javad.keypour@taltech.ee
https://orcid.org/0000-0002-2557-2967

Katharina Koch received a Ph.D. in geography in 2018 at the University of Oulu, Finland; her studies focused on EU-funded Finnish-Russian cross-border cooperation. Currently, she is a postdoctoral researcher in the Canadian Northern Corridor Program in the Energy and Environmental Policy Research Division at the School of Public Policy (University of Calgary). Her research focuses on various issues related to corridor governance, northern and Arctic security and geopolitics, and the digital divide in Canada.
katharina.koch@ucalgary.ca
https://orcid.org/0000-0003-4383-6687

Macarena Larrea-Basterra received a Ph.D. in Economics from the University of the Basque Country (UPV/EHU). She is a researcher at the Energy Lab at Orkestra–Basque Institute of Competitiveness (University of Deusto). Her research focuses on various energy and climate issues, self-consumption policies, business models with distributed energy resources, energy, climate and industrial policies, energy transition processes, environmental sustainability, and territorial

competitiveness. She has published articles on issues such as energy security, the circular economy, and green finance.
macarena.larrea@orkestra.deusto.es
https://orcid.org/0000-0002-3024-2372

Francisco José Leandro received a Ph.D. in political science and international relations from the Catholic University of Portugal in 2010. From 2016 to 2017, he took part in a postdoctoral research program on state monopolies in China—One Belt, One Road studies. In 2014, 2017, and 2020, he was awarded the Institute of European Studies in Macau (IEEM) Academic Research Grant, which is a major component of the Asia-Europe Comparative Studies Research Project. From 2014 to 2018, he was the program coordinator at the Institute of Social and Legal Studies, Faculty of Humanities at the University of Saint Joseph in Macau, China. From 2018 to 2023 he was the Associate-Dean of the Institute for Research on Portuguese-Speaking Countries at the City University of Macau (China). He is currently associate professor with habilitation in international relations at the Faculty of Social Sciences – University of Macau (China). His most recent books are *Steps of Greatness: The Geopolitics of OBOR* (2018, University of Macau), *The Challenges, Development and Promise of Timor-Leste* (2019, City University of Macau), *The Belt and Road Initiative: An Old Archetype of a New Development Model* (2020, Palgrave Macmillan), *Geopolitics of Iran* (2021, Palgrave Macmillan), *The Handbook of Special Economic Zones* (2021, IGI Global), *Disentangled Visions on Higher Education: Preparing the Generation Next* (2023, Peter Lang Publishers), and *The Palgrave Handbook of Globalization with Chinese Characteristics* (2023, Palgrave Macmillan). Leandro is a member of OBSERVARE (Observatory of Foreign Relations), which was established in 1996 as a center for studies in international relations at the Autonomous University of Lisbon, Portugal.
fleandro@um.edu.mo
https://orcid.org/0000-0002-1443-5828

Dipta Majumder is an electrical and electronics engineer with a master's degree in renewable energy. He has been working in the renewable energy sector for seven years and has managed projects in several African and Asian countries, including Bangladesh, Nigeria, Sierra Leone, and Uganda. He has provided technical assistance to organizations like UNOPS, GIZ, JICA, ADB, the World Bank Group, IDCOL (Bangladesh), and REA (Nigeria), to implement renewable energy projects. His areas of interest are solar photovoltaic technologies and off-grid rural electrification. Currently, Dipta is working as a mini-grid expert for INENSUS GmbH (Germany).
dipta12majumder@gmail.com
https://orcid.org/0000-0002-3171-030X

João Marques Cardoso is a researcher at the Center of Energy Studies of Getúlio Vargas Foundation (FGV Energia). He holds a master's degree in political science from the Federal University of the State of Rio de Janeiro (UNIRIO) and an undergraduate degree in international relations from the Federal Fluminense University (UFF).
joao.marques@fgv.br
https://orcid.org/0000-0001-5745-4757

Jaime Menéndez-Sánchez is a mining engineer from the University of Oviedo (Spain) and a predoctoral researcher at the Energy Lab of Orkestra–Basque Institute of Competitiveness (University of Deusto). He works on projects related to energy transition and sustainable mobility. He is currently working to acquire a Ph.D. in business management, knowledge, and innovation at the University of the Basque Country (UPV/EHU). He has published articles on issues such as the sustainability strategies of oil and gas companies, energy governance, and energy security.
jaime.menendez@orkestra.deusto.es
https://orcid.org/0000-0002-3189-2983

Alaz Munzur completed her Ph.D. in economics at the University of Calgary, Canada. Her research focuses on government regulation and policy on energy and the environment, international cooperation on environmental issues, and international trade. Currently, she is a research associate with the Energy and Environmental Policy Research Division at the School of Public Policy, University of Calgary. Her research, which is part of the Canadian Northern Corridor Program, focuses on the economic and environmental impact of infrastructure development and Canada's international and interregional trade.
asmunzur@ucalgary.ca
https://orcid.org/0000-0001-9251-0558

Majia Nadesan is a professor at Arizona State University. Her research examines the biopolitics (or politics of life) of energy and other key social assemblages, seeking greater transparency and democratic reform of extractive processes and effects. She has focused on energy risk governance and crisis management, along with their implications for democracy and sustainability as drawn from case examples, such as the 2010 U.S. Deepwater Horizon Oil Spill and the 2011 Fukushima nuclear crisis.
majia@asu.edu
https://orcid.org/0000-0002-2399-5587

Roopinder Oberoi is Fellow at Institute of Eminence, Delhi School of Public Policy and Governance and a Professor at the Department of Political Science, KMC, University of Delhi. She received a Ph.D. in political science from the University of Delhi. In 2012, she was awarded a postdoctoral research fellowship by the University Grant Commission of India. In 2017 she was awarded the UKIERI project by the British Council. She has authored and edited several books: *Corporate Social Responsibility and Sustainable Development in Emerging Economies* (Lexington Publisher, USA, 2015), *Globalization Reappraised: A false Oracle or a talisman?* (Vajpeyi, D and Oberoi, R, Lexington Books, USA, 2017), *Revisiting Globalization: From Borderless to Gated Globe* (Springer, UK, 2018), and *Social Enterprise in the Higher Education Sector* (Cambridge Scholars Publishing, 2020), *Contestations in Global Civil Society* (Emerald Elgar, 2022). She has published around 35 articles in peer-reviewed journals and 26 chapters in international books. She is an editor of Social Responsibility Journal (UK). She has also completed an international project on Social Enterprise and Higher Education awarded by the UK-India Education and Research Initiative (2017–2020). She has been a visiting research fellow at the University of Huddersfield UK since 2020. She is the founder of the Centre of Innovation and Social Enterprise (CISE), KMC, University of Delhi, and the Young Leader Policy Discourse Forum (YLDPF). She is also a coordinator and convenor of the 180DC KMC chapter. Her areas of specialization include political science, public policy, public administration, global governance, CSR, social enterprise, and higher education.
roberoi2019@gmail.com
https://orcid.org/0000-0003-3567-8885

Rui P. Pereira, born in 1970, holds an MA in European studies from the Portuguese Catholic University (2006–2008) and postgraduate degrees in modern China (ISCSP/UTL, 2003) and international economic relations (ISEG/UTL, 2001–2002). He also has a degree in international relations from Lusíada University of Lisbon (1989–1994). He is the head of the International Relations Division at the Directorate-General for Economic Activities of the Ministry of Economy of Portugal. He is the focal point of the Forum for Economic and Trade Cooperation between China and Portuguese-Speaking Countries (the Macau Forum). He has written several articles and chapters of books published on themes related to China. His latest book chapter (co-authored by Jorge Tavares da Silva and Rui Pereira) is "China and the Portuguese Atlantic: The BRI's last puzzle piece" (2020, pp. 389–409). This chapter appears in Leandro and Duarte. eds. *The Belt and Road Initiative—International Perspectives on an Old Archetype of a New Development Model* (Singapore: Palgrave).
rui.pereira@dgae.gov.pt
https://orcid.org/0000-0003-0442-1614

Marcelo Pereira da Cunha graduated with a degree in mechanical engineering from the Polytechnic School of the University of São Paulo in 1993, an M.Sc. in applied mathematics from the University of Campinas (Unicamp) in 2005, and a Ph.D. in energy systems planning from the University of Campinas in 2011. Marcelo is currently a professor at the Institute of Economics of Unicamp, and he works in mathematical economics and business economics. He has experience building input-output and general equilibrium models to assess socioeconomic and environmental impacts due to the insertion of new productive sectors or technological and structural changes in the economy. He mainly studies energy sectors.
mpcunha@unicamp.br
https://orcid.org/0000-0002-1027-1694

Sara Pugliese is an associate professor of EU law at the Parthenope University of Naples. She has authored articles and made contributions concerning several issues (EU environmental and cultural policy, EU defense policy, EU economic governance, EU agencies, protection of minorities, special economic zones, and joint procurements). She also wrote the volume "Il rischio nel diritto dell'Unione europea tra principi di precauzione, proporzionalità e standardizzazione." The Universidad de Jaén hosted her as an invited researcher and winner of Erasmus teaching mobility grants. She has given lectures for several degree and postgraduate courses at her university. She has also participated in numerous research projects, conferences, and editorial boards.
sara.pugliese@uniparthenope.it
https://orcid.org/0000-0002-5543-1858

Gerardo Rabinovich is an industrial engineer from Buenos Aires University (UBA) who received a Master of Sciences in Energy Economics from the Insitut d'Economie et Politiques de l'Energie (IEPE-CNRS), Grenoble University. Rabinovich is vice president of the Argentina Institute of Energy "General Mosconi" and president of the Chapter of International Association for Energy Economics of the Latin American Association of Energy Economics.
grenerg@gmail.com
https://orcid.org/0000-0002-6238-1051

Ferdous Rahman is an assistant professor of Law at Jahanagirnagar University, Bangladesh, where she teaches courses on topics such as international investment law, business law and business ethics, and economic analysis of law. She previously worked on renewable energy projects for three years for Infrastructure Development Company Ltd. (Bangladesh) as a legal expert. Currently, she is pursuing her doctoral studies at the Department of Private International Law at the University of Szeged, Hungary, with the Stipendium Hungaricum scholarship. Her research is focused on private parties' litigations against states. She has a keen

interest in researching sovereign debt, international investment law, investment dispute settlement, sovereign immunity, and sustainable development.
ferdous@juniv.edu
https://orcid.org/0000-0001-5158-5932

Gianmatteo Sabatino is a research fellow in comparative and European law at the Sino-Italian Institute of Zhongnan University of Economics and Law (Wuhan, People's Republic of China). He holds a Ph.D. in comparative and European legal studies from the University of Trento (Italy). His main research fields include comparative economic law, Chinese law, European economic governance, development planning law, and legal anthropology.
sabatinogianmatteo@gmail.com
https://orcid.org/0000-0003-4746-3443

Ana Teresa Santos is a senior data analyst and science coordinator outsourced to CHDI Foundation, Inc. She graduated with a degree in pharmaceutical medicine in 2010 and obtained her MSc degree in biomedicine in 2012 from the University of Aveiro, Portugal. She has a multidisciplinary background, holding a postgraduate degree in economy and management of science, technology, and innovation (ISEG–University of Lisbon) and earned her Ph.D. in complexity sciences (ISCTE–University Institute of Lisbon). She has been involved in multiple international projects funded by FP7 and H2020, as well as other national agencies such as FCT and ANR. Her primary research interests are in scientometrics and data-driven approaches.
ana_teresa_santis@iscte-iul.pt
https://orcid.org/0000-0002-3753-7528

Evgeniia (Jen) Sidorova, Ph.D., is a postdoctoral associate at the School of Public Policy at the University of Calgary. Her areas of expertise are the collection, documentation, and utilization of Indigenous and local knowledge in wildlife management, science, and industrial development in Canada, the US (Alaska), and Siberia, Russia. Her research also involves the analysis of environmental impact assessments in the US (Alaska) and northern Canada (NWT). Jen holds a doctorate in Political Science (International Relations and Comparative Politics) from the University of Calgary, AB, Canada; a Master of Arts from the University of Alaska Fairbanks (Arctic and Northern Studies Program, Global Environmental Policy concentration), Alaska, USA; and Bachelor of Law from North-Eastern Federal University, Yakutsk, Russia. She identifies as an Indigenous Siberian (Sakha) from Yakutsk, Russia. She spent more than seven years researching Indigenous politics in the Arctic and traditional knowledge.
evgeniia.sidorova@ucalgary.ca
https://orcid.org/0000-0002-6561-2441

João Simões received a Ph.D. in Portuguese-speaking countries studies from the City University of Macau, China, a master's degree in Chinese studies from the University of Aveiro, Portugal, and a bachelor's in electrical and computer engineering from the University of Lisbon, Portugal. He worked as a lecturer at Xi'an International Studies University, China, and is currently working in the utility sector in Macau, China.
a20092105032@cityu.mo
https://orcid.org/0000-0003-1437-5527

Jorge Tavares da Silva is an assistant professor at the University of Beira Interior (UBI), Portugal, and associate researcher at the Research Unit on Governance, Competitiveness and Public Policy (GOVCOPP) at the University of Aveiro, Portugal. He holds a Ph.D. in international relations from the University of Coimbra. He is the author of the book *BRICS and the New International Order* (Caleidoscópio, 2015) and co-author of *Role and Impact of Tourism in Peacebuilding and Conflict Transformation* (IGI Global, 2020) and Xi Jinping - *The New Helmsman of China* (in Portuguese) (Sílabas & Desafios, 2021). Many of these publications cover in detail the political, economic, and social situation in contemporary China.
jorge.tavares.silva@ubi.pt
https://orcid.org/0000-0002-2526-4745

Thijs Van de Graaf is an associate professor of international politics at the Ghent Institute for International and European Studies, Ghent University, Belgium. His research covers the intersection of energy security, climate policy and international politics.
Thijs.VandeGraaf@UGent.be
https://orcid.org/0000-0003-3372-3830

Jennifer Winter is an associate professor of economics and the scientific director of the Energy and Environmental Policy Research Division at the School of Public Policy, University of Calgary. Her research examines climate policies and the effects of government regulations and policy on energy development (and the associated consequences and trade-offs). She has advised governments in Canada in several capacities and serves on several boards and advisory groups.
jwinter@ucalgary.ca
https://orcid.org/0000-0001-6806-5263

Ana Isabel Xavier is an associate professor of international relations at UAL (Lisbon, Portugal) and deputy director and senior researcher at OBSERVARE. She holds a Ph.D. in international relations/European studies from the University of

Coimbra; her thesis was entitled "The European Union and Human Security: a crisis management global player in search of a strategic culture?"
aixavier@autonoma.pt
https://orcid.org/0000-0001-9428-104X

Faustina Fu Yip holds an MA in Middle Eastern and Mediterranean studies from King's College London and a BA in history from the University of Hong Kong. Her research topics are multidisciplinary, and she has explored the interconnectedness of global political economies, their dynamics, and how they have interacted with each other. She has a particular interest in the MENA region, their foreign policies, institutional development, and how their relations have been contextualized in the modern international order.
faustina_yip94@hotmail.com
http://orcid.org/0000-0002-5823-9984

Paulo Pereira Zagalo is a colonel of the Portuguese Army (active duty) who graduated from the War College, receiving a master's degree in military sciences. He received training in civil crisis management and in strategic, geo-economic and foresight analysis from the Portuguese National Defense Institute. Further, he is a researcher at the Professor Joaquim Veríssimo Serrão Research Center. He is also a Ph.D. candidate in the field of military sciences. Furthermore, he served at the headquarters of the European Rapid Operating Force (EUROFOR) in Florence, Italy, as an operational procedures section chief and subsequently as head of the plans branch (2005–2008). From December 2006 to June 2007, he served as deputy joint operations center and shift director in Operation ALTHEA at the EUFOR HQ in Sarajevo, Bosnia, and Herzegovina. He was also a representative of the army to the NATO working group on land capabilities (2010–2014). Recently, he worked as the coordinator of the Defense Cooperation Program in Timor-Leste (2018–2020). He is currently the head of the Department of Military Sciences at the army's Military Academy.
ppzagalo@gmail.com
https://orcid.org/0000-0001-9163-9747

www.ingramcontent.com/pod-product-compliance
Ingram Content Group UK Ltd.
Pitfield, Milton Keynes, MK11 3LW, UK
UKHW020837290926
15470UKWH00004B/1408

9 781433 191350